Ida M. Tarbell

McClure's Magazine

Napoleon Bonaparte

Ida M.Tarbell

McClure's Magazine
Napoleon Bonaparte

ISBN/EAN: 9783741198892

Manufactured in Europe, USA, Canada, Australia, Japa

Cover: Foto ©ninafisch / pixelio.de

Manufactured and distributed by brebook publishing software (www.brebook.com)

Ida M.Tarbell

McClure's Magazine

NAPOLEON THE GREAT CROSSING THE MOUNT ST. BERNARD, MAY, 1800.

Engraved by Antonio Gilberti in 1809, under the direction of Longhi, after portrait painted by David in 1805. Dedicated to the Prince Eugène Napoleon of France, Viceroy of Italy. It was soon after his return from Marengo that Napoleon expressed his desire to be painted by David. The artist had long desired this work, and seized the opportunity eagerly. He asked the First Consul when he would pose for him.

"Pose!" said Bonaparte. "Do you suppose the great men of antiquity posed for their portraits?"

"But I paint you for your time, for men who have seen you. They would like to have it like you."

"Like me! It is not the perfection of the features, a pimple on the nose, which makes resemblance. It is the character of the face that should be represented. No one cares whether the portraits of great men look like them or not. It is enough that their genius shines from the picture."

"I have never considered it in that way. But you are right, Citizen Consul. You need not pose; I will paint you without that." David went to breakfast daily after this with Napoleon, in order to study his face, and the Consul put at his service all the garments he had worn at Marengo. It is told that David mounted Napoleon on a mule for this picture, but that the General demurred. He sprang upon his horse, and, making him rear, said to the artist, "Paint me thus."

McCLURE'S MAGAZINE.

Vol. IV.   DECEMBER, 1894.   No. 1.

NAPOLEON BONAPARTE.

BY IDA M. TARBELL.

With pictures from the collection of the Hon. Gardiner G. Hubbard, who also furnishes the explanatory notes.

SECOND PAPER.

THIRTEENTH VENDÉMIAIRE.

PAUL BARRAS, revolutionist, conventionalist, member of the Directory, was one of the most influential members of the French government in 1795. When he saw the good work Napoleon was doing in the topographical bureau of the Committee of Public Safety, he resolved to be his friend. It was not long before he had an opportunity to put his *protégé's* talent to test.

In October, 1795, the government was threatened by the revolting sections. Barras, the nominal head of the defence, asked Napoleon to command the forces which protected the Tuileries, where the Convention had gone into permanent session. He hesitated for a moment. He had much sympathy for the sections. His sagacity conquered. The Convention stood for the republic; an overthrow now meant another proscription, more of the Terror, perhaps a royalist succession, an English invasion.

"I accept," he said to Barras; "but I warn you that once my sword is out of the scabbard I shall not replace it till I have established order."

It was on the night of 12th Vendémiaire that Napoleon was appointed. With incredible rapidity he massed the men and cannon he could secure at the openings into the palace and at the points of approach. He armed even the members of the Convention as a reserve. When the sections marched their men into the streets and upon the bridges leading to the Tuileries, they were met by a fire which scattered them at once.

That night Paris was quiet. The next day Napoleon was made general of division. On October 26th he was appointed general-in-chief of the Army of the Interior.

GENERAL-IN-CHIEF OF THE ARMY OF THE INTERIOR.

At last the opportunity he had sought so long and so eagerly had come.

The first use he made of his power was for his family and friends. Fifty or sixty thousand francs, assignats, and dresses go to his mother and sisters; Joseph is to have a consulship; "a roof, a table, and carriage" are at his disposal in Paris; Louis is made a lieutenant and his aide-de-camp; Lucien, commissioner of war; Junot and Marmont are put on his staff. He forgets nobody. The very day after the 13th Vendémiaire, when his cares and excite-

NAPOLEON WHILE FIRST CONSUL OF FRANCE.

"Bonaparte, 1er Consul de la Rep. Franc." Engraved in 1801 by Audouin, after a design by Bouillon.

ments were numerous and intense, he was at the Permons', where Monsieur Permon had just died. "He was like a son, a brother." This relation he tried soon to change, seeking to marry the beautiful widow Permon. When she laughed merrily at the idea, for she was many years his senior, he replied that the age of his wife was a matter of indifference to him so long as she did not *look over thirty*.

The change in Bonaparte himself was great. Up to this time he had gone about Paris "in an awkward and ungainly manner, with a shabby round hat thrust down over his eyes, and with curls (known at that time as *oreilles des chiens*) badly pow-

JOSEPHINE, THE FIRST WIFE OF NAPOLEON.

Engraved by Audouin, after Lasseret. This portrait, "Joséphine impératrice des Français, reine d'Italie," is surrounded by an elaborate frame of imperial emblems. After the divorce, Josephine's portrait was erased from the plate, and that of Marie Louise inserted.

NAPOLEON IN 1801.

Painted by A. Girard in 1801; engraved by Richomme in 1835. This is considered by many the best portrait of Napoleon painted during the consulship.

with a wan and livid complexion, bowed shoulders, and a weak and sickly appearance."

But now, installed in an elegant *hôtel*, driving his own carriage, careful of his person, received in every *salon* where he cared to go, the young general-in-chief is a changed man. Success has had much to do with this; love has perhaps had more.

JOSEPHINE DE BEAUHARNAIS.

Barras had used his influence for Napoleon in society as well as in public life,

BONAPARTE.
Engraved by Bartolozzi, R.A., an Italian engraver, resident of England, after the portrait by Appiani.

and before the 13th Vendémiaire he had been admitted to the most brilliant and influential political *salon* of the day, that of Madame Tallien. Among the women whom he met there and at Barras' own house was the Viscountess de Beauharnais (*née* Tascher de la Pagerie), widow of the Marquis de Beauharnais, guillotined on the 5th Thermidor, 1794. At the time of his death his wife was a prisoner. She owed her release to Madame Tallien, with whom she since had been on intimate terms. All Madame Tallien's circle had, indeed, become attached to Josephine de Beauharnais, especially Barras, whom she regarded as her real protector.

There was much about her that was pleasing. A creole past the freshness of youth—Josephine was thirty-two years old in 1795—she had a grace, a sweetness, a charm, that made one forget that she was

NAPOLEON WHILE FIRST CONSUL OF FRANCE.
"N. Bonaparte, 1er Consul de la République Française"—engraved by Morcoli fils, after Dallos.

not beautiful, even when she was beside such brilliant women as Madame Tallien and Madame Récamier. It was never possible to surprise her in an attitude that was not graceful. She was never ruffled nor irritable. By nature she was the perfection of ease and repose.

Artist enough to dress in clinging stuffs made simply, which harmonized perfectly with her style, and skilful enough to use the arts of the toilet to conceal defects which care and age had brought, the Viscountess de Beauharnais was altogether one of the most fascinating women in Madame Tallien's circle.

Napoleon was attracted to her from the first; but by her station, her elegance, her influence, she seemed inaccessible to him.

NAPOLEON WHILE FIRST CONSUL OF FRANCE.
"Bonaparte, premier Consul"; designed and engraved by Chataignier.

Indeed, it was after he had known Josephine some time that he sought the hand of the widow Permon.
 Though he dared not tell her his love, talents which will secure advancement; but you are isolated, without fortune and without relations. You ought to marry; it gives weight," and he asked permission

NAPOLEON BONAPARTE.

"Bonaparte": drawn from the life by T Phillips, Esq., R.A., in 180
Engraved by Edwards.

NAPOLEON.

Engraved by J B Massard, after J H Prout. Below the portrait is
printed in French and English the following legend

"His name will be resounded through all Europe and Egypt for his ruin to combat,
and yet none so for his wish·· m to r·····l"

his advice, but Napoleon frightened and wearied her by the violence of his love. A letter of hers, written at this stage of the affair, shows admirably her feelings:

"'Do you like him?' you ask. No; I do not. 'You dislike him, then?' you say. Not at all; but I am in a lukewarm state that troubles me, and which in religion is considered more difficult to manage than unbelief itself, and that is why I need your advice, which will give strength to my feeble nature. To take any positive step has always seemed most fatiguing to my creole nonchalance. I have always found it far easier to yield to the wishes of others.

"I admire the courage of the General, the extent of his information (for he speaks equally well on all subjects), the vivacity of his wit, and the quick intelligence which enables him to grasp the thoughts of others almost before they are expressed; but I am terrified, I admit, at the empire he seems to exercise over all about him. His keen gaze has an inexplicable something which impresses even our Directors; judge, then, if he is not likely to intimidate a woman. In short, just that which ought to please one—the strength of a passion of which he speaks with an energy that permits no doubt of his sincerity—is precisely that which arrests the consent that often hovers on my lips.

"Having passed my *première jeunesse*, can I hope to preserve for any length of time this violent tenderness, which in the General amounts almost to delirium? If when we are married he should cease to love me, would he not reproach me for what I had allowed him to do? Would he not regret a more brilliant marriage that he might have made? What, then, could I say? What could I do? Nothing but weep.

. . . . .

"Barras declares that if I will marry the General he will certainly secure for him the command of the Army of Italy. Yesterday Bonaparte, in speaking of this favor, which has excited a murmur of discontent in his brother officers, even though not yet granted, said to me: 'Do they think that I need protection to rise? They will be glad enough some day if I grant them mine. My sword is at my side, and with it I can go far.'

"What do you say of this certainty of success? Is it not a proof of self-confidence that is almost ridiculous? A general of brigade protecting the heads of government! I feel that it is; and yet this preposterous assurance affects me to such a degree that I can believe everything may be possible

NAPOLEON BONAPARTE.

NAPOLEON WHILE FIRST CONSUL OF FRANCE.

"Napoleon Bonaparte, Premier Consul de la République Française"—engraved by an English engraver, Dickinson, after a portrait by Gros. The original picture was given to the Second Consul, Cambacérès, by the First Consul, Bonaparte.

to this man, and with his imagination, who can tell what he may be tempted to undertake?

"But for this marriage, which worries me, I should be very gay in spite of many other things; but until this is settled one way or another, I shall torment myself."

In spite of her doubts she yielded at last, and on the 9th of March, 1796, they were married. Shortly before, Napoleon had been appointed commander-in-chief of the Army of Italy, and two days later he left his wife for his post.

NAPOLEON'S LOVE FOR HIS WIFE.

From every station on his route he wrote her passionate letters:

"Every moment takes me farther from you, and every moment I feel less able to be away from you. You are ever in my thoughts; my fancy tires itself in trying to imagine what you are doing. If I picture you sad, my heart is wrung and my grief is increased. If you are happy and merry with your friends, I blame you for so soon forgetting the painful three days' separation; in that case you are frivolous and destitute of deep feeling. As you see, I

NAPOLEON BONAPARTE.

NAPOLEON BONAPARTE.

BONAPARTE: APPOINTED COMMANDER-IN-CHIEF OF THE ARMY OF ITALY IN FEBRUARY, 1796, AND OF THE ARMY OF ENGLAND IN DECEMBER, 1797.

"*Bonaparte, nommé général en chef de l'armée d'Italie en ventôse An IV., puis général en chef de l'armée d'Angleterre, en frimaire An VI.*"—Engraved by Tassaert in 1798, after the portrait of Appiani

delicious joy of pouring out my heart. You have robbed me of more than my soul; you are the sole thought of my life. If I am worn out by all the torments of events, and fear the issue, if men disgust me, if I am ready to curse life, I place my hand on my heart; your image is beating there. I look at it, and love is for me perfect happiness; and everything is smiling, except the time that I see myself absent from my love."

THE CONDITION OF THE ARMY OF ITALY.

But Napoleon had much to occupy him besides his separation from Josephine. Extraordinary difficulties surrounded his new post. Neither the generals nor the men knew anything of their new commander

JOACHIM MURAT (1771-1815).

Engraved by Ruotte, after Gros. Murat was born in 1771, in the department of Lot. He was destined for the church, but abandoned the seminary for the army. Exalted revolutionist, he sought to change his name from Murat to *Marat* after the death of the *ami du peuple*. In 1795 he was in Paris, idle, when he made the acquaintance of Napoleon. When Barras called Napoleon to the defence of the convention, the 13th Vendémiaire, Murat was asked to aid, and for his services he was given a command in the army, and made an aide-de-camp of Napoleon in Italy. His valor in the first battles of the campaign, Montenotte, Ceva, Dego, and Mondovi, was rewarded by sending him to Paris with the first flags captured. Throughout the rest of the Italian campaign he continued to distinguish himself. In 1798 he went to Egypt. He made a brilliant cavalry charge at the battle of the Pyramids, was the first in the assault on St. Jean d'Acre, and himself took Moustapha-Pacha prisoner at the battle of Aboukir. He aided in the 18th Brumaire, and was rewarded with the command of the consular guard and the hand of Caroline Bonaparte. At Marengo he led the French cavalry, and was afterwards made governor of the Cisalpine Republic. In 1804 he was made a marshal of France, and in 1805 grand admiral, with the title of prince. He commanded the cavalry of the Grand Army in the campaign of 1805, and after Austerlitz was made grand-duke of Berg and Clèves. Murat led the cavalry at Jena, Eylau, and Friedland, and in 1808 was made general-in-chief of the French armies in Spain. Soon after he became king of Naples under the title of King Joachim Napoleon. Murat was greatly loved as a king, and effected many reforms in his kingdom. He was present in the

NAPOLEON BONAPARTE. 15

"Who is this general Bonaparte? Where has he served? No one knows anything about him," wrote Junot's father when the latter at Toulon decided to follow his artillery commander.

In the Army of Italy they were asking the same questions, and the Directory could only answer as Junot had done : "As far as I can judge, he is one of those men of whom nature is avaricious, and that she permits upon the earth only from age to age."

He was to replace a commander-in-chief who had sneered at his plans for an Italian campaign and might be expected to put obstacles in his way. He was to take an army which was in the last stages of poverty and discouragement. Their garments were in rags. Even the officers were so nearly shoeless that when they reached Milan and one of them was invited to dine at the palace of a marquise, he was obliged to go in shoes without soles and tied on by cords carefully blacked. They had provisions for only a month, and half rations at that. The Piedmontese called them the "rag heroes."

Worse than their poverty was their inactivity. "For three years they had fired off their guns in Italy only because war was going on, and not for any especial object—only to satisfy their consciences." Discontent was such that counter-revolution gained ground daily. One company had even taken the name of *Dauphin*, and royalist songs were heard in camp.

Napoleon saw at a glance all these difficulties, and set himself to conquer them. With his generals he was reserved and severe. "It was necessary," he explained afterward, "in order to command men so much older than myself." His look and bearing quelled insubordination, restrained familiarity, even inspired fear. "From his arrival," says Marmont, "his attitude was that of a man born for power. It was plain to the least clairvoyant eyes that he knew how to compel obedience, and scarcely was he in authority before the line of a celebrated poet might have been applied to him :

"'Des egaux ? dès longtemps Mahomet n'en a plus.'"

General Decrès, who had known Napoleon well at Paris, hearing that he was going to pass through Toulon, where he was stationed, offered to present his comrades. "I run," he says, "full of eagerness and joy ; the *salon* opens ; I am about to spring forward, when the attitude, the look, the sound of his voice are sufficient to stop me. There was nothing rude about him, but it was enough. From that time I was never tempted to pass the line which had been drawn for me."

Lavalette says of his first interview with him : "He looked weak, but his regard was so firm and so fixed that I felt myself turning pale when he spoke to me." Augereau goes to see him at Albenga, full of contempt for this favorite of Barras who has never known an action, determined on insubordination. Bonaparte comes out, little, thin, round-shouldered, and gives Augereau, a giant among the generals, his orders. The big man backs out in a kind of terror. "He frightens me," he tells Massena. "His first glance crushed me."

He quelled insubordination in the ranks by quick, severe punishment, but it was not long that he had insubordination. The army asked nothing but to act, and immediately they saw that they were to move. He had reached his post on March 22d ; nineteen days later operations began. The movement from that day is so rapid and so brilliant that a true notion of it is gained only in a summary.

SUMMARY OF THE ITALIAN CAMPAIGN.

On the 10th of April, 1796, he moved his army ; on the 12th he gained the battle of Montenotte ; the 13th, Millesimo ; the 15th, Dego ; the 22d, Mondovi. The Piedmontese, dazzled and terrified by his victories, put at his disposal the fortresses which commanded Piedmont, and on the 15th of May Napoleon entered Milan.

Austria, amazed and indignant, sent a new general, Würmser, to Italy. While waiting his arrival, Napoleon turned toward the south and quelled the plots against him which the Pope and the English were fomenting. By the end of July he was at Mantua, to meet Würmser The Austrian general had divided his forces into three parts, so marching as to surround the French. Napoleon saw the tactics at once, and, leaving his position before

KLÉBER, 1753 OR 1754-1800.

Engraved by G. Fiesinger, after portrait by Guérin. Jean Baptist Kléber was born at Strasburg in 1754(?). The son of a mason, he studied architecture for a time, but abandoned it to enter the military school of Munich, from which he went into the Austrian army. In 1783 he left the army to return to architecture. In 1792 he joined the revolutionary army, and served first on the Rhine, later in the Vendée, where he distinguished himself. Made general of division in the army of the North, Kléber won laurels at Fleurus, Mons, Lourain, and Maëstricht, and in the campaign of 1796. He was appointed commander-in-chief temporarily, but was recalled when about to enter Frankfort in 1797, the command being given to Hoche. Disappointed, he resigned from the army. When Napoleon went to Egypt, he asked for Kléber. In all the battles of the campaign he showed his bravery and skill; and when Napoleon left for France he transferred his command to him. The situation of the French army in Egypt soon became desperate, and Kléber was trying to negotiate with the English and Turks an honorable retirement, when Admiral Keith ordered him to give up his army as prisoners of war. Kléber published the letter in the army, with the words. "Soldiers, such insolence can be answered but by victories; prepare for combat." At Heliopolis, with eight thousand men, he met the Grand Vizir with eighty thousand, and completely conquered him. Soon after he put down a revolt in Cairo, and was beginning to reconquer and reorganize the country when he was assassinated, June 14, 1800.

NAPOLEON BONAPARTE.

NAPOLEON AT THE BATTLE OF THE PYRAMIDS, JULY 21, 1798.

Engraved by Vallot in 1838, after painting by Gros (1810). The moment chosen by the artist is that when Napoleon addressed to his soldiers that short and famous harangue, "Soldiers, from the summit of these pyramids forty centuries look down upon you." In the General's escort are Murat, his head bare and his sword clasped tightly; and after him, in order, Duroc, Sulkowski, Berthier, Junot, and Eugène de Beauharnais, then sub-lieutenant, all on horseback. On the right are Rampon, Denais, Bertrand, and Lasalle. This picture was ordered for the Tuileries, and was exhibited first in 1810. Napoleon gave it to one of his generals, and it did not reappear in Paris until 1835. It is now in the gallery at Versailles. Gros regarded this picture as his best work, and chose Vallot himself to engrave it.

Mantua, fell on one division at Lonato and defeated it on July 31st. Then, before the other two could unite, he engaged them; the first at Lonato on August 3d, the second at Castiglione on August 5th. Both battles he won.

On September 8th, at Bassano, Würmser was again defeated, escaping with but a remnant of his army, which he led into Mantua.

A new Austrian army, fifty thousand strong, under Alvinzi, was sent into Italy. With forty thousand men Napoleon met them on the Adige, and in the three-days' battle of Arcola—November 15, 16, 17—he disabled this, the second force sent against him by the Austrians since he had defeated the one he found in Italy the preceding April.

Obstinate in spite of her losses, Austria sent Alvinzi to renew the attack. He had an army of sixty-five thousand men—full twenty-five thousand more than Napoleon. Most of them were fresh troops; all of the French army was worn. On the 14th of January, 1797, the two armies met on the table-land of Rivoli. Again Alvinzi was completely routed, and this time driven into the Tyrol.

One branch of his army had been sent to relieve Würmser and was marching rapidly to Mantua. Napoleon hurried from Rivoli, overtook and defeated this relief force, and on the 2d of February, 1797, Würmser surrendered.

The Papal States and the various aristocratic parties of southern Italy were threatening to rise against the French. The spirit of independence and revolt they were bringing into the country could not but weaken clerical and monarchical institutions. An active enemy to the south would have been a serious hindrance to Napoleon, and he marched into the Papal States. A fortnight was sufficient to silence the threats of his enemies, and on February 19, 1797, he signed with the Pope the treaty of Tolentino.

In March he was again in pursuit of the Austrians. Steadily he drove them from point to point until Vienna itself was in sight, and at Leoben, in April, an armistice was signed.

On May 16th the French took possession of Venice. On October 17th, one year seven months and seven days after he left Paris, Napoleon signed the treaty of Campo Formio. By this treaty France gained the frontier of the Rhine and the Low Countries to the mouth of the Scheldt. Austria was given Venice, and a republic called the Cisalpine was formed from Reggio, Modena, Lombardy, and part of the States of the Pope.

NAPOLEON'S RULES OF WAR.

The military genius that this twenty-eight-year-old commander had shown in the campaign in Italy bewildered his enemies and thrilled his friends.

"Things go on very badly," said an Austrian veteran taken at Lodi. "No one seems to know what he is about. The French general is a young blockhead who knows nothing of the regular rules of war. Sometimes he is on our right, at others on our left; now in front, and presently in our rear. This mode of warfare is contrary to all system, and utterly insufferable."

It is certain that if Napoleon's opponents never knew what he was going to do, if his generals themselves were frequently uncertain, it being his practice to hold his peace about his plans, he himself had definite rules of warfare. The most important of these were:

"Attacks should not be scattered, but should be concentrated."

"Always be superior to the enemy at the point of attack."

"Time is everything."

To these formulated rules he joined marvellous fertility in stratagem. Thus in the begining of the campaign of 1796 Napoleon made a feint of marching toward Genoa. Beaulieu, his opponent, directed a large body of troops there. Napoleon instantly countermarched, and routed the Austrians left behind at Montenotte. This done, and before Beaulieu, moving slowly and ponderously, could join his colleague, the French had literally sprung between the two bodies, engaging and defeating first one at Millesimo, and then the other at Dego.

It was his skill in stratagem which a few days later made Beaulieu believe that Napoleon was going to cross the Po at Valenza, and induced him to place a large part of his army there. Convinced that this had been done, Napoleon sped to Piacenza, and was across the river without disturbance and on his enemy's flank, before the latter had discovered that he had changed route.

In November, when engaging Alvinzi's first army, Napoleon was in camp at Verona. The Austrians were across the Adige. Their superior position, greater numbers, and excellent artillery made a direct attack impracticable. On the night of the 12th

NAPOLEON IN THE MOSQUE AT JAFFA IN USE AS A HOSPITAL, MAY, 1799.

Engraved by Vallot, after painting by Gros. At Jaffa the plague broke out in the army. To persuade the soldiers that it was only a fever and not to be feared, Napoleon went to the hospital himself, and even touched the afflicted. In this Gros had undertaken to paint the Battle of Nazareth and the brilliant action of Junot where he broke a column of ten thousand Turks with a body of three hundred horse. Napoleon secured this artist, and made him take as subject the Pest of Jaffa. The canvas was exhibited in the *Salon* of 1804, and had an immense success. The state bought the picture for sixteen thousand francs.

NAPOLEON BONAPARTE.

AUGEREAU (1757-1816).

Engraved by Lefevre, after a design by Le Dru. Augereau, son of a Paris fruit dealer, was born in 1757. Began his military career as a carbineer in the Neapolitan army. In 1792 joined the republican army. From the army of the Pyrenees he passed to that of Italy, where his intrepidity and military talents soon won him a first place. At Lodi and Castiglione he distinguished himself, and he shared with Bonaparte the glory of Arcola. After the treaty of Campo Formio he was chosen by Napoleon to carry the flags taken from the enemy to Paris. He aided the government in the *coup d'état* of the 18th Fructidor, and it was he who arrested Pichegru. After the death of Hoche he was sent to take his place in the army of the Rhine-and-Moselle. Afterwards he was elected a member of the Council of Five Hundred. He returned to Paris about the time that Bonaparte came from Egypt, and at first he opposed him; but after the 18th Brumaire the two became friendly again, and Augereau received the command of the army of Holland. When Napoleon became emperor, Augereau was made marshal, was given the eagle of the Legion of Honor, and the title of Duke of Castiglione. He distinguished himself at Jena and Eylau, served for a time in Spain, and performed prodigies of valor at Leipsic. On the Restoration, Augereau joined Louis XVIII.; but when Napoleon returned from Elba he tried to regain his good will. The Bourbons refused him after the Hundred Days. He died in 1816.

of November he went quietly into camp. Early in the evening he gave orders to leave Verona, and took the road westward. It looked like a retreat. The French army believed so, and began to say sorrowfully among themselves that Italy was lost. When far enough from Verona to escape the attention of the enemy, he wheeled to the southeast, crossed the Adige, and in the morning was on Alvinzi's rear, where, for three days, the battle of Arcola was fought.

This fertility in stratagem, this rapidity of action, this audacity in attack, bewildered and demoralized the enemy, but it raised the enthusiasm of his imaginative Southern troops to the highest pitch.

He insisted in this campaign on one other rule: "Unity of command is necessary to assure success." After his defeat of the Piedmontese, the Directory ordered him, May 7, 1796, to divide his command with Kellermann. Napoleon answered:

"I believe it most impolitic to divide the army of Italy in two parts. It is quite as much against the interests of the republic to place two different generals over it. . . .

"A single general is not only necessary, but also it is essential that nothing trouble him in his march and operations. I have conducted this campaign without consulting any one. I should have done nothing of value if I had been obliged to reconcile my plans with those of another. I have gained advantage over superior forces and when stripped of everything myself, because persuaded that your confidence was in me. My action has been as prompt as my thought.

"If you impose hindrances of all sorts upon me, if I must refer every step to government commissioners, if they have the right to change my movements, of taking from me or of sending me troops, expect no more of any value. If you enfeeble your means by dividing your forces, if you break the unity of military thought in Italy, I tell you sorrowfully you will lose the happiest opportunity of imposing laws on Italy.

"In the condition of the affairs of the republic in Italy, it is indispensable that you have a general that has your entire confidence. If it is not I, I am sorry for it, but I shall redouble my zeal to merit your esteem in the post you confide to me. Each one has his own way of carrying on war. General Kellermann has more experience and will do it better than I, but both together will do it very badly.

"I can only render the services essential to the country when invested entirely and absolutely with your confidence."

He remained in charge, and throughout the rest of the campaign continued to act more and more independently of the Directory, even dictating terms of peace to please himself.

INFLUENCE OVER SOLDIERS AND GENERALS.

It was in this Italian campaign that the almost superstitious adoration which Napoleon's soldiers and most of his generals felt for him began. Brilliant generalship was not the only reason for this. It was due largely to his personal courage, which they had discovered at Lodi. A charge had been ordered across a wooden bridge swept by thirty pieces of cannon, and beyond was the Austrian army. The men hesitated. Napoleon sprang to their head and led them into the thickest of the fire. From that day he was known among them as the "Little Corporal." He had won them by the quality which appeals most deeply to a soldier in the ranks—contempt of death.

His addresses never failed to stir them to action and enthusiasm. They were oratorical, prophetic, and abounded in phrases which the soldiers never forgot. Such was his address at Cherasco, after the armistice with Piedmont:

"Soldiers!" he said, "in fifteen days you have gained six victories, taken twenty-one stands of colors, fifty-five pieces of cannon, and several fortresses, and conquered the richest part of Piedmont. You have made fifteen hundred prisoners, and killed or wounded ten thousand men.

"Hitherto, however, you have been fighting for barren rocks, made memorable by your valor but useless to the nation. Your exploits now equal those of the conquering armies of Holland and the Rhine. You were utterly destitute, and have supplied all your wants. You have gained battles without cannons, passed rivers without bridges, performed forced marches without shoes, bivouacked without brandy and often without bread. None but republican phalanxes—soldiers of liberty—could have borne what you have endured. For this you have the thanks of your country.

"The two armies which lately attacked you in full confidence, now fly before you in consternation. . . . But, soldiers, it must not be concealed that you have done nothing, since there remains aught to do. Neither Turin nor Milan are ours. . . . The greatest difficulties are no doubt surmounted; but you have still battles to fight, towns to take, rivers to cross. . . ."

Such was his address in March, before the final campaign against the Austrians:

"You have been victorious in fourteen pitched battles and sixty-six combats; you have taken one hundred thousand prisoners, five hundred pieces of large cannon and two thousand pieces of smaller; four equipages for bridge pontoons. The country has nourished you, paid you during your campaign, and you have beside that sent thirty millions from the public treasury to Paris. You have enriched the Museum of Paris with three hundred *chefs d'œuvre* of ancient and modern Italy, which it has taken thirty ages to produce. You have conquered the most beautiful country of Europe. The French colors float for the first time upon the borders of the Adriatic. The kings of Sardinia and Naples, the Pope, the Duke of Parma have become allies. You have chased the English from Leghorn, Genoa, and Corsica. You have yet to march against the Emperor of Austria."

NAPOLEON BONAPARTE.

VISCOUNT NELSON, DUKE OF BRONTÉ (1758-1805).

Engraved by Dick, after portrait by Knight. Nelson was born at Burnham, England. He entered the navy at twelve years of age. Was made a post-captain when twenty one years old, and during the next few years was engaged actively in the American war. After the peace of Versailles, in 1783, he served in the West Indies. When war was declared between France and England in 1793, Nelson was given command of the "Agamemnon," and sent to the Mediterranean, where he took part in the sieges of Bastia and Cadiz. At the latter place he lost an eye. For his services in the winter of 1795-96 he was made commodore, and for his daring and skill in the engagement with the Spanish off Cape St. Vincent, February 13, 1797, he received the Order of the Bath and was made admiral. It was here that Nelson led his crew with the cry, "Westminster Abbey or victory!" When Napoleon started for Egypt, Nelson was ordered to intercept him, but his squadron was crippled in a gale and Napoleon escaped. On August 1, 1798, he attacked the French fleet in the harbor of Aboukir, and destroyed all but two of the thirteen French ships. The Battle of the Nile, as this engagement is called, is considered Nelson's masterpiece, and for it he received a peerage. This victory gave encouragement to Europe to attack revolutionary France afresh. Nelson now went against Naples, where, after the French had been driven from Italy and an amnesty declared, he allowed the trial and sentence of Caracciolo, the admiral of the Neapolitan fleet a judicial murder similar to that of the Duc d'Enghien. In the spring of 1801 Nelson went to the Baltic against

His approval was their greatest joy. Let him speak a word of praise to a regiment, and they embroidered it on their banners. "I was at ease, the Thirty-second was there," was on the flag of that regiment. Over the Fifty-seventh floated a name Napoleon had called them by, "The terrible Fifty-seventh."

His displeasure was a greater spur than his approval. He said to a corps which had retreated in disorder: "Soldiers, you have displeased me. You have shown neither courage nor constancy, but have yielded positions where a handful of men might have defied an army. You are no longer French soldiers. Let it be written on their colors, 'They no longer form part of the Army of Italy.'" A veteran pleaded that they be placed in the van, and during the rest of the campaign no regiment was more distinguished.

The effect of his genius was as great on his generals as on his troops. They were dazzled by his stratagems and manoeuvres, inspired by his imagination. "*There was so much of the future in him,*" is Marmont's expressive explanation. They could believe anything of him. A remarkable set of men they were to have as followers and friends—Augereau, Masséna, Berthier, Marmont, Junot.

IMPRESSIONS OF THE ITALIAN CAMPAIGN IN PARIS.

The people and the government in Paris had begun to believe in him, as did the Army of Italy. He not only sent flags and reports of victory; he sent money and works of art. Impoverished as the Directory was, the sums which came from Italy were a reason for not interfering with the high hand the young general carried in his campaign and treaties.

Never before had France received such letters from a general. Now he announces that he has sent "twenty first masters, from Correggio to Michael Angelo;" now, "a dozen millions of money;" now, two or three millions in jewels and diamonds to be sold in Paris. In return he asks only for men and officers "who have fire and a firm resolution not to make *learned retreats.*"

The entry into Paris of the first art acquisitions made a profound impression on the people:

"The procession of enormous cars, drawn by richly caparisoned horses, was divided into four sections. First came trunks filled with books, manuscripts, . . . including the antiques of Josephus, on papyrus, with works in the handwriting of Galileo. . . . Then followed collections of mineral products. . . . For the occasion were added wagons laden with iron cages containing lions, tigers, panthers, over which waved enormous palm branches and all kinds of exotic shrubs. Afterwards rolled along chariots bearing pictures carefully packed, but with the names of the most important inscribed in large letters on the outside, as, The Transfiguration, by Raphael; The Christ, by Titian. The number was great, the value greater. When these trophies had passed, amid the applause of an excited crowd, a heavy rumbling announced the approach of massive carts bearing statues and marble groups: the Apollo Belvidere; the Nine Muses; the Laocoön; . . . The Venus de Medici was eventually added, decked with bouquets, crowns of flowers, flags taken from the enemy, and French, Italian, and Greek inscriptions. Detachments of cavalry and infantry, colors flying, drums beating, music playing, marched at intervals; the members of the newly established Institute fell into line; artists and savants; and the singers of the theatres made the air ring with national hymns. This procession marched through all Paris, and at the Champ de Mars defiled before the five members of the Directory, surrounded by their subordinate officers."

The practice of sending home works of art, begun in the Italian campaign, Napoleon continued throughout his military career, and the art of France owes much to the education thus given the artists of the first part of this century.

His agents ransacked Italy, Spain, Germany, and Flanders for *chefs-d'œuvre.* When entering a country one of the first things he did was to collect information about its chief art objects, in order to demand them in case of victory, for it was by treaty that they were usually obtained. Among the works of art which Napoleon sent to Paris were twenty-five Raphaels, twenty-three Titians, fifty-three Rubenses, thirty-three Van Dykes, thirty-one Rembrandts.

NAPOLEON'S STAR.

In Italy rose Napoleon's "star," that mysterious guide which he followed from

---

the Northern Courts, which had renewed the armed neutrality of 1780. At Copenhagen he engaged the Danish. His victory was not complete, but it broke up the league and won him the title of viscount. On the renewal of war between France and England in 1803, Nelson went to the Mediterranean, where for two years he kept the French shut in port at Toulon, while Napoleon was preparing for the invasion of England at Boulogne. In March, 1805, the French Admiral Villeneuve escaped. Nelson sought him in the Mediterranean, chased him across the Atlantic and back again, and finally, in September, 1805, found him at Cadiz. In October the French were forced to battle off Cape Trafalgar, where Nelson won a glorious victory, though at the cost of his life. His remains were conveyed to England, and interred in St. Paul's Cathedral on January 9, 1806.

NAPOLEON BONAPARTE.

"LUCIEN BONAPARTE, PRESIDENT OF THE COUNCIL OF THE FIVE HUNDRED, 18TH BRUMAIRE, 1799."

Lucien Bonaparte, born at Ajaccio, March 21, 1775, was educated in France, and returned to Corsica in 1792. Ardent revolutionist, he abandoned Paoli, and left Corsica for France. Obtaining a place at Saint Maximin, he became prominent as an agitator. Here he married Christine Boyer, his landlord's daughter. In 1793 Lucien left St. Maximin and soon after was made commissary to the army of the North, but resigned the next year. The two years following he passed in Corsica, but went to Paris in 1798, on being elected deputy to the Council of Five Hundred. He soon became prominent as a speaker, and his house was a centre for the best literary society of the capital. He was made president of the Council of Five Hundred after Napoleon's return from Egypt, and aided in the *coup d'état* of the 18th Brumaire. In the reorganization of the government Lucien was named Minister of the Interior, but he and Napoleon did not get on well, and he was sent as ambassador to Spain. Returning, he took an active part in the delicate work of the Concordat and Legion of Honor. Lucien was made senator after the consulate for life was arranged, but he made a second marriage which displeased Napoleon. He left France, settling in Rome,

NAPOLEON CROSSING THE GREAT ST. BERNARD, 1800.

Engraved by François, after a picture by Delaroche, painted in 1848, published in 1850 by F. & D. Colnaghi & co., London. "The Queen of England possesses at Osborne a reduction of this portrait made by Delaroche himself."

rather than give up his wife. Napoleon made overtures to him later, but they were refused, and he was ordered to quit the continent. He wished to go to the United States, but was captured in 1810 by an English cruiser, and taken to England, where for a time he was a prisoner. In 1814 he returned to Rome. While Napoleon was at Elba, Lucien offered him his support, and during the Hundred Days he sat in the French Chamber of Peers. After Waterloo he advised Napoleon to dissolve the Assembly and proclaim himself dictator, and it was he who suggested that the second abdication be made in favor of Napoleon's son. He parted with his brother June 29, and left France. At Turin he was arrested and kept prisoner for three months. When liberated he settled in Rome with his family, where he passed the rest of his life in literary and antiquarian labors. He died June 29, 1840. Lucien Bonaparte did some creditable literary work, including an epic poem on *Charlemagne*, studies in Etruscan vases, and most valuable, his historical *Memoires*.

Lodi to Waterloo. Here was born that faith in himself and his future, that belief that he "marched under the protection of the goddess of fortune and of war," that confidence that he was endowed with a "good genius."

He called Lodi the birthplace of this faith.

"Vendémiaire and even Montenotte did not make me believe myself a superior man. It was only after Lodi that it came into my head that I could become a decisive actor on our political field. Then was born the first spark of high ambition."

Trained in a religion full of mysticism, taught to believe in signs, guided by a "star," there is a tinge of superstition throughout his active, practical, hard-working life. Marmont tells that one day while in Italy the glass over the portrait of his wife, which he always wore, was broken. "He turned frightfully pale, and the impression upon him was most sorrowful, 'Marmont,' he said, 'my wife is very ill or she is unfaithful.'" There are many similar anecdotes to show his dependence upon and confidence in omens.

LOVE IN WAR.

In a campaign of such achievements as that in Italy there seems to be no time for love, and yet love was never more imperative, more absorbing, in Napoleon's life than during this period.

"Oh, my adorable wife," he wrote Josephine in April. "I do not know what fate awaits me, but if it keeps me longer from you, I shall not be able to endure it; my courage will not hold out to that point. There was a time when I was proud of my courage; and when I thought of the harm that men might do me, of the lot that my destiny might reserve for me, I looked at the most terrible misfortunes without a quiver, with no surprise. But now, the thought that my Josephine may be in trouble, that she may be ill, and, above all, the cruel, fatal thought that she may love me less, inflicts torture in my soul, stops the beating of my heart, makes me sad and dejected, robs me of even the courage of fury and despair. I often used to say, Man can do no harm to me who is willing to die; but now, to die without being loved by you, to die without this certainty, is the torture of hell; it is the vivid and crushing image of total annihilation. It seems to me as if I were choking. My only companion, you who have been chosen by fate to make with me the painful journey of life, the day when I shall no longer possess your heart will be that when for me the world shall have lost all warmth and all its vegetation. . . . I will stop, my sweet pet, my soul is sad. I am very tired, my mind is worn out, I am sick of men. I have good reason for hating them. They separate me from my love."

Josephine was indifferent to this strong passion. "How queer Bonaparte is!" she said coldly at the evidences of his affection which he poured upon her; and when, after a few weeks' separation, he began to implore her to join him, she hesitated, made excuses, tried in every possible way to evade his wish. It was not strange that a woman of her indolent nature, loving flattery, having no passion but for amusement, reckless expenditure, and her own ease, should prefer life in Paris. There she shared with Madame Tallien the adoration which the Parisian world is always bestowing on some fair woman. At opera and ball she was the centre of attraction; even in the street the people knew her. *Notre Dame des Victoires* was the name they gave her.

In desperation at her indifference, Napoleon finally wrote her, in June, from Tortona:

"My life is a perpetual nightmare. A black presentiment makes breathing difficult. I am no longer alive; I have lost more than life, more than happiness, more than peace; I am almost without hope. I am sending you a courier. He will stay only four hours in Paris, and then will bring me your answer. Write to me ten pages; that is the only thing that can console me in the least. You are ill; you love me; I have distressed you; you are with child; and I do not see you. . . . I have treated you so ill that I do not know how to set myself right in your eyes. I have been blaming you for staying in Paris, and you have been ill there. Forgive me, my dear; the love with which you have filled me has robbed me of my reason, and I shall never recover it. It is a malady from which there is no recovery. My forebodings are so gloomy that all I ask is to see you, to hold you in my arms for two hours, and that we may die together. Who is taking care of you? I suppose that you have sent for Hortense; I love the dear child a thousand times better since I think that she may console you a little. As for me, I am without consolation, rest, and hope until I see again the messenger whom I am sending to you, and until you explain to me in a long letter just what is the matter with you, and how serious it is. If there were any danger I warn you that I should start at once for Paris. . . . You! you!—and the rest of the world will not exist for me any more than if it had been annihilated. I care for honor because you care for it; for victory, because it brings you pleasure; otherwise, I should abandon everything to throw myself at your feet."

After this letter Josephine consented to go to Italy, but she left Paris weeping as if going to her execution. Once at Milan, where she held almost a court, she recovered her gayety, and the two were very happy for a time. But it did not last. Napoleon, obliged to be on the march, would implore Josephine to come to him here and there, and once she narrowly escaped with her life when trying to get away from the army.

Wherever she was installed she had a circle of adorers about her, and as a result she neglected writing to her husband. Reproaches and entreaties filled his letters. He begs her for only a line, and he implores her that she be less cold.

"Your letters are as cold as fifty years of age: one would think they had been written after we had been married fifteen years. They are full of the friendliness and feelings of life's winter . . . What more can you do to distress me? Stop loving me? That you have already done. Hate me? Well, I wish you would; everything degrades me except hatred; but indifference, with a calm pulse, fixed eyes, monotonous walk! . . . A thousand kisses, tender, like my heart."

It was not merely indolence and indifference that caused Josephine's neglect. It was coquetry frequently, and Napoleon, informed by his couriers as to whom she received at Milan or Genoa, and of the pleasures she enjoyed, was jealous with all the force of his nature. More than one young officer who dared pay homage to Josephine in this campaign was banished "by order of the commander-in-chief." Reaching Milan once, unexpectedly, he found her gone. His disappointment was bitter.

"I reached Milan, rushed to your rooms, having thrown up everything to see you, to press you to my heart—you were not there; you are traveling about from one town to another, amusing yourself with balls. . . . My unhappiness is inconceivable. . . . Don't put yourself out; pursue your pleasure; happiness is made for you."

It was between such extremes of triumphant love and black despair that Napoleon lived throughout the Italian campaign.

RETURN TO PARIS.

In December, 1797, he returned to Paris. His whole family were collected there,

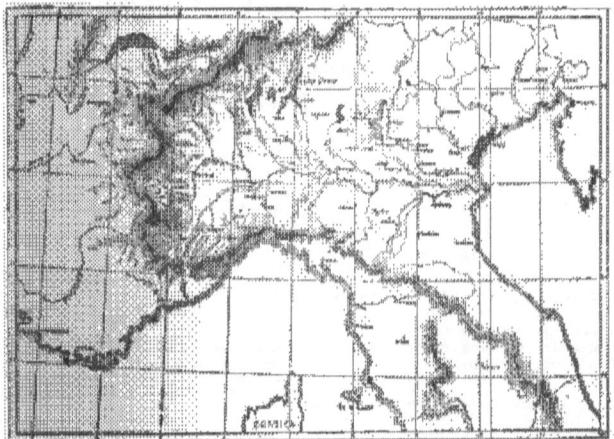

MAP OF NORTHERN ITALY, ILLUSTRATING THE NAPOLEON CAMPAIGNS OF 1796-1800—REPRODUCED, BY PERMISSION OF G. P. PUTNAM'S SONS, FROM SLOANE'S LIFE OF NAPOLEON, IN THE "HEROES OF THE NATIONS" SERIES.

forming a "Bonaparte colony," as the Parisians called it. There were Joseph and his wife; Lucien, now married to Christine Boyer, his old landlord's daughter, a marriage Napoleon never forgave; Eliza, now Madame Bacciochi; Pauline, now Madame Leclerc. Madame Letitia was in the city, with Caroline; Louis and Jerome were still in school. Josephine had her daughter Hortense, a girl of thirteen, with her. Her son Eugene, though but fifteen years old, was away on a mission for Napoleon, who, in spite of the boy's youth, had already taken him into his confidence. According to Napoleon's express desire, all the family lived in great simplicity.

The return to Paris of the commander-in-chief of the Army of Italy was the signal for a popular ovation. The Directory gave him every honor, changing the name of the street in which he lived to *rue de la Victoire*, and making him a member of the Institute; but, conscious of its feebleness, and inspired by that suspicion which since the revolution began had caused the ruin of so many men, planned to get rid of him.

Of the coalition against France, formed in 1793, one member alone remained in arms—England. Napoleon was to be sent against her. An invasion of the island was first discussed, and he made an examination of the north coast. His report was adverse, and he substituted a plan for the invasion of Egypt—an old idea in the French Government.

The Directory gladly accepted the change, and Napoleon was made commander-in-chief of the Army of Egypt. On the 4th of May he left Paris for Toulon.

To Napoleon this expedition was a merciful escape. He once said to Madame Rémusat:

"In Paris, and Paris is France, they never can take the smallest interest in things, if they do not take it in persons. . . . The great difficulty of the Directory was that no one cared about them, and that people began to care too much about me. This was why I conceived the happy idea of going to Egypt."

He was under the influence, too, of his imagination; the Orient had always tempted him. It is certain that he went away with gigantic projects—nothing less than to conquer the whole of the East, and to become its ruler and lawgiver.

"I dreamed of all sorts of things, and I saw a way of carrying all my projects into practical execution. I would create a new religion. I saw myself in Asia, upon an elephant, wearing a turban, and holding in my hand a new Koran which I had myself composed. I would have united in my enterprise the experiences of two hemispheres, exploring for my benefit and instruction all history, attacking the power of England in the Indies, and renewing, by their conquest, my relations with old Europe. The time I passed in Egypt was the most delightful period of my life, for it was the most ideal."

His friends, watching his irritation during the days before the campaign had been decided upon, said: "A free flight in space is what such wings demand. He will die here. He must go." He himself said; "Paris weighs on me like a leaden mantle."

EXPEDITION IN EGYPT, 1798-1799.

Napoleon sailed from France on May 19, 1798; on June 9th he reached Malta, and won for France "the strongest place in Europe." July 2d he entered Alexandria. On July 24th he was in Cairo, after the famous Battle of the Pyramids.

The French fleet had remained in Aboukir Bay after landing the army, and on August 1st was attacked by Nelson. Napoleon had not realized, before this battle, the power of the English on the sea. He knew nothing of Nelson's genius. The destruction of his fleet, and the consciousness that he and his army were prisoners in the Orient, opened his eyes to the greatest weakness of France.

The winter was spent in reorganizing the government of Egypt and in scientific work. Over one hundred scientists had been added to the Army of Egypt, including some of the most eminent men of the day: Monge, Geoffroy-St.-Hilaire, Berthollet, Fourier and Denon. From their arrival every opportunity was given them to carry on their work. To stimulate them, Napoleon founded the Institute of Egypt, in which membership was granted as a reward for services.

These scientists went out in every direction, pushing their investigations up the Nile as far as Philœ, tracing the bed of the old canal from Suez to the Nile, unearthing ancient monuments, making collections of the flora and fauna, examining in detail the arts and industries of the people. Everything, from the inscription on the Rosetta Stone to the incubation of chickens, received their attention.

On the return of the expedition, their researches were published in a magnificent work called " Description de l'Egypte."

The information gathered by the French at this time gave a great impetus to the study of Egyptology, and their investigations on the old Suez canal led directly to the modern work.

The peaceful work of science and law-giving which Napoleon was conducting in Egypt was interrupted by the news that the Porte had declared war against France, and that two Turkish armies were on their way to Egypt. In February he set off to Syria to meet the first.

This Syrian expedition was a failure, ending in a retreat made horrible not only by the enemy in the rear but by pestilence and heat.

The disaster was a terrible disillusion for Napoleon. It ended his dream of an Oriental realm for himself, of a kingdom embracing the whole Mediterranean for France. "I missed my fortune at St. Jean d'Acre," he told his brother Lucien afterward; and again, "I think my imagination died at St. Jean d'Acre." The words are those of the man whose discouragement at a failure was as profound as his hope at success was high.

As Napoleon entered Egypt from Syria, he learned that the second Turkish army was near the Bay of Aboukir. He turned against it and defeated it completely. In the exchange of prisoners made after the battle, a bundle of French papers fell into his hands. It was the first news he had had for ten months from France, and sad news it was: Italy lost, an invasion of Austrians and Russians threatening, the Directory discredited and tottering.

If the Oriental empire of his imagination had fallen, might it not be that in Europe a kingdom awaited him? He decided to leave Egypt at once, and with the greatest secrecy prepared for his departure. The army was turned over to Kléber, and with four small vessels he sailed for France on the night of August 22, 1799. On October 16th he was in Paris.

THE 18TH BRUMAIRE.

For a long time nothing had been heard of Napoleon in France. The people said he had been exiled by the jealous Directory. His disappearance into the Orient had all the mystery and fascination of an Eastern tale. His sudden reappearance had something of the heroic in it. He came like a god from Olympus, unheralded, but at the critical instant.

The joy of the people, who at that day certainly preferred a hero to suffrage, was spontaneous and sincere. His journey from the coast to Paris was a triumphal march. *Le retour du héros* was the word in everybody's mouth. On every side the people cried: "You alone can save the country. It is perishing without you. Take the reins of government."

At Paris he found the government waiting to be overthrown. "A brain and a sword" was all that was needed to carry out a *coup d'état* organized while he was still in Africa. Everybody recognized him as the man for the hour. A large part of the military force in Paris was devoted to him. His two brothers, Lucien and Joseph, were in positions of influence, the former president of the *cinq-cents*, as one of the two chambers was called. All that was most distinguished in the political, military, legal, and artistic circles of Paris rallied to him. Among the men who supported him were Talleyrand, Sieyès, Chénier, Roederer, Monge, Cambacérès, Moreau, Berthier, Murat.

On the 18th Brumaire, the 9th of November, 1799, the plot culminated, and Napoleon was recognized as the temporary dictator of France.

NAPOLEON AND JOSEPHINE.

The private sorrow to which Napoleon returned was as great as the public glory. During the campaign in Egypt he had learned beyond a doubt that Josephine's coquetry had become open folly, and that a young officer, Hippolyte Charles, whom he had dismissed from the Army of Italy two years before, was installed at Malmaison. The *liaison* was so scandalous that Gohier, the president of the Directory, advised Josephine to get a divorce from Napoleon and marry Charles.

These rumors reached Egypt, and Napoleon, in despair, even talked them over with Eugène de Beauharnais. The boy defended his mother, and for a time succeeded in quieting Napoleon's resentment. At last, however, he learned in a talk with Junot that the gossip was true. He lost all control of himself, and declared he would have a divorce. The idea was abandoned, but the love and reverence he had given Josephine were dead. From that time she had no empire over his heart, no power to inspire him to action or to enthusiasm.

When he landed in France from Egypt, Josephine, foreseeing a storm, started out to meet him at Lyons. Unfortunately she took one road and Napoleon another, and when he reached Paris at six o'clock in the morning he found no one at home. When Josephine arrived Napoleon refused to see her, and it was three days before he relented. Then his forgiveness was due to the intercession of Hortense and Eugène, to both of whom he was warmly attached.

But if he consented to pardon he could never give again the passionate affection which he once had felt for her. He ceased to be a lover, and became a commonplace, tolerant, indulgent, bourgeois husband, upon whom his wife, in matters of importance, had no influence. Josephine was hereafter the suppliant, but she never regained the noble kingdom she had despised.

RETURN OF PEACE.

Napoleon's domestic sorrow weakened in no way his activity and vigor in public affairs.

He realized that, if he would keep his place in the hearts and confidence of the people, he must do something to show his strength, and peace was the gift he proposed to make to the nation.

When he returned he found a civil war raging in La Vendée. Before February he had ended it. All over France brigandage had made life and property uncertain. His new régime ended it.

Two foreign enemies only remained at war with France—Austria and England. He offered them peace. It was refused. Nothing remained but to compel it. The Austrians were first engaged. They had two armies in the field, one on the Rhine, against which Moreau was sent, the other in Italy—now lost to France—besieging the French shut up in Genoa.

Moreau conducted the campaign in the Rhine countries with skill, fighting two successful battles, and driving his opponent from Ulm.

Napoleon decided that he would himself carry on the Italian campaign, but of that he said nothing in Paris. His army was quietly brought together as a reserve force; then suddenly, on May 6, 1800, he left Paris for Geneva. Immediately his plan became evident. It was nothing else than to cross the Alps and fall upon the rear of the Austrians, then besieging Genoa. Such an undertaking was a veritable *coup de théâtre*. Its accomplishment was not less brilliant than its conception. Three principal passes lead from Switzerland into Italy; Mont Cenis, the Great Saint Bernard, and the Mount Saint Gothard. The last was already held by the Austrians. The first is the westernmost, and here Napoleon directed the attention of General Melas, the Austrian commander. The central, or Mount Saint Bernard, Pass was left almost defenceless, and here the army was led across a passage surrounded by enormous difficulties, particularly for the artillery, which had to be taken to pieces and carried or dragged by the men.

Save the delay which the enemy caused the French at Fort Bard, where five hundred men stopped the entire army, Napoleon met with no serious resistance in entering Italy. Indeed, the Austrians treated the force with contempt, declaring that it was not the First Consul who led them, but an adventurer, and that the army was not made up of French, but of refugee Italians. This rumor was soon known to be false. On June 2d Napoleon entered Milan. The Austrians soon after advanced into the plains of Marengo, where, on June 14th, the battle was fought. The story of the battle is described in a picturesque narrative by a member of the army, which will appear in the next number of this magazine.

The Parisians were dazzled by the campaign. Of the passage of the Alps they said, "It is an achievement greater than Hannibal's;" and they repeated how "the First Consul pointed his finger at the frozen summits, and they bowed their heads."

At the news of Marengo the streets were lit with "joy fires," and from wall to wall rang the cries of *Vive la république*, *Vive le premier consul*, *Vive l'armée*.

The campaign against the Austrians was finished December 3, 1800, by the battle of Hohenlinden, and in February the treaty of Lunéville established peace. England was slower in coming to terms, it not being until March, 1802, that she signed the treaty of Amiens.

At last France was at peace with all the world. She hailed Napoleon as her savior, and ordered that the 18th Brumaire be celebrated throughout the republic as a solemn fête in his honor.

The country saw in him something greater than a peacemaker. She was discovering that he was to be her lawgiver, for, while ending the wars, he had begun to bring order into the interior chaos which had so long tormented the French people, to reëstablish the finances, the laws, the industries, even to harmonize the interests of rich and poor, of church and state. To Napoleon's work as a statesman and lawgiver, the next article in this series will be devoted.

NOTE. This Life of Napoleon began in the November number, and will continue through four numbers more. There will be seventy-five portraits of Napoleon in the series, and one hundred other pictures. Chosen as these pictures are from the collection of the Hon. Gardiner G. Hubbard, one of the richest Napoleon collections in existence, too much can scarcely be said in their praise.

DIKKON'S DOG.*

BY DOROTHY LUNDT.

THE distinguishing trait of Grubbins was his unexpectedness. Grubbins was Dikkon's dog.

All the cats in the old regiment could have told you that the time it was least safe to try to slip by Grubbins was when he sat gazing across the plains, apparently oblivious of everything on earth but the progress of a mule-train just fading off the distant horizon. The young and untaught kitten who attempted, at such times, to glide, with shadow-like swiftness and silence, behind Grubbins's meditative back, had a never-to-be-forgotten vision of lanky yellow legs lengthening themselves in a leap, bristling yellow hair, and glaring yellow eyes; and if that kitten got off with the loss of his ear or two-thirds of his tail, he was congratulated by his more experienced fellows.

Private McAllison was new to the old regiment, which explains his premature assumption that Grubbins was too soundly asleep to resent his tail being stepped on by a friend hastily crossing the barrack-room, or to identify that friend for purposes of reprisal. McAllison was in his stocking-feet; so that his howls, when Grubbins's teeth met through the end of his heel, were louder than they otherwise might have been. Private Mooney, his neighbor of the right-hand cot, gave up in disgust his latest attempt to get sufficiently sound asleep to forget the dismal downpour that was making out-door life impossible, and casting an untimely chill over the twilight of Christmas Eve.

"Hould up yer yellin', can't ye, ye Scotch omadahn?" said Private Mooney. "Shure it's only Grubbins's way!"

"Ma certie! It's a way wull lead Maister Grubbins to the grave that's too lang been awaitin' him; if not by meelitary execution by the Colonel's orders, then by preevate assassination!" Thus McAllison, with the polysyllabic solemnity of his nation, nursing his wounded heel, and glaring at Grubbins, who had tranquilly returned to his interrupted slumbers.

"I reckon Grubbins's grave ain't dug yet, nor the man ain't born that 'll send him to it; not while my name's Dikkon! Grubbins, ain't that so, honey?"

The gaunt yellow dog was alert and on his feet at the first syllable of his name spoken in his master's voice. He shambled heavy-footedly across to the bench where Dikkon sat, just in from a bit of fatigue duty at the stables, toasting his soaked and odorous cowhide boots at the low fire in the barrack-room stove. Grubbins laid his rough, grizzled muzzle on his master's knee, and Dikkon's brown and knotted hand fell affectionately on the dog's head. The two sat looking at each other with a look of perfect understanding and full companionship. As they sat thus, there was a curious likeness between man and dog. Dikkon's close-cropped hair was of the same dusty yellow as Grubbins's scraggy coat; chronic malaria and long exposure to every weather had brought Dikkon's complexion to much the same hue that was Grubbins's by birthright; the faded eyes of the man had an expression oddly akin to that which from the dog's eyes looked up at him—a latent gleam through a mist as of habitual drowsy apathy.

"Thet's so; ain't it, honey?" drawled Dikkon again; and Grubbins rapped his stumpy tail in fervent affirmation. "'Pears to me yo' haven't took 's much exercise as common to-day, Grubbins," went on his master. "Don't yo' feel like racin' down a cat or s'uthin', so 's to get up a moughty good appetite fer yer Christmas grub?"

The men chuckled. The idea of Grubbins's appetite requiring a tonic was a deeply humorous one. Dikkon opened the door, and Grubbins, with a short, approving sniff of the freshening air, trotted loose-leggedly across the soaked parade.

"Shure it's an appetite we'll ahl be needin' for our Chrismas grub," said Private Mooney, stretching his brawny arms with a cavernous yawn. "The mule-thrain's over due, and divil a thing for Christmas Day but bull-beef an' hard-tack, wid likely a redshkin bullet for sauce wid it!"

"Redskin bullet! Bosh! In midwinter!" Thus Corporal Perkins, newly from the Northwest.

* This story, in the McClure prize story contest, closed some months ago, was awarded the prize of one hundred and fifty dollars, the third of the five prizes offered. The author lives in Boston, Massachusetts.

"Corporal, me joy, it's forgettin' ye are that down in this suburb av Tophet there's niver a winter at ahl, and the redshkins dishport thimsilves as loively at Chris-tmas as on the sacred Fourth o' July! Shure I niver pass that clump o' brush beyant the ould shtables on a black night—an' it's black nights a-plinty we have, as see the wan that's a-shuttin' down like a box-lid this blissid minnit—widout falin' me schalp-lock a-wigglin' wid spirituous terrors!"

"But the sentries?"

"Faith, it's happined before that the divil led his own by ways onseen o' the right-eous—manio' Uncle Sam's senthries, that last—an' he'll do ut agin! I say agin, a redshkin bullet's the Christmas prisint likeliest to come the way av us poor sinners."

"Dikkon, ma lad!" Thus McAllison, stopping by Dikkon's bench to put on his rough overcoat, his injured heel well greased, and his Scotch equanimity apparently restored. "I've nae ill-will tae the bit beastie, an' forbye he but defendit the richts o' his ain tail. But I'll gie ye a hint for a Christmas gift; it was the Colonel himself was sayin' but the nicht's nicht, that the next complaint of Dikkon's dog that came tae his ears, the beastie wad hae a bullet an' a ditch, an' nae mair said!"

Dikkon sprang to his feet. A dull flush kindled under his yellow skin; the gleam in his faded eyes shone keen through their dulled indifference.

"He will, will he?" There was a savage snarl in the man's voice. "An' what mought *he* be, that's been with the old regiment only six months, an' not half the use to it then or now that my old dog——"

"Hold hard, Dikkon!" "Whisht, me boy! It's the short cut to the guard-house you're takin'!" There were grunts and exclamations of remonstrance on every side. Dikkon looked about him with a sort of bewilderment. The momentary flush and gleam were gone. He sat down again, quietly enough, and put out his feet to the fire.

"Bedad, the Colonel's bark is a dale worse nor his bite, we ahl know!" Thus Mooney, pacifically. "It's only whin his pepper-pot av a timper gits a rough shake, that he's onsafe to play wid. An' Grubbins *is* tryin' at times, his bist frinds know. Take ut lasht shpring, whin the Colonel paid the saints know what ahl for thim seeds from the North, an' whin they was comin' up umbrageous, in sails Grubbins, scoutin' afther a last year's bone he'd mis-rimimbered where he'd buried, an' in tin minnits the Colonel's vigitible garden was ploughed up more complate than the field before wan av our batteries at Chatta-nooga, four years back."

"But that didn't rile him for coppers with Grubbins's gobblin' up little Miss Marion's taffy." Thus Corporal Perkins, picking up his cap, in the general exodus toward the parade. The rain had stopped for a moment. A wild wind was angrily driving the clouds in frightened masses before it; the freshness of the outside world was good to feel, after the stuffy and smoky atmosphere of the barrack-room. "Miss Marion she's the apple o' the Colonel's eye an' the light of it; an' I pity dog or man that sets her cryin' many times as she cried the other day when Grubbins caught on to her taffy the cook had set out to cool, an'——"

"There they go now! See 'em?" Thus one of the men at the window. There was a general turning of heads.

"Faith, it's shmall blame to the Colonel," —from Mooney—"for it's a sunbame little Miss Marion carries in the eyes of her an' the heart of her; an' she kindled it from the wan that wint away wid her mother whin they laid her, an' the ould Colonel's heart wid her, in her grave a year gone!"

And indeed three-year-old Miss Marion was a winsome sight to see, as in her wee blue-hooded rain-cloak, a golden-haired kobold, she danced across the parade by her soldierly grandfather's side, smiling up confidingly in the face that never was stern for her, and leading tenderly, by a ribbon as blue as her rain-cloak or her eyes, a tiny terrier, also blue-blanketed, and mincingly remonstrant at the wet grass that brushed his dainty paws. The men approved of Miss Marion, but the terrier was not regarded with favor in barracks. "For whin I want a dog, I want a *dog*," said Private Mooney, voicing the general sentiment. "An' whin I want a ladylike rat, I don't want him pritindin' to *be* a dog, an' izpictin' to be rispected accordin'!"

The men were making their way out for a whiff of fresh air before retreat should sound. Dikkon alone had not left his place by the fire. As Mooney, last of the men, was opening the rough door, he was arrested by Dikkon's voice, sounding musingly, and as if unconscious that he spoke aloud.

"It's a moughty queer world," Dikkon said, "where an old yaller dog will stand to one man for what a pretty little baby does to another!"

DIKKON'S BROWN AND KNOTTED HAND FELL AFFECTIONATELY ON THE DOG'S HEAD.

With an Irishman's involuntary sympathy for a guessed sorrow, and an Irishman's quick appreciation of a chance to gratify a long-baffled curiosity, Mooney soundlessly closed the door, threw down his cap, and crossed toward an empty chair. After a pause:

"Manin' yersilf an' the Colonel?" said he.

"Meanin' just that. Ol' Grubbins is about as much to me, I reckon, as little Miss Marion you is to the ol' Colonel. Fer th' same reason. All that's left to me o' somethin' I loved."

Mooney stuffed the tobacco deep into his pipe, and diplomatically waited. There was a momentary break in the heavy clouds, and a late, pale yellow light shone tremulously through.

"I reckon I never told ye how I met up with Grubbins? I was in the Tennessee mountings, when we wor down there with Grant. That was in '64, years back, when I wor a volunteer. Nigh where we wor camped there wor a cabin. A girl lived thar, all alone. Her dad an' five brothers had gone into the Union army, and they never come back. Her name wor Marcella. She had right pretty blue eyes, an' a cough. I punched a man oncet for tryin' to make free with her, an' Grubbins chawed him up afterwards. Grubbins wor her dog; a five-year-old, then, an' 's ornery 's he is now. We got to be right good friends, she 'n I; afterwards, more. I hadn't nary a red but my pay; no more she. But I promised ter kem back an' marry her oncet the fightin' wor over."

Both men smoked for a time in silence.

"'Twas in May, '65, I got back there. It was a moughty purty day, with clouds like gold. The cabin do' was tight shet. An' the windows. Ez I kem up I heerd Gruhbins howl. Reckon ye never heerd a yaller dog howl?

"The neighbors hed jest took care o' her an' left her, an' gone back ter get the coffin. She had changed considerable—thin as a shadder. She hed wound grass round my ring to keep it on her finger—it wor a hoss-hair ring. I braided it from my hoss's tail.

"I stayed for the fun'ral. Grubbins an' I sot by her all day an' all night. When the grave wor filled in, Grubbins he turned an' reached up his big yaller paw ter me, an' his eyes said, 'Reckon it's we two now, ol' man?' An' I shuk his paw, an' I says, 'Yes, Grubbins, 's long as we both live.' An' when I 'listed ez a reg'lar, Grubbins 'listed 'long o' me."

"An' wid ahl his eccsyncrasities, Grubbins is a cridit to the ould rigimint!"—there was a sympathetic choke in Mooney's voice, "An'—saints be good! Phwat's that?"

It was a wild commotion on the parade ground. There were growls and snarls and doleful squeals; rushing footsteps, thwacking blows, a child's sobs, a stern and angry voice. "Take that dog away, and—" a short, enraged howl in Grubbins's unmistakable accents.

Dikkon and Mooney were in the middle of the parade. In little Maid Marion's arms, pressed close to her tear-stained face, was a squealing huddle of very muddy blue blanket, with a pathetic pink stain oozing out here and there. Grubbins, his yellow eyes afire, a stout cord round his neck, was in the grasp of a soldier who was vainly trying to combine holding the dog with a respectful salute to his colonel. The Colonel's face was gray with rage; his eyes blazed under their shaggy brows. Through the sudden silence, Marion's sobs came piteously clear.

"Take away that nasty beast—do you hear?" Thus the Colonel, tensely, between his teeth. "I've overlooked his tricks hitherto, because his master is an old soldier and a good one. But when it comes to killing my granddaughter's pet on the open parade——"

"Shure the little baste isn't dead at ahl, sorr!" Mooney had gently taken the small blue bundle, separated chewed-up blanket from chewed-up dog, and held the squealing terrier out with one hand, the other at salute; his eyes clouded and anxious. "He's just dis disfraeshured a bit, in shpots, sorr, but a shtrip or two o' plashter 'll make him as good as iver he was, sorr,—an' that's no good at ahl!" jerked Mooney, confidentially, back from his teeth to his throat. "An' Grubbins mint no harm, sorr. He'd niver sane the loike before, an' was just investigatin', an' when he found it wad bite——"

"Hold your tongue, Mooney!" thundered the Colonel, recovering the breath that the Irishman's unparalleled audacity had taken away. "Take charge of that dog!" Mooney mechanically took from the soldier the leash at whose other end Grubbins was wildly straining to reach his master. "He has done his last mischief. You will have him hanged within an hour. Not a word, I tell you!" as Mooney's lips opened in a gasp. "Come, sweetheart." The stern and angry voice fell to a caressing whisper; the Colonel lifted Marion, dog and all, and set her on his stalwart arm. "Hush, hush, dear! The bad dog shan't hurt little Fido any more. Come home, baby; come and find Christmas." As he turned, he stopped abruptly. Dikkon stood squarely facing him. The man's sallow face was dully purple with passion; his eyes gleamed tigerishly. "Take back that order, Colonel," he raved. "Give me back my old dog! Give him back, I tell you! or I'll——"

"Arrest that man!" Dikkon was in the grasp of a dozen ready hands. There was that in his eyes, as they turned on the Colonel, that had sent the men's hearts to their throats. "Clap him in the guard-house. He's probably drunk or mad. The court-martial can decide which."

The Colonel turned on his heel and strode

"TAKE AWAY THAT NASTY BEAST—DO YOU HEAR?"

off through the blackening twilight with the frightened child on his breast. As he went, there followed him the howls of a half-choked dog, as Grubbins was dragged in one direction, powerless to reach the master who was being marched off in the other.

The Colonel was in what his sister and housekeeper called a most un-Christmas-like temper throughout his dinner. "Confound the fellow!" he muttered, pacing restlessly to and fro, when dinner was done. "Why need he have given me that madman's talk? Mooney would have found a way to keep the beast safe till the men could send in a petition, and—then—of course—it being Christmas, and all—" He looked abstractedly out into the inky darkness. "Dear, dear! I believe I'm half a madman myself when Marion comes into a question. More than ever, since there have been those Apache rumors. I can't leave to carry the child North; and if, while she was here, the Indians—" he put up his hand to his forehead, suddenly damp with the starting sweat.

There rang out through the windy darkness the long-drawn howl of a dog, followed by a sharp, sudden shot, and another and another; shouts, wandering lights.

"What is that? Martha, bar the doors and windows," shouted the Colonel, hoarsely. He caught up his sword and buckled it as he ran.

Mooney had come to kindle the smoky lamp in the guard-house cell. The figure lying face downward in the bunk had stirred at sound of his heavy footsteps, and turned toward him a bloodless face, and eyes of dumb, agonized entreaty. "Shure I wud if I cud, ye poor sowl!" said Mooney; yet Dikkon had spoken no word. "It isn't to let him live. I heard the Colonel's orders. God send him such torment as he's sent me! But, Mooney, Grubbins is a soldier's dog. Yo' won't *hang* him? Oh, for the love o' God, for the sake of Christmas, *say* yo' won't *hang* him! Yo'll give him a bullet?"

Mooney gripped his hand with a firm, quick nod.

"I'm in fo' a term in the military prison, sho'. Grubbins is gittin' older every day, an' he'd be onery, missin' me, an' likely to git kicked 'round, 'mong the men. He mought as well go befo' I do. But—yo're a good shot, Mooney, but yo'll stand close, an' not let him need but one bullet?"

Another nod. Mooney shut the door softly, and went out into the dark. Left alone, Dikkon threw himself down again in his bunk, his face hidden in his arms.

"I'd like to say good-by to yo', Grubbins." The man was sobbing, thickly, dryly, without tears. "I'd have liked to ask yo' to a' told Marcella——"

The long-drawn howl that the Colonel had heard at his window, came to Dikkon's ears as he lay in the guard-house bunk. At the shot that sharply followed, the man sat upright, his face gray. "He's gone! The old dog's gone!"

Another shot.

Dikkon leaped up as they say men leap who take a bullet in the heart.

"Mooney! Yo' crazy blunderer! Yo' had to shoot *again!* Oh, my God! O Grubbins! *Grubbins?*"

He flung himself face downward on the floor. He ran his fingers hard into his ears. So he lay, half-unconscious, agonized, hearing nothing more.

The Colonel stood just without the door of the stables, all the men of the little garrison around and before him. At his feet, across the threshold, lay the body of an Indian, the face taking ghastly cleansing of its war-paint from the thin stream of blood that trickled from its temple. Three other Indians, bound hand and foot, crouched sullenly in the midst of their guard. A trooper was, with many half-choked grunts of discomfort, examining his shattered knee. The faint, far echo of galloping ponies was dying away, through the wind, over the plain.

"Let me understand this," said the Colonel. He spoke somewhat unsteadily. He was looking down at the dead Indian, at whose belt there dangled a child's scalp. It could not have been taken many months ago. The child had had golden hair.

Corporal Perkins stepped forward, saluting. "It was like this, sir. The half-breeds had probably told them Christmas was a good time to attack, the men being jolly, and careless-like. They must have crept up through the brush behind the stables. There was a board loose at the back o' the stables; this fellow"—he indicated the dead Indian—"crept through it. Their scheme was to stampede the horses first, so there'd be no way of escape. It'd ha' worked well if——"

"Well?"

"If Grubbins——"

"*Grubbins?*"

"Yis, sorr!"—it was Mooney, now, standing sheepish, at the salute. "Yer orders was to hang the dog in an hour, sorr; but when the min was a-thrimmin' the barrick-room clock wid Christmas grane, sorr, they shtopped it intoirely, sorr, an'——"

"Grubbins was in the stables? The dog gave the alarm?"

"Yis, sorr. An' he hild this divil past mischief, sorr, till the senthry——"

"Where is the dog?"

"Shure he's waitin' his doom, sorr, like his mashter in the guard-house beyant. It's quare they're both in thrimble together"—Mooney was apparently addressing the universe in general, since he never would have ventured such discourse to his

HE FLUNG HIMSELF FACE DOWNWARD ON THE FLOOR.

colonel—"for says Dikkon to me, this afthernoon, says he, 'Grubbins is to me,' says he, 'what the shwate little lady up yonder is to the Colonel,' says he—an' little did he think that but for Grubbins, this night, them divils that's gallopin' away yon might ha' been—this blissid minnit——'.

Apparently by accident, Mooney's foot touched the golden hair that fluttered from the dead Indian's belt.

"Release Dikkon!" said the Colonel, briefly. There was a queer look in the Colonel's eyes. He was very white. "Send him up to me to report. We shall want all our available men before we can round these rascals up."

"Vis, sorr. An' Grubbins, sorr?"

The Colonel looked hard in silence at Private Mooney. Then, "Don't you know how to treat the dog that saved the garrison?" said he.

"Vis, sorr. I think so, sorr," said Private Mooney.

The smoky lamp had almost burned itself out.

When a man has his fingers run hard into his ears, how is it any sound can come through? When his eyes are pressed hard against the floor, how can he see great mountains? Great mountains, with clouds drifting, majestic, above them. And a homely garden across which the cloud-shadows play. And a girl standing in the garden, with pretty, timid blue eyes upturned. And an old yellow dog, whining for notice, and importunately licking a man's clenched hands and tear-drenched, hidden face—licking and whining, and shambling eagerly all about a man who lies prone in the dust, on the guard-house floor.

"Now I'm loony, for sho'!" Dikkon whispers to himself through closed teeth. "Or p'raps it's his ha'nt. I didn't know dogs had ha'nts. They say ha'nts go away if you speak. I won't speak, I won't open my eyes. It's must as good as 'f they hadn't shot him. His tongue's *warm*. His paw's *rough*. His nails kin *scratch*. O Lord A'mighty! Take him away! Take him away! I can't bear anythin' to be so *like* Grubbins, when it's only a ha'nt!"

But the wet tongue caresses. The rough paws plead.

There are footsteps in the room, and lanterns. A dozen comrades are catching at his hand. He has no choice but to sit up and open his eyes.

"Wuz it becos the angels didn't have no wings to fit yo', Grubbins, that they fixed yo' up that-a-way?" said Dikkon.

There, in the full lantern-light, stood an old yellow dog. His neck was hung with Christmas greens. A small American flag was wired to his tail, and was wiggling joysomely. His eyes met his master's. With one mighty leap he was in his master's arms, against his master's breast.

"Come away, b'ys," said Private Mooney. "Grubbins 'll be wantin' to exh-plain matthers to Dikkon, and, begorra! we'll be in the way."

A MORNING WITH BRET HARTE.

BY HENRY J. W. DAM.

"IF I had been an artist I should have painted them," he says, referring to John Oakhurst and M'liss and Tennessee's Partner and all the other denizens of that strange literary land which he was the first to discover and describe to all the world, "If I had been an artist" is his phrase, and it sounds strange from his lips, for a more artistic personality, in thought, speech, sympathies, and methods, was never numbered among the creators of character or the observers of nature than that of the historian of the Golden Age of California, Mr. Bret Harte.

It is one of those winter mornings in London when upon parks and lawns and all the architectural distances the cold gray mist lies heavily. The sun, a preposterous ruby set in fog, looms red and high. Through the study window its radiance comes balefully, as if fleeing the dreariness of streets that stretch silent and deserted under London's Sabbath spell. Within the room, however, all is cheerfulness and warmth. The heaped-up coals make flickering traceries of shadow over walls covered with the originals of pictures and engravings which all the world has seen in certain famous books. Some of these originals will be found among the illustrations of this article, and are interesting exhibitions of the manner in which the English imagination endeavors to conceive the unfamiliar California types. The sides of the room are given up to high book-shelves. Bric-a-brac meets the eye in all directions, the mantel being covered with pretty souvenirs of continental watering-places, those guide-posts on the highway of memory by which charming acquaintances are recalled and favorite spots revisited.

BRET HARTE IN PERSON.

At the desk, surrounded by an inealculable visitation of Christmas cards, sits Bret Harte, the Bret Harte of actuality, a

BRET HARTE, FROM A PAINTING BY JOHN PETTIE, R.A. REPRODUCED BY THE KIND PERMISSION OF THE FINE ARTS SOCIETY, LONDON. PHOTOGRAPHED BY FRADELLE & YOUNG, LONDON.

gentleman as far removed from the Bret Harte of popular fancy as is the St. James Club from Mount Shasta, or a Savoy Hotel supper from the cinder cuisine of a mining camp in the glorious days of '49. Instead of being, as the reader usually conceives, one of the long-bearded, loose-jointed heroes of his Western Walhalla, he is a polished gentleman of medium height, with a curling gray mustache. In lieu of the recklessness of Western methods in dress, his attire exhibits a nicety of detail which, in a man whose dignity and sincerity were less impressive, would seem foppish. This quality, like his handwriting and other characteristic trifles, perceptibly assists one in grasping the main elements of a personality which is as harmonious as it is peculiar, and as unconventional as it is sensitive to fine shades, of whatever kind they be. Over his cigar, with a gentle play of humor and a variety of unconscious gestures which are always graceful and never twice the same, he touches upon this very subject—the impressions made upon him by his first sight of gold-hunting in

BRET HARTE IN 1869, WHILE EDITOR OF THE "OVERLAND MONTHLY." FROM A PHOTOGRAPH LOANED BY THE PRESENT PUBLISHERS OF THE "OVERLAND MONTHLY."

California, and the eye and mind which he brought to bear upon the novel scene.

BRET HARTE'S STORY OF HIS LIFE IN CALIFORNIA.

"I left New York for California," says Mr. Harte, "when I was scarcely more than a boy, with no better equipment, I fear, than an imagination which had been expanded by reading Froissart's 'Chronicles of the Middle Ages,' 'Don Quixote,' the story of the Argonauts, and other books from the shelves of my father, who was a tutor of Greek. I went by way of Panama, and was at work for a few months in San Francisco in the spring of 1853, but felt no satisfaction with my surroundings until I reached the gold country, my particular choice being Sonora, in Calaveras County.

"Here I was thrown among the strangest social conditions that the latter-day world has perhaps seen. The setting was itself heroic. The great mountains of the Sierra Nevada lifted majestic snow-capped peaks against a sky of purest blue. Magnificent pine forests of trees which were themselves enormous, gave to the landscape a sense of largeness and greatness. It was a land of rugged cañons, sharp declivities, and magnificent distances. Amid rushing waters and wild-wood freedom, an army of strong men in red shirts and top boots were feverishly in search of the buried gold of earth. Nobody shaved, and hair, mustaches, and beards were untouched by shears or razor. Weaklings and old men were unknown. It took a stout heart and a strong frame to dare the venture, to brave the journey of three thousand miles, and battle for life in the wilds. It was a civilization composed entirely of young men, for on one occasion, I remember, an elderly man—he was fifty, perhaps, but he had a gray beard—was pointed out as a curiosity in the city, and men turned in the street to look at him as they would have looked at any other unfamiliar object.

"These men, generally speaking, were highly civilized, many of them being cultured and professionally trained. They were in strange and strong contrast with their surroundings, for all the trammels and conventionalities of settled civilization had been left thousands of miles behind. It was a land of perfect freedom, limited only by the instinct and the habit of law which prevailed in the mass. All its forms were original, rude, and picturesque. Woman was almost unknown, and enjoyed the high estimation of a rarity. The chiv-

BRET HARTE IN 1871. FROM A PHOTOGRAPH TAKEN BY SARONY, NEW YORK, SHORTLY AFTER THE PUBLICATION OF "THE HEATHEN CHINEE."

airy natural to manhood invested her with ideal value when respect could supplement it, and with exceptional value even when it could not. Strong passions brought quick climaxes, all the better and worse forces of manhood being in unbridled play. To me it was like a strange, ever-varying panorama, so novel that it was difficult to grasp comprehensively. In fact, it was not till years afterwards that the great mass of primary impressions on my mind became sufficiently clarified for literary use.

"The changes of scene were constant and unexpected. Here is one that I remember very well. Clothing was hard to get in the early days, and everything that could serve was made use of. Our valley, in its ordinary aspect, had as many 'spring styles for gentlemen' as there were men to be seen. One hot summer morning, however, the old order changed. A large consignment of condemned navy outfits, purchased by a local storekeeper, had found ready sale, and the result was that the valley was filled with men, hard at work over their claims, and all dressed in white 'jumpers,' white duck trousers, and top boots. On their heads were yellow straw hats, and around their shoulders gaudy bandanna handkerchiefs of yellow, blue, red, and green patterns. Perspiration was so profuse in the hot weather that a handkerchief was as necessary to a miner as a whiskey flask or a revolver. They wore them clung loosely around their necks and falling over their chests, like the collar of some extraordinary order, and each man as he worked would now and then dab his forehead with the handkerchief and push it a little farther round. The white clothes and bright handkerchiefs against the wild background made a very novel picture, and I said something to this effect to a miner by my side. He took a look down the valley, the standpoint being one that had not occurred to him, and said: 'It does look kinder nice. Didn't know we gave ourselves away like that,' and shambled down the trail with a chuckle. Every day brought new scenes and new experiences, though I did not commit them to paper till many years afterward."

MINER, EXPRESS MESSENGER, SCHOOLMASTER, EDITOR.

"And were you taking notes for future literary work at this period?"

"Not at all. I had not the least idea at this time that any portion of literary fame awaited me. I lived their life, unthinking. I took my pick and shovel, and asked where I might dig. They said 'Anywhere,' and it was true that you could get 'color,' that is, a few grains of gold, from any of the surface earth with which you chose to fill your pan. In an ordinary day's work you got enough to live on, or, as it was called, 'grub wages.' I was not a success as a gold-digger, and it was conceived that I would answer for a Wells Fargo messenger. A Wells Fargo messenger was a person who sat

BRET HARTE IN 1871. FROM A PHOTOGRAPH BY SARONY, NEW YORK.

beside the driver on the box-seat of a stage-coach, in charge of the letters and 'treasure' which the Wells Fargo Express Company took from a mining camp to the nearest town or city. Stage robbers were plentiful. My predecessor in the position had been shot through the arm, and my successor was killed. I held the post for some months, and then gave it up to become the schoolmaster near Sonora—Sonora having by immigration attained the size and population which called for a school. For several years after this I wandered about California from city to camp, and camp to city, without any special purpose. I became an editor, and learned to set type, the ability to earn my own living as a printer being a source of great satisfaction to me, for, strange to say, I had no confidence, until long after that period, in literature as a means of livelihood. I have never in my life had an article refused publication, and yet I never had any of that confidence which, in the case of many others, does not seem to have been impaired by repeated refusals. Nearly all my life I have held some political or editorial post, upon which I relied for an income. This has, no doubt, affected my work, since it gave me more liberty to write as pleased myself, instead of endeavoring to write for a purpose, or in accordance with the views of somebody else.

"A great part of this distrust of literature as a profession arose, I think," continues Mr. Harte, and he smiles at the reminiscence, "from my first literary effort. It was a poem called 'Autumn Musings.' It was written at the mature age of eleven. It was satirical in character, and cast upon the fading year the cynical light of my repressed dissatisfaction with things in general. I addressed the envelope to the New York 'Sunday Atlas,' at that time a journal of some literary repute in New York, where I was then living. I was not quite certain how the family would regard this venture on my part, and I posted the missive with the utmost secrecy. After that I waited for over a week in a state of suspense that entirely absorbed me. Sunday came, and with it the newspapers. These were displayed on a stand in the street near our house, and held in their places—I shall never forget them—with stones. With an unmoved face, but a beating heart, I scanned the topmost copy of the 'Atlas.' To my dying day I shall remember the thrill that came from seeing 'Autumn Musings,' a poem, on the first page. I don't know that the headline type was any longer than usual, but to me it was colossal. It had something of the tremendousness of a three-sheet poster. I bought the paper and took it home. I exhibited it to the family by slow and cautious stages. My hopes sank lower and lower. At last I realized the enormity of my offence. The lamentation was general. It was unanimously conceded that I was lost, and I fully believed it. My idea of a poet—it was the family's idea also—was the Hogarthian one, born of a book of Hogarth's drawings belonging to my father. In the lean and miserable and helpless guise of 'The Distressed Poet,' as therein pictured, I saw, aided by the family, my probable future. It was a terrible experience. I sometimes wonder that I ever wrote another line of verse."

His natural tendency in that direction was too strong to be crushed, however. He has always, he says, had a weakness for humorous verse, and in that particular direction his pen is as playful as ever. All of which digression leads naturally to the "Heathen Chinee," concerning which he has several new facts to make public.

BRET HARTE. FROM A PHOTOGRAPH BY THOMAS FALL, LONDON.

BRET HARTE AT THE PRESENT TIME. FROM A PHOTOGRAPH BY ELLIOTT AND FRY, LONDON.

SOME NEW FACTS ABOUT THE "HEATHEN CHINEE."

"I was always fond of satiric verse, and the instinct of parody has always possessed me. The 'Heathen Chinee' is an instance of this, though I don't think I have told anybody, except a well-known English poet, who observed and taxed me with the fact, the story of its metrical origin. The 'Heathen Chinee' was for a time the best known of any of my writings. It was written for the 'Overland Monthly,' of which I was editor, with a satirical political purpose, but with no thought of aught else than its local effect. It was born of a somewhat absurd state of things which appealed to the humorous eye. The thrifty Oriental, who was invading California in large numbers, was as imitative as a monkey. He did as the Caucasian did in all respects, and, being more patient and frugal, did it a little better. From placer mining to card playing he industriously followed the example set him by his superiors, and took cheating at cards quite seriously, as a valuable addition to the interesting game. He cheated admirably, but, instead of winning praises for it, found himself, when caught at it, abused, contemned, and occasionally mobbed by his teachers in a way that had not been dreamt of in his philosophy. This point I put into verse. I heard nothing of it for some time, until a friend told me it was making the rounds of the Eastern press. He himself had heard a New York brakeman repeating:

Yet he played it that day upon William and me in a way I despise.'

Soon afterwards I began to hear from it frequently in a similar way. The lines were popular. The points seemed to catch the ear and hold the memory. I never intended it as a contribution to contemporary poetry, but I doubt, from the evidence I received, if I ever wrote anything more catching. The verses had, however, the dignity of a high example. I have told you of the English poet who was first to question me regarding the metre, and appreciate its Greek source. Do you remember the threnody in Swinburne's 'Atalanta in Calydon'? It occurred to me that the grand and beautiful sweep of that chorus was just the kind of thing which Truthful James would be the last man in the world to adopt in expressing his views. Therefore I used it. Listen," and he quotes, marking the accents with an amused smile:

" 'Atalanta, the fairest of women, whose name is a blessing to speak—

Yet he played it that day upon William and me in a way I despise

The narrowing Symplegades whitened the straits of Propontis with spray—

And we found on his nails, which were taper, what's frequent in tapers, that's wax.' "

He laughs over the parody in metre and goes on quoting; and as he talks of his verse and his work in general, it is evident that the humorous is one of his most fully developed literary characteristics. He still takes delight in the "Condensed Novels," and is as much in the mood for writing them to-day, at fifty-three, as he was twenty years ago. They belonged, it seems, to a kind of chrysalis period in his development, when, living in San Francisco, he wrote variously for a number of local literary periodicals, the most widely known of which was the "Golden Era." These writings, and the position which he won through them, led to the editorship of the "Californian Weekly," and finally of a magazine, the "Overland Monthly." The latter was the inducing cause of the first of that series of stories which carried his name all over the world. At the start he was most bitterly opposed. The first step was the one that cost, with him as with others. His narrative is full of interest, as a matter both of personal and of literary history.

EDITORIAL CAUTION AND "THE LUCK OF ROARING CAMP."

"I was eventually offered the editorship of a new magazine, the 'Overland Monthly,' which was about to make its first issue, and it was through the acceptance of this post that my career, generally speaking, began. As the editor of this magazine, I received for its initial number many contributions in the way of stories. After looking these over, it impressed me as a strange thing that not one of the writers had felt inspired to treat the fresh subjects which lay ready to his hand in California. All the stories were conventional, the kind of thing that would have been offered to an editor in the Atlantic States, stories of those localities and of Europe, in the customary form. I talked the matter over with Mr. Roman, the proprietor, and then wrote a story whose sole object was to give the first number a certain amount of local coloring. It was called 'The Luck of Roaring Camp.' It was a

BRET HARTE IN HIS STUDY.

BRET HARTE'S "M'LISS." FROM A PAINTING BY EDWIN LONG. REPRINTED BY KIND PERMISSION OF MESSRS. BRIDGES AND SONS, LONDON, PHOTOGRAPHED BY BRAUFITZ & YOUNG, LONDON.

single picture out of the panorama which had impressed me years before. It was put into type. The proof-reader and printer declared it was immoral and indecent. I read it over again in proof, at the request of the publisher, and was touched, I am afraid, only with my own pathos. I read it to my wife—I had married in the meantime—and it made her cry also. I am told that Mr. Roman also read it to his wife, with the same diabolically illogical result. Nevertheless, the opposition was unshaken.

"I had a serious talk with an intimate friend of mine, then the editor of the 'Alta California.' He was not personally opposed to the story, but felt that that sort of thing might be injudicious and unfavorably affect immigration. I was without a sympathizer or defender. Even Mr. Roman felt that it might imperil the prospects of the magazine. I read the story again, thought the matter over, and told Mr. Roman that if 'The Luck of Roaring Camp' was not a good and suitable story I was not a good and suitable editor for his magazine. I said that the chief value of an editor lay in the correctness of his judgment, and if his view was the true one, my judgment was clearly at fault. I am quite sure that if the decision had been left to San Francisco, the series of mining pictures that followed the first would not have been written—at least, not in that city. But the editor remained, and the story appeared. It was received harshly. The religious papers were unanimous in declaring it immoral, and they published columns in its disfavor. The local press, reflecting the pride of a young and new community, could not see why stories should be printed by their representative magazine which put the community into such unfavorable contrast with the effete civilization of the East. They would have none of it!

"A month later, however, by return of mail from Boston, there came an important letter. It was from Fields & Osgood, the publishers, and was addressed to me as editor. It requested me to hand the enclosed note to the author of 'The Luck of Roaring Camp.' The note was their offer to publish anything he chose to write, upon his own terms. This became known, and it turned the tide of criticism. Since Boston indorsed the story, San Francisco was properly proud of it. Thenceforth I had my own way without interruption. Other stories, the mining tales with which you are familiar, followed in quick succession. The numberless impressions of the earlier days were all vividly fixed in my mind, waiting to be worked up, and their success was made apparent to me in very substantial ways, though the religious press continued to suffer from the most painful doubts, and certain local critics who had torn my first story to pieces, fell into a quiet routine of stating that each succeeding story was the worst thing that had yet appeared from my pen."

"A IDYLL OF THE SIERRAS." FROM A PHOTOGRAPH BY FRADELLE & YOUNG, LONDON, OF A DRAWING BY CATON WOODVILLE.

A MORNING WITH BRET HARTE.

BRET HARTE'S FIRST MEETING WITH MARK TWAIN.

"Local color having been placed, through the dictum of the Atlantic States, at a premium," Mr. Hart continues, "the 'Overland' became what it should have been from the start, truly Californian in tone. Other writers followed my 'trail,' and the freshness and vivid life of the country found a literary expression. At that time I held a political office, the secretaryship of the San Francisco Mint. The Mint was but a few steps from the leading newspaper establishments, and as I had previously been the editor of 'The Californian,' a literary weekly, my office was a rendezvous for contributors and would-be contributors to the magazine.

"Some months before the 'Overland' appeared, George Barnes, a well-known journalist and an intimate friend of mine, walked into my office one morning with a young man whose appearance was unmistakably interesting. His head was striking. He had the curly hair, the aquiline nose, and even the aquiline eye—an eye so eagle-like that a second lid would not have surprised me —of an unusual and dominant nature. His eyebrows were very thick and bushy. His dress was careless, and his general manner one of supreme indifference to surroundings and circumstances. Barnes introduced him as Mr. Sam Clemens, and remarked that he had shown a very original talent in a number of newspaper contributions over the signature of 'Mark Twain.' We talked on different topics, and about a month afterwards Clemens dropped in upon me again.

"He had been away in the mining district on some newspaper assignment in the meantime. In the course of conversation he remarked that the unearthly laziness that prevailed in the town he had been visiting was beyond anything in his previous experience. He said the men did nothing all day long but sit around the barroom stove, spit, and 'swop lies.' He spoke in a slow, rather satirical, drawl which was in itself irresistible. He went on to tell one of those extravagant stories, and half unconsciously dropped into the lazy tone and manner of the original narrator. It was as graphic as it was delicious. I asked him to tell it again to a friend who came in, and then asked him to write it out for 'The Californian.' He did so, and when published it was an emphatic success. It was the first work of his that attracted general attention, and it crossed the Sierras for an Eastern hearing. From that point his success was steady. The story was "The Jumping Frog of Calaveras." It is now known and laughed over, I suppose, wherever the English language is spoken; but it will never be as funny to anybody in print as it was to me, told for the first time by the unknown Twain himself, on that morning in the San Francisco Mint."

HOW MUCH IS REAL IN BRET HARTE'S TALES.

Whether or not there ever really existed an innocent frog, wickedly filled with bird shot, for speculative purposes, by a designing man, it now appears that there certainly did exist a John Oakhurst, and that all the Bret Harte characters and incidents were drawn from life to a greater or less extent.

"'Greater or less' is perhaps the best way to answer the question," says their creator, thoughtfully, and this statement, like every other expression of opinion from him, is very emphatic, but very polite, in fact, almost deferential in tone. He is firm in his own conclusions, but as gentle in differing with you as an oriental potentate, who might beg you with tears in his eyes to agree with him, and complacently drowned you if you didn't.

"I may say with perfect truth," he adds, "that there were never any natural phenomena made use of in my novels of which I had not been personally cognizant, except one, and that was the bursting of the reservoir, in 'Gabriel Conroy.' But not a year had elapsed after the publication of the book before I received a letter from a man in Shasta County, California, asking how I happened to know so much about the flood that had occurred there, and stating that I had described many of its incidents to the very life. I have been credited with great powers of observation, and not a few discoveries in natural phenomena. Whether I am entitled to the credit or not, I cannot say. When I wrote, in 'The Tale of a Pony,'

'Bean pods are noisiest when dry,
And you always wink with your weakest eye,'

I did not dream that an eminent Philadelphia ophthalmologist would make this statement, which it appears is true, the subject of an essay before his society. Another eminent scientist who is interested in the elementary conditions of human nature, and the prehensile tendencies of babies' fingers, seriously corroborated my statement about the baby in 'The Luck of Roaring Camp,' which 'wrastled' with Kentuck's finger.

"My stories are true, however, not only in phenomena, but in characters. I do not pretend to say that many of my characters existed exactly as they are described, but I believe there is not one of them who did not have a real human being as a suggesting and starting point. Some of them, indeed, had several. John Oakhurst, for instance, was drawn quite closely from life. On one occasion, however, when a story in which he figures was being discussed, a friend of mine said: 'I know the original of Oakhurst—the man you took him from.'

"'Who?' said I.

"'Young L——.'

"I was astounded. As a matter of fact, the gambler as portrayed was as good a picture, even to the limp, of young L——, as of the actual original. The two men, you see, belonged to a class which had strongly marked characteristics, and were generally alike in dress and manner. And so with the others. Perhaps some of my heroes were slightly polished in the setting, and perhaps some of my heroines were somewhat idealized, but they all had an original existence outside of my brain and outside of my books. I know this, though I could not possibly tell you who the originals were or where they were found."

As Mr. Harte talks his hands become eloquent. The gestures are quiet and graceful, but arms, wrist, hands, and fingers come into continuous play. And when he finally lights upon his grievance—like every other man of note, he has a grievance—he becomes particularly earnest, and the gestures are slightly more emphatic.

HOW BRET HARTE WORKS AND DOES NOT WORK.

"I don't object to being written about as I am," he says, "but I particularly dislike being described as I am not. And, for some strange journalistic or human reason, the inventions concerning me seem to have much greater currency and vitality than the truths. Here, for instance," and he examines a pile of newspaper cuttings on the desk, "are two interesting contributions to my public history which came this morning."

The first, from "Galignani's Messenger," read as follows:

"Bret Harte cannot work except in seclusion, and when he is busy on a story he will hide himself away in some suburban retreat known only to his closest friends. Here he will rise just after dawn, be at his desk several hours before breakfast, and remain there, with an interval of an hour for a walk, the whole day."

"I meet this everywhere," said Mr. Harte, "and this," taking up a second cutting in its natural sequence :

"Bret Harte has reached a point where literary work is impossible to him except in absolute solitude. When writing he leaves his own home for suburban lodgings, where no visitor is allowed to trouble him, and where he follows a severe routine of early rising, scant diet, and steady work. It has been generally remarked that one can see this laborious regimen in his latter-day novels." This was from "The Argonaut," San Francisco,

"Now, what is diabolically ingenious in this," continues Mr. Harte, "is that those authoritative statements are

o'clock, and eat my breakfast like any other human being. I then go to work, if I have a piece of work in hand, and remain at my desk till noon. I never work after luncheon. I read my proofs with as much interest and, I think, as much care as anybody else, and yet the public is taught to believe that I never see my 'copy' after it once leaves my hands.

"If newspapers were as anxious to print facts about a man as they are to furnish information which their readers will presumably enjoy repeating, it would be different. I won, some years ago, without the slightest effort on my part, the reputation of being the laziest man in America. At first the compliment took the form of an extended paragraph deploring my fatal facility, and telling in deprecating sentences how much I could probably do if I

were not so indolent. This grew smaller and smaller, until it took a concise and easily annexable form, viz.: 'Bret Harte is the laziest man in America.' As an interesting adjunct to the personal column I read it, of course with extreme pleasure, in every paper that came habitually under my eye. Denial, of course, was of no earthly use, and the line travelled all over the country, and is doubtless still on its rounds. In the course of time, on a lecturing tour, I reached St. Joe, Missouri. I had been lecturing by night and travelling by day for ten weeks, continuously. A reporter called and desired to know what kind of soap I used—he had heard sinister rumors that it was a highly scented foreign article—my opinion of Longfellow, and various other questions of moment. I assured him that I used the soap of the hotel, and concealed nothing from him with regard to Longfellow, but begged him particularly to note the fact of my preternatural activity. He managed these facts correctly in his half-column next morning, but adorned me with a glittering diamond stud of which I had no knowledge. And in the same paper, in another column, I found a pleasant variation from the usual line. There was no allusion to my late labors. It was simply: 'Bret Harte *says* he is not the laziest man in America.' Altogether, therefore, I should perhaps think well of my friend of St. Joe, Missouri.

"Those lectures were an amusing experience," he adds, laughing. "What the people expected in me I do not know. Possibly a six-foot mountaineer, with a voice and lecture in proportion. They always seemed to have mentally confused me with one of my own characters. I am not six feet high, and I do not wear a beard. Whenever I walked out before a strange audience there was a general sense of disappointment, a gasp of astonishment that I could feel, and it always took at least fifteen minutes before they recovered from their surprise sufficiently to listen to what I had to say. I think, even now, that if I had been more herculean in proportions, with a red shirt and top boots, many of those audiences would have felt a deeper thrill from my utterances and a deeper conviction that they had obtained the worth of their money."

A MAN CAREFUL OF DETAILS IN HIS WORK AND HIS PERSON.

The conversation rambles. A polished critic, an epicurean, a man of the world, and carrying everywhere the independence of a distinct literary personality, Bret Harte talks as he writes, like a gentleman. This is a subtile attribute, but one which England never fails to recognize and value, and it is one prime cause of the popularity of his works in the United Kingdom. Continually in evidence also is his distinguishing characteristic, one which is only described by the word "nicety"—nicety in dress, nicety in speech, nicety in thought. This artistic precision and thoughtful attention to details is the most marked attribute of the man, and from it you understand the plane and power of his work. Without it, the most impressive of his stories, "The Luck of Roaring Camp," for instance, could not possibly have been written. It is rather a singular quality to be found in combination with his emotional breadth and dramatic sweep as a writer, but it is the one which finishes and polishes the whole, and it is clearly natural and inherent.

THE CIVIL WAR A GREAT OPPORTUNITY FOR AMERICAN NOVELISTS.

Perhaps the most valuable of all Mr. Harte's ideas are his opinions concerning the literary field of to-day. His views of literature as a profession are now pleasantly optimistic, possibly through the business-like way in which his interests have long been handled by that most skilful of literary agents, Mr. A. P. Watt. Contemporary life in its highest social aspects he looks upon, however, as most unpromising material for romantic treatment.

"In America," he says, "the great field is the late war. The dramatists have found and utilized it, but the novelists, the romance writers, have in it the richest possible field for works of serious import, and yet, outside of short stories, they seem to have passed it by. If I had time, nothing would please me better than to go over the ground, or portions of it, and make use of it for future work. Our war of the Revolution is not good material for cosmopolitan purposes. This country has never quite forgotten the way in which it ended. But the war of the Rebellion was our own and is our own; its dramatic and emotional aspects are infinite; and while American writers are coming abroad for scenes to picture, I am in constant fear that some Englishman or Frenchman will go to America and reap the field in romance which we should now, all local feeling having passed away, be utilizing to our own fame and profit."

"HUMAN DOCUMENTS."

BIOGRAPHICAL NOTES.

The Venerable FREDERIC WILLIAM FARRAR, D.D., F.R.S., Archdeacon of Westminster, combines in himself several kinds of eminence any one of which would be a just source of pride to an ordinary man. Besides being a high dignitary in a great Church Establishment, he is an eminent pulpit orator, an eminent scholar, and an eminent man of letters. He was born in Bombay, August 7, 1831, and is the son of a clergyman. For many years he was an assistant master in the noted school at Harrow, and then head master of Marlborough College. Having served for a time as Honorary Chaplain to the Queen, he became, in 1873, one of her Chaplains in Ordinary. In 1876 he was appointed to a canonry in Westminster Abbey and to the rectory of St. Margaret's, London. In 1883 he became Archdeacon of Westminster, and in 1890 Chaplain of the House of Commons. He has published stories, books of sermons, books of lectures, theological treatises, and philological treatises; and many of his works have been immensely popular. In 1885 he paid a visit to America, for which he has great friendliness, and received a very warm welcome. An interesting article by Dr. Farrar, entitled "The Christ Child in Art," appears on another page of this number of the magazine.

DWIGHT LYMAN MOODY was born at Northfield, Massachusetts, February 5, 1837, and until he was seventeen years old lived on a farm. He discovered remarkable ability as a missionary on removing to Chicago in 1856. A complete study of his career, by Professor Drummond, appears in another part of this number of the Magazine.

IRA DAVID SANKEY, the evangelist, was born in Edinburgh, Lawrence County, Pennsylvania, August 28, 1840. His father, a banker and an editor, and for some years a State senator, was a zealous member of the Methodist Church, and the son united with the same church at the age of fifteen. He became leader of the choir, superintendent of the Sunday school, and president of the local Young Men's Christian Association. He was at Indianapolis in 1870 as a delegate to an international convention of the Young Men's Christian Association, and there made the acquaintance of Mr. Moody, and they began that association which has since made them known to all the world. Many of the melodies which Mr. Sankey sings are of his own composition, and he has compiled a very popular book of "Sacred Songs and Solos."

ARCHDEACON FARRAR.

ARCHDEACON FARRAR.

1876. AGE 45. FROM A PHOTOGRAPH BY SAMUEL A. WALKER, LONDON.

1854. æt. 17. Mr. Moody as he appeared at the time he removed from the family farm to Boston.

1864. æt. 27.

IRA D. SANKEY IN 1860. AGE 18.

1863. AGE 23.

1875. AGE 35. FROM A PHOTOGRAPH BY W. & D. DOWNEY, LONDON, THE LATEST TAKEN OF MR. SANKEY.

MR. MOODY: SOME IMPRESSIONS AND FACTS.

By HENRY DRUMMOND, LL.D., F.R.S.E., F.G.S.

Author of "Natural Law in the Spiritual World," "The Greatest Thing in the World," "The New Evangelism," etc.

TO gain just the right impression of Mr. Moody you must make a pilgrimage to Northfield. Take the train to the wayside depot in Massachusetts which bears that name, or, better still, to South Vernon, where the fast trains stop. Northfield, his birthplace and his present home, is distant about a couple of miles, but at certain seasons of the year you will find awaiting trains a two-horse buggy, not conspicuous for varnish, but famous for pace, driven by a stout farmer-like person in a slouch hat. As he drives you to the spacious hotel—a creation of Mr. Moody's—he will answer your questions about the place in a brusque, business-like way; indulge, probably, in a few laconic witticisms, or discuss the political situation or the last strike with a shrewdness which convinces you that, if the Northfield people are of this level-headed type, they are at least a worthy field for the great preacher's energies. Presently, on the other side of the river, on one of those luscious, grassy slopes, framed in with forest and bounded with the blue receding hills, which give the Connecticut Valley its dream-like beauty, the great halls and colleges of the new Northfield which Mr. Moody has built, begin to appear. Your astonishment is great, not so much to find a New England hamlet possessing a dozen of the finest educational buildings in America—for the neighboring townships of Amherst and Northampton are already famous for their collegiate institutions—but to discover that these owe their existence to a man whose name is, perhaps, associated in the minds of three-fourths of his countrymen, not with education, but with the want of it. But presently, when you are deposited at the door of the hotel, a more astounding discovery greets you. For when you ask the clerk whether the great man himself is at home, and where you can see him, he will point to your coachman, now disappearing like lightning down the drive, and—too much accustomed to Mr. Moody's humor to smile at his latest jest—whisper, "That's him."

If this does not actually happen in your

HENRY DRUMMOND.

case, it is certain it has happened;* and nothing could more fittingly introduce you to the man, or make you realize the naturalness, the simplicity, the genuine and unaffected humanity of this great unspoilt and unspoilable personality.

MR. MOODY MUCH MISUNDERSTOOD.

Simple as this man is, and homely as are his surroundings, probably America possesses at this moment no more extraordinary personage; nor even amongst the most brilliant of her sons has any

---

* At the beginning of each of the terms, hundreds of students, many of them strangers, arrive to attend these seminaries. At such times Mr. Moody literally haunts the depots, to meet them the moment they arrive, need a friend, and give them that personal welcome which is sure to many of them than half their education. When casual visitors, mistaking perhaps the only vehicle in waiting for a public conveyance, have taken possession for themselves and their luggage, the driver, circumstances permitting, has duly risen to the occasion. The fact, by the way, that he so escapes recognition, illustrates a peculiarity. Mr. Moody, owing to a life-long resistance to the self-advertisement of the camera, is probably less known by photographs than any public man.

rendered more stupendous or more enduring service to his country or his time. No public man is less understood, especially by the thinking world, than D. L. Moody. It is not that it is unaware of his existence, or even that it does not respect him. But his line is so special, his work has lain so apart from what it conceives to be the rational channels of progress, that it has never felt called upon to take him seriously. So little, indeed, is the true stature of this man known to the mass of his generation, that the preliminary estimate recorded here must seem both extravagant and ill-considered. To whole sections of the community the mere word evangelical is a synonym for whatever is narrow, strained, superficial, and unreal. Assumed to be heir to all that is hectic in religion, and sensational in the methods of propagating it, men who, like Mr. Moody, earn this name are unconsciously credited with the worst traditions of their class. It will surprise many to know that Mr. Moody is as different from the supposed type of his class as light is from dark; that while he would be the last to repudiate the name, indeed, while glorying more and more each day he lives in the work of the evangelist, he sees the weaknesses, the narrownesses, and the limitations of that order with as clear an eye as the most unsparing of its critics. But especially will it surprise many to know that while preaching to the masses has been the main outward work of Mr. Moody's life, he has, perhaps, more, and more varied, irons in the fire—educational, philanthropic, religious—than almost any living man; and that vast as has been his public service as a preacher to the masses, it is probably true that his personal influence and private character have done as much as his preaching to affect his day and generation.

Discussion has abounded lately as to the standards by which a country shall judge its great men. And the verdict has been given unanimously on behalf of moral influence. Whether estimated by the moral qualities which go to the making up of his personal character, or the extent to which he has impressed these upon whole communities of men on both sides of the Atlantic, there is, perhaps, no more truly great man living than D. L. Moody. By moral influences in this connection I do not mean in any restricted sense religious influence. I mean the influence which, with whatever doctrinal accompaniments, or under whatever ecclesiastical flag, leads men to better lives and higher ideals; the influence which makes for noble character, personal enthusiasm, social well-being, and national righteousness. I have never heard Mr. Moody defend any particular church; I have never heard him quoted as a theologian. But I have met multitudes, and personally know, in large numbers, men and women of all churches and creeds, of many countries and ranks, from the poorest to the richest, and from the most ignorant to the most wise, upon whom he has placed an ineffaceable moral mark. There is no large town in Great Britain or

MR. MOODY: SOME IMPRESSIONS AND FACTS.

MRS. BETSEY MOODY, MOTHER OF D. L. MOODY.

Ireland, and I perceive there are few in America, where this man has not gone, where he has not lived for days, weeks, or months, and where he has not left behind him personal inspirations which live to this day; inspirations which, from the moment of their birth, have not ceased to evidence themselves in practical ways—in furthering domestic happiness and peace; in charities and philanthropies; in social, religious, and even municipal and national service.

It is no part of the present object to give a detailed account of Mr. Moody's career, still less of his private life. The sacred character of much of his work also forbids allusion in this brief sketch to much that those more deeply interested in him, and in the message which he proclaims, would like to have expressed or analyzed. All that is designed is to give the outside reader some few particulars to introduce him to, and interest him in, the man.

BOYHOOD ON A NEW ENGLAND FARM.

Fifty-seven years ago (February 5, 1837) Dwight Lyman Moody was born in the same New England valley where, as already said, he lives to-day. Four years later his father died, leaving a widow, nine children—the eldest but thirteen years of age—a little home on the mountain side, and an acre or two of mortgaged land. How this widow shouldered her burden of poverty, debt, and care; how she brought up her helpless flock, keeping all together in the old home, educating them, and sending them out into life stamped with her own indomitable courage and lofty principle, is one of those unrecorded histories whose page, when time unfolds it, will be found to contain the secret of nearly all that is greatest in the world's past. It is delightful to think that this mother has survived to see her labors crowned, and still lives, a venerable and beautiful figure, near the scene of her early

D. L. MOODY'S RESIDENCE AT NORTHFIELD, MASSACHUSETTS, LOOKING SOUTH.

battles. There, in a sunny room of the little farm, she sits with faculties unimpaired, cherished by an entire community, and surrounded with all the love and gratitude which her children and her children's children can heap upon her. One has only to look at the strong, wise face, or listen to the firm yet gentle tones, to behold the source of those qualities of sagacity, energy, self-unconsciousness, and faith which have made the greatest of her sons what he is.

Until his seventeenth year Mr. Moody's boyhood was spent at home. What a merry, adventurous, rough-and-tumble boyhood it must have been, how much fuller of escapade than of education, those who know Mr. Moody's irrepressible temperament and buoyant humor will not require the traditions of his Northfield schoolmates to recall. The village school was the only seminary he ever attended, and his course was constantly interrupted by the duties of the home and of the farm. He learned little about books, but much about horses, crops, and men; his mind ran wild, and his memory stored up nothing but the alphabet of knowledge. But in these early country days his bodily form strengthened to iron, and he built up that constitution which in after life enabled him not only to do the work of ten, but to sustain without a break through four decades as arduous and exhausting work as was ever given to man to do. Innocent at this stage of "religion," he was known in the neighborhood simply as a raw lad, high-spirited, generous, daring, with a will of his own, and a certain audacious originality which, added to the fiery energy of his disposition, foreboded a probable future either in the ranks of the incorrigibles or, if fate were kind, perchance of the immortals.

Somewhere about his eighteenth year the turning point came. Vast as were the issues, the circumstances were in no way eventful. Leaving school, the boy had set out for Boston, where he had an uncle, to push his fortune. His uncle, with some trepidation, offered him a place in his store; but, seeing the kind of nature he had to deal with, laid down certain conditions which the astute man thought might at least minimize explosions. One of these conditions was, that the lad should attend church and Sunday school. These influences—and it is interesting to note that they are simply the normal influences of a Christian society—did their work. On the surface what appears is this: that he attended church—to order, and listened with more or less attention; that he went to Sunday school, and, when he recovered his breath, asked awkward questions of his teacher; that, by and by, when he applied for membership in the congregation, he was summarily rejected, and told to wait six months until he learned a little more about it; and, lastly, that said period of probation having expired, he was duly received into communion. The decisive instrument during this period seems to have been his Sunday-school teacher, Mr. Edward Kimball, whose influence upon his charge was not merely professional, but personal and direct. In private friendship he urged young Moody to the supreme decision, and Mr. Moody never ceased to express his gratitude to the layman who met him at the parting of the ways, and led his thoughts and energies in the direction in which they have done such service to the world.

REMOVAL TO CHICAGO—RARE GIFT FOR BUSINESS.

The immediate fruit of this change was not specially apparent. The ambitions of the lad chiefly lay in the line of mercantile success; and his next move was to find a larger and freer field for the abilities for business which he began to discover in himself. This he found in the then new world of Chicago. Arriving there, with due introductions, he was soon engaged as salesman in a large and busy store, with possibilities of work and promotion which suited his taste. That he distinguished himself almost at once, goes without saying. In a year or two he was earning a salary considerable for one of his years, and his business capacity became speedily so proved that his future prosperity was assured. "He would never sit down in the store," writes one of his fellows, "to chat or read the paper, as the other clerks did when there were no customers; but as soon as he had served one buyer, he was on the lookout for another. If none appeared, he would start off to the hotels or depots, or walk the streets in search of one. He would sometimes stand on the sidewalk in front of his place of business, looking eagerly up and down for a man who had the appearance of a merchant from the country, and some of his fellow-clerks were accustomed laughingly to say: 'There is the spider again, watching for a fly.'"

The taunt is sometimes levelled at religion, that mainly those become religious teachers who are not fit for anything else. The charge is not worth answering; but it is worth recording that in the case of Mr. Moody the very reverse is the case. If Mr. Moody had remained in business, there is almost no question that he would have been to-day one of the wealthiest men in the United States. His enterprise, his organizing power, his knowledge and management of men are admitted by friend and foe to be of the highest order; while such is his generalship—as proved, for example, in the great religious campaign in Great Britain in 1873-75—that, had he

MR. MOODY: SOME IMPRESSIONS AND FACTS.

MR. MOODY'S HOUSE AT NORTHFIELD IN WINTER, LOOKING EAST.

chosen a military career, he would have risen to the first rank among leaders. One of the merchant princes of Britain, the well-known director of one of the largest steamship companies in the world, assured the writer lately that in the course of a life-long commercial experience he had never met a man with more business capacity and sheer executive ability than D. L. Moody. Let any one visit Northfield, with its noble piles of institutions, or study the history of the work conceived, directed, financed, and carried out on such a colossal scale by Mr. Moody during the time of the World's Fair at Chicago, and he will discover for himself the size, the mere intellectual quality, creative power, and organizing skill of the brain behind them.

Undiverted, however, from a deeper purpose even by the glamor of a successful business life, Mr. Moody's moral and religious instincts led him almost from the day of his arrival in Chicago to devote what spare time he had to the work of the Church. He began by hiring four pews in the church to which he had attached himself, and these he attempted to fill every Sunday with young men like himself. This work for a temperament like his soon proved too slow, and he sought fuller outlets for his enthusiasm. Applying for the post of teacher in an obscure Sunday school, he was told by the superintendent that it was scholars he wanted, not teachers, but that he would let him try his hand if he could find the scholars. Next Sunday the new candidate appeared with a procession of eighteen urchins, ragged, rowdy, and barefooted, on whom he straightway proceeded to operate. Hunting up children and general recruiting for mission halls remained favorite pursuits for years to come, and his success was signal. In all this class of work he was a natural adept, and his early experiences as a scout were full of adventure. This was probably the most picturesque period of Mr. Moody's life, and not the least useful. Now we find him tract-distributing in the slums; again, visiting among the docks; and, finally, he started a mission of his own in one of the lowest haunts of the city. There he saw life in all its phases; he learned what practical religion was; he tried in succession every known method of Christian work; and when any of the conventional methods failed, invented new ones. Opposition, discouragement, failure, he met at every turn and in every form; but one thing he never learned—how to give up man or scheme he had once set his heart on. For years this guerilla work, hand to hand, and heart to heart, went on. He ran through the whole gamut of mission experience, tackling the most difficult districts and the most adverse circumstances, doing all the odd jobs and menial work himself, never attempting much in the way of public speaking, but employing others whom he thought more fit; making friends especially with children, and through them with their dissolute fathers and starving mothers.

MR. MOODY: SOME IMPRESSIONS AND FACTS

Great as was his success, the main reward achieved was to the worker himself. Here he was broken in, moulded, toned down, disciplined, in a dozen needed directions, and in this long and severe apprenticeship he unconsciously qualified himself to become the teacher of the Church in all methods of reaching the masses and winning men. He found out where his strength lay, and where his weakness; he learned that saving men was no child's play, but meant practically giving a life for a life; that regeneration was no milk and water experience; that, as Mrs. Browning says:

"It takes a high-soul'd man
To move the masses—even to a cleaner sty."

But for this personal discipline it is doubtful if Mr. Moody would ever have been heard of outside the purlieus of Chicago. The clergy, bewildered by his eccentric genius, and suspicious of his unconventional ways, looked askance at him; and it was only as time mellowed his headstrong youth into a soberer, yet not less zealous, manhood that the solitary worker found influential friends to countenance and guide him. His activity, especially during the years of the war, when he served with almost superhuman devotion in the Christian Commission, led many of his fellow-laborers to know his worth; and the war over, he became at last a recognized factor in the religious life of Chicago. The mission which he had slowly built up was elevated to the rank of a church, with Mr. Moody, who had long since given up business in order to devote his entire time to what lay nearer his heart, as its pastor.

MR. MOODY'S SLOW DEVELOPMENT AS A PUBLIC SPEAKER.

As a public speaker up to this time Mr. Moody was the reverse of celebrated. When he first attempted speaking, in Boston, he was promptly told to hold his tongue, and further efforts in Chicago were not less discouraging. "He had never heard," writes Mr. Daniells, in his well-known biography, "of Talleyrand's famous doctrine, that speech is useful for concealing one's thoughts. Like Antony, he only spoke 'right on.' There was frequently a pungency in his exhortation which his brethren did not altogether relish. Sometimes in his prayers he would express opinions to the Lord concerning them which were by no means flattering; and it was not long before he received the same fatherly advice which had been given him at Boston—to the effect that he should keep his four pews full of young men, and leave the speaking and praying to those who could do it better." Undaunted by such pleasantries, Mr. Moody did, on occasion, continue to use his tongue—no doubt much ashamed of himself. He spoke not because he thought

DINING-ROOM, MR. MOODY'S HOUSE AT NORTHFIELD.

MR. MOODY: SOME IMPRESSIONS AND FACTS.

he could speak, but because he could not be silent. The ragged children whom he gathered round him in the empty saloon near the North Side Market, had to be talked to somehow, and among such audiences, with neither premeditation nor preparation, he laid the foundations of that amazingly direct anecdotal style and explosive delivery which became such a splendid instrument of his future service. Training for the public platform, this man, who has done more platform work than any man of his generation, had none. He knew only two books, the Bible and Human Nature. Out of these he spoke; and because both are books of life, his words were afire with life; and the people to whom he spoke, being real people, listened and understood. When Mr. Moody first began to be in demand on public platforms, it was not because he could speak. It was his experience that was wanted, not his eloquence. As a practical man in work among the masses, his advice and enthusiasm were called for at Sunday school and other conventions, and he soon became known in this connection throughout the surrounding States. It was at one of these conventions that he had the good fortune to meet Mr. Ira D. Sankey, whose name must ever be associated with his, and who henceforth shared his labors at home and abroad, and contributed, in ways the value of which it is impossible to exaggerate, to the success of his after work.

Were one asked what, on the human side, were the effective ingredients in Mr. Moody's sermons, one would find the answer difficult. Probably the foremost is the tremendous conviction with which they are uttered. Next to that is their point and direction. Every blow is straight from the shoulder, and every stroke tells. Whatever canons they violate, whatever fault the critics may find with their art, their rhetoric, or even with their theology, as appeals to the people they do their work, and with extraordinary power. If eloquence is measured by its effects upon an audience, and not by its balanced sentences and cumulative periods, then here is eloquence of the highest order. In sheer persuasiveness Mr. Moody has few equals, and rugged as his preaching may seem to some, there is in it a pathos of a quality which few orators have ever reached, an appealing tenderness which not only wholly redeems it, but raises it, not unseldom almost to sublimity. No report can do the faintest justice to this or to the other most characteristic qualities of his public speech, but here is a specimen taken almost at random: "I can imagine when Christ said to the little band around Him, 'Go ye into all the world and preach the gospel,' Peter said, 'Lord, do you really mean that we are to go back to Jerusalem and preach the gospel to those men that murdered you?' 'Yes,' said Christ, 'go, hunt up that man that spat in my face, tell him he may have a seat in my kingdom yet. Yes, Peter, go find that man that made that cruel crown of thorns and placed it on my brow, and tell him I will have a crown ready for him when he comes into my kingdom, and there will be no thorns in it. Hunt up that man that took a reed and brought it down over the cruel thorns, driving them into my brow, and tell him I will put a sceptre in his hand, and he shall rule over the nations of the earth, if he will accept salvation. Search for the man that drove the spear into my side, and tell him there is a nearer way to my heart than that. Tell him I forgive

MR. MOODY'S STUDY.

Buildings and Grounds of the Young Ladies' Seminary. Mr. Moody's Home

A VIEW FROM THE WEST SIDE OF THE CONNECTICUT RIVER, AT NORTHFIELD, MASSACHUSETTS.

him freely, and that he can be saved if he will accept salvation as a gift.'" *Tell him there is a nearer way to my heart than that*—prepared or impromptu, what dramatist could surpass the touch?

MR. MOODY'S MANNER OF PREPARING A SERMON.

His method of sermon-making is original. In reality his sermons are never made, they are always still in the making. Suppose the subject is Paul: he takes a monstrous envelope capable of holding some hundreds of slips of paper, labels it "Paul," and slowly stocks it with original notes, cuttings from papers, extracts from books, illustrations, scraps of all kinds, nearly or remotely referring to the subject. After accumulating these, it may be for years, he wades through the mass, selects a number of the most striking points, arranges them, and, finally, makes a few jottings in a large hand, and these he carries with him to the platform. The process of looking through the whole envelope is repeated each time the sermon is preached. Partly on this account, and partly because in delivery he forgets some points, or disproportionately amplifies others, no two sermons are ever exactly the same. By this method also—a matter of much more importance—the delivery is always fresh to himself. Thus, to make this clearer, suppose that after a thorough sifting, one hundred eligible points remain in the envelope. Every time the sermon is preached, these hundred are overhauled. But no single sermon, by a mere limitation of time, can contain, say, more than seventy. Hence, though the general scheme is the same, there is always novelty both in the subject matter and in the arrangement, for the particular seventy varies with each time of delivery. No greater mistake could be made than to imagine that Mr. Moody does not study for his sermons. On the contrary he is always studying. When in the evangelistic field, the batch of envelopes, bursting with fatness, appears the moment breakfast is over; and the stranger who enters at almost any time of the day, except at the hours of platform work, will find him with his litter of notes, either stuffing himself or his portfolios with the new "points" he has picked up through the day. His search for these "points," and especially for light upon texts, Bible ideas, or characters, is ceaseless, and he has an eye like an eagle for anything really good. Possessing a considerable library, he browses over it when at home; but his books are chiefly

men, and no student ever read the ever-open page more diligently, more intelligently, or to more immediate practical purpose.

To Mr. Moody himself, it has always been a standing marvel that people should come to hear him. He honestly believes that ten thousand sermons are made every week, in obscure towns, and by unknown men, vastly better than anything he can do. All he knows about his own productions is that somehow they achieve the result intended. No man is more willing to stand aside and let others speak. His search for men to whom the people will listen, for men who, whatever the meagreness of their message, can yet hold an audience, has been life-long, and whenever and wherever he finds such men he instantly seeks to employ them. The word jealousy he has never heard. At one of his own conventions at Northfield, he has been known to keep silent—but for the exercise of the duties of chairman--during almost the whole ten days' sederunt, while mediocre men—I speak comparatively, not disrespectfully—were pushed to the front.

It is at such conferences, by the way, no matter in what part of the world they are held, that one discovers Mr. Moody's size. He gathers round him the best men he can find, and very good men most of them are; but when one comes away it is always Mr. Moody that one remembers. It is he who leaves the impress upon us; his word and spirit live; the rest of us are forgotten and forget one another. It is the same story when on the evangelistic round. In every city the prominent workers in that field for leagues around are all in evidence. They crowd round the central figure like bees; you can review the whole army at once. And it is no disparagement to the others to say—what each probably feels for himself—that so high is the stature and commanding personality of Mr. Moody that there seems to be but one real man among them, one character untarnished by intolerance or pettiness, pretentiousness, or self-seeking. The man who should judge Mr. Moody by the rest of us who support his cause would do a great injustice. He makes mistakes like other men; but in largeness of heart, in breadth of view, in single-eyedness and humility, in teachableness and self-obliteration, in sheer goodness and love, none can stand beside him.

MR. MOODY'S FIRST VISIT TO GREAT BRITAIN.

After the early Chicago days the most remarkable episode in Mr. Moody's career was his preaching tour in Great Britain. The burning down of his church in Chicago severed the tie which bound him to the city, and though he still retained a connection with it, his ministry henceforth belonged to the world. Leaving his mark on Chicago, in many directions— on missions, churches, and, not least, on the Young Men's Christian Association— and already famous in the West for his success in evangelical work, he arrived in England, with his colleague Mr. Sankey, in June, 1873. The opening of their work there was not auspicious. Two of the friends who had invited them had died, and the strangers had an uphill fight. No one had heard of them; the clergy received them coldly; Mr. Moody's so-called Americanisms prejudiced the super-refined against him; the organ and the solos of Mr. Sankey were an innovation sufficient to ruin almost any cause. For some time the prospect was bleak enough. In the town of Newcastle finally some faint show of public interest was awakened. One or two earnest ministers in Edinburgh went to see for themselves. On returning they reported cautiously, but on the whole favorably, to their brethren. The immediate result was an invitation to visit the capital of Scotland; and the final result was the starting of a religious movement, quiet, deep, and

THE NORTHFIELD AUDITORIUM: COMPLETED DURING THE PRESENT YEAR, AND THE NEWEST IN THE GROUP OF SEMINARY BUILDINGS. IT HAS A SEATING CAPACITY OF THREE THOUSAND.

lasting, which moved the country from shore to shore, spread to England, Wales, and Ireland, and reached a climax two years later in London itself.

This is not the place, as already said, to enter either into criticism or into details of such a work. Like all popular movements, it had its mistakes, its exaggerations, even its grave dangers; but these were probably never less in any equally wide-spread movement of history, nor was the balance of good upon the whole ever greater, more solid, or more enduring. People who understand by a religious movement only a promiscuous carnival of hysterical natures, beginning in excitement and ending in moral exhaustion and fanaticism, will probably be assured in vain that whatever were the lasting characteristics of this movement, these were not. That such elements were wholly absent may not be asserted; human nature is human nature; but always the first to fight them, on the rare occasions when they appeared, was Mr. Moody himself. He, above all popular preachers, worked for solid results. Even the mere harvesting—his own special department—was a secondary thing to him compared with the garnering of the fruits by the Church and their subsequent growth and further fruitfulness. It was the writer's privilege as a humble camp-follower to follow the fortunes of this campaign personally from town to town, and from city to city, throughout the three kingdoms, for over a year. And time has only deepened the impression not only of the magnitude of the results immediately secured, but equally of the permanence of the after effects upon every field of social, philanthropic, and religious activity. It is not too much to say that Scotland—one can speak with less knowledge of England and Ireland—would not have been the same to-day but for the visit of Mr. Moody and Mr. Sankey; and that so far-reaching was, and is, the influence of their work, that any one who knows the inner religious history of the country must regard this time as nothing short of a national epoch. If this is a specimen of what has been effected even in less degree elsewhere, it represents a fact of commanding importance. Those who can speak with authority of the long series of campaigns which succeeded this in America, testify in many cases with almost equal assurance of the results achieved both throughout the United States and Canada.

After his return from Great Britain, in 1875, Mr. Moody made his home at Northfield, his house in Chicago having been swept away by the fire. And from this point onward his activity assumed a new and extraordinary development. Continuing his evangelistic work in America, and even on one occasion revisiting England, he spent his intervals of repose in planning and founding the great educational institutions of which Northfield is now the centre.

MR. MOODY'S SCHOOLS AT NORTHFIELD.

There is no stronger proof of Mr. Moody's breadth of mind than that he should have inaugurated this work. For an evangelist seriously to concern himself with such matters is unusual; but that the greatest evangelist of his day, not when his powers were failing, but in the prime of life, and in the zenith of his success, should divert so great a measure of his strength into educational channels, is a phenomenal circumstance. The explanation is manifold. No man sees so much slip-shod, unsatisfactory and half-done work as the evangelist; no man so learns the worth of solidity, the necessity for a firm basis for religion to work upon, the importance to the Kingdom of God of men who "weigh." The value, above all things, of character, of the sound mind and disciplined judgment, are borne in upon him every day he lives. Converts without these are weak-kneed and useless; Christian workers inefficient, if not dangerous. Mr. Moody saw that the object of Christianity was to make good men and good women; good men and good women who would serve their God and their country not only with all their heart, but with all their mind and all their strength. Hence he would found institutions for turning out such characters. His pupils should be committed to nothing as regards a future profession. They might become ministers or missionaries, evangelists or teachers, farmers or politicians, business men or lawyers. All that he would secure would be that they should have a chance, a chance of becoming useful, educated, God-fearing men. A favorite aphorism with him is, that "it is better to set ten men to work than to do the work of ten men." His institutions were founded to equip other men to work, not in the precise line, but in the same broad interest as himself. He himself had had the scantiest equipment for his life-work, and he daily lamented—though perhaps no one else ever did—the deficiency. In his journeys he constantly met young men and young women of earnest spirit,

MR. MOODY HOLDING A SERVICE ON THE HILL CALLED "NEW CALVARY," NEAR JERUSALEM, SUNDAY AFTERNOON, APRIL 28, 1892. MR. MOODY STANDS WHERE LINES DRAWN FROM THE TWO STARS AT THE MARGIN OF THE PICTURE WOULD CROSS EACH OTHER.

with circumstances against them, who were in danger of being lost to themselves and to the community. These especially it was his desire to help, and afford a chance in life. "The motive," says the "Official Handbook," "presented for the pursuit of an education is the power it confers for Christian life and usefulness, not the means it affords to social distinction, or the gratification of selfish ambition. It is designed to combine, with other instruction, an unusual amount of instruction in the Bible, and it is intended that all the training given shall exhibit a thoroughly Christian spirit. . . . No constraint is placed on the religious views of any one. . . . The chief emphasis of the instruction given is placed upon the life."

The plan, of course, developed by degrees, but once resolved upon, the beginning was made with characteristic decision; for the years other men spend in criticising a project, Mr. Moody spends in executing it. One day in his own house, talking with Mr. H. N. F. Marshall about the advisability of immediately securing a piece of property—some sixteen acres close to his door—his friend expressed his assent. The words were scarcely uttered when the owner of the land was seen walking along the road. He was invited in, the price fixed, and, to the astonishment of the owner, the papers made out on the spot. Next winter a second lot was bought, the building of a seminary for female students commenced, and at the present moment the land in connection with this one institution amounts to over two hundred and seventy acres. The current expense of this one school per annum is over fifty-one thousand dollars, thirty thousand dollars of which comes from the students themselves; and the existing endowment, the most of which, however, is not yet available, reaches one hundred and four thousand dollars. Dotted over the noble campus thus secured, and clustered especially near Mr. Moody's home, stand ten spacious buildings and a number of smaller size, all connected with the Ladies' Seminary. The education, up to the standard aimed at, is of first-rate quality, and prepares students for entrance into Wellesley and other institutions of similar high rank.

Four miles distant from the Ladies' Seminary, on the rising ground on the opposite side of the river, are the no less imposing buildings of the Mount Hermon School for Young Men. Conceived earlier than the former, but carried out later, this institution is similar in character, though many of the details are different. Its three or four hundred students are housed in ten fine buildings, with a score of smaller ones. Surrounding the whole is a great farm of two hundred and seventy acres, farmed by the pupils themselves. This economic addition to the educational training of the students is an inspiration of Mr. Moody's. Nearly every pupil is required to do from an hour and a half to two hours and a half of farm or industrial work each day, and much of the domestic work is similarly distributed. The lads work on the roads, in the fields, in the woods; in the refectory, laundry, and kitchen; they take charge of the horses, the cattle, the hogs, and the hens—for the advantage of all which the sceptical may be referred to Mr. Ruskin. Once or twice a year nearly everyone's work is changed; the indoor lads go out, the farm lads come in. Those who before entering the school had already learned trades, have the opportunity of pursuing them in leisure hours, and though the industrial department is strongly subordinated to the educational, many in this way help to pay the fee of one hundred dollars exacted annually from each pupil, which pays for tuition, board, rooms, etc.*

THE LARGE PROFITS OF THE MOODY AND SANKEY HYMN-BOOK.

The mention of this fee—which, it may be said in passing, only covers half the cost—suggests the question as to how the vast expenses of these and other institutions, such as the new Bible Institute in Chicago, and the Bible, sewing and cooking school into which the Northfield Hotel is converted in winter, are defrayed. The buildings themselves and the land have been largely the gift of friends, but much of the cost of maintenance is paid out of Mr. Moody's own pocket. The fact that Mr. Moody has a pocket has been largely dwelt upon by his enemies, and the amount and source of its contents are subjects of curious speculation. I shall suppose the critic to be honest, and divulge to him a fact which the world has been slow to learn—the secret of Mr. Moody's pocket. It is, briefly, that Mr. Moody is the owner of one of the most paying literary properties in existence. It is the hymn-book

---

* An exhaustive literature, up to date and fully describing all the Northfield institutions, splendidly edited by Mr. Henry W. Rankin, one of Mr. Moody's most wise and accomplished coadjutors, may be had at Revell's, 112 Fifth Avenue, New York.

MR. MOODY: SOME IMPRESSIONS AND FACTS. 69

MR. MOODY TIPPING THE BEGGARS IN JAFFA STREET, JERUSALEM. FROM A PHOTOGRAPH BY MR. GEORGE F. MACKAY. MR. MOODY'S COMPANION IS SELAH G. MERRILL, UNITED STATES CONSUL.

which, first used at his meetings in conjunction with Mr. Sankey, whose genius created it, is now in universal use throughout the civilized world. Twenty years ago, he offered it for nothing to a dozen different publishers, but none of them would look at it. Failing to find a publisher, Mr. Moody, with almost the last few dollars he possessed, had it printed in London in 1873. The copyright stood in his name; any loss that might have been suffered was his; and to any gain, by all the laws of business, he was justly entitled. The success, slow at first, presently became gigantic. The two evangelists saw a fortune in their hymn-book. But they saw something which was more vital to them than a fortune—that the busybody and the evil tongue would accuse them, if they but touched one cent of it, of preaching the gospel for gain. What did they do? They refused to touch it—literally even to touch it. The royalty was handed direct from the publishers to a committee of well-known business men in London, who distributed it to various charities. When the evangelists left London, a similar committee, with Mr. W. E. Dodge at its head, was formed in New York. For many years this committee faithfully disbursed the trust, and finally handed over its responsibility to a committee of no less weight and honor—the trustees of the Northfield seminaries, to be used henceforth in their behalf. Such is the history of Mr. Moody's pocket. It is pitiful to think that there are men and journals, both at home and abroad, who continue to accuse of self-seeking a man who has given up a princely fortune in noble—the man of the world would say superfluous—jealousy for the mission of his life. Once we heard far more of this. That Mr. Moody has lived it down is not the least of his triumphs.

A FOREIGN-OFFICE ROMANCE.

BY A. CONAN DOYLE.

Author of "Micah Clarke," "The Adventures of Sherlock Holmes," etc.

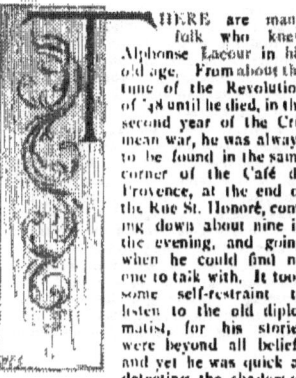

THERE are many folk who knew Alphonse Lacour in his old age. From about the time of the Revolution of '48 until he died, in the second year of the Crimean war, he was always to be found in the same corner of the Café de Provence, at the end of the Rue St. Honoré, coming down about nine in the evening, and going when he could find no one to talk with. It took some self-restraint to listen to the old diplomatist, for his stories were beyond all belief; and yet he was quick at detecting the shadow of a smile or the slightest little raising of the eyebrows. Then his huge rounded back would straighten itself, his bulldog chin would project, and his r's would burr like a kettledrum. When he got as far as "Ah, monsieur r-r-r-rit!" or "Vous ne me cr-r-r-royez pas donc!" it was quite time to remember that you had a ticket for the opera.

There was his story of Talleyrand and the three oyster-shells, and there was his utterly absurd account of Napoleon's second visit to Ajaccio. Then there was that most circumstantial romance (which he never ventured upon until his second bottle had been uncorked) of the Emperor's escape from St. Helena—how he lived for a whole year in Philadelphia, while Count Herbert de Bertrand, who was his living image, personated him at Longwood. But of all his stories there was none which was more notorious than that of his single-handed reconquest of Egypt. And yet, when Monsieur Otto's memoirs were written, it was found that there really was some foundation for old Lacour's incredible statement.

"You must know, monsieur," he would say, "that I left Egypt after Kléber's assassination. I would gladly have stayed on, for I was engaged in a translation of the Koran, and, between ourselves, I had thoughts at the time of embracing Mahometanism, for I was deeply struck by the wisdom of their views about marriage. They had made an incredible mistake, however, upon the subject of wine, and this was what the mufti who attempted to convert me could never get over. Then, when old Kléber died, and Menou came to the top, I felt that it was time for me to go. It is not for me to speak of my own capacities, monsieur, but you will readily understand that the man does not care to be driven by the mule. I carried my Koran and my papers to London, where Monsieur Otto had been sent by the First Consul to arrange a treaty of peace, for both nations were very weary of the war, which had already lasted ten years. Here I was most useful to Monsieur Otto on account of my knowledge of the English tongue, and also, if I may say so, on account of my natural capacity. They were happy days during which I lived in the Square of Bloomsbury. The climate of monsieur's country is, it must be confessed, detestable. But then, what would you have? Flowers grow best in the rain. One has but to point to monsieur's fellow-countrywomen to prove it.

"Well, Monsieur Otto, our ambassador, was kept terribly busy over that treaty, and all of his staff were worked to death. We had not Pitt to deal with, which was perhaps as well for us. He was a terrible man, that Pitt, and wherever half a dozen enemies of France were plotting together, there was his sharp-pointed nose in the middle of them. The nation, however, had been thoughtful enough to put him out of office, and we had to do with Monsieur Addington. But Milord Hawkesbury was the Foreign Minister, and it was with him that we were obliged to do our bargaining.

"You can understand that it was no child's play. After ten years of war each nation had got hold of a great deal which had belonged to the other, or to the other's allies. What was to be given back? And what was to be kept? Is this island worth that peninsula? If we do this at Venice, will you do that at Sierra Leone? If we give up Egypt to the Sultan, will you restore the Cape of Good Hope, which you have taken from our allies, the Dutch? So we wrangled and wrestled, and I have seen Monsieur Otto come back to the embassy so exhausted that his secretary and I had to help him from his carriage to the sofa. But at last things adjusted themselves, and the night came round when the treaty was to be finally signed.

"Now you must know that the one great card which we held, and which we played, played, played, at every point of the game, was that we had Egypt. The English were very nervous about our being there. It gave us a foot on each end of the Mediterranean, you see. And they were not sure that that wonderful little Napoleon of ours might not make it the base of an advance against India. So, whenever Lord Hawkesbury proposed to retain anything, we had only to reply: 'In *that* case, of course, we cannot consent to evacuate Egypt,' and in this way we quickly brought him to reason. It was by the help of Egypt that we gained terms which were remarkably favorable, and especially that we caused the English to consent to give up the Cape of Good Hope. We did not wish your people, monsieur, to have any foothold in South Africa, for history has taught us that the British foothold of one halfcentury is the British empire of the next. It is not your army or your navy against which we have to guard, but it is your terrible younger son and your man in search of a career. When we French have a possession across the seas, we like to sit in Paris and felicitate ourselves upon it. With you it is different. You take your wives and your children and you run away to see what kind of place this may be, and after that we might as well try to take that old Square of Bloomsbury away from you.

"Well, it was on the 1st of October that the treaty was finally to be signed. In the morning I was congratulating Monsieur Otto upon the happy conclusion of his labors. He was a little pale shrimp of a

man, very quick and nervous, and he was so delighted now at his own success that he could not sit still, but ran about the room chattering and laughing, while I sat on a cushion in the corner, as I had learned to do in the East. Suddenly, in came a messenger with a letter which had been forwarded from Paris. Monsieur Otto cast his eyes upon it, and then, without a word, his knees gave way and he fell senseless upon the floor.

"I ran to him, as did the courier, and between us we carried him to the sofa. He might have been dead, from his appearance, but I could still feel his heart thrilling beneath my palm.

"'What is this, then?' I asked.

"'I do not know,' answered the messenger. 'Monsieur Talleyrand told me to hurry as never man hurried before, and to put this letter into the hands of Monsieur Otto. I was in Paris at midday yesterday.'

"I know that I am to blame, but I could not help glancing at the letter, picking it out of the senseless hand of Monsieur Otto. My God, the thunderbolt that it was! I did not faint, but I sat down beside my chief and I burst into tears. It was but a few words, but they told us that Egypt had been evacuated by our troops a month before. All our treaty was undone, then, and the one consideration which had induced our enemies to give us good terms had vanished. In twelve hours it would not have mattered. But now the treaty was not yet signed. We should have to give up the Cape. We should have to let England have Malta. Now that Egypt was gone we had nothing to offer in exchange.

"But we are not so easily beaten, we Frenchmen. You English misjudge us when you think that because we show emotions which you conceal we are therefore of a weak and womanly nature. You cannot read your histories and believe that. Monsieur Otto recovered his senses presently, and we took counsel what we should do.

"'It is useless to go on, Alphonse,' said he; 'this Englishman will laugh at me when I ask him to sign.'

"'Courage!' I cried; and then, a sudden thought coming into my head, 'How do we know that the English will have news of this? Perhaps they may sign the treaty before they know of it.'

"Monsieur Otto sprang from the sofa and flung himself into my arms.

"'Alphonse,' he cried, 'you have saved me. Why should they know about it? Our news has come from Toulon to Paris and thence straight to us. Theirs will come by sea through the Straits of Gibraltar. At this moment it is unlikely that any one in Paris knows of it, save only Talleyrand and the First Consul. If we keep our secret we may still get our treaty signed.'

"Ah, monsieur, you can imagine the horrible uncertainty in which we spent the day. Never, never, shall I forget those slow hours during which we sat together, starting at every distant shout, lest it should be the first sign of the rejoicing which this news would cause in London. Monsieur Otto passed from youth to age in a day. As for me, I find it easier to go out and meet danger than to wait for it. I set forth, therefore, towards evening. I wandered here and wandered there. I was in the fencing-rooms of Monsieur Angelo, and in the salon-de-boxe of Monsieur Jackson, and in the club of Brooks, and in the lobby of the Chamber of Deputies, but nowhere did I hear any news. Still it was possible that Milord Hawkesbury had received it himself just as we had. He lived in Harley Street, and there it was that the treaty was to be finally signed that night at eight. I entreated Monsieur Otto to drink two glasses of Burgundy before he went out, for I feared lest his haggard face and trembling hands should rouse suspicion in the English Minister.

"Well, we went round together in one of the embassy's carriages about half-past seven. Monsieur went in alone, but presently, on excuse of getting his portfolio, he came out again, with his cheeks flushed with joy, to tell me that all was well.

"'He knows nothing,' he whispered, 'Ah, if the next half-hour were over!'

"'Give me a sign when it is settled,' said I.

"'For what reason?'

"'Because, until then, no messenger shall interrupt you unless he pass over my body.'

"He clasped my hand in both of his. 'I shall move one of the candles on to the table in the window,' said he, and hurried into the house, while I was left waiting beside the carriage.

"Well, if we could but secure ourselves from interruption for a single half-hour the day would be our own. I had hardly begun to form our plans when I saw the lights of a carriage coming swiftly from the direction of Oxford Street. Ah, if it should be the messenger! What could I do? I was prepared to kill him—yes, even to kill him rather than at this last moment allow our work to be undone. Thousands die to make a glorious war, why should not one die to make a glorious peace? What though they hurried me to the scaffold? I should have sacrificed myself for my country. I had a little curved Turkish knife strapped to my waist. My hand was on the hilt of it when the carriage which had alarmed me so rattled safely past me.

"But another might come. I must be prepared. Above all, I must not compromise the embassy. I ordered our carriage to move on, and I engaged what you call a hackney coach. Then I spoke to the driver and gave him a guinea. He understood that it was a special service.

"'You shall have another guinea, if you do what you are told,' said I.

"'All right, master,' said he, turning his slow eyes upon me without a trace of excitement or curiosity.

"'If I enter your coach with another gentleman, you will drive up and down Harley Street, and take no orders from any one but me. When I get out, you will carry the other gentleman to Watier's Club in Bruton Street.'

"'All right, master,' said he again.

"So I stood outside Milord Hawkesbury's house, and you can think how often my eyes went up to that window, in the hope of seeing the candle twinkle in it. Five minutes passed, and another five. Ah, how slowly they crept along! It was the first day of October, raw and cold, with a white fog crawling over the wet, shining cobblestones, and blurring the dim oil-lamps. I could not see fifty paces in either direction, but my ears were straining, straining, to catch the rattle of hoofs or the rumble of wheels. It is not a cheering place, monsieur, that street of Harley, even upon a sunny day. The houses are solid and very respectable over yonder, but there is nothing of the feminine about them. It is a city to be inhabited by males. But on that raw night, amid the damp and the fog, with the anxiety gnawing at my heart, it seemed the saddest, weariest spot in the whole wide world. I paced up and down, slapping my hands to keep them warm, and still straining my ears. And then suddenly, out of the dull hum of the traffic down in Oxford Street, I heard a sound detach itself, and grow louder and louder and clearer and clearer with every instant, until two yellow lights came flashing through the fog, and a light cabriolet whirled up to the door of the Foreign Minister. It had not stopped before a young fellow sprang out of it and hurried to the steps, while the driver turned his horse and rattled off into the fog once more.

"Ah, it is in the moment of action that I am best, monsieur. You, who only see me when I am drinking my wine in the Café de Provence, cannot conceive the heights to which I rise. At that moment, when I knew that the fruits of a ten years' war were at stake, I was magnificent. It was the last French campaign, and I, the general and army in one.

"'Sir,' said I, touching him upon the arm, 'are you the messenger for Lord Hawkesbury?'

"'Yes,' said he.

"'I have been waiting for you half an hour,' said I. 'You are to follow me at once. He is with the French Ambassador.'

"I spoke with such assurance that he never hesitated for an instant. When he entered the hackney coach and I followed him in, my heart gave such a thrill of joy that I could hardly keep from shouting aloud. He was a poor little creature, this Foreign Office messenger, not much bigger than Monsieur Otto, and I—Monsieur can see my hands now, and imagine what they were like when I was seven-and-twenty years of age.

"Well, now that I had him in my coach the question was what I should do with him. I did not wish to hurt him if I could help it.

"'This is a pressing business,' said he. 'I have a despatch which I must deliver instantly.'

"Our coach had rattled down Harley Street, but now, in accordance with my instructions, it turned and began to go up again.

"'Hullo!' he cried, 'what's this?'

"'What then?' I asked.

"'We are driving back. Where is Lord Hawkesbury?'

"'We shall see him presently.'

"'Let me out!' he shouted. 'There's some trickery in this. Coachman, stop the coach! Let me out, I say!'

"I pushed him back into his seat as he tried to turn the handle of the door. He roared for help. I clapped my palm across his mouth. He made his teeth meet through the side of it. I seized his own cravat and bound it over his lips. He still mumbled and gurgled, but the noise was covered by the rattle of our wheels. We were passing the Minister's house, and there was no candle in the window.

"The messenger sat quiet for a little, and I could see the glint of his eyes as he stared at me through the gloom. He was partly stunned, I think, by the force with which I had dashed him into his seat. And also he was pondering, perhaps, what he should do next. Presently he got his mouth partly free from the cravat.

"'You can have my watch and my purse if you will let me go,' said he.

"'Sir,' said I, 'I am as honorable a man as you are yourself.'

"'Who are you, then?'

"'My name is of no importance.'

"'What do you want with me?'

"'It is a bet.'

"'A bet! What d'you mean? Do you understand that I am on the government service, and that you will see the inside of a jail for this?'

"'That is the bet. That is the sport,' said I.

"'You may find it poor sport before you finish,' he cried. 'What is this insane bet of yours, then?'

"'I have bet,' I answered, 'that I will recite a chapter of the Koran to the first gentleman whom I should meet in the street.'

"'I do not know what made me think of it, save that my translation was always running in my head. He clutched at the door-handle, and again I had to hurl him back into his seat.

"'How long will it take?' he gasped.

"'It depends on the chapter,' I answered.

"'A short one, then, and let me go!'

"'But is it fair?' I argued. 'When I say a chapter, I do not mean the shortest chapter, but rather one which should be of average length.'

"'Help! help! help!' he squealed, and I had again to adjust his cravat.

"'A little patience,' said I, 'and it will soon be over. I should like to recite the chapter which would be of most interest to yourself.'

"He slipped his mouth free again.

"'Quick, then, quick!' he groaned.

"'The Chapter of the Camel?' I suggested.

"'Yes, yes.'

"'Or that of the Fleet Stallion?'

"'Yes, yes. Only proceed!'

"We had passed the window, and there was no candle. I settled down to recite the Chapter of the Stallion to him.

"Perhaps you do not know your Koran very well, monsieur. Well, I knew it by heart then, as I know it by heart now. The style is a little exasperating for any one who is in a hurry. But then, what would you have? The people in the East are never in a hurry, and it was written for them. I repeated it all with the dignity and solemnity which a sacred book demands, and the young Englishman he wriggled and groaned.

"'When the horses, standing on three feet and placing the tip of their fourth foot upon the ground, were mustered in front of him in the evening, he said, "I have loved the love of earthly good above the remembrance of things on high, and have spent the time in viewing these horses. Bring the horses back to me." And when they were brought back he began to cut off their legs and their——'

"It was at that moment that the young Englishman sprang at me. My God, how little can

I remember of the next few minutes! He was a boxer, this shred of a man. He had been trained to strike. I tried to catch him by the hands. Pac, pac, he came upon my nose and upon my eye. I put down my head and thrust at him with it. Pac, he came from below. But ah, I was too much for him. I hurled myself upon him, and he had no place where he could escape from my weight. He fell flat upon the cushions, and I seated myself upon him with such conviction that the wind flew from him as from a burst bellows.

"Then I searched to see what there was with which I could tie him. I drew the strings from my shoes, and with one I secured his wrists and with another his ankles. Then I tied the cravat round his mouth again, so that he could only lie and glare at me. When I had done all this, and had stopped the bleeding of my own nose, I looked out of the coach, and ah, monsieur, the very first thing which caught my eyes was that candle, that dear little candle, glimmering in the window of the Minister! Alone, with these two hands, I had retrieved the capitulation of an army and the loss of a province.

"Well, I had no time to lose, for at any moment Monsieur Otto might be down. I shouted to my driver, gave him his second guinea, and allowed him to proceed to Watier's. For myself, I sprang into our embassy carriage, and a moment later the door of the Minister opened. He had himself escorted Monsieur Otto down stairs, and now so deep was he in talk that he walked out bareheaded as far as the carriage. As he stood there by the open door there came the rattle of wheels, and a man rushed down the pavement.

"'A despatch of great importance for Milord Hawkesbury,' he cried.

"I could see that it was not my messenger, but a second one. Milord Hawkesbury caught the paper from his hand, and read it by the light of the carriage lamp. His face, monsieur, was as white as this plate before he had finished.

"'Monsieur Otto,' he cried, 'we have signed this treaty upon a false understanding. Egypt is in our hands.'

"'What!' cried Monsieur Otto. 'Impossible!'

"'It is certain. It fell to Abercromby, last month.'

"'In that case,' said Monsieur Otto, 'it is very fortunate that the treaty is signed.'

"'Very fortunate for you, sir,' cried Milord Hawkesbury, and he turned back to the house.

"Next day, monsieur, what they call the Bow Street runners were after me, but they could not run across salt water; and Alphonse Lacour was receiving the congratulations of Monsieur Talleyrand and the First Consul before ever his pursuers had got as far as Dover."

THE CHRIST CHILD IN ART.

BY ARCHDEACON FARRAR.

Being passages from a new book, entitled "The Life of Christ as represented in Art," by Archdeacon Farrar.

[In a book on "The Life of Christ as represented in Art," which Archdeacon Farrar has just published through the firm of Macmillan & Co., he says: "The representation of Christ, directly or indirectly, is the main object of Christian art in every stage, because Christian thought has turned in all epochs, and without interruption, to

THE CHRIST CHILD IN ART.

MADONNA BOLOGNA (BOTTICELLI)

source of the ready, even affectionate, reception that seems to await every word of his in both America and England. And to illustrate the text there are reproductions of the most significant and impressive of the works of Christian art, from the earliest days, when, under a reserve and reverence that pervaded the whole Christian world, and wherein there is something extremely beautiful, "Christ was only shadowed forth symbolically" in art, down to our own times, when directness and realism in the portrayal of Him have come to an extreme that can, as Dr. Farrar says, "only be regarded as degrading and profane." The result is a book very attractive and instructive to look through as well as to read.

Dr. Farrar modestly disclaims the right to speak simply as a critic, and says that he has written his book not from love of art, deep as his love of art is, but solely because he "wished to illustrate the thoughts about religion, and especially about our Saviour Jesus Christ, of which art has eternized the ever-varying phases." But it is clear that his love of art is intelligent as well as deep; for he has embodied in the book brief expositions of the principal pictures reproduced, full of sympathy and insight. The following article, after some fit introductory paragraphs, is a series of these expositions. For the exclusive privilege of using the passages of which the article is composed, and the pictures accompanying them, we are indebted to the publishers of the book, Messrs. Macmillan & Co.—EDITOR.]

THE Virgin Mary occupies a vast space in Christian art, and is inseparably mixed up with her Divine Son as an object of adoration in thousands of paintings executed between the culmination of Byzantinism and the Reformation. This fact alone shows how completely and unconsciously the art of an epoch is the reflection of its beliefs.

Very little is told us in the Gospels, and Madonna and Child, we shall have gained no insignificant glimpse into the functions and the history of art. And that for two reasons:

1. In the first place, it was a sort of *test* subject. It evidenced alike the religious feelings of individual painters, and the highest reach to which they could attain. For the Virgin is the human mother of Him who was the Word of God; and in

VIRGIN AND CHILD (MICHAEL ANGELO).

nothing elsewhere in the New Testament, about the Virgin Mary; but as the Christian ages advanced, she received greater and greater prominence in the thoughts of Christians. The apocryphal Gospels have many legends about her. The devotion with which she was regarded assumed a special development in the fourth and fifth centuries. . . .

If we can rightly appreciate the merits and defects of the chief schools and the chief painters in the representation of the painting the Virgin and Child the painter tried to show all that he could achieve in the expression of humanity at its loveliest, and of the divine in human form. Even if the inspiration of deep religious feeling is absent from the rendering of such a subject, the painter must, at the very lowest, express the sanctity of motherhood and the innocence of infancy; and to do this, and nothing more, may well tax the powers of the most consummate genius.

2. In the second place, in every new

Madonna the painter not only challenged comparison with himself, and with all his contemporaries, but with generations of artists during many centuries. Thus, as Grayer says in his admirable work, *Les Vierges de Raphael*, "legions of painters are reunited under the banner of Raphael. His Virgins are the sovereign expression of a religious idea, incessantly pursued not only during the two centuries of the Renaissance (the fourteenth and fifteenth), but also by all the Christian generations from the Catacombs down to Giotto." We find "Madonnas" from the second (?) to the fifth century. They become rare from that time till the thirteenth, but were produced by hundreds between 1294 and 1523. The manner in which the subject is treated marks every improvement of process, every change of conception, every powerful influence of individuality, every ripple on the deep ocean of religious life.

Of the Madonna Dolorosa there are two lovely specimens in our National Gallery.

One of these is the famous *tondo* of Sandro Botticelli [page 76 of this magazine]. Those who only look at his "Spring" or "Venus rising from the Sea" might think that the painter's soul was full of joy; but a picture like this shows how deep and dark were the shadows flung by the Renaissance; how terrible were the troubles stirred up by the feverish unrest of the doubts and passions which it let loose.

In this lovely picture, of which the fascination grows continually on those who gaze at it, the Virgin is giving her breast to the unweaned Child. A long-haired, youthful angel, his face full of sorrow, bows his head and folds his arms in adoration. On the other side, a second angel turns upwards his melancholy gaze towards the Mother. Her eyes and her thoughts are far away. She is not looking at the Child upon her breast; apparently she is not even thinking of Him; or, if she is,

HOLY FAMILY (FILIPPINO LIPPI).

ADORATION OF THE SHEPHERDS (CORREGGIO). THE PICTURE IS USUALLY KNOWN AS "LA NOTTE" (THE NIGHT).

she thinks only of His sufferings. Even the angels, lovely as they are, show an almost human despair in their angelic hearts. They are wholly unlike the incarnate Innocencies of Fra Angelico, with their robes of tender hues, and their many-colored, sunlit wings. Still less do they resemble the radiant child-denizens of heaven, as Dell Raphael, Francia, Carpaccio, or Bocc painted them. As we look at them, we most fancy that they will burst into "s tears as angels weep," and that such te must often have coursed each other do their pale and melancholy cheeks.

ADORATION OF THE MAGI (BERNARDINO LUINI).

Still more pathetic in its hopelessness is the expression of the Virgin. It has none of the fervent passion of maternity, none of the rapt joyance of the Magnificat; but there is an infinite yearning in the far-off gaze. As in Botticelli's Madonna in the Uffizi, this Virgin is bowed down with deepest woe. The large, open eyes seem drowned in tears, as though she were devoting herself and her Son for the human race. Yet, amid her agony, she more than keeps her beauty. "Is not the riddle of the human race contained in such pictures?" asks Gruyer. "Are not these Virgins sad with the unconquerable sadness which man everywhere carries with him, while their brow is radiant at the same time with the hope which constantly reinspires us? This need of infinitude, which momently torments and elevates us, is a sure guarantee of our immortality."

. . . .

Another of Angelo's Madonnas, which is neither religious nor domestic, is in the Uffizi at Florence [page 77]. The powerful figure of the Virgin is kneeling, and she seems to be handing Jesus over her right shoulder into the arms of the aged St. Joseph. The little St. John is walking in a road below the scene, and looks joyously back at the Holy Child. Seated on the wall behind, on either side, are five naked youths—beautiful and powerful figures, but wholly unconnected with the picture, and worse than meaningless. They are a fatal indication that the painter wished chiefly, as Vasari says, "mostrare maggiormente l'arte sua essere grandissima," to show how completely he had

THE CHRIST CHILD IN ART.

mastered the laws of perspective (to which so much attention had been directed by Paolo Uccello), and also his power to represent the nude.

The most famous picture of Correggio is *La Notte* [page 79], in the Dresden Gallery. It has all his sweetness and incontestable charm, his mastery of coloring, his sunny softness, his technical skill in chiaroscuro. The light from the Divine Child, as He lies on the straw of the manger, irradiates the happy, smiling features of the Virgin, and dazzles the astonished gaze of the humble shepherdess, who is bringing a pair of turtle-doves. A poor old shepherd is about to shroud his face with his mantle, and the splendid youth by his side turns away in rapturous astonishment. Behind the Virgin, Joseph is tethering the ass, and in the sky a group of angels of exquisite loveliness, but showing the same characteristic foreshortening which made a canon of Parma say to Correggio, after looking at his decoration of the cathedral dome, " Ci avete fatto gauzzetto di rane " (" You have made us a fricassee of frogs ").

The "Adoration of the Kings" [page 76], by Gentile da Fabriano, in the Academy at Florence, is a truly splendid work, not only rich and bright, but full of feeling. The details are magnificent, and the finish is extraordinary. The hand of the Child, resting on the bald head of the old white-bearded king, who kneels in utter lowliness to kiss His feet, is a marvel of grace, dignity, and pathos.

But there is, perhaps, no nobler "Adoration of the Magi" than the fresco by Bernardino Luini at Saronno [page 80]. The beautiful and modest Virgin is leaning against the manger wall, with the ox and ass behind her. The Holy Child with His left hand holds the edge of her veil; His little right hand blesses a grand old king in robes of ermine and golden chain, whose sword and turban are carried by a beautiful youth. Behind him is the youthful Melchior, who is represented as a fine negro; Balthazar kneels to present his offering on the other side. One of the attendants shades his eyes from the star which gleams above the stable roof. Down the hillside come others of the retinue leading horses, camels, and a giraffe. A choir of lovely child-angels sing their Christmas carols in the sky.

Mr. Holman Hunt's " Finding of Christ in the Temple " [page 81] is undoubtedly one of the most profound and deeply studied religious pictures of this or of any age, and he has treated the subject in a manner which can never be surpassed. The scene is a sort of open *loggia*, approached by steps from the Temple court, and having at one end a gilded latticework. Just outside sits a lame beggar,

and in the courtyard below we see the builders at work on Herod's yet unfinished temple, and catch a glimpse of a rejected corner-stone. At the back of this lecture-room a boy is scaring away the intrusive doves with a streamer of silk. In the distance is a seller of animals, and a family has taken a lamb from its ewe to offer at the consecration of a first-born child. The rabbis, seven in number, are seated on a semi-circular divan, and are richly dressed in Eastern costume. The nearest rabbi, blind and very aged, is clasping to his breast a roll of the Thora, and is a type of the Jewish law, already beginning to fall dead and effete in useless formalism. One of the Levite chorister boys behind him is reverently lifting a fold of the Thora covering to kiss it. Three other boys, with their musical instruments, are curiously watching the meeting of the boy Christ with His parents.

The old blind rabbi has evidently been agitated by some answer of Jesus, and the one next to him holds a phylactery in his hand, and comforts him. The next, a man in the prime of life, has been deeply and favorably struck, and has unrolled the law-scroll on his knee, while he gazes on Christ with earnest thought. The rest are less affected by what they have heard. One of them is about to drink a bowl of wine which an attendant is pouring out for him.

The boy Jesus has just caught sight of Joseph and His mother, and has risen from His seat at the feet of the doctors to salute them. The Virgin draws him towards her with a look of intense and yearning love; but His thoughts are far away. One hand lies passive in her tender grasp, the other is tightening the buckle of His girdle, while he seems to be saying, "How is it that ye sought Me? Wist ye not that I must be in My Father's House?" He is dressed in the costume which would then have been worn by a peasant boy of Galilee, except that it has a fringe. There is a natural aureole formed by the light passing through the edge of the reddish golden hair, which was a traditional element in the beauty of His ancestor David. Joseph, with his tools, stands behind the Virgin. His right hand seems to hover with infinite awe and tenderness over the shoulders of the Divine Boy.

The great aim of the painter in this picture has been to avoid all mere prettiness, all touch of effeminacy, in the figure of the boy Christ. He wished to represent Him as ready, gentle, manly; full of the most heavenly thoughts, yet meek and lowly, and desiring to be reverent to His earthly parents. He has been eminently successful. No mediæval painter—not even L. da Vinci, or Luini, or Raphael—ever painted so pure an ideal of the boy Christ, or produced any rendering of this favorite subject so thorough or so perfect. As we look at it, we can say:

"This, this is *Thou!* No idle painter's dream
Of aureoled, imaginary Christ,
Laden with attributes that make not God,
But Jesus, Son of Mary, lowly, wise,
Obedient, subject unto parents, mild,
Meek—as the meek that shall inherit earth;
Pure—as the pure in heart that shall see God."
—MISS MULOCK.

THE TAKIN' IN OF OLD MIS' LANE

By ELLA HIGGINSON.

"WELL, I guess I might 's well string them beans for dinner before I clean up," said Mrs. Bridges.

She took a large milkpan full of beans from the table, and sat down by the window.

"Isaphene," she said, presently, "what do you say to an organ an' a horse an' buggy —a horse with some style about him, that you could ride or drive, an' that 'u'd always be up when you wanted to go to town?"

"What do I say?" Isaphene was making a cake, and beating the mixture with a long-handled tin spoon. She had reddish-brown hair, that swept away from her brow and temples in waves so deep you could have lost your finger in any one of them; and good, honest, gray eyes, and a mouth that was worth kissing. She wore a blue cotton gown that looked as if it had just left the ironing table. Her sleeves were rolled to her elbows. She turned and looked at her mother as if she feared one of them had lost her senses; then she returned to the cake-beating with an air of good-natured disdain.

"Oh, you can smile an' turn your head on one side, but you'll whistle another tune before long, or I'll miss my guess. Isaphene, I've been savin' up chicken and butter money ever since we come to Puget Sound; then I've always got the money for the strawberry crop, an' for the geese an' turkeys, an' the calves, an' so on." Mrs. Bridges stopped, and, lowering her voice to a mysterious whisper, "Somebody's comin'," she exclaimed.

"Who is it?" Isaphene stood up straight, with that little quick beating, of mingled pleasure and dismay, that the cry of "Company" brings to country hearts.

"I can't see. I don't want to be caught peepin'. I can see it's a woman, though; she's just passin' the row of chrysanthums. Can't you stoop down an' peep? She won't see you 'way over there by the table."

Isaphene stooped, and peered cautiously through the wild cucumber vines that climbed over the kitchen window.

"Oh, it's Mis' Hanna!"

"My goodness! An' the way this house looks! You'll have to bring her out here in the kitchen, too. I s'pose she's come to spen' the day—she's got her bag, ain't she?"

"Yes. What'll we have for dinner? I ain't goin' to cut this cake for her. I want this for Sunday."

"Why, we've got corn' beef to boil, an' a head o' cabbage, an' these here beans; an' there's potatoes; an' watermelon perserves. An' you can make a custard pie. I guess that's a good enough dinner for her. There! She's knockin'! Open the door, can't you! Well, 'f I ever! Look at that grease spot on the floor!"

"Well, I didn't spill it."

"Who did, then, missy?"

"Well, *I* never."

Isaphene went to the front door, returning presently, followed by a tall, thin lady.

"Here's Mis' Hanna, maw," she said, with the air of having made a pleasant discovery. Mrs. Bridges got up, very much surprised to find who her visitor was, and shook hands with exaggerated delight.

"Well, I'll declare! It's really you, is it? At last? Well, set right down an' take off your things. Isaphene, take Mis' Hanna's things. My! ain't it warm, walkin'?"

"It is so." The visitor gave her bonnet to Isaphene, dropping her black mitts into it after rolling them carefully together. "But it's always nice an' cool in your kitchen." Her eyes wandered about with a look of unabashed curiosity that took in everything. "I brought my crochet with me."

"I'm glad you did. You'll have to excuse the looks o' things. Any news?"

"None perticular." Mrs. Hanna began to crochet, holding the work close to her face. "Ain't it too bad about poor old Mis' Lane?"

"What about her?" Mrs. Bridges snapped a bean into three pieces, and looked at her visitor with a kind of pleased expectancy, as if almost any news, however dreadful, would be welcome as a relief to the monotony of existence. "Is she dead?"

"No, she ain't dead; but the poor old creature 'd better be. She's got to go to the poor-farm, after all."

There was silence in the kitchen, save for the click of the crochet-needle and the snapping of the beans. A soft wind came in the window and drummed with the lightest of touches on Mrs. Bridges's temple. It brought all the sweets of the old-fashioned flower-garden with it—the mingled breaths of mignonette, stock, sweet lavender, sweet peas, and clove pinks. The whole kitchen was filled with the fragrance. And what a big, cheerful kitchen it was! Mrs. Bridges contrasted it unconsciously with the poor-farm kitchen, and almost shivered, warm though the day was.

"What's her children about?" she asked, sharply.

"Oh, her children!" said Mrs. Hanna, with a contemptuous air. "What does her children amount to, I'd like to know!"

"Her son's got a good comf'terble house an' farm."

"Well, what if he has? He got it with his wife, didn't he? An' M'lissy wont let his poor old mother set foot inside the house. I don't say as she is a pleasant body to have about—she's cross an' sick most all the time, an' childish. But that ain't sayin' her children oughtn't to put up with her disagreeableness."

"She's got a married daughter, ain't she?"

"Yes, she's got a married daughter." Mrs. Hanna closed her lips tightly together and looked as if she might say something, if she chose, that would create a sensation.

"AIN'T IT TOO BAD ABOUT POOR OLD MIS' LANE?"

THE TAKIN' IN OF OLD MIS' LANE.

"Well, ain't she got a good enough home to keep her mother in?"

"Yes, she has. But she got her home along with her husband, an' he won't have the old soul any more 'n M'lissy would."

There was another silence. Isaphene had put the cake in the oven. She knelt on the floor and opened the door very softly now and then, to see that it was not browning too fast. The heat from the oven had crimsoned her face and arms.

"Guess you'd best put a piece o' paper on top o' that cake," said her mother. "It smells kind o' burny like."

"It's all right, maw."

Mrs. Bridges looked out the window.

"Ain't my flowers doin' well, though, Mis' Hanna?"

"They are that. When I come up the walk I couldn't help thinkin' of poor old Mis' Lane."

"What's that got to do with her?" There was resentment bristling in Mrs. Bridges's tone and glance.

Mrs. Hanna stopped crocheting, but held her hands stationary in the air, and looked over them in surprise at her questioner.

"Why, she ust to live here, you know."

"She did! In this house?"

"Why, yes. Didn't you know that? Oh, they ust to be right well off 'n her husband's time. I visited here consid'rable. My! the good things she always had to eat! It makes my mouth water to think of them."

"Hunh! I'm sorry I can't give you as good as she did," said Mrs. Bridges, stiffly.

"Well, as if you didn't! You set a beautiful table, Mis' Bridges, an', what's more, that's your reputation all over. Everybody says that about you."

Mrs. Bridges smiled deprecatingly, with a faint blush of pleasure.

POOR OLD MIS' LANE.

"They do, Mis' Bridges. I just told you about Mis' Lane because you'd never think it now of the poor old creature. An' such flowers 's she ust to have on both sides that walk! Larkspurs an' sweet-williams an' bachelor's-buttons an' pumgranates an' mournin' widows, an' all kinds. Guess you didn't know she set out that pink cabbage-rose at the north end o' the front porch, did you? An' that hop-vine that you've got trained over your parlor window—set that out, too. An' that row of young alders between here an' the barn—she set them all out with her own hands; dug the holes herself. It's funny she never told you she lived here."

"Yes, it is," said Mrs. Bridges, slowly and thoughtfully.

"It's a wonder she never broke down an' cried when she was visitin' here. She can't mention the place without cryin'."

A dull red came into Mrs. Bridges's face.

"She never visited here."

"Never visited here!" Mrs. Hanna laid her crochet and her hands in her lap, and stared. "Why, she visited everywhere. That's the way she managed to keep out o' the poor-house so long. Everybody was real consid'rate about invitin' her. But I expect she didn't like to come here, because she thought so much of the place."

Isaphene looked over her shoulder at her mother, but the look was not returned. The beans were sputtering nervously into the pan.

"Ain't you got about enough, maw?" she said. "That pan seems to be gettin' hefty."

"Yes, I guess." She got up, brushing the strings off her apron, and set the pan on the table. "I'll watch the cake now, Isaphene. You put the beans on in the pot to boil. Put a piece o' that salt pork in with 'em. Better get 'em on right away. It's pret' near eleven. Ain't this oven too hot with the door shet?"

Then the pleasant preparations for dinner went on. The beans soon began to boil, and an appetizing odor floated through the kitchen. Then the potatoes were pared—big, white fellows, smooth and long—with a sharp, thin knife, round and round and round, each without a break until the whole paring had curled itself about Isaphene's pretty arm to the elbow. The cabbage was chopped finely for the cold-slaw, and the vinegar and butter set on the stove in a saucepan to heat. Then Mrs. Bridges began to set the table, covering it first with a red cloth having a white border and fringe. In the middle of the table she placed an uncommonly large, six-bottled caster.

"I guess you'll excuse a red tablecloth, Mis' Hanna. The men-folks get their shirt-sleeves so dirty out 'n the fields that you can't keep a white one clean no time."

"I use red ones myself most the time," replied Mrs. Hanna, crocheting industriously. "It saves washin'. I guess poor old Mis' Lane 'll have to see the old place after all these years; they'll take her right past here to the poor-farm."

Mrs. Bridges set on the table a white plate holding a big square of yellow butter, and stood looking through the open door, down the path, with its tall hollyhocks and scarlet poppies on either side. Between the house and the barn some wild mustard had grown, thick and tall, and was now drifting, like a golden cloud, against the pale blue sky. Butterflies were throbbing through the air, and grasshoppers were crackling everywhere. It was all very pleasan. and peaceful; while the comfortable house and barns, the wide fields stretching away to the forest, and the cattle feeding on the hillside gave a look of prosperity. Mrs. Bridges wondered how she would feel—after having loved the place—riding by to the poor-farm. Then she pulled herself together and said, sharply:

"I'm afraid you feel a draught, Mis' Hanna, settin' so close to the door."

"Oh, my, no; I like it. I like lots o' fresh air. If I didn't have six childern an' my own mother to keep, I'd take her myself."

"Take who?" Mrs. Bridges's voice rasped as she asked the question. Isaphene paused on her way to the pantry, and looked at Mrs. Hanna with deeply thoughtful eyes.

"Why, Mis' Lane—who else?—before I'd let her go to the poor-farm."

"Well, I think her children ought to be made to take care of her!" Mrs. Bridges went on setting the table with brisk, angry movements. "That's what I think about it. The law ought to take holt of it."

"Well, you see the law *has* took holt of it," said Mrs. Hanna, with a grim smile. "It seems a shame that there ain't somebody 'n the neighborhood that 'u'd take her in. She ain't much expense, but a good deal o' trouble. She's sick, in an' out o' bed, nigh onto all the time. My opinion is she's been soured by all her troubles; an' that if somebody 'u'd only take her an' be kind to her, her temper'ment 'u'd emprove wonderful. She's always mighty grateful for every little chore you do her. It just makes my heart ache to think o' her goin' to the poor-farm!"

Mrs. Bridges shut her lips tightly together; all the softness and irresolution went out of her face.

"Well, I'm sorry for her," she said, with an air of dismissing a disagreeable subject; "but the world's full o' troubles, an' if you cried over all o' them you'd be cryin' all the time. Isaphene, you go out an' blow that dinner-horn. I see the men folks ev' got the horses about foddered."

"I'm thinkin' about buyin' a horse an' buggy," she announced, with sternly repressed triumph, when the girl had gone out. "An' an organ. Isaphene's been wantin' one, an' I don't believe her paw'll ever get worked up to the pitch o' gettin' it for her. But I've got some money laid by. I'd like to see his eyes when he comes home an' finds a bran new buggy with a top an' all, an' a horse that he can't hetch to a plough, no matter how bad he wants to! I ain't sure but I'll get a phaeton."

"They ain't as strong, but they're handy to get in an' out of—'specially for old, trembly knees."

"I ain't so old that I'm trembly."

"Oh, my—no," said Mrs. Hanna, with a little start. "I was just thinkin' mebbe sometimes you'd go out to the poor-farm an' take poor old Mis' Lane for a little ride. It ain't more'n five miles, is it? She ust to have a horse an' buggy o' her own. Somehow, I can't get her off o' my mind at all to-day. I just heard about her 's I was startin' for your house."

The men came to the house, pausing on the back porch to clean their boots on the scraper, and wash their hands and faces with water dipped from the rain-barrel. Their faces shone like brown marble when they came in.

It was five o'clock when Mrs. Hanna, with a sigh, began rolling the lace she had crocheted around the spool, preparatory to taking her departure.

"—" BLESS THESE KIND PEOPLE—BLESS 'EM, OH, LORD GOD!"

"Well," she said, "I must go. I had no idy it was so late. How the time does go, talkin'. Just see how well I've done— crocheted full a yard since dinner-time! My! how pretty that hop-vine looks. 'T makes awful nice shade, too. I guess when Mis' Lane planted 't she thought

she'd be settin' under it herself to-day—she took such pleasure in it."

The ladies were sitting on the front porch. It was cool and fragrant out there. The shadow of the house reached almost to the gate now. The bees had been drinking too many sweets—greedy fellows! and were lying in the red poppies, droning stupidly. A soft wind was blowing from Puget Sound and turning over the clover leaves, making here a billow of dark green and there one of light green; it was setting loose the perfume of the blossoms, too, and sifting silken thistle-needles through the air. Along the fence was a hedge, eight feet high, of the beautiful ferns that grow luxuriantly in western Washington. The pasture across the lane was a tangle of royal color, being massed in with golden-rod, pink-weed, yarrow, purple thistles, and field daisies; the cottonwoods that lined the creek at the side of the house were snowing. There was a wild syringa near the gate, throwing out spray upon spray of white, delicately scented, gold-hearted flowers.

Mrs. Bridges arose and followed her guest into the spare bedroom.

"When they goin' to take her to the poor-farm?" she asked, abruptly.

"Day after to-morrow. Ain't it awful? It just makes me sick to think about it. I couldn't 'a' eat a bite o' dinner 'f I'd stayed at home, just for thinkin' about it. They say the poor old creature ain't done nothin' but cry an' moan sence she know'd she'd got to go."

"Here's your bag," said Mrs. Bridges. "Do you want I should tie your veil?"

"No, thanks; I guess I won't put it on. If I didn't have such a big fam'ly, an' my own mother to keep, I'd take her myself b'fore I'd see her go to the poor-house. If I had a small fam'ly an' plenty o' room, I

THE TAKIN' IN OF OLD MIS' LANE.

declare my conscience wouldn't let me rest, no way."

A dull red glow spread slowly over Mrs. Bridges's face.

"Well, I guess you needn't keep hintin' for me to take her," she said, sharply.

"*You!*" Mrs. Hanna uttered the word in a tone that was an unintentional insult; in fact, Mrs. Bridges affirmed afterward that her look of astonishment, and, for that matter, her whole air of dazed incredulity, were insulting. "I never once thought o' *you*," she said, with an earnestness that could not be doubted.

"Why not o' me?" demanded Mrs. Bridges, showing something of her resentment. "What you been talkin' about her all day for, 'f you wasn't hintin' for me to take her in?"

"I never thought o' such a thing," repeated her visitor, still looking rather helplessly dazed. "I talked about it because it was on my mind, heavy, too; an', I guess, because I wanted to talk my conscience down."

Mrs. Bridges cooled off a little, and began to drum on the bedpost with her rough fingers.

"Well, if you wasn't hintin'," she said, in a conciliatory tone, "it's all right. You kep' harpin' on the same string till I thought you was; an' it riles me awful to be hinted at. I'll take anything right out to my face, so 's I can answer it, but I won't be hinted at. But why"—having rid herself of the grievance she at once swung around to the insult—"why *didn't* you think o' me?"

Mrs. Hanna cleared her throat and began to unroll her mitts.

"Well, I don't know just why," she said, helplessly. She drew the mitts on, smoothing them well up over her thin wrists. "I don't know why. I'd thought o' most everybody 'n town—but you never come into my head *oust*. I was 's innocent o' hintin' 's a baby unborn."

Mrs. Bridges drew a long breath noiselessly.

"Well," she said absent-mindedly, "come again, Mis' Hanna. An' be sure you always fetch your work an' stay the afternoon."

"Well, I will. But it's your turn to come now. Where's Is'phene?"

"I guess she's makin' a fire 'n the cookstove to get supper."

"Well, tell her to come over an' stay all night with Julia some night."

Mrs. Bridges went into the kitchen and sat down, rather heavily, in a chair. Her face wore a puzzled expression.

"Isaphene, did you hear what we was a-sayin' in the bedroom?"

"Yes—most of it, I guess."

"Well, what do you s'pose was the reason she never thought o' me takin' Mis' Lane in?"

"Why, you never thought o' takin' her in yourself, did you?" said Isaphene, turning down the damper of the stove with a clatter. "I don't see how anybody else 'u'd think of it when you didn't yourself."

"Well, don't you think it was awful impudent in her to say that, anyhow?"

"No, I don't. She told the truth."

"Why ought they to think o' everybody takin' her exceptin' me, I'd like to know?"

"Because everybody else, I s'pose, have thought of it theirselves. The neighbors have all been chippin' in to help her for years. You never done nothin' for her, did you? You never invited her to visit here, did you?"

"No, I never. But that ain't no sayin' I wouldn't take her 's quick 's the rest of 'em. They ain't none of 'em takin' her very fast, be they?"

"No, they ain't," said Isaphene, facing her mother and looking at her steadily; "they ain't one of 'em but's got their hands full—no spare room, an' lots o' childern or their own folks to take care of."

"Hunh!" said Mrs. Bridges. She began chopping some cold boiled beef for hash.

"I don't believe I'll sleep to-night for thinkin' about it," she said, after a while.

"I won't neither, maw. I wish she wasn't goin' right by here."

"So do I."

After a long silence Mrs. Bridges said, "I don't s'pose your paw 'd hear to our takin' her in."

"I guess he'd hear to 't if we would," said Isaphene, dryly.

"Well, we can't do 't, that's all there is about it," announced Mrs. Bridges, with a great air of having made up her mind. Isaphene did not reply. She was slicing potatoes to fry, and she seemed to agree silently with her mother's decision. Presently, however, Mrs. Bridges said, in a less determined tone, "There's no place to put her exceptin' the spare room, an' we can't get along without that, no ways."

"No," said Isaphene, in a non-committal tone.

Mrs. Bridges stopped chopping and looked thoughtfully out the door.

"There's this room openin' out o' the kitchen," she said, slowly. "It's nice an' big an' sunny. It 'u'd be handy 'n winter, too, bein' right off the kitchen. But it ain't furnished."

"No," said Isaphene, "it ain't."

"An' I know your paw wouldn't furnish it."

Isaphene laughed. "No, I guess not," she said.

"Well, there's no use a-thinkin' about it, Isaphene; we just can't take her. Better get them potatoes on; I see the men-folks comin' up to the barn."

The next morning after breakfast Isaphene said suddenly, as she stood washing dishes, "Maw, I guess you better take the organ money an' furnish up that room."

Mrs. Bridges turned so sharply she dropped the turkey-wing with which she was polishing off the stove.

"You don't never mean it," she gasped.

"Yes, I do. I know we'd both feel better to take her in than to take in an organ"— they both laughed rather foolishly at the poor joke, "You can furnish the room real comfter'ble with what it 'u'd take to buy an organ; an' we can get the horse an' buggy, too."

"Oh, Isaphene, I've never meant but what you should have an organ! No, I won't never spen' that money for nothin' but an organ—so you can just shet up about it."

"I want a horse an' buggy worse, maw. We can get a horse that I can ride too. An' we'll get a phaeton, so's we can take Mis' Lane to church an 'round." Then she added, with a regular masterpiece of diplomacy, "We'll show the neighbors that when we do take people in, we take 'em in all over."

"Oh, Isaphene," said her mother, weakly, "wouldn't it just astonish 'em!"

It was ten o'clock of the following morning when Isaphene ran in and announced that she heard wheels coming up the lane. Mrs. Bridges paled a little and breathed quickly as she got her bonnet and went out to the gate. A red spring wagon was coming slowly toward her, drawn by a single horse. The driver was half asleep on the front seat. Behind, in a low chair, sat old Mrs. Lane; she was stooping over, her elbows on her knees, her gray head bowed.

Mrs. Bridges held up her hand, and the driver pulled in the not reluctant horse.

"How d'you do, Mis' Lane? I want you should come in an' visit me a while."

The old creature lifted her trembling head and looked at Mrs. Bridges; then she saw the old house, half hidden by vines and flowers, and her dim eyes filled with bitter tears.

"We ain't got time to stop, ma'am," said the driver, politely. "I'm a-takin' her to the county," he added, in a lower tone, but not so low that the old woman did not hear.

"You'll have to make time," said Mrs. Bridges, bluntly. "You get down an' help her out. You don't have to wait. When I'm ready for her to go to the county, I'll take her myself."

Not understanding in the least, but realizing, as he said afterwards, that she "meant business" and wasn't the kind to be fooled with, the man obeyed with alacrity.

"Now you lean all your heft on me," said Mrs. Bridges, kindly. She put her arm around the old woman and led her up the hollyhock path, and through the house into the pleasant kitchen.

"Isaphene, you pull that big chair over here where it's cool. Now, Mis' Lane, you set right down an' rest."

Mrs. Lane wiped the tears from her face with an old cotton handkerchief. She tried to speak, but the sobs had to be swallowed down too fast. At last she said, in a choked voice: "It's awful good in you—to let me see the old place—once more. The Lord bless you—for it! But I'm most sorry I stopped—seems now 's if I—just couldn't go on now."

"Well, you ain't goin' on," said Mrs. Bridges, while Isaphene went to the door and stood looking toward the hill with drowned eyes. "This is our little joke—Isaphene's an' mine. This'll be your home 's long 's its our'n. An' you're goin' to have this nice big room right off the kitchen, 's soon 's we can furnish it up. We'll have to put you in the spare room for a week or two, though. An' we're goin' to get a horse an' buggy—a *low* buggy, so 's you can get in an' out easy like—an' take you to church an' all 'round."

That night, after Mrs. Bridges had put Mrs. Lane to bed and told her good-night, she went out on the front porch and sat down; but presently, remembering that she had not put a candle in the room, she went back, opening the door noiselessly, not to disturb her. Then she stood perfectly still. The old creature had got out of the bed and was kneeling beside it, her face buried in her hands.

"Oh, Lord God," she was saying aloud, "bless these kind people—bless 'em, oh, Lord God! Hear a poor old mis'rable soul's prayer, an' bless 'em! An' if they've ever done a sinful thing, oh, Lord God, forgive 'em for it, because they've kep' me out o' the poor-house——"

Mrs. Bridges shut the door, and stood sobbing as if her heart would break.

"What's the matter, maw?" said Isaphene, coming up suddenly.

"Never you mind what's the matter," said her mother, sharply, to conceal her emotion. "You go to bed, missy, an' don't bother your head about what's the matter with me."

Then she went down the hall and entered her own room, and Isaphene heard the key turned in the lock.

THE OVERTHROW OF THE MOLLY MAGUIRES.

STORIES FROM THE ARCHIVES OF THE PINKERTON DETECTIVE AGENCY.

By CLEVELAND MOFFETT.

SOME twenty years ago five counties in eastern Pennsylvania were dominated, terrorized, by a secret organization, thousands strong, whose special purpose was to rob, burn, pillage, and kill. Find on the map that marvellous mineral country, as large as Delaware, which lies between the Blue Mountains on the south and the arm of the Susquehanna on the north, and there you will see what was the home of these banded outlaws, the merciless Molly Maguires. Look in Carbon County for Mauch Chunk, with its towering hills and picturesque ravines, and from there draw a line westward through Schuylkill County and into Northumberland County as far as Shamokin. This line might well be called the red axis of violence, for it cuts through Mount Carmel, Centralia, Raven Run, Mahanoy Plane, Girardville, Shenandoah, Tamaqua, Tuscarora, and Summit Hill, towns all abounding in hateful memories of the Molly Maguires. Now, on this line as a long diameter, construct an egg-shaped figure, to include in its upper boundary Wilkesbarre in Luzerne County and Bloomsburg in Columbia County, and on its lower to pass somewhat to the south of Pottsville. Your egg will be about fifty miles long and forty miles across, and will cover scores of thriving communities that once were the haunts of the murderers and ruffians who polluted with their crimes this fair treasure garden of a great State.

Such was the situation when the Centennial Exhibition was opening its gates to enthusiastic millions. A scant hundred miles separated the City of Brotherly Love from these tormented centres of violence.

But what a contrast! Here a proud metropolis was gay with flags and illuminations; there the mountains mourned in the ashes of poor men's homes. Here sounded rejoicing bells and cannons; there were heard the groans of victims butchered. Here were grand parades, and hurrahing multitudes; there lurked bands of armed assassins, defying alike the laws of man and God, and leaving behind them everywhere curses, and tears, and blood. The condition of things in Schuylkill, Carbon, Luzerne, Columbia, and Northumberland Counties, in this glorious year of grace 1876, was horrible to contemplate. And meantime the nation's orators at Philadelphia were blowing themselves red in the face at the trumpets of self-praise!

The origin and development of the Molly Maguires will always present a hard problem to the social philosopher, who will, perhaps, find some subtle relation between crime and coal. One understands the act of an ordinary murderer who kills from greed, or fear, or hatred; but the Molly Maguires killed men and women with whom they had had no dealings, against whom they had no personal grievances, and from whose death they had nothing to gain, except, perhaps, the price of a few rounds of whiskey. They committed murders by the score, stupidly, brutally, as a driven ox turns to left or right at the word of command, without knowing why, and without caring. The men who decreed these monstrous crimes did so for the most trivial reasons—a reduction in wages, a personal dislike, some imagined grievance of a friend. These were sufficient to call forth an order to burn a house where

THE OVERTHROW OF THE MOLLY MAGUIRES.

women and children were sleeping, to shoot down in cold blood an employer or fellow workman, to lie in wait for an officer of the law and club him to death. In the trial of one of them, Mr. Franklin B. Gowen described the reign of these ready murderers as a time "when men retired to their homes at eight or nine o'clock in the evening, and no one ventured beyond the precincts of his own door; when every man engaged in any enterprise of magnitude, or connected with industrial pursuits, left his home in the morning with his hand upon his pistol, unknowing whether he would again return alive; when the very foundations of society were being overturned."

In vain the officials of the Philadelphia and Reading and Lehigh Valley Railroads, whose lines spread over this region like huge arteries, offered thousands of dollars in rewards for the apprehension of the criminals. In vain Archbishop Wood, of Philadelphia, fought the Molly Maguires with the whole power of the Catholic Church, issuing an edict excommunicating all members of the organization, depriving them of all spiritual benefits, and refusing them burial in Catholic cemeteries. In vain the Catholic priests throughout the five counties, under Father Bridgeman, of Girardville, seeing that not even the Church's curse could check the course of crime, formed an organization popularly called the "Sheet Irons," which was to oppose the Molly Maguires politically and in every possible way. In vain reputable citizens in almost every town, formed and armed committees of vigilantes, who were to take the law into their own hands, inasmuch as the forces of the law were paralyzed. All was of no avail; public offices remained in the hands of ruffians; the same fierce crimes persisted; people were assaulted, robbed, and murdered with increasing frequency.

DETECTIVE McPARLAND DETAILED.

In 1873 Mr. Franklin B. Gowen, then president of the Philadelphia and Reading Railroad, took counsel with Allan Pinkerton in regard to the matter. "It was owing to Mr. Gowen," says Mr. Robert A. Pinkerton in a recent letter, "that the Molly Maguire organization was broken up. Mr. Gowen, when a young man, had been District Attorney of Schuylkill County, and, while occupying this office, had found great difficulty in convicting men accused of crimes, as the Mollys would swear to alibis for any of their members arrested. When he afterwards became the president of the Philadelphia and Reading Railroad, in order to protect its interests, and its employees, and the managers and superintendents of the mines which it owned, he found it necessary to break up this organization, and it was then he consulted Mr. Allan Pinkerton."

JAMES McPARLAND.

"I have the very man for you," said Allan Pinkerton, the man to whom he referred being James McParland. Like his employer, James McParland had become a detective by accident. For a number of years he had been occupied with irregular work, sailing the Great Lakes in the summer, and acting as coachman during the winter, when he could get employment. Early in the sixties, while he was employed in Chicago as a night watchman, Mrs. Allan Pinkerton came to know him, and interested herself in him. Through her recommendation and that of Capt. R. J. Linden, one of Allan Pinkerton's ablest lieutenants, he was given a chance to show what he could do on the Pinkerton detective force, and he was soon recognized as a young man of rare aptitude for detective work and advanced rapidly.

A few weeks after the interview between Mr. Gowen and Mr. Pinkerton, James McParland was announced to have sailed for Europe on an important mission. Only two men in the country knew that he had really set out for the terrorized region, with instructions to run down these Molly Maguire bandits, whether it took six months or six years, six hundred or six hundred thousand dollars. His orders from Allan Pinkerton were explicit:

"You are to remain in the field until every cut-throat has paid with his life for the lives so cruelly taken."

After some weeks of reconnoitring on foot through the coal regions, the young detective arrived in Pottsville, where he established himself in a boarding-house kept by a Mrs. O'Regan. There he met a man named Jennings, who volunteered to show him the sights of the city that same night. Passing a noisy drinking-place called the Sheridan House, McKenna, for that was McParland's assumed name, proposed going in. Jennings warned him as he valued his life never to cross the threshold of that place.

"It's kept by Pat Dormer," he said, "the big body-master of the Molly Maguires. He stands six feet four, weighs two hundred and fifty pounds, and is a bad man."

McPARLAND BECOMES A HERO AMONG THE MOLLY MAGUIRES.

McKenna noted his companion's frightened tone, but, far from being disturbed by these words, rejoiced to find himself so soon on the right scent. Later in the evening, having given Jennings the slip, he went back to the dangerous saloon and entered without ceremony, finding himself in the midst of a noisy company, most of them drinking, while some danced to a screaming fiddle. Things moved on rapidly enough during the next two hours. McKenna, having invited all hands to the bar, paid for a second round of drinks; and then, springing into the middle of the floor, danced a flying hornpipe, to the full approval of the assembled Irishmen, who were all Mollys. He completed the favorable impression thus made by singing a roaring song, and was then invited to a game of cards, Pat Dormer himself being his partner, against Jack Hurley and another big ruffian, named Frazer, who used to boast that he thrashed every stranger who came into camp.

"You've got six cards in your hand," said McKenna to Frazer, after a few minutes' playing; "that's too many in a game of euchre."

"You're a li——"

"Am I?" said McKenna, seizing Frazer's big hand in his sailor's grip, and making him show half a dozen cards.

The result was a fight in the hand-ball alley, which Pat Dormer lighted up especially for the purpose, the company of Mollys ranging themselves in an appreciative circle to see Frazer demolish the plucky little fellow, who, though strong and agile, was far out-classed in height and weight. In the first round Frazer caught the detective a swinging right-hander under the ear and knocked him down, while the spectators applauded. But the battle was not over yet; for McKenna's blood was up, and he was a hard hitter, his arm being nerved by the consciousness that much depended upon his victory. Six times in succession he floored the bully of Pottsville, and the seventh time Frazer fell heavily on his face and failed to get up again.

McKenna immediately became a hero. All hands insisted on treating him, and even Mrs. Dormer and her eldest daughter came forward with congratulations. In such a company friendships are made easily and quickly, and a week later the detective was on such intimate terms with the formidable Pat Dormer that he was invited to his sister's wedding, and pretended to get gloriously drunk with everybody else there. As a matter of fact, while apparently asleep on a bench, he managed to overhear some of the passwords and catch some of the signs and signals adopted by the Mollys, which he carefully practised the next day, and subsequently used with profit.

McPARLAND JOINS THE ORDER.

A little later, in December, 1873, McKenna told Dormer he was going to move on in search of a better job, and the admiring body-master gave him a letter to the desperate "Muff" Lawler, body-master of the Molly Maguire lodge at Shenandoah, a great coal centre twelve miles

THE OVERTHROW OF THE MOLLY MAGUIRES.

north of Pottsville, with a population of nearly ten thousand. This letter insured him a cordial reception, and he made such good use of his opportunities that within a few weeks he was installed as a boarder in Lawler's house, and was regarded by the Mollys who frequented Lawler's saloon as a roaring, reckless fellow, quite good enough—that is, bad enough—to be initiated into the Molly Maguires. The ceremony took place in due time over Lawler's saloon, and, after having paid for unlimited whiskey and been instructed in the signs and pass-words, McKenna was pronounced a member in full standing. And he rose in time to be secretary of a division, the Shenandoah.

An incident occurred about this time that greatly increased McKenna's prestige among the Mollys. He had accompanied "Muff" Lawler to Big Mine Run, to visit an aged Molly who was very ill. While in the sick-room, an enemy of Lawler's, Dick Flynn, the terror of the Colorado colliery, burst through the door, armed with a carving-knife and a six-shooter, and showing every intention of using them. Lawler jumped down-stairs and escaped, whereupon Flynn turned upon McKenna, and remarked with an oath that he had missed "Muff," but would kill his "Putty."

"We'll see about that," said McKenna, flashing a revolver in the man's face before he could make a move. Pale and trembling, Flynn dropped his weapon, and at a word from McKenna backed down the stairs.

"I don't like to kill you in the presence of a sick man and these ladies," said the detective. At the bottom of the stairs there was a beer-cellar, and in this the prisoner was securely locked, waiting the arrival of an officer, who took him to jail.

This display of nerve, taken with the thrashing of Frazer, gave McKenna a great reputation throughout that section; and he was soon regarded as one of the worst Mollys in the State, not only by members of the order who admired him, but by respectable citizens, who looked upon him with fear and abhorrence as a man capable of the most desperate acts. Wishing to leave no means untried that might ingratiate him still deeper in the confidence of the order, he created the impression that he had to his credit nearly all the crimes on the statute book, not excepting murder, and that the abundant supply of money he always seemed to have was the product of counterfeiting.

Having thus laid the foundation for his future work, McKenna, with a letter of recommendation from "Muff" Lawler, now began a period of wandering through the distracted counties, getting work in various mines, but never keeping one position very long. In the course of his travels, which extended over many weeks, he made the acquaintance of most of the prominent Mollys, including Jack Kehoe, of Girardville, and "Yellow Jack" Donahue, both of whom were afterwards hanged on his testimony. Everywhere he found that his reputation had preceded him, and he was received by all the Mollys with the respect which ruffians never fail to pay men whom they regard as greater ruffians than themselves. At each new stopping place he came into possession of new secrets touching crimes of the order already committed, and others that were planning, all of which he reported day by day to Allan Pinkerton.

HOW THE MOLLY MAGUIRES OPERATED.

He learned that the number of Molly Maguires in the five counties had been much exaggerated in the popular mind, through fear, and that there were not really more than three or four thousand active members of the organization, whereas it had been reported through the State that there were ten times that many. McKenna saw, however, that it was impossible to exaggerate the desperate character of these men. He found that each county was governed by a "county delegate," his territory being divided into districts, or "patches," each under a "body-master" or chief officer, who gave out the signs and pass-words to trusted members, and ordered the execution of crimes that had been decided upon. In nearly every case the body-master was the keeper of a saloon near one of the shafts, slopes, or drifts, and no autocrat ever wielded a power more

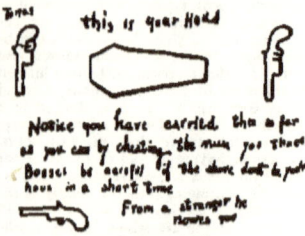

A "COFFIN-NOTICE."

irresponsible than his over all who came within his jurisdiction. In order to force the miners and workmen to buy liberally at his bar, which was usually run without a license, it was necessary for him to control their relations with the mines, and to do this he must have the superintendent absolutely in his power. If any superintendent dared to refuse the request of a body-master to hire or discharge any man, with or without reason, that superintendent's life was as good as forfeited. "Bosses" were in the same way constrained to give Mollys the best jobs —that is, the easiest —and in case of their failure to do so they were promptly made an example of with clubs or revolvers. Before killing a superintendent or a colliery "boss," the body-master would usually serve him with a "coffin-notice," a roughly written warning, bearing crudely drawn knives and revolvers, and a large coffin in the centre. Woe to the man who allowed such a notice to go unheeded! In nearly every instance he was shot or clubbed to death within a few days by unknown assailants.

A peculiar reciprocity system was in operation between the various "patches," in accordance with which, if the body-master of District No. 1 wanted a certain man killed, he would call upon the body-master of District No. 2 for men to do it; and in return for this favor, he was bound to furnish assassins for the body-master of District No. 2, whenever the latter found himself in a murderous mood. As a measure of safety, it was always arranged, if possible, to have the murders committed by men not acquainted with their victims, these being pointed out by the resident body-master. The commission of these murders was regarded as a title to distinction, and by way of pecuniary reward, it was customary, after each "accommodation" of this sort, to organize a dance and drunken revel for the benefit of the assassins. To illustrate the system: Whenever "Muff" Lawler of Shenandoah wanted a man put out of the way, he applied to Jack Kehoe of Girardville, thirteen miles to the south, for two, three, or four Mollys to do a "clean job." Kehoe would select the men, give them a special sign chosen by the two body-masters, tell them to provide themselves with firearms, and report to Lawler, whom he described accurately. Upon entering Lawler's saloon, they would throw him the sign agreed upon, whereupon he would answer and lead them to a place of concealment, usually in some lonely part of a road over which the victim would pass. There Lawler would leave them with a Molly whose duty it was to point out the "boss" or superintendent to be killed; and when he passed, the men from Girardville would shoot him down like a dog, leave his body at the roadside, and start off for home as if nothing had happened. This was a matter of weekly occurrence.

CAPTAIN J. B. LINDEN AT THE TIME OF THE MOLLY MAGUIRE TROUBLES.

AN IMPORTANT DISCOVERY.

One of the most important discoveries made by McKenna at this period was in regard to the murder of Alexander Rae, a mine superintendent, who was brutally beaten to death in October, 1868. From various hints dropped, he became convinced that a man named Manus Coll, familiarly known as "Kelly the Bum," had been in some way concerned in this crime. Coll had been a Molly for a number of years, but had been expelled from the order as being too bad even for that desperate organization. McKenna observed that Coll was constantly hanging about the saloon of Pat Hester, the Molly above mentioned, who, although a ruffian himself, had a wife who was a woman of refinement, and three intelligent and highly educated daughters, who were school teachers. McKenna remarked also that, although the women evidently loathed the presence of this drunken fellow Coll, they nevertheless treated him with a certain deference, plainly born of fear. There was no reasonable explanation of their manner, except that Coll knew of some crime committed by Hester, and so held him and his family in his power. So confident was McKenna of the justness of this conclusion that he went on a walking tour through Schuylkill and Northumberland Counties in Coll's company, hoping to draw valuable information from him. He was disappointed, however; for, although he got Coll drunk again and again, he could never draw from him any admission. Still his efforts were not in vain, for some months' later, when Coll had been imprisoned at Pottsville for burglary, McKenna suggested to Captain Linden, who had been detailed by Allan Pinkerton to serve as captain of the coal and iron police, an adroit ruse, which the captain at once proceeded to put into execution. Going to Coll's cell one day, Captain Linden said to him:

"Do you know what you told McKenna, in your drunken frolics together, about the murder of Alexander Rae?"

Coll was so completely deceived by this "bluff," that the next day he made a full confession. He said that Rae was driving along a lonely part of the road between Mount Carmel and the village of Centralia, when he was attacked by four Mollys—Pat Hester, Dooley, McHugh, and himself. Hester had suggested to them the plan, at his saloon, saying that Rae would have nineteen thousand dollars with him, which it was his custom to carry in a buggy, to pay off the men. By the merest accident Rae did not carry the money in his buggy on this particular night, having been ill and sent the money on ahead by his clerk, whom the outlaws allowed to drive by undisturbed. After drinking freely most of the night, the Mollys chosen for the murder set out at dawn on their deadly mission, and hid in the woods, where they drank more whiskey until Rae's buggy came in sight. At a signal from the picket, the assassins rushed upon their victim with drawn pistols, "Kelly the Bum" firing the first shot. Rae pleaded for his life, and handed the men his watch and sixty dollars in money, which was all he had with him. He offered to sign a check for any amount if they would spare him. The men hesitated a moment.

"What are we going to do with this man?" said one of the Mollys. McHugh answered:

"I'm not going to have a living man tagging me around," and then he fired, and some of the others fired also. Rae was only wounded, but with clubs and the butts of their revolvers, they beat him to death; his bleeding body being left beside a spring.

As the result of Coll's confession, Pat Hester, Dooley, and McHugh were subsequently tried, convicted, and hanged.

CAPTAIN J. R. LINDEN AT THE PRESENT DAY.

McPARLAND CALLED ON TO ASSIST IN THE MOLLY MAGUIRE CRIMES.

Early in 1875, Frank McAndrew, the body-master of the Shenandoah division, having been forced to go into another township to secure work, McParland, or "McKenna," was chosen as his successor, and as such was expected to furnish murderers when called upon, and in general to wield the terrible power of the organization. One of the first calls made on him was for men to destroy the Catawissa bridge on the Philadelphia and Reading Railroad, but by diplomacy he managed to have this project abandoned. He next learned of and frustrated a plan of the

Mollys to assassinate a "boss" named Forsythe; and about the same time (July, 1875), he saved the life of a young Welshman named Gomer James, whom the Mollys had planned to shoot at a night picnic near Shenandoah. Whenever McKenna learned of an outrage being planned, he immediately notified Mr. Franklin, superintendent of the Pinkerton Agency at Philadelphia, who then took measures to protect the lives or property threatened, by sending to the rescue a force of the coal and iron police, under Captain J. R. Linden. It was impossible, however, for the detective, work as he might, to prevent the continued commission of murders and assaults, for the territory actively covered by the organization was fifty or sixty miles square.

Early in July, 1875, while McKenna was still in Shenandoah, acting as a bodymaster, a shocking murder was committed by Molly Maguires at the town of Tamaqua, situated on the Little Schuylkill, some twenty miles to the east. The victim was Franklin B. Yost, a policeman, and a man who had served honorably in the civil war, and a most peaceful and worthy citizen. Hurrying to the scene of the crime, McKenna addressed himself to "Powder Keg" Carrigan, the body-master of that patch. The way in which Carrigan earned his sobriquet of "Powder Keg" well illustrates his character. Some years before, while working in a mine at Heckville, he had come into the slope one cold morning when the men were crowding around a huge salamander heaped with burning coals. He carried on his shoulder a keg of powder, and, seeing that there was no place for him at the fire, he leaned over the circle formed by his comfortable comrades, and, placing the keg of powder on the red-hot coals, remarked coolly:

"As long as you boys won't move, I'll have to make a place for myself."

The men scattered in terror right and left, whereupon Carrigan coolly lifted the keg of powder off the salamander, sat down upon it, lit his pipe, and began smoking.

McKenna was not long in learning that "Powder Keg" himself was the man at whose instigation the murder had been committed. Carrigan explained to him that they had killed the wrong man, his grievance having been not against Yost, but against another policeman, Bernard McCarron, who had aroused "Powder Keg's" enmity years before by frequently arresting him for disorderly conduct. Carrigan nursed the memory of this treatment, and when he had became a body-master at once proceeded to arrange for the killing of McCarron. Having applied to Alexander Campbell, the body-master of Landsford, Carbon County, as was customary, for two men to do a "clean job," he brought the men to a retired spot on McCarron's beat. Later in the night, when a policeman passed by, the two men shot him, according to orders, and then started for their homes. But on that night McCarron had exchanged beats with Yost, who accordingly came to a violent death, although neither the Mollys nor anyone else in the region had any but kind feelings toward him. Carrigan showed McKenna the revolver, a weapon of thirty-two caliber, with which the policeman had been killed, and explained that it had been borrowed from a Molly named Roarity by the two men, Hugh McGehan and James Doyle, who with others had done the murder. McGehan was the man who fired the fatal shot. McKenna secured the names of every man concerned in the crime, and ultimately, on his evidence, it was punished by the hanging, in Pottsville, of Hugh McGehan, Thomas Duffy, James Roarity, James Carl, and James Doyle.

TWO CLAIMANTS OF A REWARD FOR MURDER.

Following closely upon the murder of Yost, there came in August, 1875, a "Bloody Saturday," as it was called by the Mollys, when they killed on that one day, Thomas Guyther, a justice of the peace, at Gerardville, and, at Shenandoah, Gomer James, the same whose life had been saved a few weeks before by McKenna's intervention. James was a desperado himself, having some time before, while drunk, shot down an Irishman named Cosgrove, and this offence the Mollys had sworn to avenge. Angered by several failures, for which McKenna was responsible, the Mollys resolved that on this particular Saturday their plans should not miscarry. The Shenandoah firemen were giving a banquet in a public hall, and Gomer James was serving as bartender. A little before midnight, when the gayety was at its height, Thomas Hurley left his mother, who was sitting on a bench near the bar, and going up to James ordered a glass of beer. James served him promptly, whereupon Hurley threw down a nickel, and lifting the glass in his left hand, pretended to drain it. But he held a pistol, ready cocked, in the righthand pocket of his sack coat, and, while the glass was at his lips, he pulled the trigger. Then, quite unconcerned, he finished his beer, and affected to join in a search for the murderer. At the time he himself was not suspected, there being no evidence of his guilt, except an unobserved hole in his coat.

So fierce had been the desire for James's death that Jack Kehoe, the county delegate, had stated that the order would pay five hundred dollars to the man who should accomplish it. After the murder, at a meeting of the officers of the different Molly Maguire lodges of Schuylkill County, the payment of this reward came under discussion, and it then appeared that there were two claimants for the reward, Thomas Hurley and John McClaine. In order to decide between them, a committee of two was appointed; Pat Butler, a friend of McClaine's, being one, and McKenna himself, who, in his capacity of acting body-master, had taken a prominent part in the deliberations, being the other.

The following Sunday, Butler and McKenna met in a secret resort of the Mollys near Loss Creek, and there listened to the testimony of the two sides. Hurley made out an overwhelming case in his own favor, showing the pistol he had used, the hole in his coat through which the bullet had passed, and, as a culminating argument, bringing forward, triumphantly, his own mother, who was a willing witness that with her own eyes she had seen her son commit the murder. In final support of his claim Hurley declared that if the money was paid to McClaine, he would prove his pretensions by killing McClaine on the spot. The money, therefore, was paid to Hurley.

A year later, when McParland, or McKenna, related this history in the courts, it appeared that Hurley had gone to Colorado, where he was working as a miner under the name of McCabe. He had left Pennsylvania hurriedly, after an attempt to kill a saloon-keeper named James Ryle, and burn his house. Some years later Sheriff Shores of Gunnison County, Colorado, arrested him for having stabbed a young man named Clines in a fight. He was arrested as "McCabe," but on information from the East, the sheriff was able to identify him as Hurley. Taking him aside, the sheriff said, "Your time has come, Tom Hurley! McParland is on his way here to take you back to Pennsylvania."

"Who is McParland?" demanded Hurley.

"You used to know him as James McKenna."

No sooner had he heard the name than he slipped his hand under a mattress, and pulling out a razor, cut his throat from ear to ear. As he dropped dying to the floor, he said, "Mac will never get me alive."

A DEMAND MADE ON MCPARLAND TO PROVIDE MEN TO KILL A SUPERINTENDENT.

Shortly after the murder of Policeman Yost, McKenna, as acting body-master of the Shenandoah lodge, found himself in a most delicate and dangerous position. Yost had been murdered by men furnished from Lansford by the body-master there, Alexander Campbell. It was, therefore, Campbell's right to demand a return of the courtesy, which he did without delay, calling upon McKenna to furnish men to kill John P. Jones, superintendent of the Lonsdale Mine, who had refused to obey Campbell's orders, and paid no attention to several "coffin notices."

In order to gain time McKenna promised to comply with this request, but kept delaying on one pretext or another, until Campbell, grown impatient, went to Jack Kehoe, the county delegate, and got him to send a positive order to McKenna to do a "clean job" on Jones without delay. McKenna notified Captain Linden and Mr. Franklin, and at the risk of being killed himself, refused to carry out Kehoe's orders, feigning a serious illness. Then the order came again, and, to allay suspicion, he actually started for Tamaqua with several men and several bottles of whiskey, under the avowed intention of doing the appointed murder. He contrived, however, to get the men very drunk, and thus the night passed, and early next morning, leaving his companions in a drunken stupor, he set out for home, congratulating himself on having again averted a horrible crime. He had gone but a short distance through the streets of Tamaqua, when a young man, hatless and greatly excited, came riding into town on a mule at full gallop. He stopped in front of the City Marshal's office just as McKenna was passing, and called out:

"A man named John P. Jones was murdered a few minutes ago, in the presence of three hundred people,—shot down by two men."

The young man then described the murderers, and McKenna easily recognized them as a man named Doyle and a man named Kelly.

An angry crowd quickly gathered, and some of them recognizing in McKenna a

Molly Maguire leader, a movement was started forthwith to lynch him. He showed, however, his usual nerve, and, drawing two revolvers, walked through the crowd with an air that kept off attack. Although his best efforts had failed to save Jones's life, he resolved that he would, at least, secure the capture of the murderers. Going into the Columbia House he wrote a few words on slips of paper, and then came out and secretly dropped these slips in conspicuous places. One of them, he observed, was picked up by a prominent jeweller of the town, who showed it to several people near him. The words on the slip were:

"Get a spyglass; go to the monument in the Devil's Cemetery and cover the Bloomingdale Mountain."

The purpose was to give people familiar with the neighboring country a hint that would put them on the trail which McKenna knew the guilty men would take on their way from the scene of the crime. Continuing to watch the jeweller and his neighbors, McKenna saw them provide themselves with field glasses and a number of rifles, and start for the Devil's Cemetery. Then he knew that they had understood the hint, as was really the case, the result being that later in the day Kelly, Doyle, and a third man, Carrigan, were captured in the mountains while they were eating their lunch and drinking whiskey beside a spring. Kelly and Doyle were subsequently hanged, and Carrigan turned State's evidence.

THE MURDER OF THOMAS SANGER AND WILLIAM UREN.

A few days after the murder of Jones, McKenna woke up one morning at his home in Shenandoah, and discovered a notorious Molly Maguire, named Mike Doyle, lying on the bed beside him. After the free and easy manner of the fraternity, Doyle had come in quietly during the night, and thrown himself on the bed without undressing. McKenna discovered, also, a thirty-two caliber Smith and Wesson revolver lying on the table, and asked what it was for. Doyle told him that he had borrowed it from the constable of Shenandoah, Ed Monagan, and that he was going to Raven Run to "do a job" with Tom Munley, Jim McAllister, and Charlie and Jim O'Donnell.

"Who are you going to kill?" asked McKenna.

"I don't know yet," answered Doyle.

Going down into the street, they met O'Donnell, and McKenna repeated the question to him. But O'Donnell also said he did not know yet. A few hours later McKenna heard from boasting Mollys that Thomas Sanger and William Uren, two prominent citizens of Raven Run, had been murdered.

In a trial that followed ultimately, Mr. Gowen, who was one of the attorneys for the prosecution, gave the following description of the murder of Sanger:

"What is this case? On the 1st of September, 1875, Thomas Sanger, a young English 'boss' miner, a man between thirty and forty years of age, left his house in the morning to go to his daily work. Going forward in the performance of his duty, this man was confronted by an armed band of five assassins. He was shot in the arm. He turned, stumbled, and fell; then the foremost of this band came up to him as he lay upon the ground and discharged his revolver into him. Then another turned him, as he lay upon his face, over upon his back, so that he could expose a deadly part for his aim, and with calm deliberation selected a vital spot, and shot him as he lay prostrate upon the ground. His wife, from whom he had just parted, hearing his cries, rushed out and reached her husband only in time to hear his last faltering accents: 'Kiss me, Sarah, for I am dying.'"

Under the indignation aroused by this double murder, a vigilance committee attacked Charles O'Donnell in his house, shot him, and hanged his dead body to a tree. By accident they also killed O'Donnell's sister, who was near her confinement. Later, under the disclosures made by the detective, Munley and James O'Donnell were arrested, tried, convicted, and hanged.

McPARLAND SUSPECTED AND THREATENED BY BOTH SIDES.

Toward the end of 1875, the strain under which McParland had been working for eighteen months began to tell upon him, and he appealed to Allan Pinkerton to be allowed to strike the final blow. "I am sick and tired of this work," he said in one of his reports. "I hear of murder and bloodshed in all directions. The very sun to me looks crimson; the air is polluted, and the rivers seem running red with human blood. Something must be done to stop it."

Allan Pinkerton and his assistants, Mr. Franklin and Captain Linden, had already concluded that the evidence McParland had secured was sufficient, and steps were forthwith taken to close in on the murderers. McParland had still, however, many dangers to face; first from fellow-members of the order who were beginning to believe he had played them false; and then from outraged citizens, who regarded him as a monster of crime whose unceremonious killing would be a service to the State. One night, in Tamaqua, bands of armed men searched for him from house to house until morning, and would certainly have discovered and lynched him, had he not, by pretending to fall into a drunken sleep, succeeded in remaining all night in the house of a respectable citizen who was not suspected of harboring him. All the next day he remained in concealment. But at night he was about to board a coal train bound for Pottsville, when the pangs of hunger drove him into a little restaurant near the station to get a cup of coffee. There, as fate would have it, he came face to face with the man of all others in Tamaqua most eager for his life, a brother-in-law of the John P. Jones who had been assassinated shortly before. This man had spent the whole of the previous night with the party that was searching for him. He recognized McKenna at once.

"Have a drink," he said gruffly.

"I'm not drinking anything now," said McKenna, "but I'll have a cup of coffee and a sandwich."

"I'm feeling badly," said the man, looking hard into the detective's face, "and I've made up my mind to kill the first Irish scoundrel I meet."

"I'm not an Irish scoundrel," said McKenna, "but I think, to prevent trouble, I'd better kill you right here;" and into the face of the man who was not feeling well he pushed a revolver. The invalid dashed into the street, McKenna following. But McKenna soon returned and finished his coffee, and then by the next coal train went to Pottsville.

Jack Kehoe, the county delegate whose influence in the order was very great, was now busily reporting his suspicion that "James McKenna" was a detective. To meet this danger McParland boldly went straight to Kehoe, accused him of treachery, and demanded an immediate investigation. As county delegate, Kehoe instructed McKenna, who was at that time county secretary, to write notices to all the body-masters in the county to meet at Shenandoah at a given date, to conduct the investigation. He was writing the notices in a room over Kehoe's saloon, where Mrs. Kehoe was sewing, when Kehoe came in suddenly with a glass of soda for his wife, and a hot whiskey for McKenna. Having placed the two glasses on the table, he left the room, his manner showing an unusual constraint. As soon as he had gone, Mrs. Kehoe, who was a good woman at heart, and devoted to McKenna, took up the hot whiskey, threw it into the stove, and then burst into tears.

"What's the matter?" asked McKenna.

"Don't ask me," said the trembling woman.

It is certain that the whiskey was poisoned. A second attempt to poison McKenna was made the day before his trial at Shenandoah. He was lifting the drugged glass to his lips when an instinctive suspicion moved him to set it down.

On the day of the trial Jack Kehoe did not appear. He was expecting that there would be no trial; for he had engaged sixteen men to murder McKenna, and had even advanced several of them twenty-five dollars each for the service. McKenna's life was probably saved by the personal devotion of a Molly Maguire named Frank McAndrew, who told him of the plot to kill him, and swore to stand true to him, which he did. By McAndrew's aid he stole away and returned to Philadelphia, where he was warmly welcomed by Allan Pinkerton and the president of the Philadelphia and Reading Railroad, Mr. Gowen, who had entertained grave fears for his life. And there the services of McParland (alias McKenna) as a detective in the Molly Maguire cases ended; but he had still a most important service to render as a witness. At the beginning of his employment it had been agreed that he was not to be called on to testify in court; not his own safety only, but the continuation of his work, clearly requiring that he should not. And for a time the impossibility of getting other testimony to the crimes which to him were known perfectly, prevented prosecutions. But now that his real character had been discovered by the desperadoes, and he could hope no longer to hold their confidence, there remained no reason why he should not testify.

ARRESTS AND CONVICTIONS.

All being in readiness, on May 6, 1876, a number of arrests were made. The trials that followed were highly dramatic. Held as they were at the very centre of the lawless district, there was more or less danger that persons engaged in them would themselves suffer the fraternity's vengeance. Under a sense of this danger Mr. Gowen, who himself conducted the prosecutions, said in one of his speeches to the jury:

"Is there a man in this audience, looking at me now, and hearing me denounce this association, who longs to point his pistol at me? I tell him that he has as good a chance here as he will ever have again. . . . I tell him that if there is another murder committed by this organization, every one of the five hundred members of the order in this county or out of it, who connives at it, will be guilty of murder in the first degree, and can be hanged by the neck until he is dead. . . . I tell him that if there is another murder in this county by this society, there will be an inquisition for blood with which nothing that has been known in the annals of criminal jurisprudence can compare."

And here he added a cordial tribute to the faithfulness and skill of Detective McParland and his employer the Pinkerton Agency:

"And to whom are we indebted for this security, of which I now boast? To whom do we owe all this? Under the divine providence of God, to whom be all the honor and all the glory, we owe this safety to James McParland; and if there ever was a man to whom the people of this county should erect a monument, it is James McParland the detective. . . .

It is simply a question between the Molly Maguires on the one side, and Pinkerton's Detective Agency on the other; and I know too well that Pinkerton's Detective Agency will win. There is not a place on the habitable globe where these men can find refuge, and in which they will not be tracked down."

The result of the trials—which is to say the result of McParland's dangerous investigations and subsequent testimony—was the complete extermination of the order of Molly Maguires. A score or more of the desperadoes were condemned to longer or shorter terms in the penitentiary. Nineteen were hanged. Among the latter was Jack Kehoe, who had been among the first to suspect McParland of being a detective, and had expended all his power and ingenuity to get him killed and well out of the way.

LITERARY NOTES.

A NEW JUNGLE STORY BY RUDYARD KIPLING.

Mr. Kipling's stories of Indian life, his ballads, and his jungle stories, give him three separate claims to the highest distinction. As a story teller he ranks with Stevenson, while his stories of jungle life have no parallel. They are certainly a contribution to the centuries, and will be as much a part of a youth's library as Robinson Crusoe or Pilgrim's Progress.

We are glad to announce a new jungle story by Mr. Kipling, which tells of the adventures of Mowgli after he killed Shere Khan. It will be published in our next issue, with an introductory note, so that readers who have not read the other jungle stories can read this one understandingly. It follows the story entitled "Tiger! Tiger!"

PROFESSOR DRUMMOND is preparing an additional article on Mr. Moody which will probably appear in the January number.

NAPOLEON: BIOGRAPHY AND PORTRAITS.

Among many letters received in regard to the first article on Napoleon and its illustrations, we have here room for extracts from only three:

From Colonel John C. Ropes, the most eminent American student of Napoleon's history:

BOSTON, November 9, 1894.
I do congratulate you on the success of your Napoleon biography.
JOHN C. ROPES.

From the Hon. D. C. Gilman, President of Johns Hopkins University:

BALTIMORE, October 30, 1894.

DEAR SIR,—I saw not long ago, in the library of Hon. Gardiner G. Hubbard, in Washington, the extraordinary feeling I should say unique, collection of the portraits of Napoleon, and I then learned that you are to publish copies of the most significant of those portraits, in connection with an article upon them, which Miss Tarbell was then preparing. This interested me very much. It is doubtful whether portraits of any other man, of any age or land, have been taken in so many aspects, by such able artists, at such frequent intervals and through so many years. Whatever the power and fame of Napoleon are considered, you may be sure that the students of history, geography, and portraiture, by whatever motives they are governed, will be much indebted to you and to all your collaborators for making accessible to them this superb collection.

Yours truly,
D. C. GILMAN.
S. S. MCCLURE, ESQ.

From Major J. W. Powell, U. S. A., the well-known scientist, writer, and explorer:

SMITHSONIAN INSTITUTION,
BUREAU OF AMERICAN ETHNOLOGY.
WASHINGTON, November 6, 1894.

MY DEAR MCCLURE: I have just read with care, and with great interest, Miss Tarbell's first article on Napoleon. It is not only graphic, but its simplicity is high art. With the abundant illustration it constitutes a picture to live.

I am yours cordially,
J. W. POWELL.

MR. S. S. MCCLURE,
30 Lafayette Place, New York City.

EMPEROR NAPOLEON 1813

Engraved by Lefèvre, after Isabey; published December 26, 1816

McCLURE'S MAGAZINE.

Vol. IV.   JANUARY, 1895.   No. 2.

NAPOLEON BONAPARTE.

BY IDA M. TARBELL.

With engravings from the collection of the Hon. Gardiner G. Hubbard, who also furnishes the explanatory notes

THIRD PAPER.—NAPOLEON AS STATESMAN AND LAWGIVER.

THE NEW CONSTITUTION.

"NOW we must rebuild, and, moreover, we must rebuild solidly," said Napoleon to his brother Lucien the day after the *coup d'état* which had overthrown the Directory and made him the temporary dictator of France.

The first necessity was a new constitution. In ten years three constitutions had been framed and adopted, and now the third had, like its predecessors, been declared worthless. At Napoleon's side was a man who had the draft of a constitution ready in his pocket. It had been promised him that, if he would aid in the 18th Brumaire, this instrument should be adopted. This man was the Abbé Sieyès. He had been a prominent member of the Constituent Assembly, but, curiously enough, his fame there had been founded more on his silence and the air of mystery in which he enveloped himself than on anything he had done. The superstitious veneration which he had won, saved him even during the Terror, and he was accustomed to say laconically, when asked what he did in that period, "*I lived.*"

It was he who, when Napoleon was still in Egypt, had seen the necessity of a military dictatorship, and had urged the Directory to order Napoleon home to help him reorganize the government—an order which was never received.

Soon after the 18th Brumaire, Sieyès presented his constitution. No more bungling and bizarre instrument for conducting the affairs of a nation was ever devised. Warned by the experience of the past ten years, he abandoned the ideas of 1789, and declared that the power must come from above, the confidence from below. His system of voting took the suffrage from the people; his legislative body was composed of three sections, each of which was practically powerless. All the force of the government was centred in a senate of aged men. The Grand Elector, as the figurehead which crowned the edifice was called, did nothing but live at Versailles and draw a princely salary.

Napoleon saw at once the weak points of the structure, but he saw how it could be rearranged to serve a dictator. He demanded that the senate be stripped of its power, and that the Grand Elector be replaced by a First Consul, to whom the executive force should be confided. Sieyès consented, and Napoleon was named First Consul.

The whole machinery of the government was now centred in one man. "The state, it was I," said Napoleon at St. Helena. The new constitution was founded on principles the very opposite of those for which the Revolution had been made, but it was the only hope there was of dragging France from the slough of anarchy and despair into which she had fallen.

Napoleon undertook the work of reconstruction which awaited him, with courage, energy, and amazing audacity. He was

Copyright, 1894, by S. S. McClure, Limited. All rights reserved.

"NAPOLEON BONAPARTE, FIRST CONSUL OF FRANCE." 1800.

Painted by Masquerrier, who visited Paris in 1800, where he made a portrait of Napoleon. "This, on being exhibited in England, where it was the first authentic portrait of the emperor, proved a source of considerable gain to the painter." The portrait was engraved soon after his return to London, by C. Turner.

forced to deal at once with all departments of the nation's life—with the finances, the industries, the *émigrés*, the Church, public education, the codification of the laws.

THE FINANCES.

The first question was one of money. The country was literally bankrupt in 1799. The treasury was empty, and the government practised all sorts of makeshifts to get money to pay those bills which could not be put off. One day, having to send out a special courier, it was obliged to give him the receipts of the opera to pay his expenses. And, again, it was in such a tight pinch that it was on the point of sending the gold coin in the Cabinet of Medals to the mint to be melted. Loans could not be negotiated; government paper was worthless; stocks were down to the lowest. One of the worst features of the situation was the condition of the taxes. The assessments were as arbitrary as before the Revolution, and they were collected with greater difficulty.

To select an honest, capable, and well-known financier was Napoleon's first act. The choice he made was wise—a Monsieur Gaudin, afterward the Duke de Gaëte, a quiet man, who had the confidence of the people. Under his management credit was restored, the government was able to make the loans necessary, and the department of finance was reorganized in a thorough fashion.

Napoleon's gratitude to M. Gaudin was lasting. Once when asked to change him for a more brilliant man, he said:

"I fully acknowledge all your *protégé* is worth; but it might easily happen that, with all his intelligence, he would give me

nothing but fresh water, whilst with my good Gaudin I can always rely on having good crown pieces."

The famous Bank of France dates from this time. It was founded under Napoleon's personal direction, and he never ceased to watch over it jealously. More important was the reorganization of the system of taxation.

He insisted that the taxes must meet the whole expense of the nation, save war, which must pay for itself; and he so ordered affairs that never after his administration was fairly begun was a deficit known or a loan made. This was done, too, without the people feeling the burden of taxation. Indeed, that burden was so much lighter under his administration than it had been under the old regime, that peasant and workman, in most cases, probably did not know they were being taxed.

"Before 1789," says Taine, "out of one hundred francs of net revenue, the workman gave fourteen to his seignor, fourteen to the clergy, fifty-three to the state, and kept only eighteen or nineteen for himself. Since 1800, from one hundred francs income he pays nothing to the seignor or the Church, and he pays to the state, the department, and the commune but twenty-one francs, leaving seventy-nine in his pocket." And such was the method and care with which this system was administered, that the state received more than twice as much as it had before. The enormous sums which the police and tax-collectors had appropriated now went to the state. Here is but one example of numbers which show how minutely Napoleon guarded this part of the finances. It is found in a letter to Fouché, the chief of police:

"What happens at Bordeaux happens at Turin, at Spa, at Marseilles, etc. The police commissioners derive immense profits from the gaming-tables. My intention is that the towns shall reap the benefit of the tables. I shall employ the two hundred thousand francs paid by the tables of Bordeaux in building a bridge or a canal...."

A great improvement was that the taxes became fixed and regular. Napoleon wished that each man should know what he had to pay out each year. "True civil liberty depends on the safety of property," he told his Council of State. "There is none in a country where the rate of taxation is changed every year. A man who has three thousand francs income does not know how much he will have to live on the next year. His whole substance may be swallowed up by the taxes."

Nearly the whole revenue came from indirect taxes applied to a great number of articles. In case of a war which

ELISA BACCIOCHI, GRAND DUCHESS OF TUSCANY, ELDEST SISTER OF NAPOLEON (1777-1820).
Engraved by Morghen in 1814, after Cousin.

did not pay its way, Napoleon proposed to raise each of these a few centimes. The nation would surely prefer this to paying it to the Russians or Austrians. When possible the taxes were reduced. "Better leave the money in the hands of the citizens than lock it up in a cellar, as they do in Prussia."

He was cautious that extra taxes should not come on the very poor, if it could be avoided. A suggestion to charge the vegetable and fish sellers for their stalls came before him. "The public square, like water, ought to be free. It is quite enough that we tax salt and wine. . . . It would become

NAPOLEON, 1796-97.
Composed and designed by Carle Vernet; engraved by Simon.

the city of Paris much more to think of restoring the corn market."

An important part of his financial policy was the rigid economy which was insisted on in all departments. If a thing was bought, it must be worth what was paid for it. If a man held a position, he must do its duties. Neither purchases nor positions could be made unless reasonable and useful. This was in direct opposition to the old regime, of which waste, idleness, and parasites were the chief characteristics. The saving in expenditure was almost incredible. A trip to Fontainebleau, which cost Louis XVI. four hundred thousand dollars, Napoleon would make, in no less state, for thirty thousand dollars.

The expenses of the civil household,

MADAME DE STAEL (ANNE LOUISE GERMAINE NECKER, BARONNE DE STAEL-HOLSTEIN). 1810.

Engraved in 1812 by Laugier, after Gérard. Madame de Staël was born in Paris in 1766. Her father was the famous banker Necker, and her mother, Suzanne Curchod, the early love of Gibbon. She held a high position in Paris until the Terror obliged her to flee, when she went to Coppet, on Lake Geneva, where a number of her friends were continually gathered about her. She returned to Paris under the Directory, and when Napoleon returned from the Italian campaign she showed him the greatest admiration, and persisted in putting herself in his way. His dislike was so pronounced that she was irritated, and when to this personal complaint she added a more serious one—the way he was centralizing power in his hands—she became a noisy and troublesome critic of his policy. In 1803, when she came to Paris from Coppet, she was ordered not to reside within forty leagues of the city. For three years she obeyed, but in 1806 she returned to France. In 1807 the publication of "Corinne" called attention to her, and she went back to Coppet. For two years she was busy at her work on "Germany," which, when done, she published in Paris; but the whole edition of ten thousand copies was condemned as "not French," and she was forbidden to enter France. When Louis XVIII was restored, she returned to Paris but fled to Coppet at the news of Napoleon's landing. She died on July 14, 1817.

which amounted to five million dollars under the old regime, were now cut down to six hundred thousand dollars, though the elegance was no less.

THE INDUSTRIES.

A master who gave such strict attention to the prosperity of his kingdom would not, of course, overlook its industries. In fact, they were one of Napoleon's chief cares. His policy was one of protection. He would have France make everything she wanted, and sell to her neighbors, but never buy from them. To stimulate the manufactories, which in 1799 were as nearly bankrupt as the public treasury, he visited the factories himself to learn their needs. He gave liberal orders, and urged, even commanded, his associates to do the same. At one time, anxious to aid the batiste factories of Flanders, he tried to force Josephine to give up cotton goods and to set the fashion in favor of the batistes; but she made such an outcry that he was obliged to abandon the idea. For the same reason he wrote to his sister Eliza: "I beg that you will allow your court to wear nothing but silks and cambrics, and that you will exclude all cottons and muslins, in order to favor French industry."

Frequently he would take goods on consignment, to help a struggling factory. Rather than allow a manufactory to be idle, he would advance a large sum of money, and a quantity of its products would be put under government control. After the battle of Eylau, Napoleon sent one million six hundred thousand francs to Paris, to be used in this way.

NAPOLEON, EMPEROR OF THE FRENCH AND KING OF ITALY. ("NAPOLEON, EMPEREUR DES FRANÇAIS, ROI D'ITALIE.") 1805.
Engraved by Andreus, after Charles de Chatillon.

To introduce cotton-making into the country was one of his chief industrial ambitions. At the beginning of the century it was printed in all the factories of France, but nothing more. He proposed to the Council of State to prohibit the importation of cotton thread and the woven goods. There was a strong opposition, but he carried his point.

"As a result," said Napoleon to Las Cases with complacency, "we possess the three branches, to the immense advantage of our population and to the detriment and sorrow of the English; which proves that, in administration as in war, one must exercise character. . . . I occupied myself no less in encouraging silks. As Emperor, and King of Italy, I counted one hundred and twenty millions of income from the silk harvest."

In a similar way he encouraged agriculture; especially was he anxious that France should raise all her own articles of diet. He had Berthollet look into maple and turnip sugar, and he did at last succeed in persuading the people to use beet sugar; though he never convinced them that Swiss tea equalled Chinese, or that chicory was as good as coffee. The works he insisted should be carried on in regard to roads and public buildings were of great importance. There was need that something be done.

"It is impossible to conceive, if one had not been a witness of it before and after the 18th Brumaire [said the chancellor Pasquier], of the widespread ruin wrought by the Revolution. . . . There were hardly two or three main roads [in France] in a fit condition for traffic; not a single one was there, perhaps, wherein was not found some obstacle that could not be surmounted without peril. With regard to the ways of internal communication, they had been indefinitely suspended. The navigation of rivers and canals was no longer feasible.

"In all directions, public buildings, and those monuments which represent the splendor of the state, were falling into decay. It must fain be admitted that if the work of destruction had been prodigious, that of restoration was no less so. Everything was taken hold of at one and the same time, and everything progressed with a like rapidity. Not only was it resolved to restore all that required restoring in various parts of the country, in all parts of the public service, but new, grand, beautiful and useful works were decided upon, and many were brought to a happy termination. This certainly constitutes one

THE EMPEROR NAPOLEON IN HUNTING COSTUME. ("L'EMPEREUR EN PIED OU CHASSEUR À CHEVAL.")

Designed by Charlet, probably about 1834. The title is a little misleading, for the costume shown in the picture, save the boots, is the one Napoleon commonly wore, in-doors as well as out.

of the most brilliant sides of the consular and imperial regime."

In Paris alone vast improvements were made. Napoleon began the Rue de Rivoli, built the wing connecting the Tuileries and the Louvre, erected the triumphal arch of the Carrousel, the Arc de Triomphe at the head of the Champs Elysées, the column Vendôme, the Madeleine, began the Bourse, built the Pont d'Austerlitz, and ordered, commenced, or finished, a number of minor works of great importance to the city. The markets interested him particularly. "Give all possible care to the construction of the markets and to their healthfulness, and to the beauty of the Halle-aux-blés and of the Halle-aux-vins. The people, too, must have their Louvre," was his order.

THE ÉMIGRÉS.

But there were wounds in the French nation more profound than those caused by lack of credit, by neglect and corruption. The body which in 1789 had made up France had, in the last ten years, been violently and horribly wrenched asunder. One hundred and fifty thousand of the

NAPOLEON WITH THE IRON CROWN OF LOMBARDY. 1813.
Designed and engraved by Longhi, in 1813, for "Vite e Ritratti di illustri Italiani."

of about one thousand, and this number, it was arranged, should be reduced to five hundred in the course of a year. More, he provided for their wants. Most of the smaller properties confiscated by the Revolution had been sold, and Napoleon insisted that those who had bought them from the State should be assured of their tenure; but in case a property had not been disposed of, he returned it to the family, though rarely in full. In case of forest lands, not over three hundred and seventy-five acres were given back. Gifts and positions were given to many émigrés, so that the majority were

judges, and thinkers, many of whom were promptly admitted to the government.

THE CHURCH.

More serious than the amputation of the aristocracy had been that of the Church. The Revolution had torn it from the nation, had confiscated its property, turned its cathedrals into barracks, its convents and seminaries into town halls and prisons, sold its lands, closed its schools and hospitals. It had demanded an oath of the clergy which had divided the body, and caused thousands to emigrate. Not content with this, it had tried to supplant the old religion, first with a worship of the Goddess of Reason, afterwards with one of the Supreme Being.

But the people still loved the Catholic Church. The mass of them kept their crucifixes in their houses, told their beads, observed fast days. No matter how severe a penalty was attached to the observance of Sunday instead of the day which had replaced it, called the "decade," at heart the people remembered it. "We rest on the decade," said a workman once, "but we change our shirts on Sunday."

Napoleon understood the popular heart, and he proposed the reëstablishment of the Catholic Church. The Revolutionists, even his warmest friends among the generals, opposed it. Infidelity was a cardinal point in the creed of the majority of the new régime. They not only rejected the Church, they ridiculed it. Rather than restore Catholicism, they advised Protestantism. "But," declared Napoleon, "France is not Protestant; she is Catholic."

In the Council of State, where the question was argued, he said: "My policy is to govern men as the greatest number wish to be governed. . . . I carried on the war of Vendée by becoming a Catholic; I established myself in Egypt by becoming a Mussulman; I won over the priests in Italy by becoming Ultramontane. If I governed Jews I should reëstablish the temple of Solomon. . . . It is thus, I think, that the sovereignty of the people should be understood."

Evidently this was a very different way of understanding that famous doctrine from that which had been in vogue, which consisted in forcing the people to accept what each idealist thought was best, without consulting their prejudices or feelings. In spite of opposition, Napoleon's will prevailed, and in the spring of 1802 the Concordat was signed. This treaty between the Pope and France is still in force in France. It makes the Catholic Church the State church, allows the government to name the bishops, compels it to pay the salaries of the clergy, and to furnish cathedrals and churches for public worship, which, however, remain national property. The Concordat provided for the absolution of the priests who had married in the Revolution, restored Sunday, and made legal holidays of certain *fête* days. This arrangement was not made at the price of intolerance towards other bodies. The French government protects and contributes towards the support of all religions within its borders, Catholic, Protestant, Jew, or Mussulman.

The Concordat was ridiculed by many in the government and army, but undoubtedly it was one of the most statesmanlike measures carried out by Napoleon.

"The joy of the overwhelming majority of France silenced even the boldest malcontents," says Pasquier; "it became evident that Napoleon, better than those who surrounded him, had seen into the depths of the nation's heart."

It is certain that in reëstablishing the Church Napoleon did not yield to any religious prejudice, although the Catholic Church was the one he preferred. It was purely a question of policy. In arranging the Concordat he might have secured more liberal measures—measures in which he believed—but he refused them.

"Do you wish me to manufacture a religion of caprice for my own special use, a religion that would be nobody's? I do not so understand matters. What I want is the old Catholic religion, the only one which is imbedded in every heart, and from which it has never been torn. This religion alone can conciliate hearts in my favor; it alone can smooth away all obstacles."

At St. Helena he said to Las Cases:

"When I came to the head of affairs, I had already formed certain ideas on the great principles which hold society together. I had weighed all the importance of religion; I was persuaded of it, and I had resolved to reëstablish it. You would scarcely believe in the difficulties that I had to restore Catholicism. I would have been followed much more willingly if I had unfurled the banner of Protestantism. . . . It is sure that in the disorder to which I succeeded, in the ruins where I found myself, I could choose between Catholicism and Protestantism. And it is true that at that moment the disposition was in favor of the latter. But outside the fact that I really clung to the religion in which I had been born, I had the highest motives to decide me. By proclaiming Protestantism, what would I have obtained? I should have created in France two great parties about equal, when I wished there should be no longer but one. I should have excited the fury of religious quarrels, when the

NAPOLEON BONAPARTE.

NAPOLEON.

Engraved by Conslo, after Lefèvre. Lefèvre probably painted this portrait early in the career of Napoleon. It was engraved by Conslo, a celebrated mezzotint engraver, many years ago, but when finished Napoleon "did not sell." It therefore was laid aside until 1893, when this print was made.

enlightenment of the age and my desire was to make them disappear altogether. These two parties in tearing each other to pieces would have annihilated France and rendered her the slave of Europe, when I was ambitious of making her its mistress. With Catholicism I arrived much more surely at my great results. Within, at home, the great number would absorb the small, and I promised myself to treat with the latter so liberally that it would soon have no motive for knowing the difference.

"Without Catholicism saved me the Pope; and with my influences and our forces in Italy I did not despair sooner or later, by one way or another, of finishing by ruling the Pope myself."

EDUCATION.

When the Church fell in France, the whole system of education went down with her. The Revolutionary governments tried to remedy the condition, but beyond many plans and speeches little had been done. Napoleon allowed the religious bodies to reopen their schools, and thus primary instruction was soon in operation again; and he founded a number of secondary and special schools. The greatest of his educational undertakings was the organization of the University. This institution was centralized in the head of the state as completely as every other Napoleonic institution. It exists to-day but little changed—a most efficient body, in spite of its rigid state control. This university did nothing for woman.

"I do not think we need trouble ourselves with any plan of instruction for young females," Napoleon told the Council. "They cannot be brought up better than by their mothers. Public education is not suitable for them, because they are never called upon to act in public. Manners are all in all to them, and marriage is all they look to. In times past the monastic life was open to women; they

MADAME RÉCAMIER. 1800.

By Jacquet, after David. Madame Récamier (Jeanne Françoise Julie Adélaide) was born in Lyons in 1777. Her father, Jean Bernard, afterwards moved to Paris, where he saw much of society and occupied a good position. In 1793 Julie was married to Monsieur Récamier, a rich banker twenty-seven years her senior. During the Directory Madame Récamier became intimate with the members of the Bonaparte family in Paris, and Lucien fell deeply in love with her, an affection she never returned. She first met the First Consul at Lucien's in the winter of 1799-1800, and he ranked her especially. She was much attracted by his simplicity and by his kindness. In 1800 Madame Récamier's father, who was Postmaster-General, was found to be sheltering a royalist correspondence, and was arrested and imprisoned. Through the intercession of Madame Récamier, Bernadotte secured his release from the First Consul. The arrest and trial of Moreau, who was a friend of Madame Récamier, the exile of Madame de Staël, and the execution of the Duke d'Enghien, put her in opposition to the government, though she received both friends and enemies of Napoleon. In 1807 Fouché attempted to persuade her to accept a place at court, which she refused. In 1807 Madame Récamier visited Madame de Staël at Coppet, where she met Prince Augustus of Prussia, who wished to marry her. She seems to have determined once to secure a divorce and marry the Prince, but abandoned the idea because of Monsieur Récamier's distress. In 1811 she was exiled forty leagues from Paris because of her intimacy with Madame de Staël, and she did not return until after the invasion in 1814. In 1817, after Madame de Staël's death, she met Chateaubriand, with whom she remained intimately allied through the rest of her life. In 1830 Monsieur Récamier died. Sixteen years afterwards Chateaubriand became a widower. He wished to marry Madame Récamier, but she refused. She died in Paris in 1849. Of all the women of the period, no one is more interesting than Madame Récamier. Purity of character, independence of spirit, and fidelity to friends distinguished her, as well as remarkable beauty.

espoused God, and, though society gained little by that alliance, the parents gained by pocketing the dowry."

It was with the education of the daughters of soldiers, civil functionaries, and members of the Legion of Honor, who had died and left their children unprovided for, that he concerned himself, establishing schools of which the well-known one at St. Denis is a model. The rules were prepared by Napoleon himself, who insisted that the girls should be taught all kinds of housework and needlework—everything, in fact, which would make them good housekeepers and honest women.

The military schools were also reorganized at this time. Remembering his own experience at the *École Militaire*, Napoleon arranged that the severest economy should be practised in them, and that the pupils should learn to do everything for themselves. They even cleaned, bedded, and shod their own horses.

THE LEGION OF HONOR.

The destruction of the old system of privileges and honors left the government without any means of rewarding those who rendered it a service. Napoleon presented a law for a Legion of Honor, under control of the state, which should admit to its

BONAPARTE AT MALMAISON. 1803.

The title on the engraving reads: "Bonaparte, dédié à Madame Bonaparte." Engraved in 1803 by Godefroy, after Isabey. In 1798, after Josephine de Beauharnais had become Madame Bonaparte, she bought, for thirty-two thousand dollars, a property at Marly, eight miles from Paris, known as Malmaison. While Napoleon was in Egypt, Josephine spent most of her time here, gathering about her a circle of the *beaux esprits* of the day, including Bernardin de Saint Pierre, Arnault, Chénier, Talma, Gérard, Girodet, Mesdames Tallien, Regnault de Saint Jean d'Angely, the Comtesse d'Houdetot, and Fanny de Beauharnais. When Napoleon returned from Egypt he found waiting him a powerful *sedan*. After the 18th Brumaire, Malmaison was enlarged and beautified, becoming, in fact, another Trianon. Its park contained kiosks, a *dameron*, a temple of love, a theatre, fountains, lakes, and gardens, and the *château* a fine library and many valuable works of art. A few of the pictures brought to France as spoils of war were deposited at Malmaison, especially two superb Paul Potters. Napoleon is said to have always regretted, when he looked at them, that Josephine had taken them, as he wanted them for the Museum. Before the end of the consulate the Bonapartes left Malmaison for Saint Cloud, and after the Empire the place was almost entirely abandoned. When the divorce was pronounced in 1811 Josephine retired to Malmaison, where she died in 1814, three days after a visit from the Emperor Alexander, whose army had just invaded France. Napoleon visited Malmaison after his return from Elba, and spent five days there after Waterloo. Malmaison passed to Prince Eugène, who sold it to private parties in 1828. In 1861 the state bought it, and still owns it.

NAPOLEON I., EMPEROR OF THE FRENCH AND KING OF ITALY. ("NAPOLEON I*r*, EMPÉREUR DES FRANÇAIS, ROI D'ITALIE.") ABOUT 1809.

Engraved by Roger, after Gérard. Painted, probably, about 1809.

membership only those who had done something of use to the public. The service might be military, commercial, artistic, humanitarian; no limit was put on its nature; anything which helped France in any way was to be rewarded by membership in the proposed order. In fact, it was the most democratic distinction possible, since the same reward was given to all classes of services and all classes of people.

Now the Revolutionary spirit spurned all distinctions; and as free discussion was allowed on the law, there was a severe arraignment of it made. Nevertheless, it in the hands of the First Consul, and such it has remained until to-day in the hands of the government. Though it has been frequently abused, and never, perhaps, more flagrantly than by the present Republic, unquestionably the French "red button" is a decoration of which to be proud.

CODIFICATION OF THE LAWS.

The greatest civil achievement of Napoleon was the codification of the laws. Up to the Revolution, the laws of France had been in a misty, incoherent condition, feudal in their spirit, and by no means uniform

sembly had ordered them revised, but the work had only been begun. Napoleon believed justly that the greatest benefit he could render France would be to give her a complete and systematic code. He organized the force for this gigantic task, and pushed revision with unflagging energy.

His part in the work was interesting and important. After the laws had been well digested and arranged in preliminary bodies, they were submitted to the Council of State. It was in the discussions before this body that Napoleon took part. That a man of thirty-one, brought up as a soldier, and having no legal training, could follow the discussions of such a learned and serious body as Napoleon's Council of State always was, seems incredible. In fact, he prepared for each session as thoroughly as the law-makers themselves.

His habit was to talk over, beforehand generally, with Cambacérès and Portalis, two legislators of great learning and clearness of judgment, all the matters which were to come up.

"He examined each question by itself," says Roederer, "inquiring into all the authorities, times, experiences; demanding to know how it had been under ancient jurisprudence, under Louis XIV., or Frederick the Great. When a bill was presented to the First Consul, he rarely failed to ask these questions: Is this bill complete? Does it cover every case? Why have you not thought of this? Is that necessary? Is it right or useful? What is done nowadays and elsewhere?"

At night, after he had gone to bed, he

"NAPOLEON BONAPARTE, FIRST CONSUL." 1802.
Painted in 1802 by T. Phillips, Esq., R.A.; engraved by C. Turner.

on the subject. Such was his capacity for grasping an idea, that he would come to the Council with a perfectly clear notion of the subject to be treated, and a good idea of its historical development. Thus he could follow the most erudite and philosophical arguments, and could take part in them.

He stripped them at once of all conventional phrases and learned terms, and stated clearly what they meant. He had no use for anything but the plain meaning. By thus going directly to the practical sense of a thing, he frequently cleared up the ideas of the revisers themselves.

In framing the laws, he took care that they should be worded so that everybody could understand them. Thus, when a law relating to liquors was being prepared, he urged that *wholesale* and *retail* should be defined in such a way that they would be definite ideas to the people. "*Pot* and *pint* must be inserted," he said. "There is no objection to those words. An excise act isn't an epic poem."

Napoleon insisted on the greatest freedom of speech in the discussions on the laws, just as he did on "going straight to the point and not wasting time on idle talk." This clear-headedness, energy, and grasp of subjects exercised over a body of really remarkable men, developed the Council until its discussions became famous throughout Europe. One of its wisest members, Chancellor Pasquier, says of Napoleon's direction, that "it was of such a nature as to enlarge the sphere of one's ideas, and to give one's faculties all the

JOSEPHINE 1804.
Engraved by Weber in 1844; painted by Lefebre.

The highest legislative, administrative, and sometimes even political matters were taken up in it (the Council). Did we not see, for two consecutive winters, the sons of foreign sovereigns come and complete their education in its midst?"

It was the genius of the head of the state, however, which was the most impr

sive feature of the Council of State. De Molleville, a former minister of Louis XVI., said once to Las Cases:

"It must be admitted that your Bonaparte, your Napoleon, was a very extraordinary man. We were far from understanding him on the other side of the water. We could not refuse the evidence of his victories and his invasions, it is true; but Genseric, Attila, Alaric had done as much; so he made more of an impression of terror on me than of admiration. But when I came here and followed the discussions on the civil code, from that moment I had nothing but profound veneration for him. But where in the world had he learned all that? And then every day I discovered something new in him. Ah, sir, what a man you had there! Truly, he was a prodigy."

The modern reader who looks at France and sees how her University, her special schools, her hospitals, her great honorary legion, her treaty with the Catholic Church, her code of laws, her bank —the vital elements of her life, in short—are as they came from Napoleon's brain, must ask, with De Molleville, How did he do it—he a foreigner, born in a half-civilized island, reared in a military school, without diplomatic or legal training, without the prestige of name or wealth? How could he make a nation? How could he be other than the barbaric conqueror, the English and the *émigrés* first thought him?

Those who look at Napoleon's achievements, and are either dazzled or horrified by them, generally consider his power superhuman. They call it divine or diabolic, according to the feeling he inspires in them; but, in reality, the quali-

ties he showed in his career as a statesman and law-giver are very human ones. His stout grasp on subjects; his genius for hard work; his power of seeing everything that should be done, and doing it himself; his unparalleled audacity, explain his civil achievements.

The comprehension he had of questions of government was really the result of serious thinking. He had reflected from his first days at Brienne; and the active interest he had taken in the Revolution of 1789 had made him familiar with many social and political questions. His career in Italy, which was almost as much a diplomatic as a military career, had furnished him an experience upon which he had founded many notions. In his dreams of becoming an Oriental lawgiver he had planned a system of government of which

LUCIEN BONAPARTE
Engraved by Schule in 1815

NAPOLEON BONAPARTE.

MARSHAL LEFEBVRE (1755-1820) ABOUT 1796.

Engraved in 1796 by Firsinger, after Mengelberg. Lefebvre (François Joseph) was born at Ruffach in 1755, son of a miller, destined for the Church, but at eighteen he enrolled in the French guards. When the Revolution broke out he had just reached the grade of sergeant. In 1793 he was made general of brigade under Hoche, and served in the armies of the Rhine with honor until wounded in 1798, when he returned to Paris, where he was named commander of one of the military divisions. On the 18th Brumaire, Lefebvre rendered important service, and in 1800 was named for the Senate by the First Consul. In 1803 he was made a marshal and a grand officer of the Legion of Honor. In 1806 Lefebvre commanded a division of the Grand Army, and at Jena led the Imperial foot-guard. In 1807 he directed the siege of Dantzic, which lasted fifty-one days. For the capture of this town he was made Duke of Dantzic. In 1808 Lefebvre served in Spain, gaining two battles. In the war of 1809 against the Austrians he led the Bavarian army, and in 1812 was commander in chief of the Imperial Guard, at whose head he remained during the retreat from Russia. Lefebvre was made a peer of France by the Restoration, and during the Hundred Days he sat in the Imperial Chamber. When Louis XVIII. returned he deprived him, but he was recalled in 1819. He died in 1820. The marshal and his wife are altogether among the most interesting people in the Napoleonic court. Both of them were uneducated and completely impervious to culture, but of such sincerity of thought and speech, and such goodness of heart, that Napoleon valued them highly. The courtiers, however, ridiculed them incessantly, and repeated many of their blunders against etiquette and grammar. Madame Lefebvre, a kind of noble hearted Mrs. Malaprop, has been made the heroine of several French plays. The latest of these is the "Madame Sans-Gêne" of Victor Sardou, put on at the Vaudeville in Paris in the winter

NAPOLEON BONAPARTE.

MARSHAL NEY ("LE MARÉCHAL NEY, DUC D'ELCHINGEN, PRINCE DE LA MOSKOWA, PAIR DE FRANCE") 1814.

Engraved by Tardieu, after Gérard. Ney (Michel) was born at Sarrelouis in 1769; entered the army at nineteen years of age. In 1792 Ney entered the Army of the North, where he soon attracted attention by his bravery and skill, winning the title of the *Indefatigable*. In 1794 he was made chief of brigade, and two years later general of brigade. He served in the Army of the Rhine and of the Danube until the peace of Lunéville in 1801. Returning to Paris, Napoleon succeeded in attaching him to his fortunes, and sent him to Switzerland as minister plenipotentiary to propose that the Helvetian Republic be placed under the protectorate of France. When, in 1803, war was declared against England, Ney was recalled from Switzerland, where he had succeeded in his negotiations, and sent to the north to command a corps of the Army of Invasion. In 1804 he was named marshal and given the *grand cordon* of the Legion of Honor. In the campaign of 1805 against Austria, Ney played a brilliant part, as well as in those of 1806 and 1807. His audacity, military skill, and bravery won him various titles from his soldiers, such as the "Brave of Braves," the "Red Lion" (Ney's hair was red), and "Peter the Red." When Napoleon instituted his new nobility, after Tilsit, Ney was made Duke of Elchingen. During 1807 and 1808 he served in Spain, but, quarrelling with Masséna, his commander in chief, he was obliged to return to France. In the Russian campaign no one distinguished himself more than Ney. For his services at the battle of Moskowa he was made Prince of Moskowa. When Louis XVIII. was restored, Ney joined the Bourbons, and was rewarded with high honors, but at court his wife was ridiculed by the ancient nobility, until, deeply wounded, he left Paris. He was in command at Besançon when Napoleon returned from Elba, and was ordered to take his former master prisoner. Ney started, promising to "bring back Bonaparte in an iron cage"; but the enthusiasm over the imperial cause was so great that he made up his mind that the cause of the Bourbons was lost, and went over to Napoleon. He was convicted of treason, and shot in Paris, December 7, 1815.

he was to be the centre. Thus, before the 18th Brumaire made him the dictator of France, he had his ideas of centralized government all formed, just as, before he crossed the Great Saint Bernard, he had fought, over and over, the battle of Marengo with black- and red-headed pins stuck into a great map of Italy spread out on his study floor.

His habit of attending to everything himself explains much of his success. No detail was too small for him, no task too menial. If a thing needed attention, no matter whose business it was, he looked after it. Reading letters once before Madame Junot, she said to him that such work must be tiresome, and advised him to give it to a secretary.

"Later, perhaps," he said. "Now it is impossible; I must answer for all. It is not at the beginning of a return to order that I can afford to ignore a need, a demand."

He carried out this policy literally. When he went on a journey, he looked personally after every road, bridge, public building, he passed, and his letters teemed with orders about repairs here, restorations there. He looked after individuals in the same way; ordered a pension to this one, a position to that one, even dictating how the gift should be made known so as to offend the least possible the pride of the recipient.

When it comes to foreign policy, he tells his diplomats how they shall look, whether it shall be grave or gay, whether they shall discuss the opera or the political situation.

The cost of the soldiers' shoes, the kind of box Josephine takes at the opera, the style of architecture for the Madeleine, the amount of stock left on hand in the silk factories, the wording of the laws, all is his business.

He thinks of the flowers to be scattered daily on the tomb of General Régnier, suggests the idea of a battle hymn to Rouget de l'Isle, tells the artists what expression to give him in their portraits, what accessories to use in their battle pieces, orders everything, verifies everything. "Beside him," said those who looked on in amazement, "the most punctilious clerk would have been a bungler."

Without an extraordinary capacity for work, no man could have done this. Napoleon would work until eleven o'clock in the evening, and be up again at three in the morning.

Frequently he slept but an hour, and came back as fresh as ever. No secretary could keep up to him, and his ministers sometimes went to sleep in the Council, worn out with the length of the session. "Come, citizen ministers," he would cry, "we must earn the money the French nation gives us." The ministers rarely went home from the meetings that they did not find a half-dozen letters from him on their tables to be answered, and the answer must be a clear, exact, exhaustive document. "Get your information so that when you do answer me, there shall be no 'buts,' no 'ifs,' and no 'becauses,'" was the rule Napoleon laid down to his correspondents.

He had audacity. He dared do what he would. He had no conventional notions to tie him, no master to dictate to him. The Revolution had swept out of his way the accumulated experience of centuries — all the habits, the prejudices, the ways of doing things. He commenced nearer the bottom than any man in the history of the civilized world had ever done, worked with imperial self-confidence, with a conviction that he "was not like other men." He listened to others, but in the end he dared do as he would.

The centralization of France in Napoleon's

GENERAL FOY, ABOUT 1810.

Engraved by Lefèvre, after Horace Vernet. Foy (Maximilien Sébastien), born at Ham in 1775, entered the artillery school at Châlons, and assisted as lieutenant at the battle of Jemmapes. Arrested for contra-revolutionary talk, Foy was imprisoned, but was released after the 9th Thermidor. He afterwards served in the Army of the Rhine under Moreau, and made the German campaign of 1800 under Moreau. He voted against the life consulate and the empire, and showed an opposition to the growth of Imperialism which hurt his advancement. After the battle of Vimeiro in 1808 he was named general of brigade, and later general of division. He fought in Spain until the evacuation of the country. Under the restoration Foy served as an inspector-general of artillery; but he joined Napoleon on his return, fought at Waterloo, and went into retirement afterwards. In 1819 he was elected deputy, and almost at once he showed himself an orator of unusual power. He was a pure constitutionalist, and gave all his efforts to holding the Bourbons to the charter. He died in November, 1825.

hands was not to be allowed to go on without interference. Jacobinism, republicanism, royalism, were deeply-rooted sentiments, and it was not long before they began to struggle for expression.

OPPOSITION, AND HOW HE MET IT.

Early in the Consulate, plots of many descriptions were unearthed. The most serious before 1803 was that known as the "Opera Plot," or "Plot of the 3d Nivose" (December 24, 1800), when a bomb was placed in the street, to be exploded as the First Consul's carriage passed. By an accident he was saved, and, in spite of the shock, went on to the opera. Madame Junot, who was there, gives a graphic description of the way the news was received by the house:

"The first thirty measures of the oratorio were scarcely played, when a strong explosion like a cannon was heard.

BERNADOTTE. ABOUT 1798.

"'What does that mean?' exclaimed Junot with emotion. He opened the door of the *loge* and looked into the corridor. . . . 'It is strange; how can they be firing the cannon at this hour?' And then, 'I should have known it. Give me my hat; I am going to find out what it is. . . .'

"At this moment the *loge* of the First Consul opened, and he himself appeared with General Lannes, Lauriston, Berthier, and Duroc. Smiling, he saluted the immense crowd, which mingled cries like those of love with its applause. Madame Bonaparte followed him in a few seconds. . . .

"'Junot was going to enter the *loge* to see for himself the serene air of the First Consul that I had just remarked, when Duroc came up to us with troubled face and a worried air.

"'The First Consul has just escaped death,' he said quickly to Junot. 'Go down and see him; he wants to talk to you.' . . . But a dull sound commenced to spread from parterre to orchestra, from orchestra to amphitheatre, and thence to the *loges*.

"'The First Consul has just been attacked in the Rue Saint Nicaise,' it was whispered. Soon the truth was circulated in the *salle* as

Engraved by Alls. after Le Dru. Bernadotte (J. B. Jules) was born at Pau, in 1764; entered the Royal Marine at seventeen years of age, and was sergeant in 1789. In 1792 entered the Army of the North, where he served with honor. He entered the Army of Italy in 1797, and, although suspicious of Bonaparte's ambition, he served him valiantly, and was one of those sent to Paris with captured flags. Was an active supporter of the *coup d'état* of the 18th Fructidor, and was ambassador at Vienna after the treaty of Campo Formio. Bernadotte married the Désirée Clary, sister-in-law of Joseph Bonaparte, whom Napoleon, in 1795, had thought of making his wife. In 1799 he served in the Rhenish armies. He disapproved of the 18th Brumaire, but after it accepted the command of the Army of the West. In 1804 he was made marshal, and later, Prince of Ponte Corvo. In the Austrian war of 1809 Bernadotte played an important part, and again in the campaign of 1807. In 1810 the Swedish States proclaimed him prince royal and heir presumptive of Sweden. He was received as a son by Charles XIII., and during the life of that monarch Bernadotte surrounded him by a really filial care. In 1813 he entered the coalition against Bonaparte. At first he tried to act as a mediator, but this failing, he led his army against the French, defeating Ney and Oudinot, and deciding the battle of Leipsic. But he took no part in the invasion of France. In 1818, on the death of Charles XIII., he was proclaimed King of Norway and Sweden, and took the name of Charles Jean IV., though he is usually called Charles XIV. He held the throne for twenty-five years, and his son Oscar succeeded him.

the same instant, and, as by an electric shock, one and the same acclamation arose, one and the same look enveloped Napoleon, as if in a protecting love.

"What agitation preceded the explosion of national anger which was represented in that first quarter of an hour, by that crowd whose fury for so black an attack could not be expressed by words! Women sobbed aloud, men shivered with indignation. Whatever the banner they followed, they were united heart and arm in this case to show that differences of opinion did not bring with them differences in understanding honor."

It was such attempts, and suspicion of like ones, that led to the extension of the police service.

One of the ablest and craftiest men of the Revolution became Napoleon's head of police in the Consulate, Fouché. A consummate actor and skilful flatterer, hindered by no conscience other than the duty of keeping in place, he acted a curious and entertaining part. Detective work was for him a game which he played with intense relish. He was a veritable amateur of plots, and never gayer than when tracing them.

Napoleon admired Fouché, but he did not trust him, and, to offset him, formed a private police to spy on his work. He never succeeded in finding any one sufficiently fine to match the chief, who several times was malicious enough to contrive plots himself, to excite and mislead the private agents.

The system of espionage went so far that letters were regularly opened. It was commonly said that those who did not want their letters read, did not send them by post. It was difficult, however, to get officials for the post-office who

NAPOLEON BONAPARTE.

MOREAU. ABOUT 1800.

Engraved by Elizabeth G. Gerhan, after Guérin. Moreau (Jean-Victor) was born at Morlaix in 1763. Studied law at Rennes. In the troubles of the Parliament which preceded the Revolution, he showed such ability in directing a body of his comrades that he was called the "General of the Parliament." In 1792 entered the army of Dumouriez. Was made general of brigade in 1793, and general of division in 1794. Two years later received the command of the Army of the Rhine and Moselle, which he conducted with rare skill. Having seized a correspondence of the Prince of Condé and Pichegru, which proved the latter a conspirator, he concealed it out of friendship for Pichegru until after the 18th Fructidor, when the latter was arrested. For this he was retired from service for eighteen months, but returned to the Army of Italy in 1799. Returning to Paris in 1799, he first met Bonaparte, whom he aided on the 18th Brumaire. Moreau, as a reward for his services, was named general in chief of the Army of the Rhine. His campaign as the head of his new army was brilliant, ending in the great victory of Hohenlinden on December 3, 1800. Returning to Paris, he became the centre of a faction discontented with Bonaparte, and refused the title of marshal and the decoration of the Legion of Honor which the latter offered him. He was approached by agents of Louis XVIII., and was supposed to be connected indirectly with the Georges plot. Was arrested, tried, and exiled for two years. He retired to the United States, where at first he travelled extensively. Moreau settled in this country, leading a quiet life until 1813, when he was invited by the Emperor Alexander to return to Europe. With Bernadotte he prepared the plans of the campaign of 1813 and 1814, and it was by his advice that the allies refused to give general battle to Napoleon. At Dresden, on August 27, 1813, he was mortally wounded: it is said, by a French bullet.

could be always relied on; and in 1802, the Postmaster-General, M. Bernard, the father of the beautiful Madame Récamier, was found to be concealing an active Royalist correspondence, and to be permitting the circulation of a quantity of seditious pamphlets. His arrest and imprisonment made a great commotion in his daughter's circle, which was one of social and intellectual importance. Through the intercessions of Bernadotte, M. Bernard was pardoned by Napoleon. The *cab net noir*, as the department of the post-office which did this work was called, was in existence when Napoleon came to the Consulate, and he rather restricted than increased its operations. It has never been entirely given up, as many an inoffensive foreigner in France can testify.

The theatre and press were also subjected to a strict censorship. In 1800 the number of newspapers in Paris was reduced to twelve; and in three years there were but eight left, with a total subscription list of eighteen thousand six hundred and thirty. Napoleon's contempt for journalists and editors equalled that he had for lawyers, whom he called a "heap of babblers and revolutionists." Neither class could, in his judgment, be allowed safely to go free.

The *salons* were watched, and it is certain that those whose *habitués* criticised Napoleon freely were reported. One serious rupture resulted from the supervision of the *salons*, that with Madame de Staël. She had been an ardent admirer of Napoleon in the beginning of the Consulate, and Bourrienne tells several amusing stories of the disgust Napoleon showed at the letters of admiration and sentiment which she wrote him even so far back as the Italian campaign. If the secretary is to be believed, Madame de Staël told Napoleon, in one of these letters, that they were certainly create l for each other, that it was an error in human institutions that the mild and tranquil Josephine was united to his fate, that nature evidently had intended for a hero such as he, her own soul of fire. Napoleon tore the letter to pieces, and he took pains thereafter to announce with great bluntness to Madame de Staël, whenever he met her, his own notions on women, which certainly were anything but "advanced."

As the centralization of the government increased, Madame de Staël and her friends criticised Napoleon more freely and sharply than they would have done, no doubt, had she not been incensed by his personal attitude towards her. This hostility increased until, in 1803, the First Consul ordered her out of France. "The arrival of this woman, like that of a bird of omen," he said in giving the order, "has always been the signal for some trouble. It is not my intention to allow her to remain in France."

In 1807 this order was repeated, and many of Madame de Staël's friends were included in the proscription:

"I have written to the Minister of Police to send Madame de Staël to Geneva. This woman continues her trade of intriguer. She went near Paris in spite of my orders. She is a veritable plague. Speak seriously to the Minister, for I shall be obliged to have her seized by the *gendarmerie*. Keep an eye upon Benjamin Constant; if he meddles with anything I shall send him to his wife at Brunswick. I will not tolerate this ellipse."

But when one compares the policy of restriction during the Consulate with what it had been under the old régime and in the Revolution, it certainly was far in advance in liberty, discretion, and humanity. The republican government to-day, in its repression of anarchy and socialism, has acted with less wisdom and less respect for freedom of thought than Napoleon did at this period of his career; and that, too, in circumstances less complicated and critical.

INTERNAL PEACE AND PROSPERITY.

If there were still dull rumors of discontent, a *cabinet noir*, a restricted press, a censorship over the theatre, proscriptions, even imprisonments and executions, on the whole France was happy.

"Not only did the interior wheels of the machine commence to run smoothly," says the Duchesse d'Abrantès, "but the arts themselves, that most peaceful part of the interior administration, gave striking proofs of the returning prosperity of France. The exposition at the *Salon* that year (1800) was remarkably fine. Guérin, David, Gérard, Girodet, a crowd of great talents, spurred on by the emulation which always awakes the fire of genius, produced works which must some time place our school at a high rank."

The art treasures of Europe were pouring into France. Under the direction of Denon, that indefatigable *dilettanti* and student, who had collected in the expedition in Egypt more entertaining material than the whole Institute, and had written a report of it which will always be preferred to the "Great Work," the galleries of Paris were reorganized and opened two days of the week to the people. Napoleon inaugurated this practice himself. Not only was Paris supplied with galleries; those de-

EUGÈNE DE BEAUHARNAIS, NAPOLEON'S STEP-SON. ("EUGENIO NAPOLEONE, PRINCE DI FRANCIA, VICE RE D'ITALIA, 1813.")

Engraved by Longhi, after Gérard, Milan, 1813. Eugène de Beauharnais, son of Josephine Tascher de la Pagerie and the Viscount Alexandre de Beauharnais, was born in Paris in 1781. The property of his father having been confiscated, Eugène was apprenticed to a cabinet-maker, but, fortune changing, he was employed on the staff of General Hoche. After the marriage of Josephine and Bonaparte, the latter took his step-son with him into Italy, and sent him on a mission to Corfu. He accompanied General Bonaparte to Egypt, and was wounded at Saint Jean d'Acre. He rose steadily in military rank, and when the Empire was established was made prince, and in 1805, Arch-chancellor of State. When Napoleon took the iron crown, Eugène was made Viceroy of Italy. He governed his kingdom with wisdom and fidelity. In 1806 Eugène was married to a daughter of the King of Bavaria, and adopted by Napoleon, who declared that in case he had no direct heir he intended giving him the crown of Italy. When the Austrian war of 1809 broke out, an army invaded Italy, and Eugène was defeated in a first battle, but, rallying, he gained a series of victories, ending with that of Raab, which Napoleon called the "granddaughter of Marengo." It was Eugène and his sister Hortense that Napoleon charged to prepare Josephine for the divorce, and the former explained to the Senate the reasons for the act. He took so distinguished a part in the Russian campaign that Napoleon said: "Eugène is the only one who has not committed blunders in this war." In 1813 and 1814 he fought with great skill against the allies. The final overthrow of Napoleon took his kingdom from him. He retired then to the court of the King of Bavaria, his father-in-law, who made him Duke of Leuchtenberg and Prince of Eichstadt. He died in 1824 at Munich.

partment museums which surprise and delight the tourist so in France to-day were then created at Angers, Antwerp, Autun, Bordeaux, Brussels, Caen, Dijon, Geneva, Grenoble, Le Mans, Lille, Lyons, Mayence, Marseilles, Montpellier, Nancy, Nantes, Rennes, Rouen, Strasburg, Toulouse, and Tours.

The *prix de Rome*, for which there had been no money in the treasury for some time, was again reëstablished.

In literature and in music, as in art, there was a renewal of activity. A circle of poets and writers gathered about the First Consul. Paisiello was summoned to Paris to direct the opera and conservatory of music. There was a revival of dignity and taste in strong contrast to the license and carelessness of the Revolution. The *incroyable* passed away. The Greek costume disappeared from the street. Men and women began again to dress, to act, to talk according to conventional forms. Society recovered its systematic ways of doing things, and soon few signs of the general dissolution which had prevailed for ten years were to be seen.

Once more the traveller crossed France in peace; peasant and laborer went undisturbed about their work, and slept without fear. Again the people danced in the fields and "sang their songs as they had in the days before the Revolution." "France has nothing to ask from Heaven," said Regnault de Saint-Jean d'Angely, "but that the sun may continue to shine, the rain to fall on our fields, and the earth to render the seed fruitful."

LETTING IN THE JUNGLE.

By RUDYARD KIPLING,

Author of "Plain Tales from the Hills," "The Jungle Book," etc.

[" Letting in the Jungle " is a continuation of the marvellous tales of " Mowgli's Brothers " and " Tiger! Tiger ! " Those who read the first stories will remember how the tiger Shere Khan pursued a little Indian baby to the mouth of a cave, where it took refuge with Mother Wolf. The lame tiger demanded his prey, but after defying him, the pack adopted Mowgli the man cub, and he was reared as one of the jungle folk, talking their language, and hunting and living along with Bagheera the black panther, and Baloo the bear. It was when the pack revolted against Akela, the old wolf who for years had led them to battle, that Mowgli, in a fit of rage, quit the jungle. He went to live among men, but before his departure vowed never to return till he came to spread Shere Khan's hide on the Council Rock.

In the village Mowgli found his real parents, Messua and her husband, and like a dutiful son tried to conform to human habits and speech. But jungle intrigues followed him ; and when his arch enemy Shere Khan lay in wait thirsting for blood, his foster family, Mother Wolf, Grey Brother, and Akela, gave the man cub warning. Mowgli was village herder at the time, and cunningly he trapped his foe. The lame tiger was decoyed into a narrow defile, and then the angry bull buffaloes were driven at a mad pace down the gorge until they trampled the last breath out of Shere Khan's body. In the moment of Mowgli's triumph, Buldeo, the village hunter, demanded that the tiger skin be given to him for the reward it would bring. His insistence forced the man cub to call upon Akela for assistance. Obedient to orders, the old wolf sprang upon the hunter and pinned him to the ground, while Mowgli stripped off the gay hide. Seeing the beast's implicit obedience, Buldeo returned to the village, declared Mowgli a sorcerer, and when the boy returned, driving his buffaloes before him, the people stoned him from the gate. He then returned to the jungle, fulfilled his promise of carpeting the Council Rock with Shere Khan's hide, called the pack together, and after reinstating Akela as leader, he said, " Man pack and Wolf pack have cast me out. Now I will hunt alone in the jungle."—EDITOR.]

YOU will remember how, after Mowgli had pinned Shere Khan's hide to the Council Rock, he told as many as were left of the Seeonee pack that henceforward he would hunt in the jungle alone, and the four children of Mother and Father Wolf said that they would hunt with him. But it is not easy to change one's life all in one minute—particularly in the jungle. The first thing Mowgli did when the disorderly pack had slunk off, was to go to the home-cave and tell Mother Wolf and Father Wolf as much as they could understand of his adventures ; and when he made the morning sun flicker up and down the blade of his skinning-knife—the same he had skinned Shere Khan with—they said he had learned something. Then Akela and Grey Brother had to explain their share of the great buffalo-drive in the ravine, and Baloo toiled up the hill to hear all about it, and Bagheera scratched himself all over with pure delight at the way in which Mowgli had managed his war.

LETTING IN THE JUNGLE.

It was long after sunrise, but no one dreamed of going to sleep, and from time to time during the talk Mother Wolf would throw up her head and sniff a deep sniff of satisfaction as the wind brought her the smell of the tiger-skin on the Council Rock.

"But for Akela and Grey Brother here," Mowgli said at the end, "I could have done nothing. Oh, mother, mother, if thou hadst seen the black herd-bulls pour down the ravine, or hurry through the gates when the man pack flung stones at me!"

"I am glad I did not see that last," said Mother Wolf stiffly. "It is not my custom to suffer my cubs to be driven to and fro like jackals. *I* would have taken a price from the man pack, but I would have spared the woman that gave thee the milk. Yes, I would have spared her alone."

"For this reason," the Lone Wolf answered. "When that yellow thief's hide was hung up, I went back along our trail from the village, stepping in my tracks, turning aside, scratching and lying down, to make a mixed trail in case one should follow us. But when I had fouled the trail so that I myself hardly knew it again, Mang the bat came hawking between the trees, and hung up above me. Said Mang, 'The village of the man pack where they cast out the man cub hums like a hornets' nest.'"

"It was a big stone that I threw," chuckled Mowgli, who had often amused himself by throwing ripe paw-paws into a hornets' nest, and racing to the nearest pool before the hornets caught him.

"I asked of Mang what he had seen. He said the Red Flower blossomed at the gate of the village, and men sat about it carrying guns. Now *I* know, for I have good cause"— Akela looked down at the old dry scars on his flank and side— "that men do not carry guns for pleasure. Presently, Little Brother, a man with a gun follows our trail—if, indeed, he be not already on it."

HE HAD JUST TIME TO SNATCH UP HIS PAW AS THE SKINNING-KNIFE CUT DEEP INTO THE GROUND BELOW.

"Peace—peace, Raksha," said Father Wolf lazily. "Our Frog has come back again—so wise that his own father must lick his feet; and what is a cuff more or less on the head? Leave the men alone." Baloo and Bagheera both echoed, "Leave the men alone."

Mowgli, his head on Mother Wolf's side, smiled contentedly, and said that for his own part he never wished to see or hear or smell a man again.

"But what," said Akela, cocking one ear, "but what if the men do not leave thee alone, Little Brother?"

"We be *five*," said Grey Brother, looking round at the company, and snapping his jaws on the last word.

"We also might attend to that hunting," said Bagheera with a little *switch-switch* of his tail, looking at Baloo. "But why think of men now, Akela?"

"But why should he? Men have cast me out. What more do they need?" said Mowgli angrily.

"Thou art a man, Little Brother," Akela returned. "It is not for us, the Free Hunters, to tell thee what thy brethren do, or why."

He had just time to snatch up his paw as the skinning-knife cut deep into the ground below. Mowgli struck quicker than an average human eye could follow, but Akela was a wolf; and even a dog, who is very far removed from the wild wolf his ancestor, can be waked out of deep sleep by a cartwheel touching his flank, and can spring away unharmed before that wheel comes on.

"Another time," Mowgli said quietly, returning the knife to its sheath, "speak of the man pack and of Mowgli in *two* breaths, not one."

"Phff! that is a sharp tooth," said Akela,

snuffing at the blade's cut in the earth; "but living with the man pack has spoiled thy eye, Little Brother. I could have killed a buck while thou wast striking."

Bagheera sprang to his feet, thrust up his head as far as he could, sniffed, and stiffened through every curve in his body. Grey Brother followed his example quickly, keeping a little to his left to get the wind that was blowing from the right, while Akela bounded fifty yards up wind, and, half-crouching, stiffened too. Mowgli looked on enviously. He could smell things as very few human beings could, but he had never reached the hair-trigger-like sensitiveness of a jungle nose; and his three months in the smoky village had put him back sadly. However, he dampened his finger, rubbed it on his nose, and stood up to catch the upper scent, which, though it is the faintest, is the truest.

"Man," Akela growled, dropping on his haunches.

"Buldeo," said Mowgli, sitting down. "He follows our trail, and yonder is the sunlight on his gun. Look!"

It was no more than a flash of sunlight, for a fraction of a second, on the brass clamps of the old Tower musket, but nothing in the jungle winks with that flash except when the clouds race over the sky. Then a piece of mica, or a little pool, or even a highly polished leaf will flash like a heliograph. But that day was cloudless and still.

"I knew men would follow," said Akela triumphantly. "Not for nothing have I led the pack—and now?"

The four cubs, headed by Grey Brother, said nothing, but ran down hill on their bellies, melting into the thorn and underbrush as a mole melts into the earth.

"Where go ye, without word?" Mowgli called.

"H'sh! We will roll his skull here before midday!" Grey Brother answered.

"Here! Back and wait! Man does not eat man!" Mowgli shrieked.

"Who was a wolf but now? Who drove the knife at me for thinking he might be a man?" said Akela, as the four wolves turned back sullenly and dropped to heel.

"Am I to give reasons for what I choose to do?" said Mowgli furiously.

"That is a man. There speaks a man," Bagheera muttered under his whiskers. "Even so did men talk round the king's cages at Oodeypore. We of the jungle know that man is wisest of all. If we trusted our ears, we should know that of all things he is most foolish." Then raising his voice, he added, "The man cub is right in this. Men hunt in packs. To kill one, unless we know what the others will do, is bad hunting. Come, let us see what this man means towards us."

"We will not come," Grey Brother growled. "Hunt alone, Little Brother. We know our own minds. That skull would have been ready to bring by now."

Mowgli had been looking from one to the other of his friends, his chest heaving, and his eyes full of tears. But now he strode forward to the wolves, and dropping on one knee, said: "Do I not know my mind? Look at me!"

They looked uneasily; and when their eyes wandered, he called them back again and again, till their hair stood up all over their bodies, and they trembled in every limb, while Mowgli stared and stared.

"Now," said he, "of us five, which is leader?"

"Thou art leader, Little Brother," said Grey Brother, and he licked Mowgli's foot.

"Follow, then," said Mowgli; and the four followed at his heels with their tails between their legs.

"This comes of living with the man pack," said Bagheera, slipping down after them. "There is more in the jungle now than jungle law, Baloo."

The old bear said nothing, but he thought many things.

Mowgli cut across noiselessly through the jungle, at right angles to Buldeo's path, till, parting the undergrowth, he saw the old man, his musket on his shoulder, running up the trail of overnight at a dog-trot.

You will remember that Mowgli had left the village with the heavy weight of Shere Khan's hide on his shoulders, while Akela and Grey Brother trotted behind, so that the trail was very clearly marked. Presently Buldeo came to where Akela, as you know, had gone back and mixed it all up. Then he sat down and coughed and grunted and made little casts round and about into the jungle to pick it up again, and all the time he could have thrown a stone over those who were watching him. No one can be so silent as a wolf when he does not care to be heard; and Mowgli, though the wolves thought he moved very clumsily, could come and go like a shadow. They ringed the old man as a school of porpoises ring a steamer going at full speed, and as they ringed him, they talked unconcernedly; for their speech began below the lowest end of the scale that untrained human beings can hear. The other end is bounded by the high squeak of Mang the bat, which very many people cannot hear at all. From that note all the bird and bat and insect talk takes on.

"This is better than any kill," said Grey Brother as the old man stooped and peered and puffed. "He looks like a lost pig in the jungles by the river. What does he say?" Buldeo was muttering savagely.

Mowgli translated. "He says that packs of wolves must have danced round me. He says that

"EAT, OR BLOW SMOKE OUT OF HIS MOUTH. MEN ALWAYS PLAY WITH THEIR MOUTHS," SAID MOWGLI.

man's buff that they were playing. "Now what does the lean thing do?"

"Eat, or blow smoke out of his mouth. Men always play with their mouths," said Mowgli; and the silent trailers saw the old man fill and light and puff at a water-pipe, and they took good note of the smell of the tobacco, so as to be sure of Buldeo in the darkest night, if things fell out that way.

Then a little knot of charcoal-burners came down the path, and naturally halted to speak to Buldeo, whose fame as a hunter reached for at least twenty miles round. Then they all sat down he never saw such a trail in his life. He and smoked, and Bagheera and the others says he is tired." came up and watched while Buldeo

"He will be rested before he picks it up began to tell the story of Mowgli, the again," said Bagheera coolly, as he slipped devil-child, from one end to another with killed Shere Khan; and how Mowgli had turned himself into a wolf, and fought with him all the afternoon, and changed into a boy again, and bewitched Buldeo's rifle, so that the bullet turned the corner when he pointed it at Mowgli, and killed one of Buldeo's own buffaloes; and how the village, knowing him to be the bravest hunter in Seeonee, had sent him out to kill this devil-child. But, meantime, the village had got hold of Messua and her husband, who were undoubtedly the father and mother of this devil-child,—Messua he knew was a sorceress; had known it for years, but had not cared to make bad blood in the village by talking about it,—and had barricaded them in their own hut, and presently would torture them to make them confess they were witch and wizard, and then they would be beaten to death. "When?" said the charcoal-burners, because they would very much like to be present at the ceremony.

Buldeo said that nothing would be done till he returned, because the village wished him to kill the jungle boy first. After that they would dispose of Messua and her husband, and divide their lands and buffaloes among the village. Messua's husband had some remarkably fine buffaloes, too. It was an excellent thing to clear out wizards, Buldeo thought; and people who entertained wolf children out of the jungle were clearly the worst kind of witches.

"But," said the charcoal-burners, "what would happen if the English heard of it?" The English, they had heard, were a perfectly mad people, who would not let honest farmers kill witches in peace.

Why, said Buldeo, the head man of the village would report that Messua and her husband had died of snake bite. That was all arranged, and the only thing now was to kill the wolf child. They did not happen to have seen anything of such a creature? The charcoal-burners looked around cautiously, and thanked their stars they had not; but they had no doubt that so brave a man as Buldeo would find him, if any one could. The sun was getting rather low, and they had an idea that they would push on to Buldeo's village and see that wicked witch. Buldeo said that though it was his duty to kill the devil-child, he could not think of letting a party of unarmed men go through the jungle, which might produce the wolf-demon at any minute, without his escort. He, therefore, would accompany them, and if the sorcerer's child appeared—well, he would show them how the best hunter in Seeonee dealt with such things. The Brahmin, he said, had given him a charm against the creature, that made everything perfectly safe.

"What says he? What says he? What says he?" the wolves repeated every few minutes; and Mowgli translated until he came to the witch part of the story, which was a little bit beyond him, and then he said that the man and woman who had been so kind to him were trapped.

"Do men trap men?" said Bagheera.

"So he says. I cannot understand the talk. They are all mad together. What have Messua and the man to do with me that they should be put in a trap, and what is all this talk about the Red Flower? I must look to this. Whatever they would do to Messua, they will not do till Buldeo returns. . . . And so——" Mowgli thought hard, with his fingers playing round the haft of the skinning-knife, while Buldeo and the charcoal-burners went off very valiantly in single file.

"I am going hot foot back to the man pack," he said at last.

"And those?" said Grey Brother, looking hungrily after the brown backs of the charcoal-burners.

"Sing them home," said Mowgli, with a grin; "I do not wish them to be at the village gate till it is dark. Can you hold them?"

Grey Brother bared his white teeth in contempt. "We can head them round and round in circles like tethered goats—if I know men."

"That I do not need. Sing to them a little, lest they be lonely on the road; and, Grey Brother, the song need not be of the sweetest. Go with them, Bagheera, and help make that song. When the night is well down, meet me by the village. Grey Brother knows the place."

"It is no light hunting to work for a man cub. When shall I sleep?" said Bagheera yawning, though his eyes showed he was delighted with the amusement. "Me to sing to naked men! But let us see."

He lowered his head so that the sound would travel well, and cried a long, long "good hunting"—a midnight call in the afternoon which was quite awful enough to begin with. Mowgli heard it rumble and rise, and fall and die off in a creepy sort of whine behind him, and laughed to himself as he ran through the jungle. He could see the charcoal-burners huddled in a knot, with old Buldeo's gun-barrel waving like a banana-leaf to every point of the compass at once. Then Grey Brother gave the *Ya-la-hi, Yalaha!* call for the buck-driving, when the pack drives the Nilghai, the big Blue Cow, before them; and it seemed to come from the very ends of the earth, nearer and nearer and nearer, till it ended in a shriek snapped off short. The other three answered till even Mowgli could have vowed that the full pack was in full cry; and then they all broke into the magnificent morning-song in the jungle, with every turn and flourish and grace-note that a deep-mouthed wolf of the pack knows. This is a rough rendering of the song, and you must imagine what it sounds like when it breaks the afternoon hush of the jungle:

One moment past our bodies cast
No shadow on the plain ;
Now clear and black they stride our track,
And we run home again.
In morning hush, each rock and bush
Stands hard and high and raw ;
Then give the call : "*Good rest to all That keep the jungle law.*"

Ho! Get to lair! The sun's aflare
Behind the breathing grass ;
And creaking through the young bamboo,
The warning whispers pass.
By day made strange, the woods we range,
With blinking eyes we scan ;
While down the skies the wild duck cries :
"*The day—the day to man!*"

The dew is dried that drenched our hide,
Or washed about our way ;
And where we drank, the puddled bank
Is crisping into clay,
The traitor dark gives up each mark
Of stretched or hooded claw ;
Then hear the call : "*Good rest to all That keep the jungle law.*"

But no translation can give the effect of it, or the yelping scorn the four threw into every word of it as they heard the trees crash when the men hastily climbed up into the branches, and Buldeo began repeating incantations and charms. Then they lay down and slept, for, like all who live by their own exertions, they were of a methodical cast of mind ; and no one can work well without sleep.

Meantime Mowgli was putting the miles behind him at the rate of nine an hour, swinging on, delighted to find himself so fit after all those cramped months among men. The one idea in his head was to get Messua and her husband out of the trap, whatever it was, for he had a natural mistrust of traps. Later on, he promised himself, he would begin to pay his debts to the village at large. It was twilight when he saw the well-remembered grazing-grounds, and the dhak-tree where Grey Brother had waited for him on the morning that he killed Shere Khan. Angry as he was at the whole breed and community of man, something jumped up in his throat and made him catch his breath when he looked at the village roofs. He noticed that every one had come in from the fields unusually early, and that, instead of getting to their evening cooking, they gathered in a crowd under the village tree, and chattered and shouted.

HER HUSBAND . . . SAT PICKING DUST AND THINGS OUT OF HIS TORN BEARD.

"Men must always be making traps for men, or they are not content," said Mowgli. "Last night it was Mowgli—the last night seems many rains ago. To-night it is Messua and her man. To-morrow and for very many nights after, it will be Mowgli's turn again."

He crept along outside the wall till he came to Messua's hut, and looked through the window into the room. There lay Messua, gagged and bound hand and foot, breathing hard and groaning, and her husband was tied to the gayly painted bedstead. The door of the hut that opened into the street was shut fast, and three or four men were sitting with their backs to it.

Mowgli knew the manners and customs of the villagers very fairly. He argued that so long as they could eat and talk and smoke, they would not do anything else; but as soon as they had fed, they would begin to be dangerous. Buldeo would be coming in before long, and if his escort had done its duty, Buldeo would have a very interesting tale to tell. So he went in through the window, and stooping over the man and the woman, cut their thongs, pulled out the gags, and looked round the hut for some milk.

Messua was half wild with pain and fear (she had been beaten and stoned and cuffed all the morning), and Mowg'. put his hand over her mouth just in time to stop a scream. Her husband was only bewildered and angry, and sat picking dust and things out of his torn beard.

"I knew—I knew he would come," Messua sobbed at last. "Now do I *know* that he is my son;" and she hugged Mowgli to her heart. Up to that time he had been perfectly steady, but now he began to tremble all over, and that surprised him immensely.

"What are all these things? Why have they tied thee?" he asked, after a pause.

"To be put to the death for making a son of thee—what else?" said the man sullenly. "Look! I bleed."

Messua said nothing, but it was at her wounds that Mowgli looked, and they heard him grit his teeth when he saw the blood.

"Whose work is this?" said he. "There will be a price to pay."

"The work of all the village. I was too rich. I had too many cattle. *Therefore*, she and I are witches because we gave thee shelter."

"I do not understand. Let Messua tell the tale."

"I gave thee milk, Nathoo; dost thou remember?" Messua said timidly. "Because thou wast my son whom the tiger took, and because I loved thee very dearly. They said that I was thy mother, the mother of a devil, and therefore worthy of death."

"And what is a devil?" said Mowgli. "Death I have seen."

The man looked up gloomily under his eyebrows, but Messua laughed. "See!" she said to her husband. "I knew when I said that he was no sorcerer. He is my son—my son!"

"Son or sorcerer, what good will that do us?" the man answered. "We are as dead already."

"Yonder is the road to the jungle"—Mowgli pointed through the window—"and your hands and feet are free. Go, now."

"We do not know the jungle, my son, as —as thou knowest," Messua began. "I do not think that I could walk far."

"And the men and women would be upon our backs and drag us here again," said the husband.

"H'm!" said Mowgli, and he tickled the palm of his hand with the tip of his skinning-knife. "I have no wish to do harm to any one of this village—*yet*. But I do not think they will stay thee. In a little while they will have much to think of. Ah!" He lifted his head and listened to shouting and trampling outside. "So they have let Buldeo come home at last."

"He was sent out this morning to kill thee," Messua cried. "Didst thou meet him?"

"Yes—we—I met him. He has a tale to tell; of that I am certain. And while he is telling it, there is time to do much. But first I will look and see what they mean. Think where ye would go, and tell me when I come back."

He bounded through the window, and ran along again outside the wall of the village, till he came within earshot of the crowd round the peepul-tree. Buldeo was lying

MOTHER WORE STAMPED HERSELF UP ON END, AND LOOKED THROUGH THE WINDOW INTO THE DARK OF THE HUT.

"LOOK! AS I DANCE WITH MY SHADOW SO I DANCED WITH THOSE MEN."

on the ground coughing and groaning, and every one was asking him questions all at once. His hair had fallen about his shoulders; his hands and legs were skinned from climbing up trees, and he could hardly speak; but he felt the importance of his position keenly. From time to time he said something about devils and singing devils and magic enchantment, just to give the crowd a taste of what was coming. Then he called for water.

"Bah!" said Mowgli. "Chatter, chatter. Talk, talk! These men are brothers of the Bander-log. Now he must wash his mouth with water; now he must smoke; and when all that is done, he has still his story to tell. They are very wise people—men. They will leave no one to guard Messua, till their ears are stuffed with Buldeo's tales. And—I am becoming as lazy as they!"

He shook himself and glided back to the

hut. Just as he was at the window, he felt a touch on his foot.

"Mother," said he, for he knew that tongue well, "what dost thou here?"

"I heard my children singing through the woods, and I followed the one I loved best. Little Frog, I have a desire to see that woman who gave thee milk," said Mother Wolf, all wet with the dew.

"They have bound and mean to kill her. I have cut those ties, and she goes with her man through the jungle."

"I also will follow. I am old, but not yet toothless." Mother Wolf reared herself up on end, and looked through the window into the dark of the hut.

In a minute she dropped noiselessly, and all she said was, "I gave thee thy first milk; but Bagheera speaks true. Man goes to man at last."

"Maybe," said Mowgli, with a very unpleasant look on his face. "But to-night I am very far from that trail. Wait here, but do not let her see."

"*Thou* wast never afraid of *me*, Little Frog," said Mother Wolf, backing into the high grass, and blotting herself out, as she knew how.

"And now," said Mowgli cheerfully, as he came into the hut again, "they are all sitting round Buldeo, who is saying that which did not happen. When his talk is finished, they say they will assuredly come here with the Red—with fire, and burn you both. And then?"

"I have spoken to my man," said Messua. "Kanhiwara is thirty miles from here, but at Kanhiwara we may find the English——"

"And what pack are they?" said Mowgli.

"I do not know. They be white, and it is said that they govern all the land, and do not suffer people to burn or beat each other without witnesses. If we can get thither to-night, we live. Otherwise, we die."

"Live, then. No man passes the gates to-night. But what does *he* do?" Messua's husband was on his hands and knees, digging up the earth in one corner of the hut.

"It is his little money," said Messua. "We can take nothing else."

"Ah, yes! The stuff that passes from hand to hand and never grows warmer. Do they need it outside this place also?"

The man stared angrily. "He is a fool, and no devil," he muttered. "With the money I can buy a horse. We are too bruised to walk far, and the village will follow us in an hour."

"I say they will *not* follow till I choose; but the horse is well thought of, for Messua is tired." Her husband stood up and knotted the last of the rupees into his waist-belt. Mowgli helped Messua through the window, and the cool night air revived her; but the jungle in the starlight looked very dark and terrible.

"Ye know the trail to Kanhiwara?" Mowgli whispered.

They nodded.

"Good. Remember, now, not to be afraid. And there is no need to go quickly. Only—only there may be some small singing in the jungle behind you and before."

"Think you we would have risked a night in the jungle through anything less than the fear of burning? It is better to be killed by beasts than by men," said Messua's husband; but Messua looked straight at Mowgli and smiled.

"I say," Mowgli went on, just as though he were Baloo repeating an old jungle law for the hundredth time to a foolish cub, "I say that not a tooth in the jungle is bared against you; not a foot in the jungle is lifted against you. Neither man nor beast shall stay you till ye come within eyeshot of Kanhiwara. There will be a watch about you." He turned quickly to Messua, saying, "*He* does not believe, but thou wilt believe."

"Ay, surely, my son. Man, ghost, or wolf of the jungle, I believe."

"*He* will be afraid when he hears my people singing. Thou wilt know and understand. Go now, and slowly, for there is no need of any haste. The gates of this village are shut."

Messua flung herself sobbing at Mowgli's feet, but he lifted her very quickly with a shiver. Then she hung about his neck, and called him every name of blessing she could think of; but her husband looked enviously across his fields, and said: "*If* we reach Kanhiwara, and I get the ear of the English, I will bring such a lawsuit against the Brahmin and old Buldeo and the others as shall eat the village to the bone. They shall pay me twice over for my crops untilled and my buffaloes unfed, I will have a great justice."

Mowgli laughed. "I do not know what justice is; but—come next rains, and see what is left."

They went off towards the jungle, and Mother Wolf leaped from her place of hiding.

"Follow," said Mowgli, "and look to it that all the jungle knows these two are safe. Give tongue a little. I would call Bagheera."

"BAT IN THE JUNGLE, NATHU!"

"I am ashamed of thy brethren," he said, purring.

"What! Did they not sing sweetly to Buldeo?" said Mowgli.

"Too well! Too well! They made even *me* forget my pride, and, by the Broken Lock that freed me, I went singing through the jungle as though I were out wooing in the spring. Didst thou not hear us?"

"I had other game afoot. Ask Buldeo if he liked the song. But where are the four? I do not wish one of the man pack to leave the gates to-night."

"What need of the four, then?" said Bagheera, shifting from foot to foot, his eyes ablaze, and purring louder than ever. "I can hold them, Little Brother. It is killing at last? The singing and the sight of the men climbing up the trees have made me very ready. What is man that we should care for him? The naked brown digger, the hairless and toothless, the eater of earth. I have followed him all day, at noon, in the white sunlight. I herded him as the wolves herd buck. I am Bagheera! Bagheera! Bagheera! Look! As I dance with my shadow so I danced with those men." The great panther

The long, low howl rose and fell, and leaped, as a kitten leaps, at a dead leaf Mowgli saw Messua's husband flinch and whirling overhead; struck left and righ-

Bagheera to a full stop, flung back on his haunches, that quivered under him, his eyes just on the level of Mowgli's. Once more Mowgli stared as he had stared at the rebellious cubs, full into the beryl-green eyes, till the red glare behind their green went out like the light of a lighthouse shut off twenty miles across the sea; till the eyes dropped and the big head with them—dropped, lower and lower, and the red rasp of a tongue grated on Mowgli's instep.

"Brother—brother—brother!" the boy whispered, stroking steadily and lightly from the neck along the heaving back. "Be still, be still. It is the fault of the night, and no fault of thine."

"It was the smells of the night," said Bagheera penitently. "This air cries aloud to me. But how dost *thou* know?"

Of course the air round an Indian village is full of all kinds of smells; and to any creature who does nearly all his thinking through his nose, smells are as maddening as music and drugs are to human beings. Mowgli gentled the panther for a few minutes longer, and he lay down like a cat before a fire, his paws tucked under his breast, and his eyes half shut.

"Thou art of the jungle and not of the jungle," he said at last. "And I am only a black panther. But I love thee, Little Brother."

"They are very long at that council under the tree," Mowgli said, without noticing the last sentence. "Buldeo must have told many tales. They should come soon to drag the woman and her man out of the trap and put them into the Red Flower. They will find that trap sprung. Ho! ho!"

"Nay, listen," said Bagheera. "The fever is out of my blood now. Let them find *me* there! Few would leave their houses after meeting me. It is not the first time I have been in a cage, and I do not think they will tie *me* with cords."

"Be wise, then," said Mowgli laughing; for he was beginning to feel as reckless as the panther, who had glided into the hut.

"Pah!" he heard Bagheera say. "This place is heavy with man, but here is just such a bed as they gave me to lie upon in the king's cages at Oodeypore. Now I am lying down." Mowgli heard the strings of the cot crack under the great brute's weight. "By the Broken Lock that freed me, they will think they have caught big game! Come and sit beside me, Little Brother; we will give them good hunting together!"

stomach. The man pack shall not know what share I have in the sport. Make thy own hunt. I do not wish to see them."

"Be it so," said Bagheera. "Ah, now they come."

The conference under the peepul-tree had been growing noisier and noisier, at the far end of the village. It broke in wild yells and a rush up the street of men and women waving clubs and bamboos and sickles and knives. Buldeo and the Brahmin were at the head of it, but the mob was close at their heels, and they cried, "The witch and the wizard! Let us see if hot coins will make them confess! Burn the hut over their heads! We will teach them to shelter wolf devils! Nay, beat them first. Torches! More torches! Buldeo, heat the gun barrel."

There was some little difficulty with the catch of the door. It had been very firmly fastened, but the crowd tore it away bodily, and the light of the torches streamed into the room, where, lying at full length on the bed, his paws crossed and lightly hung down over one end, black as the pit and terrible as a demon, was Bagheera. There was one half minute of desperate silence, as the front ranks of the crowd clawed and tore their way back from that threshold, and in that minute Bagheera raised his head and yawned—elaborately, carefully, and ostentatiously—as he would yawn when he wished to insult an equal. The fringed lips drew back and up; the red tongue curled; the lower jaw dropped and dropped till you could see half way down the hot gullet; and the gigantic dog-teeth stood clear to the pit of the gums till they rang together, upper and under, with the snick of steel-faced wards shooting home round the edges of a safe. Next minute the street was empty; Bagheera had leaped back through the window and stood at Mowgli's side, while a yelling, screaming torrent scrambled and tumbled over one another in their panic haste to get to their own huts.

"They will not stir till the day comes," said Bagheera quietly. "And now?"

The silence of the afternoon sleep seemed to have overtaken the village, but, as they listened, they could hear the sound of heavy grain-boxes being dragged over earthen floors and set down against doors. Bagheera was quite right; the village would not stir till daylight. Mowgli sat still and thought, and his face grew darker and darker.

"What have I done?" said Bagheera, at

"Nothing but great good. Watch them now till the day. I must go sleep." And Mowgli ran off into the jungle, and dropped like a dead man across a rock, and slept and slept the day round and the night back again.

When he waked, Bagheera was at his side, and there was a newly-killed buck at his feet. Bagheera watched curiously while Mowgli went to work with his skinning knife, ate and drank, and turned over with his chin in his hands.

"The man and the woman came safe within eye-shot of Kanhiwara," Bagheera said. "Thy mother sent the word back by Chil the kite. They found a horse before midnight of the night. They were freed and went very quickly. Is not that well?"

"That is well," said Mowgli. "And thy man pack in the village did not stir till the sun was high this morning. Then they ate their food, and ran back quickly to their houses."

"Did they by chance see thee?"

"It may have been. I was rolling in the dust before the gate at dawn, and I may have sung also a little song to myself. Now, Little Brother, there is nothing more to do. Come hunting with me and Baloo. He has new hives, that he wishes to show, and we all desire thee back again as of old. Take off that look which makes even me afraid. The man and woman will not be put into the Red Flower, and all goes well in the jungle. Is it not true? Let us forget the man pack."

"They shall be forgotten in a little while. Where does Hathi feed to-night?"

"Where he chooses. Who can answer for the silent one? But why? What is there Hathi can do which we cannot?"

"Bid him and his three sons come here to me."

"But, indeed, and truly, Little Brother, it is not—it is not seemly to say 'come' and 'go' to Hathi. Remember he is the master of the jungle; and before the man pack changed the look on thy face, he taught thee the master-words of the jungle."

"That is all one. I have a master-word for him now. Bid him come to Mowgli the Frog, and if he does not hear at first, bid him come because of the sack of the fields of Bhurtpore."

"The sack of the fields of Bhurtpore," Bagheera repeated two or three times to make sure. "I go. Hathi can but be angry at the worst, and I would give a moon's hunting to hear the master-word that compels the silent one."

He went away, leaving Mowgli stabbing furiously with his skinning-knife into the earth. Mowgli had never seen human blood in his life before till he had seen and—what meant much more to him—smelt Messua's blood on the thongs that bound her. And Messua had been kind to him, and, as far as he knew anything about love, he loved Messua as completely as he hated the rest of mankind. But deeply as he loathed them, their talk, their cruelty, and their cowardice, not for anything the jungle had to offer could he bring himself to take a human life and have that terrible scent back again in his nostrils. His plan was simpler, but much more thorough; and he laughed to himself when he thought that it was one of old Buldeo's tales, told under the peepul-tree in the evening, that had put the idea into his head.

"It was a master-word," Bagheera whispered in his ear. "They were feeding by the river, and they obeyed as though they were bullocks. Look, there they come now!"

Hathi and his three sons had arrived in their usual way without a sound. The mud of the river was still fresh on their flanks, and Hathi was thoughtfully chewing the green stem of a young banana-tree that he had gouged up with his tusks. But every line in his vast body showed to Bagheera, who could see things when he came across them, that it was not the master of the jungle speaking to a man cub, but one who was afraid coming before one who was not. His three sons rolled side by side behind their father.

Mowgli hardly lifted his head as Hathi gave him "Good hunting." He kept him swinging and rocking and shifting from one foot to another for a long time before he spoke, and when he opened his mouth it was to Bagheera and not to the elephants.

"I will tell a tale that was told to me by the hunter ye hunted to-day," said Mowgli. "It concerns an elephant, old and wise, who fell into a trap, and the sharpened stake in the pit scarred him from a little above his heel to the crest of his shoulder, leaving a white mark." Mowgli threw out his hand, and as Hathi wheeled, the moonlight showed a long white scar on his side as though he had been struck with a red-hot whip. "Men came to take him from the trap," Mowgli continued, "but he broke his ropes, for he was strong, and he went away till his wound was healed. And I remember now that he had three sons. These things happened many, many rains ago, and very far away — among the fields of Bhurtpore. What came to those fields at the next reaping, Hathi?"

"They were reaped by me and by my three sons," said Hathi.

"And to the ploughing that follows the reaping?" said Mowgli.

"There was no ploughing," said Hathi.

"And to the men that live by the green crops on the ground?" said Mowgli.

"They went away."

"And to the huts in which the men slept?" said Mowgli.

"We tore the roofs to pieces, and the jungle swallowed up the walls," said Hathi.

"And what more beside?" said Mowgli.

"As much good ground as I can walk over in two nights from the east to the west, and from the north to the south as much as I can walk over in three nights, the jungle took. We let in the jungle upon five villages, and in those villages and in their lands, the grazing-ground and the soft crop grounds, there is not one man to-day who gets his food from the ground. That was the sack of the fields of Bhurtpore, which I and my three sons did; and now I ask, man cub, how the news of it came to thee?" said Hathi.

"A man told me. And now I see even Hathi can speak truth. It was well done, Hathi with the white mark; but a second time it can be done better, for the reason that there is a man to direct. Thou knowest the village of the man pack that cast me out? They are idle, senseless, and cruel; they play with their mouths, and they do not kill the weaker for food but for sport. When they are full-fed they would throw their own breed into the Red Flower. It is not well that they should live here any more. I am tired of them."

"Kill, then," said the youngest of Hathi's three sons, picking up a tuft of grass, dusting it against his forelegs, and throwing it away, while his little red eyes glanced furtively from side to side.

"What good are white bones to me?" Mowgli answered angrily. "Am I cub of a wolf to play in the sun with a raw head? I have killed Shere Khan, and his hide rots on the Council Rock; but—but I do not know where Shere Khan is gone, and my stomach is still empty. Now I will take that which I can see and touch. Let in the jungle upon that village, Hathi."

Bagheera shivered and cowered down. He could understand, if the worst came to the worst, a quick rush down the village street, and a right and left blow into a crowd, or systematic killing of men as they ploughed in the twilight; but this scheme for deliberately blotting out an entire village from the eyes of man and beast frightened him. Now he saw why Mowgli had sent for Hathi. No one but the long-lived elephant could plan and carry through such a war.

"Let them run as the men ran from the fields of Bhurtpore, till we have the rainwater for the only plough, and the noise of the rain on the thick leaves for the pattering of the spindles; till Bagheera and I lair in the house of the Brahmin, and the buck drink at the tank behind the temple. Let in the jungle, Hathi!"

"But I—but we have no quarrel with them, and it needs the red rage of great pain ere we tear down the places where men sleep," said Hathi doubtfully.

"Are ye the only eaters of grass in the jungle? Drive in your peoples. Let the deer and the pig and the nilghai look to it. Ye need never show a hand's-breadth of hide till the fields are naked. Let in the jungle, Hathi!"

"There will be no killing? My tusks were red at the sack of the fields of Bhurtpore, and I would not wake that smell again."

"Nor I. I do not wish their bones to lie on the clean earth. Let them go and find a new place. They cannot stay here. I have seen and smelt the blood of the woman that gave me food—the woman whom they would have killed but for me. Only the smell of the new grass on their doorsteps can take away that smell. It burns in my mouth. Let in the jungle, Hathi!"

"Ah!" said Hathi. "So did the scar of the stake burn on my hide till we saw the villages die under in the spring growth. Now I see. We will let in the jungle."

Mowgli had barely time to catch his breath—he was shaking all over with rage and hate—before the place where the elephants had stood was empty, and Bagheera was looking at him with terror.

"By the Broken Lock that freed me," said the black panther at last, "art thou the naked thing I spoke for in the pack! Master of the jungle, when my strength goes, speak for me—speak for Baloo—speak for us all. We are cubs before thee. Snapped twigs under foot. Fawns that have lost their doe."

The idea of Bagheera being a stray fawn upset Mowgli altogether, and he laughed and caught his breath, and sobbed and laughed again, till he had to jump into a pool to make himself stop. Then he swam round and round, ducking in and out of

WHERE HATHI LEADS THERE IS NO ROAD TO FOLLOW.

the bars of the moonlight like the frog his namesake.

By this time Hathi and his three sons had turned, each to one point of the compass, and were striding silently down the valleys a mile away. They went on and on for two days' march, that is to say, a good sixty miles, through the jungle, and every step they took and every wave of their trunks was known and noted and talked over by Mang and Chil and the monkeys and all the birds of the forest. Then they began to feed, and fed quietly for a week or so. Hathi and his sons are like Kaa the rock python. They never hurry till they have to.

At the end of that time, and no one knew who had started it, a rumor went through the jungle that there was better food and water to be found in such and such a valley. The pig—who, of course, will go to the ends of the earth for a full meal—moved first by companies, scuffling over the rocks; and the deer followed, with the little wild foxes that live on the dead and dying of the herds; and the heavy-shouldered nilghai moved parallel with the deer, and the wild buffaloes of the swamps came after the nilghai. The least little thing would have turned the scattered, straggling droves that grazed and sauntered, and drank and grazed again; but whenever there was an alarm some one would rise up and soothe them. At one time it would be Sahi the porcupine, full of news of good feed just a little farther on; at another, Mang would cry cheerily, and flap down a glade to show it was all empty; or Ikki, with his mouth full of roots, would shamble alongside a wavering line, and half frighten, half romp it clumsily back to the proper road. Very many creatures broke back, or ran away, or lost interest, but very many were left to go forward. At the end of another ten days or so the situation was this: The deer and the pig and the nilghai were milling round and round in a circle of eight or ten miles radius, while the eaters of flesh skirmished round its edge. And the centre of that circle was the village, and round the village the crops were ripening, and in the crops sat men on what they call machans—platforms like pigeon perches, made of sticks, at the top of four poles—to scare away birds and other stealers. Then the deer were coaxed no more. The eaters of flesh were close on them, and forced them forward and onward.

It was a dark night when Hathi and his three sons slipped down from the jungle and broke off the poles of the machans with their trunks, and they fell as a snapped stalk of hemlock in bloom falls, and the men that tumbled from them heard the deep breathing of the elephants in their ears. Then the vanguard of the bewildered armies of the deer broke down and flooded into the village grazing grounds and the ploughed fields, and the sharp-hoofed, rooting wild pig came with them, and what the deer left, the pig spoiled; and from time to time an alarm of wolves would shake the herds, and they would rush to and fro desperately, treading down the young barley, and cutting flat the banks of the irrigating channels. Before the dawn broke, the pressure on the outside of the circle gave way at one point. The eaters of flesh had fallen back, and left an open path to the south, and drove upon drove of buck fled along it. The others, who were bolder, lay up in the wild sal thickets to finish their meal next night.

But the work was practically done. When the villagers looked in the morning, they saw their crops were lost. And that meant death, if they did not get away; for they lived, year in and year out, as near to starvation as the jungle was near to them. When the buffaloes were sent to graze, the hungry brutes found that the deer had cleared the grazing-ground, and so wandered into the jungle, and drifted off with their wild mates; and when twilight fell, the three or four ponies that belonged to the village lay in their stables with their heads beaten in. Only Bagheera could have given those strokes, and only Bagheera would have thought of insolently dragging the last carcasses to the open street.

The villagers had no heart to light fires in the fields that night, so Hathi and his three sons went gleaning among the pump-kins and what was left of the maize; and where Hathi gleans there is no need to follow. The men decided to live on their stored seed corn until the rains had fallen, and then to take work as servants till they could catch up with the lost year; and as the grain-dealer was thinking of his well-filled crates of corn, and the prices he would levy at the sale of it, Hathi's sharp tusks were picking out the corner of his mud house, and smashing open the big wicker-chest heaped with cowdung, where the precious stuff lay.

When that last loss was discovered, it was the Brahmin's turn to speak. He had prayed to his own gods without answer. It might be, he said, that unconsciously the village had offended some one of the gods of the jungle, for beyond doubt the jungle was against them. So they sent for the head man of the nearest tribe of wandering Gonds—little, wise, and very black hunters living in the deep jungle, whose fathers came of the oldest race in India—the aboriginal owners of the land. They made the Gond welcome with what they had, and he stood on one leg, his bow in his hand, and two or three poisoned arrows stuck through his top-knot, looking half afraid and half contemptuously at the anxious villagers and their ruined fields. They wished to know whether his gods—the old gods—were angry with them, and what sacrifices should be offered. The Gond said nothing, but picked up a trail of the vine that bears the bitter wild gourd, and laced it to and fro across the temple door in the face of the staring red Hindu image. Then he pushed with his hand in the open air along the road to Kanhiwara and went back to his jungle, and watched the jungle people drifting through it.

There was no need to ask his meaning. The wild gourd would grow where they had worshipped their god, and the sooner they saved themselves the better.

But it is hard to tear a village from its moorings. They stayed on as long as any of their summer food was left to them, and they tried to gather nuts in the jungle; but shadows with glaring eyes watched them and rolled before them even at noon, and when they ran back, afraid, to their walls, on the tree trunks they had passed not five minutes before the bark would be stripped and chiselled with the stroke of some great-taloned paw. The more they kept to their village, the bolder grew the wild things that gambolled and bellowed on the grazing-grounds by the Waingunga. They had no time to patch and plaster the rear walls of the empty byres tacking on to the jungle, so the pig trampled them down, and the vines hurried after and threw their elbows over the new-won ground, and the coarse grass bristled behind the vines like the lances of a goblin army following a retreat. The single men had left earlier, and carried the news far and near that the village was doomed. Who could fight, they said, against the jungle, or the gods of the jungle, when the very cobra had left his hole in the platform under the peepul? So their little commerce with the outside world shrunk as the trodden paths across the open grew fewer and fainter; and the nightly trumpetings of Hathi and his three sons ceased to trouble them, for they had no more to lose. The crop on the ground and the seed in the ground had been taken. The outlying fields were already losing their shape, and it was time to throw themselves on the charity of the English at Kanhiwara.

Native fashion, they delayed their departure from one day to another, till the first rains caught them, and the unmended roofs let in a flood, and the grazing-ground stood ankle deep. And all nature came on with a rush after the heat of the summer. Then they waded out, men, women, and children, through the blinding hot rain of the morning, but turned naturally for one look at their homes.

They heard, as the last burdened family filed through the gate, a crash of falling beams and thatch behind the walls. Then they saw a shiny, snaky, black trunk lifted for an instant, scattering sodden thatch to and fro. It disappeared, and there was another crash, followed by a squeal. Hathi had been plucking off the roofs of the huts

as you pluck water-lilies, and a rebounding beam had hit him. It only needed this to unchain his full strength; for of all things in the jungle the wild elephant enraged is the most wantonly destructive. He kicked backwards at a mud wall that crumbled at the stroke, and, as it crumbled, melted to yellow mud under the torrent of rain. Then he wheeled and squealed and tore through the narrow streets, leaning against the huts right and left, shivering the crazy doors and crumpling up the eaves, while his three sons raged behind, as they had raged at the sack of the fields at Bhurtpore.

"The jungle will swallow these shells," said a quiet voice in the wreckage. "It is the outer wall that must lie down," and Mowgli, with the rain sluicing over his bare shoulders and arms, leaped back from a wall that was settling like a tired buffalo.

"All in good time," panted Hathi. "Oh, but my tusks were red at Bhurtpore! To the outer wall, children! With the head! Together! Again! With the tusk stab and weaken! Now!"

The four were in line side by side, and the outer wall bulged, split, and fell, and the villagers, dumb with horror, saw the savage, clay-streaked heads of the wreckers in the ragged gap. Then they fled, homeless and foodless, down the valley, as their village, smashed and overturned, shredded and tossed and trampled, melted behind them. A month later the place was a dimpled mound covered with soft green young stuff; and by the end of the rains there was the roaring jungle, in full blast, on the spot that had been under plough not six months before.

CONCERNING "SHIPS THAT PASS IN THE NIGHT."

BY BEATRICE HARRADEN,

Author of "Ships that Pass in the Night," "Things Will Take a Turn," etc.

IT has been suggested to me that I should give some short account of the writing of that little book, "Ships that Pass in the Night," which seems to have won for itself a success quite unexpected either by the publishers or myself. It was really written for the few who might perhaps care for that kind of story—a story without a plot, without a motive, without, indeed, any sort of *raison d'être*; without any striking situation or subtle development of circumstance. But the many decided that it was a story for them, too. And so in England the book leapt from one edition into another; and in America, having unfortunately been unprotected, from one piracy into another, until it has spread through the States, and is to be found in places remote and unfrequented.

fore regards itself, with justice, as self-made. It was first of all submitted to a well-known firm of publishers, who decided against it. They said that it could not possibly sell; that it was morbid and pessimistic from beginning to end; that the attempts at sentiment and pathos rang false; that there was nothing original in it. But for all that, if it had been in three volumes, they would have published it, as they admired the style and appreciated the workmanship—or words somewhat to that effect.

At that time I was possessed with the fixed idea that these gentlemen were the only publishers in the world; and that failing to meet with their approval, all chances of success were everlastingly cut off from me. So when a friend proposed

ings, and she passed it on to two or three of the farmers who came in the evenings to smoke their long clay pipes and drink the famous Green Dragon ale. They took their pipes from their mouths, gazed at me absently, and said:

"Well, to be sure, now! Who'd have thought the like of her?"

And then they returned to the topics which were more congenial to their tastes, such as turnips and potatoes and the forthcoming horse fair; and so frivolous a subject as literature was immediately dismissed from their consideration.

WHERE THE BOOK GOT ITS TITLE.

About five months later the book was published, and was reviewed in the papers unusually quickly; and I was beset with letters of inquiry concerning the origin of the words "Ships that Pass in the Night."

I myself did not know where to find them, although I had searched through many editions of Longfellow. They had been given to me many years ago, and I suppose I had borne them unconsciously in my mind all that time; and when I came to one of the last chapters of the first part of the book, where the melting of the snow had begun, and the guests of Petershof were speeding each on his own way, each in utter disregard of any one else, then those words swept across my remembrance, and I called the chapter "Ships that Speak Each Other in Passing."

When the book was finished, I could find no title for it. I thought of this, and thought of that, and then in despair I took my pen and wrote on the outside sheet, "Ships that Pass in the Night." In sending the story to the publishers, I told them that I could suggest no other title, but that of course these words would not do, only that they would serve for the present, just for the sake of calling the book something. The publishers saw no objection to the quotation, and therefore the title remained. It would be impossible to say how many letters I have received and answered about those words; and as time went on, and the book became more generally known in reading circles, the first question that was put to me personally was: "Where——" I instinctively felt what would be likely to follow, and began to wish that my ships would sink and be heard of no more. I believe that letters of inquiry still continue to be sent to me in England, but in the land of Longfellow no one needs to ask such a question—or is it, rather, that in America all the editions of Longfellow are complete?

HOW THE BOOK WAS WRITTEN.

I gathered much of the material out of which the book was built, at Petershof, a mountain health resort, probably identified by many people. I was there myself for six or seven months, and during that time was too ill to have any thoughts of writing a book or to take mental notes of the sufferers around me. It was more than a year after leaving Petershof, when I was supposed to have gained a certain amount of strength, that I was strongly urged by those who loved me to take up my writing once more, and try whether the old pleasure in the old occupation would not return.

And here perhaps it would not be out of place to say that, before falling ill, I had attained to a certain amount of quiet success, having, of course, passed through the usual round of disappointments, all of them well merited, and useful as steppingstones in the apprenticeship which every workman must have. I wrote many unsigned and some signed stories for children, and in contriving these I learnt something about the secret of concentration; and I wrote short tales for two or three of the magazines, and, finally, had the advantage of appearing in "Blackwood's Magazine." First in one direction and then another, opportunities presented themselves, but I confined myself almost entirely to the short story, for I felt, and had been told, too, that this was the best way of preparing for a longer and more sustained attempt; and I had no wish to rush headlong into a novel, and then have cause to regret my hastiness. But after waiting some time I did begin a novel, and had written about twelve chapters of it, when I was obliged to give up work, and the twelve chapters were laid on one side and afterwards burnt, a circumstance which has ever since caused me unmixed satisfaction. But to return to the book which was not burnt.

The suggestion that I should go back to my old occupation weighed heavily on me, for I was quite out of practice and out of touch; and it seemed impossible to me that I should ever manage to set down six consecutive words. I felt entirely bereft of ideas and inclination and enthusiasm; and moreover, my hand, which for some time had been entirely useless, was still a very troublesome member, often fickle and uncontrollable. But this did not fret me so much as the bereftness; it was that which made me feel that it was folly to waste the time and energy on attempts which were foregone failures. I should never have gone on with my task but for the tender solicitude of the friends to whom the little book was dedicated. It was written chiefly in their home, and I count it my greatest pleasure in remembering how deep an interest they took in every sentence, and how gratified they were when I seemed to be less dissatisfied than usual with my morning's efforts.

THE STORY CAME MAINLY AS THE PEN MOVED.

When I began my work again, I had no idea of inventing a story about Petershof; but as I bent lazily over the blank sheet of paper, memories of the Kurhaus came crowding over me, and, much to my own astonishment, the first chapter contrived itself. But that did not help me greatly, for I could not think what to make out of the characters which I had thus casually introduced on the scene; but I went on in a dull kind of way, not knowing from one sentence to another what I was going to say next. And, indeed, it was not until I arrived at the thirteenth chapter that I felt I was beginning to take hold of my people and to form some vague idea of what might possibly be done with them. But for all that, it was a very vague idea; and, indeed, the dimness of purpose pursued me to the last word of the book. The great drawback was that I could not use my hand for more than a quarter of an hour or so at a time; and in consequence of this hinderance, my work seemed to me hopelessly disconnected, done in such snatches, and without the advantage of continuous application. But, with the exception of a word here and there, I made no alterations, and the pages stand just as I originally wrote them. The second chapter in the first part, containing a few details about my heroine's life previous to her departure for Petershof, was written last of all, and gave me some trouble. I knew, of course, that I should have to account for Bernardine's existence, and refer, however briefly, to her surroundings; but I put this off to the end, shirking the difficulty until I was obliged to turn and face it. In reading novels I have always felt irritated when the author gives a long and detailed account of the back history of his characters, and I determined to try and avoid a tediousness from which I myself had so often suffered, just at a point, too, where my interest had been aroused in the present, and where the past seemed an unwelcome intrusion. So I made my second chapter as short as possible, and felt more than thankful that Bernardine had only one relation. In real life, as is well known, too many relatives are apt to be a nuisance, and difficult of management, but I have always thought that in a book they must be even worse. Crowded together in one little volume, what could anyone do with them, and what could they do with themselves in such close quarters?

With regard to the allegory of the Traveller and the Temple of Knowledge, I wrote it for the purpose of avoiding a long and delicate analysis of Bernardine's condition of mind when she discovered that she had taken a long journey in vain. It seemed to me to present the situation, and without need of any comment.

There was a chapter called "Self-cheatings: A Chapter which has Crept in Unawares"; and it followed "The One Great Sacrifice." As far as I recollect, it was a reverie of the Disagreeable Man, and it might, perhaps, have been interesting to some of the many friends who have taken so kindly to him; but for some reason or other I decided not to use it, and I have since lost it.

THE MUCH-DISCUSSED ENDING.

The ending of the story has been much criticised, and Bernardine's unexpected death favorably and unfavorably commented upon. I felt at the time that she had to die, and that it was in keeping with the irony of life that she, the stronger of the two, should be suddenly swept away. I felt, too, that she would never have got back to any real touch with life, and I was not sorry that she should be at rest. I do not at all claim that my own ending was the best or the most artistic; but of the many suggestions which have been made on the subject, I have not found one which would have helped me on satisfactorily. I can only say about my own ending, that it came so, whether for better or for worse.

An incident in connection with the description of Bernardine's last moments is perhaps worth mentioning. I had made her send one more message to the Disagreeable Man; and when the proofs of the story were forwarded to me at Mentone, where I was passing the winter, a friend helped me to correct them, and pounced like a tigress upon those extra words (on which I set great store), and tried to persuade me that they were bathos itself, and that they would spoil the chances of the book, as the critics would be sure to make fun of them—as, indeed, so she said, they ought to do. I was extremely touchy on the point, and fought obstinately for those extra words; but finally I was overcome by her arguments, and gave in. Nevertheless, I still regret that sentence, and so would the critics, especially the young and unmerciful ones, if they only knew what it contained.

As I had no definite idea of what I intended to do with my characters, notes would not have been of any use to me; but as the book grew, and my confidence with it, I remember putting down on paper the headings of some of the conversations which afterwards took place between Bernardine and Robert Allitsen. For instance, I put down: "The loneliness of most of us," "Death and our bereftness." "Our unreasonable desire for uninterrupted happiness," and so on; and then, as the opportunity presented itself, I wove these detached thoughts into the story, just where they happened to fit in best; or, rather, I should say, they arranged themselves according to their fancy.

BEATRICE HARRADEN. FROM A PHOTOGRAPH BY MUDALY
ANJUTIN, HARROGATE, ENG.

LETTERS TO THE AUTHOR FROM ALL DIRECTIONS AND OF EVERY DESCRIPTION.

I have been repeatedly asked for my favorite passages in the book, and I always turn to the words: "Saints they may not be, but, for want of a better name, saints they are to us, gracious and lovely presences." Or, if not in a serious mood, I turn to the scene between Mrs. Reffold and Bernardine, and put my finger on the words: "Where does one get the best tea?"

The chapter "Concerning the Caretakers" has, I believe, caused a great deal of amusement and irritation and anger amongst the care-takers of various health-resorts, and I have been thought by some people to be somewhat malicious in my judgment of this interesting portion of the community. I never intended to be malicious, but was merely anxious to paint a truthful picture, and I am quite sure that I have not used too strong colors. I have been comforted on this point by receiving letters of reassurance from French and German, as well as English, guests, who said that my observations coincided with their own experiences.

And this leads me to speak of the many curious letters which have reached me from all sorts and conditions of men and women—strange human documents which will always remain in my memory. I have heard from grave scholars and professors, and hurried business men who seldom pause to read a book; from people of rare culture and distinction, and people without any culture or distinction; from gay women and from tired workers; from the happy and the miserable; from Baptist ministers, and Catholics, and French *pasteurs*, and Church of England clergymen. I am always being surprised by the widely different types of readers who take up their pen and write to me so warmly about the book and so frankly about themselves. They find something in it, I suppose, which appeals to them, or which seems to apply to their own particular cases; and then they hasten to tell me that the book was written for them, and that it has sunk into their hearts. As for the gracious and gratifying words spoken and written to me by other authors, that alone has been to me a most delightful experience.

Of course I have had other kinds of letters, too—complaints about Bernardine's death; reproaches about many other things; regrets over Bernardine's way of looking at life and death, and over the general tone of pessimism and hopelessness pervading the story; whilst others have written at the same time, rejoicing over the optimism and the strong note of hope. One curious document was sent me, containing nothing but texts from the Bible, chosen to contradict some of the statements in the book; no letter came with it, and it was signed "From a Ship Passing in the Night." One letter from a lover of dogs interested me. He asked what had become of the Disagreeable Man's dog, which was never mentioned after Bernardine appeared on the scene. It is true that I had completely forgotten him. The funniest note of all came a few days ago. It was from a lady, saying that I had done a great deal for her by my book, and now she wanted to benefit me. She gave me the name of an electric battery, peculiarly helpful in cases of writer's cramp, and she asked me to order it through her, as it was the means of bringing her in a small percentage.

TRANSLATIONS.

I have been much astonished at the number of applications from both French and German translators, asking for permission to translate the book, and all of them, apparently, quite confident of its success in France and Germany. I have not yet heard whether the French version has been completed, but I understand that the German edition, by Madame Niemeyer, will be issued by Engelhorn.

These letters from foreign readers have greatly pleased me, for I feel it to be very satisfactory to have broken through the barriers of nationality; and even now, as I write, I have before me a note just received from an Italian medical student, telling me that he has translated my book into Italian, " con intelletto d'amore," with loving heart and mind, and asking for permission to publish it, and keeping all the time a great fear in his heart, so he says, lest I should have given to some one else "the right to frame those thoughts with Italian words." I am half tempted to quote his naïve and graceful letter, but it was written for me and not for the public, and so I reluctantly reserve it for myself. The Danish translation, "Skibe i Natten," done by Madame Ingeborg Kadnkiar of Copenhagen, herself a writer of some standing, appeared several months ago, and has met with a favorable reception.

"Ships" has also been put into the Braille type for the blind. I learn from many sides that sermons have been preached for and against this little volume, and more than once the text for the discourse has been taken from the allegory of "The Traveller and the Temple of Knowledge."

And so I might go on, telling of curious experiences and gracious incidents which have befallen me, and running the risk, I fear, of tiring my readers. But I cannot resist the temptation of saying that my knowledge of geography, which was always my weakest point, has considerably increased since the publication of "Ships." Obscure places in dear old England have revealed themselves to me, and kindly greetings have been sent me from mysterious corners of several countries. From lonely hill stations in India, news comes to me that the book has been read and cared for. And out here in California I have myself learned how far into the mountains it has penetrated; for the other day, on an expedition into the back country, amongst cattle ranches, and near a desolate Indian reservation, I was astonished to find a copy of it at the inn where I stayed. To my everlasting shame, very little I knew about the geography of the United States until I came here and received letters from so many places both in the East and West. Even if I forget most of what I have learnt, I shall certainly always remember that Keokuk is in Iowa. The inhabitants of that town write frequently, begging me to settle some point of dispute about the book. The last question asked was whether, in my opinion, Bernardine, if she had lived, would ever have married the Disagreeable Man. My answer was, that, so far as my understanding of her went, she would not have married him. And last week I saw it stated in the "London Era" that "Ships that Pass in the Night" had been dramatized and performed in -Keokuk!

The following lines from Matthew Arnold seem to me to contain the same idea as Longfellow's words, though not so simply stated:

"Yes, in the sea of life enisled,
 With echoing straits between us thrown,
 Dotting the shoreless watery wild,
 We mortal millions live alone.
 The islands feel the enclasping flow,
 And then their endless bounds they know."

DR. CHARLES H. PARKHURST:

HIS RECENT WORK IN MUNICIPAL REFORM.

BY F. J. EDWARDS.

DR. PARKHURST, his purpose and his methods in carrying on the work of municipal reform, were the subject of a review printed in McClure's Magazine for April, 1894. At that time it was possible to do little more than set forth something of the personal qualities of Dr. Parkhurst, and suggest why he had undertaken a work of reform in a manner unusual for a clergyman, and, it seemed at first to many persons, in some respects not wholly worthy.

DR. PARKHURST THE MORAL RULER OF NEW YORK.

At the time of the publication of that sketch Dr. Parkhurst's work was still tentative. At least it was so deemed even by many who had learned to have respect for his courage and confidence in his purpose. The fruition of the work had not been then reached, nor is the work yet fully and finally done. Nevertheless, the personal triumph, if the achievement of Dr. Parkhurst may properly be so termed, has come. Dr. Parkhurst is to-day the acknowledged moral force that directs public sentiment in New York city. Turning to him, with exquisite grace and gesture, and in the presence of many distinguished men, the Honorable Joseph H. Choate, then fresh from his highest achievement, the reconstruction of the State Constitution of New York, said: "There is Parkhurst, the moral ruler of New York."

The characterization was accepted by all present as deserved. To-day Dr. Parkhurst is in truth the moral ruler of New York. Since the review of him and his work was published in McClure's—a review which needs not, in the light of later events, to be changed in a single word or suggestion—he has revealed himself as a moral force producing actual, concrete, tremendous results, such as it is safe to say have not been gained by the power of agitation and moral suasion since the day when Hamilton persuaded the State, against its own inclination, to become a member of the Federal Union.

DR. PARKHURST'S SKILL AS AN ORGANIZER.

Perhaps the most difficult of the more recent work Dr. Parkhurst had to do was to give proper direction to the public sentiment, and bring into effective union the various influences, which had been aroused by the revelations which he and his associates were able to make. From the first Dr. Parkhurst had said, "We are aiming not so much at vice as at a system which tolerates and supports vice. We are bringing our guns to bear upon the citadels of those by whose authority, influence, and command vice flourishes, honest government is destroyed, and the community is made a spot of shame."

Therefore, when public sentiment was sufficiently aroused—after testimony had been heaped on testimony and the awful skeleton had been exposed—there was need of executive qualities of the highest order, the wisdom which distinguishes statesmanship; a capacity for handling groups of men who, while having a common object, incline to seek it by diverse ways and thereby jeopardize it; and beyond that even, the skill and strategy of the politician, who depends somewhat upon expediency, and very greatly upon organization.

It was in the way he met these new demands on him that Dr. Parkhurst made the fullest revelation of his extraordinary intellectual power. His purpose was moral. He aimed to overthrow, and to overthrow permanently, a political system which had made the administration of the city's affairs a left-handed partnership with vice and crime—an administration for spoils. In the arguments, the consultations, and the other work which the achievement of this aim involved, he showed an intellectual capacity which now even the greatest of the politicians of New York cheerfully admit would have made him, had he chosen

DR. CHARLES H. PARKHURST.

DR. PARKHURST AT 15.

DR. PARKHURST AT 20.

politics or public life as his vocation, preeminent.

THE ELEMENTS THAT HAD TO BE HARMONIZED.

In the interest and horror excited by the revelations before the investigating committee of the State Senate, the public lost sight of the extraordinary political skill with which Dr. Parkhurst was then attempting to unite into one compact, coherent, sympathetic, and well-disciplined organization all of the elements which had been aroused against the Tammany administration in New York City. It was a task of supreme difficulty. It could not have been accomplished with less than Dr. Parkhurst's generalship. The elements opposing Tammany were many. There was first the Republican party. Then there were the independents—the persons associated with the Good Government clubs and kindred organizations. There was a great body of German-American citizens, nearly all of them of Democratic inclination. There was a new organization of the Democracy, cre-

DR. PARKHURST AT 35.

ated by ex-Secretary of the Treasury Fairchild and ex-Mayor Grace. There was an independent Democratic association; and two or three others. Every one of these organizations was opposed to Tammany and to Tammany methods. But the great danger was that, fighting against the enemy each organization in its own way, the attack would be futile, and the strength which united would be irresistible would be frittered away. In each of these organizations there were very able and very ambitious men. Some of them had had long training in political organization and management. It seemed even to the shrewdest of them that it might be impossible to bring about an understanding and combination. This was the work which Dr. Parkhurst undertook. The Republican leaders before taking any action consulted with him. The German reform association spent through its representatives hours with him. The Fairchild and Grace Democracy sent delegates to him. And so he found himself in the position of an arbiter, and he realized that his suggestions were taken almost as commands. He was the moral power of the moment. Nothing was behind him but public sentiment; he was supported wholly and only by the confidence of the worthy elements in the community. That was a supreme test of the qualities which make the ablest statesman, the most successful politician. An error in counsel, a mistake in judgment, a concession to personal vanity or pride, and the union which Dr. Parkhurst sought could never be accomplished.

DR. PARKHURST'S RELATIONS WITH MR. GOFF.

Probably Dr. Parkhurst's power was best illustrated when he interfered to prevent the nomination for mayor of a man in whom he had the highest confidence, and who had been his most able lieutenant. Mr. John W. Goff had been named as a satisfactory candidate for the mayoralty nomination by the Grace Democracy and by the Committee of Seventy, an independent association representing the business and professional activities of New York. The nomination was formally tendered to Mr. Goff. It was a dazzling honor for a man who six months ago was almost unknown. Moreover, the chances were that it would not prove an empty honor. Yet Mr. Goff, in a brief, simple, courteous note, declined it. And those who had tendered it did not then know, nor does the public know yet, that it was Dr. Parkhurst's judgment more than any other influence that caused Mr. Goff to decline. Dr. Parkhurst was

persuaded that it would be a mistake for Mr. Goff to accept, and for two reasons: first, because his acceptance might prevent a union of all the elements opposing Tammany; second, because Dr. Parkhurst believed that Mr. Goff could be of more service in the work which remains to be done, and which must be continued for many months, if he were chosen to another post, that of presiding criminal judge, an office long filled by an able lawyer, but one who has been in intimate association with Tammany Hall.

DR. PARKHURST'S TRIUMPH.

Dr. Parkhurst insisted from the beginning that union was absolutely essential, and he recognized that in order to procure union the various elements must be represented upon a single anti-Tammany ticket. It seemed to him that as the Republican organization contained by far the greater number of those who would deliver votes against Tammany, the candidate for mayor might properly be chosen from that party. But he also said that any one of a score or more of Democrats would be preferable to any one of a score or more of Republicans who had no other recommendation for the mayoralty than that they had been active politicians.

Several times there seemed to be danger that union could not be effected, and in these emergencies Dr. Parkhurst showed a diplomacy which amazed the politicians with whom he was brought in contact. He spurned the proposition that he himself become a candidate, regarding the acceptance of a nomination as sure to involve him in the charge of self-interest and ambition in his reform work. Moreover, he believed that his influence would be more effective if it were still exerted through purely moral agencies. The delicate, difficult task was achieved finally. Every element in the city opposed to Tammany was brought by Dr. Parkhurst's genius and influence into enthusiastic association, and it, a tribute could be swiftly secured which would represent a considerable fortune.

THE INVALUABLE AID RENDERED BY MR. GOFF.

In the moment of his triumph, Dr. Parkhurst regards with especial fondness and approval his able assistant John W. Goff. When the first review of Dr. Parkhurst's work appeared in McClure's Magazine, Mr. Goff was known to a comparatively limited circle. There he had gained a repute not only for moral honesty, but for intellectual honesty. He thought honestly as well as acted honestly. He had served briefly as an Assistant District Attorney, and had held no other public office. Although of Irish birth, he bore in personal appearance the marks of the Saxon race. Golden-haired (before time had touched his locks), blue-eyed, and fair-cheeked, he scarcely suggested the power of the reformer which was in him. But it was known that in his brief experience in public office he had been made well aware of the vicious system that prevailed, and that he could speak of it only with loathing and contempt. The men who maintained that system often solicited him to become their associate, and he refused opportunities that would have made him comfortable even at times when he had no great promise of securing much of the good things of life.

When Mr. Goff and Dr. Parkhurst first met, they approached each other not suspiciously, but still searchingly, curiously, each determined to read the other well. There were not many interviews, however, before each discovered in the other a man of his own quality, and after a little there came perfect trust and confidence. Dr. Parkhurst turned over to Mr. Goff a great mass of testimony which his agents had collected. After this testimony had been carefully sifted, Mr. Goff, profiting by his training as a prosecutor and examiner, as well as his natural abilities, laid down a line of procedure before the Lexow Committee in-

sioner he had driven him from office. Then there came witness after witness telling under oath most startling stories of police blackmailing and persecution. Shock followed shock, as police captains, sergeants, and even inspectors were involved, until at last the community was ready to believe anything; and it seemed useless to prolong the investigation, except possibly, for the purpose of bringing guilty officers to justice. As a result of these investigations, some ten police captains, as many sergeants, and a considerable number of wardmen, or detectives, were shown to be participants in the system of blackmail. Three of these captains have since been dismissed from the force, with sergeants and wardmen as well, and some of them and others are now under indictment, and are to be prosecuted.

Mr. Goff cannot much longer take formal part in these investigations. On the 1st of January he becomes presiding criminal judge, succeeding a man who fined him for contempt because he insisted upon his rights as counsel in protecting one of Dr. Parkhurst's agents. The investigation, however, will continue on the lines laid down by Mr. Goff and Dr. Parkhurst, and it is understood that we have really had but a beginning of these exposures. Dr. Parkhurst's work, however, and that of the successful party which he organized, will he hereafter mainly that of the constructive reformer, a more difficult and delicate task, even, than the destructive reform with which Dr. Parkhurst was compelled to begin this great labor. There is to be necessary careful, prudent legislation, and the maintenance of influences that will keep public spirit alert, watchful, impressive, and sufficient.

THOMAS NAST'S SHARE IN THE OVERTHROW OF THE TWEED RING IN 1872.

IT has occurred to many persons who are familiar with the influences which procured the overthrow of the corrupt ring of which Tweed was the chief, to compare the service rendered by the artist Thomas Nast in that work with what has been done by Dr. Parkhurst in the later revolution. Excepting the fact that both men were prominent in undertakings of a similar nature, there is, after all, little to furnish a comparison. Mr. Nast's service was important. He represented in the concrete, and by the weapon of satire, the public opinion which was then making against Tweed and the vulgar thieves by whom he was surrounded. He was able to catch the spirit of the public opposition, and so suggest it by his pencil as to show the public by cartoon what it was thinking about. His most famous cartoon represented Tweed as a money-bag. With a skill which has never been equalled in this country, Nast converted, by a few strokes of his pencil, the representation of a bag of gold into a caricature of Tweed's face, and this expressed week after week what everybody had in his mind, that Tweed had, by his political power and control of the city of New York, been able to make a great fortune for himself.

The cartoons were of immense importance in thus formulating or crystallizing public opinion. It has been said that Tweed himself looked upon them as one of the most important influences in causing his downfall.

Mr. Nast is of European birth, having been born in Bavaria fifty-four years ago; but he came early to this country, and is one of the most enthusiastic and loyal of Americans. His first work as a cartoonist or a sketch-maker for the illustrated weeklies was done before the civil war. He went to England, and sketched the famous prize-fight between Heenan and Sayers, and he also followed Garibaldi during the most important of his engagements. It was by means of his pencil that America became familiar with these important events. Coming back to the United States, he became associated with the Harpers, and sprang into general fame when he began to tell in satire the story of Tweed's corruption. He became still further known by his illustrated lectures, delivered all over the county. Lately Mr. Nast has made one or two ventures of his own in illustrated journalism. He was the first of the great American cartoonists, and pointed the way for Keppler and Gillam.

THOMAS NAST IN 1855. AE. 15.

1860, AT THE TIME OF THE GARIBALDIAN CAMPAIGN. AE. 20.

1868, AT THE TIME OF GRANT'S FIRST ELECTION AS PRESIDENT. AE. 28.

1865, AT THE CLOSE OF THE WAR. AE. 25.

THE GREEN FLAG.

By A. Conan Doyle,

Author of "Micah Clarke," "The Adventures of Sherlock Holmes," etc.

WHEN Jack Conolly, of the Irish Shot-gun Brigade, the Rory of the Hills Inner Circle, and the extreme left wing of the Land League, was incontinently shot by Sergeant Murdoch of the constabulary, in a little moonlight frolic near Kanturk, his twin brother Dennis joined the British army. The countryside had become too hot for him; and, as the seventy-five shillings were wanting which might have carried him to America, he took the only way handy of getting himself out of the way. Seldom has Her Majesty had a less promising recruit, for his hot Celtic blood seethed with hatred against Britain and all things British. The sergeant, however, smiling complacently over his six feet of brawn and his fortyfour inch chest, whisked him off with a dozen other of the boys to the depot at Fermoy, whence in a few weeks they were sent on, with the spade-work kinks taken out of their backs, to the first battalion of the Royal Mallows, at the top of the roster for foreign service.

The Royal Mallows, at about that date, were as strange a lot of men as ever were paid by a great empire to fight its battles. It was the darkest hour of the land struggle, when the one side came out with crowbar and battering-ram by day, and the other with mask and with shot-gun by night. Men driven from their homes and potato-patches found their way even into the service of the government, to which it seemed to them that they owed their troubles, and now and then they did wild things before they came. There were recruits in the Irish regiments who would forget to answer to their own names, so short had been their acquaintance with them. Of these, the Royal Mallows had their full share; and, while they still retained their fame as being one of the smartest corps in the army, no one knew better than their officers that they were dry-rotted with treason and with bitter hatred of the flag under which they served.

And the centre of all the disaffection was C Company, in which Dennis Conolly found himself enrolled. They were Celts, Catholics, and men of the tenant class to a man; and their whole experience of the British government had been an inexorable landlord, and a constabulary who seemed to them to be always on the side of the rent-collector. Dennis was not the only moonlighter in the ranks, nor was he alone in having an intolerable family bloodfeud to harden his heart. Savagery had begotten savagery in the veiled civil war. A landlord with an iron mortgage weighing down upon him had small bowels for his tenantry. He did but take what the law allowed; and yet, with men like Jim Holan, or Patrick McGuire, or Peter Flynn, who had seen the roofs torn from their cottages and their folk huddled among their pitiable furniture upon the roadside, it was ill to argue about abstract law. What matter that in that long and bitter struggle there was many another outrage on the part of the tenant, and many another grievance on the side of the landowner! A stricken man can only feel his own wound, and the rank and file of the C Company of the Royal Mallows were sore and savage to the soul. There were low whisperings in barrack-rooms and canteens, stealthy meetings in public-house parlors, bandying of pass-words from mouth to mouth, and many other signs which made their officers right glad when the order came which sent them to foreign and, better still, to active, service.

For Irish regiments have before now been disaffected, and have at a distance looked upon the foe as though he might, in truth, be the friend; but when they have been put face on to him, and when their officers have dashed to the front with a wave and halloo, those rebel hearts have softened and their gallant Celtic blood has boiled with the mad joy of the fight, until the slower Britons have marvelled that they ever could have doubted the loyalty of their Irish comrades. So it would be again, according to the officers, and so it would not be if Dennis Conolly and a few others could have their way.

It was a March morning upon the eastern fringe of the Nubian desert. The sun had not yet risen; but a tinge of pink flushed up as far as the cloudless zenith, and the long strip of sea lay like a rosy ribbon along the horizon. From the coast inland stretched dreary sand-plains, dotted over with thick clumps of mimosa scrub and mottled patches of thorny bush. No tree broke the monotony of that vast desert. The dull, dusty hue of the thickets and the yellow glare of the sand were the only colors, save at one point where, from a distance, it seemed that a landslip of snow-white stones had shot itself across a low foot-hill. But as the traveller approached, he saw, with a thrill, that these were no stones, but the bleaching bones of a slaughtered army. With its dull tints, its gnarled viperous bushes, its arid barren soil, and this death streak trailed across it, it was indeed a nightmare country.

Some eight or ten miles inland the rolling plain curved upwards with a steeper slope until it ran into a line of red basaltic rock which zigzagged from north to south, heaping itself up at one point into a fantastic knoll. On this summit there stood upon that March morning three Arab chieftains—the Sheik Kadra of the Hadendowas, Moussa Wad Aburhegel, who led the Berber dervishes, and Hamid Wad Hussein, who had come northward with his fighting men from the land of the Baggaras. They had all three just risen from their praying-carpets, and were peering out, with fierce, high-nosed faces thrust forward, at the stretch of country revealed by the spreading dawn.

The red rim of the sun was pushing itself now above the distant sea, and the whole coast-line stood out brilliantly yellow against the rich deep blue beyond. At one spot lay a huddle of white-walled houses, a mere splotch in the distance; while four tiny cock-boats, which lay beyond, marked the position of three of Her Majesty's ten-thousand-ton troopers and the admiral's flagship. But it was not upon the distant town, nor upon the great vessels, nor yet upon the sinister white litter which gleamed in the plain beneath them, that the Arab chieftains gazed. Two miles from where they stood, amid the sand-hills and the mimosa scrub, a great parallelogram had been marked by piled-up bushes. From the inside of this dozens of tiny blue smoke-reeks curled up into the still morning air; while there rose from it a confused deep murmur, the voices of men and the gruntings of camels blended into the same insect buzz.

"The unbelievers have cooked their morning food," said the Baggara chief, shading his eyes with his tawny, sinewy hand. "Truly their sleep has been but scanty; for Hamid and a hundred of his men have fired upon them since the rising of the moon."

"So it was with these others," answered the Sheik Kadra, pointing with his sheathed sword towards the old battle-field. "They also had a day of little water and a night of little rest, and the heart was gone out of them ere ever the sons of the Prophet had looked them in the eyes. This blade drank deep that day, and will again before the sun has travelled from the sea to the hill."

"And yet these are other men," remarked the Berber dervish. "Well I know that Allah has placed them in the clutch of our fingers, yet it may be that they with the big hats will stand firmer than the cursed men of Egypt."

"Pray Allah that it may be so," cried the fierce Baggara, with a flash of his black eyes. "It was not to chase women that I brought seven hundred men from the river to the coast. See, my brother, already they are forming their array."

A fanfare of bugle-calls burst from the distant camp. At the same time the bank of bushes at one side had been thrown or trampled down, and the little army within began to move slowly out on to the plain. Once clear of the camp, they halted, and the slant rays of the sun struck flashes from bayonet and from gun-barrel as the ranks closed up, until the big pith helmets joined into a single long white ribbon. Two streaks of scarlet glowed on either side of the square, but elsewhere the fringe of fighting men was of the dull yellow khaki tint which hardly shows against the desert sand. Inside their array was a dense mass of camels and mules bearing stores and ambulance needs. Outside, a twinkling clump of cavalry was drawn up on each flank, and in front a thin scattered line of mounted infantry was already slowly advancing over the bush-strewn plain, halting on every eminence, and peering warily round as men might who have to pick their steps among the bones of those who have preceded them.

The three chieftains still lingered upon the knoll, looking down with hungry eyes and compressed lips at the dark steel-tipped patch. "They are slower to start than the men of Egypt," the sheik of the Hadendowas growled in his beard.

"Slower also to go back, perchance, my brother," murmured the dervish. "And yet they are not many—three thousand at the most."

"And we ten thousand, with the Prophet's grip upon our spear-hafts and his words upon our banner. See to their chieftain, how he rides upon the right and looks up at us with the glass that sees from afar! It may be that he sees this also." The Arab shook his sword at the small clump of horsemen who had spurred out from the square.

"Lo! he beckons," cried the dervish; "and see those others at the corner, how they bend and heave. Ha! by the Prophet, I had thought it!"

As he spoke, a little woolly puff of smoke spurted up at the corner of the square, and a seven-pound shell burst with a hard metallic smack just over their heads. The splinters knocked chips from the red rocks around them.

"Bismillah!" cried the Hadendowa, "if the gun can carry thus far, then ours can answer to it. Ride to the left, Moussa, and tell Ben Ali to cut the skin from the Egyptians if they cannot hit yonder mark. And you, Hamid, to the right, and see that three thousand men lie close in the wady that we have chosen. Let the others beat the drum and show the banner of the Prophet; for, by the black stone, their spears will have drunk deep ere they look upon the stars again."

A long, straggling, boulder-strewn plateau lay on the summit of the red hills, sloping very precipitously to the plain, save at one point, where a winding gully curved downwards, its mouth choked with sand mounds and olive-hued scrub. Along the edge of this position lay the Arab host, a motley crew of shock-headed desert clansmen, fierce, predatory slave-dealers of the interior, and wild dervishes from the Upper Nile, all blent together by their common fearlessness and fanaticism. Two races were there, as wide as the poles apart, the thin-lipped, straight-haired Arab, and the thick-lipped curly negro; yet the faith of Islam had bound them closer than a blood tie. Squatting among the rocks, or lying thickly in the shadow, they peered out at the slow-moving square beneath them, while women with water-skins and bags of dhoora fluttered from group to group, calling out to each other those fighting texts from the Koran which in the hour of battle are maddening as wine to the true believer. A score of banners waved over the ragged valiant crew, and among them, upon desert horses and white Bishareen camels, were the emirs and sheiks who were to lead them against the infidels.

As the Sheik Kadra sprang into his saddle and drew his sword, there was a wild whoop and a clatter of waving spears, while the one-ended war-drums burst into a dull crash like a wave upon shingle. For a moment ten thousand men were up on the rocks, with brandished arms and leaping figures. The next they were under cover, again waiting sternly and silently for their chieftain's orders. The square was less than half a mile from the ridge now, and shell after shell from the seven-pound guns was pitching over it. A deep roar on the right, and then a second one, showed that the Egyptian Krupps were in action. Sheik Kadra's hawk eyes saw that

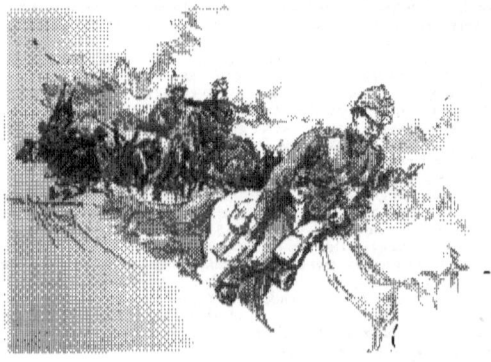

AN INSTANT LATER THEY WERE SPURRING IT FOR THEIR LIVES, CROUCHING OVER THE MANES OF THEIR HORSES.

the shells burst far beyond the mark, and he spurred his horse along to where a knot of mounted chiefs were gathered round the two guns, which were served by their captured crews.

"How is this, Ben Ali?" he cried. "It was not thus that the dogs fired when it was their own brothers in faith at whom they aimed!"

A chieftain reined his horse back, and thrust a blood-smeared sword into its sheath. Beside him, two Egyptian artillerymen with their throats cut were sobbing out their lives upon the ground.

"Who lays the gun this time?", asked the fierce chief, glaring at the frightened gunners. "Here, thou black-browed child of Shaitan, aim, and aim for thy life."

It may have been chance, or it may have been skill, but the third and fourth shells burst over the square. Sheik Kadra smiled grimly and galloped back to the left, where his spearmen were streaming down into the gully. As he joined them, a deep growling rose from the plain beneath, like the snarling of a sullen wild beast, and a little knot of tribesmen fell in a struggling heap, caught in the blast of lead from a Gardner. Their comrades pressed on over them and sprang down into the ravine. From all along the crest burst the hard sharp crackle of Remington fire.

The square had slowly advanced, rippling over the low sand-hills, and halting every few minutes to rearrange its formation. Now, having made sure that there was no force of the enemy in the scrub, it changed its direction, and began to take a line parallel to the Arab position. It was too steep to assail from the front, and if they moved far enough to the right the general hoped that he might turn it. On the top of those ruddy hills lay a baronetcy for him, and a few extra hundreds in his pension, and he meant having them both that day. The Remington fire was annoying, and so were those two Krupp guns; already there were more cacolets full than he cared to see. But on the whole he thought it better to hold his fire until he had more to aim at than a few hundreds of fuzzy heads peeping over a razor-back ridge. He was a bulky, red-faced man, a fine whist-player, and a soldier who knew his work. His men believed in him, and he had good reason to believe in them, for he had excellent stuff under him that day. Being an ardent champion of the short-service system, he took particular care to work with veteran first battalions, and his little force was the compressed essence of an army corps.

The left front of the square was formed by four companies of the Royal Wessex, and the right by four of the Royal Mallows. On either side the other halves of the same regiments marched in quarter column of companies. Behind them, on the right, was a battalion of guards, and on the left one of marines, while the rear was closed in by a rifle battalion. Two Royal Artillery seven-pound screw-guns kept pace with the square, and a dozen white-bloused sailors, under their blue-coated, tight-waisted officers, trailed their Gardner in front, turning every now and then to spit up at the draggled banners which waved over the cragged ridge. Hussars and lancers scouted in the scrub at each side, and within moved the clump of camels, with humorous eyes and supercilious lips, their comic faces a contrast to the blood-stained men who already lay huddled in the cacolets on either side. The square was now moving slowly on a line parallel with the rocks, stopping every few minutes to pick up wounded, and to allow the screw-guns and Gardner to make themselves felt. The men looked serious, for that spring on to the rocks of the Arab army had given them a vague glimpse of the number and ferocity of their foes; but their faces were set like stone, for they knew to a man that they must win or they must die, and die, too, in a particularly unlovely fashion. But most serious of all was the general, for he had seen that which brought a flush to his cheeks and a frown to his brow.

"I say, Stephen," said he to his galloper, "those Mallows seem a trifle jumpy. The right flank company bulged a bit when the niggers showed on the hill."

"Youngest troops in the square, sir," murmured the aide, looking at them critically through his eyeglass. The general glared at them too, and remarked, in the racy speech for which he was famous, that the eternally lost idiots were cackling in the ranks like a coopful of anti-Christian hens who had laid an egg which was condemned by the deity.

"Tell Colonel Flanagan to see to it, Stephen," he concluded; and the galloper sped upon his way. The colonel, a fine old Celtic warrior, was over at C Company in an instant.

"How are the men, Captain Foley?"

"Never better, sir," answered the senior captain, in the spirit that makes a Madras officer look murder if you suggest recruiting his regiment from the Punjaub.

"Stiffen them up!" cried the colonel. As he rode away a color-sergeant seemed to trip, and fell forward into a mimosa bush.

He made no effort to rise, but lay in a hemp among the thorns.

"Sergeant O'Rooke's gone, sorr," cried a voice.

"Never mind, lads," said Captain Foley.

"He's died like a soldier, fighting for his queen."

"To hell with the queen!" shouted a hoarse voice from the ranks.

But the roar of the Gardner and the typewriter-like clicker of the hopper burst in at the tail of the words. Captain Foley heard them, and subalterns Grice and Murphy heard them; but there are times when a deaf ear is a gift from the gods.

"Steady, Mallows!" cried the captain, in a pause of the grunting machine gun. "We have the honor of Ireland to guard this day."

"And well we know how to guard it, captain!" cried the same ominous voice; and there was a buzz from the length of the company.

The captain and the two "subs" came together behind the marching line.

"They seem a bit out of hand," murmured the captain.

"Bedad," said the Galway boy, "they mean to scoot like redshanks."

"They nearly broke when the blacks showed on the hill," said Grice.

"The first man that turns, my sword is through him," cried Foley, loud enough to be heard by five files on either side of him. Then, in a lower voice: "It's a bitter drop to swallow; but it's my duty to report what you think to the Chief, and have a company of Jollies put behind us." He turned away, with the safety of the square upon his mind, and before he had reached his goal the square had ceased to exist.

In their march in front of what looked like a face of cliff, they had come opposite to the mouth of the gully, in which, screened by scrub and boulders, three thousand chosen dervishes, under Hamid Wad Hussein of the Baggarras, were crouching. Tat, tat, tat, went the rifles of three mounted infantrymen in front of the left shoulder of the square, and an instant later they were spurring it for their lives, crouching over the manes of their horses, and pelting over the sand-hills, with thirty or forty galloping chieftains at their heels. Rocks and scrub and mimosa swarmed suddenly into life. Rushing black figures came and went in the gaps of the bushes. A howl that drowned the shouts of the officers, a long, quavering yell, burst from the ambuscade. Two rolling volleys from the Royal Wessex, one crash from the screw-gun firing shrapnel, and then, before a second cartridge could be rammed down, a living, glistening black wave, tipped with steel, had rolled over the gun, the Royal

Wessex had been dashed back among the camels, and a thousand fanatics were hewing and hacking in the heart of what had been the square.

The camels and mules in the centre, jammed more and more together as their leaders flinched from the rush of the tribesmen, shut out the view of the other three faces, who could only tell that the Arabs had got in by the yells upon Allah, which rose ever nearer and nearer amid the clouds of sand-dust, the struggling animals, and the dense mass of swaying, cursing men. Some of the Wessex fired back at the Arabs who had passed them, as excited Tommies will ; and it is whispered among doctors that it was not always a Remington bullet which was cut from a wound that day. Some rallied in little knots, stabbing furiously with their bayonets at the rushing spearsmen. Others turned at bay, with their backs against the camels ; and others round the general and his staff, who, revolver in hand, had flung themselves into the heart of it. But the whole square was sidling slowly away from the gorge, pushed back by the pressure at the shattered corner.

The officers and men at the other faces were glancing nervously to their rear, uncertain what was going on, and unable to take help to their comrades without breaking the formation.

"By Jove, they've got through the Wessex !" cried Grice of the Mallows.

"The divils have hurrooshed us, Tiddy," said his brother subaltern, cocking his revolver.

The ranks were breaking and crowding towards Private Conolly, all talking together as the officers peered back through the veil of dust. The sailors had run their Gardner out, and she was squirting death out of her five barrels into the flank of the rushing stream of savages.

"Oh, this bloody gun !" shouted a voice. "She's jammed again.". The fierce metallic grunting had ceased, and her crew were straining and hauling at the breech.

"This vertical feed !" cried an officer.

"The spanner, Wilson, the spanner ! Stand to your cutlasses, boys, or they're into us."

His voice rose into a shriek as he ended, for a shovel-headed spear had been buried in his chest. A second wave of dervishes lapped over the hillocks, and burst upon the machine-gun and the right front of the line. The sailors were overborne in an instant, but the Mallows, with their fighting blood aflame, met the yell of the Moslem with an even wilder, fiercer cry, and dropped two hundred of them with a single point-blank volley. The howling, leaping crew swerved away to the right, and dashed on into the gap which had already been made for them.

But C Company had drawn no trigger to stop that fiery rush. The men leaned moodily upon their Martinis. Some had even thrown them upon the ground. Conolly was talking fiercely to those about him. Captain Foley, thrusting his way through the press, rushed up to him with a revolver in his hand.

"This is your doing, you villain !" he cried.

"If you raise your pistol, capt'in, your brains will be over your coat," said a low voice at his side.

He saw that several rifles were turned on him. The two "subs" had pressed forward, and were by his side.

"What is it, then ?" he cried, looking round from one fierce mutinous face to another. "Are you Irishmen ? Are you soldiers ? What are you here for, but to fight for your country ?"

"England is no country of ours," cried several.

"You are not fighting for England. You are fighting for Ireland, and for the empire of which it is part."

"A black curse on the impire !" shouted Private McGuire, throwing down his rifle. "'Twas the impire that backed the man that druv me onto the roadside. May me hand stiffen before I draw thrigger for it."

"What's the impire to us, Captain Foley, and what's the widdy to us ayther ?" cried a voice.

"Let the constabulary foight for her."

"Ay, they'd be better imployed than pullin' a poor man's thatch about his ears."

"Or shootin' his brother, as they did mine."

"It was the impire laid my grounin' mother by the wayside. Her son will rot before he upholds it, and ye can put that in the charge sheet in the next coortmartial."

In vain the three officers begged, menaced, persuaded. The square was still moving, ever moving, with the same bloody fight raging in its entrails. Even while they had been speaking they had been shuffling backwards, and the useless Gardner, with her slaughtered crew, was already a good hundred yards from them. And the pace was accelerating. The mass of men, tormented and writhing, was trying, by a common instinct, to reach some clearer ground where they could re-form. Three faces were still intact, but the fourth had been caved in, and badly mauled, without its comrades being able to help it. The guards had met a fresh rush of the Hadendowas, and had blown back the tribesmen with a volley, and the cavalry had ridden over another stream of them, as they welled out of the gully. A litter of hamstrung horses, and haggled men behind them, showed that a spearman on his face among the bushes can show some sport to the man who charges him. But, in spite of all, the square was still reeling swiftly backwards, trying to shake itself clear of this torment which clung to its heart. Would it break, or would it re-form? The lives of five regiments and the honor of the flag hung upon the answer.

Some, at least, were breaking. The C Company of the Mallows had lost all military order, and was pushing back in spite of the haggard officers, who cursed and shoved and prayed in the vain attempt to hold them. Their captain and the "subs" were elbowed and jostled, while the men crowded towards Private Conolly for their orders. The confusion had not spread, for the other companies, in the dust and smoke and turmoil, had lost touch with their mutinous comrades. Captain Foley saw that even now there might be time to avert a disaster.

"Think what you are doing, man," he yelled, rushing towards the ringleader. "There are a thousand Irish in the square, and they are dead men if we break."

The words alone might have had little effect on the old moonlighter. It is possible that, in his scheming brain, he had already planned how he was to club his Irish together and lead them to the sea. But at that moment the Arabs broke through the screen of camels which had fended them off. There was a struggle, a screaming, a mule rolled over, a wounded man sprang up in a cacolet with a spear through him, and then through the narrow gap surged a stream of naked savages,

"THIS IS YOUR DOING, YOU VILLAIN!" HE CRIED.

mad with battle, drunk with slaughter, spotted and splashed with blood—blood dripping from their spears, their arms, their faces. Their yells, their bounds, their crouching, darting figures, the horrid energy of their spear-thrusts, made them look like a blast of fiends from the pit. And were these the allies of Ireland? Were these the men who were to strike for her against her enemies? Conolly's soul rose up in loathing at the thought.

He was a man of firm purpose, and yet at the first sight of those howling fiends that purpose faltered; and at the second it was blown to the winds. He saw a huge coal-black negro seize a shrieking camel-driver and saw at his throat with a knife. He saw a shock-headed tribesman plunge his great spear through the back of their own little bugler from Millstreet. He saw a dozen deeds of blood—the murder of the wounded, the hacking of the unarmed—and caught, too, in a glance, the good, wholesome faces of the faced-about rear rank of the marines. The Mallows, too, had faced about, and in an instant Conolly had thrown himself into the heart of C Company, striving with the officers to form the men up with their comrades.

But the mischief had gone too far. The rank and file had no heart in their work. They had broken before, and this last rush of murderous savages was a hard thing for broken men to stand against. They flinched away from the furious faces and dripping forearms. Why should they throw away their lives for a flag for which they cared nothing? Why should their leader urge them to break, and now shriek to them to re-form? They would not re-form. They wanted to get to the sea and to safety. He flung himself among them with outstretched arms, with words of reason, with shouts, with gaspings. It was useless; the tide was beyond his control. They were shredding out into the desert with their faces set for the coast.

"Bhoys, will ye stand for this?" screamed a voice. It was so ringing, so strenuous, that the breaking Mallows glanced backwards. They were held by what they saw. Private Conolly had planted his rifle stock downwards in a mimosa bush. From the fixed bayonet there fluttered a little green flag with the crownless harp. God knows for what black mutiny, for what signal of revolt, that flag had been treasured up within the corporal's tunic! Now its green wisp stood amid the rush, while three proud regimental colors were reeling slowly backwards.

"What for the flag?" yelled the private.

"My heart's blood for it!" "And mine!" "And mine!" cried a score of voices. "God bless it! The flag, boys— the flag!"

C Company were rallying upon it. The stragglers clutched at each other and pointed. "Here. McGuire. Flynn, O'Hara," ran the shoutings, "close on the flag! Back to the flag!" The three standards reeled backwards, and the seething square strove for a clearer space where they could form their shattered ranks; but C Company, grim and powder-stained, choked with enemies, and falling fast, still closed in on the little rebel ensign that flapped from the mimosa bush.

It was a good half-hour before the square, having disentangled itself from its difficulties, and dressed its ranks, began to slowly move forwards over the ground across which, in its labor and anguish, it had been driven. The long trail of Wessex men and Arabs showed but too clearly the path they had come.

"How many got into us, Stephen?" asked the general, tapping his snuff-box.

"I should put them down at a thousand or twelve hundred, sir."

"I did not see any get out again. What were the Wessex thinking about! The Guards stood well, though ; so did the Mallows."

"Colonel Flanagan reports that his front flank company was cut off, sir."

"Why, that's the company that was out of hand when we advanced."

"Colonel Flanagan reports, sir, that the company took the whole brunt of the attack, and gave the square time to re-form."

"Tell the Hussars to ride forward, Stephen," said the general, "and try if they can see anything of them. There's no firing, and I fear that the Mallows will want to do some recruiting. Let the square take ground by the right, and then advance."

But the Sheik Kadra of the Hadendowas saw from his knoll that the men with the big hats had rallied, and that they were coming back in the quiet business fashion of men whose work was before them. He took counsel with Moussa the dervish and Hussein the Baggarra, and a woe-struck man was he when he learned that the third of his men were safe in the Moslem paradise. So, having still some signs of victory to show, he gave the word, and the desert warriors flitted off unseen and unheard, even as they had come.

A red rock plateau, a few hundred spears and Remingtons, and a plain which, for the second time, was strewn with slaughtered men, was all that his day's fighting gave to the English general.

It was a squadron of Hussars which came first to the spot where the rebel flag had waved. A dense litter of Arab dead marked the place. Within, the flag waved no longer, but the rifle still stood in the mimosa bush, and round it, with their wounds in front, lay the Fenian private and the silent ranks of his Irishry. Sentiment is not an English failing, but the Hussar captain raised his hilt in a salute as he rode past the blood-soaked ring.

The British general sent home despatches to his government, and so did the chief of the Hadendowas to his, though the style and manner differed somewhat in each. "The Sheik Kadra of the Hadendowa people to Mohammed Ahmed, the chosen of Allah, homage and greeting," began the latter. "Know by this that on the fourth day of this moon we gave battle to the Kaffirs who call themselves Inglees, having with us the Chief Hussein, with ten thousand of the faithful. By the blessing of Allah we have broken them, and chased them for a mile; though, indeed, these infidels are different from the dogs of Egypt, and have slain very many of our men. Yet we hope to smite them again ere the new moon be come, to which end I trust that thou wilt send us a thousand dervishes from Omdurman. In token of our victory, I send you by this messenger a flag which we have taken. By the color it might well seem to have belonged to those of the true faith, but the Kaffirs gave their blood freely to save it, and so we think that though small it is very dear to them."

"CLOSE ON THE FLAG! BACK TO THE FLAG!"

THE BATTLE OF MARENGO.

BY JOSEPH PETIT, OF THE MOUNTED GRENADIERS OF THE CONSULAR GUARD.

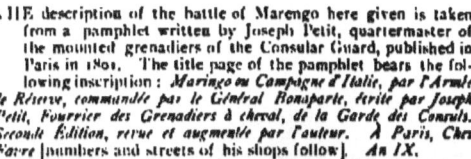

THE description of the battle of Marengo here given is taken from a pamphlet written by Joseph Petit, quartermaster of the mounted grenadiers of the Consular Guard, published in Paris in 1801. The title page of the pamphlet bears the following inscription: *Maringo ou Campagne d'Italie, par l'Armée de Réserve, commandée par le Général Bonaparte, écrite par Joseph Petit, Fourrier des Grenadiers à cheval, de la Garde des Consuls. Seconde Édition, revue et augmentée par l'auteur. A Paris, Chez Favre* [numbers and streets of his shops follow]. *An IX.*

This pamphlet is included in a remarkable series of Napoleon pamphlets owned by the Congressional Library of Washington. In addition to the description of the battle of Marengo, it gives a picturesque and rather detailed account of the passage of the Alps and of the skirmishes and adventures of the army on its march from the foot of the mountain to the battle-field. It includes also a sketch of General Desaix, a list of the rewards given for brilliant services in the campaign, and the agreement drawn up between Generals Berthier and Mélas after the victory.

The Austrians under General Mélas were in Italy besieging Genoa. Napoleon had decided to attack them on their rear, and so cut off their retreat. To do this he was obliged to cross the Alps. To hide his plan he collected at Dijon what was called the Army of the Reserve. It was a feeble force, and the Austrian spies only ridiculed it. In order to deceive the enemy as to his route, Napoleon made a demonstration near the Mont Cenis Pass, which led Mélas to believe that if the French crossed the Alps, it would be there, and consequently to send part of his troops to Turin to watch. The pass to the east of Mont Cenis, that of the Great Saint Bernard, he left but feebly defended. It was this pass Napoleon had chosen. The preparations in Switzerland for the passage were made so quietly that even in France the project was not understood. Napoleon did not leave Paris until May 6th. Two weeks later the whole army was across. Descending the valleys of the Aoste and the Po, it came into the plain of Marengo, where, defiantly confronting an army much its superior in numbers, it fought, on June 14, 1800, the great battle which M. Petit describes.—EDITOR.

THE PASSAGE OF THE GREAT SAINT BERNARD.

Bonaparte arrived at Martigny, a village of Hautvalais, situated six leagues from Mount Saint Bernard. He believed that this place, because so near the mountain, was a suitable one for preparing and directing the astonishing passage that he had resolved to make. He stayed there three days in the hospital of the monks of Mount Saint Bernard. The advance guard, commanded by General Lannes, advanced to Saint Pierre, a hamlet at the foot of the mountain. . . . On the 30th Floreal, the advance guard crossed the mountain, and at Saint Reme saw for the first time the enemy, of which we did not lose sight again until we had triumphed at Marengo. . . . The first division of the army, commanded by General Watrin, followed the advance guard. The rest did the same. . . .

SLEDDING CANNON OVER THE ALPS.

The gunners took to pieces the cannon, caissons, forges, etc. The inspector of artillery, Gassendi, had trees hollowed out into troughs. In these the cannon were slid, and five or six hundred men, according to the weight, dragged these loads. The wheels were carried on poles by hand. Sleds made expressly for this purpose carried the axles and the empty caissons. The mules were loaded with the

THE FOOT GRENADIERS OF THE CONSULAR GUARD WITHSTANDING A DEADLY CHARGE.

ammunitions, which were placed in pine cases. In this way, the army of the French Hannibal began its passage over the summit of the Alps.

To encourage this work, five or six hundred francs were given for each cannon furnished with its caisson. An entire battalion was necessary to transport these two objects. Half alone were needed to drag the loads, while the others were obliged to carry the knapsacks, guns, cartridge-boxes, cans, cooking utensils, and, most important of all, provisions for five days,—bread, meat, salt, and biscuit. The complete furnishing made a burden of from sixty to seventy pounds. Baggage was left behind at Lausanne. The Consul himself took only what was absolutely necessary.

THE WHOLE ARMY CLIMBED SINGLE FILE.

The army followed close to the advance guard. We mounted one by one. No one was tempted to pass his comrade, an imprudent attempt, the result of which would have inevitably been to bury him in the snow. The head of the army stopped frequently, and we took advantage of these frequent halts to quench our thirst by dipping biscuits in melted snow. No one would believe, unless, like us, he has climbed over the Alps, how delicious this drink is.

It took us five hours to climb from Saint Pierre to the convent. The path that we followed is more dangerous than difficult to mount. The First Consul mounted it on a mule led by a guide. He was often stopped by the caissons or cannon that the infantry was carrying up this miserable road. His presence always animated the courage of those who were working; and when they were stopped by any obstacle, his advice, listened to in great silence, was carried out with more promptness than could have been procured by anybody else, no matter how much gold he had scattered. On our arrival, each of us received a glass of wine. This liquor, although frozen, warmed us up and revived our strength. No one would have given up his glass for all the gold in Mexico.

A TERRIBLE SIX LEAGUES.

We still had six leagues to make, but six leagues that the extreme rapidity of the descent made terrible. At each step we found crevasses caused by the melting of the snow. In vain we held our horses back firmly. It did not prevent them from slipping frightfully. The men themselves, in spite of all their precautions, often fell; and if they did not get up quickly, they ran the risk of dragging their horses out of the path, and rolling with them into the frightful gulfs.

Bonaparte had entered the monastery, accompanied by the prior, who had followed us; but he stayed there only an hour, and left, urging the hermits to continue their humane work. The mules and the horses of the Consul followed us. As for him, wishing doubtless to join us by the quickest path, he took a road which a few foot soldiers were following. About the middle, the descent was so rapid that he was obliged to sit down and slide for a distance of about two hundred feet. His aides-de-camp, Duroc, Le Maroi, Merlin, and others, preceded him, and, like us, made the six leagues on foot. The crevasses into which we fell constantly made the path much more fatiguing than that we had followed in mounting. We had marched since midnight, and it was nine o'clock in the evening when we arrived, after having made fourteen leagues

DESAIX.

THE DEATH OF DESAIX.

almost without eating. The fatigue and the need we had of sleep made us easily forget our sad supper. . . .

[Having passed the summit, the army made its way down, by hard marching and with occasional light engagements, until it was received at last with great rejoicing at Milan.]

All the engagements in which we had taken part since we crossed the Saint Bernard were of small importance in comparison with the coming one. It was here [in Milan] that the First Consul addressed the

BONAPARTE'S PROCLAMATION TO THE ARMY.

"Soldiers, one of our departments was in the power of the enemy; consternation was in all the south of France; the greatest part of the Ligurian territory, the most faithful friends of the Republic, had been invaded. The Cisalpine Republic had again become the grotesque plaything of the feudal regime. Soldiers, you march, —and already the French territory is delivered! Joy and hope have succeeded in

dence to the people of Genoa. You have delivered them from their eternal enemies. You are in the capital of the Cisalpine. The enemy, terrified, no longer hopes for anything, except to regain its frontiers. You have taken possession of its hospitals, its magazines, its resources.

"The first act of the campaign is terminated. Every day you hear millions of men giving you thanks for your acts.

"But shall it be said that the French territory has been violated with impunity? Shall we allow an army which has carried fear into our families to return to its firesides? Will you run with your arms? Very well, march to the battle; forbid their retreat; tear from them the laurels of which they have taken possession; and so teach the world that the curse of destiny is on the rash who dare insult the territory of the Great People. The result of all our efforts will be spotless glory, solid peace.
[Signed]   BONAPARTE."
. . . . . .
[The battle of Montebello followed, and then Marengo.]

BEGINNING OF THE BATTLE.

The 25th Prairial [June 14th] commenced to break. A few cannon shots from the advance guard broke our slumbers. In the twinkle of an eye we were ready. At eight o'clock the enemy had not shown much vigor. They were feeling for feeble spots, and arranging their forces accordingly. At the headquarters we did not know their intentions exactly until the end of the morning. General Berthier was on the field of battle, and all through the morning the aides-de-camp came in, one after another, bringing the Consul word of the movements of the enemy. The wounded commenced to arrive, saying that the Austrians were in force.

At eleven o'clock the Consul mounted his horse and rode rapidly to the battlefield. The cannon and the musketry became heavier and heavier, and constantly approached. A great number of wounded cavalry, as well as infantry, carried and led by their comrades, were coming back. The First Consul, seeing them pass, said: "One must regret not to be wounded as they are, and not to share their suffering."

The line of the enemy reached about two leagues; for the Bormida, although rapid and deep, is, nevertheless, fordable in several places. Near the bridge the

the principal point of the action was San Stephano. From this place they were able to reach Voghéra ahead of us and cut off all retreat, so their forces were turned on this—the feeblest part. At noon we no longer had any doubt but that we were engaging the whole Austrian force; that they had accepted the battle they had refused the evening before.

Orders were given to the troops which were in the rear to come up promptly, but the corps that General Desaix commanded was still far away. The left wing, under the order of General Victor, commenced to give way. Much of the infantry retreated in disorder, and our cavalry was driven back. The fire approached. In the centre a terrible uproar was heard, and it ceased suddenly on the Bormida. An inexpressible anxiety took possession of us. Now we flattered ourselves that our troops were advancing, but the same instant we saw them retire in haste, bringing back the wounded on their shoulders. On the right wing the enemy slowly gained ground.

At that moment Bonaparte advanced to the front. He exhorted the soldiers whom he met to firmness and to courage. His presence restored confidence. More than one soldier preferred death to having him a witness of his flight. From this moment his mounted guard no longer remained near him, as before, but began to take an active part in the battle. A cloud of Austrian cavalry suddenly came into the plain and formed itself in battle array before us, concealing several pieces of light artillery, which were not long in beginning to grumble. General Berthier, who examined the movements of this column, was charged and forced to retire. General Murat, at the head of the dragoons, attacked them in the rear, protected the retreat of our infantry, and prevented the right flank of General Victor from being attacked.

THE GRENADIER GUARD BRAVELY MEETS A TERRIFIC CHARGE.

The foot grenadiers of the Consular Guard arrived at this moment, as if for a

THE FALL OF DESAIX   A REPRODUCTION OF THE ORIGINAL FRONTISPIECE OF PATIN'S PAMPHLET.

parade. They filed out in order, and marched with rapid step on the enemy, whom they met not more than a hundred steps from our front. Without artillery, without cavalry, not more than five hundred in number, they sustained the impetuous and terrible shock of a victorious army. Heedless of their small numbers, they continued to advance. Everything yielded before them. The haughty eagle hovered over them and threatened to rend them in pieces. The first bullet carried away three grenadiers and a quartermaster. Charged three times by the cavalry, shot by the infantry fifty steps away, they close in a square battalion upon their flags and their wounded, exhaust their cartridges, retire slowly in order, and rejoin our astonished rear guard.

One of the foot soldiers of the Consular Guard was left nearly dead on the battlefield at the moment of our retreat. The Austrian soldiers surrounded him and disputed the spoils. Nothing remained but his coat, which they were tearing off in spite of his cries of pain, when an Austrian colonel drove off the inhuman wretches and asked the soldier to what regiment he belonged. "I belong to the Consular Guard in front of you," answered the *chasseur*. The colonel praised the guard, sent for a surgeon, had the Frenchman's wounds dressed before him, and carried him to the ambulance.

Schmitt, the trumpeter of the grenadiers, carried away with excitement, was surrounded by several Austrians. Summoned to surrender, he answered by killing his fiercest assailant. He received several sabre strokes, his trumpet was cut off, and his arm was wounded. The pain made him drop the reins. An Austrian seized them and led him away on a gallop. Schmitt did not lose his presence of mind; driving his spurs into his horse's sides, the animal broke into a run so rapid that the Austrian was forced to abandon him, and Schmitt reached our lines. His bravery was rewarded by the gift of a trumpet of honor from the First Consul.

However, the retreat sounded on all sides. The centre was giving way; the enemy had passed and turned our wings. On the right, particularly, they were successful. On the left they were even able to reach our headquarters. The garrison of Tortone, seeing our defeat, and being less shut in, was able to escape. On all sides we were almost buried.

The Consul, always in the centre, encouraged the brave men who still defended the road and the defile which it crossed. This defile was shut in on one side by a wood, and on the other by very high and bushy vines. The village of Marengo lay to the left of this place so cruelly memorable.

THE DEAD AND DYING COVER THE EARTH.

How much blood was spilled here! How many brave men perished here! Our indomitable courage struggled ceaselessly against the constantly increasing number of our furious enemies. Our artillery, partly dismounted, had lost some guns, and the ammunition commenced to fail. Thirty pieces of cannon thundering at us cut our men in two, and, to increase the disaster, destroyed trees whose branches in their fall crushed those who had been wounded.

At four o'clock in the afternoon there remained in a radius of two leagues not over six thousand infantry, a thousand horses, and six pieces of cannon. Let no one accuse me of exaggeration in showing so terrible a falling off; the causes of it are easy to explain. A third of our army was not in condition for battle. The lack of carriages to transport the sick made another third necessary for this painful task. Hunger, thirst, fatigue, had forced a great number to withdraw. The sharpshooters for the most part had lost the direction of their regiments. That which remained of the army was occupied in defending vigorously the defile of which I have spoken, and was not aware of what was passing behind it.

BONAPARTE'S MARVELLOUS COOLNESS.

At this frightful moment, when the dead and the dying covered the earth, the Consul was constantly braving death. He gave his orders with his accustomed coolness, and saw the storm approach without seeming to fear it. Those who saw him, forgetting the danger that menaced them, said: "What if he should be killed? Why does he not go back?" It is said that General Berthier begged him to do so. General Berthier came to him to tell him that the army was giving way and that the retreat had commenced. Bonaparte said to him: "General, you do not tell me that with sufficient coolness." This greatness of soul, this firmness, did not leave him in the greatest dangers. When the Fifty-ninth Brigade reached the battle-field the action was the hottest. The First Consul advanced towards them and cried: "Come, my brave soldiers, spread your banners; the moment has come to distinguish yourselves. I count on your courage to avenge your comrades." At the moment that he pronounced these words, a bullet struck down five men. He turned with a tranquil air towards the enemy and said: "Come, my friends, charge them."

I had curiosity enough to listen attentively to his voice, to examine his features. The most courageous man, the hero the

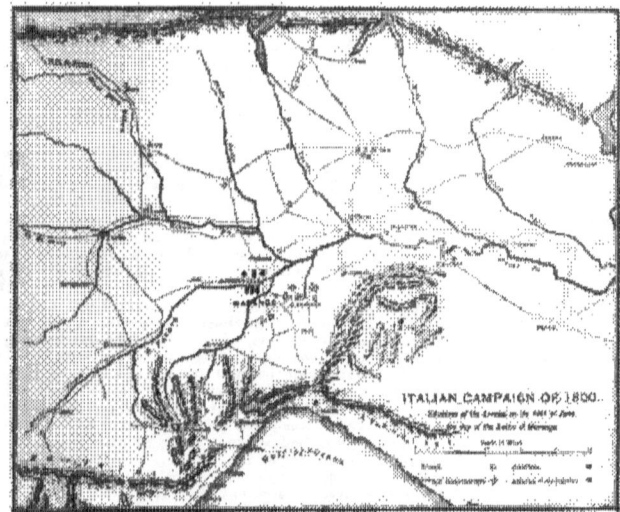

THIS MAP IS REPRODUCED FROM MR. JOHN C. ROPES'S "THE FIRST NAPOLEON," BY PERMISSION OF AND ARRANGEMENT WITH THE PUBLISHERS, MESSRS. HOUGHTON, MIFFLIN & COMPANY, BOSTON AND NEW YORK.

most eager for glory, might have been overcome in his situation without any one blaming him. But he was not. In these frightful moments, when Fortune seemed to desert him, he was still the Bonaparte of Arcola and Aboukir.

He who in these frightful circumstances would have said, "In two hours we shall have gained the battle, made ten thousand prisoners, taken several generals, fifteen flags, forty cannons; the enemy shall have delivered to us eleven-fortified places and all the territory of beautiful Italy; they will soon defile shamefaced in our ranks; an armistice will suspend the plague of war and bring back peace into our country,"— he, I say, who would have said that, would have seemed to insult our desperate situation.

How came it, then, that such prodigies were accomplished?

The enemy, not succeeding in forcing the defile where the greatest part of our troops were headed, had established a formidable line of artillery, under the protection of which it threw its infantry into the vines and into the wood. The cavalry, ar-

when we should give way, to throw themselves on our scattered ranks.

If this final misfortune had happened us, all would have been lost. The Consul would have been taken or killed. But we would rather have been hacked to pieces than survived him.

ARRIVAL OF REËNFORCEMENTS.

The hour of Victory sounded. Faithful to Bonaparte, she came at last to hover over our heads, and to act as our guide. The divisions of Monnier and Desaix came in sight. In spite of a forced march of ten leagues, they came upon a quickstep, forgetful of all their needs, thirsting only to avenge us. The great number of refugees and of wounded whom they had met might have weakened their courage, but, their eyes fixed on Desaix, they only knew how to brave dangers and fly to glory. Alas! they little thought that in an hour they would be no longer commanded by their brave general.

When we perceived these reënforcements from afar, hope and joy came back to our

with their own victory, which had cost them dear, were constantly held in check by our soldiers, who, ignorant of the succor which was coming up, had resolved, rather than fall back, to perish in this new Thermopylæ.

General Mélas, finding too great a resistance at the centre, believed that, by stretching out his wings, he could surround us or cut us off entirely. Imagining that he had sufficiently concealed his movements, and that he could hold us in place by his artillery, he arranged his forces in this way. Not being able to discover what was going on on our side, and ignorant of the reënforcements which were coming, he thus prepared for himself an inevitable defeat. Bonaparte, always at the post of honor, and whom nothing escaped, seized the opportunity.

As soon as the first battalion of Desaix's division reached the height, it was formed into a close column. The Consul, the General-in-chief, the generals, the officers of the staff, ran through the ranks, and everywhere inspired that confidence which gives birth to great successes. This operation lasted an hour, terrible to pass, for the Austrian artillery was thundering upon us, and each volley carried away whole ranks. Bullets and shells destroyed man and horses. They received death without moving from their places, and the ranks closed over the bodies of their comrades. This deadly artillery even reached the cavalry, which was drawn up behind us, as well as a large number of footmen of different corps who, encouraged by Desaix's division, which they had seen passing, had hastened back to the field of honor.

THE ENEMY OVERWHELMED.

Everything is arranged. The battalions burn with impatience. The drummer, his eye fixed upon the baton of his major, awaits the signal. The trumpeter, his arm raised, is ready to sound. The signal is given; the terrible quickstep is heard; the regiments all move together. French impetuosity, like a torrent, carries everything before it. In the twinkle of an eye the defile is crossed. The enemy is overwhelmed on all sides. Dying, living, wounded, and dead are trampled under foot.

Each leader, as he reaches the opposite side of the defile and prepares to enter the plain, arranges his division in battle array. Then it was that our line presented a formidable front. As fast as the artillery arrived, it was arranged, and vomited death on the frightened enemy. They recoil. Their immense cavalry charges with fury, but musketry, grape-shot, bayonets, stop them short. One of their caissons explodes; the terror is redoubled. The disorder which begins is hidden by thick clouds of smoke. The cries of the victor increase the terror; at last they are overwhelmed. They fall back; they fly.

Then the French cavalry threw itself into the plain, and by its boldness concealed its small numbers. It marches on the enemy without fear of being broken. At the right is Desaix at the head of his intrepid soldiers. Like a thunderbolt he seems to precede the lightning. Everything gives way before him. He crosses the ditches, the hedges; overwhelms, tramples, crushes everything in his way.

The rough ground is crossed with the same speed. The soldiers clamber headlong over the ditches, conquer every difficulty, and even dispute with their chiefs the glory of passing first.

On the left, General Victor, with the same speed, takes possession of Marengo and flies towards the Bormida, in spite of the efforts of a superior enemy whose artillery and cavalry disturb his right flank.

The centre, with less force and cavalry, under the order of General Murat, advances majestically into the plain. Murat attacks the centre of the enemy, follows up his movement, holds in check an enormous body of cavalry. The intrepid Desaix, by an oblique and quick motion, turns to the right on San Stephano, and cuts off entirely the left Austrian wing. At the same moment General Kellermann, with eight hundred horses gathered up from several regiments, compels six thousand Hungarian grenadiers to lay down their arms.

DESAIX FALLS MORTALLY WOUNDED.

Oh, grief! It is in the very moment of his triumph, after having saved his army and perhaps his country, that the friend and the model of all brave men, Desaix, is mortally wounded. He has only time to say to young Lebrun, "Go, tell the First Consul that the only regret I have is not to have done enough for posterity." With these words he expires. The First Consul, on learning this misfortune, cried out, "Why may I not weep?"

Night approached. The troops of the enemy in disorder—cavalry, infantry, artillery—were piled up, one on the other, to-

GENERAL LANNES PRESENTING THE TROPHIES OF MARENGO TO THE GOVERNMENT IN PARIS.

wards the centre and driven from the bridge into the river. The artillery, which they had withdrawn from the beginning of our success, lest it be taken, was more of a hinderance than a help to them now, for it cut off their passage. General Murat, seeing the importance of hurrying their retreat and of increasing their disorder, made us advance double quick. Already we had passed a part of their infantry which, not being able to fly as quickly as the cavalry, was about to be cut to pieces or made prisoner. Our proximity increased the confusion among the enemy. The decisive moment arrives. The trumpets sound the charge. The earth trembles. We are ready to fall on the panting infantry.

The Austrian cavalry, deciding to save the infantry, bore down upon us in a column; they pursued them to a ravine, where several were made prisoners.

Our small number; the difficulty of the land; the night which was coming on; the extreme fatigue of the horses, worn out with hunger; the numerous cavalry, under the eyes of which the action was passing, and which might have taken revenge, forbade the prudent Murat from exposing further the fruits of this glorious day.

THE BATTLE-FIELD IN THE DARKNESS.

Thus ended this memorable day. The darkness did not allow us to care for the wounded, and a great number remained on the battle-field. Austrians and French became brothers, drew near together, dragging themselves as they could, and gave each

the fields, implored our aid and awakened in our hearts that melancholy which is not unknown to the true soldier, and which is so honorable to him. Horses wandered here and there on three legs, neighing to ours as we passed. At every step we turned out of the road to avoid crushing the wounded. Further on we came upon houses which had been burned and had fallen in on the unfortunate inmates, who, half dead with fright, had concealed themselves in the cellars. The profound darkness which surrounded us made the picture still more frightful.

At last we reached headquarters. Each one camped where he could among the dead and the dying; not even their sharp cries could disturb our fatigue. The next day hunger was more imperative. I went into the court of the headquarters to try to find something to eat for myself and my horse. The horrible sight made me shudder. More than three thousand wounded French and Austrians were piled one on the other in the court, in the stables, even in the cellars and the garrets. They uttered the most lamentable cries, and even swore at the surgeons, who were not sufficient to care for them all. On every side I heard the weak voices of my comrades and friends, begging me for something to eat or to drink. All that I could do was to go and find them water in my gourd. Forgetting my own needs and those of my horse, I remained more than two hours, doing the work of a surgeon and of a nurse; and every well person did as much. From every side prisoners were being brought in. The day was intolerably long for every one. However, an event which caused many conjectures softened our uneasiness a little. An Austrian officer demanded an interview, and a French aide-de-camp departed immediately for Alexandria. General Berthier went there himself at noon. We all waited, and dared not hope what the next day we knew we had obtained. We learned then the news of an armistice, which filled the French army with joy, while the Austrians shivered with rage.

FRANCE'S PROFITS AND LOSSES FROM MARENGO.

Marengo is the glorious patrimony of all the brave men who fought there. There is not a regiment, not a soldier, who did not there reap laurels.

Who would not have fought in the Ninety-sixth Brigade? Who would not have been glad to have been in the ranks with the grenadiers, as terrible as the Greeks who met the Persian army at the pass of Thermopylæ? With those regiments that counted as many battles as days passed in Italy? What charges were given and received by our cavalry! What audacity! what intrepidity!

As well as I can compute it, the French army at the moment of battle numbered from forty to forty-five thousand men, of whom three thousand were in the cavalry. It had twenty-five to thirty pieces of cannon, two companies of light artillery.

The Austrian army, all told, was composed of from fifty-five to sixty thousand men, of whom fifteen to eighteen thousand were in the cavalry; more than eighty pieces of cannon, two hundred caissons well furnished with ammunition, and an immense quantity of war implements. It is well known that we were not embarrassed with the last; that for lack of caissons we were obliged to put our ammunition on ox-carts, and that the little we had was soon exhausted.

It cannot be denied that this victory cost the Republic dear, by the loss of a great number of its defenders and of one of its best generals. But let us remember that this was necessary to save the South from a certain invasion, and perhaps save France from a frightful devastation. Let us remember that the rights of Italy are assured, that the armistice concluded has brought about since a glorious peace; then we shall have powerful motives for putting aside our just regrets.

A LONELY SOUL.

By Marjorie Milton.

"BE you my boarder?"
The person addressed looked around with a smile at her questioner. She had just alighted from the cars at a wayside station among the hills, and there was an amused look in her dark eyes, as she answered, "If you are Miss Martha Bascom, then I be."

The other woman drew a long breath of relief. "I was so afraid," she said, "that something would happen to hinder your coming. Now, just as soon as the cars are out of sight, I'll bring round the horse, and we will go home. It's Deacon Hinds's horse, and he's dreadful afraid of railroads."

Disappearing behind the station for a moment, she presently came leading a very meek-looking animal. She held him by the bit, at arm's length, and seemed very much afraid he would step on her. It was quite evident Martha did not feel at home with horses.

The small trunk was placed in the back of the open wagon by the station-master, and, climbing up beside her driver, the boarder, whose name was Marcia Ames, presently found herself riding down a most beautiful country road.

It had been a warm June day, and the sun was still hot on the little depot platform, but as they turned into the shady highway, a cool breeze met them, laden with all the fragrance of the pines and other sweet odors of the wood. The wild roses made pink all the hedges. On one side Marcia saw a meadow white with daisies, like summer snow; and when Martha Bascom, on meeting a carriage, turned out to let it go by, her wheels crushed the mint that grew by the roadside, and the strong fragrance came to Marcia like a welcome.

acter," she thought, "and one that I shall like to study."

She saw a straight figure that disdained the support of the back of the seat; a care-worn face with grave gray eyes and a smiling mouth that did not seem to belong to the rest of the face. She was dressed in a brown checked gingham, as clean as possible; you could see the folds where it had been ironed. She wore a shade hat with strings, which were tied in a prim bow under a rather square chin.

She looked up and caught Marcia's glance.

"I hope," she said, "you won't laugh at my hat; I can't bear bonnets. I know hats are for girls; but I put strings on this, and thought they would take the curse off."

"I am not a girl," said Marcia pleasantly, "and I have a hat in my trunk. I hope you won't insist on my putting strings on it."

"Oh!" replied the other, "you can wear what you have a mind to; I don't care."

"You need not be surprised," she went on, "if folks look pretty sharp at you. You see, I didn't tell anybody I was going to take a boarder, and they don't know who you can be. I hope you will be contented. I haven't got much room, but I can give you a good bed. And I've bought a hammock for you. All the summer boarders I ever heard of loved to set in them."

And Marcia assured her she loved hammocks, and did not care for room, as she intended to live out of doors most of the time.

People *did* stare when they met them, and presently the horse was brought to a standstill by Martha before the gate of a low red house on the side of a hill, and she

front windows a table was set for two. "Her dining-room," she said to herself, "or her kitchen," as she caught sight of a small cook-stove. A door opened between the side windows, and Marcia saw a piazza with a hammock in a shady corner. There was a home-made lounge in one part of the room, and she sat down on it, thinking she would not remove her bonnet until she went to her room.

And then Martha came in; she untied her hat-strings with nervous hands.

"I don't know how to tell you," she said, "but this is all the house I've got. I know it's ridiculous for me to think of taking a boarder, but I've got to earn some money somehow, and there didn't seem to be any other way."

She held out her hands, and Marcia saw that they trembled. "I will do well by you," she went on ; "do say that you will put up with it and stay. You don't know what it will be to me."

There was something in the woman's face that touched Marcia. "She is in trouble," she thought, "and I am going to help her."

She smiled reassuringly. "If you don't think I shall crowd you," she said, "I'll stay. But you don't mean that this room is all you have?" And Martha hastened to tell her there was a bedroom where she could sleep. "I shall sleep on the lounge," she added, as she opened the door of the little sleeping-room, and Marcia went in and took off her bonnet.

It was the next morning. Martha's housework was all done ; so she took her rocking-chair out on the piazza, where her boarder was trying the new hammock, and as she rocked, she knit, and presently began to talk.

"I want to tell you all about it," she said.

"You see, this was father's house, and, when he died, he left it to brother James and me, after mother. James, he thought he would move right down here, and be wanted mother and me to live in with them, and have a chamber finished off to sleep in; but we didn't want to—we didn't like his wife over and above—and so we divided the house. Afterwards, James built on a porch on his part. They've got a dining-room and everything.

"And mother and I lived in here for a good many years. We got along real comfortable. She had her pension, and I sewed braid; but after a while they stopped bringing braid around. It was all sewed on machines in the straw shop. And then

She was silent a moment, and Marcia saw her lip quiver.

"She died, and I was all alone. James wanted me to break up and live in with them—his wife wanted this room for a parlor—but I could not ; it was home, and I knew it wouldn't be in the other part.

"The children were sassy, too ; they hadn't used mother well, and one of them called me an old maid. His mother heard him, and I looked at her, for I thought she would take him to due; but she didn't, she only laughed. And she knew," continued Martha, "all about my disappointment, too. I was going to marry Hiram Parker, and I had all my sheets and pillow-cases made, and mother and I were just going to quilt. I had five bed-quilts all ready for the bars. He wasn't sick but two weeks ; it was the typhus fever. I am sure I feel just like a widder, and I went to his funeral as chief mourner. It was real cruel for James's wife to let her boy twit me so, as if I never had a chance to be married, like old Liddy Wilber." And Martha's knitting-needles flashed brightly in the sun, and her gray eyes were almost black with the remembrance of her wrongs. Marcia murmured sympathizingly, and presently Martha went on.

"It's eight years now," she said, "since mother died, and they are always at me to give them this part of the house. I can't bear to. I've got along in spite of them, till now."

"But how could you?" said Marcia. "What did you do to get something to eat?"

The other woman looked at her a moment. "I suppose," she said, "you'll despise me, but I've worked just like a man. That field over there is mine. I planted it myself, and raised a good many things to sell. I went huckleberrying, and I sold my grass standing, for fifteen dollars, every year, and year before last I sold potatoes enough to buy me a barrel of flour and an alpaca dress. I got a man to plough the field, and I planted the potatoes myself, and hoed them, and dug them. I've got along all right till last year ; it was so dry everything dried up. There wasn't any huckleberries, and my potatoes were too little to sell. James used to put a hose in the pond and get water to water his garden, but he never put a drop on mine. They wanted me to give up, and they thought I would have to.

"I came pretty short last winter. Many a time I did not have anything to eat but tea. I used to smell it from the other part of the house, and I wanted it so bad.

"I will say I don't think James knew how poor I was; he has always been pretty good to me. And the neighbors used to invite me out to spend the afternoon. I used to be afraid, sometimes, they mistrusted how poor I was.

"I've got a splendid garden this year, but I know we may have a dry season again, and I made up my mind I *must* have a little money to fall back on. I laid awake night after night, thinking of every way folks took to earn money, and finally I thought if I could only take a lady boarder I could save most of her board in the summer; for most of folks like garden sauce and so forth, and I've got most everything planted, and they are doing well. I tried to get the schoolmarm. I went to see her, and when she heard what accommodations I could give her, she laughed at me; but she promised she would not tell anybody I asked her.

"I composed that advertisement myself, and sent it to a Boston paper, because I didn't know anybody around here that took a paper from there, and I could not bear to have anybody know I had tried to get a boarder, if I did not get one. I never saw how it looked in print," and she looked appealingly at Marcia, who told her kindly that it was very much to the point and all right.

Then they sat in silence for a while, and Marcia thought how she had read the advertisement in her city home, and laughed at it, and then suddenly determined to answer it, and find out what manner of woman Martha Bascom was. She thought over the words she had read:

"Wanted, a lady boarder, by a plain country woman, who will do the best she can. The view from the piazza is beautiful, and you will be sure to like it. Address Miss Martha Bascom, Littlefield, Mass."

And here she was, seated on the piazza. She let her eyes wander over the scene before her.

"Yes, it *is* beautiful," she thought. The house was on a hill, and she could look a long way down the valley at her feet. Field after field was outlined there; the stone walls that marked their boundaries seemed like children's work—like the playhouses her brothers used to make years ago, marking out the rooms with a row of stones. A thick growth of bushes and trees told where a river crept, and she could see the glitter of the water, here and there, between the trees.

"I don't wonder," she said to herself, "that the poor woman wanted to keep her home. I will help her all I can."

One day they were in the parlor, as Marcia called the piazza. She had hung it around with pretty shawls, and had a bright cushion in the hammock; a vine shaded one side, and Martha's thrush sang in his cage among the leaves.

"There is one thing I want to tell you," said Martha. "It don't seem right to take four dollars a week for your board. I never was so happy in my life as I have been since you come. You don't eat hardly a thing, and I haven't had but one white petticoat to wash for you since you have been here."

"And there is one thing I want to tell you," said her friend. "I always go somewhere in the country in the summer, and I never paid less than seven dollars a week for board in my life. I intend to pay you as much as that, I assure you. Four dollars a week!" she said scornfully. "It is very evident, my dear Martha, you are taking your first boarder."

Martha sat up straight in her rocking-chair; her eyes shone like diamonds, and there was a faint red in her faded cheek.

"If you stay till September and pay me seven dollars a week," she said excitedly, "I'll have me a cow. I can keep her as well as not, if I can only get her in the first place. I've got a pasture, and I can raise a lot of pumpkins and fodder corn. I know how to milk. I can make butter. Why, I can most live on her milk," and she burst into a flood of tears, and hid her face in her hands.

It seemed as if the poor woman could not talk enough about her cow, and her gratitude to the lady who had proved from the first such a godsend to her.

"I shall have something to love after you are gone," she said one day. "I got me a cat after mother died; she was real pretty, and I thought so much of her. She used to sleep on the foot of my bed, and I did not feel half so lonesome nights, if I could not sleep; for if I spoke to her, she would purr, and come up and rub herself against me. I thought there never was such a cat; but James's boys, they used to stone her whenever she went over on their side, and one day she came dragging herself home with a broken leg, and her head was hurt, too. She died before night, and I buried her under the laylock there. And I missed her so, I got me another; but that one was missing within a week, and one of the boys kept asking me what had become of my cat, and laughing in a hateful way. So I made up my mind I could not have any more pets.

"But they won't dare to hurt a cow, they are too valuable; and I could have the law on them if they did," she added grimly. "Anybody can do what they have a mind to to cats, poor things!" for Martha had never heard of the "society" with the long name."

"Let me see," said Marcia, "what kind of a cow will you get—Jersey?"

"I shall get a red and white one," said Martha. "Father used to keep a cow, and that was speckled red and white. I mean to get one just like her, if I can. What will James's folks say! I guess they'll think it will be some time before they'll have my house for a parlor."

"It beats all," said she, one day, "how little things trouble folks. Now, any great trial, like death and such, you can carry to the Lord, and He will help you bear it; but anybody feels so mean to trouble Him about the little things.

"Now, there was mother's gold beads. She always told me I should have them after her. Many a time I've put them on my neck when I was a little girl, and wished mother would give them to me then; but she would take them, and say I should have them some time.

"And when she died I was almost crazy, and James's wife, she had to see to everything.

"It was a few weeks afterwards, and I saw mother's beads on Maria's neck—that is her oldest girl. I felt dreadfully. I went out to the barn and talked to James about it. He said Maria wanted them as bad as I did, and he didn't know if she would give them up. His wife made a fuss about it, and so I did not have them.

"But it was a trial. I never had a piece of jewelry in my life but a cornelian ring. I have got that now, but I have outgrown it."

Now, Martha had a birthday that week; and James's wife was astonished, as she was getting breakfast one morning, by seeing her sister's boarder coming in. She had in her hand a beautiful gold chain. There was a locket attached, and the rhinestone in it sparkled like a diamond in the morning sun.

"Mrs. Bascom," said the lady, "I want to make a bargain with you. I want you to exchange your daughter's gold beads for this chain; it is fully as valuable, and prettier for her.

"You know it is Miss Martha's birthday to-day, and I want to give her a present. I know there is nothing she will prize like her mother's gold beads."

Both mother and child were delighted with the chain.

"I have always felt mean about those beads," said Mrs. Bascom, "but the girl wanted them so; and I'm real glad to change. Here, let me brighten them up a bit," and she hurried around after a piece of flannel and some whiting.

And so it happened, just after breakfast, as Martha was getting up from the table, Marcia Ames's white hands went lovingly around her neck, and clasped there the precious beads.

The autumn came all too soon, and the friends parted until next summer, Marcia said.

A gentle red and white cow stood by the bars in Martha's pasture, and it was on her glossy neck that Martha left the tears she shed when the stage that bore her friend away went out of sight.

For Marcia had insisted on the cow being a reality before she went away, and had named her at Martha's request. Sultana was the rather high-flown name she had bestowed upon her; and her mistress thought it just the right name, as, indeed, she would have if Marcia had called her Peter Snooks. They had a merry time when they christened the gentle creature, who calmly chewed her cud, and looked at them with her great mild eyes, as she thought to herself: "What fools these mortals be!"

I do not think Martha Bascom ever closed her eyes at night, as long as she lived, without thanking God for the friend she had found—a friend who did not forget her as the years went by.

THE DRAMATIC SEASON.

NEW PLAYS, THE OPERA, NOTABLE ACTORS, ACTRESSES, AND SINGERS OF THE YEAR.

BY EDWARD MARSHALL.

LAST night (if this article be read on any day but Monday) at least two hundred thousand dollars was paid by the people of the United States for the privilege of sitting in theatres and gazing from box or orchestra or gallery at the efforts, tragic and comic, good and bad, of play-actors to mimic life. At least twenty millions had been spent for no other purpose than to furnish buildings and their fittings for the accommodation of this portion of the public. It is safe to say that more than two million five hundred thousand dollars had been, at one time or another, devoted to the preparation of scenery and "properties" used in the presentation of last evening's entertainments, and that the men and women who took part in them had devoted no less than one-fourth of that sum to buying proper costumes for their rôles. The daily cost of moving theatrical people and things from place to place about the country is estimated at seventy-five thousand dollars, and the cost of sustenance and shelter for the players and those who go with them is not under sixty thousand dollars for every twenty-four hours at this time of year. It is fair to figure that the weekly total of salaries paid by theatrical managers will average ing the early part of this dramatic season —until February, perhaps. Later it will shrink, because many companies whose efforts fail to gain the public's approbation will disband and scatter.

These figures are not my own, precisely, and are at the best so vague—it is impossible to approach accuracy in preparing them—that they would be of no value to a statistician. Most of them were secured by cutting the estimates of a conservative theatrical manager in half. They are advanced, however, with a certainty that they are not too large.

THE GROWTH OF THE STAGE IN AMERICA.

But, even if they are not too large, they are stupendous. They offer a pretty contrast to the records of only two years more than a century ago (midwinter, 1792), when, in Boston, "about five hundred dollars" was devoted to the building of the first theatre there, veiled (because theatres and theatrical performances were prohibited by the legislature and abhorred by the governor) under the name of the "New Exhibition Hall." The governor, in fact, suppressed the performance on the night of December 5, 1792, in the midst of a rebellious riot. The first dramatic per-

JOSEPH JEFFERSON AND HIS GRANDDAUGHTER. FROM A PHOTOGRAPH BY FALK, NEW YORK.

JULIE DE LUSSAN, FROM A PHOTOGRAPH BY CONLY, BOSTON.

record exists, occurred sixty years earlier, in a hall the use of which was donated by one Rip Van Dam; and so fearful of official interference were those interested in it that pickets were posted to watch, and, if necessary, to warn.

But the nineteenth century had well begun before the theatre had gained a good foothold in America. It is even true that as late as 1833 a whole company of theatrical folk who were bold enough to attempt to give their show in Lowell, Massachusetts, (well known as a stronghold of prejudice against such things,) were arrested because they were "following no lawful and honorable profession." They barely escaped suffering violence at the hands of outraged moralists, and, in thus escaping, they were more fortunate than some of their ilk in other places. It is probable that the tolerance which theatres gained in some localities during the closing years of the eighteenth century was regarded with as much amazement by many good people of the day as are the progressions and queer matters—cleverly set aside by French wit as *fin de siècle*—which make us wonder, as the end of the nineteenth century approaches.

Nor has the evolution of the theatre and the drama in America been less astonishing in other ways. From those days when only Shakespeare was regarded worthy by cultivated folk, to these (when one is sometimes forced to fear that it is not entirely dissatisfaction with the players that keeps American theatres empty on nights when the dramas of the immortal bard are given), the gap is wider than one hundred twelve-months make in almost any other line.

America has had its share of influence on the drama of the world, and has given its quota of almost everything, good and bad, that goes to make the ingredients of dramatic history—except great plays. Good dramas have been penned with Yankee ink, but nothing, so far, that will withstand the wear of years, and last to anything approaching immortality. American lavishness has forced the managers of Europe to extravagance in playhouse and in scenery of which they would not have dreamed without the influence of this spendthrift republic. More money has been made by players here than elsewhere; and, alas! more also has been lost. When a New York manager seeks an artist in London, Paris, or Berlin, competition is abandoned. Great tales are told of individual salaries paid by enterprising American managers to European stars, and most of them should be cut in half for truth's sake; yet it is true that one actress was guaranteed a weekly income of fifteen thousand dollars, besides

JEAN DE RESZKE, FROM A PHOTOGRAPH BY NADAR, PARIS.

her expenses, during an American tour, and that operatic stipends have sometimes risen to heights truly incredible to the layman.

THE DRAMATIC SEASON OF 1894-95.

From the patriot's point of view, the season of 1894-95 offers cold comfort. Not one really notable actor, actress, or singer; not one extraordinarily good play or opera, has sprung within the year from the ranks or brains of America's sixty-five millions. There have been none and will be none but imported *pro*ductions in New York play houses and opera houses this winter, and New York is America's amusement barometer. Two of three artists of whom fine things were predicted during the opening days of last season, have failed to show any sort of whatever this year, and not one American this year has risen to real dramatic importance. The great plays which were imported from American pens have all been bad to boot.

JESSIE FREMONT. FROM A PHOTOGRAPH BY SARONY, NEW YORK.

MR. BARNES AS "PARSIFAL." FROM A PHOTOGRAPH BY B. MEREK, BERLIN.

important managers in America last year announced that thereafter he should open his theatre each season with a play written by an American, this year to be the first under this plan. A few weeks ago this manager was forced to confess his inability to secure an American play of which he thought well enough to devote to it the time and money necessary for production. He opened his theatre with a play by a foreigner. This is melancholy from the patriot's point of view. Presenting to the manager an equally sorrowful aspect is the fact that, whether times have improved or not in other lines, the business done by the theatres thus far this season has been little, if any, in excess of that done during the same months of last year—and last year was the worst for a decade.

But, as the intelligent observer looks at it, there are many things this year to rejoice over. Principal among them is the decadence— long promised —of the so-called "farce comedy," that

THE ITALIAN OPERA.

In New York the great period of the amusement year is the operatic season at the Metropolitan Opera House, although it is reasonable to believe that not one-twentieth of the habitual theatre-goers of this city have ever stepped within the lobbies of that great, brown brick pile on Broadway. For a number of years a controversy, which has driven some of its partisans to writing and printing bitter things, has been waged between the lovers of German and the lovers of Italian opera. This year this battle may be said to have been brought to a compromise, for when the end of the winter comes, both will have had extended hearings at the Metropolitan. The regular season of Italian opera is already in progress. It departs little in its features from that of a year ago. The repertory is nearly the same, and the most important change in the list of artists is the absence of the name of Calvé, who brightened the glory of the winter of '93–'94 by her matchless "Carmen," and who turned the financial scale in favor of the management. Calvé is now singing most busily in the capitals of Europe, earning her dowry, it is said, although at a smaller salary than she would have received if a quarrel with Emma Eames had not prevented her returning to America with the rest of the company. Her place in the popular fancy is quite likely to be taken by Miss Sybil Sanderson, the gifted California girl whose voice and beauty captivated Jules Massenet, the first of French operatic composers. She is an exceedingly clever woman, less impulsive than Calvé, but a great artist.

Zelie de Lussan, long a stranger to the land that gave her her first laurels, also adds strength to the Metropolitan forces. She looks something like Patti, and of late years she must have been singing considerably better than *La Diva*, for it is said that her voice has broadened and developed notably since the days when she was a treasured member of the old Boston Ideals. Both Miss de Lussan and a promising young Russian prima donna named Myra Heller will appear as "Carmen."

If "Falstaff," the bright, musical child of Verdi's old age, is produced at the Metropolitan Opera House, as it has been half promised that it shall be, the title rôle probably will be reserved for Victor Maurel, who created the part at Milan on February

NELLIE MELBA. FROM A PHOTOGRAPH BY DUPONT, BRUSSELS.

THE DRAMATIC SEASON.

THE GERMAN OPERA.

The season of German opera will begin February 25th, and will be watched with more than passing interest. It will be judged more critically, perhaps, than any other of the winter's appeals for public favor from the musical stage, for Walter Damrosch's reputation is staked upon it, and, to an extent, the immediate future of the Wagner cult in New York depends upon it. Mr. Damrosch's season will last four weeks in all, and will include only fourteen performances. After these end, the company will make short visits to Philadelphia, Chicago, and Boston, and then hasten home, with scarcely an hour to spare between their closing performance and the time of the sailing of the steamer on which they are to depart.

It was only by consenting to extraordinary concessions that the American conductor was able to get them; and it is doubtful whether Berlin would have consented to release Rosa Sucher at all, had it not been for a feeling of national pride in the effort to establish German opera in America. Mr. Damrosch has no inten-

TAMAGNO. FROM A PHOTOGRAPH BY MONTABONE, FIRENZE.

9, 1893, and who introduced it to the Parisians. The other stars of the Metropolitan constellation are Melba, Eames, Scalchi, Pol Plançon, Tamagno, and last, but not least, the brothers De Reszke.

An important step toward the declaration of American independence in music has been the training of an American chorus at the Metropolitan, to take the place of the motley collection which has been brought over from Europe in previous years,—imported not because its component parts could sing exceptionally well, but simply because they knew, in a wooden way, the music of all the operas in the Metropolitan repertory. The training of a new and native

dämmerung," "Die Meistersinger," "Lohengrin," "Tannhäuser," and "Siegfried." Mr. Damrosch, whose first ambition was to be a painter, will make the mounting of these operas his especial care. His standing as a Wagner authority is a little uncertain now, but will be well defined by the time his operatic season is half over. The effort will mark a crisis in his life.

MADAME RÉJANE AND HER FRENCH COMPANY.

The most important of all the dramatic engagements of the year will also bring a company of foreigners to America. It is that of Madame Réjane. Madame Réjane is, next to Sara Bernhardt, France's greatest actress, and is probably the best comedienne Paris has produced. She is the wife of M. Porel, who was the manager of the Odéon when he married her. This put her into the position of leading woman at the second in importance of France's state theatres; and when M. Porel left that famous place of amusement, she went with

MADAME RÉJANE. FROM A PHOTOGRAPH BY NADAR, PARIS.

tion of continuing as an operatic manager after the coming experiment. He asserts that his only aim is to induce the autocrats of grand opera in America to include in the regular Metropolitan Opera House seasons of the future, German opera, sung by German artists, as well as the works of Italian and French composers.

Besides Rosa Sucher, undoubtedly the greatest living singer of Wagner's mightiest female rôle, Mr. Damrosch will have Herr Alvary,—over whom New York waxed so enthusiastic in 1889 that his path from the stage door to his carriage was often lined with impressionable women who begged for attention from him, even going so far as to lift his cloak and kiss it,—Franz Schwarz, and Marie Brema. The last named is the Scotch woman who made a swift flight from obscurity to fame at Bayreuth last summer. It is an interesting tribute to Mr. Damrosch's judgment to note that he engaged Miss Brema before Frau Wagner heard her and brought her into great celebrity.

him to the Varieties. M. Porel and his partner, M. Carrée, known in America as a writer of comedies with M. Bisson, are the most important managers in France, and so it is not surprising that for them Victorien Sardou should write the play which is said to be his greatest comedy. That play is "Madame Sans-Gêne." It was written for Madame Réjane, and her success in it was instantaneous and world-echoing. She has played in it in London as well as in Paris, and pleased the English almost as well as she had pleased her own country's people. It is as "Madame Sans-Gêne" that she will be seen in America.

The news that Madame Réjane is coming to America to act in "Madame Sans-Gêne" must have been a severe blow to Miss Kathryn Kidder, an American actress who, early in November, produced a version of the play in English.

Next to the coming of Mme. Réjane, it is of Beerbohm Tree and his talented wife, who are also coming to America, that the greatest hints are ex-

JOHN DREW. FROM A PHOTOGRAPH BY BLACK (KEARING), BOSTON.

notable London comedy players will appear here before long in "A Bunch of Violets," a play by Mr. Sidney Grundy, which has become one of the decade's greatest successes abroad. They will also act in "A Red Lamp," by Tristram Outram; "Gringoire," and "Captain Swift."

THE NEW PLAYS.

One of Henry Arthur Jones's plays, "The Bauble Shop," is Mr. John Drew's most important medium for this year's work. It is a study of human nature, and "takes up a question." "Taking up questions" is becoming more and more popular among playwrights. "The Masqueraders" is another question play. It followed "The Bauble Shop" in New York, and is by the same author. It has already won success in England, and will undoubtedly make money, if not artistic reputation, for its author in America. Mr. Grundy has also written "The New Woman," recently produced in New York. That this has the very biggest query of the day in it, its name

THE DRAMATIC SEASON.

Another English play which is to be brought out in New York during the season, and which will afterwards tour the country, is "The Fatal Card." It was written by Haddon Chambers and B. C. Stephenson. This is looked upon as being a most astonishing melodrama, and is one of the greatest "money-makers" that have been produced in London in a long time. Much curiosity has been evinced by people who wish to know just how much of the play was written by each man. A London correspondent says that Chambers recently settled this by remarking that he had written the consonants, while Stephenson wrote the vowels.

It is agreed, at any rate, that the best work of each man was devoted to this play.

France, so far as is known, will contribute, besides "Madame Sans-Gêne," only three important new plays to the American season. One of these is "Gigolette," by Decourcelle and Tarbé. This has not even been rendered into English by an American. It was adapted by George Sims, widely celebrated as a maker of conventional English melodramas. Besides this, "A Woman's Silence," a new Sardou play, has recently been produced by Mr. Daniel Frohman's Lyceum company in New York. Another play by Sardou has been secured by Fanny Davenport. It is "The Duchess of Athens," and has been produced in Paris by Sara Bernhardt.

FANNY DAVENPORT, JEFFERSON, AND OTHER ESTABLISHED FAVORITES.

Indeed, Miss Davenport seems to be about the only American star who has in view any notable new work. Mr. W. H. Crane, early in the season, produced an ambitious revival of "Falstaff," but it was not received with favor, and he reverted to an old English comedy. Mr. Joseph Jefferson, who is America's only really great actor now, does not purpose to do anything this year which he has not done before, and Mr. Richard Mansfield has probably given us all the new material which he will show during the season in two plays neither of which has been widely successful. A most interesting event, because of the impressive scale on which it is to be executed, and because of the fact that it will, for the first time, bring to notable prominence the work of an exceedingly young, but exceedingly promising, American playwright, named Paul Kester, will be the production by Alexander Salvini of "The Moor." If "The Moor," which is a drama of the old romantic school, but which is written and will be produced on a scale of elaborateness seldom attempted, succeeds, it will mean that a very great change, and a change for the better, has come over the public taste.

ADA REHAN, FROM A PHOTOGRAPH BY ALEX. BASSANO, LONDON.

MISS REHAN AND MISS CAYVAN HOVERING ON THE STAR LINE.

Mr. Augustin Daly, who may generally be depended upon to give America one or two novelties during the course of each season, will, it is said, produce this winter an adaptation from the German of Sudermann's most recent failure—"Butterflies." It was announced early in the season that Mr. Daly's famous leading woman, Miss Ada Rehan, would leave his company and star this year, but it is now thought that this idea has been abandoned. This would have been as serious a loss to Mr. Daly as the recent resignation of Miss Georgia Cayvan from the Lyceum organization was to Mr. Daniel Frohman. Miss Cayvan, however, says that she has no thought of starring. But it would be surprising if the great success of Miss Olga Nethersole,

York some months ago with "The Transgressor," and afterwards carried big audiences into ecstasies with "Camille"), did not fill the heads of some of our able American leading women with thoughts of plays and companies of their own. A curious divergence in taste between England and America was illustrated by the reception here of "The Transgressor." In England it was popular and pronounced to be powerful. In America only the superb work of Miss Nethersole has saved it from utter failure,—a fact from which Miss Judith Berolde may draw consolation in the long illness under which she has been suffering. Early in the autumn she planned to produce "The Transgressor" herself, and her illness prevented her.

The Rosenfeld brothers, who last year encountered a settled public opinion against the production of Gerhardt Hauptmann's vision play "Hannele," will probably arouse a new and greater opposition this season

ALEXANDER SALVINI AS "JANAK," FROM A PHOTOGRAPH BY SARONY, NEW YORK.

by producing Ilario's "Christ at the Feast of the Purim." This and another play by Hauptmann include the same objectionable feature that aroused indignation at the time of the production of "Hannele"—the impersonation of Christ upon the stage. Up to the time of "Hannele's" production this had been attempted in a New York theatre but once, and that was when Salmi Morse prepared a version of the "Passion Play," which was promptly suppressed by the police.

Lacking in original work by American dramatists as the season will be, it will be still more lacking in original work by American composers and librettists. The only particularly notable matters of this sort to be offered to the public this winter are "Rob Roy," the joint work of De Koven and Smith, and "Prince Ananias," the new medium for the farce and melody of our most famous native operatic organization —the "Bostonians."

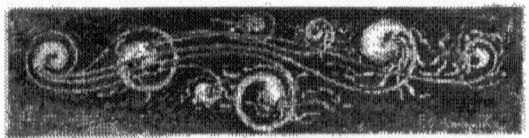

MR. MOODY: SOME IMPRESSIONS AND FACTS.

By HENRY DRUMMOND, LL.D., F.R.S.E., F.G.S.

Author of "Natural Law in the Spiritual World," "The Greatest Thing in the World," "The Ascent of Man," etc.

SECOND PAPER.

IN the year 1889 Mr. Moody broke out in a new place. Not content with having founded two great schools at Northfield, he turned his attention to Chicago, and inaugurated there one of his most successful enterprises—the Bible Institute. This scheme grew out of many years' thought. The general idea was to equip lay workers—men and women—for work among the poor, the outcast, the churchless, and the illiterate. In every centre of population there is a call for such help. The demand for city missionaries, Bible readers, evangelists, superintendents of Christian and philanthropic institutions, is unlimited. In the foreign field it is equally claimant. Mr. Moody saw that all over the country were those who, with a little special training, might become effective workers in these various spheres—some whose early opportunities had been neglected; some who were too old or too poor to go to college; and others who, half their time, had to earn their living. To meet such workers and such work the Institute was conceived.

THE BIBLE INSTITUTE IN CHICAGO.

The heart of Chicago, both morally and physically, offered a suitable site, and here, adjoining the Chicago Avenue Church, a preliminary purchase of land was made at a cost of fifty-five thousand dollars. On part of this land, for a similar sum, a three-storied building was put up to accommodate male students, while three houses, already standing on the property, were transformed into a ladies' department. No sooner were the doors opened than some ninety men and fifty women began work. So immediate was the response that all the available accommodation was used up, and important enlargements have had to be made since. The mornings at the Institute are largely given up to Bible study and music, the afternoons to private study and visitation, and the evenings to evangelistic work. In the second year of its existence no fewer than two hundred and forty-eight students were on the roll-book. In addition to private study, these conducted over three thousand meetings, large and small, in the city and neighborhood, paid ten thousand visits to the homes of the poor, and "called in" at more than a thousand saloons.

As to the ultimate destination of the workers, the statistics for this same year record the following:

At work in India are three, one man and two women; in China, three men and one woman, with four more (sexes equally divided) waiting appointment there; in Africa, two men and two women, with two men and one woman waiting appointment; in Turkey, one man and five women; in South America, one man and one woman; in Bulgaria, Persia, Burma, and Japan, one woman to each. Among the North American Indians, three women and one man. In the home field, in America, are thirty-seven men and nine women employed in evangelistic work, thirty-one in pastoral work (including many ministers who had come for further study), and twenty-nine in other schools and colleges. Sunday-school missions employ five men; home missions, two; the Young Men's Christian Association, seven; the Young Women's Christian Association, two. Five men and one woman are "singing evangelists." Several have positions in charitable institutions, others are evangelists, and twenty are teachers. It will be allowed that this is a pretty fair record for a two-years' old institute. As Mr. Moody gives it much of his time, spending many months there annually in personal superintendence, there can be little doubt as to its future.

THE NORTHFIELD TRAINING SCHOOL FOR WOMEN.

Not quite on the same lines, but with certain features in common, is still a fourth institution founded by the evangelist at Northfield about the same time. This is, perhaps, one of his most original developments—the Northfield Training School for Women. In his own work at Chicago, and in his evangelistic rounds among the churches, he had learned to appreciate the exceptional value of women in ministering to the poor. He saw, however, that women of the right stamp were not always to be found where they were needed most, and in many cases where they were to be found, their work was marred by inexperience and lack of training. He determined, therefore, to start a novel species of training school, which city churches and mission fields could draw upon, not for highly educated missionaries, but for Christian women who had undergone a measure of special instruction, especially in Bible knowledge and *domestic economy*—the latter being the special feature. The initial obstacle of a building in which to start his institute was no difficulty to Mr. Moody. Among the many great buildings of Northfield there was one which, every winter, was an eyesore to him. It was the Northfield Hotel, and it was an eye-sore because it was empty. After the busy season in summer, it was shut up from October till the end of March, and Mr. Moody resolved that he would turn its halls into lecture rooms, its bedrooms into dormitories, stock the first with teachers and the second with scholars, and start the work of the Training School as soon as the last guest was off the premises.

In October, 1890, the first term opened. Six instructors were provided, and fifty-six students took up residence at once. Next year the numbers were almost doubled, and the hotel college to-day is in a fair way to become a large and important institution. In addition to systematic Bible study, which forms the backbone of the curriculum, the pupils are taught those branches of domestic economy which are most likely to be useful in their work among the homes of the poor. Much stress is laid upon cooking, especially the preparation of foods for the sick, and a distinct department is also devoted to dressmaking. An objection was raised at the outset that the students, during their term of residence, were isolated from the active Christian work in which their lives were to be spent, and that hence the most important part of their training must be merely theoretical. But this difficulty has solved itself. Though not contemplated at the founding of the school, the living energy and enthusiasm of the students have sought their own outlets; and now, all through the winter, flying columns may be found scouring the country-side in all directions, visiting the homesteads, and holding services in hamlets, cottages, and schoolhouses.

MR. MOODY UNDENOMINATIONAL AND UNSECTARIAN IN HIS WORKS.

Like all Mr. Moody's institutions, the winter Training Home is undenominational and unsectarian. It is a peculiarity of Northfield, that every door is open not only to the Church Universal, but to the world. Every State in the Union is represented among the students of his two great colleges, and almost every nation and race. On the college books are, or have been, Africans, Armenians, Turks, Syrians, Austrians, Hungarians, Canadians, Danes, Dutch, English, French, German, Indian, Irish, Japanese, Chinese, Norwegians, Russians, Scotch, Swedish, Alaskans, and Bulgarians. These include every type of Christianity, members of every Christian denomination, and disciples of every Christian creed. Twenty-two denominations, at least, have shared the hospitality of the schools. This, for a religious educational institution, is itself a liberal education; and that Mr. Moody should not only have permitted, but encouraged, this cosmopolitan and unsectarian character, is a witness at once to his sagacity and to his breadth.

With everything in his special career, in his habitual environment, and in the traditions of his special work, to make him intolerant, Mr. Moody's sympathies have only broadened with time. Some years ago the Roman Catholics in Northfield determined to build a church. They went round the township collecting subscriptions, and by and by approached Mr. Moody's door. How did he receive them? The narrower evangelical would have shut the door in their faces, or opened it only to give them a lecture on the blasphemies of the Pope or the iniquities of the Scarlet Woman. Mr. Moody gave them one of the handsomest subscriptions on their list. Not content with that, when their little chapel was finished, he presented them with an organ. "Why," he exclaimed, when some one challenged the action, "if they are Roman Catholics, it is better they should be good Roman Catholics than bad. It is surely better to have a Catholic Church than none; and as for the organ, if they are to have music in their church, it is better to have good music. Besides," he added, "these are my own townspeople. If ever I am to be of the least use to them, surely I must help them." What the kindly feeling did for them, it is difficult to say; but what it did for Mr. Moody, is matter of local history. For, a short time after, it was rumored that he was going to build a church, and the site was pointed out by the villagers—a rocky knoll close by the present hotel. One day Mr. Moody found the summit of this knoll covered with great piles of stones. The Roman Catholics had taken their teams up the mountain, and brought down, as a return present, enough building-stone to form the foundations of his church.

Mr. Moody's relations with the Northfield people and with all the people for miles and miles around are of the same type. So far from being without honor in his own country, it is there he is honored most. This fact—and nothing more truly decisive of character can be said—may be verified even by the stranger on the cars. The nearer he approaches Northfield, the more thorough and genuine will he find the appreciation of Mr. Moody; and when he passes under Mr. Moody's own roof, he will find it truest, surest, and most affectionate of all. It is forbidden here to invade the privacy of Mr. Moody's home. Suffice it to say that no more perfect homelife exists in the world, and that one only begins to know the greatness, the tenderness, and the simple beauty of this man's character when one sees him at his own fireside. One evidence of this greatness it is difficult to omit recording. If you were to ask Mr. Moody—which it would never occur to you to do—what, apart from the inspirations of his personal faith, was the secret of his success, of his happiness and usefulness in life, he would assuredly answer, "Mrs. Moody."

THE WIDE REACH OF MR. MOODY'S LABORS.

When one has recorded the rise and progress of the four institutions which have been named, one but stands on the threshold of the history of the tangible memorials of Mr. Moody's career. To realize even partially the intangible results of his life, is not within the compass of man's power; but even the tangible results—the results which have definite visible outcome, which are capable of statistical expression, which can be seen in action in different parts of the world to-day—it would tax a diligent historian to tabulate. The sympathies and activities of men like D. L. Moody are supposed by many to be wasted on the empty air. It will surprise them to be told that he is probably responsible for more actual stone and lime than almost any man in the world. There is scarcely a great city in England where he has not left behind him some visible memorial. His progress through Great Britain and Ireland, now nearly twenty years ago, is marked to-day by halls, churches, institutes, and other buildings which owe their existence directly to his influence. In the capital of each of these countries—in London, Edinburgh, and Dublin—great buildings stand to-day which, but for him, had had no existence. In the city where these words are written, at least three important institutions, each the centre of much work and of a multitude of workers, Christian philanthropy owes to him. Young Men's Christian Associations all over the land have been housed, and in many cases sumptuously housed, not only largely by his initiative, but by his personal actions in raising funds. Mr. Moody is the most magnificent beggar Great Britain has ever known. He will talk over a millionnaire in less time than it takes other men to apologize for intruding upon his time. His gift for extracting money amounts to genius. The hard, the sordid, the miserly, positively melt before him. But his power to deal with refractory ones is not the best of it. His supreme success is with the already liberal, with those who give, or think they give, handsomely already. These he somehow convinces that their giving are nothing at all; and there are multitudes of rich men in the world who would confess that Mr. Moody inaugurated for them, and for their churches and cities, the day of large subscriptions. The process by which he works is, of course, a secret, but one half of it probably depends upon two things. In the first place, his appeals are wholly for others; for places—I am speaking of England—in which he would never set foot again; for causes in which he had no personal stake. In the second place, he always knew the right moment to strike.

HOW MR. MOODY ORGANIZED A GREAT CHARITY IN TEN MINUTES.

On one occasion, to recall an illustration of the last he had convened a great conference in Liverpool. The theme for discussion was a favorite one—"How to reach the masses." One of the speakers, the Rev. Charles Garrett, in a powerful speech, expressed his conviction that the chief want of the masses in Liverpool was the institution of cheap houses of refreshment to counteract the saloons. When he had finished, Mr. Moody called upon him to speak for ten minutes more. That ten minutes might almost be said to have been a crisis in the social history of Liverpool. Mr. Moody spent it in whispered conversation with gentlemen on the platform. No sooner was the speaker done than Mr. Moody sprang to his feet and announced that a company had been formed to carry out the objects Mr. Garrett had advocated; that various gentlemen, whom he named (Mr. Alexander Balfour, Mr. Samuel Smith, M. P., Mr. Lockhart, and others), had each taken one thousand shares of five dollars each, and that the subscription list would be open till the end of the meeting. The capital was gathered almost before the adjournment, and a company floated under the name of the "British Workman Company, Limited," which has not only worked a small revolution in Liverpool, but—what was not contemplated or wished for, except as an index of healthy business—paid a handsome dividend to the shareholders. For twenty years this company has gone on increasing; its ramifications are in every quarter of the city; it has returned ten per cent. throughout the whole period, except for one (strike) year, when it returned seven; and, above all, it has been copied by cities and towns innumerable all over Great Britain. To Mr. Garrett, who unconsciously set the ball a-rolling, the personal consequences were as curious as they were unexpected. "You must take charge of this thing," said Mr. Moody to him, "or at least you must keep your eye on it." "That cannot be," was the reply. "I am a Wesleyan; my three years in Liverpool have expired; I must pass to another circuit." "No," said Mr. Moody, "you must stay here." Mr. Garrett assured him it was quite impossible, the Methodist Conference made no exceptions. But Mr. Moody would not be beaten. He got up a petition to the Conference. It was granted—an almost unheard-of thing—and Mr. Garrett remains in his Liverpool church to this day. This last incident proves at least one thing—that Mr. Moody's audacity is at least equalled by his influence.

THE CHARACTER OF MR. MOODY'S GREATNESS.

rowed to its close. It is of small significance that one should make out this or the other man to be numbered among the world's great. But it is of importance to national ideals, that standards of worthiness should be truly drawn, and, when those who answer to them in real life appear, that they should be held up for the world's instruction. Mr. Moody himself has never asked for justice, and never for homage. The criticism which sours, and the adulation—an adulation at epochs in his life amounting to worship—which spoils, have left him alike untouched. The way he turned aside from applause in England struck multitudes with wonder. To be courted was to him not merely a thing to be discouraged on general principles; it simply made him miserable. At the close of a great meeting, when crowds, not of the base, but of the worthy, thronged the platform to press his hand, somehow he had always disappeared. When they followed him to his hotel, its doors were barred. When they wrote him, as they did in thousands, they got no response. This man would not be praised. Yet, partly for this very reason, those who love him love to praise him. And I may as well confess what has induced me, against keen personal dislike to all that is personal, to write these articles. One day, travelling in America last summer, a high dignitary of the Church in my presence made a contemptuous reference to Mr. Moody. A score of times in my life I have sailed in on such occasions, and at least taught the detractor some facts. On this occasion, with due humility, I asked the speaker if he had ever met him? He had not; and the reply elicited that the name which he had used so lightly was to him no more than an echo. I determined that, time being then denied, I would take the first opportunity of bringing that echo nearer him. It is for him these words were written.

WHITTIER'S OPINION OF MR. MOODY.

In the Life of Whittier, just published, the patronizing reference to Mr. Moody but too plainly confirms the statement with which the first article opened—that few men were less known to their contemporaries.

"Moody and Sankey," writes the poet,

good, and believe that he will reach and move some who could not be touched by James Freeman Clarke or Phillips Brooks. I cannot accept his theology, or part of it at least, and his methods are not to my taste. But if he can make the drunkard, the gambler, and the debauchee into decent men, and make the lot of their weariful wives and children less bitter, I bid him God-speed."

I have called these words patronizing, but the expression should be withdrawn. Whittier was incapable of that. They are broad, large-hearted, even kind. But they are not the right words. They are the stereotyped charities which sweet natures apply to anything not absolutely harmful, and contain no more impression of the tremendous intellectual and moral force of *the man behind* than if the reference were to the obscurest Salvation Army zealot. I shall not indorse, for it could only give offence, the remark of a certain author of world-wide repute when he read the words: "Moody! Why, he could have put half a dozen Whittiers in his pocket, and they would never have been noticed;" but I shall indorse, and with hearty good-will, a judgment which he further added. "I have always held," he said—and he is a man who has met every great contemporary thinker from Carlyle downward—"that in sheer brain-size, in the mere raw material of intellect, Moody stands among the first three or four great men I have ever known." I believe Great Britain is credited with having "discovered" Mr. Moody. It may or may not be; but if it be, it was men of the quality and the experience of my friend who made the discovery; and that so many distinguished men in America have failed to appreciate him is a circumstance which has only one explanation—that they have never had the opportunity.

An American estimate, nevertheless, meets my eye as I lay down the pen, which I gladly plead space for, as it proves that in Mr. Moody's own country there are not wanting those who discern how much he stands for. They are the notes, slightly condensed, of one whose opportunities for judging of his life and work have been exceptionally wide. In his opinion:

1. "No other living man has done so much directly in the way of uniting man to God, and in restoring men to their true centre.

2. "No other living man has done so much to unite man with man, to break down personal grudges and ecclesiastical barriers, bringing into united worship and harmonious coöperation men of diverse views and dispositions.

3. "No other living man has set so many other people to work, and developed, by awakening the sense of responsibility, latent talents and powers which would otherwise have lain dormant.

4. "No other living man, by precept and example, has so vindicated the rights, privileges, and duties of laymen.

5. "No other living man has raised more money for other people's enterprises.

6. "No other evangelist has kept himself so aloof from fads, religious or otherwise; from isms, from special reforms, from running specific doctrines, or attacking specific sins; has so concentrated his life upon the one supreme endeavor."

If one-fourth of this be true, it is a unique and noble record; if all be true, which of us is worthy even to characterize it?

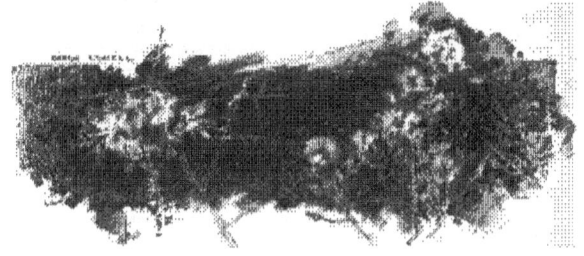

Three Men and Two Bears

Cy Warman

AN old prospecting partner of Mr. Creede's told the following story to the writer, after the discovery of the Amethyst, which lifted the discoverer into prominence, gave him fame and a bank account, and gave every adventuress who heard of his fortune a new field:

Creede and I, together with a man by the name of Chester, were prospecting in San Miguel County, Colorado, in the '80's. We had our camp in a narrow cañon by a little mountain stream. It was summer time; the berries were ripe, and bear were as thick as sheep in New Mexico. About sunset one evening I called Creede out to show him a cow which I had discovered on a steep hillside near our cabin.

The moment the Captain saw the animal he said in a stage whisper, "Bear!" I thought he was endeavoring to frighten me; but he soon convinced me that he was in earnest.

Without taking his eyes from the animal, he spoke again in the same stage whisper, instructing me to hasten and bring Chester with a couple of rifles. When I returned I gave the rifle I carried to Creede, who instructed me to climb upon a sharp rock that stood up like a church spire in the bottom of the cañon. From my high place I was to signal the sharp-shooters, keeping them posted as to the movements of the bear.

"You come with me," said Creede to Chester, who stood at his side. It occurred to me now for the first time that there was some danger attached to this sport. I couldn't help wondering what would become of me in case the bear got the best of my two partners. If the bear captured them and got possession of the only two guns in the camp, my position on that rock would become embarrassing, if not actually dangerous.

I turned to look at Chester, who did not seem to start when Creede did. Poor fellow, he was pale as a ghost. "See here," he said, addressing Creede, who was looking back, smiling and beckoning him on as he led the way down toward the noisy little creek which they must cross to get in rifle range of the bear, "I'm a man of family, an' don't see why I should run headlong into a fight with a grizzly bear. I suppose if I was a single man, I would do as you do, but when I think of my poor wife and dear little children, it makes me homesick." Creede kept smiling and beckoning with his forefinger. I laughed at Chester for being so scared. He finally followed, after asking me to look after his family in case he failed to return; just as a man would who was on his way to the Tower.

Having reached the summit of the rock, I was surprised to see the big bear coming down the hill headed for the spot where the hunters stood counselling as to how they should proceed. I tried to shout a warning to them, but the creek made such a noise falling over the rocks that they were unable to hear me.

A moment more and she hove in sight, coming down the slope on a long gallop. Probably no man living ever had such an entertainment as I was about to witness. In New York ten thousand people would pay a hundred dollars a seat to see it; but there was no time to bill the country—the curtain was up and the show was on. Creede, who was the first to see the animal, shot one swift glance at his companion, raised his rifle, a Marlin repeater, and fired. The great beast shook her head, snorted, increased her pace, and bore down upon her assailants. Again and again Creede's rifle rang out upon the evening air, and hearing no report from Chester's gun, he turned, and to his horror, saw his companion, rifle in hand, running for camp. Many a man would have wasted a shot on the deserter, but Creede was too busy with the bear, even if he had been so inclined. Less than forty feet separated the combatants when Creede turned, and at the next shot I was pleased to see the infuriated animal drop and roll upon the ground. In another second she was up again, and she looked more like a

CREEDE STOOD STILL AS A STATUE WITH ONE FOOT RESTING ON THE BODY OF THE DEAD BEAR.

ball of blood than an animal. Now she mal. One eye had been forced from the stood up for the final struggle. I saw Creede socket, and stood out like a great ball of

I did not shout now. This was the third time I had seen him kill all that same bear, and I expected her to get up again. Creede himself was not quite satisfied, for I saw him hastily filling his magazine; and it was well.

The hunter stepped up to the great dead animal and placed his feet upon her, as hunters are wont to do, when another danger confronted him.

Attracted by the shooting and the cries of the wounded bear, her mate came bounding down the slope to her rescue.

The first act had been interesting, but I confess that I was glad when the curtain dropped. Creede was tired. Even an experienced hunter could hardly be expected to go through such a performance without experiencing some anxiety. I almost held my breath as the second bear bore down upon him. Nearer and nearer he came, and Creede had not even raised his rifle to his shoulder. Now the bear was less than twenty feet away, and Creede stood still as a statue with one foot resting on the body of the dead bear.

I was so excited that I shouted to him to shoot, but he never knew it; and if he had known, it would have made no difference.

At last the bear stopped within eight feet of him, and bear-like, stood up. Now the rifle was leveled, and it seemed to me it would never go, but it did. The bullet broke the bear's neck, and he fell down dead at the hunter's feet.

WHAT IS SAID ABOUT THE "McCLURE'S" LIFE OF NAPOLEON AND ABOUT THE MAGAZINE ITSELF.

The paid monthly circulation of this magazine has increased forty thousand copies in two months. The press has been no less emphatic in its approval.

WHAT IS SAID OF THE McCLURE'S LIFE OF NAPOLEON.

A LETTER FROM ONE OF OUR READERS.

NOVEMBER 30, 1894.

EDITOR McCLURE'S MAGAZINE,
New York.

DEAR SIR,—I congratulate you on the excellence of your Napoleonic pictures and the charming biography that accompanies them.

You deserve the thanks of every student of the history of that period for having made Mr. Hubbard's superb collection accessible to the readers of your magazine, and you are well worthy of the success that evidently attends you.

I was also highly pleased with Mr. Mitchell's paper on Mr. Dana in the October number. I venture to say that a series of articles by Mr. Dana on his relations with President Lincoln and the events of his time would be valuable and very readable. I am aware that that particular period has been pretty extensively covered, but few of those who have written about it have had the advantages for observation, and none the discernment and attractive literary style, of Mr. Dana. I am prompted to make this suggestion because I read, only yesterday, an extract from an interview with him referring to an incident that occurred the night of Mr. Lincoln's second election.

Hoping you will favor your readers with such a series, I am, with the sincerest hopes for your continued success,

Respectfully yours,
P. A. PHILBIN, *Archbald, Penn.*

We are very grateful to Mr. Philbin for his kind letter. The editors of McCLURE'S MAGAZINE have every reason to believe that Mr. Dana's reminiscences of Lincoln will form part of a series of papers on Lincoln which they are planning for the magazine, and which will consist mainly of the recollections of men now living who knew Lincoln.

THE BEST SHORT LIFE OF NAPOLEON.

The success of Mr. McClure's publication has been enormous. It is a new comer among the magazines, and, of course, lost money for a time. Most good things do, to begin with. But now the presses are kept at work for six weeks (counting time by ordinary working days) to supply the demand for it, and the fortune and fame of its energetic and original publisher are assured. The Napoleon series, of which the second installment is given in McClure's Christmas number, is, by the way, the best short life of Napoleon we have ever seen, and its illustrations are admirable.—*New York Press.*

A CONTRIBUTION OF THE GREATEST VALUE.

McCLURE'S MAGAZINE begins in the November number the publication of a series of seventy-five portraits of Napoleon at successive stages in his life. This unique exhibit promises to be a contribution of the greatest value to the exhaustive study of Napoleon's career that is occupying so much attention at this time.—*Washington (D. C.) Pathfinder.*

AN ADMIRABLE LIFE OF NAPOLEON.

McCLURE'S MAGAZINE for November begins an admirable life of Napoleon, which promises to arouse the deepest interest among readers.—*Washington (D. C.) Tribune.*

PAINSTAKING AND ATTRACTIVE.

It is familiar [the Napoleon biography] with the latest as well as with older data, and is so painstaking in search that it brings out much that is new to most readers. It recognizes the scientific spirit of modern historical criticism, and is finished and attractive in style. — *Boston (Mass.) Globe.*

NAPOLEON PORTRAITS UNIQUE AND REMARKABLE.

MCCLURE'S MAGAZINE has the first part of a great pictorial life of Napoleon. The special feature of this work is the great number of rare portraits of Napoleon, his family, and his generals. In this number we have many portraits taken when he was general-in-chief of the army of Italy, and the collection is unique and remarkable. Another article in this number which will attract attention is the story of Allan Pinkerton's thwarting the assassination of Lincoln. — *Augusta (Me.) Age.*

BEST PROCURABLE PORTRAITS.

I like MCCLURE'S MAGAZINE because it is the most timely publication published but twelve times a year. If there is anything occupying the public mind, there will be something about it in MCCLURE'S, and it will be well written, and well illustrated, and loading over with interesting facts. Just at present, Napoleon is the character of the day. Of course, all of the magazines are telling much about the "war god," as the greatest fighter since his day called the First Consul. But that did not satisfy MCCLURE. When a person is much talked about, the first question asked is, "What did he look like?" That is what MCCLURE is answering. The last number presented a beautiful collection of the best procurable portraits of the "Little Corporal." They are beautiful works of art — and timely. — *Harrisburg (Pa.) Telegram.*

The Bonaparte portraits in MCCLURE'S are one of the most interesting features appearing in magazine literature this year. — *Milwaukee (Wis.) Journal.*

MCCLURE'S MAGAZINE branches out into a most interesting field with its November number in giving the first instalment of a great pictorial life of Napoleon Bonaparte. — *Piedmont (W. Va.) Herald.*

Its illustrated life of Napoleon is worth double the subscription price asked for it. — *Havre de Grace (Md.) Republican.*

MCCLURE'S for November (New York) has its own excellent condensed life of Napoleon now begun, by Ida M. Tarbell. — *Brooklyn (N. Y.) Daily Eagle.*

MCCLURE'S for November has one feature that is worth the price of the magazine. It is the portraits of Napoleon and Lincoln. — *Harrisburg (Pa.) Telegram.*

A very notable series of articles and portraits, forming a pictorial life of Napoleon, commences in the current number of MCCLURE'S MAGAZINE. The interest in the romantic career of the young Corsican soldier who became well nigh the master of Europe is perennial, and this remarkable collection of portraits, beginning with the young lieutenant of twenty-two and going on through every stage of his career up to the time when the death mask was taken at St. Helena, cannot but attract attention. — *Cambridge (Mass.) Tribune.*

Besides her pleasing style, Miss Tarbell brings to this work a three years' study of French and English history of the Napoleonic period. — *Minneapolis (Minn.) Tribune.*

Napoleon and Lincoln stand out in many portraits in the November MCCLURE'S. Napoleon had great beauty, and it is given here through many eyes. Greuze, Guérin, Le Gros, Cossia, Northcote, Appiani, Craig, with pictures of the bust by Ceracchi, give so many impressions of that conquering face that one is moved to wonder if it be possible truly to preserve the exact likeness of any one. Out of all these and the many others there grows up in time a sort of composite impression on the popular mind which stands for Bonaparte, and perhaps that composite is the truest truth. — *San Francisco Impress.*

WHAT IS SAID ABOUT THE MAGAZINE.

Although among the youngest, if not the youngest, of American magazines, MCCLURE'S is one of the most popular, and is constantly increasing its already large number of admirers. — *Augusta (Me.) Journal.*

MCCLURE'S MAGAZINE for November challenges public admiration, both in its illustrations and in its literary contents. No magazine within the past year has come to the front more rapidly in popular favor. The literary feature of MCCLURE'S for the coming year is the publication of a new life of Napoleon, with an exhaustive series of Napoleon portraits and other pictures. — *Topeka (Kan.) Democrat.*

It is seldom one is given the pleasure of reading a monthly with as much that is from the best authors as is found in MCCLURE'S for this month. — *Albany (N. Y.) Times-Union.*

The rapid success of MCCLURE'S is something phenomenal, but it has been won by pluck and perseverance. — *Philadelphia (Pa.) Ledger.*

One of the brightest magazines which finds its way to our desk is MCCLURE'S. It is only a few months old, and yet it has attained to a degree of popularity unparalleled in the history of magazines. — *Watertown (Conn.) Journal.*

There is a living personal interest in the character of literature furnished by MCCLURE'S MAGAZINE that differentiates it from any other of the monthly publications which have grown popular through years of established merit and usefulness.

There is less of miscellany, and more in the nature of biography and personal reminiscence, in MCCLURE'S than in any other of the established magazines, and it holds popular attention and interest in proportion. Men love to read about men of flesh and blood, rather than fictitious heroes. We gather more pleasure, and feel a nearer sympathy with the frailties, the failures and successes of some men we know personally, or by reputation, than we do in the imaginary events in the life of an imaginary character. The December number of MCCLURE'S furnishes quite a diverse bill of fare in its sketches of Napoleon, of Bret Harte, of Evangelist Moody, and the sensational experience of the Pinkerton detective, James McParland, who was detailed to ferret out the famous Molly Maguires.

The great interest that is kindled among reading people at this time in all that pertains to Napoleon is being met by the Tarbell papers on Napoleon, illustrated with portraits from the collection of Hon. Gardiner G. Hubbard, probably the finest private collection of Napoleon pictures in the world. — *From Editorial in the Augusta (Ga.) Chronicle.*

McCLURE'S MAGAZINE.

Vol. IV.   FEBRUARY, 1895.   No. 3.

NAPOLEON BONAPARTE.

BY IDA M. TARBELL.

With engravings from the collection of the Hon. Gardiner G. Hubbard, who also furnishes the explanatory notes.

FOURTH PAPER.—NAPOLEON THE KING-MAKER. 1803–1807.

RUPTURE OF THE TREATY OF AMIENS.

IN the spring of 1803 the treaty of Amiens, which a year before had ended the long war with England, was broken. Both countries had many reasons for complaint. Napoleon was angry at the failure to evacuate Malta. The perfect freedom allowed the press in England gave the pamphleteers and caricaturists of the country opportunity to criticise and ridicule him. He complained bitterly to the English ambassadors of this free press, an institution in his eyes impractical and idealistic. He complained, too, of the hostile *émigrés* allowed to collect in Jersey; of the presence in England of such notorious enemies of his as Georges Cadoudal; and of the sympathy and money the Bourbon princes and many nobles of the old regime received in London society. Then, too, he regarded the country as his natural and inevitable enemy. England to Napoleon was only a little island which, like Corsica and Elba, naturally belonged to France, and he considered it part of his business to get possession of her.

England, on the other hand, looked with distrust at the extension of Napoleon's influence on the Continent. Northern Italy, Switzerland, Holland, Parma, Elba, were under his protectorate. She had been deeply offended by a report published in Paris, on the condition of the Orient, in which the author declared that with six thousand men the French could reconquer Egypt; and she resented the violent articles in the official press of Paris in answer to those of the free press of England. Her aristocratic spirit, too, was irritated by Napoleon's success. She despised this *parvenu*, this "Corsican scoundrel," as Nelson called him, who had had the hardihood to rise so high by other than the conventional methods for getting on in the world which she sanctioned.

Real and fancied aggressions continued throughout the year of the peace; and when the break finally came, though both nations persisted in declaring that they did not want war, both were in a thoroughly war-like mood.

THE DESCENT ON ENGLAND.

Napoleon's preparations against England form one of the most picturesque military movements in his career. Unable to cope with his enemy at sea, he conceived the audacious notion of invading the island, and laying siege to London itself. The plan briefly was this—to gather a great army on the north shore of France, and in some port a flotilla sufficient to transport it to Great Britain. In order to prevent interference with this expedition, he would

THE EMPEROR NAPOLEON I. BESTOWING THE CROSS OF HONOR ON PRISONERS. 1804.
From a painting by David.

NAPOLEON THE GREAT ("NAPOLÉON LE GRAND") IN CORONATION ROBES. 1805.
Painted and engraved by order of the emperor. Engraved by Desnoyers, after portrait painted by Gérard in 1805

keep the English fleet occupied in the Mediterranean, or in the Atlantic, until the critical moment. Then, leading it by stratagem in the wrong direction, he would call his own fleet to the Channel to protect his passage. He counted to be in London, and to have compelled the English to peace, before Nelson could return from the chase he would have led him.

The preparations began at once. The

port chosen for the flotilla was Boulogne; but the whole coast from Antwerp to the mouth of the Seine bristled with iron and bronze. Between Calais and Boulogne, at Cape Gris Nez, where the navigation was the most dangerous, the batteries literally touched one another. Fifty thousand men were put to work at the stupendous excavations necessary to make the ports large enough to receive the flotilla. Large numbers of troops were brought rapidly into the neighborhood; fifty thousand men to Boulogne, under Soult; thirty thousand to Etaples, under Ney; thirty thousand to Ostend, under Davoust; reserves to Arras, Amiens, Saint-Omer.

The work of preparing the flat-bottomed boats, or walnut-shells, as the English called them, which were to carry over the army, went on in all the ports of Holland and France, as well as in interior towns situated on rivers leading to the sea. The troops were taught to row, each soldier being obliged to practise two hours a day, so that the rivers of all the north of France were dotted with land-lubbers handling the oar, the most of them for the first time.

In the summer of 1803, Napoleon went to the north to look after the work. His trip was one long ovation. *Le Chemin d'Angleterre* was the inscription the people of Amiens put on the triumphal arch erected to his honor, and town vied with town in showing its joy at the proposed descent on the old-time enemy.

Such was the interest of the people, that a thousand projects were suggested to help on the armament, some of them most amusing. In a learned and thoroughly serious memorial, one genius proposed that while the flotilla was preparing, the sailors be employed in catching dolphins, which should be shut up in the ports, tamed, and taught to wear a harness, so as to be driven, in the water, of course, as horses are on land. This novel cavalry was to transport the French to the opposite side of the Channel.

Napoleon not only occupied himself with the preparations at Boulogne and with keeping Nelson busy elsewhere. He had his eye on every point of the earth where he might be weak, or where he might weaken his enemy. Louisiana he sold to the United States. It gave him twelve million dollars to carry on his war, and removed a weak spot where England was sure to harass him if hostilities were prolonged. He took possession of Hanover. The Irish were promised aid in their efforts for freedom. "Provided that twenty thousand united Irishmen join the French army on its landing," France is to give them in return twenty-five thousand men, forty thousand muskets, with artillery and ammunition, and a promise that the French government will not make peace with England until the independence of Ireland has been proclaimed.

An attack on India was planned, his hope being that the princes of India would welcome an invader who would aid them in throwing off the English yoke. To strengthen himself in the Orient, he sought by letters and envoys to win the confidence, as well as to inspire the awe, of the rulers of Turkey and Persia.

PLOT AGAINST THE FIRST CONSUL.

While the preparation for the invasion was going on, the feeling against England was intensified by the discovery of a plot against the life of the First Consul. Georges Cadoudal, a fanatical royalist, who had directed the plot of the 3d Nivôse, and who had since been in England, had formed a gigantic conspiracy, having as its object nothing less than the assassination of Napoleon in broad daylight, in the streets of Paris.

He had secured powerful aid to carry out his plan. The Bourbon princes supported him, and one of them was to land on the north coast to put himself at the head of the royalist sympathizers as soon as the First Consul was killed. In this plot was associated Pichegru, who had been connected with the 18th Fructidor. General Moreau, the hero of Hohenlinden, was suspected of knowing something of it.

It came to light in time, and a general arrest was made of those suspected of being privy to it. The first to be tried and punished was the Duc d'Enghien, who had been seized in Ettenheim, in Baden, a short distance from the French frontier, on the supposition that he had been coming secretly to Paris to be present at the meetings of the conspirators. His trial at Vincennes was short, his execution immediate. There is good reason to believe that Napoleon had no suspicion that the Duc d'Enghien would be executed so soon as he was, and even to suppose that he would have lightened the sentence if the punishment had not been pushed on with an irregularity and inhumanity that recalls the days of the Terror.

The execution was a severe blow to Napoleon's popularity, both at home and

THE BATTLE OF AUSTERLITZ, DECEMBER 2, 1805.

Engraved by Godefroy in 1812, after a painting by Gérard made in 1810. Gérard chose for his picture the moment in the battle when the Russian Imperial Guard fled towards Austerlitz. Rapp, he had met and finished however, announces the victory to Napoleon. Behind the emperor are grouped the staff officers, and Roustan others taller prisoner. The picture was painted for the ceiling of the hall of the Council of State in the Tuileries. It was taken from the palace at the Restoration, and was again in Gérard, who refused to sell it to the Duke of Wellington. It is now in the historical gallery of Versailles.

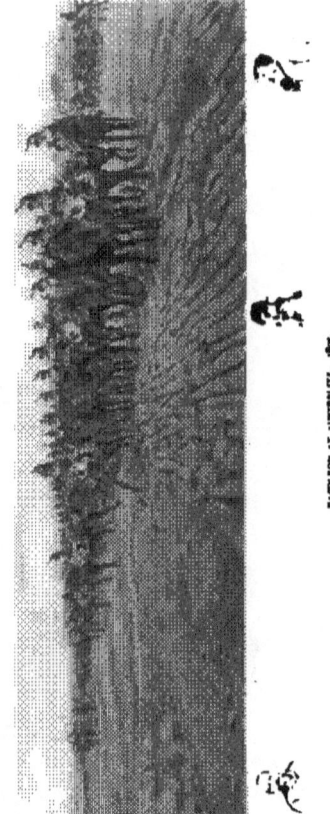

NAPOLEON AT AUSTERLITZ. 1805.

From a copyrighted etching by Jacquet, after Meissonier; reproduced by the kind permission of Mr. C. Klackner, owner of the etching. Meissonier devoted his composition from tactical descriptions of the battle. The foreground is occupied by a regiment of cuirassiers, while the emperor and staff occupy a position in the middle ground. The original picture, which forms part of the collection of the Duc d'Aumale at Chantilly, is the second upon this subject which Meissonier painted, the first having been accidentally destroyed by fire shortly after it was completed.

NAPOLEON. 1805.

Engraved by Morghen, after Gérard, in 1805. Napoleon wrote a letter thanking Morghen for the beauty of this engraving, and subsequently decorated him with the Legion of Honor.

abroad. Fouché's cynical remark was just: "The death of the Duc d'Enghien is worse than a crime; it is a blunder." Chateaubriand, who had accepted a foreign embassy, resigned at once, and a number of the old aristocracy, such as Pasquier and Molé, who had been saying among themselves that it was their duty to support Napoleon's splendid work of reorganization, went back into obscurity. In society the effect was distressing. The members of Napoleon's own household met him with averted faces and sad countenances, and Josephine wept until he

MEETING OF NAPOLEON AND FRANCIS II., EMPEROR OF AUSTRIA, AFTER THE BATTLE OF AUSTERLITZ, DECEMBER, 1805.

Engraved by Debucy, after Gros. Pointing to the nearest watchfire, Napoleon said: "I must receive your majesty in the only palace I have inhabited for two months." The emperor replied: "You make so good use of it that you must find it very pleasant."

called her a child who understood nothing of politics. Abroad there was a revulsion of sympathy, particularly in the cabinets of Russia, Prussia, and Austria.

The trial of Cadoudal and M o r e a u followed. The former with several of his accomplices was executed. Moreau was exiled for two years. Pichegru committed suicide in the Temple.

EMPEROR OF THE FRENCH.

This plot showed Napoleon and his friends that a Jacobin or royalist fanatic might any day end the life upon which the scheme of reorganization depended. It is true he had already been made First Consul for life by a practically unanimous vote, but there was need of strengthening his position and providing a succession. In March, six days after the death of the Duc d'Enghien, the Senate proposed to him that he complete his work and take the throne. In April the Council of State and the Tribunate took up the discussion. The opinion of the majority was voiced by Regnault de Saint Jean d'Angély: "It is a long time since all reasonable men, all true friends of their country, have wished that the First Consul would make himself emperor, and reëstablish, in favor of his family, the old principles of hereditary succession. It is the only means of securing permanency to the old fortune, and to the men whom merit has raised to high offices. The Republic, which I loved passionately, while I detested the crimes of the Revolution,

NAPOLEON, EMPEROR OF THE FRENCH AND KING OF ITALY ("NAPOLÉON, EMPEREUR DES FRANÇAIS, ROI D'ITALIE"), 1806.

Engraved by Arnold, after Döbling. It was at Berlin, at the time of the entry of the French army, that Döbling saw the emperor and made his portrait in colors. Masson says that all the representations of Napoleon from 1806 to 1815 were copied after this design of Döbling.

NAPOLEON BONAPARTE.

THE RIGHT HONORABLE WILLIAM PITT. 1801.

Engraved by Cardon, after Eldridge, 1801. Pitt, born May 28, 1759, was the second son of William Pitt, Earl of Chatham. Before he was fifteen, went to Cambridge, where he made a remarkable record in mathematics and the classics. He studied law in Lincoln's Inn, and at the age of twenty-one became member of Parliament. His first speech, in favor of economical reform, made a great impression. At twenty-three he was made a member of the cabinet as Chancellor of the Exchequer. At twenty-four he became Premier, with an opposition including Fox, Burke, Sheridan, and North. His courage and determination were such, on the East India Company bill, that when Parliament was dissolved, and the country appealed to, he was supported as no minister in England had been for generations. He secured the passage of several important bills, and practically did away with the opposition. When the French Revolution came on, he at first endorsed it, but was revolted by its atrocities. He tried to avoid war with France, and was only driven into it by public opinion; but his military administration was feeble. The king, George III., refusing to second his plans for Irish relief, Pitt resigned in 1801, after eighteen years of nearly absolute power. When the treaty of Amiens was broken in 1803, he appeared in Parliament again, in favor of war, and the next year was recalled to the premiership. He had great difficulty, however, with his cabinet, and Napoleon's train of victories alarmed him. At last he fell sick from his anxiety. Trafalgar aroused him, but Austerlitz struck him a blow from which he could not rally, and he died January 13, 1806. He was honored with a public funeral, and his remains were placed in Westminster Abbey.

NAPOLEON AT JENA. 1806.

After Horace Vernet. This picture of Napoleon is a fragment of a great canvas representing the battle of Jena, found in the Hall of Battles at Versailles. Vernet was commissioned by Louis Philippe to paint the great battles of France when he first conceived the idea of converting the château into an historical museum. This particular picture is one of a series, including the battles of Friedland, Jena, and Wagram. It appeared in the salon of 1836.

is now in my eyes a mere Utopia. The First Consul has convinced me that he wishes to possess supreme power only to render France great, free, and happy, and to protect her against the fury of factions." The Senate soon after proceeded in a body to the Tuileries. "You have ex-

NAPOLEON, 1804.
Engraved in 1815 by Massard, after Roullion.

tricated us from the chaos of the past," said the spokesman, "you enable us to enjoy the blessings of the present; guarantee to us the future." On the 18th of May, 1804, when thirty-five years old, Napoleon was first addressed as "sire," and congratulated on his elevation to the throne of the French people.

IMPERIAL HONORS AND ETIQUETTE.

Immediately his household took on the forms of royalty. His mother was Madame Mère; Joseph, Grand-Elector, with the title of Imperial Highness; Louis, Constable, with the same title; his sisters were Imperial Highnesses. Titles were given to all officials; the ministers were excellencies; Cambacérès and Le Brun, the Second and Third Consuls, became Arch Chancellor and Arch Treasurer of the Empire. Of his old generals, Berthier, Murat, Moncey, Jourdan, Masséna, Augureau, Bernadotte, Soult, Brune, Lannes, Mortier, Ney, Davoust, and Bessières were made marshals. The red button of the Legion of Honor was scattered in profusion. The title of *citoyen*, which had been consecrated by the Revolution, was dropped, and hereafter everybody was called *monsieur*.

Two of Napoleon's brothers, unhappily, had no part in these honors. Jerome, who had been serving as lieutenant in the navy, had, in 1803, while in the United States, married a Miss Elizabeth Patterson of Baltimore. Napoleon forbade the recording of the marriage, and declared it void. As Jerome had not as yet given up his wife, he had no share in the imperial rewards. Lucien was likewise omitted, and for a

ENTRANCE OF THE FRENCH INTO BERLIN, OCTOBER 27, 1806.

Engraved by Bartlett, after Sverbeck.

ALEXANDER I. OF RUSSIA. 1805

Alexander I. of Russia was born at St. Petersburg in 1777; ascended the throne in 1801, after the murder of his father. His first acts were remarkably liberal. He recalled the banished, opened prisons, abolished the censorship, the torture, the public sale of serfs; founded schools, reformed the code, and did much to put Russia in the line of progress Western Europe was following. He entered into the first coalition against Napoleon in 1805, and suffered a defeat at Austerlitz in December of that year. The next year the battles of Eylau and Friedland drove him to make peace with Napoleon. The negotiations of Tilsit, where this peace was signed, were the beginning of a warm personal friendship between the two emperors, and Alexander consented to aid Napoleon in his vast scheme for conquering England. The fundamental part of this scheme, the continental blockade, at last bore too heavily on the Russians, and Napoleon's occupation of Oldenburg dissatisfied Alexander. The peace was broken in 1812, and Napoleon undertook the invasion of Russia. Alexander refused to come to any terms with his former friend, and in 1813 called Europe to arms itself against France. This coalition was fatal to Napoleon, who was driven to abdicate in 1814; and Alexander, who had pictured the Bourbons by his mild treatment of them, was the main instrument in the recall of the Bourbons. At the Congress of Vienna which followed, he succeeded in obtaining assent to his confiscation of Poland. After Waterloo Alexander returned with his troops to Paris, and consented to the rigorous measures taken against the country, but opposed its dismemberment. On leaving Paris he signed the Holy Alliance with Prussia and Austria, which had no real object opposition to the liberal principles of the Revolution. Alexander fell under new influences afterwards—English and Protestant. He closed the French theatres and opened Bible societies; became, under Madame Krüdener's influence, a devout follower of her mysticism, and received a deputation of Quakers, with whom he prayed and wept. Later he became severe and suspicious. He died in 1825.

similar reason. His first wife had died in 1801, and much against Napoleon's wishes he had married a Madame Jouberthon, to whom he was deeply attached; nothing could induce him to renounce his wife and take the Queen of Etruria, as Napoleon wished. The result of his refusal was a violent quarrel between the brothers, and Lucien left France.

This rupture was certainly a grief to Napoleon. Madame de Rémusat draws a pathetic little picture of the effect upon him of the last interview with Lucien:

"It was near midnight when Bonaparte came into the room; he was deeply dejected, and, throwing himself into an arm-chair, he exclaimed in a troubled voice, 'It is all over! I have broken with Lucien, and ordered him from my presence.' Madame Bonaparte began to expostulate. 'You are a good woman,' he said, 'to plead for him.' Then he rose from his chair, took his wife in his arms, and laid her head softly on his shoulder, and with his hand still resting on the beautiful head, which formed a contrast to the sad, set countenance so near it, he told us that Lucien had resisted all his entreaties, and that he had resorted equally in vain to both threats and persuasion. 'It is hard, though,' he added, 'to find in one's own family such stubborn opposition to interests of such magnitude. Must I, then, isolate myself from every one? Must I rely on myself alone? Well! I will suffice to myself; and you, Josephine—you will be my comfort always.'"

A fever of etiquette seized on all the inhabitants of the imperial palace of Saint Cloud. The ponderous regulations of Louis XIV. were taken down from the shelves in the library, and from them a code began to be compiled. Madame Campan, who had been First Bedchamber Woman to Marie Antoinette, was summoned to interpret the solemn law, and to describe costumes and customs. Monsieur de Talleyrand, who had been made Grand Chamberlain, was an authority who was consulted on everything.

"We all felt ourselves more or less elevated," says Madame de Rémusat. "Vanity is ingenious in its expectations, and ours were unlimited. Sometimes it was disenchanting, for a moment, to observe the almost ridiculous effect that this agitation produced upon

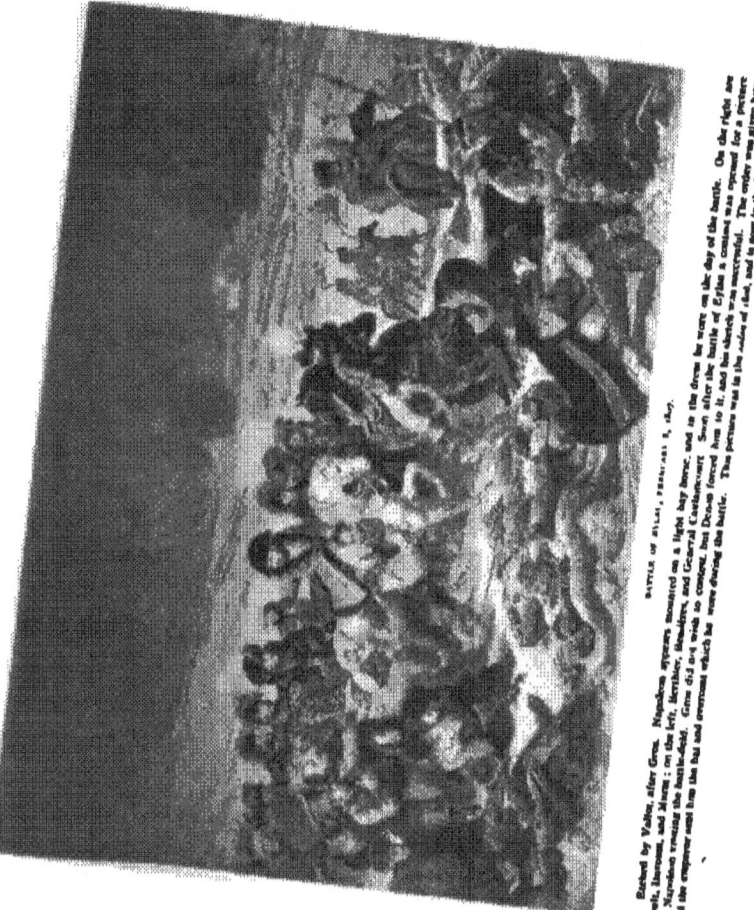

BATTLE OF AYLAU, FEBRUARY 8, 1807.

Etched by Vallot, after Gros. Napoleon appears mounted on a light bay horse, and in the dress he wore on the day of the battle. On the right are Soult, Berthier, and Murat; on the left, Berthier, Bessières, and General Corbineau. Soon after the battle of Eylau a contest was opened for a picture of Napoleon treating the battlefield. Gros did not wish to compete, but Denon forced him to it, and his sketch was accepted. The order was given him, and the composer sent him the first and prominent which he made during the battle. This picture was in the ancient club, and is now in the Louvre.

certain classes of society. Those who had nothing to do with our brand new dignities said with Montaigne, 'Let us avenge ourselves by railing at them.' Jests, more or less witty, and puns, more or less ingenious, were lavished on these new-made princes, and somewhat disturbed our brilliant visions; but the number of those who dare to censure success is small, and flattery was much more common than criticism."

No one was more severe in matters of etiquette than Napoleon himself. He studied the subject with the same attention that he did the civil code, and in much the same way. "In concert with M. de Ségur," he wrote De Champagny, "you must write me a report as to the way in which ministers and ambassadors should be received. . . . It will be well for you to enlighten me as to what was the practice at Versailles, and what is done at Vienna and St. Petersburg. Once my regulations adopted, everyone must conform to them. I am master, to establish what rules I like in France."

He had some difficulty with his old comrades-in-arms, who were accustomed to addressing him in the familiar second singular, and calling him Bonaparte, and who persisted, occasionally, even after he was "sire," in using the language of easy intimacy. Lannes was even removed for some time from his place near the emperor for an indiscretion of this kind.

THE FÊTE OF BOULOGNE.

In August, 1804, the new emperor visited Boulogne to receive the congratulations of his army and distribute decorations. His visit was celebrated by a magnificent *fête*. Those who know the locality of Boulogne, remember, north of the town, an amphitheatre-like plain, in the centre of which is a hill. In this plain sixty thousand men were camped. On the elevation was erected a throne. Here stood the chair of Dagobert; behind it the armor of Francis I.; and around rose scores of blood-stained, bullet-shot flags, the trophies of Italy and Egypt. Beside the emperor was the helmet of Bayard, filled with the decorations to be distributed. Up and down the coast were the French batteries; in the port lay the flotilla; to the right and left stretched the splendid army.

Just as the ceremonies were finished, a fleet of over a thousand boats came sailing into the harbor to join those already there, while out in the Channel English officers and sailors, with levelled glasses, watched from their vessels the splendid armament, which was celebrating its approaching descent on their shores.

CORONATION OF NAPOLEON AND JOSEPHINE.

On December 1st the Senate presented the emperor the result of the vote taken among the people as to whether hereditary succession should be adopted. There were two thousand five hundred and seventy-nine votes against; three million five hundred and seventy-five thousand for—a vote more nearly unanimous than that for the life consulate, there being something like nine thousand against him then.

The next day Napoleon was crowned at Notre Dame. The ceremony was prepared with the greatest care. Grand Master of Ceremonies de Ségur, aided by the painter David, drew up the plan and trained the court with great severity in the etiquette of the occasion. He had the widest liberty, it even being provided that "if it be indispensable, in order that the cortege may arrive at Notre Dame with greater facility, to pull down some houses," it should be done. By a master stroke of diplomacy Napoleon had persuaded Pope Pius VII. to cross the Alps to perform for him the solemn and ancient service of coronation.

Of this ceremony we have no better description than that of Madame Junot:

"Who that saw Notre Dame on that memorable day can ever forget it? I have witnessed in that venerable pile the celebration of sumptuous and solemn festivals; but never did I see anything at all approximating in splendor the spectacle exhibited at Napoleon's coronation. The vaulted roof reechoed the sacred chanting of the priests, who invoked the blessing of the Almighty on the ceremony about to be celebrated, while they awaited the arrival of the Vicar of Christ, whose throne was prepared near the altar. Along the ancient walls covered with magnificent tapestry were ranged, according to their rank, the different bodies of the state, the deputies from every city; in short, the representatives of all France assembled to implore the benediction of Heaven on the sovereign of the people's choice. The waving plumes which adorned the hats of the senators, counsellors of state and tribunes; the splendid uniforms of the military; the clergy in all their ecclesiastical pomp; and the multitude of young and beautiful women, glittering in jewels, and arrayed in that style of grace and elegance which is only seen in Paris;—altogether presented a picture which has, perhaps, rarely been equalled, and certainly never excelled.

"The Pope arrived first; and at the moment of his entering the Cathedral, the anthem *Tu es Petrus* was commenced. His Holiness advanced from the door with an air at once majestic and humble. Ere long, the firing of a cannon announced the departure of the procession from the Tuileries. From an early hour in the morning the weather had been exceeding

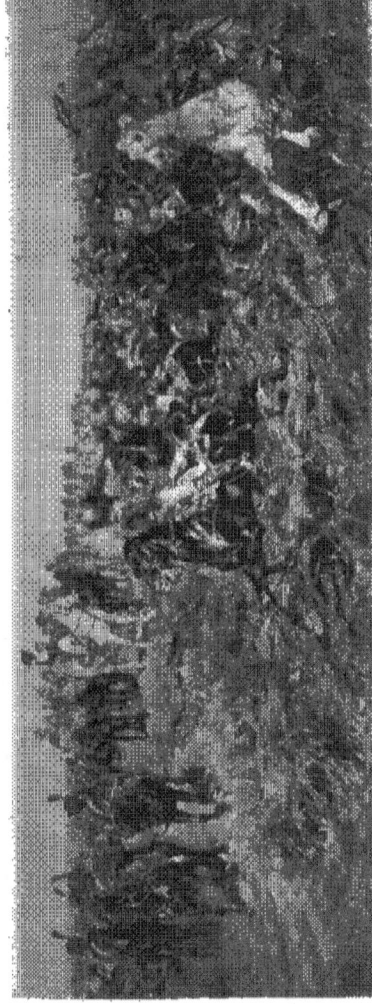

"1807." MEISSONIER AFTER FRIEDLAND.

Photographed from the original painting by Meissonier [ ] a companion piece to Meissonier's "1814." The original painting is now in the Metropolitan Museum, New York. The emperor, on a rising ground, is surrounded by his staff, amongst whom are his Marshals Soudere, Duroc, and Berthier. On his left and near Neumerly is waiting with his division for the signal to decide ; further back are seen the "Old Guard," with their grenadier caps and white breeches. Meissonier is said to have worked upon this picture for fifteen years. He modelled all the horses in wax, and every figure was drawn from the life. The painting was sold to Mr. A. T. Stewart of New York for about three hundred thousand francs (sixty thousand dollars).

unfavorable. It was cold and rainy, and appearances seemed to indicate that the procession would be anything but agreeable to those who joined it. But, as if by the especial favor of Providence, of which so many instances are observable in the career of Napoleon, the clouds suddenly dispersed, the sky brightened up, and the multitudes who lined the streets from the Tuileries to the Cathedral, enjoyed the sight of the procession without being, as they had anticipated, drenched by a December rain. Napoleon, as he passed along, was greeted by heartfelt expressions of enthusiastic love and attachment.

"On his arrival at Notre Dame, Napoleon ascended the throne, which was erected in front of the grand altar. Josephine took her place beside him, surrounded by the assembled sovereigns of Europe. Napoleon appeared singularly calm. I watched him narrowly, with a view of discovering whether his heart beat more highly beneath the imperial trappings than under the uniform of the guards; but I could observe no difference, and yet I was at the distance of only ten paces from him. The length of the ceremony, however, seemed to weary him; and I saw him several times check a yawn. Nevertheless, he did everything he was required to do, and did it with propriety. When the Pope anointed him with the triple unction on his head and both hands, I fancied, from the direction of his eyes, that he was thinking of wiping off the oil rather than of anything else; and I was so perfectly acquainted with the workings of his countenance, that I have no hesitation in saying that was really the thought that crossed his mind at that moment. During the ceremony of anointing, the Holy Father delivered that impressive prayer which concluded with these words: 'Diffuse, O Lord, by my hands, the treasures of your grace and benediction on your servant Napoleon, whom, in spite of our personal unworthiness, *we this day anoint emperor, in your name*.' Napoleon listened to this prayer with an air of pious devotion; but just as the Pope was about to take the crown, called the Crown of Charlemagne, from the altar, Napoleon seized it, and placed it on his own head. At that moment he was really handsome, and his countenance was lighted up with an expression of which no words can convey an idea.

"He had removed the wreath of laurel which he wore on entering the church, and which encircles his brow in the fine picture of Gérard. The crown was, perhaps, in itself, less becoming to him; but the expression excited by the act of putting it on, rendered him perfectly handsome.

"When the moment arrived for Josephine to take an active part in the grand drama, she descended from the throne and advanced towards the altar, where the emperor awaited her, followed by her retinue of court ladies, and having her train borne by the Princesses Caroline, Julie, Eliza, and Louis. One of the chief beauties of the Empress Josephine was not merely her fine figure, but the elegant turn of her neck, and the way in which she carried her head; indeed, her deportment altogether was conspicuous for dignity and grace. I have had the honor of being presented to many *real princesses*, to use the phrase of the Faubourg Saint-Germain, but I never saw one who, to my eyes, presented so perfect a personification of elegance and majesty. In Napoleon's countenance I could read the conviction of all I have just said. He looked with an air of complacency at the empress as she advanced towards him; and when she knelt down, when the tears, which she could not repress, fell upon her clasped hands, as they were raised to Heaven, or rather to Napoleon, both then appeared to enjoy one of those fleeting moments of pure felicity which are unique in a lifetime, and serve to fill up a lustrum of years. The emperor performed, with peculiar grace, every action required of him during the ceremony; but his manner of crowning Josephine was most remarkable: after receiving the small crown, surmounted by the cross, he had first to place it on his own head, and then to transfer it to that of the empress. When the moment arrived for placing the crown on the head of the woman whom popular superstition regarded as his good genius, his manner was almost playful. He took great pains to arrange this little crown, which was placed over Josephine's tiara of diamonds; he put it on, then took it off, and finally put it on again, as if to promise her she should wear it gracefully and lightly."

In May, 1805, Napoleon took the iron crown of Lombardy in Milan. The coronation was followed by a thorough reconstruction of this part of Italy. The new institutions of France replaced the complicated feudal arrangements which had harassed the people. Prince Eugene was made viceroy of Italy.

WAR WITH AUSTRIA.

Austria looked with jealousy on this accession of power, and particularly on this change in the institutions of her neighbor. In assuming control of the Italian and Germanic States, Napoleon gave the people his code and his methods; personal liberty, equality before the law, religious toleration, took the place of the injustice and narrowness which animated all feudal institutions. These new ideas were quite as hateful to Austria as the disturbance in the balance of power, and more dangerous to her system. Russia and Prussia felt the same suspicion of Napoleon as Austria did. All three powers were constantly incited to action against France by England, who offered unlimited gold if they would but combine with her. In the summer of 1805 Austria joined England and Russia in a coalition against France. Prussia was not yet willing to commit herself.

The great army which for so many months had been gathered around Boulogne for the descent on England, waited anxiously for the arrival of the French fleet to cover its passage. But the fleet did not come; and, though hoping until the last that his plan would still be carried out, Napoleon quietly and swiftly transferred the army of England into the Grand Army, and turned its march against his continental enemies.

Never was his great war rule, "Time is everything," more thoroughly carried out. "Austria will employ fine phrases in order to gain time," he wrote Talleyrand, "and to prevent me accomplishing anything this

MEETING OF FREDERICK WILLIAM III, KING OF PRUSSIA, NAPOLEON, AND ALEXANDER I., EMPEROR OF RUSSIA, AT TILSIT.
THE FIGURE ON THE LEFT IS FREDERICK WILLIAM; THAT ON THE RIGHT IS ALEXANDER

Engraved by Gögel, after a drawing by Wolff. The meeting occurred June 26, 1807, in the pavilion which had been erected for that purpose on the River Niemen. After Friedland the Russians crossed the Niemen ; the French camped on the banks opposite them. The first interview on the raft was between the Emperor Alexander and Napoleon alone on June 25th. The two emperors, accompanied by their staffs, started from the opposite banks at the same time ; Napoleon arrived first, passed through the tent and met Alexander. The two embraced heartily in sight of the two armies, who cheered them loudly. A second interview took place the next day, to which the Emperor Alexander brought the King of Prussia. During the time that the sovereigns at Tilsit were negotiating, the two armies kept their positions, and friendly relations grew up between them.

year ; . . . and in April I shall find one hundred thousand Russians in Poland, fed by England, twenty thousand English at Malta, and fifteen thousand Russians at Corfu. I should then be in a critical position. My mind is made up." His orders flew from Boulogne to Paris, to the German States, to Italy, to his generals, to his naval commanders. By the 28th of August the whole army had moved. A month later it had crossed the Rhine, and Napoleon was at its head.

The force which he commanded was in every way an extraordinary one. Marmont's enthusiastic description was in no way an exaggeration :

"This army, the most beautiful that was ever seen, was less redoubtable from the number of its soldiers than from their nature. Almost all of them had carried on war and had won victories. There still existed among them something of the enthusiasm and exaltation of the Revolutionary campaigns; but this enthusiasm was systematized. From the supreme chief down—the chiefs of the army corps, the division commanders, the common officers and soldiers—everybody was hardened to war. The eighteen months in splendid camps had produced a training, an *ensemble*, which has never existed since to the same degree, and a boundless confidence. This army was probably the best and the most redoubtable that modern times have seen."

The force responded to the imperious genius of its commander with a beautiful precision which amazes and dazzles one who follows its march. So perfectly had all been arranged, so exactly did every corps and officer respond, that nine days after the passage of the Rhine, the army was in Bavaria, several marches in the rear of the enemy. The weather was terrible, but nothing checked them. The emperor himself set the example. Day and night he was on horseback in the midst of his troops; once for a week he did not take off his boots. When they lagged, or the enemy harassed them, he would gather each regiment into a circle, explain to it the position of the enemy, the imminence of a great battle, and his confidence in his troops. These harangues sometimes took place in driving snowstorms, the soldiers standing up to their knees in icy slush. By October 13th, such was the extraordinary march they had made, the emperor was able to issue this address to the army:

"Soldiers, a month ago we were encamped on the shores of the ocean, opposite England, when an impious league forced us to fly to the Rhine. Not a fortnight ago that river was passed; and the Alps, the Neckar, the Danube, and the Lech, the celebrated barriers of Germany, have not for a minute delayed our march....
The enemy, deceived by our manœuvres and the rapidity of our movements, is entirely turned. . . . But for the army before you, we should be in London to-day, have avenged six centuries of insult, and have liberated the sea.

"Remember to-morrow that against the allies of England. . . .

"NAPOLEON."

Four days after this address came the capitulation of Ulm—a "new Caudine Forks," as Marmont called it. It was, as Napoleon said, a victory won by legs, instead of by arms. The great fatigue and the forced marches which the army had undergone had gained them sixty thousand prisoners, one hundred and twenty guns,

FREDERICK WILLIAM III., KING OF PRUSSIA. 1798.

Engraved by Dickenson, after a portrait painted in 1798 by Laner. Frederick William III., born August 3, 1770, was the eldest son of Frederick William II., was trained by his granduncle Frederick the Great, and succeeded to his father's throne in 1797. Public affairs were in a bad condition at that moment, but Frederick, who, although rather slow and stupid, had an honest desire to govern well, called able ministers to his aid. When the treaty of Lunéville ended the war with France in 1801, he was obliged to give up his territory on the left bank of the Rhine. He remained at peace with Napoleon until frightened by the formation of the Confederation of the Rhine in 1806. The war which followed, ending in the treaty of Tilsit, drove him from Berlin, and took away half his kingdom. But he nevertheless continued his efforts to reorganize his state. Frederick joined Napoleon for the Russian campaign, but joined the coalition of 1813. After Waterloo, he continued to improve his kingdom, though he never gave it the liberal constitution he had promised, and opposed the liberal ideas which were abroad in his later years. He died June 7, 1840.

ninety colors, more than thirty generals, at a cost of but fifteen hundred men, two-thirds of them but slightly wounded.

But there was no rest for the army. Before the middle of November it had so surrounded Vienna that the emperor and his court had fled to Brünn, seventy or eighty miles north of Vienna, to meet the Russians, who, under Alexander I., were coming from Berlin. Thither Napoleon followed them, but the Austrians retreated eastward, joining the Russians at Olmütz.

LOUISA, QUEEN OF PRUSSIA. 1798.

Engraved by Dickenson, after a portrait painted in 1798 by Lamy. Louisa, Queen of Prussia, was born March 10, 1776, in Hanover. Her father was the Duke Charles of Mecklenburg-Strelitz, and her mother a princess of Hesse Darmstadt. In 1793, she met King Frederick William III. at Frankfort. He was so enamored of her beauty and her nobility of character that he made her his wife. Queen Louise's dignity and sweetness under the reverses her kingdom suffered in the war with France, won her the love and respect of her people, and have given her a place among the most lovable and admirable women of history. She died July 19, 1810, and was buried at Charlottenburg, where a beautiful mausoleum by Rauch has been erected. In 1814 her husband instituted the Order of Louise in her honor. On March 10, 1876, the Prussians celebrated the one hundredth anniversary of her birth.

The combined force of the allies was now some ninety thousand men. They had a strong reserve, and the Prussian army was about to join them. Napoleon at Brünn had only some seventy or eighty thousand men, and was in the heart of the enemy's country. Alexander, flattered by his aides, and confident that he was able to defeat the French, resolved to leave his strong position at Olmütz and seek battle with Napoleon.

The position the French occupied can be understood if one draws a rough diagram of a right-angled triangle, Brünn being at the right angle formed by two roads, one running south to Vienna, by which Napoleon had come, and the other running eastward to Olmütz. The hypothenuse of this angle, running from northeast to southwest, is formed by Napoleon's army.

When the allies decided to leave Olmütz their plan was to march southwestward in face of Napoleon's line, and get between him and Vienna, thus cutting off what they supposed was his base of supplies (in this they were mistaken, for Napoleon had, unknown to them, changed his base from Vienna to Bohemia), separating him from his Italian army, and driving him, routed, into Bohemia.

THE BATTLE OF AUSTERLITZ.

On the 27th of November the allies advanced, and their first encounter with a small French advance guard was successful. It gave them confidence, and they continued their march on the 28th, 29th, and 30th, gradually extending a long line facing westward and parallel with Napoleon's line. The French emperor, while this movement was going on, was rapidly calling up his reserves and strengthening his position. By the first day of December Napoleon saw clearly what the allies intended to do, and had formed his plan. The events of that day confirmed his ideas. By nine o'clock in the evening he was so certain of the plan of the coming battle that he rode the length of his line, explaining to his troops the tactics of the allies, and what he himself proposed to do.

Napoleon's appearance before the troops, his confident assurance of victory, called out a brilliant demonstration from the army. The divisions of infantry raised

N. C. OUDINOT, DUC DE REGGIO. 1811.

Engraved by Forney, after Lefevre. Oudinot, Nicolas Charles, was born at Bar-le-duc in 1767, son of a merchant. Left commerce for the army, and so distinguished himself that 1792 he was made chief of battalion, and three years later general of brigade. The same year he received five wounds and was taken prisoner, remaining captive until 1796. He next served under Moreau, and in 1799 was sent to the army of Helvetia, where he distinguished himself in the battle of Zurich. Oudinot was with Masséna in the siege of Genoa (1800), and in 1805 was commander of a division of the camp of Bruges. In 1805 he received the grand cross of the Legion of Honor. In the campaign of 1805 he greatly distinguished himself at the head of ten thousand grenadiers, called the *grenadiers Oudinot*. For his services in the campaign of 1806-1807 he was made count, and in 1808 governor of Erfurt, where Napoleon presented him to Alexander I. as the *Bayard of the army*. The baton of marshal and the title of Duke of Reggio were given him after Wagram. Oudinot was wounded early in the Russian campaign, but on hearing of the disasters returned to his command, and at the terrible passage of the Beresina he performed prodigies of valor. Throughout the campaign of 1813 and the invasion the next year he was active, and only laid down arms after Napoleon's abdication. He joined Louis XVIII., and refused to leave him during the hundred days. In 1823 he served in the Spanish campaign. He was made governor of the *Invalides* in 1842, a post he held until his death in 1847.

bundles of blazing straw on the ends of long poles, giving him an illumination as imposing as it was novel. It was a happy thought, for the day was the anniversary of his coronation.

The emperor remained in bivouac all night. At four o'clock of the morning of the 2d of December he was in the saddle. When the gray fog lifted he saw the enemy's divisions arranged exactly as he had divined. Three corps faced his right—the southwest part of the hypothenuse. These corps had left a splendid position facing his centre, the heights of Pratzen.

This advance of the enemy had left their centre weak and unprotected, and had separated the body of the army from its right, facing Napoleon's left. The enemy was in exactly the position Napoleon wished for the attack he had planned.

It was eight o'clock in the morning when the emperor galloped up his line, proclaiming to the army that the enemy had exposed himself, and crying out: "Close the campaign with a clap of thunder." The generals rode to their positions, and at once the battle opened. Soult, who commanded the French centre, attacked the allies' centre so unexpectedly that it was driven into retreat. The Emperor Alexander and his headquarters were in this part of the army, and though the young czar did his best to rouse his forces, it was a hopeless task. The Russian centre was defeated and the wings divided. At the same time the allies' left, where the bulk of their army was massed in a marshy country of which they knew little, was engaged and held in check by Davoust, and their right was overcome by Lannes, Murat, and Bernadotte. As soon as the centre and right of the allies had been driven into retreat, Napoleon concentrated his forces on the left, the strongest part of his enemy. In a very short time the allies were driven back into the canals and lakes of the country, and many men and nearly all their artillery lost. Before night the routed enemy had fallen back to Austerlitz.

Of all Napoleon's battles Austerlitz was the one of which he was the proudest. It was here that he showed best the "divine side of war."

The familiar note in which Napoleon announced to his brother Joseph the result of the battle, is a curious contrast to the oratorical bulletins which for some days flowed to Paris. His letter is dated Austerlitz, December 3, 1805:

"After manœuvring for a few days I fought a decisive battle yesterday. I defeated the combined armies commanded by the Emperors of Russia and Germany. Their force consisted of eighty thousand Russians and thirty thousand Austrians. I have made forty thousand prisoners, taken forty flags, one hundred guns, and all the standards of the Russian Imperial Guard. . . . Although I have bivouacked

JEROME BONAPARTE, 1808.

"Engraved by I. G. Müller, knight, and Frederick Müller, son, engravers to his majesty the King of Wurtemberg. After a design made at Cassel by Madame Kinson." Jerome Bonaparte, youngest brother of Napoleon, was born in Ajaccio, 1784; died near Paris in 1860. Entered the navy at sixteen, and in 1801 was sent on the expedition to Santo Domingo. On his return went to the United States, where, in 1803, he married Miss Elizabeth Patterson of Baltimore. Napoleon refused to recognize this marriage, and when Jerome brought his wife to Europe in 1805, they were forbidden France. Jerome continued in the navy, and his wife went to England. In 1806 he left naval for military service, was recognized as a French prince, and made successor to the throne in event of Napoleon's leaving no male heirs. After Tilsit, Jerome was made King of Westphalia, a new kingdom having its capital at Cassel, and was married to Catherine, daughter of the King of Wurtemberg. The campaign of 1813 drove him to Paris. During the Hundred Days he sat in the chamber of peers. After the second restoration of Louis XVIII. Jerome lived in various parts of Europe, suffering at one time serious financial embarrassment, until, in 1847, he was allowed to return to Paris. After the Revolution of 1848 he was made governor of the *Invalides* and marshal. In 1850 he was president of the Imperial senate. Later the right of succession was given him and his son.

THE EMPEROR NAPOLEON IN STATE COSTUME (L'EMPEREUR EN GRAND COSTUME). 1805.

Engraved by Tardieu, after Isabey. This piece engraved by Malbeste, after Percier. Isabey became intimate with the Bonapartes during the Consulate through Hortense, whose drawing-master he had been. It was then he executed his portraits of Bonaparte at Malmaison, and the Review of the Consular Guard. He enjoyed Napoleon's favor throughout the Empire, and was charged by him to execute a series of thirty-two designs to commemorate his coronation. He was afterwards Marie Louise's drawing-master.

THE EMPRESS JOSEPHINE IN STATE COSTUME ("L'IMPÉRATRICE EN GRAND COSTUME"). 1805.
Engraved by Audouin, after a design by Isabey and Percier.

THE EMPEROR NAPOLEON IN ORDINARY COURT COSTUME ("L'EMPEREUR EN PETIT COSTUME"). 1807.
Engraved by Rihault, after a design by Isabey and Percier.

THE EMPRESS JOSEPHINE IN ORDINARY COURT COSTUME ("L'IMPÉRATRICE EN PETIT COSTUME"). 1807.
Engraved by Bilcoult, after a design by Isabey and Percier.

in the open air for a week, my health is good. This evening I am in bed in the beautiful castle of M. de Kaunitz, and have changed my shirt for the first time in eight days."

The battle of Austerlitz obliged Austria to make peace (the treaty was signed at Presburg on December 27, 1805), compelled Russia to retire disabled from the field, transformed the haughty Prussian *ultimatum* which had just been presented into humble submission, and changed the rejoicings of England over the magnificent naval victory of Trafalgar (October 21) into despair. It even killed Pitt. It enabled Napoleon, too, to make enormous strides in establishing a kingdom of the West. Naples was given to Joseph, the Batavian Republic was made a kingdom for Louis, and the states between the Lahn, the Rhine, and the Upper Danube were formed into a league, called the Confederation of the Rhine, and Napoleon was made Protector.

WAR WITH PRUSSIA AND RUSSIA.

At the beginning of 1806 Napoleon was again in Paris. He had been absent but three months. Eight months of this year were spent in fruitless negotiations with England and in an irritating correspondence with Prussia. The latter country had many grievances against Napoleon, the sum of them all being that "French politics had been the scourge of humanity for the last fifteen years," and that an "insatiable ambition was still the ruling passion of France." By the end of September war was declared, and Napoleon, whose preparations had been conducted secretly, it being given out that he was going to Compiègne to hunt, suddenly joined his army.

The first week of October the grand army advanced from southern Germany towards the valley of the Saale. This movement brought them on the flanks of the Prussians, who were scattered along the upper Saale. The unexpected appearance of the French army, which was larger and much better organized than the Prussian, caused the latter to retreat towards the Elbe. The retreating army was in two divisions; the first crossing the Saale to Jena, the second falling back towards the Unstrut. As soon as Napoleon understood these movements he despatched part of his force under Davoust and Bernadotte to cut off the retreat of the second Prussian division, while he himself hurried on to Jena to force battle on the first. The Prussians were encamped at the foot of a height known as the Landgrafenberg.

To command this height was to command the Prussian forces. By a series of determined and repeated efforts Napoleon reached the position desired, and by the morning of the 14th of October had his foes in his power. Advancing from the Landgrafenberg in three divisions, he turned the Prussian flanks at the same moment that he attacked their centre. The Prussians never fought better, perhaps, than at Jena. The movements of their cavalry awakened even Napoleon's admiration, but they were surrounded and outnumbered, and the army was speedily broken into pieces and driven into a retreat.

While Napoleon was fighting at Jena, to the right at Auerstadt, Davoust was engaging Brunswick and his seventy thousand men with a force of twenty-seven thousand. In spite of the great difference in numbers the Prussians were unable to make any impression on the French; and Brunswick falling, they began to retreat towards Jena, expecting to join the other division of the army, of whose route they were ignorant. The result was frightful. The two flying armies suddenly encountered each other, and, pursued by the French on either side, were driven in confusion towards the Elbe.

THE ENTRY INTO BERLIN—JENA, EYLAU, AND FRIEDLAND.

The entry into Berlin was one of the great spectacles of the war. One particularly touching incident of it was the visit paid to Napoleon by the Protestant and Calvinist French clergy. There were at that time twelve thousand French refugees in Berlin, owing to the revocation of the Edict of Nantes. They were received with kindness by Napoleon, who told them they had good right to protection, and that their privileges and worship should be respected.

Jena brought Napoleon something like one hundred and sixty million francs in money, an enormous number of prisoners, guns, and standards, the glory of the entry of Berlin, a great number of interesting articles for the Napoleon Museum of Paris, among them the column from the field of Rosbach, the sword, the ribbon of the black eagle, and the general's sash of Friedrich the Great, and the flags carried by his guards during the Seven Years' War. But it did not secure him peace. The King of Prussia threw himself into the arms of Russia, and Napoleon advanced boldly into Poland to meet his enemy.

The Poles welcomed the French with joy. They hoped to find in Napoleon the liberator of their country, and they poured forth money and soldiers to reënforce him. "Our entry into Varsovia," wrote Napoleon, "was a triumph, and the sentiments that the Poles of all classes show since our arrival cannot be expressed. Love of country and the national sentiment are not only entirely conserved in the heart of the people, but it has been intensified by misfortune. Their first passion, their first desire, is again to become a nation. The rich come from their *châteaux*, praying for the reëstablishment of the nation, and offering their children, their fortunes, and their influence." Everything was done during the months the French remained in Poland to flatter and aid the army.

The campaign against the Russians was carried on in Old Prussia, to the southeast of the Gulf of Dantzic, and its main engagements were, the battle of Eylau on February 8, 1807, the closest drawn and most expensive battle the emperor had so far fought; the siege of Dantzic, which capitulated in May; and the battle of Friedland, fought on June 14th. This battle, the anniversary of Marengo, was won largely by Napoleon's taking advantage of a blunder of his opponent. The French and the Russian armies were on the opposite banks of the Alle. Benningsen, the Russian commander, was marching towards Königsberg by the eastern bank. Napoleon was pursuing by the western bank. The French forces, however, were scattered; and Benningsen, thinking that he could engage and easily rout a portion of the army by crossing the river at Friedland, suddenly led his army across to the western bank. Napoleon utilized this unwise movement with splendid skill. Calling up his reënforcements he attacked the enemy solidly. As soon as the Russian centre was broken, defeat was inevitable, for the retreating army was driven into the river, and thousands lost. Many of those who did get across were pursued through the streets of Friedland by the French, and slaughtered. The battle was hardly over when Napoleon wrote to Josephine:

"FRIEDLAND, 15th *June*, 1807.

"MY FRIEND: I write you only a few words, for I am very tired. I have been bivouacking for several days. My children have worthily celebrated the anniversary of Marengo. The battle of Friedland will be just as celebrated and as glorious for my people. The whole Russian army routed, eighty guns captured, thirty thousand men taken prisoners or killed, with twenty-five generals; the Russian guard annihilated; it is the worthy sister of Marengo, Aus-

terlitz, and Jena. The bulletin will tell you the rest. My loss is not large. I successfully out-manœuvred the enemy.

"NAPOLEON."

PEACE OF TILSIT.

Friedland ended the war. Directly after the battle Napoleon went to Tilsit, which for the time was made neutral ground, and here he met the Emperor of Russia and the King of Prussia, and the map of Europe was made over.

The relations between the royal parties seem to have been for the most part amiable. Napoleon became, in fact, very fond of Alexander I. "Were he a woman I think I should make love to him," he wrote Josephine once. Alexander, young and enthusiastic, had a deep admiration for Napoleon's genius, and the two became good comrades. The King of Prussia, overcome by his losses, was a sorrowful figure in their company. It was their habit to go out every day at Tilsit on horseback, but the king was awkward, always crowding against Napoleon, beside whom he rode, and making his two companions wait for him to climb from the saddle when they returned.

Their dinners together were dull, and the emperors, very much in the style of two careless, fun-loving youths, bored by a solemn elderly relative, were accustomed after dinner to make excuses to go home early; but later they met at the apartments of one or the other, and often talked together until midnight.

Just before the negotiations were completed, Queen Louise arrived, and tried to use her influence with Napoleon to obtain at least Magdeburg. Napoleon accused the queen to Las Cases of trying to win him at first by a scene of high tragedy, but when they came to meet at dinner, her policy was quite another. "The Queen of Prussia dined with me to-day," wrote Napoleon to the empress on July 7th. "I had to defend myself against being obliged to make some further concessions to her husband; . . . " and the next day, "The Queen of Prussia is really charming; she is full of *coquetterie* towards me. But do not be jealous; I am an oilcloth, off which all that runs. It would cost me too dear to play the *galant*."

The intercessions of the queen really hurried on the treaty. When she learned that it had been signed, and her wishes not granted, she was indignant, wept bitterly, and refused to go to the second dinner to which Napoleon had invited her.

Alexander was obliged to go himself to decide her. After the dinner, when she withdrew, Napoleon accompanied her. On the staircase she stopped.

"Can it be," she said, "that after I have had the happiness of seeing so near me the man of the age and of history, I am not to have the liberty and satisfaction of assuring him that he has attached me for life? . . . "

"Madame, I am to be pitied," said the emperor gravely. "It is my evil star."

By the treaty of Tilsit the face of the continent was transformed. Prussia lost half her territory. Dantzic was made a free town. Magdeburg went to France. Hesse-Cassel and the Prussian possessions west of the Elbe went to form the kingdom of Westphalia. The King of Saxony received the grand duchy of Warsaw. Finland and the Danubian principalities were to go to Alexander in exchange for certain Ionian islands and the Gulf of Cattaro in Dalmatia.

Of far more importance than this change of boundaries was the secret treaty of Tilsit, wherein the two emperors pledged themselves to each other for nothing less than driving the Bourbons from Spain and the Braganzas from Portugal, and replacing them by Bonapartes; for giving Russia, Turkey in Europe, and as much of Asia as she wanted; for ending the temporal power of the Pope; for placing France in Egypt; for shutting the English from the Mediterranean; and for undertaking several other similar enterprises.

KING OF KINGS.

Napoleon's influence in Europe was now at its zenith. He was literally "king of kings," as he was popularly called, and the Bonaparte family was rapidly displacing the Bourbon. Joseph had been made King of Naples in 1806. Eliza was Princess of Lucques and Piombino. Louis, married to Hortense, had been King of Holland since 1806. Pauline had been the Princess Borghese since 1803; Caroline, the wife of Murat, was Grand Duchess of Cleves and Berg; Jerome was King of Westphalia; Eugene de Beauharnais, Viceroy of Italy, was married to a princess of Bavaria.

The members of Napoleon's family were elevated only on condition that they rule strictly in accordance with his plans. The interior affairs of their kingdoms were in reality centralized in his hands as perfectly as those of France. He watched the private and public conduct of his kings and nobles, and criticised them with absolute frankness and extraordinary common sense. The ground on which he protected them is well explained in the following letter, written in January, 1806, to Count Miot de Melito:

". . . You are going to rejoin my brother. You will tell him that I have made him King of Naples; that he will continue to be Grand Elector, and that nothing will be changed as regards his relations with France. But impress upon him that the least hesitation, the slightest wavering, will ruin him entirely. I have another person in my mind who will replace him should he refuse. . . . At present all feelings of affection yield to state reasons. I recognize only those who serve me as relations. My fortune is not attached to the name of Bonaparte, but to that of Napoleon. It is with my fingers and with my pen that I make children. To-day I can love only those whom I esteem. Joseph must forget all our ties of childhood. Let him make himself esteemed. Let him acquire glory. Let him have a leg broken in battle. Then I shall esteem him. Let him give up his old ideas. Let him not dread fatigue. Look at me; the campaign I have just terminated, the movement, the excitement, have made me stout. I believe that if all the kings of Europe were to coalesce against me, I should have a ridiculous paunch."

Joseph, bent on being a great king, boasted now and then to Napoleon of his position in Naples. His brother never failed to silence him with the truth, if it was blunt and hard to digest.

"When you talk about the fifty thousand enemies of the queen you make me laugh. . . . You exaggerate the degree of hatred which the queen has left behind at Naples; you do not know mankind. There are not twenty persons who hate her as you suppose, and there are not twenty persons who would not surrender to one of her smiles. The strongest feeling of hatred on the part of a nation is that inspired by another nation. Your fifty thousand men are the enemies of the French."

With Jerome, Napoleon had been particularly incensed because of his marriage with Miss Patterson. In 1804 he wrote of that affair:

". . . Jerome is wrong to think that he will be able to count upon any weakness on my part, for, not having the rights of a father, I cannot entertain for him the feeling of a father; a father allows himself to be blinded, and it pleases him to be blinded because he identifies his son with himself. . . . But what am I to Jerome? Sole instrument of my destiny, I owe nothing to my brothers. They have made an abundant harvest out of what I have accomplished in the way of glory; but, for all that, they must not abandon the field and deprive me of the aid I have a right to expect from them. They will cease to be anything for me, directly they take a road opposed to mine. If I exact so much from my brothers who have already rendered many services, if I have abandoned the one who, in mature age (Lucien), refused to follow my advice, what must not Jerome, who is still young, and who is known only for his neglect of duty, expect? If he does nothing for me, I shall see in this the decree of destiny, which has decided that I shall do nothing for him. . . ."

Jerome yielded later to his brother's wishes, and in 1807 was rewarded with the new kingdom of Westphalia. Napoleon kept close watch of him, however, and his letters are full of admirable counsels. The following is particularly valuable, showing, as it does, that Napoleon believed a government would be popular and enduring only in proportion to the liberty and prosperity it allowed the citizens.

"What the German peoples desire with impatience [he told Jerome], is that persons who are not of noble birth, and who have talents, shall have an equal right to your consideration and to public employment (with those who are of noble birth); that every sort of servitude and of intermediate obligations between the sovereign and the lowest class of the people should be entirely abolished. The benefits of the Code Napoleon, the publicity of legal procedure, the establishment of the jury system, will be the distinctive characteristics of your monarchy. . . . I count more on the effect of these benefits for the extension and strengthening of your kingdom, than upon the result of the greatest victories. Your people ought to enjoy a liberty, an equality, a well-being, unknown to the German peoples. . . . What people would wish to return to the arbitrary government of Prussia, when it has tasted the benefits of a wise and liberal administration? The peoples of Germany, France, Italy, Spain, desire equality, and demand that liberal ideas should prevail. . . . Be a constitutional king."

Louis in Holland was never a king to Napoleon's mind. He especially disliked his quarrels with his wife. The two young people had been married for state reasons, and were very unhappy. In 1807 Napoleon wrote Louis, apropos of his domestic relations, a letter which is a good example of scores of others he sent to one and another of his kings and princes about their private affairs.

"You govern that country too much like a Capuchin. The goodness of a king should be full of majesty. . . . A king orders, and asks nothing from any one. . . . When people say of a king that he is good, his reign is a failure. . . . Your quarrels with the queen are known to the public. You should exhibit at home that paternal and effeminate character you show in your manner of governing. . . . You treat a young wife as you would command a regiment. Distrust the people by whom you are surrounded; they are nobles. . . . You have the best and most virtuous of wives, and you render her miserable. Allow her to dance as much as she likes; it is in keeping with her age. I have a wife who is forty years of age; from the field of battle I write to her to go to balls, and you wish a young woman of twenty to live in a cloister, or, like a nurse, always washing her children. . . . Render the mother of your children happy. You have only one way of doing so, by showing her esteem and confidence. Un-

fortunately you have a wife who is too virtuous: if you had a coquette, she would lead you by the nose. But you have a proud wife, who is offended and grieved at the mere idea that you can have a bad opinion of her. You should have had a wife like some of those whom I know in Paris. She would have played you false, and you would have been at her feet. . . .

"NAPOLEON."

With his sisters he was quite as positive. While Josephine adapted herself with grace and tact to her great position, the Bonaparte sisters, especially Pauline, were constantly irritating somebody by their vanity and jealousy. The following letter to Pauline shows how little Napoleon spared them when their performances came to his ears:

"MADAME AND DEAR SISTER: I have learned with pain that you have not the good sense to conform to the manners and customs of the city of Rome; that you show contempt for the inhabitants, and that your eyes are unceasingly turned towards Paris. Although occupied with vast affairs, I nevertheless desire to make known my wishes, and I hope that you will conform to them.

"Love your husband and his family, be amiable, accustom yourself to the usages of Rome, and put this in your head: that if you follow bad advice you will no longer be able to count upon me. You may be sure that you will find no support in Paris, and that I shall never receive you there without your husband. If you quarrel with him, it will be your fault, and France will be closed to you. You will sacrifice your happiness and my esteem.

"BONAPARTE."

This supervision of policy, relations, and conduct extended to his generals. The case of General Berthier is one to the point. Chief of Napoleon's staff in Italy, he had fallen in love at Milan with a Madame Visconti, and had never been able to conquer his passion. In Egypt Napoleon called him "chief of the lovers' faction," that part of the army which, because of their desire to see wives or sweethearts, were constantly revolting against the campaign, and threatening to desert.

In 1804 Berthier had been made marshal, and in 1806 Napoleon wished to give him the princedom of Neufchatel; but it was only on condition that he give up Madame Visconti, and marry.

"I exact only one condition, which is that you get married. Your passion has lasted long enough. It has become ridiculous; and I have the right to hope that the man whom I have called my companion in arms, who will be placed alongside of me by posterity, will no longer abandon himself to a weakness without example. . . . You know that no one likes you better than I do, but you know also that the first condition of my friendship is that it must be made subordinate to my esteem."

Berthier fled to Josephine for help, weeping like a child; but she could do nothing, and he married the woman chosen for him. Three months after the ceremony, the husband of Madame Visconti died, and Berthier, broken-hearted, wrote to the Prince Borghese:

"You know how often the emperor pressed me to obtain a divorce for Madame de Visconti. But a divorce was always repugnant to the feelings in which I was educated, and therefore I waited. To-day Madame de Visconti is free, and I might have been the happiest of men. But the emperor forced me into a marriage which hinders me from uniting myself to the only woman I ever loved. Ah, my dear prince, all that the emperor has done and may yet do for me, will be no compensation for the eternal misfortune to which he has condemned me."

THE EMPEROR OF THE FRENCH IN 1807.

Never was Napoleon more powerful than at the end of the period we have been tracing so rapidly, never had he so looked the emperor. An observer who watched him through the Te Deum sung at Notre Dame in his honor, on his return from Tilsit, says: "His features, always calm and serious, recalled the cameos which represent the Roman emperors. He was small; still his whole person, in this imposing ceremony, was in harmony with the part he was playing. A sword glittering with precious stones was at his side, and the glittering diamond called the 'Regent' formed its pommel. Its brilliancy did not let us forget that this sword was the sharpest and the most victorious that the world had seen since those of Alexander and Cæsar."

Certainly he never worked more prodigiously. The campaigns of 1805-1807 were, in spite of their rapid movement,—indeed, because of it,—terribly fatiguing for him; that they were possible at all was due mainly to the fact that they had been made on paper so many times in his study. When he was Consul the only room opening from his study was filled with enormous maps of all the countries of the world. This room was presided over by a competent cartographer. Frequently these maps were brought to the study and spread upon the floor. Napoleon would get down upon them on all fours, and creep about, compass and red pencil in hand, comparing and measuring distances, and studying the configuration of the land. If he was in doubt about anything, he referred it to his librarian, who was expected to give him the fullest details.

Attached to his cabinet were skilful translators, whose business was not only to translate diplomatic correspondence, but to gather from foreign sources full information about the armies of his enemies. Méneval declares that the emperor knew the condition of foreign armies as well as he did his own.

The amount of information he had about other lands was largely due to his ability to ask questions. When he sent to an agent for a report, he rattled at him a volley of questions, always to the point; and the agent knew that it would never do to let one go unanswered.

While carrying on the German campaign of 1805-1807, Napoleon showed, as never before, his extraordinary capacity for attending to everything. The number of despatches he sent out was incredible. In the first three months of 1807, while he was in Poland, he wrote over seventeen hundred letters and despatches.

It was not simply war, the making of kingdoms, the direction of his new-made kings; minor affairs of the greatest variety occupied him. While at Boulogne, tormented by the failure of the English invasion and the war against Austria, he ordered that horse races should be established "in those parts of the empire the most remarkable for the horses they breed; prizes shall be awarded to the fleetest horses." The very day after the battle of Friedland, he was sending orders to Paris about the form and site of a statue to the memory of the Bishop of Vannes. He criticised from Poland the quarrels of Parisian actresses, ordered canals, planned there for the Bourse and the Odeon Theatre. This care of details went, as Pasquier says, to the "point of minuteness, or, to speak plainly, to that of charlatanism;" but it certainly did produce a deep impression upon France. That he could establish himself five hundred leagues from Paris, in the heart of winter, in a country encircled by his enemies, and yet be in daily communication with his capital, could direct even its least important affairs as if he were present, caused a superstitious feeling to rise in France, and in all Europe, that the emperor of the French people was not only omnipotent, but omnipresent.

THE WAX CAST OF THE FACE OF NAPOLEON.

THE STRANGE HISTORY OF A PRECIOUS RELIC.

By BARON DE ST. PÔL.

THIS document, practically *inédit*, is a rare and beautiful reproduction, in full face and in profile, of the real wax cast of the face and head of Napoleon I. It was engraved April 14, 1855, from a photograph taken the previous day by Bland & Sons, Fleet Street, London, the negative of which was destroyed.

But few of the memorials of Napoleon possess more dramatic interest than the wax cast in question. The average historical student knows that Dr. Arnott, who was representing Sir Hudson Lowe at the final scene, and who assisted Dr. Henry and Dr. Antommarchi at the dissection of the body, which took place early on the following morning, remained in the room with the dead body of the emperor during the night of the 5th of May; but what is not generally known is that Dr. Arnott, during two or three hours of the night, when left absolutely alone, made a cast, a solid wax cast, of the face of the emperor, which he sedulously concealed from everybody, even from Sir Hudson Lowe; and that the following morning the other doctors, and the faithful friends of the emperor, Count Bertrand, Count Montholon, and Marchand (the *valet de chambre* of Napoleon), perceiving that the face had been somewhat tampered with, a very hot discussion ensued before the taking of the plaster cast, Dr. Antommarchi accusing the English surgeon of treachery. And the accusation was more than merited, because, upon his return to Europe, Dr. Arnott hastened to Würtemberg, and offered the wax cast for sale to the king, father-in-law of King Jerome, the younger brother of Napoleon; and the work was so perfect, so beautiful, that he had no difficulty in securing three thousand pounds (fifteen thousand dollars) for it.

At the end of 1827, I forget the month, I think it was November, the wax cast was stolen from the palace of the king, and disappeared from public view until April, 1855, when a Captain Winneberger, a cashiered officer of the Bavarian army, with a very unsavory record, suddenly appeared in London with the wax cast, and exhibited it at 454 Oxford Street, attracting great crowds of people. Of course the French government at once had the case investigated, and the exhibited mask having been found to be the stolen relic, the captain was arrested. For want of proof of his complicity in the theft, Winneberger was released, and, furthermore, a sum of four thousand pounds (twenty thousand dollars) was paid to him for the return of the precious relic, which he had cleverly managed to conceal one hour before his arrest, very likely in collusion with the English detectives.

THE WRITER'S PERSONAL KNOWLEDGE OF THE CAST.

The cast was turned over to Jerome, who had hastened to London to take possession of it, and it remained his property until his death, when it reverted, by his will, to his nephew, the Emperor Napoleon III., who had paid from his own exchequer the ransom of four thousand pounds extorted by Winneberger. Prince Jerome prized this relic of his brother above all his other family souvenirs. It was still in his possession when I saw it for the first time, and I re-

WAX CAST OF THE FACE OF NAPOLEON I.—FULL FACE.

member vividly, after a lapse of thirty-five years, with what emotion I opened, with my own hands, the queer-looking box containing the cast.

"It is a beautiful likeness of my brother," said the prince, who was at that moment looking himself very solemn; "and it was a great grief, a real blow to me, when some unknown criminal carried it away from Stuttgart. But now, since we have regained possession of it, there is no probability that we will lose it again." And leaning over the cast, he pointed out to me the presence of five short hairs imbedded in the wax on the left side, about three inches from the temple; they were as fine as silk, and only slightly faded.

On two subsequent occasions I was allowed by the prince to look again upon the marvellous likeness of the great emperor. The last time was shortly before the prince's death; and a few veterans, remnants of hundreds of battle-fields, who had served with distinction under his brother, were that day his guests at a luncheon, where I occupied near him a seat of honor on the occasion of my successful examination for the degree of Bachelor of Arts. The brave General Pajol, a veteran of high repute, who had served under the emperor in different capacities since Austerlitz, and fought with the greatest gallantry during the one hundred days' campaign, was there; and, though usually a very calm and unemotional man, he exhibited that day, as did several of his comrades, the greatest feeling and passion when the box was opened, exclaiming in a voice nearly drowned in sobs : "Oh, yes! yes! it is like him! him! —our beloved and generous chief!" And looking around me at that moment, I saw tears, big tears, rolling down the weather-beaten cheeks of those sturdy men, relics themselves of another age—a real age of iron. Prince Jerome was also silently weeping. How extraordinary must have been the man who could instil such unbounded devotion and reverence into vast multitudes, and conquer so completely the

WAX CAST OF THE FACE OF NAPOLEON I.—IN PROFILE.

hearts of the noblest and bravest of a nation!

A little later, for a few years—from January, 1867, to January, 1870—I was the custodian of this interesting relic, and I had it in my own hands many times during the three years I passed under the roof of the Tuileries. It was contained in a rosewood box, known amongst us—the few privileged persons who had the entire confidence of the Emperor Napoleon III. —as the "casket." This was lined inside with metal, and was provided on the top with double glasses, which were very thick and fitted very tight. The cover was secured with a safety lock of ingenious device. The key was in my keeping.

The cast itself reposed upon a bed of white satin bordered with violet velvet strewed with the imperial bees, and the "casket" was under lock and key in a cabinet which was located on the left side of the huge desk of the emperor, between two deep windows overlooking the private garden of the palace. But having also the key of the cabinet at my disposal, I was at liberty to look at the cast at any time. I seldom indulged my curiosity, however, for the cast looked too "real" to make it a very pleasant pastime. I had strict orders never to exhibit it to the merely curious, and, as I had a perfect horror of such people, the rule was rigidly enforced.

The wax cast was burned, I suppose, with the Palace of the Tuileries, in 1871, or it may have been stolen again during the senseless and barbarian revelries of the Commune, by some "Communard," who hid it away, and who was perhaps shot himself when the army of Versailles stormed Paris, and the secret buried with him under the turf of the camp of Satory. Several times, during the dark days of exile upon British soil, the poor and unfortunate emperor mentioned to me the wax cast of his uncle, and twice told me that he looked at it for the last time the day before he left Paris for the camp of Châlons, never to return to the Tuileries again.

THE TRUMBULL PORTRAIT OF NAPOLEON.

THE portrait of Napoleon, by John Trumbull, printed on the opposite page, and now published for the first time, is from an original drawn, presumably from life or memory, in 1808. In the original, which is part of the "Trumbull Gallery of Revolutionary Sketches," owned by Professor Ed. Frossard, of Brooklyn, N. Y., the face is entirely in bold pen-and-ink work, with uniform and background finished in sepia. Under the bust is a locket containing a burning heart in a wreath of forget-me-nots, surrounded by a border of hair-work. Set in the frame beneath this is a smaller locket containing a bit of unwoven hair. On the back of the frame, which is of ebonized wood, eighteen by fifteen inches, is pasted a copy of the "New York Mirror," of August 16, 1823, containing anecdotes of Napoleon. In the upper left corner is pasted a piece of paper bearing the inscription in ink, written in Trumbull's own hand: "Napoleon at 44 with Parents Hair—his Hair in small case —J. T.;" from which it should seem that the hair in the woven border of the larger locket was that of one or the other, or both, of Napoleon's parents, and that the unwoven hair in the smaller locket was Napoleon's own.

The statement of the inscription, "Napoleon at 44," does not agree with the date on the picture, 1808, since Napoleon was not forty-four until 1813. The error is undoubtedly in the inscription, and is of a sort which anybody might fall into.

In making the portrait of Napoleon, it is not unlikely that Trumbull drew a face studied from life, though the production may have been, probably was, from memory. On several occasions he spent some time in Paris, where he enjoyed the friendship of the best people in official and artistic circles. On one occasion he dined with Talleyrand, and talked with Lucien Bonaparte, who sat beside him at table, "on the subject of his brother's wonderful success." When the Revolution was at its height, and all strangers were under suspicion, he was helped to a passport and safe conduct out of Paris by his intimate friend David, the same David whose portraits of Napoleon, painted from life, are so interesting a part of the remarkable collection now publishing in this magazine. It is not at all unlikely, therefore, that Trumbull had opportunities to study the living features of Napoleon; and, such opportunities occurring, he was not the man to neglect them. But, however produced, the portrait is certainly one of peculiar interest and value.

The original portrait is but lately dis-

NAPOLEON, DRAWN BY JOHN TRUMBULL.
Signed " J. T. 1814."

covered, and its history is a little obscure; but there is no reason to doubt its authenticity. Besides the testimony of the inscription in Trumbull's own hand, and the judgment of experts to whom the drawing has been submitted, that it is unquestionably Trumbull's work, there is further testimony to its genuineness in what is certainly known of Trumbull's life and methods. Trumbull was before all else a portrait painter, and he especially delighted in portraying the soldiers and statesmen with whom his own remarkably active career brought him into contact. Nor was it only the public men of his own country that attracted him. In the Trumbull collection preserved at Yale College is a portrait of the Duke of Wellington by him.

THE ROMANCE OF DULLTOWN.

By JAMES W. TEMPLE.

I.

DULLTOWN, as any tyro in geography can tell, is a village of a few hundred inhabitants, situated on the line of the X. Y. Z. Railroad, in the County of Blank, and State of Incognito. To describe it as a real-estate agent would do, it is the centre of a fine agricultural region, and a trading point of no mean order, judged by the staples shipped from its depot, and the merchandise sold by its several "stores" to the country people located near it. It has the regulation supply of shops, offices, and warehouses; its churches, its schools, its fine residences and humble cottages. It numbers among its population its rich man, its well-to-do tradesmen, its day-laborers, its loafers. It has its preachers, its doctors, its teachers; it has its local politicians, its office-seekers, its cranks, its weather prophets, its orators for Fourth-of-July demands and other great occasions. It has its little local squabbles, its professional jealousies, its commercial rivalries. It has its milliners, its dressmakers, its fashionable coteries and their humble imitators. It has its elections, on which days society is stirred to its profoundest depths by the struggles of Smith, Brown, and Jones to become constable, justice, assessor, or collector. It also takes a live part in greater affairs, and sends its three or four delegates to county conventions with commendable punctuality.

If, all these pointers having been given, the intelligent reader cannot locate the village or town in the writer's mind, he must be dull indeed. He can have no more data from me. It is quite possible, however, that different persons will locate it differently as I go on with an analysis of some of the peculiarities of its prominent citizens.

First, that we may show a proper respect for wealth, let us commence with the rich man of the town.

This important personage, who has now retired from active commercial pursuits, and is in the enjoyment of a dignified old age, came to the County of Blank in its early settlement. Having a little money and much shrewdness, he decided that breaking prairie and raising stock was a slow way to wealth; so he established a country store, where he could enjoy a monopoly of the trade, and whatever percentage he chose to ask on his sales, which simplified merchandising very much in those early days. He also invested some spare money in buying tax titles, having the good luck thereby to become the owner of several pieces of land forfeited by their

DULLTOWN'S RICH MAN.

former owners, under pressure of the times, to the inevitable tax laws. He also gave credit, and even made small loans, at big interest, to several farmers who owned exceptionally good farms in his vicinity, but were poor calculators; and when the times of settlement came, and the debtors failed to pay, further obliged them by extending the time, on their executing certain mortgages to secure the same, which mortgages generally swallowed farms and improvements when the times got bad, as they usually did in those days. These farms, thus falling into his hands, he either sold again, partly on time, with mortgage to secure the balance, or rented to tenants, taking, to secure the rent, chattel mortgages on the crops and teams of his renters; so that, let crops succeed or fail, he was safe; and, in fact, a failure of buyer or tenant was better to him than their success. So, in a few years he quit merchandising, and set up as banker—loaned money, shaved notes, bought and sold farms—and is now retired from active business, unless collecting rents and cutting coupons be called such, and is reaping the rewards of a well-spent life in the deference and dependence of hosts of his old neighbors, though some are ill-natured enough to associate his name with that of one Shylock of Shakespearian memory; but there are envious men everywhere, as also there are men who *will* call a spade a spade.

It would give me great pleasure to go on describing other residents of Dulltown, if I did not fear to bore the reader. I should like to describe its one lawyer, whose principal forte it was to stir up litigation in the neighborhood. I should like to sketch the two justices of the peace, dignified as owls, and as ignorant of law, but with fairly good judgment to get at the equity of cases, unless befogged by the lawyers. I should like to describe the preachers, who, filling their several appointments, came every two years, full of energy and purpose to do much good, but who found themselves confronted at the start by quarrelsome cliques within their own churches, and petty jealousies, bickerings, and scandals without, which neutralized their best efforts at reform; while social life had its castes, its "sets," and its ostracisms, which no merit in the individual, nor interest in the cause, could combat. I could describe, also, that ubiquitous personage, the "fast" young man, who punctually put in an appearance every evening at the corner restaurant, or ogled young ladies on their way to church; who, in spite of the care of the authorities, found means to keep his flask filled—and emptied —every day, and became eloquent and melodious frequently, as well as erratic in his locomotion on Saturday evenings; also that class of hangers-on of the village who seemed to have no visible means of support—those unsolved conundrums of every community, who "toil not, neither do they spin," but yet contrive to keep fat and sleek.

I could describe another class—most active in the village life of Dulltown—that class of self-constituted censors of public morals, whose duty and pleasure it seems to be to watch over the affairs of other people, much gratified to find a screw loose, or a flaw somewhere, in the running-gears of the social machine. Indeed, so zealous do they become that they grow prophetic, predicting evils they can't see; and, like the shrewd dentist in his work, if they find no cavities, try to make them. They have capital noses for faults—they assign discreditable causes for actions, good or bad; if frailty claim a victim, they "suspicioned it long ago;" if misfor-

DULLTOWN'S LAWYER.

tune overtake a neighbor, they had looked for it from his foolish management. To be first to unearth a slander, and to variegate it with fanciful decorations, is, as Scott says, the "very skimming of their life's cream."

But all these pointers will help the reader little to locate Dulltown. There are several villages we know of, possessed of like citizens; and the reader will feel like calling the writer to time, and bidding him quit generalities and "drive on with his wagon."

Well, Dulltown had its romance. Start not, incredulous reader! It is not alone the unexpected, but the improbable, that happens. Was it "probable" that a tanner of Galena, or a sheriff of Buffalo, a rail-splitter of Illinois, or a canal-boat boy of Ohio, would fill the world's highest places? Was any "good" expected to "come out of Nazareth"? So a romance is possible anywhere, even in Dulltown. For the ingredients of romance are everywhere, if properly mixed. What are they? Youth, love, ambition, hope, success. Given a poor but gallant youth for a lover; a lovely, romantic maiden, with regulation blue or hazel or dark eyes; a hard, worldly father; opportunity, in the shape of "village sociables," or other levelling and democratic assemblages, where "the rich and the poor meet together," and "the Lord is the father of them all," as the Bible says, to illustrate the levelling function of such meetings; and you have material for a romance, even in the Dulltowns of the world.

So we will prepare to mix our ingredients. Perhaps the incantation of Macbeth's witches would be a good introduction: "Double, double, toil and trouble." But it needs no mystic rhyme. "Trouble" will "double" fast enough of its own motion in such cases as this. But we will artfully adjourn our story here to the next chapter.

II.

THE Widow Brown moved into Dulltown one cold day in November of I forget what year. But no matter. "Time is not the essence of my contract." It is more essential to say that the Widow Brown was, as a neighbor said, "poor as p'ison." (This neighbor was of the class before mentioned, who deemed it their special duty to know just how poor their new neighbor was.) But poor she was, there's no denying; else she had not taken such a poor house on a back street of Dulltown, and immediately given out that she wanted work to keep her family, consisting of herself and three children. She proved to be a good needle-woman, and soon obtained work enough to keep the wolf from the door —which is easier to do in the West, even where wolves are plenty, than in big Eastern cities, they say.

A JUSTICE OF THE PEACE.

Then, she sent her two biggest children to school. John, her oldest hopeful, was sturdy, rollicking, ragged "chunk of a boy" of twelve,—ragged, but clean and well groomed; and, somehow, his rags didn't "sit heavy on his soul," to the inculcating of undue humility, for before the first school-day was over he had "licked" the son of the principal merchant in the

place for making some "profane and face-
tious remarks," as Narby would say, on the
cut and quality of his (Johnny Brown's)
trousers and jacket. The fact that the merchant's boy was a year his senior, and the
bully of the school, at once made young
Johnny "loved, feared, and respected" by
his mates—a condition some philosopher
pronounces the most desirable one possible in this vale of tears. At all events,
Johnny's ragged jacket
didn't ostracise him in
the school; and on the
playground a certain
indefinable quality of
leadership asserted it-
self, but in so pleasant
and jolly a way that
very few felt called
upon to make head
against it.

Then, Johnny Brown
had a peculiar and ori-
ginal way of mastering
his schoolbooks that
was rather remarkable
in Dulltown. For it
had been customary
there, as elsewhere, for
pupils to depend on
their t e a c h e r s to
"punch 'em up," as the
directors expressed it;
and they had got so
used to the punching-
up process, and had
considered it so good-
natured on their part
towards their teachers
to learn at all, even
with all the encourage-
ment those unfortu-
nates could give them,
that they looked on
Johnny's *voluntary*
learning of a lesson as
little less than "flat
burglary;" and some of the boldest took
occasion to remonstrate with him for truck-
ling so much to "old Whackem," the master. But Johnny had his own notions on
this, as on most matters. Besides, he had
a little mother at home whom he cared
more to please than all the people of Dulltown combined; and this unreasonable little body had, despite her poverty, pre-
sumed to entertain hopes and ambitions
for her curly-headed boy that would have
shocked the placid brains of her neighbors
almost into mental activity had they known
of them. And at the base of her plans in

THE FAST YOUNG MAN.

the boy's behalf lay a thorough education.
She knew that this, of all earthly attain-
ments, is the greatest leveller of human distinctions, the greatest help for poverty to
rise to rank and affluence; and she, a poor
needle-woman, and, on occasion, a wash-
woman, had the audacity to hope (within
her own bosom) for such a career for her
Johnny as would have surprised, and, indeed, ill pleased, some of her patrons to
whom he brought home
budgets of work done
by his hard-working
mother.

But we will skip five
years in our narrative,
only stopping to ob-
serve that our hero,
Johnny Brown, had in
that growing period
shot up from a sturdy,
curly-headed urchin of
twelve, to a rather tall,
awkward youngster of
seventeen, as self-
reliant, but much more
bashful, than on the
day he entered school
at Dulltown. It was
his good luck that the
school was presided
over d u r i n g those
years by a really capa-
ble teacher, who ac-
cepted John's unusual
c a p a c i t y as a relief
from the pond of medi-
ocrity in which he was
condemned to paddle,
and had extended the
range of his studies
much beyond the usual
limits of a d i s t r i c t
s c h o o l. To com-
pensate for this out-of-
hours instruction,
Johnny had hoed out
the "professor's" garden, chopped wood
for him winters, and generally paid back
in such currency as he had in hand for
the loan of books, mostly mathematical,
and of practical value to a young man
who had it in view to "make his brains
help his hands." For John was what is
called a "handy lad" with tools; and what
he lost in the opinion of the Dulltown folk
on the score of being a crank about "hook
larnin'," he partly redeemed by his skill in
making a bob-sled, or repairing his mother's fences and sheds. And now, on the
last day of school, if we will listen to a

THE ROMANCE OF DULLTOWN.

JOHNNY.

little talk as he is packing up his books to leave the old schoolhouse forever, we may gather something of the true "inwardness" of the boy and future man, from his conversation with a schoolmate nearly as old as himself, but certainly a thousand times prettier. She is the youngest daughter of the aforesaid rich man of the village, and we will call her Mary Van Gould, which is not a bit like her real name, but hath a moneyed sound to it, and will pass as well as another.

"Well, John," she is saying, "I suppose to-day ends your school-days among us,"—this with a half-suppressed sigh, and a rather suspicious downcasting of a pair of tell-tale eyes which the owner is determined shall tell nothing.

"Yes, Miss Van Gould," John replies, "I guess I'll have to quit studying and go to work. I should have done so a year ago, but mother wanted me to finish up surveying and trigonometry; and I was weak enough, besides, to hate to leave the school for more reasons than one," he sheepishly added. If he had been a little bolder-eyed, he might have seen a little flush and pleased smile on Mary's face as she suddenly turned away to pick up a book she didn't want a bit. But just then *he*, too, was blushing, and as anxious to hide his confusion as the lady; so no harm came of it.

But, as usual, the lady recovered herself first. "And what's your programme next, John?" she asked, with an attempted indifference in her tone that wasn't a very brilliant success; for a suspicious moisture in her eyes made her turn round again to hunt for another book. (Oh, fie! what would Mrs. Grundy of Dulltown, or what would the stately father, the gold-spectacled, dignified ex-banker and present millionaire, have thought, to have seen that tear?)

But nobody saw it; and, as I said before, no harm was done. And John went on blunderingly to tell that he hoped to obtain employment in a machine-shop in a neighboring city. He *had* thought of going to college; but lack of means, and a desire to help the folks at home a little, had determined him to seek paying work, with such chance of promotion as he might deserve. "I have taxed my mother's slender purse too long," he said; though everybody knew he had helped her every way he could, and only continued in school so long at her urgent prayer; "and now," said he, "I feel like trying my fate, and seeing whether there's anything in me that pluck and push will work out."

"Oh, John, I'm *sure* there is!" the girl answered eagerly, and then blushed at her own forward defence. "And," she continued, "you may be sure that—that you have friends here who will pray—who will heartily wish you all success, and believe in you to the end."

Now, if John had been a little more forward, and pressed things skilfully, he might, in that girl's impressible mood, have got something more explicit; but nothing was farther from his hopes and wishes. He was a poor boy, with his place in the world to make. He had nothing to

STICK IN HAND, HE SAT BETWEEN HER AND A VICIOUS STEER.

THE ROMANCE OF DULLTOWN.

offer. The pretty girl before him, generous and kindly as she was, was as far separated from him as the antipodes. He had helped her in her lessons, schoolboy fashion; he had on one occasion stood between her and considerable danger, when a herd of Texas steers were charging through the street where she was walking to school—a thing he thought little of, as, stick in hand, he got between her and a vicious steer that developed hostile intentions towards her red shawl. But when a sound lick on the horns with a good shillelah had changed the brute's mind, and sent him after the rest of the herd, Mary, pale as death, looked on the young youngster as a real hero. Well, perhaps he was, as heroes go; but heroes of romance are not generally painted in shirt-sleeves, with a torn straw hat on their heads, and in patched trousers. No, she must have been mistaken. Yet the silly girl couldn't get it out of her mind (and heart), that he was a hero; and schoolgirls take to heroes as ducks to water, as all the world knows.

Well, John and Mary parted there, with a hand-shake and a good-by, as hundreds of Johns and Marys have and will; and Mary went home to her father's elegant mansion to dream of heroes and stout boys with sticks in their hands, standing between her and danger, and then of tall, bashful youths, with unmistakable sprouting mustachios and handsome eyes, albeit they but furtively glance from under a rather fluffy hat. And John went out into the big world, with a brave heart, to try and prove himself a man.

III.

TIME flies. Gentle reader, this is not an original remark. In fact, its authorship is lost in the mists of antiquity; though there has not been an age in which the essential fact it records has not been repeated in varied shape, all either reasserting or moralizing upon the fugacious character of Time.

So we will suppose the old high-flyer to have made the circuit of three years. Dulltown has held the even tenor of its way while the seasons and the almanac

THE CHANGE OF PUBLIC MORALS.

have marked every citizen of that placid village three years older. No, not all. There are certain persons whose age does not always tally with the almanac or the family record; that is, the age they give to a curious public. These individuals, unmarried ladies generally, sometimes fail to note the earth's revolutions round the sun; but "the whirligig of Time brings in his revenges," and he has a subtle engraver, who fails not to mark his work on cheek and brow.

But to our heroine, Mary Van Gould, Time was nothing but kind. Since she had been a schoolgirl he had much improved her form, filled her cheeks, and painted them the most approved color; had given her eyes more beauty and expression, though of a more sad and thoughtful kind; and her mind had overcome the depressing influence of Dulltown society. She was the companion and joy of her father, who lacked companionship sadly since his wife had sickened and died—a prey to the universal stagnation, some said. It is a sad sight when man and wife are not society for each other. This pair had never been. He had married her for her wealth, but he got no companionship; for, though a good woman, her mind was weak and uncultivated. His library was nothing to her, nor his conversation, being often beyond her range. God help the man and wife who have no common interests to bind them together, yet are doomed to pass their lives thrown upon themselves for society!

But Mary took the place his wife was unfitted for, and became his pride, his joy, his all, as she grew older. Need it be said he grew anxious about her marrying and leaving him alone some day? And yet he was comforted by noting that, while she was pleasant and kind to all, no "bright, particular star" seemed to rise over her horizon; no one more than another of the youth of Dulltown received favor at her hands. And the old millionaire wondered at this not a little. She was young, healthy, fair, and his destined heiress. And yet she was entering her nineteenth year with a heart as indifferent as when a schoolgirl to those attractions which mean so much to young girls generally.

But one day his eyes were opened, for he had sharp eyes where his interests were touched. For one day Johnny Brown came home from New York to visit his mother and the scenes of his youth. He had gone away a stalwart lad; he came back a handsome, manly youth of past twenty, with the marks of toil and success plainly to be read on his person and in his air. Those hands had been intimate with hammer and wrench, bar and lever. His eye had the mechanical cast soon acquired by the worker in metals; his arms, the muscle of the athlete. He was a fine specimen of an intelligent American machinist; and no mother could have taken back to her arms a manlier or a more welcome wanderer from the home of his youth.

Well, John stayed at home a few weeks, visiting his friends, and welcomed by all, both as a relief from the monotony of Dulltown, and from the really friendly feeling with which every community welcomes back those who go out into the world and play a manly part therein. And there was no more appreciative or closely observant acquaintance than the ex-banker, Mr. Van Gould. His judgment of men was shrewd and unerring. He took pains to engage John in conversation—to question him on matters of business, of observation, of principle, of opinion. In fact, in his quiet way, he had thoroughly "sized up" our hero before the latter mistrusted that it was *he*, instead of his news, Mr. Van Gould was weighing. And after John had gone back to his duties in New York, to take up again his life's work, nobody in Dulltown ever suspected that the shrewd old man had inventoried him and laid him away labelled for future reference.

But of this hereafter. John and Mary met, of course, during those precious few weeks. And, as it is not in our plan to give details of love-making, which you can get from any well-constructed modern novel, I will only say that before they parted they were sworn lovers, and this despite the fact that there was a million or so dollars between them.

But they mutually agreed that it would be better not to let their engagement be known. They dreaded the opposition of her father; they knew the barrier fate had placed between them, and knew, also, that many years must elapse before young Brown could hope, with the best luck, to win means enough to demand the millionaire's daughter, with any prospect of success.

So it was a sad parting, but courageous, on both sides. Yet, "hope deferred maketh the heart sick." It was not many months before the keen eyes of the father noted a careworn look on his daughter's pretty face, and the fact that this look became more marked after the advent of the mails. He took the precaution to step to the post-office himself for the family mail, which his daughter had generally brought, and he noticed that when letters bearing a New York postmark were received by her, they were succeeded by a nervous depression she took much pains to hide.

So he proceeds to take his measures with a diabolical cunning worthy of a Malvolio. He first makes an errand to the Widow Brown's cottage. He contracts for the making of some articles of clothing, and, as he is about leaving, asks: "Ah, by the way, do you hear anything from your son John lately, madam?" He is surprised to see the widow burst into tears, and to hear her tell that a fire in his employer's factory had destroyed the plant, and all his own investment as a part owner of the stock therein, leaving John broken up, as well as thrown out of employment. And the good lady was surprised to see a hard smile pass over the millionaire's stern face, a smile of gratified malice, she was sure; and she could be sworn she heard a laugh as he stumbled down-stairs, and a remark that "it served them right, trying to deceive her old gray-haired father!"

And here the "Romance of Dulltown" properly commences, and we will warrant it to be the "first and only" romance of the kind ever recorded, so far as our researches in the much-trodden fields of fiction reveal. For, what does that inhuman

"IT WAS WEAK ENOUGH, BESIDES, TO HAVE TO LEAVE MARTHA FOR MORE REASONS THAN ONE."

parent do? He seizes her next letter, breaks the seal, reads the direction, and, I shame to say it, the contents, which were as follows:

NEW YORK, *July* 4, 18—

DEAREST MARY:

Since I wrote you last week, my affairs have taken a still more decided turn for the worse. I had hope at that date, as I told you, that my partners might save enough out of the wreck to enable us to rebuild and go on with our work; but since then, by the defection of one and the indebtedness of another, our enterprise is dead beyond hope.

Dear Mary, I write this in more pain than you can imagine. It is not the loss itself that crushes me, but the utter hopelessness of starting again with a reasonable chance of succeeding in a good many years. I will not deceive you. I am ruined financially, beyond hope of recovery until after long years of toil, and perhaps disappointment in the end. I cannot, as an honorable man, ask you to wait for me. When I had a bright prospect ahead of me, with the promise you gave me to cheer and uphold me, no man ever worked harder or more hopefully. Now I see no prospect of succeeding; and, dear as you are to me, bound up in every hope, ambition, or dream of happiness I have had on earth for years, I cannot hold you to a promise to which your heart, more than your best judgment, prompted you. Dear Mary, I give that promise back. It would be wronging you, wronging your father, nay, it would be wronging myself, to hold you on for years, hoping against hope, till the best part of your life had been lost to you, and the roses had faded from your cheeks and the joy from your life.

Mary, God only knows the pain with which I give you up! Your image has been before me ever since I left the school where we parted on the last day of the term, when I was to go forth, a green boy, to fight my way in the world. And when you so kindly

THE ROMANCE OF DULLTOWN.

gave me your "God speed." I went out to my task as bravely as ever went belted knight to win honor or his lady's favor. I knew, even then, what you were to me; but I trust I had honor enough not to try to commit you, who were so much above me in station, to any words which might seem to bind you, although even then I hoped you might not be indifferent to me. But when I seemed to be in a sure way to rise in the world; when I came back to Dulltown and found you so much lovelier than I had ever dreamed of, and, better still, as true and good as you were fair; I felt that such good fortune was beyond my deserts—that it could not be that a poor widow's son was the chosen lover of such a one as my Mary! It was too good to hope or believe, and I fear it was better than I deserved; for the fates have but given me a view of the Promised Land, to hide it again in clouds where no ray of light can penetrate.

Dear Mary, you are free. Forget me and be happy, Or remember me as one who, while he would gladly die to secure your happiness, cannot deceive you with vain hopes into wasting your youth waiting for

Your ruined and hopeless bankrupt,
JOHN BROWN.

This he reads with many a "hem!" and has to wipe his glasses two or three times, because either his indignation or some other feeling is getting away with him. Then, closing the letter and sealing it carefully, that his much-abused daughter may not suspect that it has been tampered with, he sits down and in cold blood writes to the lover of that daughter a letter, of which the following is a copy :

DULLTOWN, BLANK COUNTY, STATE OF ——
JOHN BROWN, ESQ :

Dear Sir: Having found out—no matter how, but not from my unnatural daughter—that you and she have conspired to rob me of the one treasure I value in this world ; but also that you, a co-conspirator as aforesaid, have acted what the world might call an honorable part therein; now this is to inform you that, as long as you two are so silly as to like each other, and as I find you to be a bright and honorable young fellow, you have my full consent to marry whenever you choose, with an old man's blessing to boot. But I make it one of the conditions precedent, that if you *will* go into your dirty manufacturing business, it shall be in this county, where I can live near you, and still attend to my business.

N. B. My daughter shall receive a check for one hundred thousand dollars on the day of her marriage, which I hope will be soon, for I want to see the roses bloom in those pretty cheeks again before Christmas.

P. S. You thought you were very clever, didn't you? Why, bless your silly hearts, I knew all about it ages ago! So, come home, Johnny, and I'll have the fatted calf hung up by the heels, ready for the prodigal's return.

Your future father-in-law,
THOMAS VAN GOULD.

And thus ended the "Romance of Dulltown"—or, rather, there it began in reality; for a jollier and a more perfectly happy family than the Van Gould-Brown connection would be hard to find in this world of bank failures, mail robberies, and general "cussedness." "Long may they wave!"

THE ROCK ISLAND EXPRESS ROBBERY.

STORIES FROM THE ARCHIVES OF THE PINKERTON DETECTIVE AGENCY.

BY CLEVELAND MOFFETT.

I.

ON March 12, 1886, the through express on the Rock Island road left Chicago at 10.45 P. M., with twenty-two thousand dollars in fifty and one hundred dollar bills, in the keeping of Kellogg Nichols, an old-time messenger of the United States Express Company. This sum had been sent by a Chicago bank to be delivered at the principal bank of Davenport, Iowa. In addition to the usual passenger coaches, the train drew two express cars: the first, for express only, just behind the engine; and following this, one for express and baggage. These cars had end doors, which offer the best opportunity to train robbers. Messenger Nichols was in the first car, and was duly at his work when the train stopped at Joliet, a town about forty miles west of Chicago. But at the next stop, which was made at Morris, Harry Schwartz, a brakeman, came running from Nichols's car, crying: "The messenger is dead."

The messenger's lifeless body was found lying on the floor of the car. The head had been crushed by some heavy weapon, and there was a pistol wound in the right shoulder. Apparently he had been overcome only after a hard fight. His face was set with fierce determination. His fists were clenched, and the hands and fingers cut and scratched in a curious way, while under the nails were found what proved to be bits of human flesh. The pistol wound was from a weapon of thirty-two caliber. It evidently was not the cause of the man's death, but the blows of some blunt weapon, dealt probably after the shot was fired. All who knew Messenger Nichols were surprised at the desperate resistance he seemed to have made, for he was a small, light man, not more than five feet five in height, nor weighing over one hundred and thirty pounds, and of no great credit among his fellows for pluck and courage.

WILLIAM PINKERTON.

The express car was immediately detached from the train and left at Morris, guarded by all the train crew except Schwartz, who was sent on with the train to Davenport. After the first cursory inspection no one was allowed to enter the car where Nichols lay; and nothing was known precisely as to the extent of the robbery. The safe door had been found open, and the floor of

A WIDE SEARCH THAT REVEALED NOTHING BUT A MASK.

An urgent telegram was at once sent to the Pinkertons at Chicago, and Mr. William Pinkerton, with a force of detectives, arrived at Morris on a special train a few hours later. Search parties were at once sent out in all directions along the country roads, and up and down the tracks. Hundreds of people joined in the search, for the news of the murder spread rapidly through the whole region, and not a square yard of territory for miles between Morris and Minooka Station was left unexplored. It happened that the ground was covered with snow, but the keenest scrutiny failed to reveal any significant footprints, and the search parties returned after many hours, having made only a single discovery. This was a mask found in a cattle-guard near Minooka—a mask made of black cloth, with white strings fastened at either side, one of which had been torn out of the cloth as if in a struggle.

WILLIAM PINKERTON EXAMINES THE CAR.

Meantime, Mr. Pinkerton himself entered the car and made a careful investigation. His first discovery was a heavy poker, bearing stains of blood and bits of matted hair. It was hanging in its usual place, behind the stove. The significance of this last fact was great in Mr. Pinkerton's opinion; from it he concluded that the crime had been committed by a railroad man, his reasoning being that the poker could have been restored to its usual place after such a use only mechanically, and from force of habit, and that an assailant who was not a railroad man would have left it on the floor or thrown it away.

Coming to the safe Mr. Pinkerton found that the twenty-two thousand dollars was missing, and that other papers had been hastily searched over, but left behind as valueless. Among these was a bundle of cancelled drafts that had been roughly torn open and then thrown aside. Mr. Pinkerton scarcely noticed at the moment, but had occasion to remember subsequently, that a small piece of one of these drafts was missing, as if a corner had been torn off.

All the train hands were immediately questioned, but none of their stories were in any way significant, except that of Newton Watt, the man in charge of the second car. He said that while busy counting over his way-bills and receipts he had been startled by the crash of broken glass in the ventilator overhead, and that at the same moment, a heavily built man, wearing a black mask, had entered the car and said: "If you move, the man up there will bore you." Looking up, Watt said further, he saw a hand thrust through the broken glass and holding a revolver. Thus intimidated he made no attempt to give an alarm, and the masked man presently left him under guard of the pistol overhead, which covered him until shortly before the train reached Morris, when it was withdrawn. He was able to locate the place where the crime must have been committed, as he remembered that the engine was whistling for Minooka Station when the stranger entered the car. This left about thirty minutes for the murder, robbery, and escape.

Returning to Chicago, Mr. Pinkerton investigated the character of the man Watt, and found that he had a clean record, was regarded as a trusty and efficient man, and had three brothers who had been railroad men for years and had always given perfect satisfaction. Watt's good reputation and straightforward manner were strong points in his favor, and yet there was something questionable in his story of the mysterious hand. For one thing, no footprints were found in the snow on the top of the car.

BRAKEMAN SCHWARTZ AND HIS STORY.

Brakeman Schwartz, the only man on the train who had not yet been questioned, "deadheaded" his way, in railway parlance, back from Davenport the following night on Conductor Danforth's train, and reported to Mr. Pinkerton the next morning. He was a tall, fine-looking young fellow, about twenty-seven, with thin lips and a face that showed determination. He was rather dapper in dress, and kept on his gloves during the conversation. Mr. Pinkerton received him pleasantly, and, after they had been smoking and chatting for an hour or so, he suggested to Schwartz that he would be more comfortable with his gloves off. Schwartz accordingly removed his gloves, and revealed red marks on the backs of his hands, such as might have been made by finger nails digging into them.

"How did you hurt your hands, Schwartz?" asked Mr. Pinkerton.

"Oh, I did that handling baggage night before last," explained Schwartz, and then he related incidentally that as he was on his way back to Chicago, the conductor of the train, Conductor Danforth, had discovered a valise left by somebody in one of the toilet rooms. Later in the day, Mr. Pinkerton summoned the conductor, who said that the valise was an old one, of no value; and, having no contents, he had thrown it out on an ash pile. The only thing he had found in the valise was a piece of paper that attracted his attention, because it was marked with red lines.

Examining this piece of paper carefully, Mr. Pinkerton saw that it had been torn from a money draft, and at once thought of the package in the express messenger's safe. Now, it is a remarkable fact that no human power can tear two pieces of paper in exactly the same way; the ragged fibres will only fit perfectly when the two original parts are brought together. There remained no doubt, when this test was made in the present case, that the piece of paper found on Conductor Danforth's east-bound train had been torn from the draft in the express car robbed the night before on a west-bound train. The edges fitted, the red lines corresponded, and unquestionably some one had brought that piece of paper from the one train to the other. In other words, some one connected with the crime of the previous night had ridden back to Chicago twenty-four hours later with Conductor Danforth.

Mr. Pinkerton at once ordered a search made for the missing valise, and also an inquiry regarding the passengers who had ridden on Conductor Danforth's train between Davenport and Chicago, on the night following the murder. The valise was found on the ash heap where the conductor had thrown it, and, in the course of the next few days, the detectives had located or accounted for all passengers on Conductor Danforth's train, with the exception of one man who had ridden on a free pass. The conductor could only recall this man's features vaguely; and, while some of the passengers remembered him well enough, there was no clew to his name or identity. As it appeared that no other of the passengers could have been connected with the crime, efforts were redoubled to discover the holder of this pass.

II.

THE PLUNKETT THEORY.

So great was the public interest in the crime and the mystery surrounding it, that three separate, well-organized investigations of it were undertaken. The Rock Island Railroad officials, with their detectives, conducted one; a Chicago newspaper, the "Daily News," with its detectives, another; and the Pinkertons, in the interest of the United States Express Company, a third.

Mr. Pinkerton, as we have seen, concluded that the crime had been committed by railway men. The railway officials were naturally disinclined to believe ill of their employees, and an incident occurred about this time which turned the investigation in an entirely new direction, and made them the more disposed to discredit Mr. Pinkerton's theory. This was the receipt of a letter from a convict in the Michigan City penitentiary, named Plunkett, who wrote the Rock Island Railroad officials, saying that he could furnish them with important information.

Mr. St. John, the general manager of the road, went in person to the penitentiary to take Plunkett's statement, which was in effect that he knew the men who had committed the robbery and killed Nichols, and was willing to sell this information in exchange for a full pardon, which the railroad people could secure by using their influence. This they promised to do, if his story proved true, and Plunkett then told them of a plot that had been worked out a year or so before, when he had been "grafting" with a "mob" of pickpockets at county fairs. There were with him at that time "Hutch" McCoy, James Connors (known as "Yellowhammer"), and a man named "Jeff," whose surname he did not know. These three men, Plunkett said, had planned an express robbery on the Rock Island road, to be executed in precisely the same way, and at precisely the same point on the road, as in the case in question.

AN EMINENT EDITOR TURNS DETECTIVE.

The story was plausible and won Mr. St. John's belief. It won the belief, also, of Mr. Melville E. Stone, of the "Daily News"; and forthwith, the railway detectives, working with the newspaper detectives, were instructed to go ahead on new lines, regardless of trouble or expense. Their first endeavor was to capture "Hutch" McCoy, the leader of the gang. "Hutch" was a pickpocket, burglar, and all-around thief, whose operations kept him travelling all over the United States.

The police in various cities having been communicated with to no purpose, Mr. Stone finally decided to do a thing the like of which no newspaper proprietor, perhaps, ever undertook before, that is, start out on a personal search for McCoy and his associates. With Frank Murray, one of the best detectives in Chicago, and other detectives, he went to Galesburg, where the gang was said to have a sort of headquarters. The party found there none of the men they were after, but they learned that "Thatch" Grady, a notorious criminal with whom "Dutch" McCoy was known to be in relations, was in Omaha. So they hurried to Omaha, but only to find that Grady had gone to St. Louis. Then to St. Louis went Mr. Stone and his detectives, hot on the scent, and spent several days in that city searching high and low.

A VAIN SEARCH AS FAR AS NEW ORLEANS.

The method of locating a criminal in a great city is as interesting as it is little understood. The first step is to secure from the local police information as to the favorite haunts of criminals of the class under pursuit, paying special regard in the preliminary inquiries to the possibility of love affairs; for thieves, even more than honest men, are swayed in their lives by the tender passion, and are often brought to justice through the agency of women. With so much of such information in their possession as they could gather, Mr. Stone and his detectives spent their time in likely resorts, picking up acquaintance with frequenters; and, whenever possible, turning the talk adroitly upon the man they were looking for. It is a mistake to suppose that in work like this detectives disguise themselves. False beards and mustaches, goggles and lightning changes of clothing, are never heard of except in the pages of badly informed story-writers. In his experience of over twenty-five years Mr. Murray never wore such a disguise, nor knew of any reputable detective who did. In this expedition the detectives simply assumed the characters and general style of the persons they were thrown with, passing for men of sporting tastes from the East; and, having satisfied the people they met that they meant no harm, they had no difficulty in obtaining such news of McCoy and the others as there was. Unfortunately this was not much.

After going from one city to another on various clews, hearing of one member of the gang here and another there, and in each instance losing their man, the detectives finally brought up in New Orleans. They had spent five or six weeks of time and a large amount of money, only to find themselves absolutely without a clew as to the whereabouts of the men they were pursuing. They were much discouraged when a telegram from Mr. Pinkerton told them that "Dutch" McCoy was back in Galesburg, where they had first sought him. Proceeding thither with all despatch, they traced McCoy into a saloon, and there three of them, John Smith representing the Rock Island Railroad, John McGinn for the Pinkerton agency, and Frank Murray working for Mr. Stone, with drawn revolvers captured him in spite of a desperate dash he made to escape.

McCoy's capture was the occasion of much felicitation among the people interested in the matter. Mr. St. John and Mr. Stone were confident that now the whole mystery of the express robbery would be resolved and the murderers convicted. But McCoy showed on trial that he had left New Orleans to come north only the night before the murder, and had spent the whole of that night on the Illinois Central Railroad. It also appeared that McCoy's associate, Connors, was in jail at the time of the robbery, and that the man "Jeff" was dead. Thus the whole Plunkett story was exploded.

III.

SHADOWING SCHWARTZ.

SOME time before this, the man who had ridden on the free pass, and given the detectives so much trouble, had been accidentally found by Jack Mullins, a brakeman on Conductor Danforth's train. He proved to be an advertising solicitor, employed by no other than Mr. Melville E. Stone, who would have given a thousand dollars to know what his agent knew; for the advertising man had seen the conductor bring out the valise containing the all-important fragment of the draft. But he had not realized the value of the news in his possession, and Mr. Pinkerton took good care to keep him from that knowledge. One hint of the truth to the "Daily News" people, and the whole story would have been blazoned forth in its columns, and the murderer would have taken warning. Not until he had seen the man safely on a train out from Chicago did Mr. Pinkerton breathe easily; and it was not until months later that Mr. Stone learned how near he came to getting a splendid "scoop" on the whole city and country.

The identification of the pass-holder removed the last possibility that the valise had been taken into the train by any of Conductor Danforth's passengers. And yet the valise was there! How came it there? In the course of their examination, two of the passengers had testified to having seen Schwartz enter the toilet-room during the run. Brakeman Jack Mullins stated that he had been in the same room twice that night, that the second time he had noticed the valise, but that it was not there when he went in first. Other witnesses in the car were positive that the person who entered the room last before the time when Mullins saw the valise was Schwartz. Thus the chain of proof was tightening, and Mr. Pinkerton sent for Schwartz.

SCHWARTZ AFFECTS TO PLAY DETECTIVE.

After talking with the brakeman in a semi-confidential way for some time, the detective began to question him about Watt, his fellow-trainman. Schwartz said he was a good fellow, and, in general, spoke highly of him. Mr. Pinkerton seemed to hesitate a little, and then said:

"Can I trust you, Schwartz?"

"Yes, sir."

"Well, the fact is, I am a little suspicious of Watt. You see, his story about that hand overhead does not exactly hang together. I don't want to do him any wrong, but he must be looked after. Now, my idea is to have you go about with him as much as you can, see if he meets any strangers or spends much money, and let me know whatever happens. Will you do it?"

Schwartz readily consented on the assurance that the railroad people would give him leave of absence. The next day he reported that Watt had met a man who wore a slouch hat, had unkempt red hair, and in general looked like a border ruffian. He had overheard the two talking together in a saloon on Cottage Grove Avenue, where the stranger had discussed the murder of Nichols in great detail, showing a remarkable familiarity with the whole affair. Schwartz had a sort of Jesse James theory (which he seemed anxious to have accepted), that the crime had been committed by a gang of Western desperadoes, and that this fellow was connected with them.

Mr. Pinkerton listened with interest to all this, but was less edified than Schwartz imagined, since two of his most trusted "shadows," who had been following Schwartz, had given him reports of the latter's movements, making it plain that the red-haired desperado was a myth, and that no such meeting as Schwartz described had taken place. Nevertheless, professing to be well pleased with Schwartz's efforts, Mr. Pinkerton sent him out to track the fabulous desperado. Schwartz continued to render false reports. Finally, without a word to arouse his suspicion, he was allowed to resume his work on the railroad.

The "shadows" put upon Schwartz after this, reported a suspicious intimacy between him and Watt, and a detective of great tact, Frank Jones, was detailed to get into their confidence, if possible. He was given a "run" as brakeman between Des Moines and Davenport, and it was arranged that he should come in from the west and lay over at Davenport on the same days that Schwartz and Watt laid over there, coming in from the east. Jones played his part cleverly, and was soon on intimate terms with Schwartz and Watt, taking his meals at their boarding-house and sleeping in a room adjoining theirs. They finally came to like him so well that they suggested his trying to get a transfer to their "run," between Davenport and Chicago. This was successfully arranged, and then the three men were together constantly, Jones even going to board at Schwartz's house in Chicago. About this time Schwartz began to talk of giving up railroad work, and going to live in Kansas or the Far West. It was arranged that Jones should join him and Mrs. Schwartz on a Western trip. Meantime, Schwartz applied to the company for leave of absence, on the plea that he wished to arrange some family matters in Philadelphia.

Mr. Pinkerton, being informed by Jones of Schwartz's application, used his influence to have it granted. When the young man started east, he did not travel alone. His every movement was watched and reported, nor was he left unguarded for a moment, day or night, during an absence of several weeks, in New York, Philadelphia, and other Eastern cities.

THE ART OF "SHADOWING."

To one unfamiliar with the resources and organization of a great detective system, it is incomprehensible how continuous "shadowing," day after day and week after week, through thousands of miles of journeyings, can be accomplished. The matter is made none the simpler when you know that there must be a change of "shadows" every day. However adroit the detective, his continued presence in a locality would soon arouse suspicion. The daily change of "shadows" is easy when the man under watch remains in one place; for then it is only necessary to send a new "shadow" from the central office early each morning to replace the one who "put the man to bed" the night before. But it is very different when the subject is constantly travelling about on boats or railways, and perhaps sleeping in a different town each night. Without the network of agencies, including large and small bureaus, that the Pinkertons' have gradually established all over the United States, the "shadowing" of a man in rapid flight would be impossible. As it is, nothing is easier. Schwartz, for instance, spent several days in Buffalo, where his actions were reported hour by hour, until he bought his ticket for Philadelphia. As he took the train a fresh "shadow" took it too, securing a section in the same sleeping car with him, and taking his meals at the same time Schwartz took his, either in the dining-car or at stations. No sooner had the train left the station than the Pinkerton representative in Buffalo reported by cipher despatch to the bureau in Philadelphia, whither Schwartz was going. The exact form of the despatch, which well illustrates a system in constant use in the Pinkerton bureaus, was as follows:

M. J. LINDEN, 441 CHESNUT STREET,
PHILADELPHIA, PA.

Anxious shoes sucker Brown marbles man other dropping eight arrives put grand hity marbles articles along or derby coat ship very tan sent wearing these have and is ribbon ink dust central Tuesday for dust to rice hat and and paper red yellow ink get most jewelry morning depot on.
D. ROBERTSON.

In despatches of this sort important information regarding criminals is constantly flashing over the wires, with no danger of any "leak."

Thus, from one city to another, and through every part of the country, any criminal may be "shadowed" to-day as Schwartz was "shadowed" eight years ago, one set of detectives relieving another every twenty-four hours, and the man's every word and action be carefully noted down and reported without his having the faintest suspicion that he is under observation. The task of "shadowing" a person who is traversing city streets is intrusted to men especially skilled in the art (for art it is) of seeing without being seen. This is, indeed, one of the most difficult tasks a detective is called upon to perform, and the few who excel in it are given little else to do. Where a criminal like Schwartz, upon whose final capture much depends, is being followed, two, three, or even four "shadows" are employed simultaneously, one keeping in advance, one in the rear, and two on either side. The advantage of this is that one relieves the other by change of position, thus lessening the chance of discovery, while, of course, it is scarcely possible for several "shadows" to be thrown off the trail at once. An adroit criminal might outwit one "shadow," but he could scarcely outwit four. A "shadow" on coming into a new town with a subject, reveals himself to the "shadow" who is to relieve him, by some prearranged signal, like a handkerchief held in the left hand.

The result of the "shadowing" in Schwartz's case was conclusive. No sooner was the brakeman out of Chicago than he began spending money far in excess of his income. He bought fine furniture, expensive clothing, articles of jewelry, presents for his wife, and laid in an elaborate supply of rifles, shot-guns, revolvers, and all sorts of ammunition, including a quantity of cartridges. The "shadows" found that in almost every case he paid for his purchases with fifty or one hundred dollar bills. As far as possible these bills were secured by the detectives from the persons to whom they had been paid, immediately after Schwartz's departure. It will be remembered that the money taken in the robbery consisted of fifty and one hundred dollar bills.

IV.

SCHWARTZ UNDER ARREST.

IN addition to this it was found by the investigations of detectives at Philadelphia that Schwartz was the son of a wealthy, retired butcher there, a most respectable man, and that he had a wife and child in Philadelphia, whom he had entirely deserted. This gave an opportunity to take him into custody, and still conceal from him that he was suspected of committing a worse crime. The Philadelphia wife and child were taken on to Chicago, and Schwartz was placed under arrest, charged with bigamy. Mr. Pinkerton went to the jail at once, and wishing to keep Schwartz's confidence as far as possible, assured him that this arrest was not his work at all, but that of detectives Smith and Murray, who were, as Schwartz knew, working in the interests of the railroad people, and of the Chicago "Daily News." Mr. Pinkerton told Schwartz that he still believed, as he had done all along, that Watt was the guilty man, and promised to do whatever he could to befriend Schwartz. The latter did not appear to be very much alarmed, and said that a

Philadelphia lawyer was coming on to defend him. The lawyer did come a few days later, when a bond for two thousand dollars was furnished for Schwartz's reappearance, and he was set at liberty. Matters had gone so far, however, that it was not considered safe to leave Schwartz out of jail, and he was immediately rearrested, on the charge of murder.

Whether because of long preparation for this ordeal, or because he was a man of strong character, Schwartz received this blow without the slightest show of emotion, and went back into the jail as coolly as he had come out. He merely requested that he might have an interview with his wife as soon as possible.

MRS. SCHWARTZ COMES INTO THE CASE.

Mr. Pinkerton had evidence enough against Schwartz to furnish a strong presumption of guilt, but it was all circumstantial, and, besides, it did not involve Newton Watt, whose complicity was more than suspected. From the first Mr. Pinkerton had been carefully conciliatory of the later Mrs. Schwartz. At just the right moment, and by adroit management, he got her under his direction, and by taking a train with her to Morris, and then on the next morning taking another train back to Chicago, he succeeded in preventing her from getting the advice of her husband's lawyer, who was meantime making the same double journey on pursuing trains with the design of cautioning her against speaking to Mr. Pinkerton. She had come to regard Mr. Pinkerton more as a protector than as an enemy, and he, during the hours they were together, used every device to draw from her some damaging admission. He told her that the evidence against her husband, although serious in its character, was not, in his opinion, sufficient to establish his guilt. He told her of the bills found in Schwartz's possession, of the torn piece of the draft taken from the valise, of the marks on his hands and the lies he had told. All this, he said, proved that Schwartz had some connection with the robbery, but not that he had committed the murder, or done more than assist Watt, whom Mr. Pinkerton professed to regard as the chief criminal. The only hope of saving her husband now, he impressed upon her, was for her to make a plain statement of the truth, and trust that he would use this in her husband's interest.

After listening to all that he said, and trying in many ways to evade the main question, Mrs. Schwartz at last admitted to Mr. Pinkerton that her husband had found a package containing five thousand dollars of the stolen money under one of the seats on Conductor Danforth's train, on the night of his return to Chicago. He had kept this money and used it for his own purposes, but had been guilty of no other offence in the matter. Mrs. Schwartz stuck resolutely to this statement, and would admit nothing further.

Believing that he had drawn from her as much as he could, Mr. Pinkerton now accompanied Mrs. Schwartz to the jail, where she was to see her husband. The first words she said on entering the room where he was, were, "Harry, I have told Mr. Pinkerton the whole truth. I thought that was the best way, for he is your friend. I told him about your finding the five thousand dollars under the seat of the car, and that that was all you had to do with the business."

SCHWARTZ AND HIS WIFE TELL THE WHOLE STORY TO HIDDEN AUDITORS.

Schwartz gave his wife a terrible glance as she said this, and for the first time his emotions nearly betrayed him. However, he braced himself and only admitted in a general way that there was some truth in what his wife had said. He refused positively to go into details, seemed very nervous, and almost immediately asked to be left alone with his wife. Mr. Pinkerton had been expecting this, and was prepared for it. He realized the shock that would be caused in Schwartz's mind by his wife's unexpected confession, and counted on this to lead to further admissions. It was, therefore, of the highest importance that credible witnesses should overhear all that transpired in the interview between Schwartz and his wife. With this end in view, the room where the interview was to take place had been arranged so that a number of witnesses could see and hear without their presence being suspected, and the sheriff of the county, a leading merchant, and a leading banker of the town were waiting there in readiness.

As soon as the door had closed and the husband and wife were left alone, Schwartz exclaimed:

"You fool, you have put a rope around Watt's and my neck!"

"Why, Harry, I had to tell him something, he knew so much. You can trust him."

"You ought to know better than to trust anybody."

The man walked back and forth, a prey

to the most violent emotions, his wife trying vainly to quiet him. At each affectionate touch he would brush her off roughly with a curse, and go on pacing back and forth fiercely. Suddenly he burst out :

"What did you do with that coat, the one you cut the mask out of ?"

"Oh, that's all right ; it's in the wood-shed, under the whole wood pile."

They continued to talk for over an hour, referring to the murder and robbery repeatedly, and furnishing evidence enough to establish beyond any question the guilt of both Schwartz and Watt.

Meantime, Watt had been arrested in Chicago, also charged with murder, and in several examinations had showed signs of breaking down and confessing, but in each instance had recovered himself and said nothing. The evidence of Schwartz himself, however, in the interview at the jail, taken with the mass of other evidence that had accumulated, was sufficient to secure the conviction of both men, who were condemned, at the trial, to life imprisonment in the Joliet penitentiary. They would undoubtedly have been hanged, but for the conscientious scruples of one juryman, who did not believe in capital punishment. Watt has since died, and Schwartz is now regarded as a model prisoner, his case being peculiar in this—that since he has been in the penitentiary, nearly eight years now, he has never received a letter, paper, or any communication from the outside world.

MRS. SCHWARTZ'S CONFESSION.

About a year after the trial, Schwartz's Chicago wife died of consumption. On her death bed she made a full confession to Superintendent Robertson, of the Pinkerton force. She said that her husband's mind had been inflamed by the constant reading of sensational literature of the dime novel order ; and that under this evil influence he had planned the robbery, believing that it would be easy to intimidate a weak little man like Nichols, and escape with the money without harming him. Nichols, however, had fought like a tiger up and down the car, and had finally forced them to kill him. In the fight he had torn off the mask that Mrs. Schwartz had made out of one of her husband's old coats. It was Watt who fired the pistol, while Schwartz used the poker. Schwartz had given Watt five thousand dollars of the stolen money, and had kept the rest himself. He had carried the money away in an old satchel bought for the purpose. A most unusual place of concealment had been chosen, and one where the money had escaped discovery, although on several occasions, in searching the house, the detectives had literally held it in their hands. Schwartz had taken a quantity of the cartridges he bought for his shot-gun, and emptying them, had put in each shell one of the fifty or one hundred dollar bills, upon which he had then loaded in the powder and the shot in the usual way, so that the shells presented the ordinary appearance as they lay in the drawer. The detectives had even picked out some of the shot and powder in two or three of the shells ; but, finding them so like other cartridges, had never thought of probing clear to the bottom of the shell for a crumpled-up bill.

Thus about thirteen thousand dollars lay for weeks in these ordinary looking cartridges, and was finally removed in the following way : While Schwartz was in jail, a well-known lawyer of Philadelphia came to Mrs. Schwartz one day with an order from her husband to deliver the money over to him. She understood this was to defray the expenses of the trial, and to pay the other lawyers. Superintendent Robertson remembers well the dying woman's emotion, as she made this solemn declaration, one calculated to compromise seriously a man of some standing, and belonging to an honored profession. Her body was wasted with disease, and she knew that her end was near. There was a flush on her face, and her eyes were bright with hatred as she declared that not one dollar of that money was ever returned to her, or ever used in paying the costs of her husband's trial. Nor was one dollar of it ever returned to the railroad company, or to the bank officials, who were the real owners.

LINCOLN AS COMMANDER-IN-CHIEF.*

BY ALEXANDER K. MCCLURE,

Editor of the Philadelphia "Times."

THE supreme law makes the President the commander-in-chief of the military and naval forces of the nation. This is a necessity in all well-regulated governments, as the sovereign or highest civil ruler must have supreme command of the forces of the country for the public defence. During the Revolutionary War the universal confidence that General Washington inspired made him practically the supreme director of our military operations. The supreme civil authority then was the Colonial Congress, and no one of that body could assume this high prerogative. During the war of 1812 with England, I find no instance in which President Madison exercised any authority in the direction of campaigns as commander-in-chief of the army. There was no formal commander-in-chief. Major-General Dearborn, the ranking major-general, was assigned as acting commander-in-chief, although retained in active command in the northern district. The President was conferred with very freely as to military movements, but he did not assume the responsibility of issuing orders for military movements in the field. The Mexican War presents a somewhat different phase of history. President Polk assumed the responsibility as commander-in-chief by ordering General Taylor to march from the Nueces to the Rio Grande, and thus precipitated the Mexican War without either the authority or knowledge of Congress; and later in the war, when it became necessary to enlarge the army to make an aggressive campaign on the City of Mexico, General Scott was summoned by the President to propose a plan of campaign that he should command in person. He did so, and after its approval by the President, the troops were provided, and General Scott was permitted to prosecute the campaign from Vera Cruz to the Mexican capital, without interference by orders from Washington.

INCAPACITY OF THE EARLIER COMMANDERS IN THE CIVIL WAR.

When civil war confronted us in 1861, General Scott was the hero of two wars, and recognized by the country and the world as the Great Captain of the age. Although a son of Virginia, he was thoroughly loyal to the government, and all turned to him as the bulwark of safety for our threatened country. He was believed to be the most accomplished general then living, and President Lincoln, the cabinet, and the country had absolute faith in his ability to discharge the duties of commander-in-chief, even in the extreme and appalling necessities of civil war, with consummate skill and success. It was not until active, practical operations had to be commenced for the protection of the capital and for the defence of the government, that those closest to General Scott learned the sad lesson of his utter incompetency for the new duties forced upon him. He had entirely outlived his usefulness. He had never commanded over twelve thousand men in all his lustrous record, and the magnitude of our Civil War, coming upon him when the infirmities of age enfeebled him mentally and physically, made him wholly unequal to the task. President Lincoln, always unobtrusive when he could be so consistently with his sense of duty, deferred to General Scott and his military associates. He had no plan of campaign; he sought only to attain peace with the least bloodshed and disturbance.

The first star that shed its lustre on the Union arms was that of General McClellan, the young Napoleon of the West, whose victories in Western Virginia made his name a household word. He was the first to propose a comprehensive plan for aggressive movements against the rebellion, and coming from one of the youngest soldiers of the army, it is not surprising that General Scott, with his sensitiveness as to advice from those of less experience, rejected it, and presented a comprehensive plan of his own, then known as the "Anaconda" method of crushing the rebellion. In this dispute Lincoln took no part, and probably gave little attention to it. He then clung to the hope that no such general military movements might be necessary to attain peace. His belief was that

* An address delivered before the New York Commandery of the Loyal Legion, April 5, 1893.

held by most of the prominent men of the cabinet, that a successful battle and the capture of Richmond would bring peace. He had no occasion, therefore, to exercise his authority as commander-in-chief, beyond conferring with General Scott and the Secretary of War. Had he understood the issue then as he understood it a year or more later, I hazard little in saying that the first battle of Bull Run would have been differently fought, and with almost a reasonable certainty of the defeat of the insurgents. The care with which he watched the diffusion of military forces, and the keen sagacity and tireless interest he ever manifested in the concentration of our military forces in every campaign, forbid the assumption that, had he understood the war then as he soon learned to understand it, there could have been a division of the Union forces in the Bull Run campaign to fight the united forces of the enemy. General McDowell fought the battle of Bull Run with seventeen thousand six hundred and seventy-six effective men and twenty-four guns, when he should have had some fifteen thousand additional from General Patterson's command, and from fifteen thousand to twenty thousand of the Pennsylvania Reserve Corps, then fully organized and ready for the field. I feel quite sure that had Lincoln then assumed the authority as commander-in-chief that he ever after maintained until Grant became lieutenant-general, McDowell would have commanded fully fifty thousand men at Bull Run, and would have overwhelmed the enemy and marched into Richmond. It is possible, indeed quite probable, that such an achievement would have ended the war, but it was not to be. Slavery, the author of the war, would have survived such a peace, and the great conflict of thirty years ago would have been handed down to another generation.

LINCOLN FORCED TO BECOME A REAL COMMANDER-IN-CHIEF.

Lincoln was quickened to the exercise of his full authority as commander-in-chief by the multiplied misfortunes of his generals. He accepted as commanders the men in the army most conspicuous in military service, and it was one of the saddest lessons of the war that not one of the commanders then prominent before the country and most trusted, became chieftain as the conflict progressed. The contrast between the Union and the Confederate commanders is indeed painful. The Confederate officers who started out as military leaders in the beginning of the war, as a rule were its chieftains at the close. The Johnstons, Cooper, Lee, Beauregard, Jackson, Longstreet, Hill, Kirby Smith, Ewell, Early, Bragg, Hood, Fitz Hugh Lee, Stuart, and others, either fell in the flame of battle, leading high commands, or emerged from the war with the highest distinction. On the other side, not one of the men who came out of the war with the grateful plaudits of the country as chieftains of the Union, was known to military fame when Sumter was fired upon. One by one Lincoln's commanders fell by the wayside, and he was constantly perplexed with the sense of the fearful responsibility he was compelled to assume in the assignment of commanders to the different armies. This necessity naturally called for the employment of his supreme powers, and compelled him to exercise the soundest discretion time and again, as failure followed failure in his great work of overthrowing the rebellion. Lincoln had learned the painful lesson of Scott's inability to perform the duties expected of him by the country, and on the 29th of June, 1861, he called the first council of war, which embraced his cabinet, Scott, and other military men. It was there that McDowell's plan for the advance on Manassas was decided upon. Lincoln did not advise, but assented to it, and Scott gave a reluctant assent only when he learned that it was a public necessity for the army to advance, as the term of the three months' men would soon expire. The history of that battle is known in all its details to experienced military men.

It is not surprising that a man of Lincoln's sagacity and trained practical methods should consider his responsibility as commander-in-chief after the defeat of Bull Run. He felt that he had no one to whom he could turn for counsel that he could implicitly accept, and he was equal to the occasion. On the night after the battle of Bull Run, Lincoln sought no sleep, but after gathering all the information that he could as to the situation, he devoted the hours of early morning to formulating a plan of military operations, and it is marvellous how closely that programme was followed in the long and bloody years through which the war was fought to its consummation. This was Lincoln's first distinct assumption of the duties of commander-in-chief. He wrote out in pencil, with his own hand, memoranda directing that a

LINCOLN IN 1864.

blockade should be made effective as soon as possible; that the volunteer forces at Fortress Monroe be constantly drilled and disciplined; that Baltimore be held with a firm hand; that Patterson's forces be strengthened and made secure in their position; that the forces of West Virginia continue to act under orders from McClellan;

that General Frémont push forward his work in the West, and especially in Missouri; that the Army of the Potomac be reorganized as rapidly as possible on Arlington Heights; and that new volunteers be brought forward speedily into camps for instruction. This paper bears date July 23, 1861; and on the 27th of July he added to it that when the foregoing shall have been substantially attended to, Manassas Junction and Strausburg should be seized and permanently held, with an open line from Harper's Ferry to Strausburg, and a joint movement from Cairo on Memphis, and from Cincinnati on East Tennessee, should be promptly organized. This was Mr. Lincoln's first acceptance of the necessity that called him to exercise his duties as commander-in-chief, and it will be observed that his plan of campaign fully comprehended the situation and the military necessities which arose thereafter.

The mental and physical feebleness of Scott, together with the infirmities of temper which age and disease had logically wrought, made it a necessity to have a new commander for the army. McClellan was then the only one who came with achievement to enforce his title to the general command, and he was called to Washington as commander of the Army of the Potomac. Volunteers were offered in abundance, and the one man of any country best fitted for the organization of a great army, was fortunately there to organize the army that was ever undaunted by defeat, and that in the end received the surrender of Lee at Appomattox. There was early friction between Scott and McClellan, and all the kind offices of Lincoln failed to soothe the old veteran or to make the young commander submissive to the whims of his superior. It became a supreme necessity to have Scott retired, and it was finally accomplished after much effort, but fortunately it has no detailed record in the annals of the country. The true story of Scott's retirement from the command of the army could have been written but by three men, viz.: Lincoln, Cameron, and Assistant Secretary Thomas A. Scott. They have all joined the veteran soldier in the ranks of the great majority beyond, and none will ever write the chapter on the change of the military commanders-in-chief in 1861.

LINCOLN'S DIFFERENCES WITH McCLELLAN.

From the time that Lincoln called McClellan to Washington, he tenaciously exercised his high prerogatives as commander-in-chief of the army and navy until the 8th of March, 1864, when he handed to General Grant his commission as lieutenant-general; and he was very often in conflict with his department commanders as to their operations or failure to prosecute them. His first serious trial arose with General McClellan in the fall of 1861, and that conflict was never entirely closed until McClellan was finally relieved from the command of his army after the battle of Antietam in the fall of 1862. The late fall months of 1861 were peculiarly favorable for military operations, and the administration and the entire country became impatient to have the army advance. Just when Lincoln expected a movement toward Manassas, McClellan became seriously ill, and continued so for several weeks; and after his recovery, obstacles seemed to multiply each day, until the aggressive movement was universally demanded. On the 1st of December, 1861, Lincoln requested of McClellan a plan of campaign, in which he asked how soon the army could be moved, and how many men would be required to make the advance direct to Richmond. To this McClellan replied that he could move from the 15th to the 25th, and suggested that he had another plan of campaign soon to present to the President. During McClellan's illness Lincoln assumed the responsibility of summoning Generals McDowell and Franklin in conference with him as to the movements of the army, and on the 27th of January, without consulting with any of the commanders, or even the cabinet, he issued "General War Order No. 1," directing that on the 22d of February there should be a general movement of the land and naval forces against the insurgents, of the army at Fortress Monroe, the Army of the Potomac, the Army of Western Virginia, the army in Kentucky, the army and flotilla at Cairo, and the naval forces from the Gulf of Mexico. That was followed four days later by a special order from the President to General McClellan, directing that all the disposable forces of the Army of the Potomac, after providing for the defence of Washington, be moved immediately upon Manassas Junction; that all details be in the discretion of McClellan, and the movement was to begin on the 22d of February. This was a direct order to McClellan; but believing, as he did, that it was not a wise one, he urged his objections earnestly upon the President. It was to these objections that Lincoln wrote a

LINCOLN AND McCLELLAN IN McCLELLAN'S HEADQUARTERS, FROM A PHOTOGRAPH BY BRADY.

somewhat celebrated letter to McClellan, in which he so tersely, but suggestively, discussed the difference between the Peninsula campaign, then preferred by McClellan, and the movement upon Manassas. Lincoln did not arbitrarily command; he sought to be convinced as to whether he was right or wrong, and all who knew him would bear testimony to the fact that no public man was more easily approached when his own convictions were to be questioned by sincere, intelligent men. These are his incisive inquiries to McClellan:

Has not your plan involve a greatly larger expenditure of time and money than mine?
Wherein is a victory more certain by your plan than mine?
Wherein is a victory more valuable by your plan than mine?
In fact, would it not be less valuable in this, that it would break no great line of the enemy's connections, while mine would?
In case of disaster, would not a retreat be more difficult by your plan than mine?

LINCOLN'S THOROUGH KNOWLEDGE OF ARMY MATTERS.

I cite these inquiries of Lincoln, not to show that he was either right or wrong in his judgment, but to convey a just appreciation of his careful study of the military situation at that early period of the war; his intelligent knowledge of the proposed results of campaigns, and his entire willingness to gain the best information to revise his judgment, if in error. McClellan was so tenacious as to the correctness of his Peninsula campaign, that Lincoln, after much deliberation, reluctantly yielded his convictions, and from the day that he did so he certainly sought, in every way that he could consistently with his views as to the safety of the capital, to aid McClellan in his movement. About this time Lincoln was much perplexed by another grave dispute with McClellan. Lincoln believed that it would be wise to organize the Army of the Potomac into army corps, with responsible commanders, while McClellan was unwilling to accept that method of organization, for reasons that need not here be discussed. The order of the President for the movement of the armies on the 22d of February was not obeyed, and on the 8th of March Lincoln assumed the responsibility of issuing an order to McClellan to divide the Army of the Potomac into four army corps, to be commanded by McDowell, Sumner, Heintzelmann, and Keyes, with a reserve force for the defence of Washington, under command of Wadsworth. A fifth corps was also ordered to be formed, with Banks as commander. On the same day he issued "President's General Order No. 3," directing that no change of base of operations of the Army of the Potomac should be made without leaving for the defence of Washington a sufficient force to make the capital entirely secure.

This order went to the very marrow of what is yet an unsettled dispute between the friends of Lincoln and of McClellan; but this is not the place to discuss the merits of the controversy. It necessarily withheld from direct coöperation with McClellan a considerable portion of the army that could have been utilized in the effort to capture Richmond, if it had been deemed safe to uncover Washington. McClellan advanced upon Manassas, only to find it abandoned by the enemy. A council of war was held at McClellan's quarters, Fairfax Court House, on the 13th of March, at which it was decided to proceed against Richmond by the Peninsula. The only diversity of sentiment at that council was as to whether twenty-five thousand or forty thousand men should be detached for the defence at Washington; Keyes, Heintzelmann, and McDowell favoring the smaller number, and Sumner the larger number. I should here note a circumstance that I think is not generally understood. On the 11th of March, when McClellan was advancing with his army on Manassas, Lincoln issued an order practically removing him from the office of commander-in-chief, by limiting his command only to the Army of the Potomac operating with him against Richmond. This order has been variously discussed from the different standpoints held by the friends of Lincoln and McClellan, and with the merits of the controversy I do not propose to deal. I want to say, however, that those who assume that Lincoln limited McClellan's command because of any personal prejudice against him, are in error. He appointed no successor as commander-in-chief, but obviously left the place open for him who should win it. It is evident that his difficulties with McClellan about advancing upon Richmond, and about the organization of his army, had somewhat impaired Lincoln's confidence in McClellan as commander-in-chief; but I speak advisedly when I say that he sincerely hoped that McClellan would succeed in his Richmond campaign by the capture of the Confederate capital, and thus prove his right to be restored as commander-in-chief. I know that Lincoln cherished that hope, and meant that the captor of Richmond should be made the commander-in-chief of the army. Nor is this statement without strong corroboration from circumstance. The position of commander-in-chief was not filled by Lincoln until precisely four months after McClellan had been relieved from it; namely, on the 11th of August, 1862, and just four days after McClellan's letter to

GENERAL McCLELLAN. FROM A PHOTOGRAPH BY BRADY.

the President, written at Harrison's Landing, severely criticising not only the military but the political policy of the administration.

A FATEFUL LETTER OF McCLELLAN'S.

That was a fateful letter for McClellan. It did not resolve Lincoln against the further support of McClellan, nor do I believe that it seriously prejudiced McClellan in Lincoln's estimation, as was shown by his restoration of McClellan to command after Pope's defeat soon thereafter; but it so thoroughly defined partisan lines between McClellan and the supporters of the administration, that when Lincoln called McClellan to the command of the defences of Washington, he had to do it against the united voice of his cabinet, and against the protests of almost, if not quite, a united party in Congress and in the country. However earnestly Lincoln may have desired to support McClellan thereafter, he was greatly weakened in his ability to do so. His letters to McClellan during the Peninsular campaign are an interesting study. All of them are singularly generous, and never offensive, and exhibit the sincerest desire of the President to render McClellan every support possible, without exposing Washington to what he deemed reasonable peril of capture. Only a week before this political letter was written, McClellan had addressed Stanton a long letter, in which he said: "If I save this army now, I tell you plainly that I owe no thanks to you or to any other persons in Washington. You have done your best to sacrifice this army." That McClellan, like Lincoln, did everything with the most patriotic purposes, and with intended loyalty to every duty, I do not doubt; but the issue remains now, nearly a generation after the dispute began, and is likely to continue throughout all the pages of future history.

Four days after the Harrison Landing letter was delivered to the President, Halleck was appointed commander-in-chief. The office remained vacant precisely four months, during which time there never was a doubt that Halleck would be called to the position unless McClellan should be restored. Soon after Lincoln returned from his visit to McClellan on the Peninsula, at which time McClellan's letter was delivered in person to Lincoln, Halleck urged the removal of McClellan from command; but Lincoln overruled him, and instead of ordering the Army of the Peninsula back to the support of Pope, McClellan was ordered to come with his forces. How McClellan ceased to have a command when his army was brought within the jurisdiction of General Pope, I need not stop to relate. Pope was defeated and routed and driven back into the entrenchments of Washington. In this emergency Lincoln braved the unanimous hostility of his cabinet and of his political friends by calling upon McClellan in person in Washington, and asking him to take command of the defences of the capital, which practically gave him command of the entire army while it was defending Washington. It was not a difficult matter to defend the capital with the complete system of entrenchments constructed by McClellan. There were a score of generals in the army who could have done that, but what the army needed most of all was reorganization. It was broken, dispirited, almost hopeless, and Lincoln knew that no man approached McClellan as a military organizer. To use his own language on the occasion, as quoted by Mr. Hay in his diary: "There is no one in the army who can command these fortifications, and lick these troops of ours into shape, half as well as he [McClellan] can." In this severe trial Lincoln was not forgetful of his duties of commander-in-chief. On the 3d of September, the day after assigning McClellan to the command of the defences of Washington, he issued an order to General-in-Chief Halleck, directing him to proceed with all possible despatch to organize an army for active operations, to take the field against the enemy. The Antietam campaign logically followed as Lee advanced into Maryland, and McClellan, without any special assignment, took the field against Lee, resulting in the battle of Antietam and the retreat of Lee back to Virginia.

THE LAST DAYS OF McCLELLAN'S COMMAND.

On the 28th of June Lincoln addressed a letter to Seward, in which he outlined the policy of the war in all the different departments. This was after the failure of the Peninsula campaign. It proved how thoroughly Lincoln kept in view his comprehensive strategy for the prosecution of the war. After the battle of Antietam there was continued dispute between Lincoln and McClellan, arising from what Lincoln believed to be tardiness on the part of the commander of the army to pursue the enemy. The Emancipation Proclamation speedily followed McClellan's victory at Antietam, and that rather intensified the opposing political views of the friends of Lincoln and McClellan. In a private letter written by McClellan on September 25th, and given in his own book (page 615), McClellan said: "The President's late proclamation, the continuation of Stanton and Halleck in office, rendered it almost impossible for me to retain my commission and self-respect at the same time;" and McClellan did not soften the asperities of the occasion by an address to his army, issued on the 7th of October, defining the relations of those in the military service toward the civil authorities. He said: "The remedy for political errors, if any are committed, is to be found only in the action of the people at the polls." I give these quotations to show under what grievances, whether real or assumed, McClellan suffered during this controversy; and it is not surprising that the chasm

GENERAL GRANT. FROM A PHOTOGRAPH BY BRADY IN 1863.

between the President and his general gradually widened because of the constantly increasing intensity of party prejudice against McClellan. During all this dispute Lincoln never exhibited even a shadow of resentment in anything that he said or did, so far as we have any record, and on the 13th of October he wrote an elaborate letter to McClellan, in which he temperately, but very thoroughly, discussed all the strategic lines of McClellan's prospective advance into Virginia, showing the most complete familiarity not only with the country that the army was to occupy, but with all the accepted rules of modern warfare. This controversy culminated in McClellan's removal from his command on the 5th of November, 1862, and that dated the end of his military career. He was ordered to report at Trenton for further orders, where he remained until the day of the Presidential election in 1864, when he resigned his commission, and Sheridan's appointment as his successor was announced in one of Stanton's characteristic bulletins on the following day, along with the news of McClellan's disastrous defeat for the Presidency.

LINCOLN'S SHARP REBUKE TO HOOKER.

I have given much time in this paper to Lincoln's relations with McClellan, because they present, in the strongest light, Lincoln's positive exercise of the high prerogatives of commander-in-chief of the army. Whether he did it wisely or unwisely in his protracted controversy with McClellan, cannot be here discussed, but the case of McClellan stands out most conspicuously as showing how completely Lincoln accepted and discharged the duties of the office of commander-in-chief. The most disastrous battle in which the Army of the Potomac was engaged soon followed McClellan's retirement, when Burnside was repulsed at Fredericksburg. At no stage of the war was the Army of the Potomac in such a demoralized condition as during the period from the defeat of Fredericksburg until Hooker was called to the command. Lincoln believed that some of Burnside's corps commanders were unfaithful to him, and where was he to get a commander? It is an open secret that Sedgwick, Meade, and Reynolds each in turn declined it, and the President finally turned to Hooker as the only man whose enthusiasm might inspire the demoralized army into effectiveness as an aggressive military power. That Lincoln was much distressed at the condition then existing is evident from many sources, but he makes it specially evident in a characteristic letter addressed by him to Hooker on the 26th of January, 1863, telling him of his assignment to the command of the Army of the Potomac. In this letter he says to Hooker: "I think that during General Burnside's command of the army, you have taken counsel of your ambition and thwarted him as much as you could, in which you did a great wrong to the country and to a most meritorious and honorable brother officer. I have heard, in such a way as to believe it, of your recently saying that both the army and the government needed a dictator. Of course it was not for this, but in spite of it, that I have given you the command. Only those generals who gain success can set up as dictators. What I now ask of you is military success, and I will risk the dictatorship." Hooker accepted this pointed admonition like a true soldier. His answer was : " He talks to me like a father. I shall not answer this letter until I have won a great victory." On the 11th of April Lincoln again left a record of his views as to the proper movements of the Army of the Potomac, in which he pointedly declared the true policy of making the army of Lee the objective point, instead of the Confederate capital, and from that theory he never departed. In this memorandum he said : " Our prime object is the enemy's army in front of us, and not with or about Richmond at all, unless it be incidental to the main object."

HOOKER'S SERIES OF MISFORTUNES.

I need not give in detail the result of Hooker's campaign to Chancellorsville. It was one of the most brilliant strategic movements of the war in the beginning, and one of the most strangely disastrous results at the close. On the day after Hooker's retreat back across the Rapidan the President wrote him a letter, in which there is not a trace of complaint against the commander, but clearly conveying Lincoln's profound sorrow at the result. He asked Hooker whether he had any plans for another early movement, concluding with these words : " If you have not, please inform me, so that I, incompetent as I may be, can try and assist in the formation of some plan for the army." When Lee began his movement northward toward Gettysburg, Hooker proposed to attack Lee's rear as soon as the movement was fully developed, to which Lincoln promptly replied, disapproving of the plan of attacking the enemy at Fredericksburg, which was Lee's rear, because the enemy would be in intrenchments, and, to use Lincoln's language, " so man for man worst you at that point, while his main force would, in some way, be getting an advantage of you northward." He added : " In one word, I would not take any risk of being entangled upon the river like an ox jumped half over a fence and liable to be torn by dogs front and rear without a fair chance to gore one way or kick the other." Hooker's next suggestion was to let Lee move northward, and make a swift march upon Richmond ; but this was also rejected by Lincoln because, as he says, Richmond when invested could not be taken in twenty days, and he added : " I think Lee's army and not Richmond is your sure objective point." This was on the 10th of June, 1863. On the 14th of June he again telegraphed Hooker urging him to succor Winchester, which was then threatened by the advance of Lee's army, in which he made the following quaint suggestion : " If the head of Lee's army is at Martinsburg, and the tail of it on the plank road between

Fredericksburg and Chancellorsville, the animal must be very slim somewhere. Could you not break him?" On the 16th of June he addressed a private letter to Hooker in which he spoke to him with the kind frankness so characteristic of him, gently portraying his faults and kindly pointing the way for him to act in harmony with Halleck, and all others whose aid was necessary to success. On the 27th of June Hooker was relieved from command at his own request, and Meade was charged with the responsibility of fighting the decisive battle of the war at Gettysburg. The defeat of Lee at Gettysburg decided the issue of the war. Many bloody battles were fought thereafter, but from the 4th of July, 1863, the cause of the Confederacy was a lost cause, and the man who won that battle should have been the chieftain of the war.

LINCOLN'S ATTITUDE TOWARD MEADE.

I may here properly introduce two despatches received by Lincoln from the battle-fields of Antietam and Gettysburg, which, I personally know, did much to make Lincoln distrust the capacity of both McClellan and Meade to appreciate the great purpose of the war. When Lee had retreated across the Potomac from Antietam on the 19th of September, 1862, McClellan telegraphed: "Our victory was complete. The enemy is driven back into Virginia, Maryland and Pennsylvania are now safe." Meade's congratulation to the army on the field of Gettysburg, July 4, 1863, closes as follows: "Our task is not yet accomplished, and the commanding general looks to the army for greater efforts to drive from our soil every vestige of the presence of the invader." The fact that both these commanders seemed to assume that their great work was to drive the enemy from Northern soil, impressed Lincoln profoundly. In Mr. Hay's diary Lincoln is quoted as saying, upon the receipt of this despatch: "Will our generals never get that idea out of their heads? The whole country is our soil." His theory of the war was that the enemy could be fought much more advantageously on Northern soil than in the South, as it enabled concentration of Northern forces, and diffused Southern forces in maintaining lines of supply; and before either of these battles were fought he had publicly declared his theory that Lee's army was the heart of the rebellion, and that Richmond and other important military centres would be valueless while Lee's army was unbroken. It is known that Lincoln was at first strongly inclined to censure Meade for not fighting another battle at Williamsport. I saw the President soon after that battle, and was amazed at his thorough familiarity with every highway and mountain pass which the armies had open to them. As it was near my own home I knew how accurate his information was, and he questioned me minutely as to distances and opportunities of the two armies in the race to Williamsport. When I asked him the direct question whether he was not satisfied with what Meade had accomplished, he answered in these words: "Now don't misunderstand me about General Meade. I am profoundly grateful down to the bottom of my boots for what he did at Gettysburg, but I think if I had been General Meade I would have fought another battle." He was extremely careful to avoid injustice to any of his commanders, and after fully considering the whole subject, he excused rather than justified Meade for not delivering battle to Lee at Williamsport. Had Meade done so and succeeded, he would have been the great general of the war; but there are few generals who would have fought that battle with the forces of both sides nearly equal and Lee entrenched. Had he fought it and failed, he would have been severely censured; but failing to fight, he lost his one opportunity to be the lieutenant-general of the war.

I need not refer in detail to the Pope campaign of 1862. It is known that the appointment of Pope and the creation of his department were entirely Lincoln's own acts. Without the knowledge of his cabinet he slipped off quietly to West Point to confer with General Scott, but what transpired between them no one ever learned from Lincoln. Indeed, so much were Lincoln and the country perplexed about military commanders in 1862–63 that Senator Wade conceived the idea of making himself lieutenant-general and commander of the armies, and had many supporters. In this he followed the precedent of Senator Benton during the Mexican War, who then made an earnest effort to be appointed generalissimo to supersede both Scott and Taylor in the direction of military operations in Mexico.

LINCOLN PERSONALLY ORDERS A CAMPAIGN IN TENNESSEE.

The campaign for the relief of East Tennessee was one of Lincoln's early conceptions, and in September, 1862, he went to the War Department personally and left a memorandum order for a campaign into that State. Many reasons combined to prevent early obedience to his orders, but from that time there was not a movement made in the West that Lincoln did not carefully examine and revise to hasten the relief of Tennessee; and his letter to Halleck, February 16, 1862, when Fort Donelson was about to be captured, outlined a policy of campaign to reach the heart of Tennessee. While he thus carefully revised every strategic movement, he always scrupulously avoided giving instructions which might embarrass a general fighting in a distant field. After the defeat and victory

LINCOLN AS COMMANDER-IN-CHIEF.

at Shiloh he called Halleck to the field to shield General Grant from the grossly unjust opposition that was surging against him, and in a letter to Halleck he said: "I have no instructions to give you; go ahead, and all success attend you."

The failure of the iron-clads at Charleston in 1863 was one of the sore disappointments of the war, and Lincoln's instructions, sent soon after jointly to General Hunter and Admiral Dupont, are explicit as to what they shall attempt to do. When General Banks was assigned to the department of the Gulf in 1862, with a command of twenty thousand men, Lincoln's letter to him, dated November 22d, pointedly illustrates his complete familiarity with the purposes of the campaign, and his admonitions to General Banks present a singular mixture of censure and charitable judgment. When we turn to his letter to General Grant, written July 13, 1863, after the surrender of Vicksburg, we will recall how carefully Lincoln observed all strategic movements, and also how he judged them. He was glad to confess error when the truth required it, and in his letter of thanks to Grant he told him that he believed that Grant should have moved differently, but added: "I now wish to make the personal acknowledgment that you were right and I was wrong." Early in the year 1864 Lincoln directed the movement into Florida, which resulted in the disastrous battle at Olustee, but he intended it as a political rather than as a military expedition. He in like manner directed combined military and political movements in Arkansas, Tennessee, Maryland, and Missouri. While Halleck was nominally commander-in-chief of the army, he had gradually ceased to be anything more than the chief of staff.

Lincoln is quoted in Mr. Hay's diary as saying that, although Halleck had stipulated when he accepted the position, that it should be with the full powers and responsibilities of the office, after the defeat of Pope, Halleck had "shrunk from responsibility whenever it was possible."

This brings us to the 8th of March, 1864, when Lincoln and Grant met for the first time, and Lincoln personally delivered to Grant his commission as lieutenant-general. Immediately thereafter he was assigned as commander-in-chief of the army. From that day Lincoln practically abdicated his powers as commander-in-chief, so far as they related to army movements. He had found a commander in whom he had implicit faith, and one who was fully in accord with his theory that the overthrow of Lee's army would be the overthrow of the Rebellion, and Lincoln did not conceal his purpose to impose the entire responsibility on Grant. In a letter written to Grant April 30, 1864, just before Grant's movement in the Wilderness campaign, Lincoln said: "The particulars of your plan I neither know nor seek to know. You are vigilant and self-reliant, and, pleased with these, I wish not to intrude any constraint or restraint upon you." Lincoln not only meant what he said, but he fulfilled his promise to the end. How heartily he was in accord with Grant is known to all. There never was a military or personal dispute between them, and Lincoln felt more than satisfied with the wisdom of his appointment of Grant when he received from the desperate carnage of the Wilderness the inspiring despatch: "I propose to fight it out on this line if it takes all summer." He had like faith in Sherman, and after his capture of Atlanta was more than willing to assent to Sherman's March

ALEXANDER M. McCLURE.

to the Sea, because he trusted the man who was to lead the army in that heroic movement. In his letter of congratulations to Sherman at Savannah, December 26, 1864, he told how anxious and fearful he was when Sherman left Atlanta, but added: "Remembering that 'nothing risked nothing gained,' I did not interfere. Now the undertaking being a success, the honor is all yours, for I believe none of us went farther than to acquiesce."

Soon after Sherman's march into North Carolina, Lincoln met Grant and Sherman at City Point, where the whole aspect of the war was fully discussed, and where he gave his last suggestions as commander-in-chief. They did not relate to the movement of armies but to the question of peace. The generous terms given by Grant to Lee at Appomattox were the reflex of Lincoln's suggestions at City Point, although doubtless in hearty accord with the great warrior's convictions; and Sherman, in his original agreement with Johnston for the surrender of his army, simply executed Mr. Lincoln's directions or suggestions as he understood them. The assassination of Lincoln suddenly brought a changed condition upon the country, and with it developed the intensest passions of civil war, but of these Sherman was ignorant, and he obeyed the orders of the commander-in-chief in accepting terms of surrender that became at once impracticable after Lincoln had fallen by the assassin's bullet. Thus ends the story of Abraham Lincoln as commander-in-chief in the most bloody and heroic war of modern times. I have simply presented facts, leaving for others the task of criticism; but this one fact will ever stand out conspicuously in the history of our civil war, that Lincoln was the actual commander-in-chief, from the first defeat at Manassas in July, 1861, until March, 1864, when the Silent Man of the West brought him welcome relief from that high prerogative and gave the Republic unity and peace.

A DOCTOR OF THE OLD SCHOOL.

By Ian Maclaren.

[We are enabled through the courtesy of Dodd, Mead & Company to publish herewith a short story by a new writer of great power. This story is from the book entitled "Beside the Bonnie Briar Bush," by Ian Maclaren, and it is not too much to say that Ian Maclaren is the author of whom the year 1894 will be especially proud. He is the latest of that magnificent group of writers beginning with Stevenson, and including "Q," Kipling, Doyle, Harrie, Weyman, Crockett, Hope, and others.—EDITOR.]

I.

A GENERAL PRACTITIONER.

DRUMTOCHTY was accustomed to break every row of health, except wholesome food and fresh air, and yet had reduced the Psalmist's farthest limit to an average life-rate. Our men made no difference in their clothes for summer or winter, Drumsheugh and one or two of the larger farmers condescending to a topcoat on Sabbath, as a penalty of their position, and without regard to temperature. They wore their blacks at a funeral, refusing to cover them with anything, out of respect to the deceased, and standing longest in the kirkyard when the north wind was blowing across a hundred miles of snow. If the rain was pouring at the Junction, then Drumtochty stood two minutes longer through sheer native dourness till each man had a cascade from the tail of his coat, and hazarded the suggestion, half-way to Kildrummie, that it had been "a bit scrowie;" a "scrowie" being as far short of a "shoor" as a "shoor" fell below "weet."

This sustained defiance of the elements provoked occasional judgments in the shape of a "hoast" (cough), and the head of the house was then exhorted by his women folk to "change his feet" if he had happened to walk through a burn on his way home, and was pestered generally with sanitary precautions. It is right to add that the gudeman treated such advice with contempt, regarding it as suitable for the effeminacy of towns, but not seriously intended for Drumtochty. Sandy

Stewart "napped" stones on the road in
his shirt sleeves, wet or fair, summer and
winter, till he was persuaded to retire from
active duty at eighty-five, and he spent ten
years more in regretting his hastiness and
criticising his successor. The ordinary
course of life, with fine air and contented
minds, was to do a full share of work till
seventy, and then to look after "orra"
(odd) jobs well into the eighties, and to
"slip awa" within sight of ninety. Persons
above ninety were understood to be acquitting
themselves with credit, and assumed
airs of authority, brushing aside the opinions
of seventy as immature, and confirming
their conclusions with illustrations
drawn from the end of last century.

When Hillocks' brother so far forgot
himself as to "slip awa" at sixty, that
worthy man was scandalized, and offered
laboured explanations at the "beerial."

"It's an awfu' business ony wy ye look
at it, an' a sair trial tae us a'. A' never
heard tell o' sic a thing in oor family afore,
an' it's no easy accoontin' for't.

"The gudewife was sayin' he wes never
the same sin' a weet nicht he lost himsel
on the muir and slept below a bush; but
that's neither here nor there. A'm thinkin'
he sappit his constitution thae twa
years he wes grieve (steward) aboot England.
That wes thirty years syne, but
ye're never the same aifter thae foreign
climates."

Drumtochty listened patiently to Hillocks'
apologia, but was not satisfied.

"It's clean havers aboot the muir.
Losh keep's (Lord keep us), we've a'
sleepit oot and never been a hair the waur.

"A' admit that England micht hae dune
the job; it's no cannie stravagin' (strolling)
yon wy frae place tae place, but
Drums never complained tae me as if he
hed been nippit in the Sooth."

The parish had, in fact, lost confidence
in Drums after his wayward experiment
with a potato-digging machine, which
turned out a lamentable failure, and his
premature departure confirmed our vague
impression of his character.

"He's awa noo," Drumsheugh summed
up, after opinion had time to form; "an'
there were waur roads than Drums, but
there's nae doot he wes a wee flichty."

When illness had the audacity to attack
a Drumtochty man, it was described as a
"whup," and was treated by the men with
a fine negligence. Hillocks was sitting in
the post office one afternoon when I
looked in for my letters, and the right side
of discourse was the prospects of the turnip
"breer," but he casually explained
that he was waiting for medical advice.

"The gudewife is keepin' up a dingdong
frae mornin' till nicht aboot ma face,
and a'm fair deaved (deafened), so a'm
watchin' for MacLure tae get a bottle
as he comes wast (west); yon's him noo."

The doctor made his diagnosis from
horseback on sight, and stated the result
with that admirable clearness which endeared
him to Drumtochty.

"Confoond ye, Hillocks, what are ye
ploiterin' aboot here for in the weet wi' a
face like a boiled beet? Div ye no ken
that ye've a titch o' the rose (erysipelas),
and ocht tae be in the hoose? Gae hame
wi' ye afore a' leave the bit, and send a
haflin (half-grown; a child) for some medicine.
Ye donnerd idiot, are ye ettlin (intending)
tae follow Drums afore yir time?"
And the medical attendant of Drumtochty
continued his invective till Hillocks started,
and still pursued his retreating figure with
medical directions of a simple and practical
character.

"A'm watchin', an' peety ye if ye pit aff
time. Keep yir hed the mornin', and
dinna show yir face in the fields till a' see
ye. A'll gie ye a cry on Monday—sic an
auld fule—but there's no ane o' them tae
mind anither in the hale pairish."

Hillocks' wife informed the kirkyaird
that the doctor "gied the gudeman an
awfu' clearin'," and that Hillocks "wes
keepin' the hoose," which meant that the
patient had ten breakfast, and at that time
was wandering about the farm buildings in
an easy undress with his head in a plaid.

It was impossible for a doctor to earn
even the most modest competence from a
people of such scandalous health, and so
MacLure had annexed neighbouring parishes.
His house—little more than a cottage—stood
on the roadside among the
pines towards the head of our Glen, and
from this base of operations he dominated
the wild glen that broke the wall of the
Grampians above Drumtochty—where the
snowdrifts were twelve feet deep in winter,
and the only way of passage at times was
the channel of the river—and the moorland
district westwards till he came to the Dunleith
sphere of influence, where there were
four doctors and a hydropathic. Drumtochty
in its length, which was eight miles,
and its breadth, which was four, lay in his
hand; besides a glen behind, unknown to
the world, which in the night time he visited
at the risk of life, for the way thereto was

treacherous bogs. And he held the land eastwards towards Muirtown so far as Geordie. The Drumtochty post travelled every day, and could carry word that the doctor was wanted. He did his best for the need of every man, woman, and child in this wild, straggling district, year in, year out, in the snow and in the heat, in the dark and in the light, without rest, and without holiday for forty years.

One horse could not do the work of this man, but we liked best to see him on his old white mare, who died the week after her master, and the passing of the two did our hearts good. It was not that he rode beautifully, for he broke every canon of art, flying with his arms, stooping till he seemed to be speaking into Jess's ears, and rising in the saddle beyond all necessity. But he could ride faster, stay longer in the saddle, and had a firmer grip with his knees, than any one I ever met, and it was all for mercy's sake. When the reapers in harvest time saw a figure whirling past in a cloud of dust, or the family at the foot of Glen Urtach, gathered round the fire on a winter's night, heard the rattle of a horse's hoofs on the road, or the shepherds, out after the sheep, traced a black speck moving across the snow to the upper glen, they knew it was the doctor, and, without being conscious of it, wished him God speed.

Before and behind his saddle were strapped the instruments and medicines the doctor might want, for he never knew what was before him. There were no specialists in Drumtochty, so this man had to do everything as best he could, and as quickly. He was chest doctor and doctor for every other organ as well; he was accoucheur and surgeon; he was oculist and aurist; he was dentist and chloroformist, besides being chemist and druggist. It was often told how he was far up Glen Urtach when the feeders of the threshing mill caught young Burnbrae, and how he only stopped to change horses at his house, and galloped all the way to Burnbrae, and flung himself off his horse and amputated the arm, and saved the lad's life.

"You wud hae thocht that every meenut was an hour," said Jamie Soutar, who had been at the threshing, "an' a'll never forget the puir lad lying as white as deith on the floor o' the loft, wi' his head on a sheaf, an' Burnbrae haudin' the bandage licht an' prayin' a' the while, and the mither greetin' in the corner.

"'Will he never come?' she cries, an' a'

"'The Lord be praised!' said Burnbrae, and a' slippit doon the ladder as the doctor came skelpin' intae the close, the foam fleein' frae his horse's mooth.

"'Whar is he?' wes a' that passed his lips, an' in five meenuts he hed him on the feedin' board, and wus at his wark—sic wark, neeburs—but he did it weel. An' ae thing a' thocht rael thochtfu' o' him : he first sent aff the laddie's mither tae get a bed ready.

"'Noo that's feenished, and his constitution 'ill dae the rest,' and he carried the lad doon the ladder in his airms like a bairn, and laid him in his bed, and waits aside him till he wes sleepin', and then says he : 'Burnbrae, yir a gey lad never tae say "Collie, will ye lick?" for a' hevna tasted meat for saxteen hoors.'

"It was michty tae see him come intae the yaird that day, neeburs; the verra look o' him wes victory."

Jamie's cynicism slipped off in the enthusiasm of this reminiscence, and he expressed the feeling of Drumtochty. No one sent for MacLure save in great straits, and the sight of him put courage in sinking hearts. But this was not by the grace of his appearance, or the advantage of a good bedside manner. A tall, gaunt, loosely made man, without an ounce of superfluous flesh on his body, his face burned a dark brick colour by constant exposure to the weather, red hair and beard turning grey, honest blue eyes that looked you ever in the face, huge hands with wrist bones like the shank of a ham, and a voice that hurled his salutations across two fields, he suggested the moor rather than the drawing-room. But what a clever hand it was in an operation, as delicate as a woman's; and what a kindly voice it was in the humble room where the shepherd's wife was weeping by her mun's bedside. He was "ill pitten thegither" to begin with, but many of his physical defects were the penalties of his work, and endeared him to the Glen. That ugly scar that cut into his right eyebrow and gave him such a sinister expression, was got one night Jess slipped on the ice and laid him insensible eight miles from home. His limp marked the big snowstorm in the fifties, when his horse missed the road in Glen Urtach, and they rolled together in a drift. MacLure escaped with a broken leg and the fracture of three ribs, but he never walked like other men again. He could not swing himself into the saddle without making two

and snow drifts for forty winters without a touch of rheumatism. But they were honorable scars, and for such risks of life men get the Victoria Cross in other fields. MacLure got nothing but the secret affection of the Glen, which knew that none had ever done one-tenth as much for it as this ungainly, twisted, battered figure, and I have seen a Drumtochty face soften at the sight of MacLure limping to his horse.

Mr. Hopps earned the ill-will of the Glen forever by criticising the doctor's dress, but indeed it would have filled any townsman with amazement. Black he wore once a year, on Sacrament Sunday, and, if possible, at a funeral; topcoat or water-proof never. His jacket and waistcoat were rough homespun of Glen Urtach wool, which threw off the wet like a duck's back, and below he was clad in shepherd's tartan trousers, which disappeared into unpolished riding boots. His shirt was grey flannel, and he was uncertain about a collar, but certain as to a tie which he never had, his beard doing instead, and his hat was soft felt of four colors and seven different shapes. His point of distinction in dress was the trousers, and they were the subject of unending speculation.

"Some threep (declare) that he's worn thae eedentical pair the last twenty year, an' a' mind masel (myself) his gettin' a tear ahint, when he was crossin' oor palin', and the mend's still veesible."

"Ithers declare 'at he's got a wab o' claith, and hes a new pair made in Muirtown aince in the twa year maybe, and keeps them in the garden till the new look wears aff."

"For ma ain pairt," Soutar used to declare, "a' canna mak up my mind, but there's ae thing sure, the Glen wud not like tae see him withoot them; it wud be a shock tae confidence. There's no muckle o' the check left, but ye can aye tell it, and when ye see thae breeks comin' in ye ken that if human pooer can save yir bairn's life it 'ill be dune."

The confidence of the Glen—and tributary states—was unbounded, and rested partly on long experience of the doctor's resources, and partly on his hereditary connection.

"His father was here afore him," Mrs. Macfadyen used to explain; "atween them they've had the countyside for weel on tae a century; if MacLure disna understand oor constitution, wha dis, a' wud like tae ask?"

For Drumtochty had its own constitution and a special throat disease, as became a parish which was quite self-contained between the woods and the hills, and not dependent on the lowlands either for its diseases or its doctors.

"He's a skilly man, Doctor MacLure," continued my friend Mrs. Macfadyen, whose judgment on sermons or anything else was seldom at fault; "an' a kindhearted, though o' coorse he hes his faults like us a', an' he disna tribble the Kirk often.

"He aye can tell what's wrang wi' a body, an' maistly he can put ye richt, an' there's nae new-fangled wys wi' him; a blister for the ootside an' Epsom salts for the inside dis his wark, an' they say there's no an herb on the hills he disna ken.

"If we're tae dee, we're tae dee; an' if we're tae live, we're tae live," concluded Elspeth, with sound Calvinistic logic; "but a'll say this for the doctor, that whether yir tae live or dee, he can aye keep up a shairp meisture on the skin.

"But he's no verra ceevil gin ye bring him when there's naethin' wrang," and Mrs. Macfadyen's face reflected another of Mr. Hopps' misadventures of which Hillocks held the copyright.

"Hopps' laddie ate grosarts (gooseberries) till they hed to sit up a' nicht wi' him, and naethin' wud do but they maun hae the doctor, an' he writes 'immediately' on a slip o' paper.

"Weel, MacLure had been awa a' nicht wi' a shepherd's wife Dunleith wy, and he comes here withoot drawin' bridle, mud up tae the een.

"'What's a dae here, Hillocks?' he cries; 'it's no an accident, is't?' and when he got aff his horse he cud hardly stand wi' stiffness and tire.

"'It's nane o' us, doctor; it's Hopps' laddie; he's been eatin' ower mony berries.'

"If he didna turn on me like a tiger.

"'Div ye mean tae say——'

"'Weesht, weesht,' an' I tried tae quiet him, for Hopps wes comin' oot.

"'Well, doctor,' begins he, as brisk as a magpie, 'you're here at last; there's no hurry with you Scotchmen. My boy has been sick all night, and I've never had one wink of sleep. You might have come a little quicker, that's all I've got to say.'

"'We've mair tae dae in Drumtochty than attend tae every bairn that hes a sair stomach,' and a' saw MacLure wes roosed.

"'I'm astonished to hear you speak. Our doctor at home always says to Mrs. 'Opps. "Look on me as a family friend.

Mrs. 'Opps, and send for me though it be only a headache.'"

"'He'd be mair sparin' o' his offers if he hed four an' twenty mile tae look aifter. There's naething wrang wi' yir laddie but greed. Gie him a guid dose o' castor oil and stop his meat for a day, an' he 'ill be a' richt the morn.'

"'He 'ill not take castor oil, doctor. We have given up those barbarous medicines.'

"'Whatna kind o' medicines hae ye noo in the Sooth?'

"'Well, you see, Dr. MacLure, we're homœopathists, and I've my little chest here,' and oot Hopps comes wi' his boxy.

"'Let's see 't,' an' MacLure sits doon and taks oot the bit bottles, and he reads the names wi' a lauch every time.

"'Belladonna; did ye ever hear the like? Aconite; it cowes a'. Nux Vomica. What next? Weel, ma mannie,' he says tae Hopps, 'it's a fine ploy, and ye 'ill better gang on wi' the Nux till it's dune, and gie him ony ither o' the sweeties he fancies.

"'Noo, Hillocks, a' maun be aff tae see Drumsheugh's grieve (steward), for he's doon wi' the fever, an' it's tae be a teuch fecht (hard fight). A' hinna time tae wait for dinner; gie me some cheese an' cake in ma haund, and Jess 'ill tak a pail o' meal an' water.

"'Fee; a'm no wantin' yir fees, man; wi' a' that boxy ye dinna need a doctor; na, na, gie yir siller tae some puir body, Maister Hopps,' an' he was doon the road as hard as he cud lick."

His fees were pretty much what the folk chose to give him, and he collected them once a year at Kildrummie fair.

"Weel, doctor, what am a' awin' ye for the wife and bairn? Ye 'ill need three notes for that nicht ye stayed in the hoose an' a' the veesits."

"Havers," MacLure would answer, "prices are low, a'm hearing; gie's thirty shillings."

"No, a'll no, or the wife 'ill tak ma ears off," and it was settled for two pounds.

Lord Kilspindie gave him a free house and fields, and one way or other, Drumsheugh told me, the doctor might get in about one hundred and fifty pounds a year, out of which he had to pay his old housekeeper's wages and a boy's, and keep two horses, besides the cost of instruments and books, which he bought through a friend in Edinburgh with much judgment.

There was only one man who ever complained of the doctor's charges, and that was the new farmer of Milton, who was so good that he was above both churches, and held a meeting in his barn. (It was Milton the Glen supposed at first to be a Mormon, but I can't go into that now.) He offered MacLure a pound less than he asked, and two tracts, whereupon MacLure expressed his opinion of Milton, both from a theological and social standpoint, with such vigour and frankness that an attentive audience of Drumtochty men could hardly contain themselves.

Janie Soutar was selling his pig at the time, and missed the meeting, but he hastened to condole with Milton, who was complaining everywhere of the doctor's language.

"Ye did richt tae resist him; it 'ill maybe roose the Glen tae mak a stand; he fair hauds them in bondage.

"Thirty shillings for twal veesits, and him no mair than seeven mile awa, an' a'm telt there werena mair than four at nicht.

"Ye 'ill hae the sympathy o' the Glen, for a' body kens yir as free wi' yir siller as yir tracts.

"West't 'Beware o' gude warks' ye offered him? Man, ye chose it weel, for he's been collectin' sae money thae forty years, a'm feared for him.

"A've often thocht oor doctor's little better than the Gude Samaritan, an' the Pharisees didna think muckle o' his chance aither in this warld or that which is tae come."

II.

THROUGH THE FLOOD.

DR. MACLURE did not lead a solemn procession from the sick bed to the dining-room, and give his opinion from the hearth-rug with an air of wisdom bordering on the supernatural, because neither the Drumtochty houses nor his manners were on that large scale. He was accustomed to deliver himself in the yard, and to conclude his directions with one foot in the stirrup; but when he left the room where the life of Annie Mitchell was ebbing slowly away, our doctor said not one word, and at the sight of his face her husband's heart was troubled.

He was a dull man, Tammas, who could not read the meaning of a sign, and labored under a perpetual disability of speech; but love was eyes to him that day, and a mouth.

"Is't as bad as yir lookin', doctor? tell's the truth: wull Annie no come through?"

A DOCTOR OF THE OLD SCHOOL.

and Tammas looked MacLure straight in the face, who never flinched his duty or said smooth things.

"A' wud gie onything tae say Annie hes a chance, but a' daurna; a' doot yir gaein' tae lose her, Tammas."

MacLure was in the saddle, and as he gave his judgment, he laid his hand on Tammas's shoulder with one of the rare caresses that pass between men.

"It's a sair business, but ye 'ill play the man and no vex Annie; she 'ill dae her best, a'll warrant."

"An' a'll dae mine," and Tammas gave MacLure's hand a grip that would have crushed the bones of a weakling. Drumtochty felt in such moments the brotherliness of this rough-looking man, and loved him.

Tammas hid his face in Jess's mane, who looked round with sorrow in her beautiful eyes, for she had seen many tragedies, and in this silent sympathy the stricken man drank his cup, drop by drop.

"A' wesna prepared for this, for a' aye thocht she wud live the langest. . . . She's younger than me by ten years, and never wes ill. . . . We've been mairit twal year laist Martinmas, but it's juist like a year the day. . . . A' wes never worthy o' her, the bonniest, snoddest (neatest), kindliest lass in the Glen. . . . A' never cud mak oot hoo she ever lookit at me, 'at hesna hed ae word tae say aboot her till it's ower late. . . . She didna cuist (cast) up tae me that a' wesna worthy o' her, no her, but aye she said, 'Yir ma ain gudeman, and nane cud be kinder tae me.' . . . An' a' wes minded tae be kind, but a' see noo mony little trokes a' micht hae dune for her, and noo the time is bye. . . . Naebody kens hoo patient she wes wi' me, and aye made the best o' me, an' never pit me tae shame afore the fouk. . . . An' we never hed ae cross word, no ane in twal year. . . . We were mair nor man and wife, we were sweethearts a' the time. . . . Oh, ma bonnie lass, what 'ill the bairnies an' me dae withoot ye, Annie?"

The winter night was falling fast, the snow lay deep upon the ground, and the merciless north wind moaned through the close as Tammas wrestled with his sorrow dry-eyed, for tears were denied Drumtochty men. Neither the doctor nor Jess moved hand or foot, but their hearts were with their fellow creature, and at length the doctor made a sign to Marget Howe, who had come out in search of Tammas, and now stood by his side.

"Dinna mourn tae the brakin' o' yir hert, Tammas," she said, "as if Annie an' you hed never luved. Neither death nor time can pairt them that luve; there's naethin' in a' the warld sae strong as luve. If Annie gaes frae the sicht o' yir een she 'ill come the nearer tae yir hert. She wants tae see ye, and tae hear ye say that ye 'ill never forget her nicht nor day till ye meet in the land where there's nae pairtin'. Oh, a' ken what a'm sayin', for it's five year noo sin George gied awa, an' he's mair wi' me noo than when he wes in Edinburo' and I wes in Drumtochty."

"Thank ye kindly, Marget; thae are gude words and true, an' ye hev the richt tae say them; but a' canna dae without seein' Annie comin' tae meet me in the gloamin' an' gaein' in an' oot the hoose, an' hearin' her ca' me by ma name, an' a'll no can tell her that a' luve her when there's nae Annie in the hoose.

"Can naethin' be dune, doctor? Ye savit Flora Cammil, and young Burnbrae, an' yon shepherd's wife Dunleith wy, an' we were a' sae prood o' ye, an' pleased tae think that ye hed keepit deith frae anither hame. Can ye no think o' somethin' tae help Annie, and gie her back tae her man and bairnies?" and Tammas searched the doctor's face in the cold, weird light.

"There's nae pooer in heaven or airth like luve," Marget said to me afterwards; "it maks the weak strong and the dumb tae speak. Oor herts were as water when Tammas's words, an' a' saw the doctor shake in his saddle. A' never kent till that meenut hoo he hed a share in a'body's grief, an' carried the heaviest wecht o' a' the Glen. A' peetied him wi' Tammas lookin' at him sae wistfully, as if he hed the keys o' life an' deith in his hands. But he wes honest, and wudna hold oot a false houp tae deceive a sore hert or win escape for himsel'."

"Ye needna plead wi' me, Tammas, to dae the best a' can for yir wife. Man, a' kent her lang afore ye ever luved her; a' brocht her intae the world, and a' saw her through the fever when she wes a bit lassikie; a' closed her mither's een, and it wes me hed tae tell her she wes an orphan, an' nae man wes better pleased when she got a gude husband, and a' helpit her wi' her fower bairns. A've naither wife nor bairns o' ma own, an' a' coont a' the fouk o' the Glen ma family. Div ye think a' wudna save Annie if I cud? If there wes a man in Muirtown 'at cud dae mair for her, a'd have him this verra nicht, but a' the doctors in Perthshire are helpless for this tribble.

"Tammas, ma puir fallow, if it could avail, a' tell ye a' wud lay doon this auld worn-oot ruckle o' a body o' mine juist tae see ye baith sittin' at the fireside, an' the bairns roond ye, conthy an' canty again; but it's no tae be, Tammas, it's no tae be."

"When a' lookit at the doctor's face," Marget said, "a' thocht him the winsomest man ta' ever saw. He wes transfigured that nicht, for a'm judging there's nae transfiguration like luve."

"It's God's wull an' maun be borne, but it's a sair wull for me, an' a'm no ungratefu' tae you, doctor, for a' ye've dune and what ye said the nicht," and Tammas went back to sit with Annie for the last time.

Jess picked her way through the deep snow to the main road, with a skill that came of long experience, and the doctor held converse with her according to his wont.

"Eh, Jess, wumman, yon wes the hardest wark a' hae tae face, an' a' wud raither hae ta'en ma chance o' anither row in a Glen Urtach drift than tell Tammas Mitchel his wife wes deein'.

"A' said she cudna be cured, and it wes true, for there's juist ae man in the land fit for't, and they micht as weel try tae get the mune oot o' heaven. Sae a' said naethin' tae vex Tammas's hert, for it's heavy eneuch withoot regrets.

"But it's hard, Jess, that money wull buy life after a', an' if Annie wes a duchess her man wudna lose her; but bein' only a puir cottar's wife, she maun dee afore the week's oot.

"Gin we hed him the morn there's little doot she wud be saved, for he hesna lost mair than five per cent. o' his cases, and they 'ill be puir toon's craturs, no strappin' women like Annie.

"It's oot o' the qnestion, Jess, sae burry up, lass, for we've hed a heavy day. But it wud be the grandest thing that was ever dune in the Glen in oor time if it could be managed by hook or crook."

"We 'ill gang and see Drumsheugh, Jess; he's anither man sin' Geordie Hoo's deith, and he wes aye kinder than fouk kent;" and the doctor passed at a gallop through the village, whose lights shone across the white frost-bound road.

"Come in by, doctor; a' heard ye on the road; ye 'ill hae been at Tammas Mitchell's; hoo's the gudewife? a' doot she's sober."

"Annie's deein', Drumsheugh, an' Tammas is like tae brak his hert."

"That's no lichtsome, doctor, no lichtsome ava (at all), for a' dinna ken ony man in Drumtochty sae bund up in his wife as Tammas, and there's no a bonnier wumman o' her age crosses oor kirk door than Annie, nor a cleverer at her wark. Man, ye 'ill need tae pit yir brains in steep. Is she clean beyond ye?"

"Beyond me and every ither in the land but ane, and it wud cost a hundred guineas tae bring him tae Drumtochty."

"Certes, he's no blate (backward); it's a fell chairge for a short day's work; but hundred or no hundred we 'ill hae him, an' no let Annie gang, and her no half her years."

"Are ye meanin' it, Drumsheugh?" and MacLure turned white below the tan.

"William MacLure," said Drumsheugh, in one of the few confidences that ever broke the Drumtochty reserve, "a'm a lonely man, wi' naebody o' ma ain blude tae care for me livin', or tae lift me intae ma coffin when a'm deid.

"A' fecht awa at Muirtown market for an extra pund on a beast, or a shillin' on the quarter o' barley, an' what's the gude o't? Burnbrae gaes aff tae get a goon for his wife or a buke for his college laddie, an' Lachlan Campbell 'ill no leave the place noo withoot a ribbun for Flora.

"Ilka man in the Kildrummie train has some bit fairin' in his pooch for the fouk at hame that he's bocht wi' the siller he won.

"But there's naebody tae be lookin' oot for me, an' comin' doon the road tae meet me, and daffin' (joking) wi' me aboot their fairing, or feeling ma pockets. Ou ay, a've seen it a' at ither hooses, though they tried tae hide it frae me for fear a' wud lauch at them. Me lauch, wi' ma cauld, empty hame!

"Yir the only man kens, Weelum, that I aince luved the noblest wumman in the Glen or onywhere, an' a' luve her still, but wi' anither luve noo.

"She hed given her heart tae anither, or a've thocht a' micht hae won her, though nae man be worthy o' sic a gift. Ma hert turned tae bitterness, but that passed awa beside the brier bush whar George Hoo lay yon sad simmer time. Some day a'll tell ye ma story, Weelum, for you an' me are auld freends, and will be till we dee."

MacLure felt beneath the table for Drumsheugh's hand, but neither man looked at the other.

"Weel, a' we can dae noo, Weelum, gin

we haena mickle brichtness in oor ain hames, is tae keep the licht frae gaein' oot in anither hoose. Write the telegram, man, and Sandy 'ill send it aff frae Kildrummie this verra nicht, and ye 'ill hae yir man the morn."

"Yir the man a' coonted ye, Drumsheugh, but ye 'ill grant me ae favor. Ye 'ill lat me pay the half, bit by bit—a' ken yir wullin' tae dae't a'—but a' haena mony pleesures, an' a' wud like tae hae ma ain share in savin' Annie's life."

Next morning a figure received Sir George on the Kildrummie platform whom that famous surgeon took for a gillie, but who introduced himself as "MacLure of Drumtochty." It seemed as if the East had come to meet the West when these two stood together, the one in travelling furs, handsome and distinguished, with his strong, cultured face and carriage of authority, a characteristic type of his profession ; and the other more marvellously dressed than ever, for Drumsheugh's topcoat had been forced upon him for the occasion, his face and neck one redness with the bitter cold ; rough and ungainly, yet not without some signs of power in his eye and voice, the most heroic type of his noble profession. MacLure compassed the precious arrival with observances till he was securely seated in Drumsheugh's dogcart—a vehicle that lent itself to history—with two full-sized plaids added to his equipment—Drumsheugh and Hillocks had both been requisitioned—and MacLure wrapped another plaid round a leather case, which was placed below the seat with such reverence as might be given to the Queen's regalia. Peter attended their departure full of interest, and as soon as they were in the fir woods MacLure explained that it would be an eventful journey.

"It's a' richt in here, for the wind disna get at the snaw, but the drifts are deep in the Glen, and th'ill be some engineerin' afore we get tae oor destination."

Four times they left the road and took their way over fields, twice they forced a passage through a slap in a dyke, thrice they used gaps in the paling which MacLure had made on his downward journey.

"A' seleckit the road this mornin', an' a' ken the depth tae an inch ; we 'ill get through this steadin' here tae the main road, but oor worst job 'ill be crossin' the Tochty.

"Ye see the bridge hes been shaken' wi' this winter's flood, and we dauma venture on it, sae we hev tae ford, and the snaw's been melting up Urtach way. There's nae

doot the water's gey big, an' it's threatenin' tae rise, but we 'ill win through wi' a warstle.

"It micht be safer tae lift the instruments oot o' reach o' the water ; wud ye mind haddin' (holding) them on yir knee till we're ower? an' keep firm in yir seat in case we come on a stane in the bed o' the river."

By this time they had come to the edge, and it was not a cheering sight. The Tochty had spread out over the meadows, and while they waited they could see it cover another two inches on the trunk of a tree. There are summer floods, when the water is brown and flecked with foam, but this was a winter flood, which is black and sullen, and runs in the centre with a strong, fierce, silent current. Upon the opposite side Hillocks stood to give directions by word and hand, as the ford was on his land, and none knew the Tochty better in all its ways.

They passed through the shallow water without mishap, save when the wheel struck a hidden stone or fell suddenly into a rut ; but when they neared the body of the river MacLure halted, to give Jess a minute's breathing.

"It 'ill tak ye a' yir time, lass, an' a' wud raither be on yir back ; but ye never failed me yet, and a wumman's life is hangin' on the crossin'."

With the first plunge into the bed of the stream the water rose to the axles, and then it crept up to the shafts, so that the surgeon could feel it lapping in about his feet, while the dogcart began to quiver, and it seemed as if it were to be carried away. Sir George was as brave as most men, but he had never forded a Highland river in flood, and the mass of black water racing past beneath, before, behind him, affected his imagination and shook his nerves. He rose from his seat and ordered MacLure to turn back, declaring that he would be condemned utterly and eternally if he allowed himself to be drowned for any person.

"Sit doon," thundered MacLure ; "condemned ye will be suner or later gin ye shirk yir duty, but through the water ye gang the day."

Both men spoke much more strongly and shortly, but this is what they intended to say, and it was MacLure that prevailed.

Jess trailed her feet along the ground with cunning art, and held her shoulder against the stream ; MacLure leant forward in his seat, a rein in each hand, and his eyes fixed on Hillocks, who was now standing up to the waist in the water, shouting directions and cheering on horse and driver.

"Haud tae the richt, doctor; there's a hole yonder. Keep oot o't for ony sake. That's it; yir daein' fine. Steady, man, steady. Yir at the deepest; sit heavy in yir seats. Up the channel noo, an' ye 'll be oot o' the swirl. Weel dune, Jess, weel dune, auld mare! Mak straicht for me, doctor, an' a'll gie ye the road oot. Ma word, ye've dune yir best, baith o' ye this mornin'," cried Hillocks, splashing up to the dogcart, now in the shallows.

"Sail, it wes titch an' go for a meenut in the middle; a Hielan' ford is a kittle (hazardous) road in the snaw time, but ye're safe noo.

"Gude luck tae ye at Westerton, sir; nane but a richt-hearted man wud hae riskit the Tochty in flood. Ye're boond tae succeed aifter sic a graund beginnin'," for it had spread already that a famous surgeon had come to do his best for Annie, Tammas Mitchell's wife.

Two hours later MacLure came out from Annie's room and laid hold of Tammas, a heap of speechless misery by the kitchen fire, and carried him off to the barn, and spread some corn on the threshing floor and thrust a flail into his hands.

"Noo we've tae begin, an' we 'ill no be dune for an oor, and ye've tae lay on without stoppin' till a' come for ye, an' a'll shut the door tae haud in the noise, an' keep yir dog beside ye, for there maunna be a cheep aboot the hoose for Annie's sake."

"A'll dae onything ye want me, but if——if——"

"A'll come for ye, Tammas, gin there be danger; but what are ye feared for wi' the Queen's ain surgeon here?"

Fifty minutes did the flail rise and fall, save twice, when Tammas crept to the door and listened, the dog lifting his head and whining.

It seemed twelve hours instead of one when the door swung back, and MacLure filled the doorway, preceded by a great burst of light, for the sun had arisen on the snow.

His face was as tidings of great joy, and Elspeth told me that there was nothing like it to be seen that afternoon for glory, save the sun itself in the heavens.

"A' never saw the marrow o't, Tammas, an' a'll never see the like again; it's a' ower, man, without a hitch frae beginnin' tae end, and she's fa'in' asleep as fine as ye like."

"Dis he think Annie . . . 'ill live?"

"Of coorse he dis, and be aboot the hoose inside a month; that's the gude o' bein' a clean-bluided, weel-livin'——

"Preserve ye, man, what's wrang wi' ye? it's a mercy a' keppit ye, or we wud hev hed anither job for Sir George.

"Ye're a' richt noo; sit doon on the strae. A'll come back in a whilie, an' ye 'ill see Annie juist for a meenut, but ye maunna say a word."

Marget took him in and let him kneel by Annie's bedside.

He said nothing then or afterwards, for speech came only once in his lifetime to Tammas, but Annie whispered, "Ma ain dear man."

When the Doctor placed the precious bag beside Sir George in our solitary first next morning, he laid a cheque beside it and was about to leave.

"No, no," said the great man. "Mrs. Macfadyen and I were on the gossip last night, and I know the whole story about you and your friend.

"You have some right to call me a coward, but I'll never let you count me a mean, miserly rascal," and the cheque with Drumsheugh's painful writing fell in fifty pieces on the floor.

As the train began to move, a voice from the first called so that all in the station heard:

"Give's another shake of your hand, MacLure; I'm proud to have met you; you are an honour to our profession. Mind the antiseptic dressings."

It was market day, but only Jamie Soutar and Hillocks had ventured down.

"Did ye hear yon, Hillocks? Hoo dae ye feel? A'll no deny a'm lifted."

Halfway to the Junction Hillocks had recovered, and began to grasp the situation.

"Tell's what he said. A' wud like to hae it exact for Drumsheugh."

"Thae's the eedentical words, an' they're true; there's no a man in Drumtochty disna ken that, except ane."

"An' wha's that, Jamie?"

"It's Weelum MacLure himsel. Man, a've often girned that he said fecht awa for us,a', and maybe dee before he kent that he had githered mair luve than ony man in the Glen.

"'A'm prood tae hae met ye,' says Sir George, an' him the greatest doctor in the land. 'Yir an honour tae oor profession.'

"Hillocks, a' wudna hae missed it for twenty notes," said James Soutar, cynic-in-ordinary to the parish of Drumtochty.

PORTRAITS OF ROBERT LOUIS STEVENSON.
BORN NOVEMBER 13, 1850; DIED DECEMBER 3, 1894.

AGE 20 MONTHS, 1852.

AGE 6, 1857.

AGE 14, 1865.

PORTRAITS OF ROBERT LOUIS STEVENSON.

AGE 21. 1870.

AGE 24. 1875.

AGE 34. 1884.

PORTRAITS OF ROBERT LOUIS STEVENSON.

A VIEW SHOWING THE YACHT "CASCO"—THE SMALLER OF THE TWO VESSELS IN THE FOREGROUND.

STEVENSON IN THE SOUTH SEA.

BY WILLIAM CHURCHILL.

ROBERT LOUIS STEVENSON won more than the honor of being regarded by his own people the first of romancers in the English tongue. He was acknowledged by all Samoa, where his last, and by no means his least happy and fruitful, years were spent, to be *Tusitala*, the teller of stories. It is no light honor ; it is not easily won. A man must have tales to tell, and art wherewith to make the telling notable, before he can win the approval of these Samoans, as they sit in the evening circles, in the cool trade breezes, and as the hospitable cigarette passes from lip to lip.

Any *Tusitala*, for there are several, ranks high in the simple state of the Samoans. Every chief of village has his orator, the man who, in meetings of the people, or in conference with people of other towns, presents the royal purpose. With the feathered wand which is the ensign of his rank, he stands before his chief, and in full voice, and with skill of words, presents his case. He must be an orator, a pleader, a master of speech, able to force the unwilling, to lead the ready, to spur the hesitating ; to win by argument where argument holds, by sophistry, by any rhetorical art, so he win. This much is required of an ordinary village *Tusitala*. More is necessary when one is the master of speech for a chief. Then there is the *Tusitala* for the poor puppet whom Germans or consuls will allow to be the king of the Samoan people. But higher than them all, above every talking man, above the German company, and above the consuls themselves, the Samoan people placed the master of our romance, making him as well the master of theirs. From Savaii to Manono, up the heights of Upolu, and down in the bays of Tutuila, *Tusitala* meant Robert Louis Stevenson in the speech of the gentle islanders.

STEVENSON'S WIDE SEARCH FOR HEALTH.

In 1888 Mr. Stevenson was hunting the earth for the spot of land and climate which meant life for him, if haply there were left any life to one so far gone in health as he. He had tried the Mediterranean countries until he saw that health lay not there. He had sought the Adirondacks in the hope of recovering strength, but the balsamic airs of the forests of the North Woods had proved as worthless as the reek of the orange groves. Driven ever farther afield in search of climate, he came to California in that year. He knew what those cloudless skies and that transparent air were ; that is all set down in the "Silverado Squatters." But for once the climate of a State which is all climate failed to work good. Somewhere on the earth he hoped there might be a place wherein he could live and breathe with comfort, or at least with absence of the pain which was racking him. Beyond the

Golden Gate lay the islands of the South Sea. He made his choice happily, it proved, for it added years of comfort, even of activity, to the life of a man who seemed scarce worth a month's purchase. He chose the South Sea.

It was then that I made his acquaintance, an acquaintance since renewed and maintained by letters, with such difficulty as lies in the fact that a question might be asked and answered in say half a year, if luck was good. I was called in as being somewhat of an expert in the South Sea, having, indeed, but lately come off several years of voyaging among the islands.

Mr. Stevenson, when I first saw him in his room in the Occidental Hotel in San Francisco, was sitting up in bed, not rightly able to speak for the cold that oppressed him, haggard from the illness that was sapping him, thin, pale, and wan. The first sight was something more than of a man with the blankets and counterpanes hunched up about him; it was an impression of flowing black hair, keen eyes, and a wonderful interlacing of taper fingers. At this time he

was so hoarse that his voice had none of the charm which was really one of the most marked attributes of the man. More pleasant days, and strength growing in the nervous hope that the South Sea might indeed yield him what was nowhere else for him on earth, gave chances to hear that voice as it really was—gentle, deep, sympathetic. But those fingers—long, sinewy, sinuous, never resting, but rubbing each the other as if there were a mania of the nerves in their tips! Those who have never seen Stevenson's hand may form some idea of the fingers from the so-called "watermelon seed" picture, in which one of the forefingers, resting against the face, seems to reach up into the hair.

STEVENSON, FROM A PHOTOGRAPH TAKEN IN SAMOA BY DAVIS.

STEVENSON EAGER FOR INFORMATION ABOUT THE SOUTH SEA.

At this first meeting he seemed eager for all that might be told of the mysteries of the South Sea. He asked about the voyages of the old voyagers; he sought to know what were the traders of to-day, and this in one breath. Again he caught at the name of "Bully" Hayes, the last pirate of the Pacific, and lumped with him the mystery of "La Perouse." Names of islands and of groups were, of course, all new to him, and he asked again and again where they lay and how they were pronounced. But in everything he was, more than anything else, wistful to hear of the unmixed islanders—what was their life and what sort of people they might be. At odd times Mrs. Stevenson would come in and caution him not to use his voice so much. Then he would settle himself back upon the pillows and say: "Tell me something that takes a long time telling." It took time, this first telling of the South Sea, for which he was every moment more strongly making up his mind; the session was no short one. And this first was followed by others, in which he showed the same zest to learn every fact attainable concerning the island realm that lay in the great ocean on whose verge he was.

He chose the South Sea. It was a generous choice; he chose it all. He selected no particular region of ocean in a sweep that is the very broadest to be found on the earth, except where the great southern ocean sweeps unbroken about the Antarctic Pole and frets the ice. He picked out no one island of the thousands, reef-girt and palm-crowned, in those warm waters. He took them all in one vision of health, and made his plans to go to the South Sea wherever the winds would carry him. He is not the only man on whom the spell of the South Sea has thus wrought; even the "beach-combers" bear witness to its magic, and here and there some have come out of the South Sea and long to go back.

STEVENSON CHARTERS THE YACHT "CASCO."

In the harbor of San Francisco was the schooner yacht "Casco," owned by Dr. Merritt of Oakland. In England and here in New York many men had offered their

MRS. R. L. STEVENSON.

yachts to Mr. Stevenson, not only men who knew him by word of mouth, but even men who had never met him outside of their libraries. But this yacht-owner held certain very definite views on the general subject of literature. He looked upon "Harriers Burned Away" as the highest mark in fiction, and he was oppressed with the idea that men who wrote books must be making a pretty poor living of it. Furthermore, he had never heard of Stevenson, and had never seen one of his books. He was one of the men whom you would like to drop into the middle of the "New Arabian Nights," and watch him try to make sense out of what he was reading. Anyway, he had the sense of his kind to drive a shrewd bargain when he was asked to give a charter-party of the "Casco." The hire must be all paid into bank beforehand, there must be no loop-hole for bottomry in foreign ports, all cost of repairs must rest on Stevenson, and Dr. Merritt's own sailing master must go as captain in order to see that all went well. Even with all these restrictions the charter was accomplished, and the Stevenson party began to put the "Casco" in readiness for a voyaging to nowhere in particular. The yacht was a roomy, two-masted schooner, cabin aft, galley and lockers amidships, and forecastle forward, all under a flush deck. She had been in the South Seas once before, and had proved herself not only a weatherly boat, but quite comfortable in a sea.

I was present at the ceremony when

STEVENSON IN 1893. FROM A PHOTOGRAPH TAKEN IN AUSTRALIA.

she went into commission. She was lying in Oakland Creek, at her usual berth, and the stores were being rattled aboard. I had brought down a bunch of much-marked charts, and several volumes of note-books of experiences in the South Sea, for the use of the voyagers. The cabin was a scene of disorder. Mattresses were heaped where it was not reasonable to suppose any one could sleep in a sea way; the places where the mattresses should have been were filled with a mixed assortment of clothing and cabin stores. To any but a seaman it would have seemed a hopeless task to attempt to restore order. The cabin hatch was darkened, and Stevenson came down the companion, assisted by his step-son Lloyd Osbourne. Stevenson managed to find an uneasy seat on a barrel of cabin flour, and began to yield up personal property from capacious pockets.

STEVENSON'S FIRST VOYAGE INTO THE SOUTH SEA.

This first voyage stretched away to the south and into the fine weather. The "Casco," with the Stevenson party aboard —Mr. and Mrs. Stevenson and Lloyd Osbourne—touched at the Marquesas, and then bore away for Tahiti. The log—I had it afterward and published it—showed

RECEPTION-ROOM AND STAIRWAY IN STEVENSON'S SAMOA HOUSE.

uninterrupted sailing, with little incident by the way. Between the Marquesas and Tahiti there was some rough weather, and a topmast was sprung, which delayed them for repairs when they reached Papeete. Here the cook ran away, and it became necessary to replace him. The successor seems to have been a very poor cook in-

THE STEVENSON PARTY AT BANQUET AS GUESTS OF KING KALAKAUA, HAWAII.

deed. Then they bore away northward to Honolulu, a voyage of nasty weather. At Honolulu the yacht was given up and sent back to San Francisco. Here, or at Waikiki, the party stayed with Mrs. Strong, Lloyd Osbourne's sister. There was for them, as for all who choose to stay at the watering-place of the Hawaiian capital, much of pleasure here, and the tarrying was prolonged.

But the dry weather came, and it is not a pleasant season in the Hawaiian Islands. Then, too, Stevenson had not yet seen all the South Sea, but only a little stretch of its eastern edge. He wanted more. Then it was he formed the scheme of taking a great moral show through the islands. This plan he essayed to carry out with the assistance of Osbourne and Strong. It centred around a stereopticon, which Strong was to manage; a lecture, based on the slides they were able to collect, a feature of the entertainment which Stevenson fancied came in his own line; and a general supervision of the whole affair, which was to be Osbourne's share in the enterprise. This plan was reluctantly laid aside, by reason of the incomprehensibility to any South Sea audience of Stevenson's lectures. In place of this scheme they engaged a trading schooner to take them a trip through the Line Islands. Then, for the first time, Stevenson learned to look with respect upon a cockroach, for he met with experiences, as every one must who chooses a trading schooner for passage along the Line in the Pacific. If there is any objurgation of the cockroach in any of Stevenson's South Sea tales, as indeed there is, it is all founded on this experience in the island trader "Equator."

LANDING IN SAMOA TO ABIDE.

This cruise ended in Apia, and there in Samoa the Stevenson family have lived ever since. Once, in our talks about the South Sea, Mr. Stevenson asked if there was any place there where a man might live if the land suited him. It led me to a description of a small plateau on Upolu, in the rear of Apia, a narrow shelf upon the mountain side, where the paths ran much like ladders, where there were three springs of water, where the view over the ocean was ever restful, and stopped short of the North Pole only by reason of the earth's swelling round. His memory must have stored away the description, for the place in mind was Vailima, his home in Samoa.

What Stevenson thought of his discourse in San Francisco about the South Sea, toward which his inclination was set, may be found in the early chapters of his story of "The Wrecker." Others less under the charm of the islands perhaps preferred him as a Scot rather than as a Samoan. For an instance, I have a letter from Andrew Lang, who writes: "I prefer him on his native heather. I sent him materials for a Prince Charlie tale; he began it, I believe, but whether he will do it I don't know." It may be that this is one of the two which he has left behind him. At any rate, "Catriona" has shown that even under the sonorous cocoanuts a Scot may write a tale of moor and heather.

ROBERT LOUIS STEVENSON: DIED DECEMBER 3D, 1894

THE world might have been prepared for the announcement of Stevenson's death, for every one knew that he had long been an invalid, exiled by poor health to a distant Pacific island. But the abounding vitality of his books rendered it hard for us to think of him and death together. He had lived and wrought long enough to prove himself the master story-teller of his generation, and, perhaps, the greatest prose-writer of the century; but his actual accomplishment gave promise of yet greater things to come. Thus the first thought of many lovers of his books, upon hearing of his death, may have been of the great loss to literature. But we venture to believe that the final realization that he was gone brought a yet keener pang, as of personal bereavement, for Stevenson so saturated his books with his winning individuality as to establish a sort of companionship between himself and his readers.

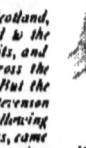

This sense of personal loss is naturally most acute in Scotland, the land of his nativity. Scotland gave him to the world, and to the end he remained a faithful son, preserving the traditions, traits, and accents that have dominated all the literature produced across the border from the time of Blind Harry down to his own day. But the Scotch voice had fallen all but silent in literature when Stevenson began to speak, and for a season he stood almost alone. Following him, however, and perhaps stimulated by his genius and success, came other Scotchmen of talent, who formed a notable group of writers, all, like Stevenson, devoted to their native land, and embodying this devotion in stories or sketches of Scottish character or founded upon stirring events and periods in Scottish history. Earliest in this group came Mr. J. M. Barrie with "A Window in Thrums" and "The Little Minister;" a few years later Mr. S. R. Crockett published "The Stickit Minister" and "The Raiders." These books were Scotch to the marrow, and, like all true Scottish things, sincere, wholesome, virile. Mr. Stevenson welcomed these writers with the enthusiasm of a Highlander for his clansmen, and sought out opportunities to offer them the testimony of his loving appreciation. Within a few months another has made himself one of the distinguished fraternity, Mr. Ian Maclaren, author of "Beside the Bonnie Brier Bush." If Mr. Stevenson saw this book he must have discerned its Scottish traits, for they are as indisputable as the plaids and bagpipes.

We count ourselves fortunate in that we are able to present to our readers this month the tributes which these three Scotchmen have paid to their dead chieftain.

[The three articles following, printed from advance sheets of "The Bookman," by permission of Messrs. Dodd, Mead & Co., are copyrighted, and receive here their first authorized publication in America.]
Copyright, 1895, by Dodd, Mead & Co.

SCOTLAND'S LAMENT.

BY J. M. BARRIE,

Author of "A Window in Thrums," "The Little Minister," etc.

HER hands about her brows are pressed,
She goes upon her knees to pray,
Her head is bowed upon her breast,
And oh, she's sairly failed the day!

SCOTLAND'S LAMENT.

Her breast is old, it will not rise,
Her tearless sobs in anguish choke,
God put His finger on her eyes,
And then it was her tears that spoke.

"I've ha'en o' brawer sons a flow,
My Walter mair renown could win,
And he that followed at the plough,
But Louis was my Benjamin!

"Ye sons wha do your little best,
Ye writing Scots, put by the pen,
He's deid, the ane abune the rest,
I winna look at write again!

"It's sune the leave their childhood drap,
I've ill to ken them, gaen me grey,
But aye he climbed intil my lap,
Or pu'd my coats to mak me play.

"He egged me on wi' mirth and prank,
We hangit gowans on a string,
We made the doakens walk the plank,
We mairit snails withoot the ring.

"'I'm auld,' I pant, 'sic ploys to mak,
To games your mither shouldna stoup.'
'You're gey an' auld,' he cries me back,
'That's for I like to gar you loup!'

"O' thae bit ploys he made sic books,
A' mithers cam to watch us playing;
I feigned no to heed their looks,
But fine I kent what they was saying!

"At times I lent him for a game
To north and south and east and west,
But no for lang, he sune cam hame,
For here it was he played the best.

"And when he had to cross the sea,
He wouldna lat his een grow dim,
He bravely dree'd his weird for me,
I tried to do the same for him.

"Ahint his face his pain was sair,
Ahint hers grat his waefu' mither;
We kent that we should meet nae mair,
The ane saw easy thro' the ither.

"For lang I've watched wi' trem'ling lip,
But Louis ne'er sin syne I've seen,
The greedy island keept its grip,
The cauldriff oceans rolled atween.

"He's deid, the ane abune the rest,
Oh, wae, the mither left alane!
He's deid, the ane I loo'ed the best,

Her breast is old, it will not rise,
Her tearless sobs in anguish choke,
God put His finger on her eyes,
It was her tears alone that spoke.

Now out the lights went stime by stime,
The towns crept closer round the kirk,
Now all the firths were smoored in rime,
Lost winds went wailing thro' the mirk.

A star that shot across the night
Struck fire on Pala's mourning head,
And left for aye a steadfast light,
By which the mother guards her dead.

"The lad was mine!" Erect she stands,
No more by vain regrets oppress't,
Once more her eyes are clear; her hands
Are proudly crossed upon her breast.

ROBERT LOUIS STEVENSON.

BY S. R. CROCKETT,

Author of "The Stickit Minister," "The Raiders," etc.

SITTING alone by the sea in the mid days of November, I wrote a little article on what I loved most in the works of Robert Louis Stevenson, and it was set in type for the January "Bookman." In itself a thing of no value, it pleased me to think that in his far island my friend would read it, and that it might amuse him. I have tried and failed to revise it in the gloom of the night that has come so swiftly to those who loved him. But it would not do.

How could one alter and amend the light sentences with the sense of loss in one's heart? How sit down to write a "tribute" when one has slept, and started, and awaked all night with the dull ache that lies below Sleep saying all the time, "Stevenson is dead! Stevenson is dead!"?

It is true also that I have small right to speak of him. I was little to him; but then he was very much to me. He alone of mankind saw what pleased him in a little book of boyish verses.

Seven years ago he wrote to tell me so. He had a habit of quoting stray lines from it in successive letters to let me see that he remembered what he had praised. Yet he was ever as modest and brotherly as if I had been the great author and he the lad writing love verses to his sweetheart.

Without reproach and without peer in friendship, our king-over-the-water stood first in our hearts because his own was full of graciousness and tolerance and chivalry.

I let my little article be just as I wrote it for his eye to see, before any of us guessed that the dread hour was so near the sounding which should call our well-beloved "home from the hill."

BANK HOUSE, PENICUIK, MIDLOTHIAN.
December 19, 1894.

MR. STEVENSON'S BOOKS.

In sunny Samoa, more thousands of miles away than the ungeographical can count, sits "The Scot Abroad." For thus Burton the historian, sane, sage, and wise, wrote of Mr. Robert Louis Stevenson be- fore his time. It is the wont of Scotland that her sons, for adventure or merchandise, should early expatriate themselves. The ships of the world in all seas are engineered from the Clyde, and a "doon-

[NOTE—This article was written apropos of the publication of the first volume of the complete Works of Robert Louis Stevenson: Edinburgh edition (limited to 1000 copies). Published in America by Charles Scribner's Sons.]

the-watter" accent is considered as necessary as lubricating oil, in order that the plunging piston rods may really enjoy their rhythmic dance. If you step ashore anywhere "east of Suez and the Ten Commandments," ten to one the first man of your tongue who greets you will hail in the well-remembered accent of the Scotch gardener who chased you out of the strawberry plots of your unblessed youth.

But to us who "stop at home, on flowery beds of ease," made aware of ourselves only when the east wind blows and we think that we are back in St. Andrews, the typical "Scot Abroad" is neither Burton's Gentleman Companion at Arms nor the oily chief engineer, but Mr. Stevenson.

On high in a cool bowery room on the hillside, looking down on the league-long rollers forming themselves to be hurled on the shore, sits one with his heels on the coco-matting of Samoa, but his head over the Highland border. The chiefs gathered for palaver (or whatever they are pleased to call hunkering-and-blethering out there), and they tell the Tale-teller of heads taken and plantations raided. And he stays his pen and arbitrates, or he "leaves for the front," as though he were plenipotentiary of the Triple Alliance. But all the while it is James More Macgregor who is marching out arrayed in a breech-clout and a Winchester "to plunder and to ravish"— or carry off an heiress lass from the lowlands, as was good Macgregor use-and-wont.

They call the beautiful new complete "Stevenson" which Mr. Sidney Colvin and Mr. Charles Baxter have contrived and organized, the "Edinburgh" edition, because, though the stars of the tropics glow like beacons, and in Apia the electric light winks a-nights like glowworms amid a wilderness of green leaves, yet to the lad who sits aloft there are still "no stars like the Edinburgh street lamps." But my own local enthusiasms are duller, for the last night I was in Edinburgh I saw a wind (Rajputana and Edinburgh are the only two places where you can see wind) —I saw a wind, with the bit between its teeth, run off with itself down that romantic wall of hotels, which in the night looks like the thunder-battered wall of the Dungeon of Buchan. I saw it snatch out a dozen gaps in the converging perspective of the gaslamps, and bring down the chimney-cans clashing on the pavement like forest leaves in a November blast. So Mr. Stevenson, who does not live there, "for love and euphony," names his collected edition (to which be all good luck and fostering breezes) "The Edinburgh Edition." I have just seen the first volume, which in its brightness and beauty seemed a summary of all the perfections, and whose print recalls that in which the early novels of Scott were set up. Mr. Hole's portrait suffers a little from the excessive size of the hands, but in spite of this is by far the most characteristic and Stevensonian portrait ever done, and represents him exactly as his friends remember him at the most productive period his genius has yet known.

To me the most interesting thing in Mr. Stevenson's books is always Mr. Stevenson himself. Some authors (perhaps the greatest) severely sit with the more ancient gods, and serenely keep themselves out of their books. Most of these authors are dead now. Others put their personalities in, indeed ; but would do much better to keep them out. Their futilities and pomposities, pose as they may, are no more interesting than those of the chairman of a prosperous limited company. But there are a chosen few who cannot light a cigarette or part their hair in a new place without being interesting. Upon such in this life, interviewers bear down in shoals with pencils pointed like spears ; and about them as soon as they are dead—lo ! begins at once the "chatter about Harriet."

Mr. Stevenson is of this company. Rarest of all, his friends have loved and praised him so judiciously that he has no enemies. He might have been the spoiled child of letters. He is only "all the world's Louis." The one unforgivable thing in a checkered past is that at one time he wore a black shirt, to which we refuse to be reconciled on any terms.

But when he writes of himself, how supremely excellent is the reading. It is good even when he does it intentionally, as in "Portraits and Memories." It is better still when he sings it, as in his "Child's Garden." He is irresistible to every lonely child who reads and thrills, and reads again to find his past recovered for him with effortless ease. It is a book never long out of my hands, for only in it and in my dreams when I am touched with fever, do I grasp the long, long thoughts of a lonely child and a hill-wandering boy —thoughts I never told to any ; yet which Mr. Stevenson tells over again to me as if he read them off a printed page.

I am writing at a distance from books and collections of Stevensoniana, so that

I cannot quote, but only vaguely follow the romancer through some of his incarnations. Of course every romancer, consciously or unconsciously, incarnates himself, especially if he writes his books in the first person. It is he who makes love to the heroine; he who fights with the Frenchman "who never can win"; he who climbs the Mountain Perilous with a dirk between his teeth.

But Mr. Stevenson writes the fascination of his personality into all his most attractive creations, and whenever I miss the incarnation, I miss most of the magic as well. Jim Hawkins is only "the Lantern Bearer" of North Berwick Links translated into the language of adventure on the high seas—the healthier also for the change. I love Jim Hawkins. On my soul I love him more even than Alan Breck. He is the boy we should all like to have been, though no doubt David Balfour is much more like the boys we were—without the piety and the adventures. I read Stevenson in every line of "Treasure Island." It is of course mixed of Erraid and the island discovered by Mr. Daniel Defoe. But we love anything of such excellent breed, and the crossing only improves it. Our hearts dance when Mr. Stevenson lands his cut-throats, with one part of himself as hero and the other as villain. John Silver is an admirable villain, for he is just the author genially cutting throats. Even when he pants three times as he sends the knife home, we do not entirely believe in his villany. We expect to see the murdered seaman about again and hearty at his meals in the course of a chapter or two. John is a villain at great expense and trouble to himself; but we like him personally, and are prepared to sit down and suck an apple with him, even when he threatens to stove in our "thundering old blockhouse and them as dies will be the lucky ones." In our hearts we think the captain was a little hard on him. We know that it is Mr. Stevenson all the time, and are terrified exactly like a three-year-old who sees his father take a rug over his head and "be a bear." The thrill is delicious, for there is just an off chance that after all the thing may turn out to be a bear; but still we are pretty easy that at the play's end the bearskin will be tossed aside, the villain repent, and John Silver get off with a comfortable tale of pieces of eight.

No book has charted more authentically the topographical features of the kingdom of Romance than "Treasure Island." Is that island in the South or in the North Atlantic? Is it in the "Spanish main"? What *is* the Spanish main? Is it in the Atlantic at all? Or is it a jewel somewhere in the wide Pacific, or strung on some fringe of the Indian Ocean? Who knows or cares? Jim Hawkins is there. His luck, it is true, is something remarkable. His chances are phenomenal. His imagination, like ours, is running free, and we could go on for ever hearing about Jim. We can trust Jim Hawkins, and void of care we follow his star.

Oh, for one hour of Jim in the "Wrecker" to clear up the mystery of the many captains, or honest and reputable John Silver to do for the poor Scot down below in a workmanlike manner when he came running to him, instead of firing as it were "into the brown" till that crying stopped—a touch for which we find it hard to forgive Mr. Stevenson—pardon, Mr. Lloyd Osbourne.

Again, Alan Breck is ever Alan, and bright shines his sword; but he is never quite Jim Hawkins to me. Nor does he seem even so point-device in "Catriona" as he was in the round house or with his foot on the heather. But wherever Alan Breck goes or David Balfour follows, thither I am ready to fare forth, unquestioning and all-believing.

But when I do not care very much for any one of Mr. Stevenson's books, it is chiefly the lack of Mr. James Hawkins that I regret. Jim in doublet and hose—how differently he would have sped "The Black Arrow!" Jim in trousers and top hat—he would never have been found in the "Black Box," never have gone out with Huish upon the "Ebb Tide." John Silver never threw vitriol, but did his deeds with a knife in a gentlemanly way, and that was because Jim Hawkins was there to see that he was worthy of himself. Jim would never have let things get to such a pass as to require Attwater's bullets splashing like hail in a pond over the last two pages to settle matters in any sort of way.

I often think of getting up a petition to Mr. Stevenson (it is easy to get a round Robin) beseeching "with sobs and tears" that he will sort out all his beach-combers and Yankee captains, charter a rakish saucy-sailing schooner, ship Jim Hawkins as ship's boy or captain (we are not particular), and then up anchor with a Yo-Ho, Cheerily for the Isle of our Heart's Desire, where they load Long Toms with pieces of eight, and, dead or alive, nobody minds Ben Gunn.

IN MEMORIAM: R. L. S.

By Ian Maclaren,

Author of "Beside the Bonnie Brier Bush," etc.

WHEN one came in with omens of sadness on his face and told us that Stevenson was dead, each man had a sense of personal bereavement. None of us had ever seen him, save one—and that was long ago; none of us had ever read a letter of his writing, save one, and he ransacked his memory for the least word. We had no "eagle's feather" to show; there was nothing between this man and us save the mystical tie that binds a writer and his readers in the kingdom of letters. He had led us in through the ivory gate, and shown us things eye had not seen; and all his service had been given at a great cost of suffering. Filled with the enthusiasm of his art, he beat back death time after time, and only succumbed like J. R. Green and Symonds, his brethren in letters and affliction, after he had achieved imperishable fame, "*monumentum ære perennius.*"

Mr. Stevenson had not to complain, with Sir Thomas More, that readers of books were so "unkind and ungenial that though they take great pleasure and delectation in the work, yet, for all that, they cannot find in their hearts to love the author thereof;" for though he was exiled from his native land, yet he lived in the heart of every reading man, not only because he was a great writer, but also because he was a good man with faith in God and man.

Fourteen years ago our author laid down in the "Fortnightly Review" the two duties incumbent on any man who enters on the business of writing—"truth to the fact and a good spirit in the treatment." One dares to say without relate to-day, that he fulfilled his own conditions, for he saw life whole and he wrote of it with sympathy. He brought also to his task a singular genius, which gave him an almost solitary place. It was difficult to name a living artist in words that could be compared with him who reminded us at every turn of Charles Lamb and William Hazlitt. There are certain who compel words to serve them and never travel without an imperial body guard; but words waited on Stevenson like "humble servitors," and he went where he pleased in his simplicity because every one flew to anticipate his wishes. His style had the thread of gold, and he was the perfect type of the man of letters—a humanist whose great joy in the beautiful was annealed to a fine purity by his Scottish faith; whose kinship was not with Boccaccio and Rabelais, but with Dante and Spenser. His was the magical touch that no man can explain or acquire; it belongs to those only who have drunk at the Pierian spring. There is a place at the marriage feast for every honest writer, but we judge that our master will go to the high table and sit down with Virgil and Shakespeare and Goethe and Scott.

The mists of his native land and its wild traditions passed into his blood so that he was at home in two worlds. In one book he would analyze human character with such weird power that the reader shudders because a stranger has been within his soul; in another he hurries you along a breathless story of adventure till your imagination fails for exhaustion. Never did he weary us with the pedantry of modern problems. Nor did he dally with foul vices to serve the ends of purity. Nor did he feed

"A gibing spirit
Whose influence is begot of that loose grace
Which shallow laughing hearers give to fools."

One subject he approached late in his work, but we are thankful he has at least given Barbara Grant and Catriona. What he might have done one can only imagine, who expected another Portia from his hands. He was buried far from the land he loved, but they chose his grave well on the mountain top, and his funeral has been described already, save that his disciples were not there.

"'This man decided not to live, but know;
Bury this man there?'
'Here—here's his place, where meteors shoot, clouds form,
Lightnings are loosened,
Stars come and go! Let joy break with the storm,
Peace let the dew send!
Lofty designs must close in like effects:
Loftily lying
Leave him—still loftier than the world suspects,
Living and dying.'"

IN THE STOKE-HOLE.
(See page 301.)

McCLURE'S MAGAZINE.

Vol. IV.   MARCH, 1895   No. 4.

AN OCEAN FLYER.

ABOVE AND BELOW THE WATER LINE.

Notes of a first voyage on an Atlantic Liner.

AT midnight seventy-two fires were lighted under the nine big boilers of the great steamship, and shortly after a cloud of yellow smoke, rolling from the huge stacks, was floating over the bosom of the bay.

In their various homes and hotels a thousand prospective travellers slept and dreamed of their voyage on the morrow.

By daybreak the water evaporating into steam fluttered through the indicators, and as early as six A.M., people were seen collecting about the docks, while a fussy little hoisting-engine worked away, lifting freight from the pier. At seven a few eager passengers came to the ship's side, anxiously inspecting her, and an hour later were going aboard.

Officers in uniform paced the decks, guarded the gangways to keep intruders back, and others of the crew, in citizen's clothes, mingled freely in the crowd, having a sharp eye out for suspicious characters.

The departure of a great trans-oceanic liner from port has the effect of a crisis upon those participating in the event. An air of suppressed excitement pervades the scene, making it one of peculiar interest. The restless, listless, laughing, melancholy, well-dressed, and slouchy multitude assembled on the decks and in the brilliant saloons afford entertainment for the most casual observer. Familiarity never dulls the edge of its entertainment, and the strain increases momentarily as time wears on.

Finally the steam-gauge pointer advances to the hundred mark. Noise and confusion wax wilder. The ship's crew is busy from captain to meanest sailor, until at ten o'clock, thirty minutes before sailing, the sound of hurrying feet is lost in a deafening hum of human voices. All visitors are now refused admittance, except perhaps a messenger with belated letters, packages, or flowers for people on board.

The little hoister fairly flies about in a heroic effort to lift everything that is at loose ends, and store it away in the ship's hold. The pier is invisible, buried beneath a multitude of peering people.

All being ready, the captain is notified, and at his signal the first engineer pulls the lever and starts the little engine whose work it is to open the throttle. The steam shoots out from the big boilers into the great cylinders, screws begin to revolve, and the "Fürst Bismarck," with one thousand passengers, three thousand tons of coal, and three thousand pounds of ice cream, clears her landing.

Hundreds of handkerchiefs flutter in the morning sunshine, and hundreds of people shout adieu, while many in the swaying throng smile through a mist of tears, following with eager eyes the trail of the vanishing ship.

I suppose the keenest sensation of an observant traveller, who for the first time settles himself for a voyage across the Atlantic, is one of sheer amazement. It matters not how much he has read of modern ocean greyhounds, his surprise is the same. Looking about, he realizes that whatever of marvel and beauty await him in foreign lands, nothing can so peremp-

Copyright, 1895, by S. S. McClure, Limited. All rights reserved.

torily demand his astonished admiration as the noble craft which transports him from the new country to the old.

To call them floating palaces is not a wholly unsatisfactory description of these wonderful steamships. But though the title tells of splendid luxury above the water line, it gives no hint of the marvellous power below, where man and machinery combine to conquer not only time and distance, but even the very forces of nature herself.

When the problem of inducing people to go by thousands and tens of thousands upon trans-oceanic voyages was first seriously considered, it presented itself as a question of how to unite safety, comfort, and reasonable rates with speed and financial profit to ship owners. The steamer might be as safe as you please, but if the journey consumed an unreasonable space of time, and implied discomfort and privation, then weary ones seeking rest and recreation refused to intrust themselves to the sea. This being the case, ship constructors were ordered to build with a view to minimising as far as possible the differences between life on land and life on sea. The travelling public, accustomed to the magnificent luxury of modern hostelries, withheld their patronage until ocean transports were able to offer an equal degree of ease and splendor.

THE VOYAGER SURPRISED AT THE SPACE HE HAS.

The novice aboard a big steamship like the "Fürst Bismarck," looks wonderingly around the broad sweep of the deck, where swarms of people wander about as comfortably as on spacious city streets. He sees wide doorways opening into great halls, and grand staircases descending into vast depths. And if he follows the stairway, he finds himself wandering through beautiful rooms, into complicated hallways. He is struck with the apparent disregard of those very narrow limitations of space which he has always associated with ships. There seems to be plenty of room, length and breadth, height and depth. As he investigates farther, he grasps the idea of the hugeness and magnificence of this iron-walled cavern.

Next to the lavish use of space, he is impressed by the apparent disregard of cost. He has paid into the steamship office a sum of money that would not be extravagant for board and lodgings in a first-class Fifth Avenue hotel for the same length of time. Yet here he is not only housed and fed in princely style, but is given transportation of the most difficult and costly kind. And he has the free use of all the rich luxuriousness of dining and smoking and music saloons, of library and writing-room. He is in a palace—for it is the palace idea that comes to him first—and, while his sleeping quarters may be small, he still has the privileges of all its great apartments.

THE DINING-ROOM AND THE TABLE.

Another source of unexpected delight to the uninitiated voyager aboard a great ship, is the quality of food and service. He gazes round in admiration at the noble dining-hall, with its tasteful walls, ornate ceiling, and generous mahogany table surrounded by comfortable chairs. There is a broad divan running the length and breadth of the room, port-holes are draped with silk and lace, chandeliers give forth a

DISMISSING THE PILOT.

THE CAPTAIN ON THE BRIDGE.

flood of tempered light, while here and there, under a pretty bracket, is a desk or cosy nook, tempting one to either work or play.

In the ship's huge refrigerators, meat, fruit, butter, and all perishable foods are solidly frozen, and these great ice-boxes offer a generous variety, including all the delicacies of the season that can be procured on either side of the Atlantic.

There is a *chef*, a most skilful, well-paid person, assisted by from a dozen to a score of under cooks, and by a small army of carvers and scullions.

The chief steward has been with the Hamburg-American Company twenty-seven years, and will probably stay as long as he cares to remain. There are eighty-four other stewards who report directly or indirectly to the chief. The passengers are divided into three classes: first cabin, second cabin, and steerage, so that three separate and complete kitchens and dining-rooms are kept up. The food furnished for the steerage passengers is better than one would expect when we consider that the company carries them over three thousand miles and keeps them on board seven days for eighteen dollars.

The food and service in the second cabin is better than the average three dollars a day American hotel. In the first cabin saloon it is perfect. Everything about the ship, after true German fashion, has a military air. The stewards file in in regular order, and when a change is made they all march out, keeping time to the band, and making, with their neat uniforms and snow-white gloves, a goodly sight to see.

The regular dinner consists of from seven to ten courses, and is fit for the emperor. The wines and ales are excellent, and, what surprises every one, they are forty per cent. cheaper than in New York.

In addition to the regular meals, at eight o'clock every evening they serve tea in the main saloon to all who care to indulge in that stimulant. After that, at nine o'clock, the band gives a concert in the second-cabin saloon, which is always attended by many of the first-cabin passengers. There the people sit about the tables and eat the daintiest little sandwiches, and some of them drink the delightful Hamburg beer, while the band plays.

If you are sick and remain in your berth, the room-steward will call half a dozen times a day to ask you what you want to eat. If you remain on deck, the deck-steward will bring you an excellent dinner without any extra charge.

WHERE YOU LODGE.

If you can afford to ignore expense, spacious apartments can be had in the big deck staterooms with their private baths, wide soft beds, and abundance of place for trunk and traps. But even in the staterooms in the depths of the ship there is a delightful display of that ingenuity which has labored for the comfort of the passengers everywhere; the conveniences for making the toilet are so compact, yet so effective; and, as everywhere else, there is splendid service. The boots comes in the night and looks to your shoes; the room-steward comes in the morning to see whether you are in good condition, or need something to set you right for your toilet; the bath-steward makes ready your bath and calls you for it; and you may leave your things about, and pay no attention to keys, because there is small chance of theft. Then there are the baths, no meagre basin of water, but big marble tubs where a hot and cold plunge is always ready.

The problem of exercise, a serious one for those taking long sea voyages, is partially solved by the broad decks running almost the full length of these mighty ships. They remind one of the great highways of a city; at night, when illuminated with electric lamps, all view of the sea cut off by darkness, then the illusion is complete, and one can fancy one's self strolling up and down a gay avenue. Those who are not walking or dancing, lounge along the rail, or range themselves in rows against the wall, commenting on the chattering throng as it surges by. All the while there is the strong, keen, joyous sea-air blowing in fresh as from some newly-created world; the day having its changing view of sun or storm upon the face of the many-colored sea, the darkness its mysterious midnight shadows and strange soothing sounds.

So much for the splendid idleness, gay pleasurings, and happy, care-free lives of passengers who, having paid their money, are served, watched over, and amused during every hour of these luxurious journeys. But there is another and even more interesting side to the picture. Below the water line, genius has labored successfully to insure safety and speed for the careless people overhead.

The ladders that lead down into the shadowy regions of fire, heat, smoke, and sweat are steep as the vessel's side, and very narrow. They are arranged in short

THE ENGINE-ROOM—STARTING THE SHIP.

THE CHIEF ENGINEER'S CABIN.

lengths, connecting the successive gradations, not much larger, some of them, than good-sized broilers. And to make the difficulty greater, these ladders, always vertical, face now one way, now another, so that in squeezing through the manholes for each fresh descent, one has to swing to right and left, monkey-like. Imagine this downward journey in a storm.

FOUR FATHOMS AND MORE BELOW THE LEVEL OF THE SEA.

Now we are at the bottom of the ship, four fathoms and more below the level of the Atlantic, and separated from the ocean below by a space of only four feet. This space forms a false bottom, a water-tight compartment, never opened except for occasional inspection, and filled with ballast, the ballast being water. The upper bottom is built of solid steel plates so strongly ribbed together that, though the outside bottom should be torn away, the ship would still float on serenely. Brushed in at the side by the nose of a man-of-war or a submerged rock, she would still

be held afloat by her thirteen air-tight compartments, any nine of which, intact, will keep her out of danger. "It is almost impossible for this ship to sink," says the chief engineer, and one comes to believe him.

On this second floor of the ship, over the tightly sealed water compartment, spread out the vital organs of the "Fürst Bismarck." The entire length of five hundred and two feet is divided between the engine-rooms aft, with the huge shafts that turn the twin propellers, and the stoke-hole forward, occupying nearly two-thirds of the ship's vast cellar, and filled with boilers, furnaces, and coal-bunkers. There are three rows of boilers and three rows of coal-bunkers, dividing the stoke-hole into six parallel spaces, all equally black, and all running from one side of the vessel to the other. The "Fürst Bismarck" shows everywhere divisions into three—a trinity of power—three watches, from twelve to four, from four to eight, from eight to twelve; three gangs of stokers, trimmers, and greasers; three great cylinders for the engines; three great cranks for each propeller shaft; three rows of boilers, as we have seen; and over these last, marking their exact location for the idlers on the decks, three yellow smokestacks.

"Look, now, we are coming to the boilers!" my guide exclaims.

A glare of light breaks into our faces as we emerge from the tunnel. Behind us is the iron wall of bunkers, black and cold. Before us is a wall of fire, twelve glowing craters, whose round red mouths, two feet in diameter, open and close with automatic, weighted doors as six stokers feed them. They seem to snap their jaws for coal. The two walls are parallel and stretch from port to starboard; they are about twelve feet apart and form one of the streets in furnaceland. The iron floor is heaped with piles of ashes, slag, and fresh coal, which latter keeps arriving in the wagons. At the men's feet lie iron implements, long bars and rakes, some of them red-hot at the ends.

Suddenly a man in the shadow puts a whistle to his lips and sounds three calls. The six stokers respond instantly. Every furnace-door flies open. Two men at the right and two at the left begin shovelling furiously, while two men in the middle lift their forty-pound lances and thrust them into the mass of fire. Having buried the lances eight feet deep in the coals, the men throw their weights full upon the ends as levers, and lift the whole bank of fire several inches. Then they draw out the lances; leaving a black hole through the fire into which the draft is sucked with an increasing roar. Three times they thrust the lances; each time they break up the fires, first at the right, then at the left, and then down the centre. When they have finished, their grimy faces are streaked with sweat, their bodies are steaming. In the pauses of their work they plunge their heads in buckets of water, and take deep draughts from bottles of red wine.

NINE HUGE BOILERS AND SEVENTY-TWO HOT FURNACES.

Resting on the twelve furnaces are three huge boilers which rise with great curving cylinders, rivet-studded, ending somewhere in the darkness far above; one peers up vainly to make out the tops. Each of these boilers could receive in its enormous girth four Broadway cable cars, and the three fill the width of the ship, their iron sides pressed close together. They are about twenty feet in length, and underneath their farther end, in the next stoke-hole space, burn twelve other furnaces equal in size to those before us, making eight roaring fires to one boiler, or twenty-four furnaces to the three. And each furnace able to take in half a ton of coal at a gulp!

The man with the whistle is one of the three *Oberheizers* on duty for each watch, there being nine of them in all, with nine gangs of men. Each *Oberheizer* directs twelve stokers, who feed the twenty-four furnaces under the row of boilers, six at one end, six at the other, each tending two fires. But there is more than the one row of boilers; the "Fürst Bismarck" has three, or nine boilers in all. And so there are always, night and day, down in her dark cellars, thirty-six stokers and their chiefs,

UPPER ENGINE-ROOM.

working like demons at seventy-two furnaces, which blaze red-hot or white-hot from the moment the steamer sails until her landing.

Now, bending our heads, we enter another passage, darker and narrower than the former, traversing the space between two boilers.

Here is greater animation, for twelve stokers are firing on this street, six for the row of boilers under which we have just passed, and six on the other side for the second row. No Oberheizer is in sight, but from the far side of the second row of boilers sounds at intervals the whistle which directs the second gang, while the whistle of the Oberheizer in the first street comes through the tunnel behind us.

Now the signal from the latter sounds sharp and imperious. The two men at either extremity of the line spring for the fire-rakes, while the two in the middle grasp their shovels. Then for five minutes they struggle with the fires, those in the centre throwing in great lumps of coal, those on the ends shaping up the burning firebeds.

WATERING THE BOILERS — CLEANING THE FURNACES.

The stoker's work is not limited to caring for the fires, he has also to keep constant watch on the boiler-gauges, letting in fresh water from the reservoir whenever the long, dusty glass tubes show that it is needed—about twice an hour. Every day the nine boilers change into steam one hundred tons of water, which is carried back to the reservoir from the condenser, and used over and over again.

The refuse, after being removed from the furnaces, is shovelled into large buckets. These are attached to chains let down through the air-shafts, and at the cry, "Heave up!" or "Hieve-op!" the engine on the deck above is set in motion, winding up the chains, and presently the waste of the furnaces is dumped into the ocean.

Not only must stokers be men of excellent bodily strength, but considerable skill is required in their work. It takes some time to learn the handling of the lances, and the proper use of the fire-rakes calls for special knowledge. When the coal is first shovelled into the furnaces, it is thrown as far back as possible, to the point of extreme combustion. Then, after breaking it up, the rakes are used to draw back the fuel now fully ignited, so as to form a curving mound near the mouth of the furnace, the highest point being about two feet back from the door. It has been found by experiment that this arrangement of the coal gives the hottest flame, and the strongest draft up through the boilers.

It is fair to say that everything that can be done to mitigate the hardships of life in the stoke-hole has been done by the steamship companies. It was to lessen the strain of their work that the stokers and trimmers were allowed to divide their working day of eight hours into two stretches of four hours each. The best quality of food is given them, with plenty of meat and fresh vegetables, and they are allowed double rations of wine and kümmel four times a day, practically all they care to drink.

It has been proposed to introduce on steamships the mechanical stoker now coming into more or less use on land. But it seems doubtful if this can ever be done. The constant shifting of the angle of a vessel's floor would interfere with the automatic feeding of any machine as yet constructed.

THE COAL IT COSTS TO INCREASE SPEED.

Few people understand the enormous increase required in the amount of coal burned to get a comparatively slight increase in a vessel's speed. For example, suppose the propellers were turning fifty-seven times to the minute, and it was desired to make them turn fifty-eight times instead. This would only make the ship go about three ship-lengths farther in a day. But it would require the burning of five more tons of coal a day. The formula accepted by the engineers is that the coal burned varies as the cube of the speed attained. One of the chief engineers of the Hamburg Line gave me the following estimate of the various amounts of coal required to produce varying rates of speed, and in this the varying proportion between the increase in coal burned and the increase in speed is at once apparent. The "Bismarck" could be driven at the rate of twelve knots an hour by burning ninety tons of coal a day. By burning twice as much coal a day—that is one hundred and eighty tons—her speed would be advanced to only sixteen knots an hour, a gain of but one-third. By increasing the coal burned to three hundred tons a day the rate of gain in speed is even less, the speed being then twenty knots an hour. It is calculated that if enough

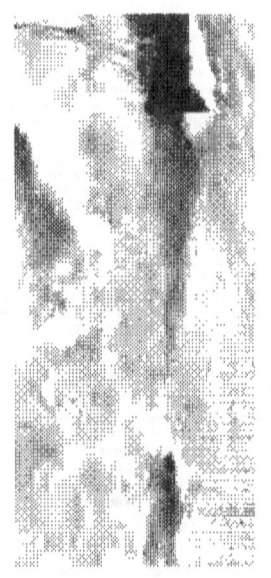

coal were burned and enough extra furnaces and firemen put in to double the present horse-power of this steamship, the result would be only to shorten her time across the Atlantic by a scant half-day. Thus much more is meant than one realizes when the newspapers inform us that a steamer has beaten the Atlantic record even by an hour or two. It has cost hundreds of tons of coal, thousands of dollars in boilers, furnaces, and machinery, and strain on human beings such as no one can easily conceive of who is not more or less familiar with the stoke-hole.

THE FIFTY-FIVE ENGINES.

Let us look now into the engine-room, the real heart of the vessel, where all the steam brought from the nine huge boilers hurls itself against the pistons in six huge cylinders, three to turn the propeller on the port side, three to turn the one on the starboard side. Of these three pairs of cylinders, the first pair are forty-three inches in diameter, and work a pressure of eleven atmospheres. The second pair are sixty-seven inches in diameter, with a pressure of four atmospheres. The third pair are low pressure cylinders, one hundred and six inches in diameter, with one atmosphere pressure, and a vacuum equal in working power to one atmosphere. Many visits are necessary to the engine-room before one becomes familiar enough with the place to appreciate its marvels. The first effect is merely stunning. One understands nothing, fails to trace any sequence of cause and effect, and only recognizes a stupendous turning of giant cranks, a piling up of enormous masses of metal all bright and oily, a wilderness of immense steel stanchions, levers, and cylinders, great wheels, great curving pipes, great pistons, the whole weighing hundreds of tons, and all apparently turning and pounding without beginning or end.

Three men, the engineer, his assistant, and a greaser, are the whole force required at one time in each engine-room, and they never seem to be particularly busy. When all is well, as it always is, the engineer has nothing more to do than turn a little wheel now and then, or open and shut some valves. Quite child's play one would think. It seems ridiculous that he should manage these giant powers about him literally with a turn of the hand. There on the floor is a little lever which, turned one way or the other, lets the whole Atlantic Ocean into the great condensers. Turn it over so, and tons of salt water are rushing into those great pipes. Having served its purpose in condensing the steam, this salt water is discharged overboard from the vessel's sides with a great spurting.

Here is the little wheel, only a foot in diameter, which will stop or start the great ship by a few turns. A woman could work it.

Beside this wheel is the telegraph connected with the bridge where the captain stands, a needle indicating on the dial the order to be executed. At the bottom of the dial, where the figure six is on a clock, is printed the word "halt." Then, on one side, in German, are the words "steady," "slow," "halt," and "full." When the needle points on this side it means to go ahead as indicated; when it points on the other side, where there are corresponding words, it means to reverse the engines and go backward.

HOW THE SHIP IS SHUT INTO WATER-TIGHT COMPARTMENTS.

Between the two sets of orders on the telegraph dial I noticed one special word, *Schotten zu*, and asked the engineer what that meant.

"That," he answered, "is one of the most important signals of all. It is given twice in twenty-four hours on every day of every voyage, but we never know when it will come, day or night. It is the signal to close the great iron doors that separate the water-tight compartments in the engine-rooms; they can all be closed within a minute of the giving of the signal. That is what we practise every day."

The engineer proceeded to show me these iron doors and explain their working. In each partition in the engine-room is an opening about the size of an ordinary low doorway through which the men pass in their daily work.

Each set of boilers with the underlying furnaces may be quite shut off from the rest of the ship, and each engine-room may be shut off from the other.

The whole hull of the ship is divided by twelve massive partitions of iron and steel which no force would crush through. There are, therefore, thirteen water-tight compartments, and the ship would float on undisturbed, even if three or four of them were stove in and filled with water.

The method of closing the compartments is beautifully simple. A heavy iron door, sliding between heavy wheels, is always poised above the opening, held in place by

THE STEERAGE DECK.

an iron pin which has only to be loosened to let the door slide downward and close by its own weight. These doors are so heavily built that in the daily manœuvres it takes two men four minutes, working with all their might at ratchet and wheel, to hoist them to their places. Whenever the signal "*Schotten zu*" is received by the engineer, a sharp whistle call rings through all the gloomy regions below, and the men spring to their posts like firemen, for they never know whether there is really danger or whether it is merely the usual practice. At a second signal, the two men stationed at each door loosen the pins, which allows the wheels to turn, and, in a few seconds, the thirteen water-tight compartments are secured.

"I will tell you another thing," said the engineer, "which shows the perfection of our system. The captain himself on the deck, or any officer, can, by a single movement of a lever, cause every one of these doors to close. Thus, you see, that even should the men be panic-stricken and fail to respond to the call, the ship would still be safe."

I asked the engineer how long it would take to stop the "Bismarck" going through mid-ocean at full speed.

"We have never made a full test of that point," he said, "but I think I could stop her within six lengths without reversing the engines. If I reversed the engines I might stop her in three lengths, say within half a minute."

"Would that be in time to save a man who had gone overboard?" I asked.

The engineer shook his head. "I am afraid not. I am very skeptical of being able to save anyone who has jumped or fallen from the ship. In many years' experience I have never known a case of such a rescue. Of course I am speaking now of large steamers with propellers. You see, the person who goes overboard is almost always drawn in by the suction of the ship, and struck by the revolving screw. Of course that means death. If a man jumped straight off the stern, and as far out as possible, so as to clear the blades, and then if he could keep afloat long enough, he might be picked up by a boat. That's about the only chance. But usually people who jump from a ship wish to die."

THE STEAM STEERING APPARATUS.

The "man at the wheel," who "puts her over" to starboard or port, grasping the handles of a great wheel with either hand as a pilot is seen to do on a ferryboat, is, as most readers are no doubt aware, not to be found on the great steamships. There is still the wheel. On the "Fürst Bismarck" it is a double wheel, six feet in diameter,

AN OCEAN FLYER.

HURRICANE DECK AND VENTILATORS.

and so heavy that four men with all their strength can scarcely manage it in easy weather, while eight men are required to steer with it in a storm. This, however, is only for use in an emergency; its great spokes being never even touched unless some accident happens to the steam steering apparatus usually employed. What really steers the ship is the strength seventy-five horse-power engine pla the steering-room, at the extreme the ship, where the emergency w wheel is also placed. This engin means of small cogged wheels and a sive iron chain, turns a great iron placed horizontally either to the rig the left. This iron wheel is as wide as a house, and weighs many tons. Its upright axis passes down through the bottom of the ship, and is fitted to the rudder, which swings beneath the propellers, and, like them, seems ridiculously small as the final recipient and agent of such enormous power. The steering-wheel never makes a complete revolution on its axis, but only turns a few degrees to the right or the left as the engine is directed. When the steam is allowed to rush in on one side of the pistons, the wheel turns one way, and when the steam is let in on the other side, the wheel turns in the other way. All that the captain or officer on the bridge does in steering the ship is, with the guidance of a dial, to open or close the valves which let the steam into the cylinders of the steering-engine. They seem to be steering the ship by their own effort, but really they are doing nothing more than pull the reins on one side or the other to direct the giant of steam who steers for them.

IN THE SHAFT-ROOM.

The last thing one comes to working aft in exploring the bottom of a ship, is the shaft-room, through which the twin axes pass from the cranks of the engines to the great screws that project behind. Not many ocean travellers have entered this room or been able to form an idea of the enormous size of these propeller shafts. Each one of them is nearly two feet in diameter and one hundred and forty-two feet in length. Each is made of the toughest steel, and is in eight sections, screwed together with elaborate couplings. Each averages a ton in weight for every foot of length; that is, ten feet of each shaft weighs ten tons, and the whole shaft weighs, with the couplings, nearly one hundred and fifty tons. They are painted white, and so uniform is their coating, and so true do they run in their bearings, that as one watches them spin around they seem scarcely to be moving at all. As a matter of fact, though, when the vessel is running at full speed they turn about seventy-five times in a minute, and it is with strange sensations that one stands in this long, low room with its bare, white-painted iron walls, and feels, only a few feet beyond the iron partition, the tremendous impact of those swift-turning screws against the plunging, surging water, kicking, as it were, at the great Atlantic with the force of sixteen thousand horses.

It is always an advantage to have steamers with twin propellers, because should anything happen to the steering apparatus or to the rudder, the ship may be steered with absolutely no danger, by simply reversing one screw, and going

SOLID COMFORT IN THE SMOKE-ROOM.

MAKING FAST AN AWNING.

ahead with the other, the effect being the same as when a rowboat is guided by holding one oar still and working the other. But there are other advantages of the twin-screw system. It secures the longitudinal bulkhead, a solid steel partition which runs from stem to stern and divides the ship into halves. Each side is fully equipped with an independent set of engines and boilers and shaft and screw. An accident to the machinery on one side, therefore, in no wise affects the other, which will continue its work and propel the ship with only slightly diminished speed.

Thus marvellously constructed and equipped, the ocean "flyer" makes her appointed voyage swiftly and securely, in any sort of weather, accommodating within her ample walls the life above and the life below—the two as widely separated as two worlds. And the personal equipment is no less remarkable than the mechanical, skill and scrupulous attention marking it everywhere. The captain on his bridge; the chief engineer in his luxurious oak-finished office, surrounded by easy chairs and soft couches, and burnished dials and indicators; and all under them, have, night or day, but one thought, one duty,— to see that all is well. And in consequence, rarely, almost never, is it otherwise than well.

THE LORD OF CHATEAU NOIR.

BY A. CONAN DOYLE,

Author of "Micah Clarke," "The Adventures of Sherlock Holmes," etc.

IT was in the days when the German armies had broken their way across France, and when the shattered forces of the young republic had been swept aside to the north of the Aisne and to the south of the Loire. Three broad streams of armed men had rolled slowly but irresistibly from the Rhine, now meandering to the north, now to the south, dividing, coalescing, but all uniting to form one great lake round Paris. And from this lake there welled out smaller streams, one to the north, one southward to Orleans, and a third westward into Normandy. Many a German trooper saw the sea for the first time when he rode his horse girth-deep into the waves at Dieppe.

Black and bitter were the thoughts of Frenchmen when they saw this wale of dishonor slashed across the fair face of their country. They had fought, and they had been overborne. That swarming cavalry, those countless footmen, the masterful guns—they had tried and tried to make head against them. In battalions their invaders were not to be beaten. But man to man, or ten' to ten, they were their equals. A brave Frenchman might still make a single German rue the day that he had left his own bank of the Rhine. Thus, unchronicled amid the battles and the sieges, there broke out another war, a war of individuals, with foul murder upon the one side and brutal reprisal upon the other.

Colonel von Gramm of the Twenty-fourth Posen Infantry had suffered severely during this new development. He commanded in the little Norman town of Les Andelys, and his outposts stretched amid the hamlets and farmhouses of the district round. No French force was within fifty miles of him, and yet morning after morning he had to listen to a black report of sentries found dead at their posts, or of foraging parties which had never returned. Then the colonel would go forth in his wrath, and farmsteadings would blaze and villages tremble, but next morning there was still that same dismal tale to be told. Do what he might, he could not shake off his invisible enemies. And yet it should not have been so hard, for from certain signs in common, in the plan and in the deed, it was certain that all these outrages came from a single source.

Colonel von Gramm had tried violence and it had failed. Gold might be more successful. He published it abroad over the countryside that five hundred francs would be paid for information. There was no response. Then eight hundred. The peasants were incorruptible. Then, goaded on by a murdered corporal, he rose to a thousand, and so bought the soul of François Rejane, farm laborer, whose Norman avarice was a stronger passion than his French hatred.

"You say that you know who did these crimes?" asked the Prussian colonel, eying with loathing the blue-bloused, rat-faced creature before him.

"Yes, Colonel."

"And it was——?"

"Those thousand francs, Colonel——"

"Not a sou until your story has been tested. Come! who is it who has murdered my men?"

"It is Count Eustace of Chateau Noir."

"You lie!" cried the colonel, angrily. "A gentleman and a nobleman could not have done such crimes."

The peasant shrugged his shoulders. "It is evident to me that you do not know the count. It is this way, Colonel. What I tell you is the truth, and I am not afraid that you should test it. The Count of Chateau Noir is a hard man—even at the best time he was a hard man. But of late he has been terrible. It was his son's death, you know. His son was under Douay, and he was taken, and then in escaping from Germany he met his death. It was the count's only child; and, indeed, we all think that it has driven him mad. With his peasants he follows the German armies. I do not know how many he has killed, but it is he who cuts the cross upon the foreheads, for it is the badge of his house."

It was true. The murdered sentries had each had a saltier cross slashed across their brows, as by a hunting-knife. The colonel bent his stiff back and ran his forefinger over the map which lay upon the table.

"The Chateau Noir is not more than four leagues," he said.

"Three and a kilometre, Colonel."

"You know the place?"

"I used to work there."

Colonel von Gramm rang the bell.

"Give this man food, and detain him," said he to the sergeant.

"Why detain me, Colonel? I can tell you no more."

"We shall need you as guide."

"As guide! But the count! If I were to fall into his hands! Ah, Colonel!——"

The Prussian commander waved him away. "Send Captain Baumgarten to me at once," said he.

The officer who answered the summons was a man of middle age, heavy-jawed, blue-eyed, with a curving yellow mustache, and a brick-red face which turned to an ivory-white where his helmet had sheltered it. He was bald, with a shining, tightly stretched scalp, at the back of which, as in a mirror, it was a favorite mess joke for the subalterns to trim their mustaches.

As a soldier he was slow, but reliable and brave. The colonel could trust him where a more dashing officer might be in danger.

"You will proceed to Chateau Noir tonight, Captain," said he. "A guide has been provided. You will arrest the count and bring him back. If there is an attempt at rescue, shoot him at once."

"How many men shall I take, Colonel?"

"Well, we are surrounded by spies, and our only chance is to pounce upon him before he knows that we are on the way. A large force will attract attention. On the other hand, you must not risk being cut off."

"I might march north, Colonel, as if to join General Goeben. Then I could turn down this road which I see upon your map, and get to Chateau Noir before they could hear of us. In that case, with twenty men——"

"Very good, Captain. I hope to see you with your prisoner to-morrow morning."

It was a cold December night when Captain Baumgarten marched out of Les Andelys with his twenty Poseners, and took the main road to the northwest. Two miles out he turned suddenly down a narrow, deeply rutted track, and made swiftly for his man. A thin, cold rain was falling, swishing among the tall poplar trees and rustling in the fields on either side. The captain walked first with Moser, a veteran sergeant, beside him. The sergeant's wrist was fastened to that of the French peasant, and it had been whispered in his ear that, in case of an ambush, the first bullet fired would be through his head. Behind

THE FRENCHMAN HELD UP A REVOLVER WHICH HE GRASPED IN HIS RIGHT HAND.

them the twenty infantrymen plodded along through the darkness, with their faces sunk to the rain, and their boots squeaking in the soft, wet clay. They knew where they were going, and why, and the thought upheld them; for they were bitter at the loss of their comrades. It was a cavalry job, they knew, but the cavalry were all on with the advance, and, besides, it was more fitting that the regiment should avenge its own dead men.

It was nearly eight when they left Les Andelys. At half-past eleven their guide stopped at a place where two high pillars, crowned with some heraldic stone-work, flanked a huge iron gate. The wall in which it had been the opening had crumbled away, but the great gate still towered above the brambles and weeds which had overgrown its base. The Prussians made their way round it, and advanced stealthily under the shadow of a black tunnel of oak branches up the long avenue which was still cumbered by the leaves of last autumn. At the top they halted and reconnoitred.

The black chateau lay in front of them. The moon had shone out between two rain-clouds, and threw the old house into silver and shadow. It was shaped like an L, with a low-arched door in front, and lines of small windows like the open ports of a man-of-war. Above was a dark roof, breaking at the corners into little, round, overhanging turrets, the whole lying silent in the moonshine, with a drift of ragged clouds blackening the heavens behind it. A single light gleamed in one of the lower windows.

The captain whispered his orders to his men. Some were to creep to the front door, some to the back. Some were to watch the east, and some the west. He and the sergeant stole on tiptoe to the lighted window.

It was a small room into which they looked, very meanly furnished. An elderly man, in the dress of a menial, was reading a tattered paper by the light of a guttering candle. He leaned back in his wooden chair, with his feet upon a box, while a bottle of white wine stood with a half-filled tumbler upon a stool beside him. The sergeant thrust his needle-gun through the glass, and the man sprang to his feet with a shriek.

"Silence for your life! The house is surrounded, and you cannot escape. Come round and open the door, or we will show you no mercy when we come in."

"For God's sake, don't shoot! I will open it! I will open it!" He rushed from the room with his paper still crumpled up in his hand. An instant later, with a groaning of old locks and a rasping of bars, the low door swung open, and the Prussians poured into the stone-flagged passage.

"Where is Count Eustace de Chateau Noir?"

"My master? He is out, sir."

"Out at this time of night? Your life for a lie."

"It is true, sir. He is out."

"Where?"

"I do not know."

"Doing what?"

"I cannot tell. No, it is no use your cocking your pistol, sir. You may kill me, but you cannot make me tell you that which I do not know."

"Is he often out at this hour?"

"Frequently."

"And when does he come home?"

"Before daybreak."

Captain Baumgarten rasped out a German oath. He had had his journey for nothing, then. The man's answers were only too likely to be true. It was what he might have expected. But, at least, he would search the house and make sure. Leaving a picket at the front door and another at the back, the sergeant and he drove the trembling butler in front of them, his shaking candle sending strange flickering shadows over the old tapestries and the low oak-raftered ceilings. They searched the whole house from the huge stone-flagged kitchen below to the dining-hall on the second floor, with its gallery for musicians, and its panelling black with age; but nowhere was there a living creature. Up in an attic they found Marie, the elderly wife of the butler, but the owner kept no other servants; and of his own presence there was no trace.

It was long, however, before Captain Baumgarten had satisfied himself upon the point. It was a difficult house to search. Thin stairs, which only one man could ascend at a time, connected lines of tortuous corridors. The walls were so thick that each room was cut off from its neighbor. Huge fire-places yawned in each, while the windows were six feet deep in the wall. Captain Baumgarten stamped with his feet, and tore down curtains, and struck with the pommel of his sword. If there were secret hiding-places he was not fortunate enough to find them.

"I have an idea," said he, at last, speaking in German to the sergeant. "You will place a guard over this fellow, and make sure that he communicates with no one."

"Yes, Captain."

"And you will place four men in ambush at the front and at the back. It is likely enough that daybreak our bird may come back to the nest."

"And the others, Captain?"

"Let them have their suppers in the kitchen. This fellow will serve you with meat and wine. It is a wild night, and we shall be better here than on the country road."

"And yourself, Captain?"

"I will take my supper up here in the

dining-hall. The logs are laid, and we can light the fire. You will call me if there is any alarm. What can you give me for supper—you?"

"Alas! monsieur, there was a time when I might have answered, 'What you wish.' But now it is all that we can do to find a bottle of new claret and a cold pullet."

"That will do very well. Let a guard go about with him, Sergeant, and let him feel the end of a bayonet if he plays us any tricks."

Captain Baumgarten was an old campaigner. In the Eastern provinces, and, before that, in Bohemia, he had learned the art of quartering himself upon the enemy. While the butler brought his supper in, he occupied himself in making his preparations for a comfortable night. He lit the candelabrum of ten candles upon the centre-table. The fire was already burning up, crackling merrily, and sending spurts of blue pungent smoke out into the room. The captain walked to the window and looked out. The moon had gone in again, and it was raining heavily. He could hear the deep sough of the wind, and see the dark gloom of the trees, all swaying in one direction. It was a sight which gave a zest to his comfortable quarters, and to the cold fowl and the bottle of wine which the butler had brought up for him. He was tired and hungry after his long tramp; so he threw his sword, his helmet, and his revolver-belt down upon a chair, and fell to eagerly upon his supper. Then, with his glass of wine before him, and a cigar between his lips, he tilted his chair back and looked about him.

He sat within a small circle of brilliant light which gleamed upon his silver shoulder-straps and drew out his terra-cotta face, his heavy eyebrows, and yellow mustache. But outside that circle things were vague and shadowy in the old dining-hall. Two sides were oak-panelled, and two were hung with faded tapestry, across which huntsmen and dogs and stags were still dimly streaming. Above the fire-place were rows of heraldic shields, with the blazonings of the family and its alliances, the fatal saltier cross breaking out on each of them.

Four paintings of old seigneurs of Chateau Noir faced the fireplace, all men with hawk noses and bold, high features, so like each other that only the dress could distinguish the crusader from the cavalier of the Fronde. Captain Baumgarten, heavy with his repast, lay back in his chair, looking up at them through the cloud of his tobacco smoke, and pondering over the strange chance which had sent him, a man from the Baltic coast, to eat his supper in the ancestral hall of these proud Norman chieftains. But the fire was hot and the captain's eyes were heavy. His chin sank slowly upon his chest, and the ten candles gleamed upon the broad white scalp.

Suddenly a slight noise brought him to his feet. For an instant it seemed to his dazed senses that one of the pictures opposite had walked from its frame. There, beside the table, and almost within arm's length of him, was standing a huge man, silent, motionless, with no sign of life save his fierce, glinting eyes. He was black-haired, olive-skinned, with a pointed tuft of black beard, and a great fierce nose towards which all his features seemed to run. His cheeks were wrinkled like a last year's apple, but his sweep of shoulder and bony, corded hands told of a strength which was unsapped by age. His arms were folded across his arching chest, and his mouth was set in a fixed smile.

"Pray, do not trouble yourself to look for your weapons," he said, as the Prussian cast a swift glance at the empty chair in which they had been laid. "You have been, if you will allow me to say so, a little indiscreet to make yourself so much at home in a house every wall of which is honeycombed with secret passages. You will be amused to hear that forty men were watching you at your supper. Ah! What then!"

Captain Baumgarten had taken a step forward with clenched fists. The Frenchman held up a revolver which he grasped in his right hand, while with his left he hurled the German back into his chair.

"Pray keep your seat," said he. "You have no cause to trouble about your men. They have already been provided for. It is astonishing, with these stone floors, how little one can hear what goes on beneath. You have been relieved of your command, and have now only to think of yourself. May I ask what your name is?"

"I am Captain Baumgarten of the Twenty-fourth Posen Regiment."

"Your French is excellent, though you incline, like most of your countrymen, to turn the 'p' into a 'b.' I have been amused to hear them cry, 'Ayez bitié sur moi!' You know, doubtless, who it is who addresses you."

"The Count of Chateau Noir."

"Precisely. It would have been a misfortune if you had visited my chateau and I had been unable to have a word with you.

I have had to do with many German soldiers, but never with an officer before. I have much to talk to you about."

Captain Baumgarten sat still in his chair. Brave as he was, there was something in this man's manner which made his skin creep with apprehension. His eyes glanced to right and to left, but his weapons were gone, and in a struggle he saw that he was but a child with this gigantic adversary. The count had picked up the claret bottle and held it to the light.

"Tut! Tut!" said he. "And was this the best that Pierre could do for you? I am ashamed to look you in the face, Captain Baumgarten. We must improve upon this."

He blew a call upon a whistle which hung from his shooting-jacket. The old man servant was in the room in an instant.

"Chambertin from bin fifteen," he cried, and a minute later a gray bottle, streaked with cobwebs, was carried in as a nurse bears an infant. The count filled two glasses to the brim.

"Drink," said he. "It is the very best in my cellars, and not to be matched between Rome and Paris. Drink, sir, and be happy! There are cold joints below. There are two lobsters fresh from Honfleur. Will you not venture upon a second and more savory supper?"

The German officer shook his head. He drained his glass, however, and his host filled it once more, pressing him to give an order for this or that dainty.

"There is nothing in my house which is not at your disposal. You have but to say the word. Well, then, you will allow me to tell you a story while you drink your wine. I have so longed to tell it to some German officer. It is about my son, my only child Eustace, who was taken, and died in escaping. It is a curious little story, and I think I can promise you that you never will forget it.

"You must know, then, that my boy was in the artillery, a fine young fellow, Captain Baumgarten, and the pride of his mother. She died within a week of the news of his death reaching us. It was brought by a brother officer who was at his side throughout, and who escaped, while my lad died. I want to tell you all that he told me.

"Eustace was taken at Weissenburg on the 4th of August. The prisoners were broken up into parties, and sent back into Germany by different routes. Eustace was taken upon the 5th to a village called Lauterburg, where he met with kindness from the German officer in command. This good colonel had the hungry lad to supper, offered him the best he had, opened a bottle of good wine, as I have tried to do for you, and gave him a cigar from his own case. Might I entreat you to take one from mine?"

The German again shook his head. His horror of his companion had increased as he sat watching the lips that smiled and the eyes that glared.

"The colonel, as I say, was good to my boy; but, unluckily, the prisoners were moved next day across the Rhine to Ettlingen. They were not equally fortunate then.

"The officer who guarded them was a ruffian and villain, Captain Baumgarten. He took a pleasure in humiliating and ill-treating the brave men who had fallen into his power. That night, upon my son's answering fiercely back to some taunt of his, he struck him in the eye like this."

The crash of the blow rang through the hall. The German's face fell forward, his hand up, and blood oozing through his fingers. The count settled down in his chair once more. "My boy was disfigured by the blow, and this villain made his appearance the object of his jeers. By the way, you look a little comical yourself at the present moment, Captain, and your colonel would certainly say that you had been getting into mischief. To continue, however, my boy's youth and his destitution—for his pockets were empty—moved the pity of a kind-hearted major, and he advanced him ten napoleons from his own pocket without security of any kind. Into your hands, Captain Baumgarten, I return these ten gold pieces, since I cannot learn the name of the lender. I am grateful from my heart for this kindness shown my boy.

"The vile tyrant who commanded the escort accompanied the prisoners to Durlach, and from there to Carlsruhe. He heaped every outrage upon my lad, because the spirit of the Chateaux-Noirs would not stoop to turn away his wrath by a feigned submission. Ay, this cowardly villain, whose heart's blood shall still clot upon this hand, dared to strike my son with his open hand, to kick him, to tear hairs from his moustache—to use him thus—and thus—and thus!"

The German writhed and struggled. He was helpless in the hands of this huge giant whose blows were raining upon him. When at last, blinded and half-senseless, he staggered to his feet, it was only to be

THE OFFICERS, PALE BUT FIRM, FOLDED HIS ARMS AND STARED DEFIANTLY AT THE MAN WHO TORTURED HIM.

hurled back again into the great oaken chair. He sobbed in his impotent anger and shame.

"My boy was frequently moved to tears by the humiliation of his position," continued the count. "You will understand when I say that it is a bitter thing to be helpless in the hands of an insolent and remorseless enemy. On arriving at Carlsruhe, however, his face, which had been wounded by the brutality of his guard, was bound up by a young Bavarian subaltern, who was touched by his appearance. I regret to see that your eye is bleeding so. Will you permit me to bind it with my silk handkerchief?"

He leaned forward, but the German dashed his hand aside. "I am in your power, you monster!" he cried. "I can endure your brutality, but not your hypocrisy."

The count shrugged his shoulders. "I am taking things in their order, just as they occurred," said he. "I was under vow to tell it to the first German officer with whom I could talk *tête-à-tête*. Let me see, I had got as far as the young Bavarian at Carlsruhe. I regret extremely that you will not permit me to use such slight skill in surgery as I possess. At Carlsruhe my lad was shut up in the old caserne, where he remained for a fortnight.

The worst pang of his captivity was that some unmannerly cur in the garrison would taunt him with his position as he sat by his window in the evening. That reminds me, Captain, that you are not quite situated upon a bed of roses yourself, are you, now? You came to trap a wolf, my man, and now the beast has you down, with his fangs in your throat. A family man, too, I should judge, by that well-filled tunic. Well, a widow the more will make little matter, and they do not usually remain widows long. Get back into the chair, you dog!

"Well, to continue my story, at the end of a fortnight my son and his friend escaped. I need not trouble you with the dangers which they ran or the privations which they endured. Suffice it to say that to disguise themselves they had to take the clothes of two peasants, whom they waylaid in a wood. Hiding by day and travelling by night, they had got as far into France as Remilly, and were within a mile—a single mile, Captain—of crossing the German lines, when a patrol of Uhlans came right upon them. Oh! it was hard, was it not, when they had come so far and were so near to safety?" The count blew a double call upon his whistle, and three hard-faced peasants entered the room.

"These must represent my Uhlans," said he. "Well, then, the captain in command, finding that these men were French soldiers in civilian dress within the German lines, proceeded to hang them without trial or ceremony. I think, Jean, that the centre beam is the shortest."

The unfortunate soldier was dragged from his chair to where a noosed rope had been flung over one of the huge oaken rafters which spanned the room. The cord was slipped over his head, and he felt its harsh grip round his throat. The three peasants seized the other end, and looked to the count for his orders.

The officer, pale but firm, folded his arms and stared defiantly at the man who tortured him.

"You are now face to face with death, and I perceive from your lips that you are praying. My son was also face to face with death, and he prayed also. It happened that a general officer came up, and he heard the lad praying for his mother, and it moved him so—he being himself a father—that he ordered his Uhlans away, and he remained with his aide-de-camp only beside the condemned men. And when he heard all the lad had to tell, that he was the only child of an old family, and that his mother was in failing health, he threw off the rope as I throw off this, and he kissed him on either cheek as I kiss you, and he bade him go as I bid you go; and may every kind wish of that noble general, though it could not stave off the fever which slew my son, descend now upon your head."

And so it was that Captain Baumgarten, disfigured, blinded, and bleeding, staggered out into the wind and the rain of that wild December dawn.

F. MARION CRAWFORD: A CONVERSATION.

Recorded by Robert Bridges,

Author of "Overheard in Arcady," etc.

THERE is no need to localize this conversation with F. Marion Crawford, for he is equally at home in a dozen great cities of the world. The readers of his books do not need any particular background to explain the man; he is a thorough cosmopolite. But personally I have always thought of Mr. Crawford as working in a grotto under the cliffs of Sorrento, with the flashing waters of the bay shining through the arched opening, and the little waves playing on the white sand, almost at his feet. There I have often imagined him sitting before a little square and much-worn table of pine, with nothing on it but reams of paper and a bottle of ink, and on one corner, near his hand, a teapot, under which the pale blue flame is always burning. I have pictured him there, day after day, drinking unnumbered cups of tea, and summoning out of the dark recesses of the grotto the strange and romantic company who are his familiars—Paul Patoff, Dr. Claudius, Saracinesca, Gouache, Mr. Isaacs, Ram Lal, Marzio, Zoroaster. They spring from the darkness, talk with him awhile, disappear and reappear, forming dramatic groups and doing daring deeds. And, while they come and go, he is always writing, writing, imperturbably writing, even when talking with them. I do not know where I first got this idea, but I think I can trace it to a chapter in "To Leeward" and a chance newspaper paragraph. At any rate, I have been a firm believer in that grotto for many years, and I want to continue to believe in it. Since I have known Mr. Crawford personally, I have carefully avoided asking him about it, for I don't want to destroy the illusion, if it is one, and I don't believe it *is* an illusion. With each new novel of his that I have read, I have seen the grotto grow a little larger, the darkness become more populous. I used to think that on some sunny day I should be rowed across the bay of Sorrento (perhaps by one of the "Children of the King"), and should be landed from the little boat at the very mouth of the cave; and then I should introduce myself to Mr. Crawford, and be asked to have a cup of tea and a smoke. When we had talked a while, I hoped he would summon his familiars from the darkness to smoke and talk with us. That is where and how this conversation should have taken place.

But there are some things that even a romantic novelist cannot do, though Thackeray said that "anything you like happens in Fable-land." So we were compelled to talk in a room, in the heart of New York, which had little in it except books, and a big chair, and a blaze of cannel-coal in the grate. If you fill the big chair with Mr. Crawford, smoking an English bull-dog pipe in which is some of

F. MARION CRAWFORD, 1894. FROM A PHOTOGRAPH BY SARONY.

all the background that is needed for this conversation.

MR. CRAWFORD'S CHILDHOOD AND YOUTH.

"You know," he said, "that my father, Thomas Crawford, was a Scotch-Irishman, born in the West of Ireland, and brought to this country when very young. His father acquired a small business in New York which supported him comfortably, and he wished his son, my father, to take part in it; but the boy had a strong artistic bent, and of his own initiative went to a wood-carver to learn his trade. Later, wishing still greater freedom for his skill, he learned marble carving, and, by a curious coincidence, he designed the handsome mantels in the house of Mr. Ward, his future father-in-law, at the corner of Bond Street and Broadway. This and other of his work was so remarkable that my grandfather and his friends determined that he should have the best opportunities to study sculpture, and he was sent to Rome, where he was a pupil of the great Thorwaldsen. While a young sculptor in Rome, gaining recognition every day, he met Miss Louisa Ward, who was travelling with Dr. Samuel G. Howe and his wife, Julia Ward Howe. They fell in love and were married, and made Rome their home. I am the youngest of their four children. When I was about two years old (in 1856) I was sent to this country, and lived with some kinsfolk on a farm near Bordentown, New Jersey. Among the earliest things that I remember is my great delight in watching the coming and going of the trains of cars as they shot across the farm near the old house. My father died in London in 1857,

I was taken back to Italy, where all my youth was spent."

I asked Mr. Crawford to tell me about his education as a boy. It seemed to recall a host of pleasant recollections.

"Most of my boyhood was spent under the direction of a French governess. Not only did I learn that language from her, but all of my studies, geography, arithmetic, etc., were taught me in French, and I learned to write it with great readiness as a mere boy, because it was the language of my daily tasks. The consequence is that to this day I write French with the ease of English. There have been times when I knew that I had lost some of my facility in speaking French, through long absence from the country; but the acquirement of writing it is always with me, which shows the value of early impressions in that direction."

I remembered hearing St. Paul's School men speak of the days when Mr. Crawford was a student at Concord, New Hampshire, and I asked him when he had been there.

"I was about twelve years old," he said, "when I was sent over to America again, and went to St. Paul's. There I found that the fact that I had been taught Latin by a natural, and not an artificial method, gave me a great advantage. My Latin tutor in Rome was a man whose ideas of learning that language were most original then, although they have since become more common in certain systems. I remember that my first lesson in Latin was to read one of the very short letters of Cicero, only two or three lines. We began by reading, and, as a consequence, I was interested from the very first lesson. You know that in Rome you are surrounded with Latin inscriptions on the public buildings and monuments, so that the whole language had a reality to me that it could hardly have to an American boy, especially one who has learned it by way of the rudiments of grammar. I made some good friends at St. Paul's, whom I see from time to time here and in Europe."

We had a long talk about the various steps in his education, which seemed to be full of pleasant memories for Mr. Crawford. He recalled his student days with a clergyman in the English village of Hatfield Regis, and the gayer life at Trinity College, Cambridge, where he went in for boating, and, incidentally, for mathematics. "They thought I was a mathematician in those days," he said. "Then followed student days at Karlsruhe and Heidelberg, from 1874 to 1876. "Of course," he said, "I learned my German in those days—learned to speak it readily; but I have never acquired the ability to write it as fluently as I do French. In fact, I always use the Roman characters when I write German."

NEWSPAPER WORK IN INDIA.

"And then," he continued, "I studied at the University of Rome (1876–78), and I had a tutor who taught me Sanskrit, and interested me in Buddhism and other Oriental mysteries. There came a time when my people lost a great deal of money, and I was in a quandary what to do. This tutor advised me to take an opportunity to go to

"ROBERT BRIDGES—'BROCK.'"

India and learn Sanskrit, and then I could come back and easily get a good professorship. So, with the enthusiasm of youth, I borrowed one hundred pounds, and sailed for Bombay. But money seemed to be as hard to earn in Bombay as elsewhere. I tried in vain for all sorts of positions. I wrote occasionally articles for a Bombay newspaper, and made the acquaintance of the editor, but these were not enough to replenish my stock of money. One day I found myself reduced to my last two pounds, and I could not see where more was coming from; but I was young and strong, and I said that if the worst came, I could enlist in the British army, and have plenty of adventure, and food and clothes. I sat down and wrote a letter of application to the proper officer, sealed and

MR. CRAWFORD'S VILLA ON THE EDGE OF THE CLIFF AT SORRENTO, SEEN FROM THE SEA. DRAWN BY E. BIONDI, SORRENTO.

stamped it, and held it in readiness to mail when I should find that there was nothing else to be done. The next day I received a letter from the editor of the 'Bombay Gazette,' asking me to call. When I presented myself, he said that he had received a letter from the proprietor of the 'Allahabad Indian Herald,' asking whether he could send him immediately a good man to take charge of that paper. He explained to me that it was a very difficult undertaking, as I should have to do all the editorial work myself; that Allahabad was a thousand miles away; and that, in certain seasons, the climate was disagreeable and dangerous. Nevertheless, he asked me would I go? 'Would a duck swim?' I said, and started immediately. I found that the paper was a daily, issued every afternoon. I was my own news collector, managing editor, and editorial writer. I wrote a leading article and several editorial paragraphs that, too, in daily journalism, an occupation in which I had had no experience whatever."

I said that it reminded me of a story of Kipling's.

"Yes," he replied, "'The Man who would be King,'—that is it exactly. I always read Kipling with a flood of recollections of India, so true are his stories to the reality. Of course," he said, "I picked up a great deal about Buddhism and other Oriental lore, and it was at Simla that I met the original of Mr. Isaacs—a real man whose name was Jacobs. Of him I shall tell you by and by. For eighteen months I edited the 'Indian Herald,' and I think it was the hardest work that I have ever done. By and by, in 1880, I returned to Italy, and there I again found myself without means or work, so I took passage on an old steamer for America, early in 1881. I was the only cabin passenger on board.

turned in between the headlands toward the harbor, the high waves swamped us. We clung to the boat, and, as luck would have it, a launch came along just then and picked us up. After we had refitted at Bermuda, we sailed away toward New York, and finally reached here in March. I liked the sea and I liked adventure, and so the voyage did not seem as bad as it might have been."

"You should put that voyage in a story," I suggested, thinking of some of Kipling's tales of the sea; and it is curious, by the way, that Mr. Crawford, with all his love of the sea, has never written a regular sea-story, although there are several chapters in "Dr. Claudius" describing an ocean voyage.

It was about this time, when he was twenty-seven years of age, that Mr. Crawford entered Harvard as a special student, and took Professor Lanman's course in Sanskrit. He lived between New York and Boston, sometime in one city and sometime in the other, from December, 1882, to May, 1883, and contributed special articles to periodicals. He wrote book reviews and articles on philosophical themes. "I got so far," he said, "as to receive one hundred dollars for an article. Of course it was a precarious living, but there was always Uncle Sam (Samuel Ward) to whom I could go."

HOW MR. CRAWFORD CAME TO WRITE HIS FIRST NOVEL.

"And now tell me," I said, "the true story of how you came to write 'Mr. Isaacs.' I have read different versions of it."

"It has once or twice been told correctly," said Mr. Crawford, "and this is exactly how it happened: On May 5, 1882, Uncle Sam asked me to dine with him at the New York Club, which was then in the building on Madison Square now called the Madison Square Bank building. It goes without saying that we had a good dinner if it was ordered by Uncle Sam. We had dined rather early, and were sitting in the smoking-room, overlooking Madison Square, while it was still light. As was perfectly natural we began to exchange stories while smoking, and I told him, with a great deal of detail, my recollections of an interesting man whom I had met in Simla. When I had finished he said to me, 'That is a good two-part magazine story, and you must write it out immediately.' He took me around to his apartments, and that night I began to write the story of 'Mr. Isaacs.' Part of the first chapter was written afterwards, but the rest of that chapter and several succeeding chapters are the story that I told to Uncle Sam. I kept at it from day to day, getting more interested in the work as I proceeded, and from time to time I would read a chapter to Uncle Sam. When I got through the original story, I was so amused with the writing of it that it occurred to me that I might as well make Mr. Isaacs fall in love with an English girl, and then I kept on writing, to see what would happen. By and by I remembered a mysterious Buddhist whom I had once met in India, and so I introduced him, to still further complicate matters. I went to Newport to visit my aunt, Mrs. Julia Ward Howe, while I was in the midst of the story, and continued it there. It was on June 13, 1882, while in her home, that I finished the last chapter of 'Mr. Isaacs;' and, Uncle Sam appearing in Newport at that time, I read him the part of the story which he had not heard. 'You will give it to me,' he said; 'I shall try and find a publisher.' He had for many years frequented the book store of Macmillan, and was well acquainted with the elder George Brett. He took the manuscript to Mr. Brett, who forwarded it to the English house, and in a short time it was accepted."

"Having tasted blood," said Mr. Crawford, "I began, very soon after finishing 'Mr. Isaacs,' to write another story for my own amusement—'Dr. Claudius.' Late in November I was advised by Messrs. Macmillan that, in order to secure an English, as well as an American, copyright, I must be on English soil on the day of publication. So I went to St. John's, New Brunswick, where I had a very pleasant time, and continued to write the story of 'Dr. Claudius,' which I finished in December. 'Mr. Isaacs' was published on December 6th, and I, of course, knew nothing about its reception. However, toward the end of the month, I started on my return journey to the United States, and when I arrived in Boston, on the day before Christmas, and stepped out of the train, I was surprised beyond measure to find the railway news-stands almost covered with great posters announcing 'Mr. Isaacs.' The next morning, at my hotel, I found a note awaiting me from T. B. Aldrich, then editor of the 'Atlantic Monthly,' asking me for an interview, at which he proposed that I write a serial for his magazine. I felt confident then, and do now, that ' Dr.

Claudius' would not be a good serial story. However, I promised that he should have a serial, and began soon after to write 'The Roman Singer,' which was completed in February, 1883."

MR. CRAWFORD'S RAPIDITY—A NOVEL WRITTEN IN TEN DAYS.

This led me to ask Mr. Crawford about the rapidity with which he worked. "I was told the other day," I said, "that you wrote 'The Three Fates' in seven days."

"No," he replied; "that would have been a physical impossibility. As a matter of fact, I was not very well, and spent a whole summer writing it from time to time. One of my stories, however, 'Marzio's Crucifix,' which is not a long novel, I wrote in ten days, in its original form, as it appeared serially. Afterwards two chapters were added for book publication. 'The Tale of a Lonely Parish' I wrote in twenty-four days—one chapter a day, of about five thousand words. Both of those stories were easy to write, because I was perfectly familiar with the background of each. I had once studied silver-carving with a skilled workman, and the idea suggested itself to me to write a story about an atheist who should put his life and soul into the carving of a crucifix. With that for a motive, the story wrote itself. In the case of 'The Lonely Parish,' I found myself with a promise unredeemed, given to my publishers, for a novel at a certain date; I had already sold the novel which I intended for them to a magazine, for serial publication. So I looked around in my memory for some spot which was thoroughly familiar to me as a background for my novel—so familiar that I need not invent details, but simply call them up from my memory. I immediately thought of the little village of Hatfield Regis in Hertfordshire, where I was sent as a pupil to a clergyman. I lifted that little village bodily out of my memory, and put it into my story, even to the extent of certain real names and localities."

The life of Mr. Crawford, from the success of "Mr. Isaacs" to the present day, has been one of hard literary work. He sailed for Italy in May, 1883, spent most of the year 1884 in Constantinople, where he was married to a daughter of General Berdan, and in 1885 went back to Italy and to Sorrento, where his villa is, and where he has lived ever since, with the exception of his two visits to America in 1893 and 1894. In these thirteen years he has produced twenty-five novels, and his popularity continues unabated.

MRS. CRAWFORD AND HER CHILDREN BEFORE THE CRAWFORD VILLA AT SORRENTO. DRAWN BY G. DE SANCTIS, SORRENTO.

MR. CRAWFORD'S MANNER OF WORKING.

"What," I asked, "is the germ of a novel for you?"

"It is a character, and not a situation, which generally suggests a novel to me. I think that in most cases my characters are portraits of real people in imaginary situations; that is why they cannot be recognized by the originals, because they are out of their usual environment. There are two exceptions to this way of conceiving a novel; as I have already told you, 'The Tale of a Lonely Parish' and 'Marzio's Crucifix' were suggested to me by the real background."

"Won't you tell me," I asked, "how you go to work to construct a novel?"

"Since my first novel or two, I always see the end of the story from the start. When I have thought it over in this way, I take a large sheet of paper, and, having decided on the size of the book, I make up my mind that it shall have—say twenty-four chapters. Along the left margin I mark the numbers of these chapters, one under the other, a line for each. If it is to be in three volumes, as most of my novels are in England, I place a horizontal mark after each eight chapter numbers. That indicates the volume. Then, after the manner of a playwright choosing what he calls his 'curtain situation,' I decide on the culminating incident in each volume, and also decide in which chapter it shall fall, and place a catch-word indicating that situation on the line with the chapter number. Then I fill in for the other chapters a catch-word or phrase which indicates the minor incidents in succession that culminate in the major incident. Of course all these things do not come at once, and I may fill in, from time to time, after I have begun the novel. But when the skeleton is comparatively complete, I begin to work. Along the right-hand margin I write down the calendar of the novel, as it may be called, from day to day. If it is a novel in which the action takes place in a very short time, I write down not only the day of the month and week, but the hour of the day, so that the action of the story may move logically. With this skeleton of the novel before me, I write with great rapidity. I have found that if I write a novel slowly my conception of the leading characters may change from week to week, so that in the end the novel is not so forcible or so complete as those written rapidly."

"Do you ever dictate?" I asked.

"I dictated one novel under stress of circumstances, and I do not think that I shall ever dictate another, for I consider it a relative failure."

"You are oftenest thought of, I think, as the author of the Saracinesca group of stories. Could you tell me how you planned them?"

"I think the origin of the stories was a walk I took, in the interior of Italy, with

THE STUDY IN MR. CRAWFORD'S HOUSE AT SORRENTO. DRAWN BY G. DE SANCTIS, SORRENTO.

MR. CRAWFORD IN 1895.

a tutor, when I was a boy—the region in which I have placed the Saracinesca estates. When I wrote the first novel of the series, I did not intend a group; but the plan grew upon me, and the first story was received so kindly that I decided to continue the history through several generations, and make it, in a sense, representative of the life of the nobility of a certain class in modern Italy. Personally, I do not think it is very successful, though my critics are very kind toward the series, and the readers seem to like them. The book, of all my novels, which has most reality for me, is 'Pietro Ghisleri;' and I may say, by the way, that the book which I enjoyed most in the writing is 'Mr. Isaacs.'"

"You have been writing a group of New York novels, in which the fortunes of a family are elaborated after the manner of your Saracinesca series?"

"Yes; I worked very hard at the group, and the first of the series, 'Katharine Lauderdale,' has already gone through many editions. The second, which has been running as a serial in 'The Ladies' Pictorial' of London, is called 'The Ralstons.' Some of the characters also appear in my little novel of Bar Harbor, 'Love in Idleness.' In the serial which I have been writing for 'The Century,' 'Casa Braccio,' I have introduced characters from both the Italian and American groups of novels."

This ended our conversation. The impression left on my mind was of delightful converse with a virile, strong, intellectual man, whose imagination and emotions are the obedient servants of a dominating will; above all things, a man of the world in the best sense, and a scholar in the best sense, whose knowledge is a delight to him, whose contact with people in great cities has broadened and deepened his serious views of life; a man with that poise of body and mind which assures one that at forty his work as a novelist has hardly reached maturity, but that the best of it lies in the future.

NAPOLEON BONAPARTE.

BY IDA M. TARBELL.

With engravings from the collection of the Hon. Gardiner G. Hubbard, who also furnishes the explanatory notes.

FIFTH PAPER.

THE CONTINENTAL BLOCKADE.

WHEN Napoleon, in 1805, was obliged to abandon the descent on England and turn the magnificent army gathered at Boulogne against Austria, he by no means gave up the idea of one day humbling his enemy. Persistently throughout the campaigns of 1805-1807 his despatches and addresses remind Frenchmen that vengeance is only deferred.

In every way he strives to awaken indignation and hatred against England. The alliance which has compelled him to turn his armies against his neighbors on the Continent, he characterizes as an "unjust league fomented by the hatred and gold of England." He tells the soldiers of the Grand Army that it is English gold which has "transported the Russian army from the extremities of the universe" to fight them. He charges the horrors of Austerlitz upon the English. "May all the blood shed, may all these misfortunes, fall upon the perfidious islanders who have caused them! May the cowardly oligarchies of London support the consequences of so many woes!" From now on, all the treaties he makes are drawn up with a view to humbling "the eternal enemies of the Continent."

Negotiations for peace went on, it is true, in 1806, between the two countries. Napoleon offered to return Hanover and Malta. He offered several things which belonged to other people, but England refused all of his combinations; and when, a few days after Jena, he addressed his army, it was to tell them: "We shall not lay down our arms until we have obliged the English, those eternal enemies of our nation, to renounce their plan of troubling the Continent and their tyranny of the seas."

A month later—November 21, 1806—he proclaimed the famous Decree of Berlin, his future policy towards Great Britain. As she had shut her enemies from the sea, he would shut her from the land. The "continental blockade," as this struggle of land against sea was called, was only using England's own weapon of war; but it was using it with a sweeping audacity, thoroughly Napoleonic in conception and in the proposed execution. Henceforth, all communication was forbidden between the British Isles and France and her allies. Every Englishman found under French authority—and that was about all Europe —was a prisoner of war. Every dollar's worth of English property found within Napoleon's boundaries, whether it belonged to rich trader or inoffensive tourist, was prize of war. If one remembers the extent of the seaboard which Napoleon at that moment commanded, the full peril of this menace to English commerce is clear. From St. Petersburg to Trieste there was not a port, save those of Denmark and Portugal, which would not close at his bidding. At Tilsit he and Alexander had entered into an agreement to complete this seaboard, to close the Baltic, the Channel, the European Atlantic, and the Mediterranean to the English. This was nothing else than asking Continental Europe to destroy her commerce for their sakes.

There were several serious uncertainties in the scheme. What retaliation would England make? Could Napoleon and Alexander agree long enough to succeed in dividing the valuable portions of the continents of Europe, Asia, and Africa? Would the nations cheerfully give up the English cottons and tweeds they had been buying, the boots they had been wearing, the cutlery and dishes they had been using? Would they cheerfully see their own products lie uncalled for in their warehouses, for the sake of aiding a foreign monarch— although the most brilliant and powerful on earth—to carry out a vast plan for crushing an enemy who was not their enemy? It remained to be seen.

In the meantime there was the small

"NAPOLEON BONAPARTE." 1806.

Engraved by Lupton, after Lefevre; published in London in 1816. "I prefer this to David's celebrated picture."—G. G. H.

part of the coast line remaining independent to be joined to the portion already blockaded to the English. There was no delay in Napoleon's action. Denmark was ordered to choose between war with England and war with France. Portugal was notified that if her ports were not closed in forty days the French and Spanish armies would invade her. England gave a drastic reply to Napoleon's measures. In August she appeared before Copenhagen, seized the Danish fleet, and for three days bombarded the town. This unjustifiable attack on a nation with which she was at peace horrified Europe, and it supported the emperor in pushing to the uttermost the Berlin Decree. He made no secret of his determination. In a diplomatic audience at Fontainebleau, October 14, 1807, he declared:

"Great Britain shall be destroyed. I have the means of doing it, and they shall be employed. I have three hundred thousand men devoted to this object, and an ally who has three hundred thousand to support them. I will permit no nation to receive a minister from Great Britain until she shall have renounced her maritime usages and tyranny; and I desire you, gentlemen, to convey this determination to your respective sovereigns."

Such an alarming extent did the blockade threaten to take, that even our minister to France, Mr. Armstrong, began to be nervous. His diplomatic acquaintances told him cynically, "You are much favored, but it won't last;" and, in fact, it was not long before it was evident that the United States was not to be allowed to remain neutral. Napoleon's notice to Mr. Armstrong was clear and decisive:

"Since America suffers her vessels to be searched, she adopts the principle that the flag does not cover the goods. Since she recognizes the absurd blockades laid by England, consents to having her vessels incessantly stopped, sent to England, and so turned aside from their course, why should the Americans not suffer the blockade laid by France? Certainly France is no more blockaded by England than England by France. Why should Americans not equally suffer their vessels to be searched by French ships? Certainly France recognizes that these measures are unjust, illegal, and subversive of national sovereignty; but it is the duty of nations to resort to force, and to declare themselves against things which dishonor them and disgrace their independence."

WAR WITH PORTUGAL.

The attempt to force Portugal to close her ports caused war. In all but one particular she had obeyed Napoleon's orders: she had closed her ports, detained all Englishmen in her borders, declared war; but her king refused to confiscate the property of British subjects in Portugal. This evasion furnished Napoleon an excuse for refusing to believe in the sincerity of her pretensions. "Continue your march," he wrote to Junot, who had been ordered into the country a few days before (October 12, 1807). "I have reason to believe that there is an understanding with England, so as to give the British troops time to arrive from Copenhagen."

Without waiting for the results of the invasion, he and the King of Spain divided up Portugal between them. If their action was premature, Portugal did nothing to gainsay them; for when Junot arrived at Lisbon in December, he found the country without a government, the royal family having fled in fright to Brazil. There was only one thing now to be done; Junot must so establish himself as to hold the country against the English, who naturally would resent the injury done their ally. From St. Petersburg to Trieste, Napoleon now held the seaboard.

THE SPANISH THRONE GIVEN TO A BONAPARTE.

But he was not satisfied. Spain was between him and Portugal. If he was going to rule Western Europe he ought to possess her. There is no space here to trace the intrigues with the weak and vicious factions of the Spanish court, which ended in Napoleon's persuading Charles IV. to cede his rights to the Spanish throne and to become his pensioner, and Ferdinand, the heir apparent, to abdicate; and which placed Joseph Bonaparte, King of Naples, on the Spanish throne, and put Murat, Charlotte Bonaparte's husband, in Joseph's place.

From beginning to end the transfer of the Spanish crown from Bourbon to Bonaparte was dishonorable and unjustifiable. It is true that the government of Spain was corrupt. No greater mismanagement could be conceived, no more scandalous court. Unquestionably the country would have been far better off under Napoleonic institutions. But to despoil Spain was to be false to an ally which had served him for years with fidelity, and at an awful cost to herself. It is true that her service had been through fear, not love. It is true that at one critical moment (when Napoleon was in Poland, in 1807) she had tried to escape; but, nevertheless, it remained a fact that for France Spain had lost colonies, sacrificed men and money, and had

NAPOLEON ON HORSEBACK. ABOUT 1814.
Etched by Rust, after Meissonier. The original picture is now in the Walters gallery, at Baltimore.

seen her fleet go down at Trafalgar. In taking her throne, Napoleon had none of the excuses which had justified him in interfering in Italy, in Germany, in Holland, in Switzerland. This was not a conquest of war, not a confiscation on account of the perfidy of an ally, not an attempt to answer the prayers of a people for a more liberal government.

If Spain had submitted to the change, she would have been purchasing good government at the price of national honor. But Spain did not submit. She, as well as all disinterested lookers-on in Europe, was revolted by the baseness of the deed. No one has ever explained better the feeling which the intrigues over the Spanish throne caused than Napoleon himself:

"I confess I embarked badly in the affair," he told Las Cases at St. Helena. "The immorality of it was too patent, the injustice far too cynical, and the whole thing too villainous; hence I failed. The attempt is seen now only in its hideous nudity, stripped of all that is grand, of all the numerous benefits which I intended. Posterity would have extolled it, however, if I had succeeded, and rightly, perhaps, because of its great and happy results."

It was the Spanish people themselves, not the ruling house, who resented the transfer from Bourbon to Bonaparte.

No sooner was it noised through Spain that the Bourbons had really abdicated, and Joseph Bonaparte had been named king, than an insurrection was organized simultaneously all over the country. Some eighty-four thousand French troops were scattered through the peninsula, but they were powerless before the kind of warfare which now began. Every defile became a battleground, every rock hid a peasant, armed and waiting for French stragglers, messengers, supply parties. The remnant of the French fleet escaped from Trafalgar, and now at Cadiz, was forced to surrender. Twenty-five thousand French soldiers laid down their arms at Baylen, but the Spaniards refused to keep their capitulation treaties. The prisoners were tortured by the peasants in the most barbarous fashion, crucified, burned, sawed asunder. Those who escaped the popular vengeance were sent to the Island of Cabrera, where they lived in the most abject fashion, half-starved, uncared for, unclad. It was only in 1814 that the remnant of this army was released.

The new king was only able to reach his capital by sending an advance army ahead to clear the way, and a week later he was obliged to flee to Vittoria.

The misfortunes in Spain were followed by greater ones in Portugal. Junot was defeated by an English army at Vimeiro in August, 1808, and capitulated on condition that his army be taken back to France without being disarmed.

NAPOLEON PREPARES FOR SPAIN.

Napoleon, amazed at this unexpected popular uprising in Spain, and angry that the spell of invincibility under which his armies had fought, was broken, resolved to undertake the Peninsular war himself.

But before a campaign in Spain could be entered upon, it was necessary to know that all the inner and outer wheels of the great machine he had devised for dividing the world and crushing England were working perfectly.

Since the treaty of Tilsit he had done much at home for this machine. The finances were in splendid condition. Public works of great importance were going on all over the kingdom; the court was luxurious and brilliant, and the money it scattered, pleased and encouraged the commercial and manufacturing classes. Never had *fêtes* been more brilliant than those which welcomed Napoleon back to Paris in 1807; never had the season at Fontainebleau been gayer or more magnificent than it was that year.

All of those who had been instrumental in bringing prosperity and order to France were rewarded in 1807 with splendid gifts from the indemnities levied on the enemies. The marshals of the Grand Army received from eighty thousand to two hundred thousand dollars apiece; twenty-five generals were given forty thousand dollars each; the civil functionaries were not forgotten; thus M. de Ségur received forty thousand dollars as a sign of the emperor's gratification at the way he had administered etiquette to the new court.

It was at this period that Napoleon founded a new nobility as a further means of rewarding those who had rendered brilliant services to France. This institution was designed, too, as a means of reconciling old and new France. It created the titles of prince, duke, count, baron, and knight; and those receiving these titles were at the same time given domains in the conquered provinces, sufficient to permit them to establish themselves in good style.

The drawing up of the rules which were to govern this new order occupied the gravest men of the country, Cambacérès, Saint-Martin, d'Hauterive, Portalis, Pasquier. Among other duties they had to prepare the armorial bearings. Napoleon refused to allow the crown to go on the new escutcheons. He wished no one but himself to have a right to use that symbol. A substitute was found in the panache, the number of plumes showing the rank.

Napoleon used the new favors at his command freely, creating in all, after 1807, forty-eight thousand knights, one thousand and ninety barons, three hundred and eighty-eight counts, thirty-one dukes, and three princes. All members of the old nobility who were supporting his government were given titles, but not those which they formerly held. Naturally this often led to great dissatisfaction, the bearers of ancient names preferring a lower rank which had been their family's for centuries to one higher, but unhallowed by time and tradition. Thus Madame de Montmorency rebelled obstinately against being made a

NAPOLEON.

Engraved in 1841 by Louis, after a painting made in 1837 by Delaroche, now in the Standish collection, and called the "Snuff-box." Probably the finest engraving ever made of a Napoleon portrait.

countess,—she had been a baroness under the old regime,—and, as the Montmorencys claimed the honor of being called the *first Christian barons*, she felt justly that the old title was far more proud than any new one Napoleon could give her. But a countess she had to remain.

In his efforts to win for himself the services of all those whom blood and fortune had made his natural supporters, the

JOSEPHINE, EMPRESS OF THE FRENCH AND QUEEN OF ITALY. ("JOSÉPHINE, IMPÉRATRICE DES FRANÇAIS ET REINE D'ITALIE.") 1805.
Designed by Bosgard.

emperor tried again to reconcile Lucien. In November, 1807, Napoleon visited Italy, and at Mantua a secret interview took place between the brothers. Lucien, in his memoirs, gives a dramatic description of the way in which Napoleon spread the kingdoms of half a world before him and offered him his choice.

"He struck a great blow with his hand in the middle of the immense map of Europe which was extended on the table, by the side of which we were standing. 'Yes, choose,' he said; 'you see I am not talking in the air. All this is mine, or will soon belong to me; I can dispose of it already. Do you want Naples? I will take it from Joseph, who, by the by, does not care for it; he prefers Morfontaine. Italy,—the most beautiful jewel in my imperial crown?

NAPOLEON THE GREAT ("NAPOLEON LE GRAND"). 1812.
Engraved by Mecou, after a portrait painted in 1812 by Isabey.

Eugene is but viceroy, and, far from despising it, he hopes only that I shall give it to him, or, at least, leave it to him if he survives me; he is likely to be disappointed in waiting, for I shall live ninety years. I must, for the perfect consolidation of my empire. Besides, Eugene will not suit me in Italy after his mother is divorced. Spain? Do you not see it falling into the hollow of my hand, thanks to the blunders of my dear Bourbons, and to the follies of your friend, the Prince of Peace? Would you not be well pleased to reign there, where you have been only ambassador? Once for all, what do you want? Speak! Whatever you wish, or can wish, is yours, if your divorce precedes mine.'"

"NAPOLEON BONAPARTE." 1812.

"Engraved, with permission, by Robert Cooper, from the original whole length picture painted by Mr. David, his chief painter of Paris. London. Published January, 1815."

Until midnight the two brothers wrestled with the questions between them. Neither would abandon his position; and when Lucien finally went away, his face was wet with tears. To Méneval, who conducted him to his inn in the town, he said, in bidding him carry his farewell to the emperor, "It may be forever." It was not. Seven years later the brothers met again, but the map of Europe was forever rolled up for Napoleon.

THE ERFURT MEETING.

The essential point in achieving the Tilsit plan was, however, the fidelity of Alexander; and Napoleon resolved, before going into the Spanish war, to meet the Emperor of Russia. This was the more needful, because Austria had begun to show signs of hostility.

The meeting opened in September, 1807, at Erfurt in Saxony, and lasted a month.

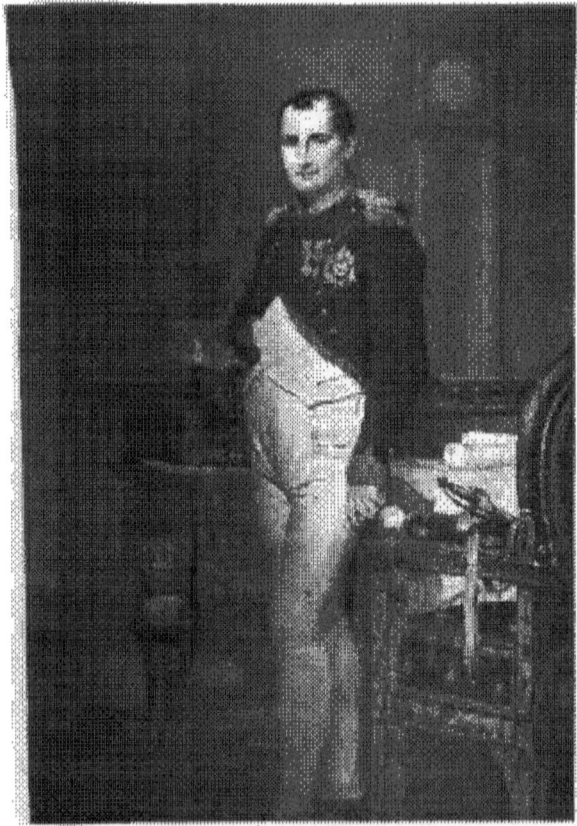

NAPOLEON, 1812.
Engraved by Levogier in 1833, from the etching by Volkel, after portrait painted by David in 1812.

Napoleon acted as host, and prepared a splendid entertainment for his guests. The company he had gathered was most brilliant. Beside the Russian and French emperors, with ambassadors and suites, were the Kings of Saxony, Bavaria, and Würtemberg, the Prince Primate, the Grand Duke and Grand Duchess of Baden, the Dukes of Saxony, and the Princes of the Confederation of the Rhine.

The palaces where the emperors were entertained, were furnished with articles from the *Garde-Meuble* of France. The leading actors of the *Théâtre Français* gave the best French tragedies to a house where there was, as Napoleon had promised Talma, a "parterre full of kings." There was a hare hunt on the battle-field of Jena, to which even Prince William of Prussia was invited, and where the party breakfasted on the spot where Napoleon had bivouacked in 1806, the night before the battle. There were balls where Alexander danced, "but not I," wrote the emperor to Josephine; "forty years are forty years." Goethe and Wieland were both presented to Napoleon at Erfurt, and the emperor had long conversations with them.

In the midst of the gayeties Napoleon and Alexander found time to renew their Tilsit agreement. They were to make war and peace together. Alexander was to uphold Napoleon in giving Joseph the throne of Spain, and to keep the continent tranquil during the Peninsular war. Napoleon was to support Alexander in getting possession of Finland, Moldavia, and Wallachia. The two emperors were to write and sign a letter inviting England to join them in peace negotiations.

This was done promptly; but when England insisted that representatives of the government which was acting in Spain in the name of Ferdinand VII. should be admitted to the proposed meeting, the peace negotiations abruptly ended. Under the circumstances Napoleon could not, of course, recognize that government.

NAPOLEON IN SPAIN.

The emperor was ready to conduct the Spanish war. His first move was to send into the country a large body of veterans from Germany. Before this time the army had been made up of young recruits upon whom the Spanish looked with contempt. The men, inexperienced and demoralized by the kind of guerilla warfare which was waged against them, had become discouraged. The worst feature of their case was that they did not believe in the war. That brave story-teller Marbot relates frankly how he felt.

"As a soldier I was bound to fight any one who attacked the French army, but I could not help recognizing in my inmost conscience that our cause was a bad one, and that the Spaniards were quite right in trying to drive out strangers who, after coming among them in the guise of friends, were wishing to dethrone their sovereign and take forcible possession of the kingdom. This war, therefore, seemed to me wicked, but I was a soldier, and I must march or be charged with cowardice. The greater part of the army thought as I did, and like me, obeyed orders all the same."

The appearance of the veterans and the presence of the emperor at once put a new face on the war; the morale of the army was raised, and the respect of the Spaniards inspired.

The emperor speedily made his way to Madrid, though he had to fight three battles to get there, and began at once a work of reorganization. Decree followed decree. Feudal rights were abolished, the inquisition was ended, the number of convents was reduced, the custom-houses between the various provinces were done away with, a political and military programme was made out for King Joseph. Many bulletins were sent to the Spanish people. In all of them they are told that it is the English who are their enemies, not their allies; that they come to the Peninsula not to help, but to inspire to false confidence, and to lead them astray. Napoleon's plan and purpose cannot be mistaken.

"Spaniards, [he proclaimed at Madrid] your destinies are in my hands. Reject the poison which the English have spread among you; let your king be certain of your love and your confidence, and you will be more powerful and more happy than ever. I have destroyed all that was opposed to your prosperity and greatness; I have broken the fetters which weighed upon the people; a liberal constitution gives you, instead of an absolute, a tempered and constitutional monarchy. It depends upon you that this constitution shall become law. But if all my efforts prove useless, and if you do not respond to my confidence, it will only remain for me to treat you as conquered provinces, and to find my brother another throne. I shall then place the crown of Spain on my own head, and I shall know how to make the wicked tremble; for God has given me the power and the will necessary to surmount all obstacles."

But a flame had been kindled in Spain which no number of even Napoleonic bulletins could quench—a fanatical frenzy inspired by the priests, a blind passion of patriotism. The Spaniards wanted their own, even if it was feudal and oppressive. A constitution which they had been forced to accept, seemed to them odious and shameful, if liberal.

The obstinacy and horror of their resistance was nowhere so tragic and so heroic as at the siege of Saragossa, going on at the time Napoleon, at Madrid, was issuing his decrees and proclamations. Saragossa had been fortified when the insurrection against King Joseph broke out. The town was surrounded by convents, which were turned into forts. Men, women, and children took up arms, and the priests, cross in hand, and dagger at the belt, led them. No word of surrender was tolerated within the walls. A Spaniard sent by Napoleon to treat, was assailed by the mob at the first word of submission he spoke, and for nearly a year lay in a dungeon. The peasants of the vicinity were quartered in the town, each family being given a house

FINAL SCENE BETWEEN HAYGARN AND POZZIES BEFORE THE DUKE'S. MOTHER, POZZIES'S DAUGHTER, STANDS BEHIND HER.

Etched by Gilli after Dichart.

MARIE LOUISE (NAPOLEON'S SECOND WIFE) IN ROYAL ROBES. 1810.
"Marie Louise, Archiduchesse d'Autriche, Impératrice, Reine, et Régente." Engraved by Mecou, after Isabey.

to defend. Nothing could drive them from their posts.

The French, exasperated by this stubborn resistance, resolved to blow up the town, inch by inch. "While a house was being mined, and the dull sound of the rammers warned them that death was at hand, not one left the house which he had sworn to defend, and we could hear them singing litanies. Then, at the moment the

THE KING OF ROME (SON OF NAPOLEON AND MARIE LOUISE). 1811.
Engraved by Desnoyers, after Gérard. "His Majesty the King of Rome. Dedicated to her Majesty Imperial and Royal, Marie Louise."

walls flew into the air and fell back with a crash, crushing the greater part of them, those who had escaped would collect about the ruins, and sheltering themselves behind the slightest cover, would recommence their sharpshooting."

For such resistance there was no end but extermination. For the first time in his career Napoleon had met sublime popular patriotism, a passion before which diplomacy, flattery, love of gain, force, lose their power.

It was for but a short time that the emperor could give his personal attention to the Spanish war. Certain wheels in his great machine were not running right. At its very centre, in Paris, there was friction among certain influential persons. The

NAPOLEON, MARIE LOUISE, AND THE KING OF ROME (NAPOLEON'S SON). APRIL 1, 1815.
Artist unknown.

peace of the Continent, necessary to the Peninsular war, and which Alexander had guaranteed, was threatened.

PLOTTING OF TALLEYRAND AND FOUCHÉ.

Two unscrupulous and crafty men, both of them of singular ability, caused the interior trouble. These men were Talleyrand and Fouché. The latter we saw during the Consulate as Minister of Police. Since that time he has been once dismissed from office because of his knavery, and restored, largely for the same quality. His cunning was too valuable to dispense with. The former, Talleyrand, made Minister of Foreign Affairs in 1799, had handled his negotiations with the extraordinary skill for which he was famous, until, in 1807, Napoleon's mistrust of his duplicity, and Talleyrand's own dislike of the details of his position, led to the portfolio being taken from him, and he being made Vice-Grand-Elector. He evidently expected, in making this change, to remain in reality as powerful as ever with Napoleon. The knowledge that the emperor was dispensing with his services made him resentful, and his devotion to the imperial cause fluctuated according to the attention he received.

Now, Napoleon's course in Spain had been undertaken at the advice of Talleyrand, largely, and he had repeated constantly, in the early negotiations, that France ought not to allow a Bourbon to remain enthroned at her borders. Yet, as the affair went on, he began slyly to talk against the enterprise. At Erfurt, where Napoleon had been impolitic enough to take him, he initiated himself into Alexander's good graces, and prevented Napo-

"NAPOLEON IN HIS CABINET." THE CHILD AT HIS SIDE IS HIS SON, THE KING OF ROME.
The manuscript on the floor of the cabinet bears the date "1811." Engraved by Weber, after Steuben.

leon's policy towards Austria being carried out. When Napoleon returned to Spain, Talleyrand and Fouché, who up to this time had been enemies, became friendly, and even appeared in public, arm in arm. If Talleyrand and Fouché had made up, said the Parisians, there was mischief brewing.

Napoleon was not long in knowing of their reconciliation. He learned more, that the two crafty plotters had written Murat that in the event of " something happening," that is, of Napoleon's death or overthrow, they should organize a movement to call him to the head of affairs;

that, accordingly, he must hold himself ready.

Napoleon returned to Paris immediately, removed Talleyrand from his position at court, and at a gathering of high officials, treated him to one of those violent harangues with which he was accustomed to flay those he would disgrace and dismiss.

"You are a thief, a coward, a man without honor; you do not believe in God; you have all your life been a traitor to your duties; you have deceived and betrayed everybody; nothing is sacred to you; you would sell your own father. I have handed you down with gifts, and there is nothing you would not undertake against me. Thus for the past ten months you have been shameless enough, because you supposed, rightly or wrongly, that my affairs in Spain were going astray, to say to all who would listen to you that you always blamed my undertakings there, whereas it was you yourself who first put it into my head, and who persistently urged it. And that man, *that unfortunate* [he was thus designating the Duc d'Enghien], by whom was I advised of the place of his residence? Who drove me to deal cruelly with him? What, then, are you aiming at? What do you wish for? What do you hope? Do you dare to say? You deserve that I should smash you like a wineglass. I can do it, but I despise you too much to take the trouble."

All of this was undoubtedly true, but, after having publicly said it, there was but one safe course for Napoleon — to put Talleyrand where he could no longer continue his plotting. He made the mistake, however, of leaving him at large.

WAR WITH AUSTRIA.

The disturbance of the continental peace came from Austria. Encouraged by Napoleon's absence in Spain, and the withdrawal of troops from Germany, and urged by England to attempt again to repair her losses, Austria had hastily armed herself, hoping to be able to reach the Rhine before Napoleon could collect his forces and reach her. Napoleon met Austria now as in 1805. On the 12th of April he learned in Paris that the Austrians had crossed the Inn. One month later, the 12th of May, he wrote from Schönbrunn, after a series of victories, "We are masters of Vienna."

The two desperate battles of Essling and Aspern followed, and the French retired to the island of Lobau in the Danube, just below Vienna, where soon Prince Eugene, who had driven out and nearly destroyed the Austrian army which had invaded Italy, joined the emperor. On the 2d of July the Danube was passed, and the battle of Wagram on the 6th completed the defeat of the Austrians.

When, on the 22d, Napoleon replied to the Emperor of Austria's request to treat for peace, he told him:

"If the fourth treaty of peace, succeeding those of Campo Formio, Lunéville, and Presburg, can be the last, secure in a durable manner the tranquillity of the Continent, and protect it from the clamors and intrigues of England, I shall regard this moment as most fortunate; for, in the four wars which your majesty has waged against France, the last three were superfluous, and advantageous only to England."

This peace was concluded in October. Austria was forced to give up Trieste and all her Adriatic possessions, to cede territory to Bavaria and to the Grand Duchy of Warsaw, and to give her consent to the continental system.

It could hardly be expected that Austria would accept such a treaty as final, yet Napoleon went home from Schönbrunn more confident than ever that the great continental peace he so much desired was near at hand. So sincerely did he believe in it that he had begun to prepare to celebrate it, ordering that a splendid temple of Janus, to cost eight million dollars, should be begun on the heights of Montmartre, where the new church of the *Sacré Cœur* now stands, and that in it should be made the first solemn proclamation of peace.

JOSEPHINE DIVORCED.

To further this peace, to prevent plots among his subordinates who would aspire to his crown in case of his sudden death, and to assure a succession which would carry out his organization, he now decided to take a step long in mind—to divorce Josephine, by whom he no longer hoped to have heirs.

In considering Napoleon's divorce of Josephine, it must be remembered that stability of government was of vital necessity to the permanency of the Napoleonic institutions. Napoleon had turned into practical realities most of the reforms demanded in 1789. True, he had done it by the exercise of despotism, but nothing but the courage, the will, the audacity of a despot could have aroused the nation in 1799. These institutions, Napoleon felt, had been so short a time in operation that in case of his death they would easily topple over, and his kingdom go to pieces like Alexander's. If he could leave an heir, this disaster would, he believed, be averted.

Then, would not a marriage with a for-

NAPOLEON. 1814.

Facsimile of a drawing by Girodet-Trioson, made from life in the emperor's private chapel, March 4, 1812. ("Facsimile d'un Dessin de Girodet-Trioson, fait d'après nature à la chapelle de l'empereur le 4 Mars, 1812.") Engraved by Maile. Published in London in 1827 by H. G. Jones. It is thought to give a more correct delineation of Napoleon than do the paintings by Lefevre, David, and Isabey, who were the royal painters, and painted, under the instructions of Napoleon, to make him look like the Cæsars. There were two designs by Girodet. Of the one given above, Maile's engraving is the only copy known. The other contains three heads, one of which is a sleeping Napoleon. It was made only a month later, at the château of St. Cloud.

eign princess calm the fears of his continental enemies? Would they not see in moniously to the system of government which prevailed on the Continent?

lutions, save the splendid organization he had created, and put France in greater harmony with her environment. It is to misunderstand Napoleon's scheme, to attribute this divorce simply to a gigantic egotism. To assure his dynasty, was to assure France of liberal institutions. His glorification was his country's. In reality, there were the same reasons for divorcing Josephine that there had been for taking the crown in 1804.

Josephine had long feared a separation. The Bonapartes had never cared for her, and even so far back as the Egyptian campaign had urged Napoleon to seek a divorce. Unwisely, Josephine had not sought in her early married life to win their affection any more than she had sought to keep Napoleon's; and when the emperor was crowned, they had done their best to prevent her coronation. When, for state reasons, the divorce seemed necessary, Josephine had no supporters where she might have had many.

Her grief was more poignant because she had come to love her husband with a real ardor. The jealousy from which he had once suffered she now felt, and Napoleon certainly gave her ample cause for it. Her anxiety was well known to all the court, the secretaries Bourrienne and Méneval, and Madame de Rémusat being her special confidants. Since 1807 it had been intense, for it was in that year that Fouché, probably at Napoleon's instigation, tried to persuade the empress to suggest the divorce herself as her sacrifice to the country.

After Wagram it became evident to her that at last her fate was sealed ; but though she beset Méneval and all the members of her household for information, it was only a fortnight before the public divorce that she knew her fate. It was Josephine's own son and daughter, Eugene and Hortense, who broke the news to her; and it was on the former that the cruel task fell of indorsing the divorce in the Senate in the name of himself and his sister.

Josephine was terribly broken by her disgrace, but she bore it with a sweetness and dignity which does much to make posterity forget her earlier frivolity and insincerity.

"I can never forget," says Pasquier, "the evening on which the discarded empress did the honors of her court for the last time. It was the day before the official dissolution. A great throng was present, and supper was served, according to custom, in the gallery of Diana, on a number of little tables. Josephine sat at the centre one, and the men went around her, waiting for that particularly graceful nod which she was in the habit of bestowing on those with whom she was acquainted. I stood at a short distance from her for a few minutes, and I could not help being struck with the perfection of her attitude in the presence of all these people who still did her homage, while knowing full well that it was for the last time ; that in an hour she would descend from the throne, and leave the palace never to reënter it. Only women can rise superior to such a situation, but I have my doubts as to whether a second one could have been found to do it with such perfect grace and composure. Napoleon did not show so bold a front as did his victim."

There is no doubt but that Napoleon suffered deeply over the separation. If his love had lost its illusion, he was genuinely attached to Josephine, and in a way she was necessary to his happiness. After the ceremony of separation, he was to go to St. Cloud, she to Malmaison. While waiting for his carriage, he returned to his study in the palace. For a long time he sat silent and depressed, his head on his hand. When he was summoned he rose, his face distorted with pain, and went into the empress's apartment. Josephine was alone.

When she saw the emperor, she threw herself on his neck, sobbing aloud. He pressed her to his bosom, kissing her again and again, until, overpowered with emotion, she fainted. Leaving her to her women, he hurried to his carriage.

Méneval, who saw this sad parting, remained with Josephine until she became conscious ; and when he went, she begged him not to let the emperor forget her, and to see that he wrote her often.

"I left her," that naïve admirer and apologist of Napoleon goes on, "grieved at so deep a sorrow and so sincere an affection. I felt very miserable all along my route, and I could not help deploring that the rigorous exactions of politics should violently break the bonds of an affection which had stood the test of time, to impose another union full of uncertainty."

Josephine returned to Malmaison to live, but Napoleon took care that she should have, in addition, another home, giving her Navarre, a château near Evreux, some fifty miles from Paris. She had an income of some six hundred thousand dollars a year, and the emperor showed rare thoughtfulness in providing her with everything she could want. She was to deny herself nothing, take care of her health, pay no attention to the gossip she heard, and never doubt of his love. Such were the constant recommendations of the frequent letters he wrote her. Sometimes he went to see her, and he told her all the details of his life. It is certain that the emperor neglected no opportunity of comforting Josephine.

JOSEPH BONAPARTE IN HIS CORONATION ROBES. 1808.
Engraved by C. S. Pradier in 1813, after Gérard.

and that she, on her side, believed in his affection, and accepted her lot with resignation and kindliness.

MARRIAGE OF NAPOLEON AND MARIE LOUISE.

Over two years before the divorce a list of the marriageable princesses of Europe had been drawn up for Napoleon. This list included eighteen names in all, the two most prominent being Marie Louise of Austria, and Anna Paulowna, sister of Alexander of Russia. At the Erfurt conference the project of a marriage with a Russian princess had been discussed, and Alexander had favored it; but now that an attempt was made to negotiate the affair, there were numerous delays, and a general lukewarmness which angered Napoleon. Without waiting for the completion of the Russian negotiations, he decided on Marie Louise.

The marriage ceremony was performed in Vienna on March 12, 1810, the Archduke Charles acting for Napoleon. The Emperor first saw his new wife some days later on the road between Soissons and Compiègne, where he had gone to meet her in most unimperial haste, and in contradiction to the pompous and complicated ceremony which had been arranged for their first interview. From the first he was frankly delighted with Marie Louise. In fact, the new empress was a most attractive girl, young, fresh, modest, well-bred, and innocent. She entirely filled Napoleon's ideal of a wife, and he certainly was happy with her.

Marie Louise in marrying Napoleon had felt that she was a kind of sacrificial offering, for she had naturally a deep horror of the man who had caused her country so much woe; but her dread was soon dispelled, and she became very fond of her husband.

Outside of the court the two led an amusingly simple life, riding together informally early in the morning, in a gay Bohemian way; sitting together alone in the empress's little *salon*, she at her needlework, he with a book. They even indulged now and then in quiet little larks of their own, as one day when Marie Louise had attempted to make an omelet in her apartments. Just as she was completely engrossed in her work, the emperor came in. The empress tried to conceal her culinary operations, but Napoleon detected the odor.

"What is going on here? There is a singular smell as if something was being fried. What, you are making an omelet! Bah! you don't know how to do it. I will show you how it is done."

And he set to work to instruct her. They got on very well until it came to tossing it, an operation Napoleon insisted on performing himself, with the result that he landed it on the floor.

BIRTH OF THE KING OF ROME.

On March 20, 1811, the long-desired heir to the French throne was born. It had been arranged that the birth of the child should be announced to the people by cannon shot; twenty-one if it were a princess, one hundred and one if a prince. The people who thronged the quays and streets about the Tuileries waited with inexpressible anxiety as the cannon boomed forth: one—two—three. As twenty-one died away the city held its breath; then came twenty-two. The thundering peals which followed it were drowned in the wild enthusiasm of the people. For days afterward, enervated by joy and the endless *fêtes* given them, the French drank and sang to the King of Rome.

In all these rejoicings none were so touching as at Navarre, where Josephine, on hearing the cannon, called together her friends and said, "We, too, must have a *fête*. I shall give you a ball, and the whole city of Evreux must come and rejoice with us."

Napoleon was the happiest of men. He devoted himself to his son with pride and tenderness, playing with him in the park, teaching him to ride, keeping him with him in his study even while the most important business was going on, and frequently throwing everything aside to lie down on the floor and romp with him. Reports of the boy's condition appear frequently in his letters; he even allowed him to be taken without the empress's knowledge to Josephine, who had begged to see him.

CAUSES OF DISCONTENT WITHIN FRANCE.

"This child in concert with our Eugène will constitute our happiness and that of France," so Napoleon had written Josephine after the birth of the King of Rome, but it soon became evident that he was wrong. There were causes of uneasiness and discontent in France which had been operating for a long time, and which were only aggravated by the apparent solidity that an heir gave to the Napoleonic dynasty.

First among these was religious disaffection. Towards the end of 1808, being doubtful of the Pope's loyalty, Napoleon had sent French troops to Rome; the spring following, without any plausible excuse, he had annexed four Papal states to the kingdom of Italy; and in 1809 the Pope had been made a prisoner at Savona. When the divorce was asked, it was not the Pope, but the clergy of Paris, who had granted it. When the religious marriage of Marie Louise and Napoleon came to be celebrated, thirteen cardinals refused to appear; the "black cardinals" they were thereafter called, one of their punishments for non-appearance at the wedding being that they could no longer wear their red gowns. To the pious all this friction with the fathers of the Church was a deplorable irritation. It was impossible to show contempt for the authority of Pope and cardinals and not wound one of the

BERNADOTTE.

Engraved by Furnager, after Guérin. Bernadotte (see note, page 124. "McClure's Magazine" for January, 1895) was born at Pau, in 1764; entered the Royal Marine at seventeen years of age; in 1792 entered the Army of the North; and in 1797 the Army of Italy. He married the Désirée Clary, sister-in-law of Joseph Bonaparte, whom Napoleon, in 1795, had thought of making his wife. In 1804 he was made marshal and later, Prince of Ponte-Corvo. In 1810 the Swedish States proclaimed him prince royal and heir-presumptive of Sweden. He was received as a son by Charles XIII., and in 1818, on the death of Charles XIII, he was proclaimed King of Norway and Sweden, and took the name of Charles Jean IV., though he is usually called Charles XIV. He held the throne for twenty-five years, and his son Oscar succeeded him.

deepest sentiments of France, and one which ten years before Napoleon had braved most to satisfy.

There was another terrible burden on the people—a tax of blood and muscle— the conscription. Napoleon had formulated and attempted to make tolerable the principle born of the Revolution, which declared that every male citizen of age owed the state a service of blood in case it needed him. The wisdom of his management of the conscription had prevented discontent until 1807; then the draft on life had begun to be arbitrary and grievous. The laws of exemptions were discarded. The "only son of his mother" no longer remained at

TALLEYRAND.

Engraved by Desnoyers, after Gérard. Talleyrand-Périgord (Charles Maurice de) (1754-1838) was educated for the Church, and in 1788 was made Bishop of Autun. He was active in the Revolution, and being struck with Napoleon's talents in Italy, hastened to win his favor. He became Napoleon's most important adviser, but later turned against him, and became his most subtle enemy. After the surrender of Paris, it was Talleyrand who secured from Alexander the declaration that he would treat neither with Napoleon nor with any member of his family. He became Louis XVIII.'s Minister of Foreign Affairs. Soon after Waterloo he lost his position as Minister of Foreign Affairs, but the Revolution of 1830 restored him to favor, and he was sent to London as ambassador. In 1834 he left diplomatic life at his own request, and returned to Paris, where he died in 1838.

her side. The father whose little children were motherless must leave them; aged and helpless parents no longer gave immunity. Those who had bought their exemption by heavy sacrifices were obliged to go. Persons whom the law made subject to conscription in 1807, were called out in 1806; those of 1808, in 1807. So far was this premature drafting pushed, that the armies were said to be made up of "boy soldiers," weak, unformed youths, fresh from school, who dropped out in the march, and wilted in a sun like that of Spain.

At the rate at which men had been killed, however, there was no other way of keeping up the army. Between 1804 and 1811 one million seven hundred thousand men had perished in battle. What wonder that now the boys of France were pressed into service! At the same time the country was overrun with the lame, the blind, the broken-down, who had come back from war to live on their friends or on charity. It was not only the funeral crape on almost every door which made Frenchmen hate the conscription, it was the crippled men whom they met at every corner.

Without, the continental blockade was causing serious trouble between Napoleon and the kings he ruled. In spite of all his efforts English merchandise penetrated everywhere. The fair at Rotterdam in 1807 was filled with English goods. They passed into Italy under false seals. They came into France on pretence that they were for the empress. Napoleon remonstrated and threatened, but he could not check the traffic. The most serious trouble caused by this violation of the Berlin Decree was with Louis the King of Holland. In 1808 Napoleon complained to his brother that more than one hundred ships passed between his kingdom and England every month, and a year later he wrote in desperation, "Holland is an English province."

The relations of the brothers grew more and more bitter. Napoleon resented the half support Louis gave him, and as a punishment he took away his provinces, filled his forts with French troops, threatened him with war if he did not break up the trade. So far did these hostilities go that in the summer of 1810 King Louis abdicated in favor of his son and retired to Austria. Napoleon tried his best to persuade him at least to return into French territory, but he refused. This break was the sadder because Louis was the brother for whom Napoleon had really done most. With him he had shared, as a poor artillery lieutenant, his bed and board and spending money.

Joseph was not happier than Louis. The Spanish war still went on, and no better than in 1808. Joseph, humbled and unhappy, had even prayed to be freed of the throne.

The relations with Sweden were seriously strained. Since 1810 Bernadotte had been by adoption the crown prince of that country. Although he had emphatically refused, in accepting the position, to agree never to take up arms against France, as Napoleon wished him to do, he had later consented to the continental blockade, and had declared war against England; but this declaration both England and Sweden considered simply as a *façon de parler*. Napoleon, conscious that Bernadotte was not carrying out the blockade, and irritated by his persistent refusal to enter into French combinations, and pay tribute to carry on French wars, had suppressed his revenues as a French prince—Bernadotte had been created Prince of Ponte-Corvo in 1806—had refused to communicate with him, and when the King of Rome was born had sent back the Swedish decoration offered. Finally, in January, 1812, French troops invaded certain Swedish possessions, and the country concluded an alliance with France and Russia.

With Russia, the "other half" of the machine, the ally upon whom the great plan of Tilsit and Erfurt depended, there was such a bad state of feeling that, in 1812, it became certain that war would result. Causes had been accumulating upon each side since Erfurt. Alexander feared that Napoleon was getting ready to restore Poland. He was offended by the haste with which his ally had dismissed the idea of marriage with his sister and had taken up Marie Louise. He complained of the changes of boundaries in Germany. Napoleon saw with irritation that English goods were admitted into Russia. He remembered that she had not supported him loyally in 1809. He was suspicious, too, of the good understanding which seemed to be growing between Sweden, Russia, and England.

As soon as war seemed inevitable, Napoleon signed treaties with Austria and Prussia, and on the 9th of May, 1812, left Paris for Dresden, the centre of his army.

The force he had brought to the field showed graphically the extension and the character of the France of 1812. The "army of twenty nations," the Russians called the host which was preparing to meet them, and the expression was just. The Grand Army, as the active body was called, numbered, to quote the popular figures, six hundred and seventy-eight thousand men, and, with reserves, the whole force numbered one million one hundred thousand. It is sure that this is an exaggerated number, though certainly over half a million men entered Russia.

With this imposing army at his command, Napoleon believed that he could compel Alexander to support the continental blockade, for come what might that system must succeed. The continental blockade had become, as its inventor proclaimed, *the fundamental law of the empire*.

Until he crossed the Nieman, Napoleon preserved the hope of being able to avoid war. Numerous letters to the Russian emperor, almost pathetic in their overtures, exist. But Alexander never replied. The Grand Army was doomed to make the Russian campaign.

An Alpine Pass on Ski.

by A Conan Doyle

Author of "Micah Clarke," "The Adventures of Sherlock Holmes," etc.

HERE is nothing peculiarly malignant in the appearance of a pair of ski. They are two strips of elm wood, eight feet long, four inches broad, with a square heel, turned-up toes, and straps in the centre to secure your feet. No one, to look at them, would guess at the possibilities which lurk in them. But you put them on, and you turn with a smile to see whether your friends are looking at you, and then the next moment you are boring your head madly into a snowbank, and kicking frantically with both feet, and half-rising, only to butt viciously into that snowbank again, and your friends are getting more entertainment than they had ever thought you capable of giving.

THE SURPRISES IN A PAIR OF SKI.

This is when you are beginning. You naturally expect trouble then, and you are not likely to be disappointed. But as you get on a little, the thing becomes more irritating. The ski are the most capricious things upon the earth. One day you cannot go wrong with them; on another, with the same weather and the same snow, you cannot go right. And it is when you least expect it that things begin to happen. You stand on the crown of a slope, and you adjust your body for a rapid slide; but your ski stick motionless, and over you go on your face. Or you stand upon a plateau which seems to you to be as level as a billiard table, and in an instant, without cause or warning, away they shoot, and you are left behind, staring at the sky. For a man who suffers from too much dignity a course of Norwegian snow-shoes would have a fine moral effect.

Whenever you brace yourself for a fall, it never comes off. Whenever you think yourself absolutely secure, it is all over with you. You come to a hard ice slope at an angle of seventy-five degrees, and

ZIGZAGGING UP A HILL.

you zigzag up it, digging the side of your ski into it, and feeling that if a mosquito settles upon you, you are gone. But nothing ever happens, and you reach the top in safety. Then you stop upon the level to congratulate your companion, and you have just time to say, "What a lovely view is this!" when you find yourself standing upon your two shoulder-blades, with your ski tied tightly round your neck. Or, again, you may have had a long

Copyright, 1894, by A. Conan Doyle.

outing without any
misfortune at all,
and, as you shuffle
back along the road,
you stop for an in-
stant to tell a group
in the hotel veranda
how well you are get-
ting on. Something
happens—and they
suddenly find that
their congratulations
are addressed to the
soles of your ski.
Then, if your mouth
is not full of snow,
you find yourself
muttering the names
of a few Swiss vil-
lages to relieve your
feelings. " Ragatz!"
is a very handy word,
and may save a scan-
dal.

But all this is in
the early stage of ski-
ing. You have to shuffle along the level,
to zigzag, or move crab fashion, up the
hills, to slide down without losing your
balance, and, above all, to turn with facility.
The first time you try to turn, your friends
think it is part of your fun. The great
ski flapping in the air has the queerest
appearance — like an
exaggerated nigger
dance. But this sud-
den whisk round is
really the most nec-
essary of accomplish-
ments; for only so can
one turn upon the
mountain side without
slipping down. It
must be done without
ever presenting one's
heels to the slope, and
this is the only way.

THE SKI MAKES MOUN-
TAIN CLIMBING EASY.

But granted that a
man has perseverance,
and a month to spare,
in which to conquer
all these early difficul-
ties, he will then find
that skiing opens up a
field of sport for him
which is, I think,

LA FRAMEN.

unique. This is not
appreciated yet, but
I am convinced that
the time will come
when hundreds of
Englishmen will
come to Switzerland
for the skiing season
in March and April.
I believe that I may
claim to be the first,
save only two Switz-
ers, to do any moun-
tain work (though on
a modest enough
scale) on snow-
shoes; but I am cer-
tain that I will not,
by many a thousand,
be the last.

The fact is that it
is easier to climb an
ordinary peak, or to
make a journey over
the higher passes, in
winter than in sum-
mer, if the weather is only set fair. In
summer you have to climb down as well as
to climb up, and the one is as tiring as the
other. In winter your trouble is halved,
as most of your descent is a mere slide. If
the snow is tolerably firm, it is much easier
also to zigzag up it on ski, than to clam-

THE LITTLE FOOTSTEPS ON THE SNOW.

her over boulders, under a hot summer sun. The temperature, too, is more favorable for exertion in winter; for nothing could be more delightful than the crisp, pure air on the mountains, though glasses are, of course, necessary to protect the eyes from the snow-glare.

A SKI MOUNT OF OVER NINE THOUSAND FEET.

Our project was to make our way from Davos to Arosa, over the Furka Pass, which is over nine thousand feet high. The distance is not more than from twelve to fourteen miles as the crow flies, but it has only once been done in winter. Last year the two brothers Dranger made their way across on ski. They were my companions on the present expedition, and more trustworthy ones no novice could hope to have with him. They are both men of considerable endurance, and even a long spell of my German did not appear to exhaust them.

We were up before four in the morning, and had started at half past for the village of Frauenkirch, where we were to commence our ascent. A great pale moon was shining in a violet sky, with such stars as can only be seen in the tropics or the higher Alps. At quarter past five we turned from the road, and began to plod up the hill-sides, over alternate banks of last year's grass, and slopes of snow. We carried our ski over our shoulders, and our ski-boots slung round our necks, for it was good walking where the snow was hard, and it was sure to be hard wherever the sun had struck it during the day. Here and there, in a hollow, we floundered into and out of a soft drift up to our waists; but on the whole it was easy going, and as much of our way lay through fir woods, it would have been difficult to ski. About half past six, after a long, steady grind, we emerged from the woods, and shortly afterwards passed a wooden cowhouse, which was the last sign of man which we were to see until we reached Arosa.

OVER ROLLING SNOW-FIELDS.

The snow being still hard enough upon the slopes to give us a good grip for our feet, we pushed rapidly on,

over rolling snow-fields with a general upward tendency. About half past seven the sun cleared the peaks behind us, and the glare upon the great expanse of virgin snow became very dazzling. We worked our way down a long slope, and then coming to the corresponding hill-side with a northern outlook, we found the snow as soft as powder, and so deep that we could touch no bottom with our poles. Here, then, we took to our snow-shoes, and zigzagged up over the long white haunch of the mountain, pausing at the top for a rest. They are useful things the ski; for, finding that the snow was again hard enough to bear us, we soon converted ours into a very comfortable bench, from which we enjoyed the view of a whole panorama of mountains, the names of which my readers will be relieved to hear I have completely forgotten.

The snow was rapidly softening now, under the glare of the sun, and without our shoes all progress would have been impossible. We were making our way along the steep side of a valley, with the mouth of the Furka Pass fairly in front of us. The snow fell away here at an angle of from fifty to sixty degrees; and as this steep incline, along the face of which we were shuffling, sloped away down until it ended in absolute precipice, a slip might have been serious. My two more experienced companions walked below me for the half mile or so of danger, but soon we found ourselves upon a more reasonable slope, where one might fall with impunity. And now came the real sport of snow-shoeing. Hitherto we had walked as fast as boots would do, over ground where no boots could pass. But now we had a pleasure which boots can never give. For a third of a mile we shot along over gently dipping curves, skimming down into the valley without a motion of our feet. In that great untrodden waste, with snow-fields bounding our vision on every side, and no marks of life save the track of chamois and of foxes, it was glorious to whiz along in this easy fashion. A short zigzag at the bottom of the slope brought us, at half past nine, into the mouth of the pass; and we could see the little toy hotels of Arosa,

TURNING—AN ADEPT.

away down among the fir woods, thousands of feet beneath us.

THE SKI A SHOE OR A SLED AT YOUR PLEASURE.

Again we had a half mile or so, skimming along with our poles dragging behind us. It seemed to me that the difficulty of our journey was over, and that we had only to stand on our ski and let them carry us to our destination. But the most awkward place was yet in front. The slope grew steeper and steeper until it suddenly fell away into what was little short of being sheer precipices. But still that little, when there is soft snow upon it, is all that is needed to bring out another possibility of these wonderful slips of wood. The brothers Branger agreed that the place was too difficult to attempt with the ski upon our feet. To me it seemed as if a parachute was the only instrument for which we had any use; but I did as I saw my companions do. They undid their ski, lashed the straps together, and turned them into a rather clumsy toboggan. Sitting on these, with our heels dug into the snow, and our sticks pressed hard down behind us, we began to move down the precipitous face of the pass. I think that both my comrades came to grief over it. I know that they were as white as Lot's wife at the bottom. But my own troubles were so pressing that I had no time to think of them. I tried to keep the pace within moderate bounds by pressing on the stick, which had the effect of turning the sledge sideways, so that one skidded down the slope. Then I dug my heels hard in, which shot me off backwards, and in an instant my two ski, tied together, flew away like an arrow from a bow, whizzed past the two Brangers, and vanished over the next slope, leaving their owner squattering in the deep snow.

DESCENDING A STEEP SLOPE.

It might have been an awkward accident in the upper field, where the drifts are twenty or thirty feet deep. But the steepness of the place was an advantage now, for the snow could not accumulate to any very great extent upon it. I made my way down in my own fashion. My tailor tells me that Harris tweed cannot wear out. This is a mere theory, and will not stand a thorough scientific test. He will find samples of his wares on view from the Furka Pass to Arosa, and for the remainder of the day I was happiest when nearest the wall.

However, save that one of the Brangers sprained his ankle badly in the descent, all went well with us, and we entered Arosa at half-past eleven, having taken exactly seven hours over our journey. The resi-

ASTONISHING THE NATIVES.

dents at Arosa, who knew that we were coming, had calculated that we could not possibly get there before one, and turned out to see us descend the steep pass just about the time when we were finishing a comfortable luncheon at the Seehof. I would not grudge them any innocent amusement, but still I was just as glad that my own little performance was over before they assembled with their opera glasses. One can do very well without a gallery when one is trying a new experiment on ski.

LA TOUSSAINT.

A STORY FROM THE MEMOIRS OF A MINISTER OF FRANCE.

BY STANLEY J. WEYMAN,

Author of "A Gentleman of France," "My Lady Rotha," etc.

TOWARDS the autumn of 1601, I was one day leaving the hall at the Arsenal, after giving audience to such as wished to see me, when Maignan came after me and detained me; reporting that a gentleman who had attended early, but had later gone into the garden, was still in waiting. While Maignan was still speaking, the stranger himself came up, with some show of haste, but none of embarrassment; and, in answer to my salutation and inquiry what I could do for him, handed me a letter. He had the air of a man not twenty, his dress was a trifle rustic; but his strong and handsome figure set off a face that would have been pleasing but for a something fierce in the aspect of his eyes. Assured that I did not know him, I broke the seal of his letter and found that it was from my old flame Madame de Bray, who, as Mademoiselle de St. Mesmin, had come so near to being my wife.

The young man proved to be her brother, whom she commended to my good offices, the impoverishment of the family being so great that she could compass no more regular method of introducing him to the world, though the house of St. Mesmin is truly respectable and, like my own, allied to several of the first consequence.

"So you have come to Paris to make your fortune?" I said.

"Yes, sir," he answered.

"And what are the tools with which you propose to do it?" I continued, between jest and earnest.

"That letter, sir," he answered simply; "and failing that, two horses, two suits of clothes, and two hundred crowns."

"You think that those will suffice?" I said, laughing.

"With this, sir," he answered, touching his sword; "and a good courage."

I could not but stand amazed at his coolness; for he spoke to me as simply as to a brother.

"Well," I said, after considering him, "I do not think that I can help you much immediately. I should be glad to know, however, what plans you have formed for yourself."

"Frankly, sir," he said, "I thought of this as I travelled; and I decided that fortune can be won by three things—by gold, by steel, and by love. The first I have not, and for the last I have a better use. Only the second is left, I shall be Crillon."

I looked at him in astonishment; for the assurance of his manner exceeded that of his words. But I did not betray the feeling. "Crillon was one in a million," I said dryly.

"So am I," he answered.

I confess that the audacity of this reply silenced me. Bidding him come to me in a week, I hinted that in Paris his crowns would find more frequent opportunities of leaving his pockets than his sword its sheath.

He parted from me with this, seeming perfectly satisfied with his reception; and marched away with the port of a man who expected adventures at every corner, and was prepared to make the most of them. Apparently he did not take my hint greatly to heart, however; for when I next met him, within the week, he was fashionably dressed, his hair in the mode, and his com-

Copyright, 1895, by Stanley J. Weyman.

pany as noble as himself. I made him a sign to stop, and he came to speak to me.

"How many crowns are left?" I said jocularly.

"Fifty," he answered, with perfect readiness.

"What!" I said, pointing to his equipment with something of the indignation I felt, "has this cost the balance?"

"No," he answered. "On the contrary, I have paid three months' rent in advance and a month's board at Zaton's; I have added two suits to my wardrobe, and I have lost fifty crowns on the dice."

"You promise well!" I said.

He shrugged his shoulders quite in the fashionable manner. "Always courage!" he said; and he went on, smiling.

I was walking at the time with M. de Saintonge, and he muttered, with a sneer, that it was not difficult to see the end, or that within the year the young braggart would sink to be a gaming-house bully. I said nothing, but I confess that I thought otherwise; the lad's disposition of his money and his provision for the future seeming to me so remarkable as to set him above ordinary rules.

From this time I began to watch his career with interest, and I was not surprised when, in less than a month, something fell out that led the whole court to regard him with a mixture of amusement and expectancy.

One evening, after leaving the King's closet, I happened to pass through the east gallery at the Louvre, which served at that time as the outer antechamber, and was the common resort as well of all those idlers who, with some pretensions to fashion, lacked the *entrée*, as of many who with greater claims preferred to be at their ease. My passage for a moment stilled the babel which prevailed. But I had no sooner reached the farther door than the noise broke out again; and this with so sudden a fury, the tumult being augmented by the crashing fall of a table, as caused me at the last moment to stand and turn. A dozen voices crying simultaneously, "Have a care!" and "Not here! not here!" and all looking the same way, I was able to detect the three principals in the *fracas*. They were no other than M. de St. Mesmin, Barradas—a low fellow, still remembered, who was already what Saintonge had prophesied that the former would become—and young St. Germain, the eldest son of M. de Cian.

I rather guessed than heard the cause of the quarrel, and that St. Mesmin, putting into words what many had known for years and some made their advantage of, had accused Barradas of cheating. The latter's fury was, of course, proportioned to his guilt; an instant challenge while I looked was his natural answer. This, as he was a consummate swordsman, and had long earned his living as much by fear as by fraud, should have been enough to stay the greediest stomach; but St. Mesmin was not content. Treating the knave, the word once passed, as so much dirt, he transferred his attack to St. Germain, and called on him to return the money he had won by betting on Barradas.

St. Germain, a young spark as proud and headstrong as St. Mesmin himself, and possessed of friends equal to his expectations, flung back a haughty refusal. He had the advantage in station and popularity; and by far the larger number of those present sided with him. I lingered a moment in curiosity, looking to see the accuser with all his boldness give way before the almost unanimous expression of disapproval. But my former judgment of him had been correctly formed. So far from being browbeaten or depressed by his position, "You must return my money!" he kept on saying monotonously. "You must return my money. This man cheated, and you won my money. You must pay or fight."

"With a dead man?" St. Germain replied, gibing at him.

"No, with me."

"Barradas will spit you!" the other scoffed. "Go and order your coffin, and do not trouble me."

"I shall trouble you. If you did not know that he cheated, pay; and if you did know, fight."

"I know?" St. Germain retorted fiercely. "You madman! Do you mean to say that I knew that he cheated?"

"I mean what I say!" St. Mesmin returned stolidly. "You have won my money. You must return it. If you will not return it, you must fight."

I should have heard more, but at that moment the main door opened, and two or three gentlemen who had been with the King came out. Not wishing to be seen watching the brawl, I moved away and forgot St. Mesmin for the time, and only recalled him next morning when Saintonge, being announced, came into my room in a state of great excitement, and almost with his first sentence brought out his name.

"Barradas has not killed him then?"

"YOU MUST PAY OR FIGHT."

I said, reproaching myself in a degree for my forgetfulness.

"No! He, Barradas!" Saintonge answered.

"No?" I exclaimed.

"Yes!" he said. "I tell you, M. le Marquis, he is a devil of a fellow—a devil of a fellow! He fought, I am told, just like Crillon; rushed in on that rascal and fairly beat down his guard, and had him pinned to the ground before he knew that they had crossed swords!"

"Well," I said, "there is one scoundrel the less. That is all."

"Ah, but that is not all!" my visitor replied more seriously. "It should be,

"What! St. Germain!" I said.

"No!" M. de Saintonge answered, prolonging the sound to the utmost. "St. Mesmin!"

"Oh," I said, "I see."

"Yes," the Marquis retorted pettishly, "but I don't. I don't see. And I beg to remind you, M. de Rosny, that this lad is my wife's second cousin through her stepfather, and that I shall resent any interference with him. I have spent enough and done enough in the King's service to have my wishes respected in a small matter such as this; and I shall regard any severity exercised towards my kinsman as a direct offence to myself. Whereas M. de Clan, he will fight St. Germain, and kill or be killed, is that the King's affair that he need interfere? I ask for no interference," M. de Saintonge continued bitterly, "only for fair play and no favor. And for M. de Clan, who has never done anything but thwart the King, for him to come now, and —faugh! it makes me sick."

"Yes," I said dryly; "I see."

"You understand me?"

"Yes," I said, "I think so."

"Very well," he replied haughtily—he had gradually wrought himself into a passion—"be good enough to bear my request in mind then; and my services also. I ask no more, M. de Rosny, than is due to me and to the King's honor."

And with that, and scarcely an expression of civility, he left me.

Saintonge could scarcely have cleared the gates before his prediction was fulfilled. His enemy arrived hot foot, and entered to me with a mien so much lowered by anxiety and trouble that I hardly knew him. Saintonge had rightly anticipated his request; the first, he said, with a trace of his old pride, that he had made to the King in eleven years; his son, his only son and only child—the single heir of his name!

"But," I said, "your son wishes to fight, M. de Clan?"

He nodded.

"And you cannot hinder him?"

He shrugged his shoulders grimly. "No," he said; "he is a St. Germain."

"Well, that is just my case," I answered. "You see this young fellow St. Mesmin was commended to me, and is, in a manner, of my household; and that is a fatal objection. I cannot possibly act against him in the manner you propose. You must see that; and for my wishes, he respects them less than your son regards yours."

M. de Clan rose, trembling a little on his legs, and glaring at me out of his fierce old eyes. "Very well," he said, "it is as much as I expected. Times are changed—and faiths—since the King of Navarre slept under the same bush with Antoine St. Germain on the night before Cahors! I wish you good-day, M. le Marquis."

I need not say that my sympathies were with him, and that I would have helped him if I could; but believing that he who places any consideration before the King's service is not fit to conduct it, I did not see my way to thwart M. de Saintonge in a matter so small. And the end justified my inaction; for the duel, taking place that evening, resulted in nothing worse than a serious, but not dangerous, wound which St. Mesmin, fighting with the same fury as in the morning, contrived to inflict on his opponent.

For some weeks after this I saw little of the young firebrand, though from time to time he attended my receptions and invariably behaved to me with a modesty which proved that he placed some bounds to his presumption. I heard, moreover, that M. de Saintonge, in acknowledgment of the triumph over the St. Germains which he had afforded him, had taken him up; and that the connection between the families being publicly avowed, the two were much together.

Judge of my surprise, therefore, when one day, a little before Christmas, M. de Saintonge sought me at the Arsenal, and, drawing me aside into the garden, broke into a furious tirade against the young fellow.

"But," I said, in immense astonishment, "what is this? I thought that he was a youngman quite to your mind; and ——"

"He is mad!" he answered.

"Mad?" I said.

"Yes, mad!" he repeated, striking the ground violently with his cane. "Stark mad, M. de Rosny. He does not know himself! What do you think—but it is inconceivable. He proposes to marry my daughter! This penniless adventurer honors Mademoiselle de Saintonge by proposing for her!"

"He has, of course, seen Mademoiselle?"

M. de Saintonge nodded.

"At your house, doubtless?"

"Of course!" he replied, with a snap of rage.

"Then I am afraid it is serious," I said.

He stared at me, and for an instant I thought that he was going to quarrel with me. Then he asked me why.

I was not sorry to have this opportunity of at once increasing his uneasiness, and requiting his arrogance. "Because," I said, "this young man appears to me to be very much out of the common. Hitherto, whatever he has said he would do, he has done. If you will take my advice, you will proceed with caution."

M. de Saintonge, receiving an answer so little to his mind, was almost bursting with rage. "Proceed with caution!" he cried. "You talk as if the thing could be entertained, or as if I had cause to fear the coxcomb! On the contrary, I intend to teach him a lesson. A little confinement will cool his temper. You must give me a letter, my friend, and we will clap him in the Bastille for a month or two."

"Impossible," I said firmly, "quite impossible, M. le Marquis."

M. de Saintonge looked at me, frowning. "How?" he said arrogantly. "Have my services earned no better answer than that?"

"You forget," I replied. "Let me remind you that less than a month ago you asked me not to interfere with St. Mesmin; and at your instance I refused to accede to M. de Clan's request that I would confine him. You were then all for non-interference, M. de Saintonge, and I cannot blow hot and cold. Besides, to be plain with you," I continued, "even if that were not the case, this young fellow is in a manner under my protection; which renders it impossible for me to move against him. If you like, however, I will speak to him."

"Speak to him!" M. de Saintonge cried. He was breathless with rage. He could say no more.

Within a week M. de St. Mesmin's pretension to the hand of Mademoiselle de Saintonge was first in the attention of all Paris. The young lady, whose reputation and the care which had been spent on her breeding, no less than her gifts of person and character, deserved a better fate, attained in a moment a notoriety far from enviable; rumor's hundred tongues alleging, and probably with truth—for what father can vie with a gallant in a maiden's eyes?—that her inclinations were all on the side of the pretender.

Wherever Mademoiselle's presence was to be expected, St. Mesmin appeared, dressed in the extreme of the fashion, and wearing either a favor made of her colors or a glove which he asserted that she had given him. Throwing himself in her road on every occasion, he expressed his passion by the most extravagant looks and gestures; and protected from the shafts of ridicule alike by his self-esteem and his prowess, did a hundred things that rendered her conspicuous and must have covered another than himself with inextinguishable laughter.

In these circumstances M. de Saintonge began to find that the darts which glanced off his opponent's armour were making him their butt; and that he, who had valued himself all his life on a stately dignity and a pride almost Spanish, was rapidly becoming the laughing-stock of the Court. His rage may be better imagined than described, and doubtless his daughter did not go unscathed. But the ordinary contemptuous refusal which would have sent another suitor about his business, was of no avail here; he had no son, while St. Mesmin's recklessness rendered the boldest unwilling to engage him. Saintonge found himself, therefore, at his wits' end, and in this emergency bethought him again of a *lettre de cachet*. But the King proved as obdurate as his minister.

Thus repulsed, the Marquis made up his mind to carry his daughter into the country; but St. Mesmin meeting this with the confident assertion that he would abduct her within a week, wherever she was confined, Saintonge, desperate as a baited bull, and trembling with rage—for the threat was uttered at Zamet's and was repeated everywhere—avowed equally publicly that since the King would give him no satisfaction he would take the law into his own hands.

At this juncture, however, an unexpected ally, and one whose appearance increased Saintonge's rage to an intolerable extent, took up St. Mesmin's quarrel. This was young St. Germain, who, quitting his chamber, was to be seen everywhere on his antagonist's arm. The old feud between the St. Germains and Saintonges aggravated the new; and more than one brawl took place in the streets between the two parties. St. Germain never moved without four armed servants; he placed others at his friend's disposal; and wherever he went he loudly proclaimed what he would do if a hair of St. Mesmin's head were injured.

This seemed to place an effectual check on M. de Saintonge's purpose; and my surprise was great when, about a week later, the younger St. Germain burst in upon me one morning, with his face inflamed with anger and his dress in disorder; and proclaimed, before I could rise or speak, that St. Mesmin had been murdered.

"How?" I said, somewhat startled. "And when?"

"By M. de Saintonge! Last night!" he answered furiously. "But I will have justice; I will have justice, M. de Rosny, or the King——"

I checked him as sternly as my surprise would let me; and when I had a little abashed him—which was not easy, for his temper vied in stubbornness with St. Mesmin's—I learned the particulars. About ten o'clock on the previous night St. Mesmin had received a note, and, in spite of the remonstrances of his servants, had gone out alone. He had not returned nor been seen since, and his friends feared the worst.

"But on what grounds?" I said, astonished to find that that was all.

"What!" St. Germain cried, flaring up again. "Do you ask on what grounds? When M. de Saintonge has told a hundred what he would do to him! What he would do—do, I say? What he has done!"

"Pooh!" I said. "It is some assignation, and the rogue is late in returning."

"An assignation, yes," St. Germain retorted; "but one from which he will not return."

"Well, if he does not, go to the Chevalier de Guet," I answered, waving him off. "Go! do you hear? I am busy," I continued. "Do you think that I am keeper of all the young sparks that bay the moon under the citizens' windows? Be off, sir!"

He went reluctantly, muttering vengeance; and I, after rating Maignan soundly for admitting him, returned to my work, supposing that before night I should hear of St. Mesmin's safety. But the matter took another turn, for while I was at dinner the captain of the watch came to speak to me. St. Mesmin's cap had been found in a by-street near the river, in a place where there were marks of a struggle; and his friends were furious.

Before noon next day M. de Clan, whose interference surprised me not a little, was with me to support his son's petition ; and at the King's *levée* next day St. Germain accused his enemy to the King's face, and caused an angry and indecent scene in the chamber.

When a man is in trouble foes spring up,

"HE . . . RUSHED IN ON THAT RASCAL AND FAIRLY BEAT DOWN
HIS GUARD."

as the moisture rises through the stones before a thaw. I doubt if M. de Saintonge was not more completely surprised than any by the stir which ensued, and which was not confined to the St. Germains' friends, though they headed the accusers. All whom he had ever offended, and all who had ever offended him, clamored for justice; while St. Mesmin's faults being forgotten and only his merits remembered, there were few who did not bow to the general indignation, which the young and gallant, who saw that at any moment his fate might be theirs, did all in their power to foment. Finally, the arrival of St. Mesmin the father, who came up almost broken-hearted, and would have flung himself at the King's feet on the first opportunity, roused the storm to the wildest pitch. I saw the King and gave him advice. This was to summon Saintonge, the St. Germains, and old St. Mesmin to his presence and effect a reconciliation; or, failing that, to refer the matter to the Parliament.

He agreed with me and chose to receive them next day at the Arsenal. I communicated his commands, and at the hour named we met, the King attended by Roquelaure and myself. But if I had flattered myself that the King's presence would secure a degree of moderation and reasonableness I was soon undeceived.

"For shame, gentlemen, for shame!" the King said, gnawing his mustachios after a fashion he had when in doubt. "I take Heaven to witness that I cannot say who is right! But this brawling does no good. The one fact we have is that St. Mesmin has disappeared."

"Yes, sire; and that M. de Saintonge predicted his disappearance," St. Germain cried, impulsively. "To the day and almost to the hour."

"I gather, M. de Saintonge," the King said, turning to him, mildly, "that you did use some expressions of that kind."

"Yes, sire, and did nothing upon them," he answered resentfully. But he trembled as he spoke. He was an older man than his antagonist, and the latter's violence shook him.

"But does M. de Saintonge deny," St. Germain broke out afresh before the King could speak, "that my friend had made him a proposal for his daughter? and that he rejected it?"

"I deny nothing!" Saintonge cried, fierce and trembling as a baited animal. "For that matter, I would to Heaven he had had her!" he continued bitterly.

"Ay, so you say now," the irrepressible St. Germain retorted, "when you know that he is dead!"

"I do not know that he is dead," Saintonge answered. "And, for that matter, if he were alive and here now, he should have her. I am tired; I have suffered enough."

"What! Do you tell the King," the young fellow replied incredulously, "that if St. Mesmin were here you would give him your daughter?"

"I do—I do!" the other exclaimed passionately. "To be rid of him, and you, and all your crew!"

"Tut, tut!" the King said. "Whatever betides, I will answer for it, you shall have protection and justice, M. de Saintonge. And do you, young sir, be silent. Be silent, do you hear! We have had too much noise introduced into this already."

He proceeded then to ask certain details, and particularly the hour at which St. Mesmin had been last seen. Notwithstanding that these facts were in the main matters of common agreement, some wrangling took place over them; which was only brought to an end at last in a manner sufficiently startling. The King with his usual thoughtfulness had bidden St. Mesmin be seated. On a sudden the old man rose; I heard him utter a cry of amazement, and following the direction of his eyes I looked towards the door. There stood his son!

At an appearance so unexpected a dozen exclamations filled the air; but to describe the scene which ensued or the various emotions that were evinced by this or that person, as surprise or interest or affection moved them, were a task on which I am not inclined to enter. Suffice it that the foremost and the loudest in these expressions of admiration was young St. Germain; and that the King, after glancing from face to face in puzzled perplexity, began to make a shrewd guess at the truth.

"This is a very timely return, M. de St. Mesmin," he said dryly.

"Yes, sire," the young impertinent answered, not a whit abashed.

"Very timely, indeed."

"Yes, sire. And the more as St. Germain tells me that M. de Saintonge in his clemency has reconsidered my claims; and has undertaken to use that influence with Mademoiselle which——"

But on that word M. de Saintonge, comprehending the *ruse* by which he had been overcome, cut him short; crying out in a rage that he would see him in perdition first. However, we all immediately took the Marquis in hand, and made it our business to reconcile him to the notion; the King even making a special appeal to him, and promising that St. Mesmin should never want his good offices. Under this pressure, and confronted by his solemn undertaking, Saintonge at last and with reluctance gave way. At the King's instance, he formally gave his consent to a match which effectually secured St. Mesmin's fortunes, and was as much above anything the young fellow could reasonably expect as his audacity and coolness exceeded the common conceit of courtiers.

THE NEW TREATMENT OF DIPHTHERIA.

BY HERMANN M. BIGGS, M.D., OF THE NEW YORK HEALTH DEPARTMENT.

FEW subjects related to modern medicine have aroused greater interest or attracted wider attention than the discovery of the new method for the treatment of diphtheria, and, from a humanitarian standpoint, few discoveries have been so full of promise as this. Judged by scientific standards it seems hardly possible to attach too much importance to this discovery, for it is a reduction to a practical form, in the treatment of disease, of the results obtained from many long series of experimental investigations. It is not only the most important application of some of the discoveries of modern bacteriology to the specific treatment of disease, but it also forms a foundation upon which, possibly, may be built up a system for both the prevention and specific treatment of all infectious diseases.

The announcement of the discovery of tuberculin (Koch's lymph) for the treatment of tuberculosis aroused, perhaps, greater interest, and produced greater excitement, than the announcement of the discovery of diphtheria anti-toxine, and the new remedy has been constantly compared in its nature and action to tuberculin, very much to its discredit. There is really only the most superficial resemblance between tuberculin and diphtheria anti-toxine. In the one case (tuberculin) the disease, tuberculosis, or consumption, was to be cured by temporarily intensifying the morbid process by the use of a substance which, in itself, was capable of doing great harm. In the other case, on the contrary (the diphtheria anti-toxine), the remedy not only is apparently quite devoid of injurious effects, and may be administered without any apprehension as to the results, but, in favorable cases, it almost at once renders the individual insusceptible to the poison which causes the disease, and thus arrests it. In the one case (tuberculin) the remedy was a poison produced by the tubercle bacillus in its growth; in the other (diphtheria anti-toxine), the remedy is obtained from animals which have been inoculated with the poison produced by the diphtheria bacillus. In the latter instance, the harmful effects which the diphtheria poison produces, are borne by the animals which are inoculated, and which furnish anti-toxine, and not by human beings who are subjected to the treatment.

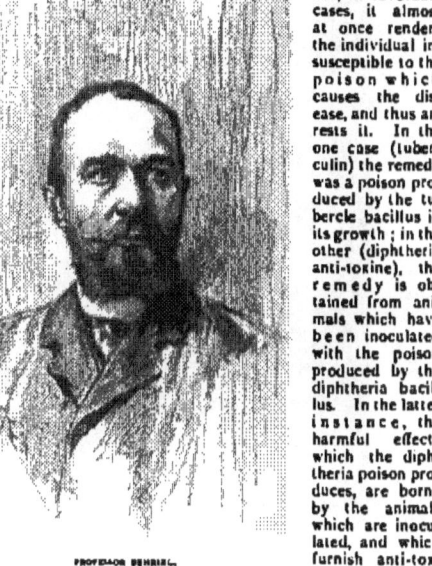

PROFESSOR BEHRING.

Sufficient time has not yet elapsed to form an accurate estimate of the exact value of the diphtheria anti-toxine in the prevention and treatment of diphtheria, but that it is of *great* value, and constitutes an immense advance upon any other method of treatment, has been fully demonstrated.

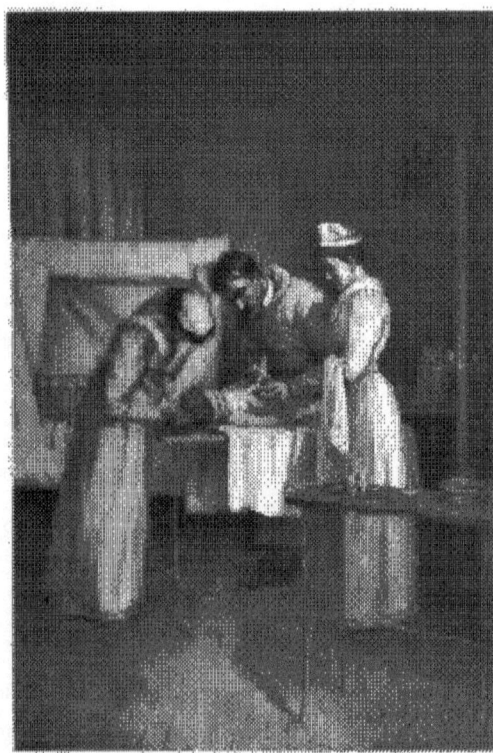

ADMINISTERING THE DIPHTHERIA ANTI-TOXINE.

There is good reason to believe that with a fuller knowledge of the best methods for its employment diphtheria may be brought almost absolutely under control.

THE EXPERIMENTS THAT LED TO THE DISCOVERY.

A number of series of experimental observations regarding the nature and causation of diphtheria preceded the discovery. Klebs were more carefully studied by Loeffler, were cultivated outside the living body, and diphtheria, or a disease resembling it, was reproduced in animals by inoculating them with the cultures of this germ. Loeffler was unable, however, to reproduce the various forms of paralysis which frequently follow diphtheria, but Roux and Yersin, in Paris, in 1888, succeeded in reproducing artificially, by the inoculation of animals with cultures of the

diphtheria toxine) with which they also produced paralysis in animals. Then Behring and Kitasato, in Berlin, found that by the inoculation of animals with the poison obtained from cultures of the diphtheria bacillus they could be gradually rendered extraordinarily insusceptible to both the poison and the diphtheria bacilli themselves. They further showed that this insusceptibility or immunity was due to the formation and presence in the blood of some substance which it has not been possible to separate chemically, and which is known as the diphtheria anti-toxine, or, from its wonderful action, the curative serum. Then followed experiments by Behring, Ehrlich, and other observers in Germany, and Roux in Paris, experiments designed to make this discovery practically available for the prevention and treatment of diphtheria in the human being.

The first important results of these experiments were published in the early part of last year, and they showed a striking diminution in the mortality, in a series of cases of diphtheria subjected to the new treatment. The results obtained in these first cases have been more than confirmed by subsequent experiences in the treatment of this disease. In order to gain an intelligent conception of the nature of the new treatment, it is necessary to know something of certain facts regarding the infectious diseases which underlie it. It has been long known that in many infectious diseases one attack grants a more or less complete insusceptibility, or, as it is called, immunity, to future attacks. The same individual rarely has two attacks of small-pox or scarlet fever, because the first attack has given nearly or complete immunity to the disease.

It has been the endeavor in many bacteriological studies of different infectious diseases, to devise or to discover some means or method by which immunity to these diseases can be artificially induced in animals and in man. These investigations have met with considerable success. In vaccination for small-pox, immunity to small-pox is produced in human beings by inoculation, through vaccination, with the virus of cow-pox, which is a closely allied disease occurring in cattle. Pasteur some years ago succeeded in conferring immunity on cattle and sheep to anthrax, or splenic fever (a disease which sometimes occurs in human beings), by inoculating them with cultures of the anthrax germ, whose virulence had been partially attenuated by the application of heat. In Pasteur's prophylactic treatment for hydrophobia, immunity is conferred by successive inoculations with a virus of constantly increasing strength, the first inoculations being made with a virus having little or no virulence. In this case the virus is obtained from the spinal cords of rabbits which have died from rabies after inoculation. The virulence of the virus in the cords is attenuated by drying for varying periods of time. A spinal cord which has been dried for fourteen days is by this process deprived of its virulence, and those which have been dried a shorter period have proportionately greater virulence.

DR. ROUX.

In the production of the diphtheria anti-toxine, a high degree of immunity is first conferred on animals by successive inoculations with larger and larger amounts of the diphtheria *toxine*, the smaller doses giving tolerance to the succeeding larger doses; this tolerance being due to the formation in the blood of *anti*-toxine. In the prevention of diphtheria by the use of the anti-toxine, a certain proportion of the immunity which has been conferred upon animals, is transferred from the immunized animal to the individual. This is done by the injection under the skin of a given amount of blood serum, *curative serum*, which contains the anti-toxine, and which is derived from an immunized animal. The amount of insusceptibility conferred by these injections is proportionate to the amount of blood serum that is thus introduced, and the degree of insusceptibility to diphtheria which the animal from which it was obtained has acquired. In the treatment of diphtheria by anti-toxine, the same immunity is transferred, and is almost immediately produced in the individual, by the introduction of this curative serum; and as the individual by its introduction is rendered relatively or absolutely immune to the disease, the disease is at once partially or completely arrested.

The results which have been obtained from the treatment of diphtheria by the new remedy, are far better than have ever been obtained by any other method. Speaking generally for the children's hospitals in Europe and in this country, it has been found that, with other methods of treatment, from 40 to 55 per cent. of the cases of diphtheria occurring in children under five years of age die. With the new method of treatment, this mortality has been reduced first to 25 per cent., then to 15 per cent., to 13 per cent., 11 per cent., and it has been said that in the last series of cases treated by Roux the mortality was only 8 per cent. The striking influence upon the mortality from this disease brought about by the use of anti-toxine, is shown in the reduced death-rate in Paris during the last few months as compared with the corresponding months of previous years. Tables are appended which show the number of deaths from diphtheria for each week during 1894, and the mortality for each month during the last five years.* The influence of the use of this agent on the death-rate from diphtheria, as shown by these tables, constitutes, in my opinion, an exhibit of the saving of life by a new remedy so extraordinary as to be without a parallel in the history of medicine. No such results have ever before been obtained, and the cumulative results, as shown by these statistics, are no more remarkable than are the immediate effects frequently seen in individual cases produced by the administration of the curative serum. The results are so extraordinary as to seem almost incredible to those who have been familiar with the usual course of diphtheria and the effects of remedies on it.

In the large majority of cases, when the anti-toxine is administered during the first twenty-four or forty-eight hours of the disease, and sometimes also during the third or fourth day, the effects are most striking. If the temperature has been elevated to perhaps one hundred and three or one hundred and four degrees, it falls to normal or nearly normal within a few hours, the extension of the membrane in the throat is arrested, and the swelling and soreness in part or entirely disappear. If the membrane is only on the surface, is of recent formation and is not very thick, and has not as yet involved the substance of the tissue, it will often entirely separate within the first twenty-four hours after the injection, and convalescence is at once established. In the most severe cases, and in those where the remedy is not administered until later in the course of the disease, the influence is usually less marked, and it becomes necessary to administer the remedy a second, a third, or even a fourth time, at intervals of twelve to twenty-four hours. There are, however, a few cases of diphtheria, especially those complicated with septic infection, which die, even if the remedy is used early in the course of the disease. The complications which are common during the course of diphtheria and following it, with other methods of treatment, are far less frequent and less

PROFESSOR EHRLICH.

severe, and in the cases which are treated early they are almost entirely obviated.

The production of anti-toxine requires considerable time, a high grade of technical skill, and is attended with very considerable expense. The cost of the remedy in this country up to the present time has been excessive. Where it could be obtained at all, the price has been from three to twelve dollars a dose, depending upon the strength of the serum. The prices have now been very much reduced, and probably there will be a still further reduction, as the supply is more nearly equal to the demand; but under all conditions it must be a comparatively expensive remedy. In France, the production of it has already been placed under the control of the government. It is produced only at the Pasteur Institute in Paris, under the supervision of Dr. Roux, and it is furnished from this institution to the whole of France, under certain restrictions and regulations, without charge. It cannot be bought or exported. In Germany, up to the present time, the largest supplies come from two sources; that produced under the supervision of Pro-

fessors Behring and Ehrlich, and that produced under the supervision of Dr. Aronson. The former has been produced either at the Institute for Infectious Diseases in Berlin (the amount there being only limited in quantity, and intended for experimental purposes, and for use in the hospitals connected with the institution), or by a manufacturing firm at Hoechst-am-Main. The latter, that produced under the supervision of Dr. Aronson, comes from the pharmaceutical house of Schering. Almost all that has reached this country within the last three months is the Behring product, and up to the 20th of January altogether amounted to perhaps one thousand two hundred vials. Larger consignments are now expected. In this country, measures were taken some months ago by the New York City Health Department, and more recently by the health departments of other cities, and by some private parties, for the home production of anti-toxine. That prepared in this country under the supervision of the New York City Health Department has, at the time of writing, been already employed in more than one hundred and fifty cases, and the mortality in cases thus treated has been about twelve per cent.

It does not seem, with such knowledge as we now have, as if too great enthusiasm regarding the importance of this discovery were possible. It apparently places at once within our control the means for the restriction of the most dreaded and most fatal disease of childhood—a disease which appeared only a few years ago, and which has been rapidly increasing in frequency and mortality all over the civilized world. In New York City alone, during 1894, there were over two thousand two hundred deaths reported as due to this malady. Aside from the direct practical advantage which is to be derived from the use of anti-toxine, the discovery of this new method for the treatment of an infectious disease opens a great field for study and investigation, where there is the brightest promise that other discoveries may be made which will place all infectious diseases as completely within our control as it seems probable now will be the case with diphtheria.

SYRINGE USED IN ADMINISTERING THE ANTI-TOXINE, SHOWN AT ABOUT HALF ITS REAL SIZE.

DIPHTHERIA ANTI-TOXINE—ITS PRODUCTION.

By WILLIAM H. PARK, M.D., OF THE NEW YORK HEALTH DEPARTMENT.

THE anti-toxine of diphtheria is a substance derived from the blood of animals, chiefly horses, which have been rendered immune to the action of the diphtheria bacilli, through repeated injections of their toxines. The first steps in its preparation are carried on in the bacteriological laboratory, ending with the final storage of the perfected toxines; and the later ones in the stables and laboratories connected with them, ending with the bottling of the curative serum.

THE PREPARATION OF THE DIPHTHERIA TOXINES.

The toxines are the poisonous chemical compounds produced and set free by the growth of the diphtheria bacilli. They are powerful irritants to the living cells of the body. It is owing to their poisonous action that the general system is so prostrated in diphtheria, and the membrane produced in the throat. Chemically they are such complicated substances that it has been impossible to secure them in a pure state. The first step in the preparation of the toxines is to secure a number of pure cultures of diphtheria bacilli. These bacilli, proven by Loeffler and other investigators to be the cause of diphtheria, are found uniformly in the gray membrane seen in the throat in diphtheria, and they persist for a time in the healthy throats of persons convalescent from that disease. Recent investigation has also shown that they are frequently present in the throat secretions of healthy persons who have been in contact with diphtheria. They remain here inactive till some disturbance makes the lining membrane of the throat vulnerable to their attack, much as grains of wheat would remain unchanged upon a dry soil until a rain produced the proper conditions for their growth. The first of the photographs shows us a number of colonies of diphtheria bacilli, slightly magnified, growing on the surface of nutrient agar jelly. The many thousands of bacilli contained in each of the colonies are too slightly magnified to be seen individually. The following three photographs show the bacilli from three different cases of diphtheria. The amount of magnification can be appreciated by those who are not bacteriologists, by stating that a man equally magnified would appear twice as large as Mount Washington.

EXAMINING CULTURES FROM SUSPECTED CASES OF DIPHTHERIA, NEW YORK CITY HEALTH DEPARTMENT.

If a visitor should stop at our laboratory any morning at an early hour, he would notice a large number of little tubes containing sterilized solid blood serum. If he looked closely, he would see on the surface of the serum in each of the tubes a growth of bacteria. Upon inquiry he would find that each of the tubes had been inoculated the previous day from the membrane in the throat of a suspected case of diphtheria, and that they were now being examined in order to determine, by the presence or absence of the bacilli, which of the cases were, and which were not, diphtheria. A few of the tubes which contain abundant bacilli, and which appear to have been inoculated from severe cases, are selected to furnish bacilli for the toxine. By the method of plate cultures, the diphtheria bacilli from each of the tubes are obtained free from mixture with other bacteria. A number of test tubes, which have been previously filled with nutrient alkaline bouillon, plugged with cotton and sterilized, are now inoculated with the bacilli, several tubes being injected with the bacilli derived from each of the cases. These tubes are now placed in an incubator and kept at the temperature of the human body, and allowed to develop for two days.

Experience has demonstrated that strong toxines are most apt to be produced from bacilli which have great virulence or disease-producing power. From the appearance of the bacilli it is impossible to tell the amount of virulence which they possess, and we are therefore forced to use living animals to obtain this information. For this purpose guinea-pigs are used, since they possess the qualifications of being easily raised and of reacting always in about the same degree to a given dose of the diphtheria germs.

Having, then, selected, weighed, and described for future identification a number of these guinea-pigs, we inject, under the skin of each, a certain quantity of the broth containing the living diphtheria bacilli. In a little animal weighing three hundred grams (about half a pound) we would inject, perhaps, one one-hundredth of a cubic centimetre, or one-fifth of a drop; in another would be injected one-half, and in a third one-quarter of this quantity.

By keeping the animals under observation a few days, we are enabled to detect just how large a quantity of the bouillon containing the living bacilli from each of the cultures is needed to destroy the life of the animal. When this has been determined, we select four or five of the most virulent cultures to use for the production of the toxines. We have to try a number of cultures, because it is found that among bacilli of equal virulence in animals, some will produce more toxines than others in the bouillon.

To produce the toxines, the bacilli must have access to the oxygen of the air. The usual method of cultivating in flasks plugged with cotton does not give as free passage to the air as is desirable for the quick production of the toxines. A more rapid process, recommended by Roux, is therefore adopted for many of the cultures. It consists in growing the bacilli in a

PSEUDO-DIPHTHERIA COCCI, ONE HUNDRED AND TWENTY-FIVE TIMES THE NATURAL SIZE.

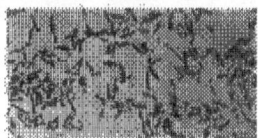

DIPHTHERIA BACILLI, ONE THOUSAND TIMES THE NATURAL SIZE.

CHARACTERISTIC DIPHTHERIA BACILLI, ONE THOUSAND TIMES THE NATURAL SIZE.

draught of moist air. For this purpose large flat-bottom flasks, provided with side tubes for the inlet and exit of air, are filled to a depth of one inch with bouillon and sterilized in a steam chamber. Into each of the flasks are then injected a few cubic centimetres of very virulent bacilli. The flasks are finally placed in one of the many large incubators and kept at thirty-seven degrees centigrade for twenty-four hours. If a good growth develops, the flasks are connected by one of the side-tubes with an exhaust pump. The air which is drawn out one side is sucked in at the other, first having been moistened by passing through a layer of water in a wash bottle. Strong toxines may be prepared in this way in from two to four weeks, about half the time needed by the older but much simpler method.

DIPHTHERIA ANTI-TOXINE—ITS PRODUCTION.

A CORNER OF THE ANIMAL ROOM, SHOWING THE GUINEA PIGS IN THEIR CAGES.

kept, and which are furnishing the supply of anti-toxine, we notice the stalls are large and well ventilated, and that the horses look well and seem comfortably housed. At present there are forty-two horses under treatment. The expenses are shared equally by the Health Department of New York City, and by the New York "Herald." These horses are as carefully tended as patients in a hospital. Twice a day their temperature is taken, and frequently their pulse also. They are taken out daily for exercise, and they are weighed once a week. Their general health is watched over with the greatest care by trained veterinarians.

At the end of this time, small quantities of the bouillon containing the toxines are withdrawn and tested in guinea-pigs. The toxines are tested in the animal in exactly the same way as the bacilli. The bouillon contained in those flasks which has been proven to contain sufficient toxine is removed from the incubator and, after filtering, is placed in large dark-colored glass jars to which one-half per cent. of carbolic acid has been added for a preservative, and stored in a dark room at an even temperature until needed.

The horses selected must be perfectly healthy, but may have slight deformities or blemishes, which, although detracting from their value for other purposes, do not in any way injure the purity of their blood, or diminish their ability to furnish anti-toxine. Having selected then a number of horses, we begin by injecting a small

SOWING TOXINE IN HORSES TO PRODUCE ANTI-TOXINE.

This toxine is now ready for injection into the horses, or other animals, which are to be used for the production of anti-toxine.

Upon entering the stable in which the horses having been longest under

amount, say one-half of a cubic centimetre (ten drops), of the toxine, which, when injected to the amount of one-tenth of a cubic centimetre, is sufficient to kill a half-grown guinea-pig in thirty-six to forty-eight hours.

The horses differ greatly in their reaction to the injections. Some have a marked rise of temperature, refuse their food, develop a large local swelling, become stiff and sore, and show, in every way, that they have been profoundly affected. Other horses receiving the same amount of poison, show little or no disturbance. The doses of toxine can be more quickly increased in horses which show no reaction than in those more sensitive, and they are thus more fitted for the quick production of anti-toxine. Some horses are so sensitive that they succumb to even very small doses of toxine, if they are frequently repeated.

From day to day the horses are observed, and as soon as the temperature has fallen to the normal, and the local swelling has subsided, a slightly larger dose of the toxine is injected. Thus from week to week, the injections increase in size and frequency until, in the course of three to five months, we are enabled to inject the less sensitive horses with a thousand times the original dose, without its producing any local or constitutional symptoms. When we can introduce from two hundred to three hundred cubic centimetres of strong toxine into the horse without producing serious symptoms, we can feel pretty certain that the horse's blood contains anti-toxine in sufficient amount to be used for healing purposes.

The horse is prepared for bleeding by having the skin of the neck over the jugular vein shaved, cleansed with soap and water, and as thoroughly as possible disinfected. To obtain the blood we use a small canula about one-fourth of an inch in diameter, having a sharp-pointed end. To the opposite end is attached a rubber tube of moderate size, about two feet in length. At the end of this a small glass tube six inches long is attached. To receive the blood we use small flasks containing from one to four pints. The mouths of these flasks have previously been covered with paper, or plugged with cotton, and sterilized by dry heat.

When we are all ready to bleed the horse, the animal is led into a well-lighted and clean room, held both by the bridle and by the small twitch which is twisted about the upper lip. Before introducing the canula into the jugular vein of the horse, a small incision about two inches in length is made directly over the vein. While an assistant presses upon the jugular lower down in the neck, to cause it to fill with blood, the sharp-pointed end of the canula is pushed through the connective tissue covering the vein, and through the walls of the vein itself until it has passed well within the lumen of the vessel. When this occurs a good stream of blood will immediately flow through the canula and rubber tube into the vessel held to receive the blood. Vessel after vessel is thus filled, until six to twelve pints have

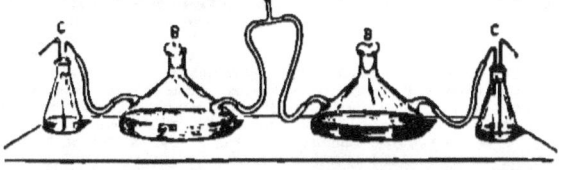

ARRANGEMENT OF FLASKS IN INCUBATOR. THE AIR, PASSING THROUGH THE WATER IN THE WASH BOTTLES C C, BECOMES MOISTENED BEFORE PASSING INTO THE FLASKS B B, WHERE THE BACILLI ARE GROWING IN BOUILLON.

been procured. The amount of blood depends upon the size and condition of the horse. The horse itself hardly minds the operation, frequently nibbling its hay during the process.

These flasks containing the blood are now stored for from two to four days in the ice-chest in the laboratory connected with the stable, until the clot has thoroughly squeezed out the serum. This serum contains dissolved in it the anti-toxine. It must always be remembered that it is the anti-toxine, and not the serum which contains it, that is curative in diphtheria.

There are a number of ways employed by different investigators to determine the amount of anti-toxine contained in any given sample of blood serum. There are two principal methods, of which the others are mostly modifications. The first is chiefly employed in Germany and was devised by Professor Behring. In this meth-

DIPHTHERIA ANTI-TOXINE—ITS PRODUCTION.

od we take a sufficient amount of bouillon containing the poison or toxine of the diphtheria bacilli, which has been proven by numerous tests to be ten times the amount sufficient to kill a guinea-pig weighing two hundred and fifty to three hundred grams. To this amount of poison we add varying amounts of the serum to be tested as to its strength in anti-toxine. The toxine and anti-toxine are thus injected together. Each animal of a series, therefore, receives the same amount of toxine, but a different amount of serum.

After a few days we are enabled to tell from the results of these injections just how much of the given sample of serum was sufficient to save the life of a guinea-pig which had received ten times a fatal dose. If one-tenth of a cubic centimetre of this sample of serum sufficed to save the life of a guinea-pig, it was called by Behring a normal anti-toxine solution, and one cubic centimetre of this comprised one unit of anti-toxine. If one-tenth of this amount or one one-hundredth of a cubic centimetre was sufficient to produce this curative result, this solution of anti-toxine was called a ten-fold normal solution.

The other method is one chiefly employed by Dr. Roux and his co-laborers. In this method we inject into a number of animals varying amounts of the serum containing the anti-toxine; twelve hours afterward we inject into these animals a sufficient quantity of living virulent diphtheria bacilli to kill an unprotected animal in thirty-six hours. Here by injecting the anti-toxine before the bacilli, we immunize the animals, and it is found that we are enabled to protect the lives of the guinea-pigs by very much smaller quantities of anti-toxine than if we injected the anti-toxine and bacilli together. The strength of the anti-toxine in the serum is estimated upon the percentage of serum required to protect the life of the guinea-pig compared to its weight. Thus, if we found that a guinea-pig weighing five hundred grams (the size usually selected by Roux) required one five-hundredth of its weight of the serum (one cubic centimetre) to be protected from the poisonous effects of the test dose, we would label the strength of that anti-toxine serum at five hundred, because one part of this serum protected five hundred parts of animal. If another sample of serum contained one hundred times as much anti-toxine, one part would protect fifty thousand parts of guinea-pigs, and the strength of this serum would be fifty thousand. Serum of this strength is the weakest that should be used in treatment.

If we consider closely the results obtained in testing anti-toxine, we may learn a truth which is of great importance. It has been found, that a very small quantity of anti-toxine suffices to save the life of an animal, when injected some hours before the introduction of the poison of diphtheria. A much larger quantity is necessary when the poison and anti-toxine are injected together, and a still greater quantity is required if the poison is injected before the anti-toxine. If the curative anti-toxine is delayed too long, no amount will suffice to rescue the animal. The evidence thus brought out experimentally has proven true at the bedside. Cases of diphtheria injected with anti-toxine in the first twenty-four hours of the disease, recovered in a manner almost marvellous. Those injected during the height of the disease show usually marked improvement, while those injected toward the end of the disease show little or none.

DRAWING FROM THE HORSE THE BLOOD CONTAINING THE ANTI-TOXINE.

THE LORD'S DAY.

By the Right Hon. W. E. Gladstone, M. P.

THE citadel of Christianity is in these days besieged all round its circuit. There is one point, however, in that circumference where the defence presents to us certain particularities. That point is the article of Sabbath, or, more properly, of Lord's Day, observance. And the particularities are two, widely separated from one another. The first is, that among the forces employed in defence there are important auxiliaries who put wholly out of view the revealed sanction and the properly Christian motive; who are not, and do not profess to be, available for the work of active defence in other parts of the precinct. The other peculiarity is this: that very many of those defenders whose motive and profession are not secular, but distinctly religious, are singularly ill-equipped with consistent or perspicuous ideas of the subject, and, what is more, that in their ordinary practice they systematically and very largely make over large portions of the day, if not to secular occupations and amusements, yet to secular thought and conversation. This is done without deliberate or conscious insincerity; yet we must all feel that when the margin between profession and practice has become, and is allowed to remain, enormous, real insincerity lies perilously near.

As to the first head, we have a class, or more than a class, who view the subject entirely from the natural or secular side, but who still believe, with a greater or less vivid clearness of conviction, that a periodical day of rest, which they reasonably associate with the one day in seven now become so venerable from its associations as well as its origin, is a necessity of health, as well for the brain of man as for the general fabric of his body; but at any rate, and in the highest degree, for corporeal health and vigor as commonly understood. I assume, and also very strongly believe, this to be generally true, although I am not aware that the opinion has ever been made the subject of sanitary statistics. It would, however, be interesting, if it were found practicable, to test the question through the case of that limited proportion of the British community who do not in one way or another enjoy at the least some considerable amount of relief from labor, bodily and mental, on the consecrated day, by a definite exhibition of results on health, through comparing their experiences with those of the community at large. This idea seems to be largely held among the masses of the people, apart from, as well as in connection with, the ideas of religious duty and of spiritual health. Even the most devout may thus think and feel without any inconsistency. It is probably both knowledge of, and participation in, this conception, which has greatly helped the continuance of Sabbath legislation, nay, the increase of its stringency, in the particular of public-houses, and the notable caution and self-restraint of the House of Commons as to administrative changes recommended on the ground of mental recreation and improvement for the people. There can be no reason why the firmest believers in the Christian character and obligation of the day should not thankfully avail themselves of the aid derived from alliance with this secondary but salutary sentiment.

When we approach the second head, it becomes needful to separate between ideas and practice. As to ideas, it can hardly be said that in our own country, of which alone I speak, the general mind is possessed with any conception, at once accurate and clear, of the religious ground on which we are to observe the Sunday. There is a hazy, but still practical and by no means superficial, impression that in some way or other it has to do with the original command delivered through Moses, so often recited in our churches, and backed there by the definite petition that God will incline our hearts "to keep this law." We do not in due proportion weigh or measure two facts which bear materially on the case. Two changes have indeed been imported into this law; one of them into its form, the other into its spirit. The first has been altered, by translation of the Commandment, from the seventh day of the week to the first; the second, by imparting to it a positive and affirmative, in addition to its originally negative and prohibitory, sense. I am not aware that that restricted signification has been relaxed—and it has certainly been kept in very full view by the Church and by the State of England—but the ascent that the Fourth Commandment of the Decalogue has made, and the development and expansion that it has received under the Christian dispensation, have not been so prominently put forward. Hence, perhaps, it is that we have but imperfectly grasped what is implied in what we familiarly call the observance of Sunday. Possibly there may have been a concurring cause for this defect in the indisposition of many minds, after the crisis of the Reformation, to recognise any action of the Church apart from Scripture. It is difficult, in a tranquil survey of the whole case, to exclude from it some admission of such action. But, so far as it has existed, it has been in obvious furtherance of the mind of the Bible, and it may equitably be considered not as raising any question as between clergy and laity, but as expressing the harmonious coöperation of the entire Christian community.

The auxiliary evidence which the Old Testament supplies to support the Fourth Commandment is ample. And it was fortified by secondary institutions, such as the "preparation of the Sabbath," and the limitation of the Sabbath Day's journey. It was not relaxed by our Lord, who lived obediently under the conditions of the older covenant, and whom we are evidently to understand, on some marked occasions, not as impairing the Commandment, but as protesting against and cancelling an artificial and extravagant stiffness in its interpretation. Cruden (*in loc.*) observes that the word "Sabbaths" included the great festivals of the Jews. But the obligatory force of the Fourth Commandment as touching the seventh day is destroyed by the declaration of St. Paul (Colossians ii. 16) that we are liable to be judged or coerced by none in respect of Sabbath days. This command was addressed, as is obvious, especially to Jews who had become Christians; so that it applies with an even enhanced force to us who have never been under the obligations of the Mosaic law.

The opinion which required a great sabbatarian strictness, has in all likelihood been largely consequent upon the Reformation; and, without much critical investigation of the case, has rested practically upon the Fourth Commandment of the Decalogue as it stands. It did not, however, arise at once out of the great movement, even in Scotland, where it eventually attained to a pitch of rigor, and exhibited a tenacity of life, probably greater than in any other Christian country. If we measure things not as they were divinely intended, nor as they are in themselves, but as they are subjectively entertained, it might be a question whether the Scottish Sabbath was not for two hundred years a greater Christian sacrament, a larger, more vital, and more influential fact in the Christianity of the country, than the annual, or sometimes semi-annual, celebration of the Lord's Supper, or the initiatory rite of baptism, or both together. I remember that when, half a century ago, ships were despatched from Scottish ports to South Australia, then in its infancy, laden with well-organized companies of emigrants, I read in the published account of one of them that perfect religious toleration was established as the rule on board, but that with regard to a fundamental article of religion like the Sabbath, every one was of course required to observe it. Many anecdotes might be given which illustrate the same idea; an idea open to criticism, but one with which the Presbyterian Church cannot well afford to part, without some risk to the public power and general influence of religion.

The seventh day of the week has been deposed from its title to obligatory religious observance, and its prerogative has been carried over to the first; under no direct precept of Scripture, but yet with a Biblical record of facts, all supplied by St. John, which go far towards showing that among the Apostles themselves, and therefore from apostolic times, the practice of divine worship on the Lord's Day has been continuously and firmly established. The Christian community took upon itself to alter the form of the Jewish ordinance; but this was with a view to giving larger effect to its spiritual purpose. The seventh day had been ordained as the most appropriate, according to the Decalogue, for commemorating the old creation. The advent of our Lord introduced us to a chain of events, by which alone the benefits of the old creation were secured to us, together with the yet higher benefits of the new. The series of these events culminated in the Resurrection. With the Resurrection began for the Saviour Himself a rest from all that was painful in the process of redemption, as on the seventh day there had begun a rest from the constructive labors that had brought the visible world into existence and maturity.

The seventh day was the festival of the old life, accompanied with an exemption from its divinely appointed burdens. The first day was the festival of the new life, and was crowned with its constant and joyous exercise. The ordinances of joint worship exhibit one particular form of that exercise. The act of the Church or Christian community in altering the day was founded on this broad and solid analogy; and was also, as has been said, warranted by the evidence of apostolic practice.

On the day of Resurrection itself, in the evening, the disciples were solemnly assembled, with the doors shut for "fear of the Jews" (St. John xx. 19), and the Lord, in His risen body, appeared among them, to confer on them their great mission (xx. 21–23). Again, on the eighth day, or, as we should term it, seven days after the great day of the Resurrection, we have a similar assembly, and a like appearance, which records the confirmation of the faith of St. Thomas (xx. 26–28). The same Apostle who had linked together thus markedly these three occasions, introduces the Apocalypse to us with a proem that shows his deep sense of its dignity and importance; and next proceeds to localize it, first in place, by describing the isle of Patmos as the scene, and then in time, by specifying that he was "in the Spirit on the Lord's Day" (Rev. i. 9, 10). We may, after all this, admit that the aggregate of evidence for the obligation of meeting together for worship on the Christian Sabbath, or Lord's Day, is not literally homogeneous; but we must assert and insist that its several parts are in keeping one with another, and that its combined force is conclusive. No Christian can entertain a reasonable doubt as to the solidity of the foundations on which the established tradition and practice rest.

But it remains to consider the portion of the subject on which the prevailing conceptions are the most lame and incomplete.

We dismiss the question of the authority for the Lord's Day. There remains the further question, What is the nature and amount of the religious observance due to it? Is it, apart from works of charity and necessity, which I set aside and cover by an assumption all along, the setting aside of worldly business, either in part or altogether? Is it an attendance on public worship, in quantity penuriously admitted, frugally and jealously doled out? Is the demand of duty, is the religious appetite satisfied, by the resort (be it more punctual or less) to a single service, by thus becoming what an old friend of mine wit- tily calls "a oncer; or can our bounty stand the drain on attention, and on available hours, of two regular services of the Church? Are we to deal with the question how much of the Lord's Day shall be given to service associated with its name in the spirit in which the commander of a capitulating fortress deals with the incoming force, when he works for a maximum of indulgence, a minimum of concession, and tempers his thrift only by a prudent care to avoid a rupture? Or, if the question be not too audacious, is all this haggling and huxtering upon quantities and portions beside the purpose, and is there not open to us, for the determination of all controversy, and for marking out the lines of duty, "a more excellent way"— a way not to be ascertained by embarking on any voyage of fanciful investigation, but simply by examining the first elements of the case?

May it not be that the Apostles, and the community which they guided, saw that they had to deal with the Fourth Commandment, and that the course dictated to them by the essential bearings of the case was not to abrogate, nor to contract, nor in any manner to disparage it, but (so to speak) to transform it from within outwards; to stand upon the analogy which it suggested, and to supply the obvious application to the enlarged and altered position? The change from the seventh day to the first was one which could not be arbitrarily made. So it appears, as we were justly told at the recent Parliament of Religions in America by the representative of one leading strain of Jewish thought, M. Pereira Mendez; who, on behalf of the strict Mosaists, declared that they could not accept a first day "Sabbath."[*] We can; and the authority which is on our side, has also reason at its back. The old Sabbath was the festival of rest from labor with the hand; a festival of the body, or natural life; a festival negative in its character, for its fundamental conception was simply a conception of what man was *not* to do. The Redeemer, like the Creator, had His work, and had His rest from His work; this was on the Resurrection Day, and the Apostles and the Church instituted the festival of the new life, as the Creator had (and surely from the beginning) appointed the festival of the old.

The festival of the new life! Not merely of the act of our Lord's rising, which had

[*] "Indian Church Quarterly Review," October, 1894, p. 388.

for its counterpart the act of the Creator's resting; but of the life, and the employments of the life, which in His Resurrection body He then began. Here comes into view a point not only of difference, but of contrast. The Fourth Commandment enjoined not a life, but a death; and all that may now be thought to require a living observance of the day is not read in, but (as the lawyers say) read into it. But the celebration of the Lord's Day is the unsealing of a fountain-head, a removal of the grave-clothes from the man found to be alive, the opening of a life spontaneous and continuous. It reminds me of the arm of a Highland river which the owner of the estate dammed up with a sluice on all ordinary days, but on special days he removed the barrier, and the waters flowed. And flowed how long? Until the barrier was replaced. Not for a measured half hour or hour, but as long as they were free to flow; and not by propulsion from without, but by native impulse from within. And in like manner the question for the Christian is not how much of the Lord's Day shall we give to service directly divine. If there be any analogous question it is, rather, how much of it shall we withhold? A suggestion to which the answer obviously is, as much, and as much only, as is required by necessity and by charity or mercy. These are undoubtedly terms of a certain elasticity, but they are quite capable of sufficient interpretation by honest intention and an enlightened conscience. If it be said that religious services are not suited for extension over the whole day, and could only lead to exhaustion and reaction, I would reply that the business of religion is to raise up our entire nature into the image of God, and that this, properly considered, is a large employment—so large; that it might be termed as having no bounds. But the limit will be best determined by maintaining a true breadth of distinction between the idea of the new life and the work of the old. All that admits the direct application of the new spirit, all that most vividly brings home to us the presence of God, all that savors most of emancipation from this earth and its *hic centum catenæ*, is matter truly proper to the Lord's Day; and what it is in each case the rectified mind and spirit of the Christian must determine. What is essential is that to the new life should belong the flower and vigor of the day. We are born on each Lord's Day morning into a new climate, a new atmosphere; and in that new atmosphere (so to speak), by the law of a renovated nature, the lungs and heart of the Christian life should spontaneously and continuously drink in the vital air.

It may perhaps be said that this view of the subject disparages the Christian life of the other six days of the week. A fatal objection, if only the fact were so. But I believe that, if we search the matter to the bottom, it is found difficult or impossible to reach any other firm foundation for the observance of the Lord's Day. The counter idea is to give a certain portion of the day to work associated with the new life, and to withhold the rest. On what authority, what groundwork of principle, does such an idea rest for its warrant? There is no allocation of a portion, of a *quantum*, of time weekly for such a purpose, commanded in the Old Testament, none in the New, none in the known practice and tradition of the Church. Would it not seem that this plan savors of will-worship, rather than the other? The observance of the Lord's Day by spiritual service rests, in its inner soul and meaning, not on a mere injunction, but on a principle.

Does, then, that principle import any dishonor to the general law of love, obedience, and conformity to the divine commands, which embraces all days alike without preference or distinction of degree? It does nothing of the kind. The service of God in this world is an unceasing service, without interval or suspense. But, under the conditions of our physical, intellectual, and social life, a very large portion of that service is necessarily performed within the area which is occupied by this world and its concerns, and within which every Christian grace finds perpetual room for its exercise: but for its exercise under circumstances not allowing the ordinary man, unless in the rarest cases, that nearness of access to the things of God, that directness of assimilation to the divine life, which belongs to a day consecrated by spiritual service. So the grace and compassion of our Lord have rescued from the open ground of worldly life a portion of that area and have made upon it a vineyard seated on a very fruitful hill, and have fenced it in with this privilege, that, whereas for our six days' work the general rule of direct contact must for the mass of men be with secular affairs, within this happy precinct there is provided, even for that same mass of men, a chartered emancipation; and the general rule is reversed in favor of a direct contact with spiritual things.

I do not enter upon the question how

far the considerations here stated bear upon the case of festivals other than the Lord's Day. They do not, all of them, seem to fall into the same category, one with another, by reason of the great difference between the determining epochs of the incarnate life of our Lord and some minor commemorations. None of them are in precise correspondence with the case of the Lord's Day, though by analogy they are carried very near its substance, and fully correspond with its occasion; so that we are at once reminded of that similar case in the Hebrew records, where the great annual festivals of the Israelites are held to be sometimes comprised under the description of Sabbaths.

Neither do I advert, as I write for our own insular case, to diversities of idea and practice prevailing in branches of the Christian Church other than our own.

Finally, the very last idea that I should desire to convey is that the idea of the Lord's Day which has here been suggested, is novel or original. The case is rather thus; it is an idea which, through the want of precision in the habitual thoughts of men, has fallen into the shade, and given place to other ideas presented in a shape more sharply defined. I cannot here do better than take refuge under the authority of one of the very greatest doctors of the Church, I mean Saint Augustine. In many places he touches upon the Sabbath. Our Sabbath, he says, is in the heart; in the peace of Christian hope. It is the work of God, not our own.* Our "Sabbatism" is an entry upon that life "which eye hath not seen, nor ear heard, neither hath the heart of man conceived;"

it is the bliss of immortality.* Its fundamental idea is "rest"—rest inhabited by sanctification. *Ibi sanctificatio, quia ibi Spiritus Dei.*† The soul can have rest only in God; and the love of God is perfect sanctification, the Sabbath of Sabbaths.‡ "Even now my Father works," says our Lord. Yes, but not in carnal work; and here is the removal of the veil.§ This is the rest promised to the faithful in doing good works,‖ and walking in newness of life, even as God works while He rests. What chiefly brings the people together on the day of rest is hunger for the word of God.¶ The fulness of divine benediction and sanctification is the highest Sabbath.** The Lord's Day anticipates the time when we shall rest and see, see and love, love and praise, in the end that has no end.†† It is undeniable that throughout Saint Augustine treats the day as a whole, that he postulates an entire withdrawal from worldly occupation, and that he regards this as the basis of a rest and of an activity which prefigure both of these in heaven. In more than one place, too, censuring a contemporaneous Jewish laxity, he declares that useful labor on the Day of Rest would be preferable to the frivolities of recreation. And now, having brought Saint Augustine before the reader to explain the basis of Lord's Day observance, I feel that there can be no more appropriate moment for withdrawing myself from his attention.

* St. Augustine *Enarr.* in Psalms xci.

† *Ibid.* Serm. 9:5, on the Octave of Easter.
‡ Serm. 8, on the Ten Plagues.
§ Serm. 33, on Psalm xlviii.
‖ *De Genes.* Book 4.
¶ *De Genes. ad lit.*; Book IV.
** Serm. 128, on John 5.
†† *De Civ. Dei*, xxii. 4.
‡‡ *Ibid.* 5.

"HUMAN DOCUMENTS."

THE RIGHT HON. W. E. GLADSTONE, M. P.

Mr. GLADSTONE was born at Liverpool, December 29, 1809. He has been a member of the House of Commons almost continuously since 1832; and when he resigned the office of prime minister a year ago, on account of his advanced age, he was serving in it for the fourth time. His first premiership extended from December, 1868, to February, 1874; the second, from April, 1880, to June, 1885; the third, from February to August, 1886; and the fourth, from August, 1892, to March, 1894. Here are nearly thirteen years; and as in England a prime minister retires the moment the country is not with him, they tell in a word what a power in the land Mr. Gladstone has been.

PORTRAITS OF GLADSTONE.

MR. GLADSTONE IN 1839. AGE 29.

From a life portrait by Bradley. At this time Mr. Gladstone was of the Opposition in the House of Commons, and acting under the leadership of Sir Robert Peel.

MR. GLADSTONE IN 1852. AGE 43.

From a photograph by Samuel A. Walker, London. In 1851 Mr. Gladstone left the Conservative, or Tory party, with which he had theretofore acted, and this year, 1852, in the "Coalition" Ministry of Lord Aberdeen, he became for the first time Chancellor of the Exchequer, an office for which he has many times proved unequalled fitness.

MR. GLADSTONE IN 1859. AGE 49.
From a photograph by Samuel A. Walker, London. This year, under Lord Palmerston, Mr. Gladstone became a second time Chancellor of the Exchequer.

PORTRAITS OF GLADSTONE

PORTRAITS OF GLADSTONE.

MR. GLADSTONE IN 1866. AGE 56.
From a photograph by Samuel A. Walker, London June 18, 1866. Mr. Gladstone, then in his first experience as leader of the House of Commons, suffered defeat on a reform bill, by the Tories under Disraeli.

MR. GLADSTONE IN 1880. AGE 70.

From a photograph by Samuel A. Walker, London. This year the Liberals recovered a lost majority in Parliament, Mr. Gladstone himself making a famous campaign, and securing election by a famous majority, in Midlothian. Disraeli (now Lord Beaconsfield) and his cabinet resigned, and Mr. Gladstone again became prime minister.

MR. GLADSTONE AND HIS GRANDSON (SON OF HIS ELDEST SON, THE LATE W. H. GLADSTONE). 1890. AGE 80.

From a portrait painted by McClure Hamilton, and presented by the ladies of England, Scotland, Wales, and Ireland to Mrs Gladstone as a souvenir of hers and Mr. Gladstone's golden wedding, celebrated the year before (1889).

MR. GLADSTONE AT 83, WITH HIS GRANDDAUGHTER DOROTHY DREW.

From a photograph by Valentine & Sons, Dundee, taken at Hawarden (Mr. Gladstone's country home), October 13, 1893. At this time Parliament was adjourned, for a month or two after long and excited debates on the subject of Home Rule for Ireland.

MR. GLADSTONE, HAWARDEN, OCTOBER 13, 1893. AGE 83.
From a photograph by Valentine & Sons, Dundee.

A BLIZZARD.

By Mrs. E. V. Wilson.

IT was a sod house, a little two-roomed affair, with a low roof, and narrow, deep-set windows and doors. Far as the eye could reach, on either side, stretched the broad prairie, with not a tree or a house in sight. Yet the group gathered in front of the lone house seemed happy enough. There were four persons—husband, wife, and their two children. The husband was seated in a big wagon to which were harnessed two good horses, the wife standing near, one chubby babe in her arms, another, a wee toddler, clinging to her dress, and coaxing to "go with papa."

"Well, Maggie, I must be off," said the husband, picking up the reins and settling himself comfortably. "Never mind, baby," to the little one, "papa will bring something pretty to his girlie. Don't be lonesome, wife ; I'll be back before night. You know we must have coal and other things. Good-by."

"Good-by, Tom," said the wife ; so, with a word to the horses, her husband drove rapidly off in the direction of the little town, ten miles distant, where they procured their necessary supplies.

For a little while Margaret Grant watched the wagon. Then, as it disappeared from her sight behind one of the great billows that, wave-like, cover the great plains, she entered the room, closing the door behind her, and, sitting down, employed herself with caring for her little ones. How long she had been thus employed she did not notice until the striking clock warned her of the flight of time. The baby had fallen asleep in her lap ; the other little one, a three-year-old, was busy piling cobs and then upsetting them on the floor. She laid the sleeping child on the bed, and replenishing the fire, which was burning low, went to the door, and, opening it, looked out long and earnestly. Surely the wind was rising and the sky growing gray with clouds. Her heart sank. "He ought not to have gone," she murmured ; "but then the coal is nearly out, and the flour, too." She sighed, and, closing the door, went about her work.

Only the spring before they had come West, built their home, cultivated a little patch of ground, entered their one hundred and sixty acres, and, with youth and health and loving hearts, resolved to make to themselves an abiding place. Her thoughts went back to the home they had left. Somehow she felt depressed. She was not homesick, surely. Tom had often left her and the children for a day, and now she knew he had been compelled to go, for they must have fuel and food. The weather had been so fine, and he so busy breaking ground for his spring crop, that he had already put it off too long. She opened the door again. A few flakes of snow were falling. It was getting colder ; the wind was higher. Her heart grew heavy. The baby woke and cried, and the little girl was hungry. She tenderly cared for them, but she could not eat. The food choked her. How dark it was getting, and the clock said two P. M.! She looked from the window. How fast the snow was falling! She could see nothing else. "Oh, Tom," she thought, "what a cold, cold ride you will have!" Only a cold ride ; no thought of danger crossed her mind. She had heard of the terrible storms on the prairies, but this snowfall, surely, surely, it was not dangerous. But how cold it was getting. She poured more fuel into the stove, and opening the back door, thought she would go to the little sod stable and attend to the cow before night came on ; but she could not see ; the snow blinded her. Then a sudden feeling of helplessness and terror filled her. Closing the door she sank on her knees and tried to pray.

Night came without bringing her husband. Toward morning she sank into an uneasy slumber, and was awakened by strange noises, a stamping as of many feet, and the air seemed filled with strange, unearthly sounds. She sprang up and opened the door. The snow was still falling, but all round her door it was tramped down by the hoofs of the great crowd of cattle that struggled and bellowed, pushing their way forward, drifting with the wind. They did not notice the open door. She could only see those in front of her, but she knew by the sounds there were many of them. Going to the opposite window, the same great, brown, horned beasts greeted her eyes. It seemed to her hours passed before the noise died away, and then, how awful the silence that reigned!

Days passed. A week went by. The storm ceased, the sun shone, and the dwellers in the little town ten miles away bethought them of the settler who had driven out of town with a load of coal at noon the day the blizzard set in. They had warned him, but he would go. Wife and children were alone, he said, with scanty supply of food and fuel. Men shook their heads and women sighed, but while the storm—an unusual one even there—lasted, nothing could be done, and for some days the deep snow was impassable. But when at last a morning dawned bright and mild, a half dozen sturdy fellows set out on their difficult task. On foot, working their way step by step through great drifts, they went, making, in spite of every effort, but a couple of miles; then they were compelled to return home exhausted and half frozen. Next day they set out again, and just before nightfall reached their destination. No sign of life was there. They knocked. No answer came. Pushing the door open they entered, and, oh, sorrowful sight! on the bed, dead babies held close in her arms, lay the dead mother. A scrap of paper on the table, with a pencil near it, attracted the attention of one of the men. Picking it up, he read with a faltering voice: "Good-by, Tom. I have done all I could. If you are out in this dreadful storm, God help you. I will go to bed with the children." The letters were straggling and faint, as if the stiffening fingers could scarcely be guided. Tears rose to the eyes of the men as they looked at the bed, and then out on the snow-covered plain. Somewhere out there, they knew, the body of the husband and father lay. And a few weeks later he was found, not a hundred yards from his home. He had striven to reach his loved ones, for he had taken the horses from the wagon, ridden on some distance, then had dismounted, and tried to make his way on foot. But all in vain. The flying snow had blinded him. There were no landmarks. Confused, frozen, he had fallen and died so near his house that his voice could have been heard if he had called aloud.

Ah! these great wide plains! Since the days when first men crossed them going in search of gold, leaving the bones of comrades to bleach upon them, how many tragedies have been enacted there, tragedies of which the world knows nothing! Some day, "when the waste places bloom and the desert has become a garden," children will listen with wondering eyes to tales like this, and ask can they be true!

GEORGE DU MAURIER.
From a photograph by Fradelle & Young, taken for McClure's Magazine at Mr. Du Maurier's house

McClure's Magazine.

Vol. IV.   APRIL, 1895.   No. 5.

THE AUTHOR OF "TRILBY."

AN AUTOBIOGRAPHIC INTERVIEW WITH MR. GEORGE DU MAURIER.

The illustrations in this article are from photographs made especially for McClure's Magazine.

BY ROBERT H. SHERARD.

AS I crossed the heath, I passed a group of devout people to whom, standing among them, a Salvation Army girl, with an inspired face, was preaching with great fervor. I did not stay to listen to her, for George du Maurier had appointed me to meet him at his house at three on that Sunday afternoon. But as I went my way, I heard the words: "Never you envy even those who seem most to be envied in this world, for in even the happiest life . . ." and that was all.

Du Maurier's house is in a quiet little street that leads from the open heath down to the township of Hampstead, a street of few houses and of high walls, with trees everywhere, and an air of seclusion and quiet over all. The house stands on the left hand as one walks away from the heath, and is in the angle formed by the quiet street and a lane which leads down to the high road. It is a house of bricks overgrown with ivy, with angles and protrusions, and in the little garden which is to the left of the entrance door stands a large tree. The front door, which opens straight on to the street, is painted white, and is fitted with brass knockers of unblemished brilliance. As one enters the house, one notices on the wall to the left, just after the threshold is crossed, the original of one of Du Maurier's drawings in "Punch," a drawing concerning two "millionnairesses," with the text written beneath the picture in careful, almost lithographic penmanship.

"That was where I received my training in literature," said Du Maurier. "So Anstey pointed out to me the other day, when I told him how surprised I was at the success of my books, considering that I had never written before. 'Never written!' he cried out. 'Why, my dear Du Maurier, you have been writing all your life, and the best of writing-practice at that. Those little dialogues of yours, which week after week you have fitted to your drawings in 'Punch,' have prepared you admirably. It was *précis* writing, and gave you conciseness and repartee and appositeness, and the best qualities of the writer of fiction.' And," added Du Maurier, "I believe Anstey was quite right, now that I come to think of it."

The waiting-room, or hall, is under an arch, to the right of the passage which leads from the door to the staircase, a cosy corner on which a large model of the Venus of Milo looks down. "There is my great admiration," said Du Maurier in the evening, as he pointed to the armless goddess, and went on to repeat what Heine has said, and mentioned Heine's desire for the Venus's armless embrace.

DU MAURIER IN HIS STUDY.

It was in his study that Du Maurier received me, a large room on the first floor,

Copyright, 1895, by S. S. McClure, Limited. All rights reserved.

with a square bay window overlooking the quiet street on the right, and a large window almost reaching to the ceiling, and looking in the direction of the heath, facing the door. It is under this window, the light from which is toned down by brown curtains, that Du Maurier's table stands, comfortably equipped and tidy. On a large blotting-pad lay a thin copybook, open, and one could see that the right page was covered with large, round-hand writing, whilst on the left page there were, in smaller, more precise penmanship, corrections, emendations, addenda. In a frame stood a large photograph of Du Maurier, and on the other side of the inkstand was a pile of thin copy-books, blue and red. "A fortnight's work on my new novel," said Du Maurier.

A luxurious room it was, with thick carpets and inviting arm-chairs, the walls covered with stamped leather, and hung with many of the master's drawings in quiet frames. In one corner a water-color portrait, by Du Maurier, of Canon Ainger, and, from the same brush, the picture of a lady with a violin, on the wall to the left of the decorative fireplace, from over which, in the place of honor, another, smaller, model of the armless Venus looks down. To the right is a grand piano, and elsewhere other furniture of noticeable style, and curtains, screens, and ornaments. A beautiful room, in fact, and within it is none of the litter of the man of letters or of the painter.

It was here that I first saw Du Maurier, a quiet man of no great stature, who at the first sight of him impresses one as a man who has suffered greatly, haunted by some evil dream or disturbing apprehension. His welcome is gentle and kindly, but he does not smile, even when he is saying a clever and smile-provoking thing. "You must smoke. One smokes here. It is a studio." Those were amongst the first words that Du Maurier said, and there was hospitality in them and the freemasonry of letters.

DU MAURIER'S FAMILY.

"My full name is George Louis Palmella Busson du Maurier, but we were of very small nobility. My name Palmella was given to me in remembrance of the great friendship between my father's sister and the Duchesse de Palmella, who was the wife of the Portuguese ambassador to France. Our real family name is Busson; the 'Du Maurier' comes from the Chateau le Maurier, built some time in the fifteenth century, and still standing in Anjou or Maine, but a brewery to-day. It belonged to our cousins the Auberys, and in the seventeenth century it was the Auberys who wore the title of Du Maurier; and an Aubery du Maurier who distinguished himself in that century was Louis of that name, who was French ambassador to Holland, and was well liked of the great king. The Auberys and the Bussons married and inter-married, and I cannot quite say without referring to family papers—at present at my bank—when the Bussons assumed the territorial name of Du Maurier; but my grandfather's name was Robert Mathurin Busson du Maurier, and his name is always followed, in the papers which refer to him, by the title *Gentilhomme verrier*—gentleman glass-blower. For until the Revolution glass-blowing was a monopoly of the *gentilhommes*; that is to say, no commoner might engage in this industry, at that time considered an art. You know the old French saying:

'Pour souffler un verre
Il faut être gentilhomme.'"

"A year or two ago," continued Du Maurier, "I was over in Paris with Burnand and Furniss, and we went into Notre Dame, and as we were examining some of the gravestones with which one of the aisles is in places laid, I came upon a Busson who had been buried there, and on the stone was carved our coat-of-arms, but it was almost all effaced, and there only remained, clearly distinguishable, the black lion, my black lion." It may be added that the Busson genealogy dates from the twelfth century. Du Maurier, though, does not take the subject of descent too seriously. "One is never quite sure," he says, with the shadow of a smile, "about one's descent. So many accidents occur. I made use of many of the names which occur in the papers concerning my family history, in 'Peter Ibbetson.'

"My father was a small *rentier*, whose income was derived from our glass-works in Anjou. He was born in England, for his father had fled to England to escape the guillotine when the Revolution broke out, and they returned to France in 1816. My grandmother was a *bourgeoise*. Her name was Bruaire, and she descended from Jean Bart, the admiral. My grandfather was not a rich man. Indeed, whilst he was in England he had mainly to depend on the liberality of the British Government, which allowed him a pension of twenty

MR. DU MAURIER'S HOUSE ON HAMPSTEAD HEATH.

pounds a year for each member of his family. He died in the post of schoolmaster at Tours.

CHILDHOOD AND YOUTH.

"My mother was an Englishwoman, and was married to my father at the British Embassy in Paris, and I was born in Paris, on March 6, 1834, in a little house in the Champs-Elysées. It bore the number 80. It was afterwards sold by my father, and has since been pulled down. I often look at the spot when I am in Paris and am walking down the Champs-Elysées, and what I most regret at such times are the pine trees which in my childhood used to be there—very different from the miserable, stumpy avenue of to-day. It is a dis-illusion which comes upon me with equal force at each new visit, for I remember the trees, and the trees only. Indeed, I only lived in the house of my birth for two years, for in 1836 my parents removed to Belgium, and here I remember with peculiar vividness a Belgian man-servant of ours, called Francis. I used to ask him to take me in his arms and to carry me down-stairs to look at some beautiful birds. I used to think that these were real birds each time that I looked at them, although, in fact, they were but painted on the panes, and I had been told so. I remember another childish hallucination. I used to sleep in my parents' room, and when I turned my face to the wall, a door in the wall used to open, and a *charbonnier*, a coal-man, big and black, used to come and take me up and carry me down a long, winding staircase, into a kitchen, where his wife and children were, and treated me very kindly. In truth, there was neither door, nor *charbonnier*, nor kitchen. It was an hallucination; yet it possessed me again and again.

"We stayed three years in Belgium, and when I was five years old I went with my parents to London, where my father took a house—the house which a year later was taken by Charles Dickens—1 Devonshire Terrace, Marylebone Road. Of my life here I best remember that I used to go out riding in the park, on a little pony, escorted by a groom, who led my pony by a strap, and that I did not like to be held in leash this way, and tried to get away. One day when I was grumbling at the groom, he said I was to be a good boy, for there was the Queen surrounded by her lords; and he added: 'Master Georgie, take off your hat to the Queen and all her lords.' And then cantered past a young woman surrounded by horsemen. I waved my hat, and the young woman smiled and kissed her hand to me. It was the Queen and her equerries.

"We only stayed a year in Devonshire Terrace, for my father grew very poor. He was a man of scientific tastes, and lost his money in inventions which never came to anything. So we had to wander forth again, and this time we went to Boulogne, and there we lived in a beautiful house at the top of the Grande Rue. I had sunny hours there, and was very happy. It is a part of my life which I shall describe in one of my books.

"Much of my childhood is related in 'Peter Ibbetson.' My favorite book was the 'Swiss Family Robinson,' and next, 'Robinson Crusoe.' I used to devour these books.

DU MAURIER A LATE SPEAKER.

"I was a late speaker. My parents must have thought me dumb. And one day I surprised them all by coming out with a long sentence. It was, '*Papa est allé chez le boucher pour acheter de la viande pour maman,*' and so astonished everybody."

George du Maurier has recently again astonished everybody in a similar way, coming forth loud and articulate and strong, after a long silence, which one fancied was to be forever prolonged.

"We used to speak both French and English at home, and I was brought up in both languages.

"From Boulogne we went to Paris, to live in an apartment on the first floor of the house No. 108 in the Champs-Elysées. The house still stands, but the ground floor is now a *café*, and the first floor is part of it. I feel sorry when I look up at the windows from which my dear mother's face used to watch for my return from school, and see waiters bustling about and my home invaded.

"I went to school at the age of thirteen, in the Pension Froussard, in the Avenue du Bois de Boulogne. It was kept by a man called Froussard, a splendid fellow, whom I admired immensely and remember with affection and gratitude. He became a deputy after the Revolution of 1848. He was assisted in the school-work by his son, who was also one of the heroes of my youthful days, another splendid fellow. I was a lazy lad, with no particular bent, and may say that I worked really hard for one year. I made a number of friends, of course, but of my comrades at the Pension Froussard, only one distinguished himself in after life. He was a big boy, two years my senior. His name was Louis Becque de Fouquière. He distinguished himself in literature, and edited André Chénier's poems. His life has recently been written by Anatole France.

"Yes, I am ashamed to say that I did not distinguish myself at school. I shall write my school life in my new novel 'The Martians.' At the age of seventeen I went up for my *bachot*, my baccalaureate degree, at the Sorbonne, and was plucked for my written Latin version. It is true that my nose began to bleed during the examination, and that upset me, and, besides, the professor who was in charge of the room had got an idea into his head that I had smuggled a 'crib' in, and kept watching me so carefully that I got nervous and flurried. My poor mother was very vexed with me for my failure, for we were very poor at that time, and it was important that I should do well. My father was then in England, and shortly after my discomfiture he wrote for me to join him there. We had not informed him of my failure, and I felt very miserable as I crossed, because I thought that he would be very angry with me. He met me at the landing at London Bridge, and, at the sight of my utterly woe-begone face, guessed the truth, and burst out into a roar of laughter. I think that this roar of laughter gave me the greatest pleasure I ever experienced in all my life.

A CONTEST FOR DU MAURIER BETWEEN SCIENCE AND THE ARTS.

"You see my father was a scientific man, and hated everything that was not science, and despised all books, the classics not less than others, which were not on scientific subjects. I, on the other hand, was fond of books—of some books, at least. When I was quite a boy, I was enthusiastic about Byron, and used to read out 'The Giaour' and 'Don Juan' to my mother for hours together. I knew the shipwreck scene in 'Don Juan' by heart, and recited it again and again; and though my admiration for Byron has passed, I still greatly delight in that magnificent passage. I can recite every word of it even now. Then came Shelley, for whom my love has lasted, and then Tennyson, for whom my admiration has never wavered, and will last all my life, though now I qualify him with Browning. Swinburne was a revelation to me. When his 'Poems and Ballads' appeared, I was literally frantic about him, but that has worn off.

"My father, then, never reproached me for my failure in the *bachot* examination, indeed, never once alluded to it. He had made up his mind that I was intended for a scientist, and determined to make me one. So he put me as a pupil at the Birkbeck Chemical Laboratory of University College, where I studied chemistry under Dr. Williamson. I am afraid that I was a most unsatisfactory pupil, for I took no interest at all in the work, and spent almost all my time in drawing caricatures. I drew all my life, I may say; it was my favorite occupation and pastime. Dr. Williamson thought me a very unsatisfactory student at chemistry, but he was greatly amused with my caricatures, and we got on very well together.

"My ambition at that time was to go in for music and singing, but my father objected very strongly to this wish of mine, and invariably discouraged it. My father, I must tell you, possessed himself the sweetest, most beautiful voice that I have ever heard; and, if he had taken up singing as a profession, would most certainly have been the greatest singer of his time. Indeed, in his youth he had studied music for some time at the Paris Conservatoire,

THE DRAWING-ROOM IN MR. DU MAURIER'S HOUSE.
From a photograph by Fradelle & Young, London.

but his family objected to his following the profession, for they were Legitimists and strong Catholics, and you know in what contempt the stage was held at the beginning of this century. It is a pity, for there were millions in his throat.

"We were all musical in our family: my father, my sister (the sister who married Clement Scott, a most gifted pianiste), and then myself. I was at that time crazy about music, and used to practise my voice wherever and whenever I could, even on the tops of omnibuses. But my father always discouraged me. I remember one night we were crossing Smithfield Market together, and I was talking to my father about music. 'I am sure that I could become a singer,' I said, 'and if you like I will prove it to you. I have my tuning-fork in my pocket. Shall I show you my A?'

"'Yes,' said my father, 'I should like to hear your idea of an A.' So I sang the note. My father laughed. 'Do you call that an A? Let me show you how to sing it.' And then and there rang out a note of music, low and sweet at the outset, and swelling as it went, till it seemed to fill all Smithfield with divine melody. I can never forget that scene, never; the dark night, the lonely place, and that wave of the sweetest sound that my ears have ever heard.

"Sometime later my father relented and gave me a few music lessons. I won him over by showing him a drawing which I had produced in Williamson's class-room, in which I was represented bowing gracefully in acknowledgment of the applause of an audience whom I had electrified with my musical talents. Music has always been a great delight to me, and until recently I could sing well. But I have spoiled my voice by cigarette-smoking.

"My poor father, I may add, as I am speaking of his musical powers, died—in my arms—as he was singing one of Count de Segur's drinking songs. He left this world almost with music on his lips.

"I remained at the Birkbeck Laboratory for two years, that is to say till 1854, when my father, who was still convinced that I had a great future before me in the pursuit of science, set me up on my account in a chemical laboratory in Bard's Yard, Bucklersbury, in the city. The house is still there; I saw it a few days ago. It was a fine laboratory, for my father being a poor man naturally fitted it up in the most expensive style, with all sorts of instruments. In the midst of my brightly-polished apparatus here I sat, and in the long intervals between business drew and drew.

"The only occasion on which the sage of Bard's Yard was able to render any real service to humanity was when he was engaged by the directors of a company for working certain gold mines in Devonshire which were being greatly 'boomed,' and to which the public was subscribing heavily, to go down to Devonshire to assay the ore. I fancy they expected me to send them a report likely to further tempt the public.

MR. DU MAURIER AT HIS DRAWING-TABLE.
From a photograph by Fradelle & Young, London.

If this was their expectation they were mistaken; for after a few experiments, I went back to town and told them that there was not a vestige of gold in the ore. The directors were of course very dissatisfied with this statement, and insisted on my returning to Devonshire to make further investigation. I went and had a good time of it down in the country, for the miners were very jolly fellows; but I was unable to satisfy my employers, and sent up a report which showed the public that the whole thing was a swindle, and so saved a good many people from loss.

ADOPTS ART AS A PROFESSION—THE LOSS OF HIS EYE.

"My poor father died in 1856, and at the age of twenty-two I returned to Paris and went to live with my mother in the Rue Paradis-Poissonnière. We were very poor, and very dull and dismal it was. However, it was not long before I entered upon what was the best time of my life. That is when, having decided to follow art as a profession, I entered Gleyre's studio to study drawing and painting. Those were my joyous Quartier Latin days, spent in the charming society of Poynter, Whistler, Armstrong, Lamont, and others. I have described Gleyre's studio in 'Trilby.' For Gleyre I had a great admiration, and at that time thought his 'Illusions Perdues' a veritable masterpiece, though I hardly think so now.

"My happy Quartier Latin life lasted only one year, for in 1857 we went to Antwerp, and here I worked at the Antwerp Academy under De Keyser and Van Lerius. And it was on a day in Van Lerius's studio that the great tragedy of my life occurred."

The voice of Du Maurier, who till then had been chatting with animation, suddenly fell, and over the face came an indefinable expression of mingled terror and anger and sorrow.

"I was drawing from a model, when suddenly the girl's head seemed to me to dwindle to the size of a walnut. I clapped my hand over my left eye. Had I been mistaken? I could see as well as ever. But when in its turn I covered my right eye, I learned what had happened. My left eye had failed me; it might be alto-

MR. DU MAURIER'S STUDIO IN HIS HOUSE AT HAMPSTEAD HEATH.
From a photograph by Pradelle & Young, London.

gether lost. It was so sudden a blow that I was as thunderstruck. Seeing my dismay, Van Lerius came up and asked me what might be the matter; and when I told him, he said that it was nothing, that he had had that himself, and so on. And a doctor whom I anxiously consulted the same day comforted me, and said that the accident was a passing one. However, my eye grew worse and worse, and the fear of total blindness beset me constantly."

It was with a movement akin to a shudder that Du Maurier spoke these words, and my mind went back to what I had heard from the girl-preacher as I crossed the heath, as in the same low tones and with the same indefinable expression he continued:

"That was the most tragic event of my life. It has poisoned all my existence."

Du Maurier, as though to shake off a troubling obsession, rose from his chair, and walked about the room, cigarette in hand.

"In the spring of 1859 we heard of a great specialist who lived in Düsseldorf, and we went to see him. He examined my eyes, and he said that though the left eye was certainly lost, I had no reason to fear losing the other, but that I must be very careful, and not drink beer, and not eat cheese, and so on. It was very comforting to know that I was not to be blind, but I have never quite shaken off the terror of that apprehension.

MAKING HIS OWN WAY IN LIFE.

"In the following year I felt that the time had come for me to earn my own living, and so one day I asked my mother to give me ten pounds to enable me to go to London, and told her that I should never ask her for any more money. She did not want me to go, and as to never asking for money, she begged me not to make any such resolution. Poor woman, she would have given me her last penny. But it happened that I never had occasion to ask her assistance; on the contrary, the time came when I was able to add to the comforts of her existence.

"My first lodging in London was in Newman Street, where I shared rooms with Whistler. I afterwards moved to rooms in Earl's Terrace, in the house where Walter Pater died. I began contributing to 'Once a Week' and to 'Punch' very soon after my arrival in London, and shockingly bad my drawing was at the time. My first drawing in 'Punch' appeared in June, 1860, and represented Whistler and myself going into a photographer's studio. The photographer is very angry with us for smoking, and says that his is not an ordinary studio, where one smokes and is disorderly.

"My life was a very prosperous one from the outset in London. I was married in 1863, and my wife and I never once knew financial troubles. My only trouble has been my fear about my eyes. Apart from that I have been very happy."

As Du Maurier was speaking, his second son, Charles, a tall, handsome youth of distinguished manners, entered the room.

"Ah, that is the 'Mummer,' as we call him," said Du Maurier. "Charles is playing in 'Money' at the Garrick, and doing well. He draws three pounds a week, and that's more than my eldest son, who is in the army, is earning."

The conversation turned on the stage. "When I went to consult my old friend John Hare about letting Charles go on the stage," said Du Maurier, "Hare said that provided one can get to the top of the tree, the stage is the most delightful profession; but that for the actor who only succeeds moderately, it is the most miserable, pothouse existence imaginable.

CONNECTION WITH "PUNCH"—A GLIMPSE OF THACKERAY.

"Most of the jokes in 'Punch' are my own, but a good many are sent to me, which I twist and turn into form. But Postlethwaite, Buntborne, Mrs. Ponsonby Tomkyns, Sir Gorgeous Midas, and the other characters associated with my drawings, are all my own creations,

"I have made many interesting friends during my long life in London, and the lecture which I have delivered all over England contains many anecdotes about them. I never met Charles Dickens to speak to him, and only saw him once; that was at Leech's funeral. Thackeray I also met only once, at the house of Mrs. Sartoris. Mrs. Sartoris, who was Adelaide Kemble, and Hamilton Aïdé, who knew of my immense admiration for Thackeray, wanted to introduce me to him, but I refused. I was too diffident. I was so little, and he was so great. But all that evening I remained as close to him as possible, greedily listening to his words. I remember that during the evening an American came up to him—rather a common sort of man—and claimed acquaintance. Thackeray received him most cordially, and invited him to dinner. I envied that American. And my admiration for Thackeray increased when, as it was getting late, he turned to his two daughters, Minnie and Annie, and said to them, '*Allons, mesdemoiselles, il est temps de s'en aller*,' with the best French accent I have ever heard in an Englishman's mouth.

"Leech was, of course, one of my intimates; my master, I may say, for to some extent my work was modelled on his. I spent the autumn of the year which preceded his death with him at Whitby. He was not very funny, but was kind, amiable, and genial, a delightful man.

"I shall never forget the scene at his funeral. Dean Hole was officiating, and as the first sod fell with a sounding thud on the coffin of our dear, dear friend, Millais, who was standing on the edge of the grave, burst out sobbing. It was as a signal, for, the moment after, each man in that great concourse of mourners was sobbing also. It was a memorable sight."

NOVEL-WRITING—THE PLOT OF "TRILBY" OFFERED TO HENRY JAMES.

Then, going on to speak of his literary work, Du Maurier said, "Nobody more than myself was surprised at the great success of my novels. I never expected anything of the sort. I did not know that I could write. I had no idea that I had had any experiences worth recording. The circumstances under which I came to write are curious. I was walking one evening with Henry James up and down the High Street in Bayswater—I had made James's acquaintance much in the same way as I have made yours. James said that he had great difficulty in finding plots for his stories. 'Plots!' I exclaimed, 'I am full of plots;' and I went on to tell him the plot of 'Trilby.' 'But you ought to write that story,' cried James. 'I can't write,' I said, 'I have never written. If you like the plot so much you may take it.' But James would not take it; he said it was too valuable a present, and that I must write the story myself.

"Well, on reaching home that night I set to work, and by the next morning I had written the first two numbers of 'Peter Ibbetson.' It seemed all to flow from my pen, without effort, in a full stream. But I thought it must be poor stuff, and I determined to look for an omen to learn whether any success would attend this new departure. So I walked out into the garden, and the very first thing that I saw was a large wheelbarrow, and that comforted me and reassured me; for, as you will remember, there is a wheelbarrow in the first chapter of 'Peter Ibbetson.'

"Some time later I was dining with Osgood, and he said, 'I hear, Du Maurier, that you are writing stories,' and asked me to let him see something. So 'Peter Ibbetson' was sent over to America and was accepted at once. Then 'Trilby' followed, and the 'boom' came, a 'boom' which surprised me immensely, for I never took myself *au sérieux* as a novelist. Indeed, this 'boom' rather distresses me when I reflect that Thackeray never had a 'boom.' And I hold that a 'boom' means nothing as a sign of literary excellence, nothing but money."

Du Maurier writes at irregular intervals, and in such moments as he can snatch from his "Punch" work. "For," he says, "I am taking more pains than ever over my drawing." And so saying, he fetched an album in which he showed me the elaborate preparation, in the way of studies and sketches, for a cartoon which was to appear in a week or two in his paper. One figure, from a female model, had been drawn several times. There was here the infinite capacity for taking pains. "I usually write on the top of the piano, standing, and I never look at my manuscript as I write, partly to spare my eyes, and partly because the writing seems literally to flow from my pen. My best time is just after lunch. My writing is frequently interrupted, and I walk about the studio and smoke, and then back to the manuscript once more. Afterwards I revise, very carefully now, for I am taking great pains with my new book. 'The Martians' is to be a very long book, and I cannot say when it will be finished."

A summons from Mrs. du Maurier to the drawing-room, where tea was served, here interrupted the conversation. A comfortable room, with amiable people whom one seemed to recognize. Over the mantel three portraits of Du Maurier's children, by himself. "*Les voilà*," he said, not without pride. Above these a water-color picture of the character of the drawings in "Punch." "It has been hawked round all over America and England," said Du Maurier of this picture, "at exhibitions and places, but nobody would buy it."

A MAN AT HIS BEST AFTER FORTY.

Over the fire in the comfortable room the conversation touched on many things.

DU MAURIER'S "SIGNATURE" AS CARVED, ALONG WITH THE SIGNATURES OF OTHER MEMBERS OF THE "PUNCH" STAFF, ON THE TABLE FROM WHICH THE WEEKLY "PUNCH" DINNER IS EATEN.

"Every book which is worth anything," said Du Maurier, "has had its original life." And again, "I think that the best years in a man's life are after he is forty. So Trollope used to say. Does Daudet say so too? A man at forty has ceased to hunt the moon. I would add that in order to enjoy life after forty, it is perhaps necessary to have achieved, before reaching that age, at least some success." He spoke of the letters he has been receiving since the "boom," and said that on an average he received five letters a day from America, of a most flattering description. "Some of my correspondents, however, don't give a man his 'du,'" he remarked, with a shadow of a smile.

Du Maurier speaks willingly and enthusiastically about literature. He is an ardent admirer of Stevenson, and quoted with gusto the passage in "Kidnapped" where the scene between David Balfour and Cluny is described. "One would have to look at one's guests," he said, "before inviting them, if not precisely satisfied with one's hospitality, to step outside and take their measure. Imagine me proposing such an arrangement to a giant like Val Prinsep."

The day on which he is able to devote most time to writing is Thursday. "*C'est mon grand jour.*" On Wednesdays he is engaged with a model; a female model comes every Friday.

It is characteristic of the man that he should work with such renewed application at his old craft, in spite of the fact that circumstances have thrown wide open to him the gates of a new career.

He reminds one as to physique, and in certain manifestations of a very nervous temperament, of another giant worker, whose name is Émile Zola.

But he is altogether original and himself, a strong and striking individuality, a man altogether deserving of his past and present good fortune.

RECOLLECTIONS OF CAPTAIN WILKIE.

A STORY OF AN OLD OFFENDER.

BY A. CONAN DOYLE.

"WHO can he be?" thought I, as I watched my companion in the second-class carriage of the London and Dover Railway.

I had been so full of the fact that my long-expected holiday had come at last, and that for a few days, at least, the gayeties of Paris were about to supersede the dull routine of the hospital wards, that we were well out of London before I observed that I was not alone in the compartment. In these days we have all pretty well agreed that "three is company and two is none" upon the railway. At the time I write of, however, people were not so morbidly sensitive about their travelling companions. It was rather an agreeable surprise to me to find that there was some chance of whiling away the hours of a tedious journey. I therefore pulled my cap down over my eyes, took a good look from beneath it at my vis-a-vis, and repeated to myself: "Who can he be?"

I used rather to pride myself on being able to spot a man's trade or profession by a good look at his exterior. I had the advantage of studying under a master of the art, who used to electrify both his patients and his clinical classes by long shots, sometimes at the most unlikely of pursuits; and never very far from the mark. "Well, my man," I have heard him say, "I can see by your fingers that you play some musical instrument for your livelihood, but it is a rather curious one; something quite out of my line." The man afterwards informed us that he earned a few coppers by blowing "Rule Britannia" on a coffee-pot, the spout of which was pierced to form a rough flute. Though a novice in the art, I was still able to astonish my ward companions on occasion, and I never lost an opportunity of practising. It was not mere curiosity, then, which led me to lean back on the cushions and analyze the quiet middle-aged man in front of me.

I used to do the thing systematically, and my train of reflections ran somewhat in this wise: "General appearance, vulgar; fairly opulent and extremely self-possessed; looks like a man who could out-chaff a bargee, and yet be at his ease in middle-class society. Eyes well set together and nose rather prominent; would be a good long-range marksman. Cheeks flabby, but the softness of expression redeemed by a square-cut jaw and a well-set lower lip. On the whole, a powerful type. Now for the hands—rather disappointed there. Thought he was a self-made man by the look of him, but there is no callous in the palm and no thickness at the joints. Has never been engaged in any real physical work, I should think. No tanning on the backs of the hands; on the contrary, they are very white, with blue projecting veins and long, delicate fingers. Couldn't be an artist with that face, and yet he has the hands of a man engaged in delicate manipulations. No red acid spots upon his clothes, no ink stains, no nitrate of silver marks upon the hands (this helps to negative my half-formed opinion that he was a photographer). Clothes not worn in any particular part. Coat made of tweed, and fairly old; but the left elbow, as far as I can see it, has as much of the fluff left on as the right, which is seldom the case with men who do much writing. Might be a commercial traveller, but the little pocketbook in the waistcoat is wanting, nor has he any of those handy valises suggestive of samples."

I give these brief headings of my ideas merely to demonstrate my method of arriving at a conclusion. As yet I had obtained nothing but negative results; but now, to use a chemical metaphor, I was in a position to pour off this solution of dissolved possibilities and examine the residue. I found myself reduced to a very limited number of occupations. He was neither a lawyer nor a clergyman, in spite of a soft felt hat, and a somewhat clerical cut about the necktie. I was wavering now between pawnbroker and horsedealer; but there was too much character about his face for the former, and he lacked that extraordinary equine atmosphere which hangs about the latter even in his hours of relaxation; so I formed a provisional diagnosis of betting man of methodistical persuasions, the latter clause being inserted in deference to his hat and necktie.

Pray, do not think that I reasoned it out like this in my own mind. It is only now, sitting down with pen and paper, that I can see the successive steps. As it was, I had formed my conclusion within sixty seconds of the time when I drew my hat down over my eyes and uttered the mental ejaculation with which my narrative begins.

I did not feel quite satisfied even then with my deduction. However, as a leading question would—to pursue my chemical analogy—act as my litmus paper, I determined to try one. There was a "Times" lying by my companion, and I thought the opportunity too good to be neglected.

"Do you mind my looking at your paper?" I asked.

"Certainly, sir, certainly," said he most urbanely, handing it across.

I glanced down its columns until my eye rested upon the list of the latest betting.

"Hullo!" I said, "they are laying odds upon the favorite for the Cambridgeshire. But perhaps," I added, looking up, "you are not interested in these matters?"

"Snares, sir!" said he violently; "wiles of the enemy! Mortals are but given a few years to live; how can they squander them so? They have not even an eye to their poor worldly interests," he added in a quieter tone, "or they would never back a single horse at such short odds with a field of thirty."

There was something in this speech of his which tickled me immensely. I suppose it was the odd way in which he blended religious intolerance with worldly wisdom. I laid the "Times" aside with the conviction that I should be able to spend the next two hours to better purpose than in its perusal.

"You speak as if you understood the matter, at any rate," I remarked.

"Yes, sir," he answered; "few men in England understood these things better in the old days before I changed my profession. But that is all over now."

"Changed your profession?" said I, interrogatively.

"Yes; I changed my name, too."

"Indeed?" said I.

"Yes; you see, a man wants a real fresh start when his r''s become opened, so he has a new deal all round, so to speak. Then he gets a fair chance."

There was a short pause here, as I seemed to be on delicate ground in touching on my companion's antecedents, and he did not volunteer any information. I broke the silence by offering him a cheroot.

"No, thanks," said he; "I have given up tobacco. It was the hardest wrench of all, was that. It does me good to smell the whiff of your weed. Tell me," he added suddenly, looking hard at me with his shrewd gray eyes, "why did you take stock of me so carefully before you spoke?"

"It is a habit of mine," said I. "I am a medical man, and observation is everything in my profession. I had no idea you were looking."

"I can see without looking," he answered. "I thought you were a detective, at first; but I couldn't recall your face at the time I knew the force."

"Were you a detective, then?" said I.

"No," he answered, with a laugh; "I was the other thing—the detected, you know. Old scores are wiped out now, and the law cannot touch me; so I don't mind confessing to a gentleman like yourself what a scoundrel I have been in my time."

"We are none of us perfect," said I.

"No; but I was a real out-and-outer. A 'fake,' you know, to start with, and afterwards a 'cracksman.' It is easy to talk of these things now, for I've changed my spirit. It's as if I was talking of some other man, you see."

"Exactly so," said I. Being a medical man, I had none of that shrinking from crime and criminals which many men possess. I could make all allowances for congenital influence and the force of circumstances. No company, therefore, could have been more acceptable to me than that of the old malefactor; and as I sat puffing at my cigar, I was delighted to observe that my air of interest was gradually loosening his tongue.

"Yes; I'm converted now," he continued, "and of course I am a happier man for that. And yet," he added wistfully, "there are times when I long for the old trade again, and fancy myself strolling out on a cloudy night with my jimmy in my pocket. I left a name behind me in my profession, sir. I was one of the old school, you know. It was very seldom that we bungled a job. We used to begin at the foot of the ladder, the rope ladder, if I may say so, in my younger days, and then work our way up, step by step, so that we were what you might call good men all through."

"I see," said I.

"I was always reckoned a hard-working, conscientious man, and had talent, too; the very cleverest of them allowed that. I began as a blacksmith, and then did a little engineering and carpentering, and then I took to sleight-of-hand tricks, and then to picking pockets. I remember, when I was home on a visit, how my poor old father used to wonder why I was always hovering around him. He little knew that I used to clear everything out of his pockets a dozen times a day, and then replace them, just to keep my hand in. He believes to this day that I am in an office in the City. There are few of them could touch me in that particular line of business, though."

"I suppose it is a matter of practice?" I remarked.

"To a great extent. Still, a man never quite loses it, if he has once been an adept—excuse me; you have dropped some cigar ash on your coat," and he waved his hand politely in front of my breast, as if to brush it off. "There," he said, handing me my gold scarf pin, "you see I have not forgot my old cunning yet."

He had done it so quickly that I hardly saw the hand whisk over my bosom, nor did I feel his fingers touch me, and yet there was the pin glittering in his hand. "It is wonderful," I said as I fixed it again in its place.

"Oh, that's nothing! But I have been in some really smart jobs. I was in the gang that picked the new patent safe. You remember the case. It was guaranteed to resist anything; and we managed to open the first that was ever issued, within a week of its appearance. It was done with graduated wedges, sir, the first so small that you could hardly see it against the light, and the last strong enough to prize it open. It was a clever managed affair."

"I remember it," said I. "But surely some one was convicted for that?"

"Yes, one was nabbed. But he didn't split, nor even let on how it was done. We'd have cut his soul out if—" He suddenly damped down the very ugly fires which were peeping from his eyes. "Perhaps I am boring you, talking about these old wicked days of mine?"

"On the contrary," I said, "you interest me extremely."

"I like to get a listener I can trust. It's a sort of blow-off, you know, and I feel lighter after it. When I am among my brethren I dare hardly think of what has gone before. Now I'll tell you about another job I was in. To this day, I cannot think about it without laughing."

I lit another cigar, and composed myself to listen.

"It was when I was a youngster," said he. "There was a big City man in those days who was known to have a very valuable gold watch. I followed him about for several days before I could get a chance; but when I did get one, you may be sure I did not throw it away. He found, to his disgust, when he got home that day, that there was nothing in his fob. I hurried off with my prize, and got it stowed away in safety, intending to have it melted down next day. Now, it happened that this watch possessed a special value in the owner's eyes because it was a sort of ancestral possession—presented by his father on coming of age, or something of that sort. I remember there was a long inscription on the back. He was determined not to lose it if he could help it, and accordingly he put an advertisement in an evening paper, offering thirty pounds reward for its return, and promising that no questions should be asked. He gave the address of his house, 31 Caroline Square, at the end of the advertisement. The thing sounded good enough, so I set off for Caroline Square, leaving the watch in a parcel at a public house which I passed on the way. When I got there, the gentleman was at dinner; but he came out quick enough when he heard that a young man wanted to see him. I suppose he guessed who the young man would prove to be. He was a genial-looking old fellow, and he led me away with him into his study.

"'Well, my lad,' said he, 'what is it?'

"'I've come about that watch of yours,' said I. 'I think I can lay my hands on it.'

"'Oh, it was you that took it!' said he.

"'No,' I answered; 'I know nothing whatever about how you lost it. I have been sent by another party to see you about it. Even if you have me arrested you will not find out anything.'

"'Well,' he said, 'I don't want to be hard on you. Hand it over, and here is my check for the amount.'

"'Checks won't do,' said I; 'I must have it in gold.'

"'It would take an hour or so to collect in gold,' said he.

"'That will just suit,' I answered, 'for I have not got the watch with me. I'll go back and fetch it, while you raise the money.'

"I started off and got the watch where

I had left it. When I came back, the old gentleman was sitting behind his study table, with the little heap of gold in front of him.

"'Here is your money,' he said, and pushed it over.

"'Here is your watch,' said I.

"He was evidently delighted to get it back; and after examining it carefully, and assuring himself that it was none the worse, he put it into the watch-pocket of his coat with a grunt of satisfaction.

"'Now, my lad,' he said, 'I know it was you that took the watch. Tell me how you did it, and I don't mind giving you an extra five-pound note.'

"'I wouldn't tell you in any case,' said I; 'but especially I wouldn't tell you when you have a witness hid behind that curtain.' You see, I had all my wits about me, and it didn't escape me that the curtain was drawn tighter than it had been before.

"'You are too sharp for us,' said he, good-humoredly. 'Well, you have got your money, and that's an end of it. I'll take precious good care you don't get hold of my watch again in a hurry. Good night—no; not that door,' he added as I marched towards a cupboard. 'This is the door,' and he stood up and opened it. I brushed past him, opened the hall door, and was round the corner of the square in no time. I don't know how long the old gentleman took to find it out, but in passing him at the door, I managed to pick his pocket for the second time, and next morning the family heirloom was in the melting-pot, after all. That wasn't bad, was it?'"

The old war-horse had evidently forgotten all about his conversion now. There was a tone of triumph in the conclusion of his anecdote which showed that his pride in his smartness far surpassed his repentance of his misdeeds. He seemed pleased at the astonishment and amusement I expressed at his adroitness.

"Yes," he continued with a laugh, "it was a capital joke. But sometimes the fun lies all the other way. Even the sharpest of us come to grief at times. There was one rather curious incident which occurred in my career. You may possibly have seen the anecdote, for it got into print at the time."

"Pray let me hear it," said I.

"Well, it is hard lines telling stories against one's self, but this was how it happened: I had made a rather good haul, and invested some of the swag in buying a very fine diamond ring. I thought it would be something to fall back upon when all the ready was gone and times were hard. I had just purchased it, and was going back to my lodgings in the omnibus, when, as luck would have it, a very stylishly-dressed young lady came in and took her seat beside me. I didn't pay much attention to her at first; but after a time something hard in her dress knocked up against my hand, which my experienced touch soon made out to be a purse. It struck me that I could not pass the time more profitably or agreeably than by making this purse my own. I had to do it very carefully; but I managed at last to wriggle my hand into her rather light pocket, and I thought the job was over. Just at this moment she rose abruptly to leave the 'bus, and I had hardly time to get my hand with the purse in it out of her pocket without detection. It was not until she had been gone some time that I found out that in drawing out my hand in that hurried manner the new and ill-fitting ring had slipped over my finger and remained in the young lady's pocket. I sprang out and ran in the direction in which she had gone with the intention of picking her pocket once again. She had disappeared, however; and from that day till this I have never set eyes on her. To make the matter worse, there was only four pence half-penny in coppers inside the purse. Sarve me right for trying to rob such a pretty girl; still, if I had that two hundred quid now I should not be reduced to—Good heavens, forgive me! What am I saying?"

He seemed inclined to relapse into silence after this; but I was determined to draw him out a little more, if I could possibly manage it. "There is less personal risk in the branch you have been talking of," I remarked, "than there is in burglary."

"Ah!" he said, warming to his subject once again, "it is the higher game which is best worth aiming at. Talk about sport, sir, talk about fishing or hunting! Why, it is tame in comparison! Think of the great country house with its men-servants and its dogs and its firearms, and you with only your jimmy and your centre bit, and your mother wit, which is best of all. It is the triumph of intellect over brute force, sir, as represented by bolts and bars."

"People generally look upon it as quite the reverse," I remarked.

"I was never one of those blundering life-preserver fellows," said my companion. "I did try my hand at garroting once;

but it was against my principles, and I gave it up. I have tried everything. I have been a bedridden widow with three young children; but I do object to physical force."

"You have been what?" said I.

"A bedridden widow. Advertising, you know, and getting subscriptions. I have tried them all. You seem interested in these experiences," he continued, "so I will tell you another anecdote. It was the narrowest escape from penal servitude that ever I had in my life. A pal and I had gone down on a country beat—it doesn't signify where it was—and taken up our headquarters in a little provincial town. Somehow it got noised abroad that we were there, and householders were warned to be careful, as suspicious characters had been seen in the neighborhood. We should have changed our plans when we saw the game was up; but my chum was a plucky fellow, and wouldn't consent to back down. Poor little Jim! He was only thirty-four round the chest, and about twelve at the biceps; but there is not a measuring-tape in England could have given the size of his heart. He said we were in for it, and we must stick to it; so I agreed to stay, and we chose Morley Hall, the country house of a certain Colonel Morley, to begin with.

"Now this Colonel Morley was about the last man in the world that we should have meddled with. He was a shrewd, coolheaded fellow, who had knocked about and seen the world, and it seems that he took a special pride in the detection of criminals. However, we knew nothing of all this at that time; so we set forth hopefully to have a try at the house.

"The reason that made us pick him out among the rest was that he had a good-for-nothing groom, who was a tool in our hands. This fellow had drawn up a rough plan of the premises for us. The place was pretty well locked up and guarded, and the only weak point we could see was a certain trap-door, the padlock of which was broken, and which opened from the roof into one of the lumber-rooms. If we could only find any method of reaching the roof, we might force a way securely from above. We both thought the plan rather a good one, and it had a spice of originality about it which pleased us. It is not the mere jewels or plate, you know, that a good cracksman thinks about. The neatness of the job and his reputation for smartness are almost as important in his eyes.

"We had been very quiet for a day or two, just to let suspicion die away. Then we set out one dark night, Jim and I, and got over the avenue railings and up to the house without meeting a soul. It was blowing hard, I remember, and the clouds were hurrying across the sky. We had a good look at the front of the house, and then Jim went round to the garden side. He came running back in a minute or two in a great state of delight. 'Why, Bill,' he said, gripping me by the arm, 'there never was such a bit of luck! They've been repairing the roof or something, and they've left the ladder standing.' We went round together, and there, sure enough, was the ladder towering above our heads, and one or two laborers' hods lying about, which showed that some work had been going on during the day. We had a good look round, to see that everything was quiet, and then we climbed up, Jim first and I after him. We got to the top, and were sitting on the slates, having a bit of a breather before beginning business, when you can fancy our feelings to see the ladder that we came up by suddenly stand straight up in the air, and then slowly descend until it rested in the garden below. At first we hoped it might have slipped, though that was bad enough; but we soon had that idea put out of our heads.

"'Hullo, up there!' cried a voice from below.

"We craned our heads over the edge, and there was a man, dressed, as far as we could make out, in evening dress, and standing in the middle of the grass plot. We kept quiet.

"'Hullo!' he shouted again. 'How do you feel yourself? Pretty comfortable, eh? Ha! ha! You London rogues thought we were green in the country. What's your opinion now?'

"We both lay still, though feeling pretty considerably small, as you may imagine.

"'It's all right; I see you,' he continued. 'Why, I have been waiting behind that lilac bush every night for the last week, expecting to see you. I knew you couldn't resist going up that ladder, when you found the windows were too much for you.—Joe! Joe!'

"'Yes, sir,' said a voice, and another man came from among the bushes.

"'Just you keep your eye on the roof, will you, while I ride down to the station and fetch up a couple of constables?—Au revoir, gentlemen! You don't mind waiting, I suppose?' And Colonel Morley—for it was the owner of the house himself—

strode off; and in a few minutes we heard the rattle of his horse's hoofs going down the avenue.

"Well, sir, we felt precious silly, as you may imagine. It wasn't so much having been nabbed that bothered us, as the feeling of being caught in such a simple trap. We looked at each other in blank disgust, and then, to save our lives, we couldn't help bursting into laughter at our own fix. However, it was no laughing matter; so we set to work going around the roof, and seeing if there was a likely water-pipe or anything that might give us a chance of escape. We had to give it up as a bad job; so we sat down again, and made up our minds to the worst. Suddenly an idea flashed into my head, and I groped my way over the roof until I felt wood under my feet. I bent down and found that the colonel had actually forgotten to secure the padlock! You will often notice, as you go through life, that it is the shrewdest and most cunning man who falls into the most absurd mistakes; and this was an example of it. You may guess that we did not lose much time, for we expected to hear the constables every moment. We dropped through into the lumber-room, slipped downstairs, tore open the library shutters, and were out and away before the astonished groom could make out what had happened. There wasn't time enough to take any little souvenir with us, worse luck. I should have liked to have seen the colonel's face when he came back with the constables and found that the birds were flown."

"Did you ever come across the colonel again?" I asked.

"Yes; we skinned him of every bit of plate he had, down to the salt-spoons, a few years later. It was partly out of revenge, you see, that we did it. It was a very well-managed and daring thing, one of the best I ever saw, and all done in open daylight, too."

"How in the world did you do it?" I asked.

"Well, there were three of us in it—Jim was one—and we set about it in this way: We wanted to begin by getting the colonel out of the way, so I wrote him a note purporting to come from Squire Brotherwick, who lived about ten miles away, and was not always on the best of terms with the master of Morley Hall. I dressed myself up as a groom, and delivered the note myself. It was to the effect that the squire thought he was able to lay his hands on the scoundrels who had escaped from the colonel a couple of years before, and that if the colonel would ride over they would have little difficulty in securing them. I was sure that this would have the desired effect; so, after handing it in, and remarking that I was the squire's groom, I walked off again, as if on the way back to my master's.

"After getting out of sight of the house, I crouched down behind a hedge; and, as I expected, in less than a quarter of an hour the colonel came swinging past me on his chestnut mare. Now, there is another accomplishment I possess which I have not mentioned to you yet, and that is, that I can copy any handwriting that I see. It is a very easy trick to pick up if you only give your mind to it. I happened to have come across one of Colonel Morley's letters some days before, and I can write so that even now I defy an expert to detect a difference between the hands. This was a great assistance to me now, for I tore a leaf out of my pocket-book and wrote something to this effect:

"'As Squire Brotherwick has seen some suspicious characters about, and the house may be attempted again, I have sent down to the bank, and ordered them to send up their bank-cart to convey the whole of the plate to a place of safety. It will save us a good deal of anxiety to know that it is in absolute security. Have it packed up and ready, and give the bearer a glass of beer.'

"Having composed this precious epistle, I addressed it to the butler, and carried it back to the Hall, saying that their master had overtaken me on the way and asked me to deliver it. I was taken in and made much of down-stairs, while a great packing case was dragged into the hall, and the plate stowed away, among cotton-wool and stuffing. It was nearly ready, when I heard the sound of wheels upon the gravel, and sauntered round just in time to see a business-like closed car drive up to the door. One of my pals was sitting very demurely on the box, while Jim, with an official-looking hat, sprang out and bustled into the hall.

"'Now then,' I heard him say, 'look sharp! What's for the bank? Come on!'

"'Wait a minute, sir,' said the butler.

"'Can't wait. There's a panic all over the country, and they are clamoring for us everywhere. Must drive on to Lord Blackbury's place, unless you are ready.'

"'Don't go, sir!' pleaded the butler. 'There's only this one rope to tie. There, it is ready now. You'll look after it, won't you?'

"'That we will. You'll never have any more trouble with it now,' said Jim, helping to push the great case into the car.

"'I think I had better go with you and see it stowed away in the bank,' said the butler.

"'All right,' said Jim, nothing abashed. 'You can't come in the car, though, for Lord Blackbury's box will take up all the spare room. Let's see; it's twelve o'clock now. Well, you be waiting at the bank door at half-past one, and you will just catch us.'

"'All right; half-past one,' said the butler.

"'Good-day,' cried my chum; and away went the car, while I made a bit of a short cut and caught it around a turn of the road. We drove right off into the next county, got a down-train to London, and before midnight the colonel's silver was fused into a solid lump."

I could not help laughing at the versatility of the old scoundrel. "It was a daring game to play," I said.

"It is always the daring game which succeeds best," he answered.

At this point the train began to show symptoms of slowing down, and my companion put on his overcoat and gave other signs of being near the end of his journey.

"You are going on to Dover?" he said.

"Yes."

"For the Continent?"

"Yes."

"How long do you intend to travel?"

"Only for a week or so."

"Well, I must leave you here. You will remember my name, won't you? John Wilkie. I am pleased to have met you. Is my umbrella behind you?" he added, stretching across. "No; I beg your pardon. Here it is in the corner;" and with an affable smile, the ex-cracksman stepped out, bowed, and disappeared among the crowd upon the platform.

I lit another cigar, laughed as I thought of my late companion, and lifted up the "Times," which he had left behind him. The bell had rung, the wheels were already revolving, when, to my astonishment, a pallid face looked in at me through the window. It was so contorted and agitated that I hardly recognized the features which I had been gazing upon during the last couple of hours. "Here, take it," he said, "take it. It's hardly worth my while to rob you of seven pounds four shillings, but I couldn't resist once more trying my hand;" and he flung something into the carriage and disappeared.

It was my old leather purse, with my return ticket, and the whole of my travelling expenses. His newly awakened conscience had driven him to instant restitution.

THE WIND AT SEA.

By Mrs. T. H. Huxley.

I woke in the night with the wailing
    Of voices, now shrill and now deep;
I thought of the ships that were sailing,
    Of mothers and wives who must weep.

I saw the mad ocean let fly
    Its army of waters, and men
Dragged down in their terror to die,
    Far, far away from our ken.

Thousands and thousands of cries
    From ages ago I can hear
In the shrieks of the wind as it flies;
    I shudder and tremble with fear.

Wild Wind! that but late was consenting
    With Death in his dark jubilee,
Sad voiced, you are surely lamenting
    The deeds you have done on the sea?

NAPOLEON AT FONTAINEBLEAU THE EVENING AFTER HIS ABDICATION, APRIL 11, 1814.
François, after Delaroche, 1845.

NAPOLEON BONAPARTE.

BY IDA M. TARBELL.

With engravings from the collection of the Hon. Gardiner G. Hubbard, who also furnishes the explanatory notes.

SIXTH PAPER.—LAST CAMPAIGNS; WATERLOO; ST. HELENA.

THE ADVANCE OF THE ARMY OF TWENTY NATIONS.

IF one draws a triangle, its base stretching along the Nieman from Tilsit to Grodno, its apex on the Elbe, he will have a rough outline of the "army of twenty nations" as it lay in June, 1812. Napoleon, some two hundred and twenty-five thousand men around him, was at Kowno, hesitating to advance, reluctant to believe that Alexander would not make peace.

When he finally moved, it was not with the precision and swiftness which had characterized his former campaigns. When he began to fight it was against new odds. He found that his enemies had been studying the Spanish campaigns, and that they had adopted the tactics which had so nearly ruined his armies in the Peninsula; they refused to give him a general battle, retreating constantly before him; they harassed his separate corps with indecisive contests; they wasted the country as they went. The people aided their soldiers as the Spaniards had done. "Tell us only the moment, and we will set fire to our dwellings," said the peasants.

By the 12th of August Napoleon was at Smolensk, the key of Moscow. At a cost of twelve thousand men killed and wounded, he took the town, only to find, instead of the well-victualled shelter he hoped, a smoking ruin. The French army had suffered frightfully from sickness, from scarcity of supplies, and from useless fighting on the march from the Nieman to Smolensk. They had not had the stimulus of a great victory; they began to feel that this steady retreat of the enemy was only a fatal trap into which they were falling. Every consideration forbade them to march into Russia so late in the year, yet on they went towards Moscow, over ruined fields and through empty villages. This terrible pursuit lasted until September 7th, when the Russians, to content their soldiers, who were complaining loudly because they were not allowed to engage the French, gave battle at Borodino, the battle of the Muskova as the French call it.

THE BATTLE OF BORODINO.

At two o'clock in the morning of this engagement Napoleon issued one of his stirring bulletins:

"Soldiers! Here is the battle which you have so long desired! Henceforth the victory depends upon you; it is necessary for us. It will give you abundance, good winter quarters, and a speedy return to your country! Behave as you did at Austerlitz, at Friedland, at Vitebsk, at Smolensk, and the most remote posterity will quote with pride your conduct on this day; let it say of you: *He was at the great battle under the walls of Moscow.*"

The French gained the battle of Borodino, at a cost of some thirty thousand men, but they did not destroy the Russian army. Although the Russians lost fifty thousand men, they retreated in good order. Under the circumstances, a victory which allowed the enemy to retire in order was of little use. It was Napoleon's fault, the critics said; he was inactive; but it was not sluggishness which troubled Napoleon at Borodino. He had a new enemy—a headache. On the day of the battle he suffered so that he was obliged to retire to a ravine to escape the icy wind. In this sheltered spot he paced up and down all day, giving his orders from the reports brought him, for he could see but a portion of the field.

THE BURNING OF MOSCOW.

Moscow was entered on the 15th of September. Here the French found at last food and shelter, but only for a few hours. That night Moscow burst into flames, set on fire by the authorities, by whom it had been abandoned. It was three days before the fire was arrested. It would cost Russia two hundred years of time, two hundred millions of money, to repair the loss which she had sustained, Napoleon wrote to France.

Suffering, disorganization, pillage, followed the disaster. But Napoleon would not retreat. He hoped to make peace. Moscow was still smoking when he wrote a long description of the conflagration to Alexander. The closing paragraph ran:

"I wage war against your Majesty without animosity; a note from you before or after the last battle would have stopped my march, and I should even have liked to have sacrificed the advantage of entering Moscow. If your Majesty retains some remains of your former sentiments, you will take this letter in good part. At all events, you will thank me for giving you an account of what is passing at Moscow."

RETREAT FROM MOSCOW.

"I will never sign a peace as long as a single foe remains on Russian ground," the Emperor Alexander had said when he heard that Napoleon had crossed the Nieman. He kept his word in spite of all Napoleon's overtures. The French position grew worse from day to day. No food, no fresh supplies; the cold increasing, the army disheartened, the number of Russians around Moscow growing larger. Nothing but a retreat could save the remnant of the French. It began on October 19th, one hundred and fifteen thousand men leaving Moscow. They were followed by forty thousand vehicles loaded with the sick and with what supplies they could get hold of. The route was over the fields devastated a month before. The Cossacks harassed them night and day, and the cruel Russian cold dropped from the skies, cutting them down as a storm of scythes. Before Smolensk was reached, thousands of the retreating army were dead.

Napoleon had ordered that provisions and clothing should be collected at Smolensk. When he reached the city he found that his directions had not been obeyed. The army, exasperated beyond endurance by this disappointment, fell into complete and frightful disorganization, and the rest of the retreat was like the falling back of a conquered mob.

There is no space here for the details of this terrible march and of the frightful passage of the Beresina. The terror of the cold and starvation wrung cries from Napoleon himself.

"Provisions, provisions, provisions," he wrote on November 29th from the right bank of the Beresina. "Without them there is no knowing to what horrors this undisciplined mass will not proceed."

And again: "The army is at its last extremity. It is impossible for it to do anything, even if it were a question of defending Paris."

The army finally reached the Nieman. The last man over was Marshal Ney. "Who are you?" he was asked. "The rear guard of the Grand Army," was the sombre reply of the noble old soldier.

Some forty thousand men crossed the river, but of these there were many who could do nothing but crawl to the hospitals, asking for "the rooms where people die." It was true, as Desprez said, the Grand Army was dead.

A CARICATURE, 1812.

Published in England; printed in English French, and German, and distributed widely on the Continent about the time of the retreat from Russia. This is the only caricature of many I own that has seemed worthy of republication or of a place in my collection. A book entitled "English Caricature, A Satire on Napoleon," was published in London in 1884, containing illustrations.

PASSAGE OF THE BERESINA, NOVEMBER, 1812.

Engraved by Adlard, after Langlois. "The greater part of the army had crossed the river; the camp followers and stragglers remained heedless of the commands of Napoleon to retire, when suddenly the Russian artillery appeared on the hill in the rear, and began firing upon the camp followers. A rush was made for the bridge, and vast numbers were drowned."

NAPOLEON IN 1814.

This portrait has never been published before. It is from a drawing in the collection of Colonel John C. Ropes, of Boston — a study made in 1814 for a snuff-box.

THE MALET CONSPIRACY.

It was on this horrible retreat that Napoleon received word that a curious thing had happened in Paris. A general and an abbé, both political prisoners, had escaped, and actually had succeeded in the preliminaries of a *coup d'état* overturning the empire, and substituting a provisional government.

They had carried out their scheme simply by announcing that Napoleon was dead, and by reading a forged proclamation from the senate to the effect that the imperial government was at an end and a new one begun. The authorities to whom these conspirators had gone had with but little hesitation accepted their orders. They had secured twelve hundred soldiers, had locked up the prefect of police, and had taken possession of the Hôtel de Ville.

The foolhardy enterprise went, of course, only a little way, but far enough to show Paris that the day of easy revolution had not passed, and that an announcement of the death of Napoleon did not bring at once a cry of "Long live the King of Rome!" The news of the Malet conspiracy was an astonishing revelation to Napoleon himself of the instability of French public sentiment. He saw that the support on which he had depended most to insure his institutions, that is, an heir to his throne, was set aside at the word of a worthless agitator. The impression made on his generals by the news was one of consternation and despair. The emperor read in their faces that they believed his

NAPOLEON AND THE POPE IN CONFERENCE AT FONTAINEBLEAU.
Engraved by Robinson, after a painting made in 1836 by Wilkie.

good fortune was waning. He decided to go to Paris as soon as possible.

On December 5th he left the army, and after a perilous journey of twelve days reached the French capital.

EXPLAINING THE RETREAT FROM MOSCOW.

It took as great courage to face France now as it had taken audacity to attempt the invasion of Russia. The grandest army the nation had ever sent out was lying behind him dead. His throne had tottered for an instant in sight of all France. Hereafter he could not believe himself invincible. Already his enemies were suggesting that since his good genius had failed him once, it might again.

No one realized the gravity of the position as Napoleon himself, but he met his household, his ministers, the council of state, the senate, with an imperial self-confidence and a *sang froid* which are awe-inspiring under the circumstances. The horror of the situation of the army was not known in Paris on his arrival, but reports came in daily until the truth was clear to everybody. But Napoleon never lost countenance. The explanations necessary for him to give to the senate, to his allies, and to his friends, had all the serenity and the plausibility of a victor—a victor who had suffered, to be sure, but not through his own rashness or mismanagement. The following quotation from a letter to the King of Denmark illustrates well his public attitude towards the invasion and the retreat from Moscow:

"The enemy were always beaten, and captured neither an eagle nor a gun from my army. On the 7th November the cold became intense; all the roads were found impracticable; thirty thousand horses perished between the 7th and the 16th. A portion of our baggage and artillery wagons was broken and abandoned; our soldiers, little accustomed to such weather, could not endure the cold. They wandered from the ranks in quest of shelter for the night, and, having no cavalry to protect them, several thousands fell into the hands of the enemy's light troops. General Sanson, chief of the topographic corps, was captured by some Cossacks while he was engaged in sketching a position. Other isolated officers shared the same fate. My losses are severe, but the enemy cannot attribute to themselves the honor of having inflicted them. My army has suffered greatly, and suffers still, but this calamity will cease with the cold."

To every one he declared that it was the Russians, not he, who had suffered. It was their great city, not his, which was burnt; their fields, not his, which were devastated. They did not take an eagle, did not win a battle. It was the cold, the Cossacks, which had done the mischief to the Grand Army; and that mischief? Why, it would be soon repaired. "I shall be back on the Nieman in the spring."

But the very man who in public and private calmed and reassured the nation, was sometimes himself so overwhelmed at the thought of the disaster which he had just witnessed, that he let escape a cry which showed that it was only his indomitable will which was carrying him through; that his heart was bleeding. In the midst of a glowing account to the legislative body of his success during the invasion, he suddenly stopped. "In a few nights everything changed. I have suffered great losses. They would have broken my heart if I had been accessible to any other feelings than the interest, the glory, and the future of my people."

PREPARATIONS FOR A NEW CAMPAIGN.

In the teeth of the terrible news coming daily to Paris, Napoleon began preparations for another campaign. To every one he talked of victory as certain. Those who argued against the enterprise he silenced peremptorily. "You should say," he wrote Eugene, "and yourself believe, that in the next campaign I shall drive the Russians back across the Nieman." With the first news of the passage of the Beresina chilling them, the senate voted an army of three hundred and fifty thousand men; the allies were called upon; even the marine was obliged to turn men over to the land force.

But something besides men was necessary. An army means muskets and powder and sabres, clothes and boots and headgear, horses and cannons and caissons; and all these it was necessary to manufacture afresh. The task was gigantic; but before the middle of April it was completed, and the emperor was ready to join his army.

The force against which Napoleon went in 1813 was the most formidable, in many respects, he had ever encountered. Its strength was greater. It included Russia, England, Spain, Prussia, and Sweden, and the allies believed Austria would soon join them. An element of this force more powerful than its numbers was its spirit. The allied armies fought Napoleon in 1813 as they would fight an enemy of freedom. Central Europe had come to feel that further French interference was intolerable. The war had become a crusade. The extent of this feeling is illustrated by an incident in the Prussian army. In the war of 1812 Prussia was an ally of the French, but at the end of the year General Yorck, who commanded a Prussian division, went over to the enemy. It was a dishonorable action from a military point of view, but his explanation that he deserted as "a patriot acting for the welfare of his country" touched Prussia; and though the king disavowed the act, the people applauded it.

Throughout the German states the feeling against Napoleon was bitter. A veritable crusade had been undertaken against him by such men as Stein, and most of the youth of the country were united in the *Tugendbund*, or League of Virtue, which had sworn to take arms for German freedom.

When Alexander followed the French

"Ice."

Engraved by John Jacquet, after Meissonier. In his preparation for this picture, we are told that "Meissonier, dressed in an old coat of the emperor's, and mounted in a saddle on a Norman-top, in the failing snow of a gloomy winter's day, studied himself as a mirror, and therefrom painted in the sombre tints laid by the winter atmosphere on the flush of the face, and the flakes of snow fallen on the cross-sleeve."

THE ABDICATION OF NAPOLEON, SIGNED AT FONTAINEBLEAU, APRIL 11, 1814.

Artist unknown. A very rare and fine proof. The form of the abdication was: "The allied powers having proclaimed that the Emperor Napoleon Bonaparte is the only obstacle to the re-establishment of the peace of Europe, the Emperor Napoleon, faithful to his oath, declares that he renounces, for himself and his heirs, the thrones of France and Italy, and that there is no personal sacrifice, even that of Life, which he is not ready to make for the interests of France. Done at the palace of Fontainebleau, April 11, 1814."

across the Nieman, announcing that he came bringing "deliverance to Europe," and calling on the people to unite against the "common enemy," he found them quick to understand and respond.

Thus, in 1813 Napoleon did not go against kings and armies, but against peoples. No one understood this better than he did himself, and he counselled his allies that it was not against the foreign enemy alone that they had to protect themselves, "There is one more dangerous to be feared—the spirit of revolt and anarchy."

THE CAMPAIGN OF 1813.

The campaign opened May 2, 1813, southwest of Leipsic, with the battle of Lützen. It was Napoleon's victory, though he could not follow it up, as he had no cavalry. The moral effect of Lützen was excellent in the French army. Among the allies there was a return to the old dread of the "monster." By May 8th the French occupied Dresden; from there they crossed the Elbe, and on the 21st fought the battle of Bautzen, another incomplete victory for Napoleon. The next day, in an engagement with the Russian rear guard, Marshal Duroc, one of Napoleon's warmest and oldest friends, was killed. It was the second marshal lost since the campaign began, Bessières having been killed at Lützen.

The French occupied Breslau on June 1st, and three days later an armistice was signed, lasting until August 10th. It was hoped that peace might be concluded during this armistice. At that moment Austria held the key to the situation. The allies saw that they were defeated if they could not persuade her to join them. Napoleon, his old confidence restored by a series of victories, hoped to keep his Austrian father-in-law quiet until he had crushed the Prussians and driven the Russians across the Nieman. Austria saw her power, and determined to use it to regain territory lost in 1805 and 1809, and Metternich came to Dresden to see Napoleon. Austria would keep peace with France, he said, if Napoleon would restore Illyria and the Polish provinces, would send the Pope back to Rome, give up the protectorate of

NAPOLEON BONAPARTE.

the Confederation of the Rhine, restore Naples and Spain. Napoleon's amazement and indignation were boundless.

"How much has England given you for playing this rôle against me, Metternich?" he asked.

A semblance of a congress was held at Prague soon after, but it was only a mockery. Such was the exasperation and suffering of Central Europe that peace could only be reached by large sacrifices on Napoleon's part. These he refused to make. There is no doubt but that France and his allies begged him to compromise; that his wisest counsellors advised him to do so. But he repulsed with irritation all such suggestions. "You bore me continually about the necessity of peace," he wrote Savary. "I know the situation of my empire better than you do; no one is more interested in concluding peace than myself, but I shall not make a dishonourable peace, or one that would see us at war again in six months. . . . These things do not concern you."

By the middle of August the campaign began. The French had in the field some three hundred and sixty thousand men. This force was surrounded by a circle of armies, Swedish, Russian, Prussian, and Austrian, in all some eight hundred thousand men. The leaders of this hostile force included, besides the natural enemies of France, Bernadotte, heir-apparent to the throne of Sweden, who had fought with Napoleon in Italy, and General Moreau, the hero of Hohenlinden. Moreau was on Alexander's staff. He had reached the army the night that the armistice expired, having sailed from the United States on the 21st of June, at the invitation of the Russian emperor, to aid in the campaign against France. He had been greeted by the allies with every mark of distinction. Another deserter on the allies' staff was the eminent military critic Jomini. In the ranks were stragglers from all the French corps, and the Saxons were threatening to leave the French in a body, and go over to the allies.

The second campaign of 1813 opened

NAPOLEON'S RETURN FROM THE ISLAND OF ELBA, MARCH, 1815.

Engraved by George Sanders, after Steuben. Soon after landing in France, Napoleon met a battalion sent from Grenoble to arrest his march. He approached within a few paces of the troop, and throwing up his surtout, exclaimed: "If there be amongst you a soldier who would kill his general, his emperor, let him do it now! Here I am!" The cry "Vive l'Empereur!" burst from every lip. Napoleon threw himself among them, and taking a veteran private, covered with chevrons and medals, by the whiskers, said, "Speak honestly, old moustache; couldst thou have had the heart to kill thy emperor?" The man dropped his ramrod into his piece to show that it was uncharged, and answered, "Judge if I could have done them much harm; all the rest are the same."

BLÜCHER.

Gebhard Leberrecht von Blücher, Prince of Wahlstadt, was born in 1742, and died in 1819. He distinguished himself as a cavalry officer in the wars against the French, and was made major general. In 1813 he was appointed commander-in-chief of the Prussian army, and defeated Marshal Macdonald, and, later, Marshal Marmont. He was made field marshal in 1813, and he led the Prussian army which, sixty thousand strong, invaded France in 1814. On the renewal of the war in 1815 he commanded the Prussian army, was defeated at Ligny, June 16th, but reached Waterloo in time to decide the victory.

brilliantly for Napoleon, for at Dresden he took twenty thousand prisoners, and captured sixty cannon. The victory turned the anxiety of Paris to hopefulness, and their faith in Napoleon's star was further revived by the report that Moreau had fallen, both legs carried off by a French bullet. Moreau himself felt that fate was friendly to the emperor. "That rascal Bonaparte is alway lucky," he wrote his wife, just after the amputation of his legs.

But there was something stronger than luck at work: the allies were animated by a spirit of nationality, indomitable in its force, and they were following a plan which was sure to crush Napoleon in the long run.

It was one laid out by Moreau; a general battle was not to be risked, but the corps of the French were to be engaged one by one, until the parts of the army were disabled. This plan was carried out. In turn Vandamme, Oudinot, Macdonald, Ney, were defeated, and in October the remnants of the French fell back to Leipsic. Here the horde that surrounded them was suddenly enlarged. The Bavarians had gone over to the allies.

The three days' battle of Leipsic exhausted the French, and they were obliged to make a disastrous retreat to the Rhine, which they crossed November 1st. Ten days later the emperor was in Paris.

THE CONDITION OF FRANCE.

The situation of France at the end of 1813 was deplorable. The allies lay on the right bank of the Rhine. The battle of Vittoria had given the Spanish boundary to Wellington, and the English and Spanish armies were on the frontier. The allies which remained with the French were not to be trusted. "All Europe was marching with us a year ago," Napoleon said; "today all Europe is marching against us." There was despair among his generals, alarm in Paris. Besides, there seemed no human means of gathering up a new army. Where were the men to come from? France was bled to death. She could give no more. Her veins were empty.

"This is the truth, the exact truth, and such is the secret and the explanation of all that has since occurred," says Pasquier. "With these successive levies of conscriptions, past, present, and to come, with the Guards of Honor, with the brevet of sub-lieutenant forced on the young men appertaining to the best families, after they had escaped the conscript lot, or had supplied substitutes in conformity with the provisions of the law, there did not remain a single family which was not in anxiety or in mourning."

Yet hedged in as he was by enemies, threatened by anarchy, supported by a fainting people, Napoleon dallied over the peace the allies offered. The terms were not dishonorable. France was to retire, as the other nations, within her natural boundaries, which they designated as the Rhine, the Alps, and the Pyrenees. But the emperor could not believe that Europe, whom he had defeated so often, had power to confine him within such limits. He could not believe that such a peace would be stable, and he began preparations for resistance. Fresh levies of troops were made. The Spanish frontier he attempted to secure by making peace with Ferdinand, recognizing him as king of Spain. He tried to settle his trouble with the Pope.

While he struggled to simplify the situation, to arouse national spirit, and to gather reinforcements, hostile forces multiplied and closed in upon him. The allies crossed the

NAPOLEON THE EVENING BEFORE WATERLOO. (BARLEY.)

Rhine. The *corps législatif* took advantage of his necessity to demand the restoration of certain rights which he had taken from them. In his anger at their audacity, the emperor alienated public sympathy by dissolving the body. "I stood in need of something to console me," he told them, "and you have sought to dishonor me. I was expecting that you would unite in mind and deed to drive out the foreigner; you have bid him come. Indeed, had I lost two battles, it would not have done France any greater evil." To crown his evil day, Murat, Caroline's husband, now king of Naples, abandoned him. This betrayal was the more bitter because his sister herself was the cause of it. Fearful of losing her little glory as queen of Naples, Caroline watched the course of events until she was certain that her brother was lost, and then urged Murat to conclude a peace with England and Austria.

This accumulation of reverses coming upon him as he tried to prepare for battle, drove Napoleon to approach the allies with proposals of peace. It was too late. The idea had taken root that France, with Napoleon at her head, would never remain in her natural limits; that the only hope for Europe was to crush him completely. This hatred of Napoleon had become almost fanatical, and made any terms of peace with him impossible.

CAMPAIGN OF 1814.

By the end of January, 1814, the emperor was ready to renew the struggle. The day before he left Paris he led the empress and the king of Rome to the court of the Tuileries, and presented them to the National Guard. He was leaving them what he held dearest in the world, he told them. The enemy were closing around; they might reach Paris; they might even destroy the city. While he fought without to shield France from this calamity, he prayed them to protect his priceless trust left within. The nobility and sincerity of the feeling that stirred the emperor were unquestionable; tears flowed down the cheeks of the men to whom he spoke, and for a moment every heart was animated by the old emotion, and they took with eagerness the oath he asked.

The next day he left Paris. The army he commanded did not number more than sixty thousand men. He led it against a force which, counting only those who had crossed the Rhine, numbered nearly six hundred thousand.

In the campaign of two months which followed, Napoleon several times defeated the allies. In spite of the terrible disadvantages under which he fought, he nearly drove them from the country. In every way the campaign was worthy of his genius. But the odds against him were too tremendous. The saddest phase of his situa-

"MARENGO," NAPOLEON'S WAR-HORSE, LAST RIDDEN BY HIM AT THE BATTLE OF WATERLOO, AND AFTERWARDS THE PROPERTY OF CAPTAIN HOWARD.

Painted and engraved by James Ward, R. A. The skeleton of "Marengo" is now preserved in the museum of the Royal United Service Institution, London, and stands under the picture painted by Ward from which this engraving is taken. "A head of Marengo, made into a snuff-box, makes its eightly round after dinner at the Queen's Guard in St. James's Palace. In the lid is the legend : 'Hoof of Marengo, barb charger of Napoleon, ridden by him at Marengo, Austerlitz, Jena, Wagram, in the Russian campaign, and finally at Waterloo.' Around the hoof the legend continues : 'Marengo was wounded in the near hip at Waterloo, where his master was on him in the hollow road in advance of the French position. He had been wounded before in many battles.'"

THE DUKE OF WELLINGTON.
Engraved by Forster in 1818, after Gérard, 1814.

tion was that he was not seconded. The people, the generals, the legislative bodies, everybody not under his personal influence seemed paralyzed. Augereau, who was at Lyons, did absolutely nothing, and the following letter to him shows with what energy and indignation Napoleon tried to arouse his stupefied followers.

"NOGENT, 21st *February*, 1814.

". . . What! six hours after having received the first troops coming from Spain you were not in the field! Six hours' repose was sufficient. I wrote the action of Nangis with a brigade of dragoons coming from Spain, which, since it left Bayonne, had not unbridled its horses. The six battalions of the division of Nîmes want clothes, equipment, and drilling, say you. What poor reasons you give me there, Augereau! I have destroyed eighty thousand enemies with conscripts having nothing but knapsacks! The National Guards, say you, are pitiable. I have four thousand here, in round hats, without knapsacks, in wooden shoes, but with good muskets, and I get a great deal out of them. There is no money, you continue; and where do you hope to draw money from? You want wagons; take them wherever you can. You have no magazines; this is too ridiculous. I order you, twelve hours after the reception of this letter, to take the field. If you are still Augereau of Castiglione, keep the command; but if your sixty years weigh upon you, hand over the command to your senior general. The country is in danger, and can be saved by boldness and good-will alone. . . . "NAPOLEON."

The terror and apathy of Paris exasperated him beyond measure. To his great disgust, the court and some of the counsellors had taken to public prayers for his safety. "I see that instead of sustaining the empress," he wrote Cambacérès, "you discourage her. Why do you lose your head like that? What are these *miserere* and these prayers forty hours long at the chapel? Have people in Paris gone mad?"

The most serious concern of Napoleon in this campaign was that the empress and the king of Rome should not be captured. He realized that the allies might reach Paris at any time, and repeatedly he instructed Joseph, who had been appointed lieutenant-general in his absence, what to do if the city was threatened.

"Never allow the empress or the king of Rome to fall into the hands of the enemy. . . . As far as I am concerned, I would rather see my son slain than brought up at Vienna as an Austrian prince; and I have a sufficiently good opinion of the empress to feel persuaded that she thinks in the same way, as far as it is possible for a woman and a mother to do so. I never saw Andromaque represented without pitying Astyanax surviving his family, and without regarding it as a piece of good fortune that he did not survive his father."

Throughout the two months there were negotiations for peace. They varied according to the success or failure of the emperor or the allies. Napoleon had reached a point where he would gladly have accepted the terms offered at the close of 1813. But those were withdrawn. France must come down to her limits in 1789. "What!" cried Napoleon, "leave France smaller than I found her? Never."

The frightful combination of forces closed about him steadily, with the deadly precision of the chamber of torture, whose adjustable walls imperceptibly, but surely, draw together, day by day, until the victim is crushed. On the 30th of March Paris capitulated. The day before, the regent Marie Louise with the king of Rome and her suite had left the city for Blois. The allied sovereigns entered Paris on the 1st

NAPOLEON ARMEEING ON THE "BELLEROPHON," IN THE NIGHT OF JULY 13-14, 1815.

Designed and engraved by Baugean. "The fate of war," said Napoleon, "has brought me to the house of my bitterest foe; but I count on his generosity." And he wrote to the regent of England: "Royal Highness: A prey to the factions which divide my country and to the enmity of the greatest powers of Europe, I have terminated my public career, and I come like Themistocles to seat myself at the hearth of the British people. I place myself under the protection of its laws, which I claim from your Royal Highness as the most powerful, the most constant, and the most generous of my enemies."

NAPOLEON ON BOARD THE "BELLEROPHON."
Engraved by Slavin, after Orchardson.

HOUSE INHABITED BY NAPOLEON AT ST. HELENA BEFORE HE OCCUPIED "LONGWOOD."
From a recent photograph.

of April. As they passed through the streets, they saw multiplying, as they advanced, the white cockades which the *grandes dames* of the Faubourg St. Germain had been making in anticipation of the entrance of the foreigner, and the only cries which greeted them as they passed up the boulevards were, "*Long live the Bourbons! Long live the sovereigns! Long live the Emperor Alexander.*"

NAPOLEON AT FONTAINEBLEAU.

The allies were in Paris, but Napoleon was not crushed. Encamped at Fontainebleau, his army about him, the soldiers everywhere faithful to him, he had still a large chance of victory, and the allies looked with uneasiness to see what move he would make. It was due largely to the wit of Talleyrand that the standing ground which remained to the emperor was undermined. That wily diplomat, whose place it was to have gone with the empress to Blois, had succeeded in getting himself shut into Paris, and, on the entry of the allies, had joined Alexander, whom he had persuaded to announce that the allied powers would not treat with Napoleon nor with any member of his family. This was eliminating the most difficult factor from the problem at the start. By his fine tact Talleyrand brought over the legislative bodies to this view.

From the populace Alexander and Talleyrand feared nothing; it was too exhausted to ask anything but peace. Their most serious difficulty was the army. All over the country the cry of the common soldiers was, "Let us go to the emperor."

"The army," declared Alexander, "is always the army; as long as it is not with you, gentlemen, you can boast of nothing. It is the army which represents the French nation, and if it is not won over, what can you accomplish that will endure?"

Every influence of persuasion, of bribery, of intimidation, was used with soldiers and generals. They were told in phrases which could not but flatter them: "You are the most noble of the children of the country, and you cannot belong to the man who has laid it waste, has delivered it up without arms and defenceless, who has sought to render your name a byword among nations, who would, perhaps, have compromised your glory, if a man who is not even a Frenchman could ever tarnish the honor of your arms and the generosity of our soldiers. You are no longer the soldiers of Napoleon; the senate and all France release you from your oaths."

The older officers on Napoleon's staff at Fontainebleau were unsettled by adroit communications sent from Paris. They were made to believe that they were fighting against the will of the nation and of their comrades. When this disaffection had become serious, one of Napoleon's oldest and most trusted associates, Marment, suddenly deserted. He led the vanguard of the army. This treachery took away the last hope of the imperial cause, and on April 11, 1814, Napoleon signed the act of abdication at Fontainebleau. The act ran:

"The allied powers having proclaimed that the Emperor Napoleon Bonaparte is the only obstacle to the reëstablishment of peace in Europe, the Emperor Napoleon, faithful to his oath, declares that he renounces, for himself and his heirs, the thrones of France and Italy, and that there is no personal sacrifice, even that of his life, which he is not ready to make in the interest of France.
"Done at the Palace of Fontainebleau, 11th April, 1814."

FAREWELL TO THE OLD GUARD.

For only a moment did the gigantic will waver under the shock of defeat, of treachery, and of abandonment. Uncertain of the fate of his wife and child, himself and his family denounced by the allies, his army scattered, he braved everything until Marmont deserted him, and he saw one after another of his trusted officers join his enemies; then for a moment he gave up the fight and tried to end his life. The poison he took had lost its full force, and he recovered from its effects. Even death would have none of him, he groaned.

But this discouragement was brief. No sooner was it decided that his future home should be the island of Elba, and that its affairs should be under his control, than he began to prepare for the journey to his little kingdom with the same energy and zest which had characterized his triumphal journeys as emperor.

It was on the 20th of April that he left the palace of Fontainebleau. As he passed through the court of the *Cheval Blanc* he paused to say farewell to the members of his Guard, some twelve hundred men gathered there.

"Soldiers of the Old Guard [he said], I bid you farewell. For the last twenty years we have trod together the road of honor and glory. Recently, as in the days of prosperity, you have showed yourselves to be models of bravery and fidelity. With men like you our cause was not lost; but war would have been interminable; there would have been civil war, and the misfortunes of France would have been increased. I have, therefore, sacrificed all our interests to those of the country. I leave you. My friends, continue to serve France. Her happiness was my only thought; it will always be the object of my wishes. Do not pity my fate; if I have consented to survive, it is to be useful to your glory. I wish to write the story of the great things which we have done together. Farewell, my children! I would gladly press you all to my heart; let me at least embrace your standard! . . ."

At these words, General Petit, seizing an eagle, advanced. Napoleon received the general in his arms and kissed the

LONGWOOD, NAPOLEON'S HOUSE AT ST. HELENA.

colors. The silence which the scene inspired was broken only by the sobs of the soldiers. Napoleon, making a visible effort to stifle his emotion, continued with a firm voice:

"Farewell, once more, my old comrades! Let this last kiss pass into your hearts!"

NAPOLEON AT ELBA.

A week later, from Frejus, he sent his first address to the inhabitants of Elba:

"Circumstances having induced me to renounce the throne of France, sacrificing my rights to the interests of the country, I reserved for myself the sovereignty of the island of Elba, which has met with the consent of all the powers. I therefore send you General Drouot, so that you may hand over to him the said island, with the military stores and provisions, and the property which belongs to my Imperial domain. Be good enough to make known this new state of affairs to the inhabitants, and the choice which I have made of their Island for my sojourn in consideration of the mildness of their manners and the excellence of their climate. I shall take the greatest interest in their welfare.

"NAPOLEON."

The Elbans received their new ruler with all the pomp which their means and experience permitted. The entire population celebrated his arrival as a *fête*. The new flag which the emperor had chosen—white ground with red bar and three yellow bees—was unfurled, and saluted by the forts of the nation and by the foreign vessels in port. The keys of the chief town of the island were presented to him, a *Te Deum* was celebrated. If these honors seemed poor and contemptible to Napoleon in comparison with the splendor of the *fêtes* to which he had become accustomed, he gave no sign, and played his part with the same seriousness as he had when he received his crown.

His life at Elba was immediately arranged methodically, and he worked as hard and seemingly with as much interest as he had in Paris. The affairs of his new state were his chief concern, and he set about at once to familiarize himself with all their details. He travelled over the island in all directions, to acquaint himself with its resources and needs. At one time he made the circuit of his domain, entering every port, and examining its condition and fortifications. Everywhere that he went he planned and began works which he pushed with energy. Fine roads were laid out; rocks were levelled; a palace and barracks were begun. From his arrival his influence was beneficial. There was a new atmosphere at Elba, the islanders said.

The budget of Elba was administered as rigidly as that of France had been, and the little army was drilled with as great care as the Guards themselves. After the daily review of his troops, he rode on horseback, and this promenade became a species of reception, the islanders who wanted to consult him stopping him on his route. It is said that he invariably listened to their appeals.

Elba was enlivened constantly during Napoleon's residence by tourists who went out of their way to see him. The major-

LONGWOOD: ANOTHER VIEW.
From a recent photograph.

NAPOLEON'S LAST DAY.
From a sculpture by Vela, in the Versailles Museum.

ity of these curious persons were Englishmen; with many of them he talked freely, receiving them at his house, and letting them carry off bits of stone or of brick from the premises as souvenirs.

His stay was made more tolerable by the arrival of Madame *mère* and of the Princess Pauline and the coming of twenty-six members of the National Guard who had crossed France to join him. But his great desire that Marie Louise and the king of Rome should come to him was never gratified. It is told by one of his companions on the island, that he kept carefully throughout his stay a stock of fireworks which had fallen into his possession, planning to use them when his wife and boy should arrive, but, sadly enough, he never had an occasion to celebrate that event.

FROM ELBA TO PARIS.

While to all appearances engrossed with the little affairs of Elba, Napoleon was in fact planning the most dramatic act of his life. On the 26th of February, 1815, the guard received an order to leave the island. With a force of eleven hundred men the emperor passed the foreign ships guarding Elba, and on the afternoon of the 1st of March landed at Cannes on the Gulf of Juan. At eleven o'clock that night he started towards Paris. He was trusting himself to the people and the army. If there never was an example of such audacious confidence, certainly there never was such a response. The people of the South received him joyfully, offering to sound the tocsin and follow him *en masse*. But Napoleon refused; it was the soldiers upon whom he called.

"We have not been conquered [he told the army]. Come and range yourselves under the standard of your chief; his existence is composed of yours; his interests, his honor, and his glory are yours. Victory will march at double-quick time. The eagle with the national colors will fly from steeple to steeple to the towers of Notre Dame. Then you will be able to show your scars with honor; then you will be able to boast of what you have done; you will be the liberators of the country. . . ."

At Grenoble there was a show of resistance. Napoleon went directly to the soldiers, followed by his guard.

"Here I am; you know me. If there is a soldier among you who wishes to kill his emperor, let him do it."

"Long live the emperor!" was the answer; and in a twinkle the six thousand men had torn off their white cockades and replaced them by old and soiled tricolors. They drew them from the inside of their caps, where they had been concealing them since the exile of their hero. "It is the same that I wore at Austerlitz," said one as he passed the emperor. "This," said another, "I had at Marengo."

From Grenoble the emperor marched to Lyons, where the soldiers and officers went over to him in regiments. The royalist leaders who had deigned to go to Lyons to exhort the army found themselves ignored; and Ney, who had been ordered from Besançon to stop the emperor's advance, and who started out promising to "bring back Napoleon in an iron cage," surrendered his entire division. It was impossible to resist the force of popular opinion, he said.

From Lyons the emperor, at the head of what was now the French army, passed by Dijon, Autun, Avallon, and Auxerre to Fontainebleau, which he reached on March 19th. The same day Louis XVIII. fled from Paris.

The change of sentiment in these few days was well illustrated in a French paper which, after Napoleon's return, published the following calendar gathered from the royalist press.

February 25.—"The *exterminator* has signed a treaty offensive and defensive. It is not known with whom.

February 26.—"The *Corsican* has left the island of Elba.

March 1.—"*Bonaparte* has debarked at Cannes with eleven hundred men.

DEATH MASK OF NAPOLEON, MADE BY DR. ANTOMMARCHI AT ST. HELENA, 1821.

Calamatta, 1834. Calamatta produced the mask from the cast taken by Dr. Antommarchi, the physician of Napoleon at St. Helena, in 1834, grouping around it portraits (chiefly from Ingrés's drawings) of Madame Dudevant and others.

March 7.—"*General Bonaparte* has taken possession of Grenoble.

March 10.—"*Napoleon* has entered Lyons.

March 19.—*The emperor* reached Fontainebleau to-day.

March 19.—"*His Imperial Majesty* is expected at the Tuileries to-morrow, the anniversary of the birth of the king of Rome."

Two days before the flight of the Bourbons, the following notice appeared on the door of the Tuileries:

"*The emperor begs the king to send him no more soldiers; he has enough.*"

WATERLOO.

"What was the happiest period of your life as emperor?" O'Meara asked Napoleon once at St. Helena.

"The march from Cannes to Paris," he replied immediately.

His happiness was short-lived. The overpowering enthusiasm which had made that march possible could not endure. The bewildered factions which had been silenced or driven out by Napoleon's reappearance recovered from their stupor. The royalists, exasperated by their own Louise had succumbed to foreign influences and had promised never again to see her husband.

If the allies had allowed the French to manage their affairs in their own way, it is probable that Napoleon would have mastered the situation, difficult as it was. But this they did not do. In spite of his promise to observe the treaties made after his abdication, to accept the boundaries fixed, to abide by the Congress of Vienna, the coalition treated him with scorn, affecting to mistrust him. He was the disturber of the peace of the world, a public enemy; he must be put beyond the pale of society,

NAPOLEON AS HE LAY IN DEATH. ["NAPOLEON UT IN MORTE ORCUBUIT."]
Dedicated, "with permission, to the Countess Bertrand, by her obliged and most obedient servant, William Rubidge. Taken at St. Helena in presence of Countess Bertrand, Count Montholon, etc." Engraved by H. Meyer, London, after W. Rubidge, and published August, 1821.

flight, reorganized, and the Vendée was soon in arms. Strong opposition developed among the liberals. It was only a short time before a reaction followed the delirium which Napoleon's return had caused in the nation. Disaffection, coldness, and plots succeeded. In face of this revulsion of feeling, the emperor himself underwent a change. The buoyant courage, the amazing audacity which had induced him to return from Elba, seemed to leave him. He became sad and preoccupied. No doubt much of this sadness was due to the refusal of Austria to restore his wife and child, and to the bitter knowledge that Marie and they took up arms, not against France, but against Napoleon. France, as it appeared, was not to be allowed to choose her own rulers.

The position in which Napoleon found himself on the declaration of war was one of exceeding difficulty, but he mastered the opposition with all his old genius and resources. Three months after the landing at Cannes he had an army of two hundred thousand men ready to march. He led it against at least five hundred thousand men.

On June 15th, Napoleon's army met a portion of the enemy in Belgium, near

NAPOLEON BONAPARTE.

Brussels, and on June 16th, 17th, and 18th were fought the battles of Ligny, Quatre Bras, and Waterloo, in the last of which he was completely defeated. The limits and nature of this sketch do not permit a description of the engagement at Waterloo. The literature on the subject is perhaps richer than that on any other subject in military science. Thousands of books discuss the battle, and each succeeding generation takes it up as if nothing had been written on it. But while Waterloo cannot be discussed here, it is not out of place to notice that among the reasons for its loss are certain ones which interest us because they are personal to Napoleon. He whose great rule in war was "time is everything," lost time at Waterloo. He who had looked after everything which he wanted well done, neglected to assure himself of such an important matter as the exact position of a portion of his enemy. He who once had been able to go a week without sleep, was ill. Again, if one will compare carefully the Bonaparte of Guérin (see MCCLURE'S for November, page 473) with the Napoleon of Lefevre (March, page 325), he will understand, at least partially, why the battle of Waterloo was lost.

The defeat was complete; and when the emperor saw it, he threw himself into the battle in search of death. As eagerly as he had sought victory at Rivoli, Marengo, Austerlitz, he sought death at Waterloo. "I ought to have died at Waterloo," he said afterwards; "but the misfortune is that when a man seeks death most he cannot find it. Men were killed around me, before, behind—everywhere. But there was no bullet for me."

He returned immediately to Paris. There was still force for resistance in France. There were many to urge him to return to the struggle, but such was the condition of public sentiment that he refused. The country was divided in its al-

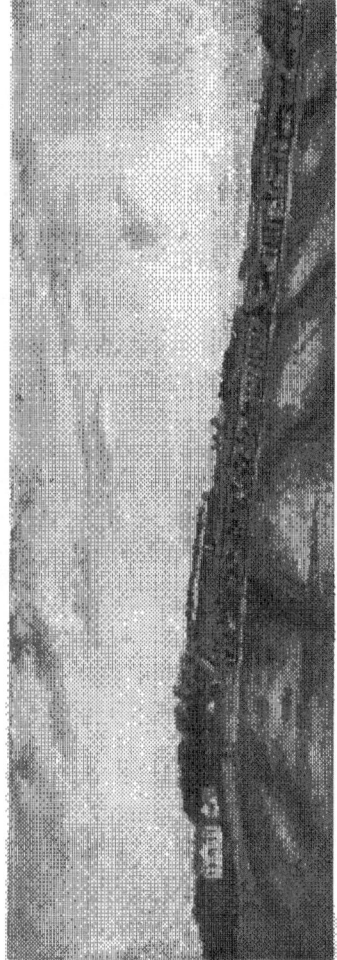

FUNERAL PROCESSION OF NAPOLEON.

Drawn by Captain Marryat. "As the procession proceeded from old Longwood along the edge of Rupert's Valley, the troops stood drawn up with arms reversed, and after it had passed, followed up in the rear."

legiance to him; the legislative body was frightened and quarrelling; Talleyrand and Fouché were plotting. Besides, the allies proclaimed to the nation that it was against Napoleon alone that they waged war. Under these circumstances Napoleon felt that loyalty to the best interest of France required his abdication, and he signed the act anew, proclaiming his son emperor under the title of Napoleon II.

SURRENDER TO THE ENGLISH.

Leaving Paris, the fallen emperor went to Malmaison, where Josephine had died only thirteen months before. A few friends joined him—Queen Hortense, the Duc de Rovigo, Bertrand, Las Cases, and Méneval. He remained there only a few days. The allies were approaching Paris, and the environs were in danger. Napoleon offered his services to the provisional government, which had taken his place, as leader in the campaign against the invader, promising to retire as soon as the enemy was repulsed, but he was refused. The government feared Napoleon, in fact, more than it did the allies, and urged him to leave France as quickly as possible.

On June 29th, a week after his return to Paris from Waterloo, he left Malmaison for Rochefort. His desire was to go to the United States, but the coast was so guarded by the English that there was no escape. Two courses were open—to call upon the country and renew the conflict, or seek an asylum in England. He resolved at last to give himself up to the English, and sent the following note to the regent :

"ROYAL HIGHNESS: Exposed to the factions which divide my country and to the hostility of the greatest powers of Europe, I have closed my political career. I come, like Themistocles, to seek the hospitality of the British nation. I place myself under the protection of their laws, which I claim from your Royal Highness as the most powerful, the most constant, and the most generous of my enemies.
"NAPOLEON."

ENGLISH HOSPITALITY.

On the 15th of July he embarked on the English ship, the "Bellerophon," and a week later he was at Plymouth.

Napoleon's surrender to the English was made with full confidence in their hospitality; but the "Bellerophon" was no sooner in the harbor of Plymouth than it became evident that he was regarded not as a guest, but as a prisoner. Armed vessels surrounded the ship he was on; extraordinary messages were hurried to and fro; sinister rumors ran among the crew. The Tower of London, a desert isle, the ends of the earth, were talked of as the hospitality England was preparing.

The British government no sooner realized that it had its hands on Napoleon than it was seized with a species of panic.

A VIEW GIVING A GLIMPSE, IN THE CENTER, OF NAPOLEON'S TOMB AT ST. HELENA.

From a recent photograph.

All sense of dignity, all notions of generosity, all feelings of hospitality, were drowned in hysterical resentment. The English people as a whole did not share the government's terror. The general feeling seems to have been similar to that which Charles Lamb expressed to Southey: "After all, Bonaparte is a fine fellow, as my barber says, and I should not mind standing bare-headed at his table to do

THE TOMB OF NAPOLEON AT ST. HELENA.

Engraved by Sutherland, after Captain Marryat. Napoleon "was interred, according to his own request, under some willow trees, near a spring to which he had been accustomed to send daily for the water used at his table."

But the government could see nothing but menace in keeping such a force as Napoleon within its limits. It evidently took Lamb's whimsical suggestion, that if Napoleon were at Hampton the people might some day eject the Brunswick in his favor, in profound seriousness. On July 30th, it sent a communication to *General Bonaparte*—the English henceforth refused him the title of emperor, though permitting him that of general, not reflecting probably that if one was spurious the other was, since both had been conferred by the same authority—notifying him that as it was necessary that he should not be allowed to disturb the repose of England any longer, the British government had chosen the island of St. Helena as his future residence, and that three persons with a surgeon would be allowed to accompany him. A week later he was transferred from the "Bellerophon" to the "Northumberland," and was *en route* for St. Helena, where he arrived in October, 1815.

The manner in which the British carried out their decision was irritating and unworthy. They seemed to feel that guarding a prisoner meant humiliating him, and offensive and unnecessary restrictions were made which wounded and enraged Napoleon.

EFFECT OF EXILE ON NAPOLEON.

The effect of this treatment on Napoleon's character is one of the most interesting studies in connection with the man, and, on the whole, it leaves one with increased respect and admiration for him. He received the announcement of his exile in indignation. He was not a prisoner, he was the guest of England, he said. It was an outrage against the laws of hospitality to send him into exile, and he would never submit voluntarily. When he became convinced that the British were inflexible in their decision, he

NAPOLEON'S TOMB AT ST. HELENA.
From a recent photograph

thought of suicide, and even discussed it with Las Cases. It was the most convenient solution of his dilemma. It would injure no one, and his friends would not be forced then to leave their families. It was the easier because he had no scruples which opposed it. The idea was finally given up. A man ought to live out his destiny, he said, and he decided that his should be fulfilled.

The most serious concern Napoleon felt in facing his new life was that he would have no occupation. He saw at once that St. Helena would not be an Elba. But he resolutely made occupations. He sought conversation, studied English, played games, began to dictate his memoirs. It is to this admirable determination to find something to do that we owe his clear, logical commentaries, his essays on Cæsar, Turenne, and Frederick, his sketch of the Republic, and the vast amount of information in the journals of his devoted comrades, O'Meara, Las Cases, Montholon.

But no amount of forced occupation could hide the desolation of his position. The island of St. Helena is a mass of jagged, gloomy rocks; the nearest land is six hundred miles away. Isolated and inaccessible as it is, the English placed Napoleon on its most sombre and remote part—a place called Longwood, at the summit of a mountain, and to the windward. The houses at Longwood were damp and unhealthy. There was no shade. Water had to be carried some three miles.

The governor, Sir Hudson Lowe, was a tactless man, with a propensity for bullying those whom he ruled. He was haunted by the idea that Napoleon was trying to escape, and he adopted a policy which was more like that of a jailer than of an officer. In his first interview with the emperor he so antagonized him that Napoleon soon refused to see him. Napoleon's antipathy was almost superstitious. "I never saw such a horrid countenance," he told O'Meara. "He sat on a chair opposite to my sofa, and on the little table between us there was a cup of coffee. His physiognomy made such an unfavorable impression upon me that I thought his evil eye had poisoned the coffee, and I ordered Marchand to throw it out of the window. I could not have swallowed it for the world."

Aggravated by Napoleon's refusal to see him, Sir Hudson Lowe became more annoying and petty in his regulations. All free communication between Longwood and the inhabitants of the island was cut off. The newspapers sent Napoleon were mutilated; certain books were refused; his letters were opened. A bust of his son brought to the island by a sailor was withheld for weeks. There was incessant haggling over the expenses of his establishment. His friends were subjected to constant annoyance. All news of Marie Louise and of his son was kept from him.

It is scarcely to be wondered at that Napoleon was often peevish and obstinate under this treatment, or that frequently, when he allowed himself to discuss the governor's policy with the members of his suite, his temper rose, as Montholon said, "to thirty-six degrees of fury." His situation was made more miserable by his ill-health. His promenades were so guarded by sentinels and restricted to such limits that he finally refused to take exercise, and after that his disease made rapid marches.

DEATH IN MAY, 1821.

Before the end of 1820 it was certain that he could not live long. In December of that year the death of his sister Eliza was announced to him. "You see, Eliza has just shown me the way. Death, which had forgotten my family, has begun to strike it. My turn cannot be far off." Nor was it. On May 5, 1821, he died.

His preparations for death were like him—methodical. During the last fortnight of April all his strength was spent in dictating to Montholon his last wishes. He even dictated, ten days before the end, the note which he wished sent to Sir Hudson Lowe to announce his death. The articles he had in his possession at Longwood he had wrapped up and ticketed with the names of the persons to whom he wished to leave them. His will remembered numbers of those whom he had loved or who had served him. Even the Chinese laborers he had employed about the place were remembered. "Do not let them be forgotten. Let them have a few score of napoleons."

The will included a final word on certain questions on which he felt posterity ought distinctly to understand his position. He died, he said, in the apostolical Roman religion. He declared that he had always been pleased with Marie Louise, whom he besought to watch over his son. To this son, whose name recurs repeatedly in the will, he gave a motto—*All for the French people*. He died prematurely, he said, assassinated by the English oligarchy. The unfortunate results of the invasion of France he attributed to the treason of Marmont, Augereau, Talleyrand, and Lafayette. He defended the death of the Duc d'Enghien. "Under similar circumstance I should act in the same way." This will is sufficient evidence that he died as he had lived, courageously and proudly, and inspired by a profound conviction of the justice of his own cause. In 1822 the French courts, though, declared it void.

They buried him in a valley beside a spring he loved, and though no monument but a willow marked the spot, perhaps no other grave in history is so well known. Certainly the magnificent mausoleum which marks his present resting place in Paris has never touched the imagination and the heart as did the humble willow-shaded mound in St. Helena.

NAPOLEON'S CHARACTER.

The peace of the world was insured. Napoleon was dead. But though the echo of his deeds was so loud and so majestic in the ears of France and England that they tried every device to turn it into discord or to drown it by another and a newer sound, the ignoble attempt was never entirely successful, and the day will come when personal and partisan considerations will cease to influence judgments on this mighty man. For he was a mighty man. One may be convinced that the fundamental principles of his life were despotic; that he used the noble ideas of personal liberty, of equality, and of fraternity as a tyrant; that the whole tendency of his civil and military system was to concentrate power in a single pair of hands, never to distribute it where it belongs, among the people; one may feel that he frequently sacrificed personal dignity to a theatrical desire to impose on the crowd as a hero of classic proportions, a god from Olympus; one may groan over the blood he spilt. But he cannot refuse to acknowledge that no man ever comprehended more clearly the splendid science of war; he cannot fail to bow to the genius which conceived and executed the Italian campaign, which fought the classic battles of Austerlitz, Jena, and Wagram. These deeds are great epics. They move in noble, measured lines, and stir us by their might and perfection. It is only a genius of the most magnificent order which could handle men and materials as Napoleon did.

He is even more imposing as a statesman. When one confronts the France of 1799, corrupt, crushed, hopeless, false to the great ideas she had wasted herself for, and watches Napoleon firmly and steadily bring order into this chaos, give the country work and bread, build up her broken walls and homes, put money into her pocket and restore her credit, bind up her wounds and call back her scattered children, set her again to painting pictures and reading books, to smiling and singing, he has a Napoleon greater than the warrior.

Nor were these civil deeds transient. France to-day is largely what Napoleon made her, and the most liberal institutions of continental Europe bear his impress. It is only a mind of noble proportions which can grasp the needs of a people, and a hand of mighty force which can supply them.

But he was greater as a man than as a warrior or statesman; greater in that rare and subtile personal quality which made men love him. Men went down on their knees and wept at sight of him when he came home from Elba—rough men whose hearts were untrained, and who loved naturally and spontaneously the thing which was lovable. It was only selfish, warped, abnormal natures, which had been stifled by etiquette and diplomacy and self-interest, who abandoned him. Where nature lived in a heart, Napoleon's sway was absolute. It was not strange. He was in everything a natural man: his imagination, his will, his intellect, his heart were native, untrained. They appealed to unworldly men in all their rude, often brutal, strength and sweetness. If they awed them, they won them.

This native force of Napoleon explains, at least partially, his hold on men; it explains, too, the contrasts of his character. Never was there a life lived so full of lights and shades, of majors and minors. It was a kaleidoscope, changing at every moment. Beside the most practical and commonplace qualities are the most idealistic. No man ever did more drudgery, ever followed details more slavishly; yet who ever dared so divinely, ever played such hazardous games of chance? No man ever planned more for his fellows, yet who ever broke so many hearts? No man ever made practical realities of so many of liberty's dreams, yet it was by despotism that he swept away feudal abuses and gave liberal and beneficent laws. No man was more gentle, none more severe. Never was there a more chivalrous lover until he was disillusioned;

a more affectionate husband even when faith had left him; yet no man ever trampled more rudely on womanly delicacy and reserve.

He was valorous as a god in danger, loved it, played with it; yet he would turn pale at a broken mirror, cross himself if he stumbled, fancy the coffee poisoned at which an enemy had looked.

He was the greatest genius of his time, perhaps of all time, yet he lacked the crown of greatness—that high wisdom born of reflection and introspection which knows its own powers and limitations, and never abuses them; that fine sense of proportion which holds the rights of others in the same solemn reverence which it demands for its own.

THE END.

Note.—With this paper the sketch of the life of Napoleon properly ends, though there are two papers yet to follow; one in the May number, on "The Second Funeral of Napoleon, in 1840," and one in the June number, on "Napoleon and America." In concluding the sketch, I want to acknowledge my indebtedness to the librarians of the Congressional Library, at Washington, D. C. These gentlemen labor at present under the greatest disadvantages, owing to the overcrowded condition of their rooms; nevertheless the student is served with an intelligence and good will for which I, at least, cannot be too grateful. My sincerest thanks are due also to Mr. Gardiner G. Hubbard, whose advice and suggestions have been invaluable.—I. M. T.

THE LIFE OF NAPOLEON
By MISS IDA M. TARBELL,

which has been running in this magazine, will be published complete in Number One of McCLURE'S QUARTERLY, and will be ready in April. The volume will contain all of the articles, with much important additional matter, and many new pictures.

THE TEXT. Miss Tarbell has proved herself to be a brilliant historical writer. She has made skilful use of memoirs, letters and papers recently made accessible by the investigations of the best foreign Napoleon students. She has told Napoleon's wonderful career as it has not been told before in popular form, and she has given pictures of his personal life, habits, methods of work and thought, that are masterly in simplicity and vividness.

THE PICTURES. There are over 200 illustrations from the works of the most eminent painters, sculptors and engravers of the century, including practically all of the masterpieces of art relating to Napoleon, his family and his military and political achievements. In illustrating this volume the publishers have supplemented the splendid set of Napoleon engravings generously placed at their service by the Hon. Gardiner G. Hubbard, with many new pictures from the State collections of France, the private galleries of the Bonaparte princes, and other collections no less notable.

THE NAPOLEON QUARTERLY forms a pictorial biography that cannot possibly be surpassed, for the publishers have had the unusual privilege of access to the great Napoleon collections of the world, and have therefore been able to select the most authentic, the most interesting, and the most beautiful Napoleon pictures that were made in Napoleon's lifetime or have been made since.

The book will be printed on specially made enamelled paper with wide margins and bound in paper covers of handsome design. It will be sold everywhere for fifty cents a copy.

THE POLLOCK DIAMOND ROBBERY.

STORIES FROM THE ARCHIVES OF THE PINKERTON DETECTIVE AGENCY.

BY CLEVELAND MOFFETT.

ON a Friday night, November 4, 1892, with thirteen men in the smoker, a train on the Sioux City and Pacific Railroad drew out of Omaha at six o'clock, and started on its eastward run. Among these thirteen, sitting about half way down the aisle, enjoying a good cigar, was Mr. W. G. Pollock of New York, a travelling salesman for W. L. Pollock & Co., of the same city, one of the largest diamond firms in America. In the inside pocket of his vest he carried fifteen thousand dollars' worth of uncut diamonds, while a leather satchel on the seat beside him contained a quantity of valuable stones in settings.

On the front seat of the car, just behind the stove, sat a stolid-looking young man, who would have passed for a farmer's lad. He seemed scarcely over twenty, having neither beard nor mustache, and a stranger would have put him down as a rather stupid, inoffensive fellow. Compared with Mr. Pollock he was slighter in build, although an inch or so taller. As he sat there staring at the stove, the passenger in the seat behind him, J. H. Shaw, an Omaha well-digger, a bluff, hearty man of social instincts, tried to draw him into conversation; but the young fellow only shook his head sulkily, and the well-digger relapsed into silence. Presently, as the train was approaching California Junction, the young man on the front seat rose and started down the aisle. Curiously enough, he now wore a full beard of black hair five or six inches long. No one paid any attention to him until he stopped at Mr. Pollock's seat, drew a revolver, and said loud enough for everyone in the car to hear him:

"Give me them diamonds."

Then, without waiting for a reply, he shifted the revolver to his left hand, drew a slungshot from his coat-pocket, and struck Mr. Pollock with it over the head such a heavy blow that the bag burst, and the shot rolled upon the floor. Then he said again: "Give me them diamonds."

Realizing that the situation was desperate, Mr. Pollock took out his pocket-book and handed it to his assailant, saying: "I have only a hundred dollars; here it is."

Pushing back the pocket-book as if unworthy of his attention, the man aimed his revolver coolly at Mr. Pollock's right shoulder and fired. Then he aimed at the left shoulder and fired. Both bullets hit; and were followed by two more, which went whizzing by the diamond merchant's head on either side, missing him, perhaps by accident, but probably by design, as the men were not three feet apart.

By this, the other people in the car had disappeared under the seats like rats into their holes. To all intents and purposes Mr. Pollock was alone with his assailant. The latter evidently knew where the diamonds were secreted, for, ripping open his victim's vest, he drew out the leather wallet in which they were enclosed, and stuffed it into his pocket. Wounded though he was, Mr. Pollock now grappled with the thief, who, using the butt of his revolver as a weapon, brought down fearful blows on Pollock's head. The latter, however, was game to the end, and, getting into the aisle, fought the robber up and down the car, until a crushing blow at last laid Mr. Pollock senseless on the floor.

With perfect self-possession and without hurry the thief walked back down the aisle to Mr. Pollock's seat, and took one of the two leather bags lying there, by mistake choosing, though, the one that did not contain the mounted diamonds. Then he went to the end of the car, pulled the bell-rope, and, as the train began to slacken its speed in response to this signal, jumped off the steps, rolled down a bank fifteen feet high, and disappeared.

Sharing apparently in the general consternation and terror inspired by the young fellow, the conductor, instead of holding the train to pursue the thief, signalled the engineer to go ahead, and no effort was made for a capture until the train reached California Junction, several miles farther on. Meanwhile the panic-stricken passengers recovered at their leisure their composure and their seats. Had but one of his fellow-travellers gone to the assistance of Mr. Pollock, the robber might easily have been overpowered. As it was, he all but murdered his man, plundered him of his diamonds, and escaped without the slightest interference. When his pistol was picked up, near the spot where he left the train, it was found that in the struggle the cylinder had caught, so that it would have been impossible to discharge the two chambers remaining loaded. Thus eleven able-bodied men were held in a state of abject terror by one slender lad, who at the last was practically unarmed.

At California Junction the wounded diamond merchant was carried from the train, and taken back to Omaha that same night. Mr. Pollock being a member of the Jewelers' Protective Union, a rich and powerful organization, established some years ago for the protection of jewelry salesmen against thieves, was entitled to its aid. The association keeps the Pinkerton Agency constantly retained for its service. And here it is worthy of note that there never has been a salesman robbed during the twelve years the association has been in existence that the stolen property has not been recovered and the thief sent to prison. One of the strictest rules of the association is to compromise or compound with a thief under no circumstances, but prosecute to the end. In this instance the case was immediately reported to Mr. William A. Pinkerton, at Chicago, with instructions to secure the robber and bring him to justice, no matter what the cost might be.

When the Pinkerton men reached the scene of the robbery, the robber had vanished as completely as if he had been whisked off to another planet. To be sure, farmers in the neighborhood brought rumors of the stealing of horses, of a strange man sleeping in the woods, and of a desperate-looking character seen limping along the road. But all this came to nothing, except to establish, what seemed probable, that the diamond thief had fled back to Omaha. A patient and exhaustive search in Omaha resulted in nothing. The man was gone, and the diamonds were gone; that was all anybody knew.

What made the case more difficult was the uncertainty as to the robber's personal appearance; for some of the passengers testified to one thing, and some to another. The black beard was a cause of confusion; only one witness besides Mr. Pollock remembered that the man wore such a beard. Mr. Pollock, however, was positive as to this particular, and it seemed as if he ought to know. It was also impossible to decide, from conflicting statements, whether the robber had a mustache or not, and whether it was dark or light in color. The fact is, the passengers had been so thoroughly frightened at the time of the assault that the credibility of their testimony was much to be questioned,

Mr. Pollock reported that for several weeks previous to the robbery he had suspected that he was being followed. He also reported that on the day of the robbery he had been in the shop of Sonnenberg, the largest pawnbroker in Omaha, and that while he was there two noted Western gamblers had entered the shop and been presented to him by Sonnenberg as possible customers. He had made a trade of some diamonds with one of the men, and in the course of the negotiations had shown his entire stock. While the trade was in progress a negro on the premises had noticed, lounging about the front of the shop, a man in a slouch hat, who suggested the robber. From these circumstances it was decided that the robbery might be the work of an organized gang, who had been waiting their opportunity for many days, and had selected one of their number to do the actual deed.

All his life it had been Mr. Pinkerton's business to study criminals and understand their natures. He knew that a crime like this one was as much beyond the power of an ordinary criminal as the strength of Sandow is beyond that of the ordinary man. Let a robber be ever so greedy of gold, reckless of human life, and indifferent to consequences, he would still think many times before declaring war to the death upon twelve men in a narrow car, on a swiftly moving train. This was surely no novice in crime, reasoned Mr. Pinkerton, but a man whose record would already show deeds of the greatest daring; a brave fellow, though a bad one. And even among the well-known experienced criminals there must be very few who were capable of this deed.

Mr. Pinkerton, therefore, set himself to studying the bureau's records and rogue's gallery to first pick out these few. Page after page of photographs was turned over, drawer after drawer of records was searched through, and at last a dozen or more men were decided upon as sufficiently preëminent to merit consideration in connection with the present case.

Photographs of these dozen or so were speedily struck off, and submitted by the detectives to all the men who had been in the smoking-car at the time of the robbery, to the conductor of the train and the train-men, to other passengers, to farmers and

THE POLLOCK DIAMOND ROBBERY.

THE THIEF . BROUGHT DOWN FEARFUL BLOWS ON MR. POLLOCK'S HEAD.

others who might have seen the robber while making his escape, and to various people in Omaha. The result was startling. Conductor D. M. Ashmore, without hesitation, selected from the dozen or more photographs one as that of the robber. Mr. Shaw, the Omaha well-digger, who had sat just behind the robber, selected the same photograph, and was positive it pictured the man he had tried to talk to. Other passengers also picked out this photograph, as did various persons who had caught sight of the man as he escaped.

The portrait thus chosen by common accord was that of Frank Bruce, one of the most desperate burglars of the younger generation in the country, and it seemed only necessary now to find Bruce, to have the problem solved. Many days were spent, and hundreds of dollars, in searching for him. Dozens of cities were visited, and every conceivable effort made to get on his track, but it was not until his pursuers were almost weary of the chase that he was finally discovered living quietly in Chicago, on Cottage Grove Avenue, near 36th Street, where he was operating with another high-class burglar, "Billy" Boyce.

Requisition papers were at once procured from the Governor of Iowa on the Governor of Illinois, and men were sent to take Bruce into custody, when the "shadows" reported that he and Boyce had left for Milwaukee, where, of course, the requisition papers were valueless. Fortunately, that same night they attempted a burglary in Milwaukee, for which they were arrested and held for ninety days. This gave the Chicago detectives abundant time to identify Bruce as the missing robber.

Mr. Pinkerton himself went at once to Milwaukee, saw Bruce in the jail, heard his story, verified its essential facts, and within two days, to his own complete disappointment, and in spite of himself, had proved a complete alibi for Bruce. To satisfy himself in this connection, Mr. Pinkerton brought Conductor Ashmore and Mr. Shaw to Milwaukee, and pointed Bruce out to them; and, after looking carefully at him, both men declared they had made a mistake in identifying his picture, and that Bruce was not the robber.

With Bruce clear, the detectives were again without a suspect, and almost without a clue. Just here, however, Mr. Pinkerton recalled that on a trip to the West, some three years previous, to investigate the case of a man arrested at Reno, Nevada, on a charge of "holding up" a faro bank, and while stopping over in Salt Lake City, Utah, he had run across some "sporting" men in that city with whom he was well acquainted, and, on his telling them where he was going and what his business was, one of them, whom Mr. Pinkerton had known for years, had said: "Why, the man at Reno is innocent. The men who committed that robbery are in this city. One of them is a smooth-faced boy, about twenty years of age, and the other is a heavy-set, dark-complexioned fellow, with a dark mustache. They are the intimate friends and companions of Jack Denton, the well-known gambler of Salt Lake; and only a short time ago, in Salt Lake, they entered a house through a rear door, wearing masks, and compelled two ladies, who were just returned from a ball, to give up a large amount of diamonds."

Though not interested in this particular robbery, Mr. Pinkerton had mentally jotted down the intimacy of Jack Denton with this class of people; and he recalled it now in connection with the fact that Jack Denton was one of the two gamblers to whom Pollock had exposed his diamonds at Sonnenberg's pawnshop in Omaha. He at once decided to secure definite information in regard to the boy who had been with Denton at Salt Lake three years earlier. Proceeding immediately to Salt Lake City, and making cautious inquiries, he learned that the boy in question, since he first heard of him, had been arrested and convicted of robbery at Ogden, Utah, and sentenced to one year's term in the penitentiary. An investigation at the penitentiary disclosed that the young man had given the name of James Burke, had served out his sentence under that name, and had been released about one month previous to the Pollock robbery.

Denton, in the meantime, had left Salt Lake and gone to Omaha to make it his home. The boy Burke, argued the detectives, had naturally followed his friend to that point. An accurate description of Burke was got from the records of the Utah penitentiary, and some idea of him and his friends was derived from the officials of the prison. But where to find him in the whole great West was a question.

Inquiries at Salt Lake developed the further fact that Burke had had one intimate friend there, a man named Marshall P. Hooker. Hooker had now, however, left Salt Lake and removed to Denver. For a man of his class, Hooker was unusually talkative, and was known by "crooks" throughout the country as "Windy" Hooker. Plans were made for keeping a watch on him and on Jack Denton, in the hope, by "shadowing" the movements of these two, of ultimately locating Burke.

Through the free talk of Hooker, reported back to the detective, it was soon learned that Burke was known by the alias of "Kid" McCoy, and that he had recently been operating on the Pacific coast in "holding up" faro banks, and had also been concerned in two large robberies, one at Lincoln, Nebraska, and the other at Sacramento, California. His whereabouts at that time, however, were unknown.

Much time had now elapsed since the robbery, and the sensation caused by it had died out. Jack Denton and his friends seldom spoke of it, and Hooker never spoke of it unless the subject was introduced to him. Both men were extremely shy of strangers, and it was almost impossible for a detective to draw them out, as anybody who introduced the subject of the robbery was at once looked upon with suspicion. For the purpose of creating further talk upon the subject, Mr. Pinkerton caused to be inserted in the Omaha papers an advertisement as follows:

"Five hundred dollars will be paid for any information leading up to the identification of the party who robbed William G. Pollock on the Sioux City and Pacific train, November 4, 1892. [Signed] WILLIAM A. PINKERTON, Paxton House, Omaha, Nebraska."

This at once attracted the attention of

THE POLLOCK DIAMOND ROBBERY.

the local newspaper men, and when Mr. Pinkerton arrived in Omaha he was interviewed by all the papers in the city in regard to the robbery. Thus interest in the robbery was at once renewed. Denton and the other persons under suspicion commenced talking of the matter again, none more freely than Hooker.

The latter was then in Denver. Mr. Pinkerton instructed Mr. James McParland, Denver superintendent of the Pinkerton Agency, to send for him, and say to him that he had understood that he (Hooker) could throw some light on the robbery, and that a large sum of money would be paid him for the information he gave. Mr. Pinkerton explained to Mr. McParland that Hooker would lie to him, and endeavor to get the money by giving him false information, but to listen patiently to what he had to say, and lead him on as far as possible without giving him any money. This done, Mr. Pinkerton further predicted Hooker would go back to his cronies and boast of the way he was fooling Pinkerton, and how much money he expected to get; and that eventually, through his boastings, he would prove the means of locating Burke, alias McCoy.

And so, precisely, it fell out. Some of Hooker's companions were Pinkerton detectives, although Hooker did not know them as such, and they in time reported back that Burke was really the Pollock robber; that after committing the robbery he had gone back to Omaha, and from there had gone to Denver. From Denver he went to Salt Lake, and visited a prisoner in the Salt Lake penitentiary with whom he was intimate, gave this prisoner some money, and went from Salt Lake west to the Pacific coast.

Mr. Pinkerton next instructed that the record be examined for daring "hold-ups" that might have occurred in the country lately traversed by Burke. It was then found that a faro bank at Colorado City, a small place between Manitou Springs and Colorado Springs, had been entered late at night by a masked robber, who compelled the dealer and other persons to hold up their hands, took the money in the drawer and escaped; that later on a similar robbery had been perpetrated at San Bernardino, California; that later still the pool house of James Malone, a noted gambler at Tacoma, Washington, had been treated in the same manner; and, finally, that a light or pane of glass in a jewelry store at Sacramento had been smashed in, and a tray of diamonds snatched from the window by a daring thief. And all of those deeds, Mr. Pinkerton learned ultimately through Hooker's talk, had been done by Burke.

The watch on Denton at Omaha developed little, if anything, except that a close companionship existed between him and Sonnenberg, the pawnbroker.

During the summer of 1893, learning that an intimate friend of Burke's, a burglar who had served time with him in the Utah penitentiary, was confined in jail at Georgetown, Texas, Mr. Pinkerton decided to go and interview this man and see if he could get any trace, through him, of the robber. In the meantime he instructed the detectives at Omaha and Denver to keep a particularly close watch on Jack Denton and Hooker.

On Mr. Pinkerton's arrival in Austin, Texas, he found awaiting him despatches from Superintendent McParland of the Denver Agency, stating that through Hooker's talk they had learned that "Kid" McCoy, or Burke, had been arrested at Eagle, Colorado, with a kit of burglar tools in his possession, and was then in jail at Leadville, Colorado.

Mr. Pinkerton at once telegraphed to have Conductor Ashmore and Mr. Shaw the well-digger sent to Leadville to see if they could identify the prisoner. Word was also sent to New York for Mr. Pollock to do the same. He also instructed Superintendent McParland at Denver to send his assistant, J. C. Fraser, to watch the case, so that if McCoy gave bail, or attempted to escape from the Leadville jail, they could be ready with a warrant for his arrest on account of the Pollock robbery.

Having wired these instructions, Mr. Pinkerton proceeded on his journey to Georgetown, Texas, where he called on McCoy's former prison associate in the Utah penitentiary, but was unable to get him to tell anything about McCoy, though he volunteered, if Mr. Pinkerton would furnish him a bond and get him out of his Texas scrape, to go to Omaha and compel the "fence" who had received the diamonds to turn back the property. But the rule of the Jewellers' Protective Union was to get the thief first and the property afterwards; so no treaty was made with the Texas prisoner.

Mr. Pinkerton now went to Kansas City, and found awaiting him there despatches from Superintendent McParland of the Denver Agency, stating that Conductor Ashmore and Messrs. Shaw and Pollock had positively identified the prisoner James Burke, alias "Kid" McCoy, as the man who assaulted and robbed Mr. Pollock of his diamonds. Burke winced perceptibly when he saw Conductor Ashmore and Mr. Shaw, and went fairly wild when confronted by Mr. Pollock. Requisition papers were obtained from the Governor of the State of Iowa on the Governor of Colorado, and the Colorado offence being a minor one, Burke was turned over to Assistant Superintendent Fraser and another detective, to be taken to Logan, Harrison County, Iowa. Before leaving Leadville, Mr. Fraser was confidentially warned by the sheriff of the county that he could not be too careful of his prisoner; for that Burke, through a friend of the sheriff, had made a proposition to the sheriff to pay him a thousand dollars if he would secretly furnish him with a revolver when he left the jail, his design being, with this revolver, to either "hold up" or kill the two detectives who had him in custody, and make his escape from the train.

On trial at Logan, Iowa, the man was easily convicted, and was sentenced to imprisonment for a term of seventeen years.

MR. HALL CAINE.

MR. HALL CAINE, whose novel "The Manxman" is one of three or four novels that made the year 1894 a particularly brilliant one in English fiction, is himself a Manxman by descent, though reared in Liverpool. He was born in 1853, and, like his brother novelist, Thomas Hardy, was educated for an architect. But at about twenty he turned to journalism. When he was about twenty-five, and while he was yet in Liverpool, he came into a close friendship with Dante Gabriel Rossetti, and this led, a year or two later, to his going up to London. One of his first books was his "Recollections of Rossetti," which was followed by various ventures in literary criticism, including "Cobwebs of Criticism," "Sonnets of Three Centuries," and by a "Life of Coleridge." While producing these early works Mr. Caine was reviewing on the "Athenæum" and the "Academy," and writing leaders daily in "The Liverpool Mercury." But in time he grew discontented with reviewing, as most men do on whom it devolves as a constant task, and, deciding "that nobody would go on writing about other people's writing who could do original writing himself," he resolved "to live on little and earn nothing" until he had produced a novel. He was now thirty.

Of the writing of this novel, "The Shadow of a Crime," he has himself given an interesting account. "Settled in a little bungalow of three rooms in a garden near the beach at Sandown, in the Isle of Wight," he fell to. "Shall I," says he, "ever forget the agony of the first efforts? . . . It took me nearly a fortnight to start that novel, sweating drops as of blood at every fresh attempt. I must have written the first half volume four times at the least. After that I saw the way clearer, and got on faster. At the end of three months I had written nearly two volumes, and then in good spirits I went up to London."

But in London a lawyer friend suggested to the author an important addition. "To work this fresh interest into my theme," Mr. Caine continues, "half of what I had written would need to be destroyed! It was destroyed; . . . and after two months more I got well into the third volume."

From all this it should seem that a tougher task than Mr. Caine had had in his first novel could scarcely fall to him. But he says, concluding his account of it: "Every book that I have written since has offered yet greater difficulties. Not one of the little series but has at some moment been a despair to me. There has always been a point of the story at which I have felt confident that it must kill me. I have written six novels (that is to say, about sixteen), and sworn as many oaths that I would never begin another. Three times I have thrown up commissions in sheer terror of the work ahead of me. Yet here I am at this moment (like half a dozen of my fellow-craftsmen) with contracts in hand which I cannot get through before the end of 1894."

For a time Mr. Caine had a pretty home in the Lake Country, made famous by Coleridge, Southey, and Wordsworth; but several years ago he cast in his lot with his brother Manxmen, and now lives in the Isle of Man, inhabiting there the ancient Greeba Castle, a rather more generous housing than the three-room bungalow in which his first novel was written.

HALL CAINE AT 24, WHEN HE WROTE HIS FIRST NOVEL. FROM A PHOTOGRAPH BY ROBINSON & THOMPSON, LIVERPOOL.

HALL CAINE AT 36, 1889. FROM A PHOTOGRAPH BY G. P. ABRAHAM, KESWICK.

HALL CAINE AT 30, 1883.

HALL CAINE AT 40, 1893.

HALL CAINE AT 38, 1891. FROM A PHOTOGRAPH BY G. P. ABRAHAM, KESWICK.

444 MR. HALL CAINE.

HALL CAINE AT 37. 1891. FROM A PHOTOGRAPH BY BARRAUD, LONDON.

GREEBA CASTLE, HALL CAINE'S RESIDENCE IN THE ISLE OF MAN. FROM A PHOTOGRAPH BY
AXEL IRWIN, DOUGLAS, ISLE OF MAN.

TAMMANY.

The Founding of the Society.—A Political Organization from the Start.—Its Part in the Early Politics of the Nation.—Great Men who belonged to Tammany and used its Influence.—The Erie Canal Fight.—Jackson's Nomination.

By E. J. Edwards.

With portraits and other illustrations.

I.

TWELVE days after Washington took the oath of office as President, a political organization was created in New York City that was the beginning of the Tammany Society. It professed to represent democracy, or, as then it was called, the republican principle. For fifty years it kept a sway that was, on the whole, fairly used in our game of empire as played by the two political parties. It gave the hint of the power that lies in a body of men who act with a common purpose and under willing discipline. Taking example by it, many similar associations were formed, although Washington, in one of his messages, expressed disapproval of such methods of politics as characterized these associations. The democracy which Jefferson's name suggests was not created by it. That impulse came with the birth of the nation. But in a feeble, groping way the organizers of Tammany sought to set up something which would balk the Federalists and the aristocrats; something which would give the plain people a fair chance to be equal in fact, as they were in name, with those who had the prestige of wealth, family, association, or political influence. That purpose was gained; and when the Democratic-Republican party, a name which Tammany has kept as its own from that day to this, had become preëminent in State and Nation, Tammany, still supporting the Federal administration, was beset by internal quarrels, the bitterness and malignity of which were so intense that we at this day wonder that they did not cause more blood than Hamilton's to be shed.

As New York was the capital for the time, there the first of American political organizations was made. Tammany was the heir of the spirit of the Sons of Liberty of the Revolutionary War. It was kin in some of its purposes, at least, to those who were then beginning the revolution in France. It was enthusiastic in its support and approval of that revolution. Indeed, a misty legend has been handed down from generation to generation in the Hall that the suggestion came from Jefferson himself, who, called from France to Washington's cabinet, was pained to see that aristocracy, English in its impulse, and fostered by the "Society of the Cincinnati," was rooting itself so early in our national life. To crush that impulse, at least to fetter it, Jefferson gave the hint, and Tammany with its tomahawk stood facing the Cincinnati and its sword.

Another of the many doubtful tales of those days of birth gives to John Trumbull, a poet of some fame and suspected wit, such honor as is due the founder of Tammany. Trumbull's humorous fancy did hit upon the name, and that, very likely,

THOMAS JEFFERSON.
From a portrait by Gilbert Stuart.

was all his service. St. George's, St. David's, St. Andrew's Societies (but no St. Patrick's till many years had passed) flourished in New York, and Trumbull said jokingly, if the tradition be true : " Let us call ours for St. Tammany, since the Tories and Loyalists should not have a monopoly of all the saints in the calendar."

GREATER EQUALITY IN GOVERNMENT AND SOCIETY WAS TAMMANY'S EARLIEST AIM.

William Mooney, an upholsterer, but, like many of the mechanics of that day, keenly interested in politics, suggested that there be brought together in an association those who dreaded the aristocracy, and who suspected that the purpose of Hamilton was to force the government into something like a limited monarchy. Mooney found a good many mechanics and merchants who thought as he did, and so a common purpose, the grouping impulse, rather than any cunning planning of one man for personal advancement, brought some of the ablest political and personal foes of Hamilton and Jay together, and, with some mystery of oaths and ritual, the pipe of peace, the feathered headdress, even the painted face and leathern costume, with wampum for its ornament, these men were bound in one association as the Tammany Society, or Columbian Order. That is the chartered body. It is the core of Tammany. Legally it is not Tammany Hall. Really it is the same thing ; and in what is to be said of the growth, the power, the shifting of the organization from its first purpose, which was fairly political, to its later methods, which typify almost all those evil and lurking tendencies that led De Tocqueville somewhat to doubt the permanence of the Republic, the Tammany Society and Tammany Hall will be spoken of as two names for the same thing.

It should be said now, however, that the common view that in the beginning Tammany was purely a benevolent and kindly association, is far from correct. Such purpose was set forth in the formal organization; but politics, and the politics of the Republican-Democracy, was from the first and for fifty years the abiding purpose. Governor George Clinton had other channels than a political association through which to send his streams of benevolence, and he was one of the early Tammany. Robert Yates was too grim and stern to use as a means for charity an organization which was formed " to connect in indissoluble bonds of friendship American brethren of known attachments to the political rights of human nature and the liberties of the country," a quotation which is word and letter from the first constitution of Tammany. John Lansing, cunning politician, and Melancthon Smith, impetuous one, did not play politics and practise the gentler graces at the same time. Philip Hone, father of Philip who was called the first gentleman of New York, and Cortlandt Van Buren and Gabriel Furman and John Burger may have been generous men, and were among the representative citizens of New York, but the Tammany they organized meant something else than philanthropy ; it meant politics.

These and some others, meeting upon the banks of the Hudson at that place where now the greater ocean steamships lie when safe in port, sat in their mock wigwams on the 12th of May, 1789, smoked the calumet each in turn, swore enmity to aristocracy and privileged classes, and fealty to the principle of pure republicanism, and with that simple ritual set up a political institution sometimes of the highest value, often honorably used, often cruelly, and which, second only to the institution of slavery, has been chief among the perils of the Republic, and perhaps its greatest shame.

Reading the story of Tammany without bias, keeping the mind free from the personal prejudices likely to be created by the most amazing and abhorrent revelations, it is hard to escape the conviction that some such story as that of Tammany was sure to be told as part of the history of the first century of the Republic. Given the peculiar opportunities and conditions then prevailing, and either Tammany or some other band of men was bound to take advantage of them. And in one sense these very things were to be the last test of the moral fibre of a newly-created nation, and of the soundness and purity of the national life.

TAMMANY'S HORROR OF CORRUPTION, SAVE AT HOME.

At the centennial celebration of Tammany Hall, on July 4, 1889, that organization seemed to be the finest, most perfect flower that had ever come from the development of bodies of men acting from a common political purpose. Its discipline was greater than that of an army, for it seldom knew deserters. It controlled nearly a hundred and twenty thousand citizens, who obeyed without a murmur the command of that one who was in author-

THE FIRST TAMMANY HALL, ERECTED IN 1811.
The same building, enlarged, is now the office of "The Sun," corner of Park Row and Frankfort Street.

ity. It controlled, with a single exception, every department of New York City. Mr. Bourke Cockran was the orator of the day, and among the truths which he uttered was this: "If corruption prevails among the people, liberty will become a blighting curse, subversive of order." Among those who applauded with vigor this sentiment were men then doing corrupt acts which five years later were exposed as part of an all-pervasive system that had corroded the department of police.

Mr. Cockran also declared, "Corruption once begun, decay is inevitable, irresistible; the destruction of the Republic is immediate, immeasurable, irredeemable, since history does not record a case of a popular government which has been arrested in its downward course." Yet the orator in saying these words was pronouncing sentence for constructive treason upon many members of the organization who then heard him. They were at that time permitting, encouraging, developing, perhaps the most perfect and far-reaching system of political and pecuniary corruption modern history has recorded.

The orator insisted that Tammany had served the nation well, because it had put up barriers against the dangerous currents of plutocracy. Yet he was addressing a political organization numbering more than one hundred thousand, commanding an annual payroll of nearly twelve millions of dollars, or five times as much as the budget of England in Queen Anne's time, and controlling an annual expenditure of nearly forty millions.

The orator insisted that to Tammany was due very much of the influence which had prevented a strong centralized government. Yet one man who heard Mr. Cockran had but to nod his head, and one hundred thousand votes would be delivered for this candidate; or to shake his head, and the same number would be cast against that one.

The orator spoke of the glorious influence of Tammany in resisting the tendency to undue accumulation of wealth. Yet some of those who clapped their hands were men who had accumulated wealth with a swiftness almost unparalleled, men who a few years before had been humble mechanics—one an engine driver, one a horse-car driver, one a carpet-layer, a score or more saloon-keepers, two or three professional gamblers—and they had gained their wealth after association with, and influence in, Tammany Hall.

These malign and desperate influences are the growth of the later Tammany. The earlier years of the organization were doubtless devoted in good faith to exactly those purposes named by Mr. Cockran. At the same time these earlier years were characterized by politics of such intensity, such malignity of personal pursuit, such desperate endeavor to crush great men, as to us now would seem appalling.

PARTY POLITICS TAMMANY'S FIRST CONCERN FROM THE OUTSET.

Tammany Hall after its organization in 1789 revealed its political purpose by the prompt association with it of Governor Clinton. It also seems to have had a notion of doing something for the commercial development of New York City. It happened that within a year after its organization, when William Pitt Smith was Grand Sachem, it held a council with the Creek Indians, out of which came a treaty of peace, and one which tended to develop trade between the Indian tribes of the interior and New York. Upon that council some of those who were distinguished as the ablest of the opponents of Hamilton and the Federal party looked with interest, giving indirectly their approval to this officiousness of the infant organization. Governor Clinton, Mayor Duane, and Jefferson himself were present as spectators, and many years later Jefferson wrote of it as one of the most interesting occasions at which it had been his privilege to be present.

The political impulse of the organization must have been very strong from the beginning. Josiah Ogden Huffman, one of the ablest members of a family distinguished nearly one hundred years for intellectual ability, became Grand Sachem two years after the organization. And what powerful men were associated with him! There was Melancthon Smith, now almost forgotten, then of great influence. And a young man impetuous, obstinate, vain, fractious, but revealing a brilliancy of intellect which caused the men of that time to look upon him with respect, and say, "He is to be one of our great men,"—young De Witt Clinton, nephew of the Governor,—was associated with Tammany, almost from the first step which he took in politics. Later the most violent, persistent, malignant, and powerful measures were adopted by Tammany Hall to crush De Witt Clinton; measures which in this State, at least, split the Democratic party. It is some indication of the intensity of the opposition to De Witt Clinton, that, while Tammany supported the recommendations of his uncle the Governor in favor of a canal from Lake Champlain to the Hudson, Tammany fought from the beginning the Erie Canal project which is De Witt Clinton's chief claim for remembrance, and fought it solely because it was his. A little later—the record does not show the exact time—one of the subtlest men of the Revolutionary time, Aaron Burr, whose intellectual powers had they been tempered with some moral purpose would have made him one of the immortals, became associated with Tammany.

HAMILTON AND FEDERALISM THE SPECIAL OBJECTS OF TAMMANY'S DISLIKE.

Therefore it was made plain, not only in New York, but elsewhere, that there had sprung up in New York City organized opposition to Hamilton, to his aristocratic Society of the Cincinnati, and to his purpose perfectly to organize and make permanent the influence of the Federal party. There can be no doubt that this opposition was at bottom honest. Hamilton, at the time of the organization of Tammany, was perhaps at his highest pinnacle of success. He was Secretary of the Treasury, and he had such patronage as the office at that time furnished. John Jay, his intimate and political sympathizer, was Chief Justice. The Livingstons, the Schuylers, the Jays, and others who composed such social aristocracy as existed at that time, were all Federalists; all distrusted an absolute republican form of government. The influence of the Society of the Cincinnati, which was very great, served Hamilton and the Federalists. The early Tammany antagonized the Federalists because the leaders of that society believed that pure republicanism was possible; and they feared that it was the purpose of the Federalists so to direct the new government that it should either become a limited monarchy or else a government of the aristocratic classes. Governor George Clinton set that stern face

GEORGE CLINTON.
From a portrait in the State Library at Albany.

The society was the first to cause the Declaration of Independence to be read upon July 4th, followed by speeches of exultation. As it was the first to do this, so it is now the last of formal organizations to celebrate the Fourth in this way. These ceremonies then had their value, although the speeches seem now to be nothing but absurdly bombastic rhetoric. They kept the national spirit at white heat, and as the Union had been reluctantly established, that was a good thing to do. That should be named among the worthy services of Tammany.

With the passing of Washington to private life, the crystallizing of the opposing forces into symmetrical parties was bound to come. The Tammany of Hoffman and Duane and Smith and others, extending as it did from 1789 to 1796, made the coming of it easier, perhaps earlier, than might otherwise have been the case.

TAMMANY BEGINS EARLY TO DIVIDE ITS OWN PARTY.

of his, surmounted as it was by the most marvellous arrangement of hair that ever appeared on the head of any American, against the Federalistic tendency. He opposed Hamilton's scheme for a national bank, and the Tammany Society supported him. Yet Clinton was in favor of internal improvements, for he recommended the Champlain Canal as early as 1791, and that project Tammany seems earnestly to have supported.

It is hard to tell exactly what Burr's relations to the politics of that day were. He always called himself a Democrat-Republican, yet he certainly acted with the Federalists upon one occasion, although not an important one. He was sent to the United States Senate in 1791, although he seems not to have been exactly a Democrat, and certainly not in any close association with the Federalists.

The years between the organization of Tammany and the Presidential election of 1796 seem to have been characterized mainly by emotional and sentimental politics on the part of the early Tammany. The society had a gift for what in these later years is called spread-eagleism. The national bird rarely screamed elsewhere as it did at the early meetings of this society, and it continues to scream at Tammany's Fourth of July celebrations.

From 1796 until 1828 Tammany was in the thick of the excited and angry politics which prevailed during that entire era. That interval of time properly marks the first of the epochs in which Tammany's influence was important, and, at times, mas-

DANIEL D. TOMPKINS.
From a portrait by J. W. Davis.

terful, in the politics of the Nation and State.

It has been said that New York politics are the most mysterious, the most difficult to understand, of any which the Nation has known since its foundation. But if they have been directed and developed in mysterious ways in these later years, they are certainly almost as difficult to comprehend for the period extending from Jefferson's to Jackson's time as were the cuneiform inscriptions when first discovered. It is only in a general way that the relations of Tammany to the politics of the time can be set forth. The intriguing, the secret play of personal ambition and personal revenge, the secretive methods used to crush this or that man who had gained political influence, and seemed to be forging ahead, cannot at this time be revealed, since these things were not fully revealed then. But enough is plain, from a careful reading of the records of Tammany and the history of the time, to show two purposes of the organization. One was to give steadfast and enthusiastic support to the national administration of the Democratic and Republican party which began with Jefferson; the other purpose was to break down certain powerful Democratic leaders, and to build up others. In other words, there were factional and personal quarrels, intense, fierce, to us inexplicable in their bitterness and vindictiveness; quarrels between men who professedly belonged to the same party.

THE MALIGN INFLUENCE OF AARON BURR IN TAMMANY.

The first of these quarrels was developed in Burr's time. Unmatched for suavity, polish, trickery, and a masterly capacity for playing on the passions and weaknesses of men, Burr became openly associated with Tammany in 1796, or thereabouts. We need no clearer proof that the society was at that time in the possession or the promise of power than Burr's association with it gives. The Federalist strength was at that time great enough in the State to secure the election of John Jay as Governor. But in New York City, under Tammany's influence, the Federal power had been broken. De Witt Clinton, then with Tammany, had been appointed Mayor of New York, and Edward Livingston—in fact, all the members of the brilliant family of that name—abandoned the Federal party, joined the Democratic-Republican, and became associated with Tammany Hall.

The Tammany Society of that time met in a tavern. The society itself seemed not greatly to have flourished. At the meetings where the rituals were done, sometimes less than a dozen members of the order attended. But while the society itself was small, there gathered about it most of those who were of influence in the Democratic party, and it was in this way that Tammany Hall, as distinguished from the Tammany Society, was developed. The increase in strength must have been very rapid after the election of John Adams, in 1796. The alien and sedition laws intensified the opposition to the Federalists, and in 1797 the Democratic party, as we shall hereafter call it, under the leadership of those associated with Tammany, carried New York City by one thousand majority, elected Aaron Burr and De Witt Clinton to the legislature, and began, through the use of patronage as well as by fairer politics, to extend its influence throughout the State.

Burr, however, nearly wrecked the local organization, or, at least, put in great peril the influence of Tammany. He secured a charter from the legislature, ostensibly for the creation of a company to supply New

AARON BURR.
From a portrait by John Vanderlyn.

ALEXANDER HAMILTON,
From a portrait by John Trumbull

York City with pure water. During the excitement caused by the Parkhurst revelations in the fall of 1894, there were dug up in the vicinity of the Court House, where the sessions of the committee were held, pieces of the old wooden water-pipes which were laid by that company, called the Manhattan Company. One of these wooden pipes lay for some days exposed to the view of those who attended the meetings at which the monstrous revelations of the later Tammany were being made. It was the visible evidence of the first legislative trickery of the Tammany Society. Concealed in that charter was one provision which enabled Burr and his Democratic associates to organize the Manhattan Bank, Burr and his Tammany associates controlled the stock. The public indignation was intense. That anger was due in part to the belief of the community that it had been cheated by a legislative trick, and in part to its fear that the power which this bank could exercise would perhaps be dangerous, or at least costly, to the community.

Therefore, in the election of 1799, the Democratic party lost the prestige which it had gained in the elections of 1797 and 1798. The Federalists hoped that by reason of this tricky charter the Democracy would lose the State in the approaching presidential election. This fear was not justified, however, Burr managing the bank, and men as well, with exceeding tact, so that there was no opposition to the placing of his name upon the national ticket with that of Jefferson, the understanding being that Jefferson would be chosen President and Burr Vice-President.

IT THROWS OVER BURR AND GROWS
RAPIDLY IN POWER.

Tammany turned upon Burr soon after he entered the office of Vice-President. It accused him of conspiring with some members of Congress to defeat in the House of Representatives the election of Jefferson, and to secure his own, to the presidential office. The society, in order the more surely to destroy Burr, called George Clinton from his retirement, and in 1802 reelected him Governor, and Clinton distributed the patronage in such manner as to aid Tammany and the more completely to thwart Burr. In addition to that, De Witt Clinton was sent the same year to the United States Senate, a post which he resigned in 1804, to become

JOHN JAY,
From a portrait by C. W. Peale.

Mayor of New York. The story which recites the part Tammany played in aiding to drive Burr from power, although he had a few years before been one of the conspicuous men associated with the Hall, is full of the incidents which make exciting historical romance.

With Burr gone, with the Federal party absolutely annihilated, as it was after the election of Jefferson, it was inevitable that the Democracy of New York, and especially the Tammany organization, should begin factional contests. In some way, too vague now to trace, the bitter hostility which had been developed in Tammany against Burr was transferred to De Witt Clinton. Clinton, it is true, was reappointed Mayor in 1807, in spite of the opposition of Tammany. His uncle the Governor having been chosen Vice-President for Jefferson's second term, thus keeping a Tammany man in that office, Morgan Lewis, who became Governor, and was in more or less close relations with Tammany, removed De Witt Clinton from the mayoralty. That was in 1807. But that handsome, fascinating, brilliant, but superficial young man whom Tammany had discovered, and through whose influence in part he was sent to Congress, Daniel D. Tompkins, having been chosen Governor in 1807, and being a shrewd politician, caused the reappointment of Clinton as Mayor. The younger Clinton then seemed to have Tammany in his control. He was Mayor, earning as much as twelve thousand dollars; he was chosen Senator in the State legislature, and he was a member of the Governor's Council.

De Witt Clinton, however, had given Tammany plausible public reasons for opposing him, since he took his stand with those who resisted fiercely the embargo laws passed in President Madison's first administration. Tammany gave to President Madison the steady and important support which it had with enthusiasm yielded to Jefferson. There came a trying time when that support was valuable, perhaps decisive. It matched, in 1811, that secretive influence which was expressed by the gathering of the New England Federalists in Hartford in the historic Hartford Convention, where first secession was suggested. The embargo laws had made New England all Federal again. De Witt Clinton's influence and the commercial impulse of New York were likely to create strong opposition in New York State. That tendency Tammany opposed and overcame.

TAMMANY'S SOCIAL STANDING IN THE EARLY DAYS.

It was at this time that the society's prestige had become so great that it was able to secure money enough to pay the cost of building its own Tammany Hall. Colonel Rutgers, one of the great merchants, raised as much as twenty-eight thousand dollars, and with this money the new building was erected in 1811. Such a sum of money as that was, in those days, looked upon as a magnificent subscription, and it surely indicates not only the po-

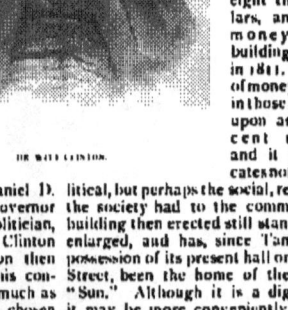

DE WITT CLINTON.

litical, but perhaps the social, relation which the society had to the community. The building then erected still stands, although enlarged, and has, since Tammany took possession of its present hall on Fourteenth Street, been the home of the New York "Sun." Although it is a digression, yet it may be more conveniently stated here than elsewhere that after the building of the new Tammany Hall in 1811, and for some twenty years, the society had important social relations. At the celebration of the centennial of the establishment of the government in 1889, and again at the time of the naval display in 1892, in which the ships of many nations took part in New York waters, it was said that Tammany had at last gained supreme social distinction, because, on the former occasion, Mr. Grant, Mayor at that time, led in the promenade at the official ball a lady who has been distinguished as the chief of New York society leaders; and because, on the latter occasion, the wife of one of the greater sachems of Tammany Hall bestowed luxurious entertainment upon distinguished officers of the foreign vessels.

These ceremonies, however, were either wholly or partly official, and the function being ended the relations established by it ceased. Tammany in these later years of the century has never gained such distinction as is implied in recognition by what is called society. On the other hand, prominent association with that organization has seemed to act as a bar-sinister. Only one man, and he a bachelor, has been equally identified in recent years with Tammany and also with what is deemed the higher social circle.

But in those days when Tammany took possession of its permanent home, it possessed undoubted social influence. Many of its members were leading merchants and men of wealth. The fact that in building the new hall the plans called for a ball-room, the like of which had not till then been constructed in New York City, is proof enough that Tammany tempered its politics with social delights. The traditions, too, of its entertainments hint at its social sway. It never had such prestige as was shared by the families of the Federalists, or the descendants of the Tories and Loyalists of the Revolution. That social circle included the Schuylers, the Hamiltons, Van Rensselaers, and the Fish family. But the Tammany of the first twenty-five years of the present century was surely a social influence, nor did it lose that character fully until new forces were developed at a later time in the organization.

MARTIN VAN BUREN.

HEARTY SUPPORT OF MADISON AND THE WAR ON ENGLAND.

In 1811, when Tammany took possession of its new hall, the society, both formally and by individual endeavor, gave to President Madison the support which he courted for his determination to make war with Great Britain. The society called public meetings, and they were enthusiastic ones. A year later, when war had been begun, it welcomed with delirious joy the news of every victory of the American forces on land or of our warships at sea. It created a splendid public sentiment. Its bird of freedom never screamed louder; and when the war was ended it was Tammany that received the commissioners of peace, Clay, Gallatin, and Adams, on their return from Ghent, honoring these commissioners with the finest banquet that had been given in New York up to that day.

In 1812 a new, and what was to be a mighty, personal leader appeared among the politicians of New York — Martin Van Buren. He was always in some association more or less close with Tammany, and yet his first important act was to support the nomination, made through political cunning and by the legislature, of De Witt Clinton for the Presidency in opposition to Madison in 1812. Tammany was bound to bolt that nomination. Mr. Van Buren did not look upon it as a wise one, but said that it had been properly made, and that it was dangerous for any portion of a party to bolt a regular nomination. Tammany respected Van Buren; nevertheless it bolted Clinton at the polls, at least, and although Clinton did receive the electoral votes of New York and some other States, yet his relation to the national canvass was, after all, insignificant.

With Madison again elected, with Tompkins still in the Governor's chair, with Tammany's prestige and influence in New York City supreme, the society seemed determined to make one final effort absolutely to crush De Witt Clinton. It caused his removal from the Mayor's office, and it secured the appointment of its Grand Sachem, John Ferguson, for Mayor. It seemed to have done its work well. De Witt Clinton was reduced to such condition that he was obliged to turn to his pen for support. He seemed to be a political outcast ; and two years later a Tammany man, Cadwallader Colden, was appointed Mayor, and Tammany was strengthened by the accession of such men as Ogden Edwards and General Root.

TAMMANY'S OPPOSITION TO DE WITT CLINTON AND THE ERIE CANAL.

It was personal ambition, secret intrigue, and almost inconceivable maliciousness of hatred, that brought about a combination of Democrats and half Federalists which, in 1817, in spite of Tammany, brought De Witt Clinton to the Governor's chair. He was Governor, but he was almost powerless, since he had little support in his council and almost none in his legislature. Tammany again tried to defeat him in 1820 with Vice-President Tompkins as its candidate for Governor, but Clinton had so large a following (called the Clintonians) that he was able to secure reëlection, mainly because the central and western parts of the State were enthusiastic for his Erie Canal project.

That great public work, one which gave to Tammany later opportunities, and created an influence which developed the newer Tammany, was persistently and vindictively opposed by Tammany Hall from the day that De Witt Clinton suggested it. Although it claimed to be in favor of every measure that would tend to develop the city of New York, its record is that of a steadfast opponent of that project which gave New York City its first mighty impulse towards its position of commercial metropolis.

In 1820 Van Buren, who with his foxy cunning had cultivated Tammany and yet not greatly offended the Clintonians, excepting in one instance, was elected United States Senator. Van Buren did not agree with Tammany as to the Presidential candidate of 1824. The best evidence is that he was then in favor of the election of William H. Crawford to the Presidency. Tammany's first impulse was in favor of John Quincy Adams, who was one of the few New England men of note who had supported the Embargo Act.

The politics which caused a sufficient number of the New York legislature to choose a majority of Adams electors are as mysteriously involved as an Egyptian labyrinth. One thing only is evident, and that is that the politicians were playing at cross purposes, some of them inspired by motives which at this day it is impossible to fathom. This much is clear, that Tammany, on the whole, supported Adams. But it repudiated him soon after he became President. Van Buren then determined that Jackson was the available candidate of the Democratic party for 1828, and in this opinion Tammany heartily agreed. With Jackson's election, in 1828, with Van Buren as Secretary of State, with the influence of the administration and the distribution of patronage so used as to give favor to Tammany, and with an alliance sometimes direct, sometimes concealed, with the Albany regency, Tammany had taken the position of the commanding political influence of the State. As it was in 1826, three years before Jackson's administration, that the Erie Canal was fully opened to business, we see the organization at the beginning of Jackson's first term, in 1829, the recognized friend of the President and his administration, and therefore in a position to take advantage of the swift and great development of trade and commerce which the Erie Canal was sure to cause, and in that position it stood at the end of the first forty years of its existence, looking with confidence to the future, where new and greater opportunities were sure to appear.

[Succeeding papers will carry the history of Tammany on through the time of the " Plug Uglies," the " Bowery Boys," the Tweed Ring, John Kelly, and finally Croker, concluding with an account of the exposures by the Lexow Committee, and the present uprising, under the leadership and inspiration of Dr. Parkhurst, against Tammany rule. — EDITOR.]

"WHERE IGNORANCE IS BLISS."

BY ROBERT BARR.

THE splendid steamship "Adamant," of the celebrated Cross Bow Line, left New York on her February trip under favorable auspices. There had just been a storm on the ocean, so there was every chance that she would reach Liverpool before the next one was due.

Captain Rice had a little social problem to solve at the outset, but he smoothed that out with the tact which is characteristic of him. Two Washington ladies—official ladies—were on board, and the captain, old British sea-dog that he was, always had trouble in the matter of precedence with Washington ladies. Captain Rice never had any bother with the British aristocracy, because precedence is all set down in the bulky volume of "Burke's Peerage," which the captain kept in his cabin, and so there was no difficulty. But a republican country is supposed not to meddle with precedence. It wouldn't, either, if it weren't for the women.

So it happened that Mrs. Assistant-Attorney-to-the-Senate Brownrig came to the steward and said that, ranking all others on board, she must sit at the right hand of the captain. Afterwards, Mrs. Second-Adjutant-to-the-War-Department Digby came to the same perplexed official and said she must sit at the captain's right hand, because in Washington she took precedence over everyone else on board. The bewildered steward confided his woes to the captain, and the captain said he would attend to the matter. So he put Mrs. War-Department on his right hand and then walked down the deck with Mrs. Assistant-Attorney and said to her ;

"I want to ask a favor, Mrs. Brownrig. Unfortunately I am a little deaf in the right ear, caused, I presume, by listening so much with that ear to the fog horn year in and year out. Now, I always place the lady whose conversation I wish most to enjoy on my left hand at table. Would you oblige me by taking that seat this voyage? I have heard of you, you see, Mrs. Brownrig, although you have never crossed with me before."

"Why, certainly, captain," replied Mrs. Brownrig ; "I feel especially complimented."

"And I assure you, madam," said the polite captain, "that I would not for the world miss a single word that," etc.

And thus it was amicably arranged between the two ladies. All this has nothing whatever to do with the story. It is merely an incident given to show what a born diplomat Captain Rice was and is to this day. I don't know any captain more popular with the ladies than he, and besides he is as good a sailor as crosses the ocean.

Day by day the good ship ploughed her way toward the east, and the passengers were unanimous in saying that they never had a pleasanter voyage for that time of the year. It was so warm on deck that many steamer chairs were out, and below it was so mild that a person might think he was journeying in the tropics. Yet they had left New York in a snow storm with the thermometer away below zero.

"Such," said young Spinner, who knew everything, "such is the influence of the Gulf Stream."

Nevertheless, when Captain Rice came down to lunch the fourth day out his face was haggard and his look furtive and anxious.

"Why, captain," cried Mrs. Assistant-Attorney, "you look as if you hadn't slept a wink last night."

"I slept very well, thank you, madam," replied the captain. "I always do."

"Well, I hope your room was more comfortable than mine. It seemed to me too hot for anything. Didn't you find it so, Mrs. Digby?"

"I thought it very nice," replied the lady at the captain's right, who generally found it necessary to take an opposite view from the lady at the left.

"You see," said the captain, "we have many delicate women and children on board and it is necessary to keep up the temperature. Still, perhaps the man who attends to the steam rather overdoes it. I will speak to him."

Then the captain pushed from him his untasted food and went up on the bridge,

NOTE.—This story, along with others by Robert Barr, is about to be published in a volume entitled, "The Face and the Mask:" The Frederick A. Stokes Co., New York.

casting his eye aloft at the signal waving from the masthead, silently calling for help to all the empty horizon.

"Nothing in sight, Johnson?" said the captain.

"Not a speck, sir."

The captain swept the circular line of sea and sky with his glasses, then laid them down with a sigh.

"We ought to raise something this afternoon, sir," said Johnson; "we are right in their track, sir. The 'Fulda' ought to be somewhere about."

"We are too far north for the 'Fulda,' I am afraid," answered the captain.

"Well, sir, we should see the 'Vulcan' before night, sir. She's had good weather from Queenstown."

"Yes. Keep a sharp lookout, Johnson."

"Yes, sir."

The captain moodily paced the bridge with his head down.

"I ought to have turned back to New York," he said to himself.

Then he went down to his own room, avoiding the passengers as much as he could, and had the steward bring him some beef-tea. Even a captain cannot live on anxiety.

"Steamer off the port bow, sir," rang out the voice of the lookout at the prow. The man had sharp eyes, for a landsman could have seen nothing.

"Run and tell the captain," cried Johnson to the sailor at his elbow; but as the sailor turned, the captain's head appeared up the stairway. He seized the glass and looked long at a single point on the horizon.

"It must be the 'Vulcan,'" he said at last.

"I think so, sir."

"Turn your wheel a few points to port and bear down on her."

Johnson gave the necessary order and the great ship veered around.

"Hello!" cried Spinner, on deck. "Here's a steamer. I found her. She's mine."

Then there was a rush to the side of the ship. "A steamer in sight!" was the cry, and all books and magazines at once lost interest. Even the placid, dignified Englishman who was so uncommunicative rose from his chair and sent his servant for his binocular. Children were held up and told to be careful, while they tried to see the dim line of smoke so far ahead.

"Talk about lane routes at sea," cried young Spinner, the knowing. "Bosh, I say. See! we're going directly for her. Think what it might be in a fog! Lane routes! Pure luck, I call it."

"Will we signal to her, Mr. Spinner?" gently asked the young lady from Boston.

"Oh, certainly," answered young Spinner. "See, there's our signal flying from the masthead now. That shows them what line we belong to."

"Dear me, how interesting," said the young lady. "You have crossed many times, I suppose, Mr. Spinner."

"Oh, I know my way about," answered the modest Spinner.

The captain kept the glasses glued to his eyes. Suddenly he almost let them drop.

"My God! Johnson," he cried.

"What is it, sir?"

"*She's* flying a signal of distress, *too!*"

The two steamers slowly approached each other and, when nearly alongside and about a mile apart, the bell of the "Adamant" rang to stop.

"There, you see," said young Spinner to the Boston girl, "she is flying the same flag at her masthead that we are."

"Then she belongs to the same line as this boat?"

"Oh, certainly," answered Mr. Cocksure Spinner.

"Oh, look! look! look!" cried the enthusiastic Indianapolis girl who was going to take music in Germany.

Everyone looked aloft and saw running up to the masthead a long line of fluttering, many-colored flags. They remained in place for a few moments and then fluttered down again, only to give place to a different string. The same thing was going on on the other steamer.

"Oh, this is too interesting for anything," said Mrs. Assistant. "I am just dying to know what it all means. I have read of it so often but never saw it before. I wonder when the captain will come down. What does it all mean?" she asked the deck steward.

"They are signalling to each other, madam."

"Oh, I know *that*. But what *are* they signalling?"

"I don't know, madam."

"Oh, see! see!" cried the Indianapolis girl, clapping her hands with delight. "The other steamer is turning round."

It was indeed so. The great ship was thrashing the water with her screw, and gradually the masts came in line and then her prow faced the east again. When this had been slowly accomplished the bell on the "Adamant" rang full speed ahead, and then the captain came slowly down the ladder that led from the bridge.

"Oh, captain, what does it all mean?"

"WHERE IGNORANCE IS BLISS."

"Is she going back, captain? Nothing wrong, I hope."

"What ship is it, captain?"

"She belongs to our line, doesn't she?"

"Why is she going back?"

"The ship," said the captain slowly, "is the 'Vulcan,' of the Black Howling Line, that left Queenstown shortly after we left New York. She has met with an accident. Ran into some wreckage, it is thought, from the recent storm. Anyhow there is a hole in her, and whether she sees Queenstown or not will depend a great deal on what weather we have and whether her bulkheads hold out. We will stand by her till we reach Queenstown."

"Are there many on board, do you think, captain?"

"There are thirty-seven in the cabin and over eight hundred steerage passengers," answered the captain.

"Why don't you take them on board, out of danger, captain?"

"Ah, madam, there is no need to do that. It would delay us, and time is everything in a case like this. Besides, they will have ample warning if she is going down, and they will have time to get everybody in the boats. We will stand by them, you know."

"Oh, the poor creatures," cried the sympathetic Mrs. Second-Adjutant. "Think of their awful position. May be engulfed at any moment. I suppose they are all on their knees in the cabin. How thankful they must have been to see the 'Adamant.'"

On all sides there was the profoundest sympathy for the unfortunate passengers of the "Vulcan." Cheeks paled at the very thought of the catastrophe that might take place at any moment within sight of the sister ship. It was a realistic object lesson on the ever-present dangers of the sea. While those on deck looked with new interest at the steamship plunging along within a mile of them, the captain slipped away to his room. As he sat there, there was a tap at his door.

"Come in," shouted the captain.

The silent Englishman slowly entered.

"What's wrong, captain?" he asked.

"Oh, the 'Vulcan' has had a hole stove in her and I signalled——"

"Yes, I know all that, of course, but what's wrong *with us?*"

"With us?" echoed the captain blankly.

"Yes, with the 'Adamant?' What has been amiss for the last two or three days? I'm not a talker, nor am I afraid any more than you are, but I want to know."

"Certainly," said the captain. "Please

MISSED LETTING THE SIGNALS.

shut the door, Sir John."

. . . .

Meanwhile there was a lively row on board the "Vulcan." In the saloon Captain Flint was standing at bay with his knuckles on the table.

"Now, what the devil's the meaning of all this?" cried Adam K. Vincent, member of Congress.

A crowd of frightened women were standing around, many on the verge of hysterics. Children clung, with pale faces, to their mother's skirts, fearing they knew not what. Men were grouped with anxious faces, and the bluff old captain fronted them all.

"The meaning of all *what*, sir?"

"You know very well. What is the meaning of our turning round?"

"It means, sir, that the 'Adamant' has eighty-five saloon passengers and nearly five hundred intermediate and steerage passengers who are in the most deadly danger. The cotton in the hold is on fire, and they have been fighting it night and day. A conflagration may break out at any moment. It means, then, sir, that the 'Vulcan' is going to stand by the 'Adamant.'"

A wail of anguish burst from the frightened women at the awful fate that might be in store for so many human beings so near to them, and they clung closer to their children and thanked God that no such danger threatened them and those dear to them.

"And, sir," cried the Congressman, "do you mean to tell us that we have to go against our will—without even being consulted—back to Queenstown?"

"I mean to tell you so, sir."

"Well, by the gods, that's an outrage, and I won't stand it, sir. I must be in New York by the 27th. I won't stand it, sir."

"I am very sorry, sir, that anybody should be delayed."

"Delayed? Hang it all, why don't you take the people on board and take 'em to New York? I protest against this, I'll bring a lawsuit against the company, sir."

"Mr. Vincent," said the captain sternly, "permit me to remind you that *I* am captain of this ship. Good afternoon, sir."

The Congressman departed from the saloon exceeding wroth, breathing dire threats of legal proceedings against the line and the captain personally, but most of the passengers agreed that it would be an inhuman thing to leave the "Adamant" alone in mid-ocean in such terrible straits.

"Why didn't they turn back, Captain Flint?" asked Mrs. General Weller.

"Because, madam, every moment is of value in such a case, and we are nearer Queenstown than New York."

And so the two steamships, side by side, worried their way toward the east, always within sight of each other by day, and with the rows of lights in each visible at night to the sympathetic souls on the other. The sweltering men poured water into the hold of the one and the pounding pumps poured water out of the hold of the other, and thus they reached Queenstown.

. . . .

On board the tender that took the passengers ashore at Queenstown from both steamers two astonished women met each other.

"Why! *Mrs.—General—*WELLER!!! You don't mean to say you were on board that unfortunate 'Vulcan!'"

"For the land's sake, Mrs. Assistant Brownrig! Is that really *you?* Will wonders never cease? Unfortunate, did you say? Mighty fortunate for you, I think. Why! weren't you just frightened to death?"

"I was, but I had no idea anyone I knew was on board."

"Well, you were on board yourself. That would have been enough to have killed me."

"On board myself? Why, what *do* you mean? I wasn't on board the 'Vulcan.' Did you get any sleep at all after you knew you might go down at any moment?"

"My sakes, Jane, what *are* you talking about? *Down* at any moment? It was you that might have gone down at any moment or, worse still, have been burnt to death if the fire had got ahead. You don't mean to say you didn't know the 'Adamant' was on fire most of the way across?"

"*Mrs.—General—Weller!!* There's some *horrible* mistake. It was the 'Vulcan.' Everything depended on her bulkheads, the captain said. There was a hole as big as a barn door in the 'Vulcan.' The pumps were going night and day."

Mrs. General looked at Mrs. Assistant as the light began to dawn on both of them.

"Then it wasn't the engines, but the pumps," she said.

"And it wasn't the steam, but the fire," screamed Mrs. Assistant. "Oh, dear, how that captain lied, and I thought him such a nice man, too. Oh, I shall go into hysterics, I know I shall."

"I wouldn't if I were you," said the sensible Mrs. General, who was a strong-minded woman; "besides, it is too late. We're all pretty safe now. I think both captains were pretty sensible men. Evidently married, both of 'em."

Which was quite true.

THE BANK OF ENGLAND.

By HENRY J. W. DAM.

THE Bank of England on the 27th of last July reached the two hundredth anniversary of its birth. For two centuries it has been, as it is to-day, the greatest bank in the world, and the governing factor in the enormous financial operations which, having their origin in London, reach out to every part of the globe in which civilization guarantees the protection of invested capital, and valuable natural products or popular necessities offer opportunities for the creation or collection of wealth. It began business on the 27th of July, 1694. It was founded by a group of rich city merchants, William Patterson, a shrewd Scotsman, being the leading spirit. The subscriptions to the capital were received in the Mercers' Chapel, where the bank's operations were conducted until the end of the year. From the Mercers' Chapel the bank moved to Grocers' Hall, where it had its home for forty years, first occupying its present premises in Threadneedle Street in 1735.

The whole of the capital of £1,200,000 ($6,000,000) was promptly loaned to the government, to meet the pressing necessities of King William. In return for this loan, Parliament passed an act " levying new duties on the tonnage, for the benefit of such loyal persons as should advance money for carrying on the campaign against the French." This enactment, passed on the 16th of July, 1694, created the institution, and gave to the "Governor and Company of the Bank of England" a peculiarly favorable charter, which has been from time to time renewed, modified, and systematized, though its original fundamental idea has never been changed. The relation thus established between the government and the bank was peculiar, but that it has proved successful is evinced by its continued extension. The debt originally owed to the bank by the government has increased, in the lapse of two centuries, from £1,200,000, with interest at eight per cent. per annum, to £11,000,000 ($55,000,000), with interest at two and three-fourths per cent. per annum, and is the foundation stone of the bank's solidity. The bank building has expanded as the business has increased, until it now covers the whole area between Threadneedle Street, Princes Street, Lothbury and Bartholomew Lane, a space of over three acres, upon which its windowless brown stone walls, only one story in height, rise with an aspect of massive impenetra-

DAVID POWELL, GOVERNOR OF THE BANK OF ENGLAND. FROM A PHOTOGRAPH BY WALERY, LONDON.

bility, unique among banks, and quite awe-inspiring in its way.

$600,000,000 IN A SPACE OF LESS THAN FOUR ACRES.

The site of the Bank of England bears an estimated annual value of £70,000. This sum, if capitalized at three per cent., would represent a gross value of £2,100,000. Estimating the buildings, vaults, printing and weighing machines, etc., at £400,000 more, it will be seen that the "plant" of the bank must be worth over $12,000,000. Add to this the average amount of bullion, coin, securities, and unissued notes usually held, and you have the gigantic sum of £120,000,000 sterling, or $600,000,000, all heaped on a space of less than four acres. Nowhere else in the world is there such an aggregation of actual and potential wealth within so small an area.

In its early days the bank employed fifty-four clerks, and the yearly salary list amounted to £4,300, the chief accountant and the secretary receiving £250 each.

At the present time the total number of employees is about fifteen hundred, the salaries and wages amounting to over £300,000 per year, and the pensions to nearly £50,000. The present price of Bank of England £100 shares is £332, making the capital of £14,553,000 worth £48,315,960, or about $240,000,000. The usual dividend distributed is equal to ten per cent. on the original capital. The solidity of the bank is thus shown to be, in the opinion of investors, equal to that of the British Government, as the yield on bank shares at the enhanced price, and on Consols, is nearly the same—two and three-fourths per cent.

HOW THE BANK IS MANAGED.

The bank is managed by twenty-four directors, in addition to the governor and deputy-governor; and they, by their committees, have full cognizance of all the bank's transactions, and full governing power in all respects. The governors are selected annually as candidates by the directors from among themselves, though they are elected by the stockholders. The governor receives £2,000, the deputy-governor £1,500, and the directors £500 a year each for their services. A chief official resides within the bank's walls, and he or his deputy is supposed to be always on the premises. Clerks of standing and character are also selected to remain at the bank every night during the year, and on Sundays and bank holidays. A guard of soldiers is on duty every night, marching from the Tower, and they are assisted by a body of watchmen, formed of porters and workmen, fully trained in case of fire or other emergency.

Under the general name of the Bank of England have been grouped, ever since its start, three separate institutions, each of which has been complete in itself, and distinct in its operations from any other, since the passage of the Act of 1844. These are, first, "the National Debt Department," which occupies the Bartholomew Lane side, and conducts the issue of all government loans and the payment of dividends on its own stock, on national bonds, and other securities controlled by the bank. The second is the "Issue Department," occupying the centre of the Threadneedle

HOUSE OF SIR JOHN HOUBLON, THE SITE OF THE BANK OF ENGLAND.

COURTYARD ENTRANCE TO THE ISSUE AND DIVIDEND DEPARTMENTS.

Street side, and having for its scope the issue of bank notes, their printing, cancellation and redemption, and the numberless transactions in the issue and receipt of the gold coin and bullion by which the note issue is mainly guaranteed. The third is the "Government and General Banking Department," on the Princes Street side, in which all the banking functions of a national treasury and the ordinary business of an ordinary commercial bank are separately carried on. These departments, with the spacious offices of the officials and the cancellation and printing departments, occupy the whole street floor. Below this is a basement equal in area to the floor above it, and containing three acres of vaults and store rooms, in which all the gold and the enormous aggregation of records which have accumulated in the bank's history are stored.

A journey through the bank has long been a privilege largely sought by tourists and provincial visitors; and though the permits have been greatly restricted of late, through anarchic disturbances and newspaper criticism, it is all the more requested and enjoyed by the favored few. After passing through the main entrance in Threadneedle Street, you come upon an inner court guarded by a gorgeous functionary in a black velvet cocked hat and a long gown of braided scarlet, who has something of the gaudiness of a Brazilian parrot, but is much less inclined to enter into conversation. He has great dignity and a wand of office, which jointly wave you towards the inner door which gives upon the Issue Department.

THE ISSUE DEPARTMENT.

This is a large square room with counters on all its sides, at which all the gold or notes paid into the bank by the general public are received. Anybody can here exchange notes for gold, or *vice versa*, and all the bags of sovereigns from other banks, or from abroad, are here paid in. Its only peculiar feature is that anyone paying in a note is asked to indorse it on the back. This is for tracing purposes, which will be discussed later on.

All the sovereigns and half-sovereigns received here immediately undergo, in a large room adjoining, the ordeal of the weighers, or separators. These are small brass boxes, perhaps a cubic foot in size, with glass sides. In the centre of the brass top is a small round hole, a little larger than the sovereign, which is filled by the round plate of a delicate balance. Upon this balance the sovereigns or half-sovereigns, according to the machine, slide, one at a time, by their own weight from an inclined half-tube, in which they are placed by the handful, forming a long inclined cylinder of gold coins. As each coin weights the balance, the latter sinks. If the coin be of standard weight the balance sinks far enough for a tiny steel finger, moving to the left, to tilt the coin off down a tube into a receptacle below. If the coin be light in weight, the balance does not sink so far, and the coin is caught by a second finger, moving in the opposite direction, which tilts it into a receptacle on the right. These machines work automatically and perfectly, and save an amount of labor which can only be imagined, testing thirty million pieces per annum. The room contains sixteen of them, all working silently and regularly by atmospheric engine power, under the care of a single employee. The light coins are immediately split in half and returned to the mint, while those of standard weight remain in circulation.

The Issue Department is so distinct in its operations from the others that it could be just as well conducted in a separate building. It is required by law to issue a weekly statement, and this statement,

THE GORGEOUS FUNCTIONARY WHO GUARDS THE INNER COURT.

hung at its door, shows, on this special day, that the outstanding note issue, translated into dollars, amounts to $220,570,825. This indebtedness is guaranteed, according to the statement, by the debt owing from the government to the amount of $55,075,500; other securities to the amount of $28,922,000, and $142,570,825 in coin and bullion now in the vaults. Gold in bars is received by the Issue Department, and paid for in notes, at the rate of £3. 17s. 9d. per ounce of twenty-two parts of pure gold out of twenty-four. This price is three half-pence below the market value of gold per ounce, and is consequently less by that proportion than the seller would receive in coin after it had passed through the mint. He would lose the interest on it, however, while it was being coined; and the discount arrangement, which is a convenient one for both parties, yields the bank an annual profit of £15,000. For the privilege of issuing the notes, and for the exemption of duty upon them, the bank pays the government about £200,000 per annum. Per contra, the amount paid by the government for the management of the national debt, according to the act of 1892, is £325 per million, up to £500,000,000, and £100 per million for the remainder. This now aggregates about the sum above mentioned, £200,000 per year.

The Issue Department practically manages itself, presenting no complications in the ordinary course of business. As every bank-note issued beyond the amount of

£16,700,000 is represented by bullion in the vaults, and the £16,700,000 is invested in government securities, no risk can possibly occur until the issue of bank-notes is reduced to this amount; and even then the conversion of the liability would be easy.

Passing through the Issue Department, you enter the main corridor, leading to the court-room or bank-parlor, where the general courts of proprietors, as well as the weekly courts of directors, are held. It is notable on account of three exquisite and antique chimney-pieces, and the doorways at either end are columned archways of the finest workmanship and most imposing effect. The western archway leads into the directors' library of financial and economical works—a vaulted apartment, decorated in renaissance style. The governors' and deputy-governors' rooms are also in this part of the building, the latter containing a selection of weapons formerly kept for bank defence.

THE ISSUE, PAYMENT, AND CANCELLATION OF BANK OF ENGLAND NOTES.

Passing these apartments and their attendant offices, including that of the chief cashier, you come to the secretary's office, where a polite messenger in a heliotrope coat and top hat takes charge of you for the conventional round. He conducts you first to the accountants' bank-note office, which, with the printing department above it, is on the Princes Street side. No note, out of the fifty or sixty thousand now issued daily, is ever issued twice. If, as a depositor, you should draw any amount in notes at the bank and pay them back into your account ten minutes afterward, they would be cancelled. So, also, any other notes received by you from any other bank in London are always new ones, crisp from the Bank of England presses of the day before. The signature is cut off immediately a note is paid in, and the Cancellation Department proceeds to file them in their regular order, taking notice and keeping account of all notes which have not been returned.

One of the curiosities of this department is a twenty-five-pound note, which was paid in after being out for one hundred and eleven years. The bank-note library is also here, with albums containing old bank-notes of various large amounts, with the names of the noblemen for whom they were

H LATIMER BROWN 1894

issued. There is, also, the million-pound bank-note, a bit of paper which, in its day, was worth $5,000,000, and was issued for convenience in closing an undertaking of unusual moment. The records of this department are of invaluable assistance in checking forgery, and the cancelled notes, which are kept for a period of about five years before being burned, are constantly under examination by Scotland Yard detectives in search of stolen money, or by other people whose notes have been lost. The strange stories of single notes which this department can furnish are many, and are ready-made plots for any number of romances, but they are too numerous to be told in this article. A more important question, and one often raised, is whether or not a Bank of England note, which mainly composes the national currency, is invariably good for its face. As a matter of fact, whether lost or stolen, the note will always be paid at the bank.

THE BANK HONORS EVEN STOLEN NOTES.

This point was finally settled many years ago by the theft of £20,000 in notes by the principal clerk in one of the London banks. He escaped to Holland, and there disposed of the notes to a Jew. The theft, with the numbers of the notes, was widely advertised for six months. After that period the Jew appeared with them and demanded payment, which was refused. He went to the Exchange and raised an outcry. The bank, he said, had refused to pay its own notes, and was clearly insolvent. In a very few minutes a clerk appeared to invite him back to the cashier's office, and his claim, as well as the question which it raised, was settled for all time.

Thence came the habit of requesting all persons presenting notes in the Issue Department to indorse them. The custom is for every person who reports his loss of a note to pay half a crown (sixty cents), and for this sum the bank guarantees to send to him the name or names of whoever may present the stolen money. Nearly all the stolen notes in England are returned through bookmakers. These gentlemen do business on race courses, and have no means of tracing persons who deal with them. They suffer no loss through the stolen paper, and are very generally used in this way by the thieves.

One of the directors in 1740 deposited $150,000, and took a single note, filled out by the cashier, in return. He went home, laid the note on the mantelpiece, and fell asleep. It disappeared. He believed it had fallen into the fire, made an affidavit to this effect, and received $150,000 more, giving a guarantee that if the note was found he would assume its responsibility. Thirty years afterward, the man having in the meantime died, the note was presented, and the bank had to pay it; and as the man's estate had long been divided, the bank lost the money.

HOW THE NOTES ARE PRINTED.

The notes are printed in a long and narrow printing room, in which a dozen machines of similar construction are in full action. Their denominations vary from £5 to £1,000, the largest note now printed. They cost about two-thirds of a cent each. A single impression completes the note, specially numbered, dated, and signed by the cashier. The notes are delivered in pairs, slid upon a small table at the back of the press, where an employee stands to examine each one and see that it is correctly numbered and perfectly printed. The numbers run backward, so that the notes of each bundle of ten thousand lie in their natural order when they are taken away. Thus, the two notes on each sheet are numbered, say 67168 and 77168, and the next pair are 67167 and 77167. The bundles are cut in two by an ordinary cutter, and it thus happens that every Bank of England note has three rough edges and one clean one. Great reliance, as a check upon counterfeiting, is placed upon the paper itself, the engraving, as compared with the American bank-note standard, being less elaborate. The paper, specially made from pure linen rags, is strangely thin and remarkably tough, has a peculiar shade of whiteness impossible to describe, and is printed in indelible black ink of a special manufacture. The paper is made by a secret process at a special mill, which time out of mind has been the property of the Portal family. The note to-day is practically the same as it ever has been, and its apparent simplicity offers a great temptation to counterfeiters out of employment.

THE BANK'S LOSSES BY COUNTERFEITING AND FORGERY.

The known losses of the bank through counterfeiting, mount up, in the two hundred years of its history, among the millions. The first offence of this kind against

PRINTING FIVE-POUND NOTES.

the bank was in 1758. A young man named Richard William Vaughan, to show his lady-love how easily he could make money, counterfeited twenty notes, and gave them to her, she thriftily taking them to the bank. What was done with Richard William nobody appears to know, but there is a general consensus of opinion that he never did it again.

Forgery does not seem to have attained the dignity of a public industry until 1797, when the one-pound notes were issued. For six years previous to this date there had been only one execution, forgery in those days being a capital offence. In the six years succeeding, however, eighty-five forgers were put to death. Executions continued, but forgery thrived until justices were compelled, by the long death roll, to take a more lenient view. Finally, in 1830, the convictions for forgery in a single year amounted to three hundred and twenty, and the death penalty, on the petition of N. M. Rothschild; Overend, Gurney & Company; and a man named Sanderson, the three biggest names in the city, along with other merchants, was finally abrogated. In 1784, "Old Patch," the son of an old-clothes dealer, and the ex-partner of Foote the comedian in a brewery, took £200,000 from the bank by forgeries, making his own ink, paper, and press, and he hung himself when arrested. Astlett, in 1803, embezzled Exchequer bills to the value of £342,000. Fauntleroy, a banker, in 1824, obtained £360,000 by forging powers of attorney for the sale of consols, and was hung at Newgate. In the general jubilee throughout the city over the proclamation of peace with the American Republic, in 1783, fourteen forged £50 notes were cashed unnoticed; and for years in the early part of this century, the bank's annual loss by counterfeits was a figure of many thousands of pounds. Forgeries to-day are rare. The machinery of detection is perfect, and the system of numbering, as well as the perpetual use by all banks of freshly printed Bank of England notes, presents insurmountable obstacles to "smashers."

THE ELABORATE SWINDLE CONDUCTED BY THE BIDWELLS.

The most sensational episode in the history of forgeries on the Bank of England was that of the Bidwells. While the total amount of money out of which they defrauded the bank was not as large as had been obtained by other great swindlers, the scale on which they were operating, the systematic cleverness with which the *coup* had been arranged, and the wonderful skill with which a large number of forgeries had been executed, and passed by the bank, showed clearly that but for an accidental discovery through carelessness on their part, the amount of their frauds might easily have mounted into the millions. I am assured by a gentleman who was cognizant of the state of feeling in the bank at the time that when the first discovery was made, there was only one word to express it, and that was consternation. The scope of the swindle was so wide, that for a day or two all confidence in commercial paper, upon which the bulk of trade is conducted, was in suspension, because the paper of so many substantial firms, including written and stamped indorsements of many kinds, had been so perfectly imitated as to defy detection.

The enterprise and its success were almost entirely due to the genius of George Bidwell, though he was ably assisted by his brother Austin, George McDonald, and, in a subsidiary way, by a young American whom they cabled for, by the name of Noyes. They came to England well supplied with money, the proceeds of forgery, and had a well-defined idea of what they proposed to do.

The first thing necessary was to obtain a banking account with the bank, and this was cleverly managed by Austin, through a first-class firm of West End tailors, who had an account at the West End branch of the bank. Austin told them he was going to Ireland, and wished to deposit a large amount of money. They obliged him by introducing him to the bank, and he deposited $6,000, and $5,000 on the day following. A transaction of $40,000, which he then induced the bank to carry through for him, removed all doubts as to his solidity, and Mr. Frederick Albert Warren, which name he assumed, was known to be a client who might deal to any amount without exciting suspicion.

Even with this advantage, George, who was buying commercial paper in Holland, and vainly endeavoring to "do" the Dutch business men, did not see his way clearly, until a small transaction through the Barings in London showed McDonald the whole inside of the system by which the commercial paper, usually bills at three months, of all reputable and substantial firms, passed from hand to hand and bank to bank without the slightest inquiry as to drawer and acceptor, until it came due. McDonald telegraphed for George, who came at once to London, and the three went to work.

They bought all the first class bills they could get, laid in a complete outfit of ink, stamps, and paper, and went to work drawing commercial bills, accepting them, indorsing them, and producing results which were never questioned by anybody, and probably would not have been till they fell due, but for the error mentioned.

In the meantime Austin opened another account, at the Continental Bank, as Mr. Charles Johnson Horton. He pretended to be an American who had come over to build Pullman palace cars at Birmingham, and from Birmingham nearly all the forged bills were sent to the bank, and discounted for Mr. "Warren." By means of the Continental Bank account, they were enabled to obtain large amounts in notes, which, if they had taken them from the Bank of England and immediately turned them back into gold, as was their plan, in the same bank, would have excited suspicion.

MORE "BOODLE" THAN THE SWINDLERS KNEW WHAT TO DO WITH.

Once started, the plan worked without a hitch. They made one or two preliminary trials, and finding that the forgeries were not questioned, sent down, on January 21, 1872, a batch amounting to $21,000. The money was paid, the bank discounting the bills without a word, and filing them away for presentation when due. A few days later, February 4th, they sent the second batch, of $55,360, with the same result. They quickly followed this up, at short intervals, with batches of $23,210 on February 10th, $73,480 on February 13th, $73,430 on February 20th, $96,265 on February 24th, and $121,325 on February 28th. Their system was perfect, and their confidence was great. The first of the forged bills did not fall due until March 25th. They were exchanging notes from the Continental Bank into gold at the Bank of England at the rate of $50,000 per day, and carrying the gold to their rooms near Piccadilly Circus, and did this until they became "sick of carrying the stuff." At the same time they were buying United States bonds through Jay Cooke & Company, $220,000 in these securities being afterwards recovered in a trunk full of dirty linen sent by George Bidwell to New York.

All being ready, they were preparing their grand stroke. They proposed to take an indefinite amount, something between half a million and a million in one day, and then leave the country. An oversight, however, proved their ruin. In the batch of $131,325, there were two bills on which the acceptance by B. W. Blydenstein was not dated. The clerk who received them thought this merely an oversight, and on March 1st sent the bills to Mr. Blydenstein for the correction. He promptly pronounced them forgeries, and the bank was aghast.

THE SWINDLERS ENTRAPPED BY THEIR OWN BUNGLING.

The notification of Scotland Yard was a matter of a few minutes, and Noyes, who had been regularly and formally indentured as "Horton's" clerk, was arrested as he entered the Continental Bank to draw the money. Even then all preparations for discovery were so perfect that the quartet would have escaped but for a second oversight. George, who was watching, saw the arrest. He sent word without delay to McDonald and Austin. Austin fled, George fled, and McDonald fled. Noyes proved to be all they had expected of him. He was to receive only five per cent of the profits, but he resolutely held to his story, refused to betray them under promise of freedom, and took a sentence of penal servitude for life rather than turn traitor. He held to his first statement that he was merely a clerk, and knew nothing of the transactions.

There would have been no means of discovering the connection between the three, but for a piece of clean blotting-paper in McDonald's lodgings, upon which he had blotted a note to George just before he went away without notifying his landlady, and thereby exciting her suspicion. The police knew that the Bidwells were in England, and flashed George Bidwell's description in all directions. He was hunted through Ireland, and caught, after an exciting chase, in Scotland. Austin was captured in Havana, and McDonald in New York. All four were tried, and sentenced to penal servitude for life on August 26, 1873, but were released, after fourteen years' imprisonment, on tickets-of-leave, George and Austin coming out of Woking in 1887. The only thing about the whole plot which the English have never been able to understand is, that forgers who had so much money to start with should have taken the chances of further crime.

THE GENERAL BANKING DEPARTMENT.

After passing through the departments occupied with printing and cancellation, you come to the one most familiar to the public in the daily routine of city finance, viz., the General Banking Department. This is a spacious apartment, looking in all respects like an ordinary banking-room, at the Princes Street corner, facing the Royal Exchange. This department has two distinct branches, the first of which is the Public Drawing Office. This has charge of all public or government accounts, and is practically a national treasury. It receives all the money collected throughout the country as taxes, customs, excise duties, etc.; and all payments made on account of the public service are

DIVIDEND ROOM.

AUTOMATIC WEIGHT TESTING MACHINE.

made through orders issued upon it, and paid over its counters.

The second branch, the Private Drawing Office, is devoted entirely to private accounts. Any person properly introduced to the chief cashier may open an account here, though the business which he offers must, in the opinion of the cashier, be a remunerative one. No stipulated cash balance is required, but, according to a rough calculation, the account to be regarded as desirable must yield an average of sixpence per check cashed throughout the year. All the London banks have drawing accounts at the Bank of England, which is essentially the bankers' bank. This creates some criticism of its system of management, since its directors, chosen according to custom, are always merchants and never bankers.

A special room is reserved for the drawing bankers, and here the vast daily exchanges of the London banks are conducted as a valuable aid to the Clearing House. The number of private accounts in the Private Drawing Office is about five thousand, and the average total balances is about £21,000,000 ($105,000,000).

The subsidiary departments in this branch of the bank are numerous. They include the Bill Office, in which all bills of exchange belonging to customers or discounted by the bank, are kept sorted and arranged, so as to be presented without fail at maturity; and the Securities Office. This receives for safe custody all mortgage and debenture shares belonging to customers of the bank who wish to deposit them. The interest is collected as it falls due, coupons are cut off, sold, or collected, as may be desired, and the proceeds credited to the customer's drawing account. A separate branch of this department is also the Discount Office, the bank employing a certain amount of its usual deposits in this customary line of banking business.

THE NATIONAL DEBT DEPARTMENT.

The National Debt Department occupies the Bartholomew Lane side, and under its popular title of the Dividend Room is well known to the two hundred and seventy thousand owners of national securities, who now exchange coupons there for notes or coin. This department, occupying ten rooms, pays quarterly the interest on £655,000,000 ($3,300,000,000) of government stock, and at other periods the interest on the colonial securities held by the bank, all of a public or semi-public character. The most interesting room in this department is the Stock Office Library. Here are stored in almost limitless number all the stock ledgers, transfer books, dividend books, power of attorney cases, and other volumes and documents which have accumulated in the past two hundred years. There are about sixty-five thousand of these in all, so systematically arranged that reference can be made to any one of them in a very short time. The most remarkable feature about them is their excellent state of preservation, and by means of them the whole of any government loan can be traced from its present possessors to the original holders, the title of any holder, at any period, being thus clearly established. The staff in this department numbers one hundred and seventy-five men, and seventeen hundred books are in constant use.

The most important general function fulfilled by the bank is that of regulating the money market by establishing the standard rate of discount. This is altered, weekly or daily, whenever circumstances call for a change. After estimating the probable movements of bullion during the next few days, the bank announces the lowest rate per annum at which it will discount the best secured bills of its regular customers. Much higher rates are required by it and other banks for trade bills, according to the standing of drawer and acceptor. The bank rate does not absolutely govern other banks, as many of them, when money is plenty, often discount well secured paper at figures below that of the Bank of England. As the stock of gold diminishes, the bank rate goes up, and descends as gold becomes more plentiful. At any period of commercial uneasiness, when the reserve is likely to be unduly diminished, the governors use their discretion, with the advice of the court of directors, in selling securities, or raising the rate of discount, or both.

CRISES IN THE HISTORY OF THE BANK.

The bank has had a number of crises in its history, though these were mainly confined to its early years. From its start it was bitterly opposed by the goldsmiths, who, in 1696, when it was but two years old, formed a conspiracy to break it. They quickly collected a large sum of its notes, and organized a run, one man alone demanding $150,000 in coin. The bank could not pay, and sent them to Parliament for redress, though it continued to pay ordinary demands. Great excitement followed, and the bank was compelled to issue a call to its proprietary. By this means it paid twenty per cent. of the claims, indorsed this on the notes, and returned them to the holders. At this time the notes fell to twenty-four per cent. discount.

In 1707 another crisis arose, through the fears of invasion, and the bank's paper fell so low that Child and Hoare, the two most prominent private bankers, refused to honor it. Then it was that many noblemen, including the Dukes of Marlborough, Newcastle, and Somerset, drove in hasty state to the bank, their coaches laden down with golden guineas, through which all claims were successfully met. As a return for this, the Bank of England not long

afterwards attacked Child's bank. They collected between £500,000 and £600,000 of Child's receipts, which then passed current as certified checks do at present, and, without warning, sent a clerk to demand this money. Child, who had begun life as an apprentice, and had risen to the first position among private bankers, was not caught napping. He had obtained from the Duchess of Marlborough a single check upon the Bank of England for £700,000, which, representing three and a half millions of dollars, would compare very favorably with the large checks of nowadays. When the clerk appeared at Child's, his clerk was sent to the Bank of England. Child began paying with his own money, but in a few minutes replaced it with fresh Bank of England notes, and the *coup* fell through.

It was in the 1707 crisis that the bank, to gain time, began paying in silver. It had a line of its own men, who, as fast as they were paid their shillings and sixpences, passed out and deposited the money, again joining the line with more notes. By this means the outside claimants were kept in check until the needed coin arrived. Queen Anne also intervened to help the bank in this crisis, allowing it six per cent. interest on a large amount in sealed bills.

THE BANK'S WHOLESOME POWER IN TIMES OF PANIC.

The essential point in the Bank of England system is one which is even now much debated, though bankers generally aver that it has worked remarkably well. This is the suspension by Parliament, when necessary, of the bank's charter, thereby allowing it to issue any amount of notes, for which extra issue the government, by its action, becomes morally, if not legally, responsible. This is a safety-valve, the calming effect of which, in a panic, since panics arise largely from the lack of ready money, is wonderful. The relation of the bank to financial affairs in the city has always been of a maternal character, and its intervention has on several occasions had a most salutary effect.

The first instance of this was in 1772, on the failure of Neale & Co. The ensuing panic was quickly ended by the bank's action. The great South Sea Bubble of 1720, in which that company's shares rose from a hundred to a thousand pounds, and then collapsed, was an occasion in which the bank held aloof, and was itself not at all injured. Its management, always conservative, had foreseen the outcome, and, moreover, the South Sea company had been its rival in bidding for a government concession which the company obtained at a ruinous figure. Consequently, the bank refused assistance, and the effect of the crash upon the public was disastrous in the widest and highest degree.

This panic was the outcome of the maddest period of speculation that the city ever saw. Company-promoting nowadays is legitimate business compared to it. Among eighty-six companies registered or patented on July 18, 1720, were the following: For a Wheel (or Perpetual Motion, £1,000,000; for Importing Walnut Trees from Virginia, £2,000,000; for Making Looking-Glasses, £2,000,000; for Importing Timber from Wales, £2,000,000; for Improving the Manufacture of Iron and Steel, £4,000,000. The company for transmuting quicksilver into a malleable metal, and Puckle's company for making square cannon balls and bullets, were capitalized equally heavily; but the happiest illustration of the public's greed for speculation was the work of an individual who advertised "A Company for carrying on an Undertaking of Great Advantage, but Nobody to know What It Is. Capital, £500,000, in five thousand shares of £100 each, each share paying £100 per annum." A deposit of two pounds per share was asked, and, incredible as it may seem, one thousand shares were taken and £2,000 paid between ten o'clock in the morning and three in the afternoon. The list then closed, and the promoter left for the Continent.

When the Barings were in difficulties in 1891, the bank averted a great panic. Many banks were heavy holders of the Baring paper, and the suspension of more than one, with a strain on many, was inevitable, unless the Barings were sustained. The bank quickly interviewed about thirty other bankers, and asked if the latter would guarantee it against loss if it assumed the £22,000,000 ($110,000,000) which the Barings owed. The guarantee was given, some of the banks insuring as high as £750,000 each. The panic ended, and the undertaking, particularly in view of a recent sale of £4,000,000 of the securities, has turned out much better than was hoped. No less serviceable in its way was the bank in the far greater panic of 1866, though in this case it assumed no responsibility whatever on behalf of the failing concerns.

THE GREAT PANIC OF 1866.

In the spring of that year a generally rotten state of financial affairs, and, as has latterly been the case in the United States, a very great extension of trade without the provision of an adequate pecuniary reserve, culminated in such a panic as London had not seen since the bursting of the South Sea Bubble. In March, 1866, Harned's bank at Liverpool stopped payment, with liabilities of $17,500,000. Business progressed in an uncertain and tremulous state until May; rumors of all kinds over like giant trees in a storm. In addition to all the contracting and other business firms which suspended, thirteen banks between May 10th and June 6th closed their doors, with aggregate liabilities exceeding $200,000,000.

The enormous sums paid across counters during the panic were never calculated. The Bank of England paid out $61,125,000 in five days. Another great bank paid out $10,000,000 in six hours. Tremendous as was the disaster, its demoralizing effect, the panic proper, was checked as if by magic. In the midst of the madness that

THE BANK GARDEN.

increased the general trepidation; uncertainty grew darker and darker; the bank raised its rate of discount steadily until, on May 3d, it reached eight per cent.; and then, in consequence of a court decision concerning only a petty $300,000, the great mercantile and financing house of Overend, Gurney & Company collapsed with a crash that, figuratively speaking, was heard all over the financial world. They had failed for the very respectable sum of $55,000,000.

The City, of course, went raving mad. For a time no banker, merchant, or citizen knew whether he was a millionaire or a pauper. Great commercial houses toppled followed the suspension of Overend, Gurney & Company, there came the news that Gladstone, then Chancellor of the Exchequer, had suspended the charter of the Bank of England. This was a suspension of a different character, and merchants dropped upon their knees upon the pavements and thanked God for Gladstone and the bank. All the money wanted was at hand, and the terrible need was met. So composing was the mere announcement, that not a single extra note was printed. Confidence was restored, and the succeeding failures were taken with comparative quietude.

AFTERWARDS.

BY IAN MACLAREN.

HE received the telegram in a garden when he was gazing on a vision of blue, set in the fronds of a palm, and listening to the song of the fishers as it floated across the bay.

"You look so utterly satisfied," said his hostess, in the high, clear voice of Englishwomen, "that I know you are tasting the luxury of a contrast. The Riviera is charming in December; imagine London, and Cannes is paradise."

As he smiled assent in the grateful laziness of a hard-worked man, his mind was stung with the remembrance of a young wife swathed in the dreary fog, who, above all things, loved the open air and the shining of the sun.

Her plea was that Bertie would weary alone, and that she hated travelling; but it came to him quite suddenly that this was always the programme of their holidays—some Mediterranean villa full of clever people for him, and the awful dulness of that Bloomsbury street for her; or he went North to a shooting lodge, where he told his best stories in the smoking-room, after a long day on the purple heather; and she did her best for Bertie at some watering-place, much frequented on account of its railway facilities and economical lodgings. Letters of invitation had generally a polite reference to his wife—"If Mrs. Trevor can accompany you, I shall be still more delighted;"—but it was understood that she would not accept.

"We have quite a grudge against Mrs. Trevor, because she will never come with her husband; there is some beautiful child who monopolizes her," his hostess would explain on his arrival; and Trevor allowed it to be understood that his wife was quite devoted to Bertie, and would be miserable without him.

When he left the room it was explained, "Mrs. Trevor is a hopelessly quiet person, what is called a 'good wife,' you know.

"The only time she dined with us, Tottie Fribby!—he was a Theosophist then, it's two years ago—was too amusing for words, and told us what incarnation he was going through.

"Mrs. Trevor, I believe, had never heard of Theosophy, and looked quite horrified at the idea of poor Tottie's incarnation.

"'Isn't it profane to use such words?' she said to me. So I changed to skirt dancing, and would you believe me, she had never seen it?

"What can you do with a woman like that? Nothing remains but religion and the nursery. Why do clever men marry those impossible women?"

Trevor was gradually given to understand, as by an atmosphere, that he was a brilliant man wedded to a dull wife, and there were hours—his worst hours—when he agreed.

"*Cara mia, cara mia*," sang the sailors; and his wife's face, in its perfect refinement and sweet beauty, suddenly replaced the Mediterranean.

Had he belittled his wife, with her wealth of sacrifice and delicate nature, beside women in spectacles who wrote on the bondage of marriage, and leaders of fashion who could talk of everything, from horse-racing to palmistry?

He had only glanced at her last letter; now he read it carefully:

"The flowers were lovely, and it was so mindful of you to send them, just like my husband. Bertie and I amused ourselves arranging and rearranging them in glasses, till we had made our tea-table lovely. But I was just one little bit disappointed not to get a letter—you see how exacting I am, sir. I waited for every post, and Bertie said, 'Has father's letter come yet?' When one is on holiday, writing letters is an awful bore; but just a line to Bertie and me. We have a map of the Riviera, and found out all the places you had been at in the yacht; and we tried to imagine you sailing on that azure sea, and landing among those silver olives. I am so grateful to every one for being kind to you, and I hope you will enjoy yourself to the full. Bertie is a little stronger, I'm sure; his cheeks were quite rosy to-day for him. It was his birthday on Wednesday, and I gave him a little treat. The sun was shining brightly in the forenoon, and we had a walk in the Gardens, and made believe that it was Italy! Then we went to Oxford Street, and Bertie chose a regiment of soldiers for his birthday present. He wished some guns so much that I allowed him to have them as a present from you. They only cost one-and-sixpence, and I thought you would like him to have something. Jane and he had a splendid game of hide-and-seek in the evening, and my couch was the den, so you see we have our own gayety in Bloomsbury.

"Don't look sulky at this long scribble and say,

'What nonsense women write!' for it is almost the same as speaking to you, and I shall imagine the letter all the way till you open it in the sunshine.

"So untie and kiss my name, for this comes with my heart's love from

"Your devoted wife,
"MAUD TREVOR.

"P. S.—Don't be alarmed because I have to rest; the doctor does not think that there is any danger, and I'll take great care."

"A telegram." It was the shattering of a dream. "How wicked of some horrid person! Business ought not to be allowed to enter paradise. Let's hope it's pleasure; perhaps some one has won a lot of money at Monte Carlo, and wishes us to celebrate the affair."

"Whom's it for? Oh! Mr. Edward Trevor; then it's a brief by telegraph, I suppose. Some millionaire's will case, and the Attorney-General can't manage it alone. What a man he is, to have briefs in holiday time.

"There it is, but remember, before you open it, that you are bound to remain here over Christmas at any rate, and help us with our theatricals. My husband declares that a successful barrister must be a born actor." . . .

An hour later Trevor was in the Paris express, and for thirty hours he prayed one petition, that she might live till he arrived. He used to have a berth in the Wagon Lit as a matter of course, and had begun to complain about the champagne in the dining-car; but the thought of comfort made him wince on this journey, and he twice changed his carriage, once when an English party would not cease from badinage that mocked his ears, and again because a woman had brown eyes with her expression of dog-like faithfulness. The darkness of the night after that sunlit garden, and the monotonous roar of the train, and the face of smiling France covered with snow, and the yeasty waters of the Channel, and the moaning of the wind, filled his heart with dread.

Will that procession of luggage at Dover never come to an end? A French seaman —a fellow with earrings and a merry face—appears and reappears with maddening regularity, each time with a larger trunk. One had X. Y. on it in big white letters. Why not Z. also? Who could have such a name? That is a lady's box, black and brown, plastered with hotel labels. Some bride, perhaps . . . they are carrying the luggage over his heart. Have they no mercy?

The last piece is in, and the sailors make a merry group at the top of the gangway. They look like Bretons, and that fellow is laughing again—some story about a little child; he can just hear "*Ma petite*." . . .

"Guard, is this train never to start? We're half an hour late already."

"Italian mail very heavy, sir; still bringing up bags; so many people at Riviera in winter, writing home to their friends." . . .

How cruel every one is! He had not written for ten days. Something always happened, an engagement of pleasure. There was a half-finished letter; he had left it to join a Monte Carlo party.

"Writing letters—home, of course, to that idolized wife. It's beautiful, and you are an example to us all; but Mrs. Trevor will excuse descriptions of scenery; she knows you are enjoying yourself."

Had she been expecting that letter from post to post, calculating the hour of each delivery, identifying the postman's feet in that quiet street, holding her breath when he rang, stretching her hand for a letter, to let it drop unopened, and bury her face in the pillow? Had she . . . waiting for a letter that never came? Those letters that he wrote from the Northern Circuit in that first sweet year, a letter a day, and one day two—it had given him a day's advantage. Careful letters, too, though written between cases, with bits of description and amusing scenes. Some little sameness towards the end, but she never complained of that, and even said those words were the best. And that trick he played—the thought of the postman must have brought it up—how pleasant it was, and what a success! He would be his own letter one day, and take her by surprise. "A letter, ma'am," the girl said—quite a homely girl, who shared their little joys and anxieties—and then he showed his face with apologies for intrusion. The flush of love in her face, will it be like that to-night, or . . . What can be keeping the train now? Is this a conspiracy to torment a miserable man?

He thrusts his head out of the window in despair, and sees the guard trying to find a compartment for a family that had mistaken their train.

The husband is explaining, with English garrulity, at the station hearing, what an inconvenience it would have been, had they gone in the Holborn Viaduct carriages.

"Half an hour's longer drive, you know, and it's very important we should get home in time; we are expected . . ."

For what? Dinner, most likely. What did it matter when they got home, to-day or next year? Yet he used to be angry if he were made late for dinner. They come into his compartment, and explain the situation at great length, while he pretends to listen.

A husband and wife returning from a month in Italy, full of their experiences; the Corniche Road, the palaces of Genoa, the pictures in the Pitti, St. Peter's at Rome. Her first visit to the Continent, evidently; it reminded them of a certain tour round the Lakes in '80, and she withdrew her hand from her husband's as the train came out from the tunnel. They were not smart people—very pronounced middle-class— but they were lovers, after fifteen years.

They forgot him, who was staring on the bleak landscape with white, pinched face.

"How kind to take me this trip. I know how much you denied yourself, but it has made me young again;" and she said "Edward." Were all these coincidences arranged? Had his purgatorio begun already?

"Have you seen the 'Globe,' sir? Bosworth, M. P. for Pedlington, has been made a judge, and there's to be a keen contest."

"Trevor, I see, is named as the Tory candidate—a clever fellow, I've heard. Do you know about him? He's got on quicker than any man of his years.

"Some say that it's his manner; he's such a good sort, the juries cannot resist him, a man told me—a kind heart goes for something even in a lawyer. Would you like to look . . .

"Very sorry; would you take a drop of brandy? No? The passage was a little rough, and you don't look quite up to the mark."

Then they left him in peace, and he drank his cup to the dregs.

It was for Pedlington he had been working and saving, for a seat meant society and the bench, perhaps . . . What did it matter now?

She was to come and sit within the cage when he made his first speech, and hear all the remarks.

"Of course it will be a success, for you do everything well, and your wife will be the proudest woman in London.

"Sir Edward Trevor, M.P. I know it's foolish, but it's the foolishness of love, dear, so don't look cross; you are everything to me, and no one loves you as I do."

What are they slowing for now? There's no station. Did ever train drag like this one?

Off again, thank God. . . . If she only were conscious, and he could ask her to forgive his selfishness.

At last, and the train glides into Victoria. No, he had nothing to declare; would they let him go, or they might keep his luggage altogether.

Some vision was ever coming up; and now he saw her, kneeling on the floor and packing that portmanteau, the droop of her figure, her thin white hands.

He was so busy that she did these offices for him—tried to buckle the straps even; but he insisted on doing that. It gave him half an hour longer at the Club. What a brute he had been. . . .

"Do anything you like with my things. I'll come to-morrow . . . as fast as you can drive."

Huddled in a corner of the hansom so that you might have thought he slept, this man was calculating every foot of the way, gloating over a long stretch of open, glistening asphalt, hating unto murder the immovable drivers whose huge vans blocked his passage. If they had known, there was no living man but would have made room for him . . . but he had not known himself. . . . Only one word to tell her he knew now.

As the hansom turned into the street he bent forward, straining his eyes to catch the first glimpse of home. Had it been day-time the blinds would have told their tale; now it was the light he watched.

Dark on the upper floors; no sick light burning . . . have mercy . . . then the blood came back to his heart with a rush. How could he have forgotten?

Their room was at the back for quietness, and it might still be well. Someone had been watching, for the door was instantly opened, but he could not see the servant's face.

A doctor came forward and beckoned him to go into the study. . . .

It seemed as if his whole nature had been smitten with insensibility, for he knew everything without words, and yet he heard the driver demanding his fare, and noticed that the doctor had been reading the evening paper while he waited; he saw the paragraph about that seat.

What work those doctors have to do. . . .

"An hour ago . . . we were amazed that she lived so long; with any other woman it would have been this morning; but she was determined to live till you came home.

"It was not exactly will-power, for she was the gentlest patient I ever had; it was"—the doctor hesitated—a peremptory Scotchman hiding a heart of fire beneath a coating of ice—" it was simply love."

When the doctor had folded up the evening paper, and laid it on a side table, which took some time, he sat down opposite that fixed, haggard face, which had not yet been softened by a tear.

"Yes, I'll tell you everything; perhaps it will relieve your mind; and Mrs. Trevor said you would wish to know, and I must be here to receive you. Her patience and thoughtfulness were marvellous.

"I attend many very clever and charming women, but I tell you, Mr. Trevor, not one has so impressed me as your wife ... Her self-forgetfulness passed words; she thought of every one except herself. Why, one of the last things she did was to give directions about your room; she was afraid you might feel the change from the Riviera. But that is by the way, and these things are not my business.

"From the beginning I was alarmed, and urged that you be sent for; but she pledged me not to write; you needed your holiday, she said, and it must not be darkened with anxiety.

"She spoke every day about your devotion and unselfishness; how you wished her to go with you, but she had to stay with the boy. . . .

"The turn for the worse? It was yesterday morning, and I had Sir Reginald at once. We agreed that recovery was hopeless, and I telegraphed to you without delay.

"We also consulted whether she ought to be told, and Sir Reginald said, 'Certainly; that woman has no fear, for she never thinks of herself, and she will want to leave messages.'

"'If we can only keep her alive till to-morrow afternoon,' he said; and you will like to remember that everything known to the best man in London was done. Sir Reginald came back himself unasked to-day, because he remembered a restorative that might sustain the failing strength. She thanked him so sweetly that he was quite shaken; the fact is, that both of us would soon have played the fool. But I ought not to trouble you with these trifles at this time, only as you wanted to know all. . . .

"Yes, she understood what we thought before I spoke, and only asked when you would arrive. 'I want to say "Good-by,"' and then I will be ready;' but perhaps . . .

"'Tell you everything?' That is what I am trying to do, and I was here nearly all day, for I had hoped to fulfil her wish.

"No, she did not speak much, for we enjoined silence and rest as the only chance; but she had your photograph on her pillow, and some flowers you had sent.

"They were withered, and the nurse removed them when she was sleeping; but she missed them, and we had to put them in her hands, 'My husband was so thoughtful.'

"This is too much for you, I see; it is simply torture. Wait till to-morrow. . . .

"Well, if you insist. Expecting a letter ... yes ... let me recollect ... No, I am not hiding anything, but you must not let this get upon your mind.

"We would have deceived her, but she knew the hour of the Continental mails, and could detect the postman's ring. Once a letter came, and she insisted upon seeing it in case of any mistake. But it was only an invitation for you, I think, to some country house.

"It can't be helped now, and you ought not to vex yourself; but I believe a letter would have done more for her than . . . What am I saying now?

"As she grew weaker she counted the hours, and I left her at four full of hope. 'Two hours more and he'll be here,' and by that time she had your telegram in her hand.

"When I came back the change had come, and she said, 'It's not God's will; bring Bertie.'

"So she kissed him, and said something to him, but we did not listen. After the nurse had carried him out—for he was weeping bitterly, poor little chap—she whispered to me to get a sheet of paper and sit down by her bedside. . . . I think it would be better . . . very well, I will tell you all.

"I wrote what she dictated with her last breath, and I promised you would receive it from her own hand, and so you will. She turned her face to the door and lay quite still till about six, when I heard her say your name very softly, and a minute afterwards she was gone, without pain or struggle." . . .

She lay as she had died, waiting for his coming, and the smile with which she had said his name was still on her face. It was the first time she did not color with joy at his coming, that her hand was cold to his touch. He kissed her, but his heart was numbed, and he could not weep.

Then he took her letter and read it beside that silence.

"DEAREST: They tell me now that I shall not live to see you come in and to cast my arms once more round your neck before we part. He kind to Bertie, and remember that he is delicate and shy. He will miss me, and you will be patient with him for my sake. Give him my watch, and do not let him forget me. My locket with your likeness I would like left on my heart. You will never know how much I have loved you, for I could never speak. You have been very good to me, and I want you to know that I am grateful; but it is better perhaps that I should die, for I might hinder you in your future life. Forgive me because I came short of what your wife should have been. None can ever love you better. You will take these poor words from a dead hand, but I shall see you, and I shall never cease to love you, to follow your life, to pray for you—my first, my only love."

The fountains within him were broken, and he flung himself down by the bedside in an agony of repentance.

"Oh, if I had known before; but now it is too late, too late!"

For we sin against our dearest not because we do not love, but because we do not imagine.

THE PIERRE LOTI OF PRIVATE LIFE.

HIS LUXURIOUS HOME—HIS METHODS OF WORK AS A NAVAL LIEUTENANT AND A NOVELIST.

BY MADAME ADAM.

IF one wishes for thorough acquaintance with the author of "Azayde," "Mariage de Loti," "Spahi," "Fleurs d'Ennui," "Pêcheur d'Islande," "Madame Chrysantheme," "Roman d'un Enfant," "Fantôme d'Orient," and of "Matelot"—if, I say, one wishes for an intimate knowledge of Pierre Loti, he needs but to seek for him in his works. Few writers more than he have looked at life through themselves. Just as he sees with his own eyes the incomparable picture which he sets before us, so he judges through his own experiences; his heroes pass through the same sorrows which he has suffered, and are struck by the same shocks which he has received. Those who live in intimate communion with the life of Pierre Loti can give double names to the faces of all his characters; and I will add that it is by his own family, by his most intimate friends, that he is most admired, for they only can appreciate the degree of art with which he enhances reality. It is likewise true that I have heard worthy praise of Pierre Loti's descriptions only from those who themselves had seen the places which he described.

In the first pages of the "Romance of a Child" Pierre Loti reveals to us the double nature which prompted him to observe himself from his childhood. His first recollection of these observations is curious, and is one which, by looking backward, we may all duplicate closely. He was not more than two years old, and he sees himself at nightfall in a large, low room, with his beloved aunt Claire at his side, before the fire. He looks deeply into the flames, which communicate their ardor to his childish imagination. He bounds and dances; he whirls about till he is giddy. For the first time he is conscious to the point of intoxication of the exhilaration of life, and yet he is a looker-on at his own transports; he observes them, and coldly passes judgment on his own exaltation. To me all of Pierre Loti is in this first scene. Never in time to come is he to experience the irresistible sway of enthusiasm without self-analysis, and he must ever feel the measure of the inadequacy of this process.

Of extreme sensibility, dreaming of that which lies beyond sight in all things, Pierre Loti is ever searching out two things in life —his own sensations and those which he may be able to call forth in others. Doubtless he is not always engaged in weighing himself, is not striking a balance between the exigencies of his heart and those of his art, and yet he suffers unconsciously from being an artist at the same time as a man. He can never be satisfied with what he comes across, real things being always inferior to those realized by an incomparable imagination like his.

AN EXCEPTIONAL CHILD WITH A TASTE FOR MUSIC.

Loti was an exceptional child; not, perhaps, in those manifestations which are the ground of his family pride in him, but in point of originality and imagination. I have often talked with his sister, who is much older than he, and she is inexhaustible in the relation of striking anecdotes of the child and of the very young man. Inventive beyond expression, he made games which delighted his young comrades, es-

PIERRE LOTI IN THE COSTUME OF A MEMBER OF THE FRENCH ACADEMY.

pecially the little girls, and he was already a social centre. He grouped about him those of both sexes who nourished his own intelligence. He told touching stories, of which his little friends could never hear enough; he built little theatres, composed plays and acted them; he busied himself with making collections, and enlisted the passionate sympathy of all about him, so that they took part in his researches.

A musician at a very early age, he developed in the members of his family a love of the beautiful in all its forms. Flowers, landscapes, nature, filled him with delight, and it was often difficult to arouse him from ecstatic contemplation. He dreamed of a life other than the one he saw lived about him, and he persuaded himself and his friends that he was some hero, whose part he often played to the verge of danger, when he had his strength or his agility to prove; and he thus entered on that extraordinary education which, unaided, he gave himself, and which has made of him a gymnast, even an acrobat, a passionate lover of all physical exercises.

What a singular medley of characteristics we find in Pierre Loti! A dreamer to the point of absorption in dreaming, so active as to be fond of the *tour de force*. All this gives Pierre Loti the aspect of a man of well-balanced, cool spirit, and at the same time of a certain supple inflexibility which is peculiar to himself.

Pierre Loti speaks little, and listens but for an instant. Devoted to his friends, he takes interest in all that renders them either joyful or sad; but spare him empty phrases, the slow lengths of a story that could be told in a few words. His eyes soon take on that look, directed inward, which it is so difficult to recall or to catch again. It cannot be said that he has a happy nature. He is disturbed to excess by an enemy; he instantly scrutinizes an agreeable event, and looks at the dark side of it; it is almost true that he suffers more from the discordance of one jealous or evil-speaking person in the concert of praises which rise before him than he enjoys from the full harmony of that concert.

Among the rarest of the artistic qualities with which Pierre Loti is endowed, is one which gives pleasure to all who approach him; that is, the exquisite and truly incomparable taste which enables him to turn the smallest object to account in giving character to a decoration. The slightest drapery, a vase, furniture disposed in a certain manner, and you say to yourself: "I am in such a country," or "I find myself back in another century." What in France is called "style" in the arrangement of interiors reaches the same perfection in Loti as his ability to render what he sees. In reading one of his descriptions it is impossible not to see what he has seen. On entering a *salon* or a room with whose decoration he has been occupied, one has a precise representation of the time and of the country which he has sought to recall.

LOTI'S FAMILY HOME.

The paternal residence at Rochefort is the most astonishing habitation imaginable. Small in appearance, in a street of a provincial city, it is impossible to foretell what will be seen on entering within. The very small façade attracts no attention. One enters a narrow, roofed passage, which communicates with another passage, also narrow, but without a roof, which is called the garden; there are low walls, allowing the windows of the upper story to enjoy a view of the adjoining gardens, otherwise I do not know how they would be lighted.

The first drawing-room in Loti's house is a modern room, richly furnished, very elegant, and altogether of the fashion of to-day; but this drawing-room looks out on a pagoda—not an imitation, but a real pagoda—brought back piecemeal from the island of Formosa. Loti and his comrade, Jean Dargène, went night after night, at the risk of their lives, to bring away some portion of it, before demolishing it altogether, to carry it home to France. Thus bit by bit Loti had traced its smallest detail, and was enabled to reconstruct it with such exactitude that it gives one the sensation of having been instantly transported to the scenes which witnessed both the glory and the sufferings of our great Admiral Courbet. Pierre Loti made the campaign of the isles of Formosa on the "Triomphante." From the pagoda we ascend a little stairway which leads to a Turkish *salon* of such strikingly original character that the impression made upon one who has once entered it can never be forgotten. It copies the interior of an Arabian dwelling with such scrupulous fidelity that I do not exaggerate when I say that in spite of the poetry and grace of every detail, in spite of the richness of the arabesque, the shimmering of the hangings, the attraction of the furnishings, which all invite to *far niente*, and the incomparable beauty of the carpets, of which Loti possesses a choice collection, a woman there feels the oppressive anguish of a prison.

From the Turkish apartment one passes, by stairways leading back to the front of the house, to Madame Pierre Loti's own room, of which you could scarcely conjecture the style. It is a bed-chamber of the First Empire. A mahogany bed with brasses which are veritable gems, hangings of yellow rep with blue borders, long chairs, easy chairs, footstools, pier tables, *bibelots*, ceilings adorned with enormous golden honey-bees in relief; the decoration of the chimney-pieces, the writing-table, all the small objects, everything, absolutely everything, is executed with the most absolute exactitude and scrupulousness of style.

But here is Loti's chamber, the room of a Breton peasant. The bed is very high, with tall posts of oak, and curtains of red and white checked cotton; there is a tall dresser, and an ancient oaken table, which, with its little basin and ewer of water, serves as washstand. The floor is tiled. There is a pair of sabots at the foot of the bed. Here we find ourselves in Brittany, at home with the *Pêcheur d'Islande*, after having traversed the First Empire, and Turkey and China.

But we go down-stairs now, cross the garden, and ascend again, to enter a mediæval dining-room, which is a most beautiful, most radiant room, and is, even among so many astonishing things, by far the greatest wonder of the house. Loti was three years in finding and putting in place the wainscoting and the loggia. The banners and window glass he had copied from old models; the table, in the shape of a horseshoe, and the immense chimney-piece, he found. One might think himself in a hall untouched by time, in the recesses of the oldest of the châteaux of Beauce.

A GRAND FÊTE GIVEN BY LOTI.

It was for the inauguration of this admirable apartment that Loti gave to forty selected guests a *fête* Louis XI., which we can never forget.

He had written or given verbally to us all the design and color of our costumes, so that each of us might contribute to the perfect harmony of the general effect which he had planned.

The preparation for this *fête* had acquired such fame in the city of Rochefort that the loungers in the streets fully expected to see me brought in a chariot drawn by oxen, and that I would alight *en costume*. How shall I give an idea of an entertainment on which Loti and two young pupils of Jacob de Charles had

INTERIOR OF PIERRE LOTI'S PAGODA.

lavished their efforts during six months? The viands and drinks had been the subjects of much research; the former had been frequently essayed during a long period of time, and the latter were carefully made ready in advance, that they might most perfectly reproduce the sensations enjoyed by our ancestors.

Loti had discovered in an isle of La Charente two old musicians who played airs of that by-gone time. One of them was more than eighty years old, and he died of the joyous excitement of the occasion, a few days after his triumph. In the anteroom, as we entered, we saw the body of a man swinging from a gallows. Scarcely were we seated at the tables when the sound of trumpets announced the arrival of a troop of Saracenic prisoners. Since we were in *joy et festin*, we bestowed pardon on them, and they seated themselves in our company. It was a surprise that wrung cries of terror from me, to feel a trapdoor rising under my feet, and to see thus admitted a band of acrobats, who proceeded to execute most curious feats of strength and agility. Meantime we continued to feast; foods and drinks were set before us in long succession; it would take a volume to describe it all. Adrien Marie, a friend of ours, had come from Paris with a tall greyhound which never left his side, and he had put on the disguise of a fool. He was one of the most amusing features of the evening. But it would be impossible to mention all the details of that unique entertainment. I will speak only of the ceremonious entry of a superb roast peacock, with tail spread, carried on the shoulders of four squires, and preceded by a band of musicians playing the traditional peacock's march.

After dinner there was a dance that was especially applauded—the torch dance—in which young girls wrapped in long muslin veils, and young men, danced the dance of the torches. The smoking flames flitting about the white draperies, outlining the intricacies of the figures of the dance, kept us in constant fear of danger; and, at the same time, the sensation of witnessing a sacred dance, revived after the lapse of centuries of neglect, aroused our enthusiasm.

PIERRE LOTI IN EARLY COSTUME AS "OSIRIS"

The illustration will enable you to judge of Loti's manner of composing a costume. It represents his attire at an entertainment of mine, in which each guest was to come in the costume of some famous character, and then to play his part during the evening. Thus Osiris was brought into conversation with Cleopatra, Charlotte Corday with Marat, Charles the First with Cromwell, a grisette with Nero, Adrienne Lecouvreur with Scapin, and Mahomet with Pourceaugnac. Pierre Loti came as the Fisher of Iceland to a garden party which I gave at the Abbage de Gif.

HOW HE APPORTIONS HIS WORK EACH DAY.

Pierre Loti is evidently never idle. Since I have to speak of him only in private life, I need not linger to describe his manner of writing. It is, moreover, perfectly simple, and can be described in a word. In the morning Lieutenant Julien Viand is wholly devoted to his work or to his study, or to his service as a mariner. If he has command of a vessel, as soon as he rises he is occupied with his men; he either questions the second in command, summoning him to his house for the report, or he goes in person to inspect his vessel; for when he is Lieutenant Viand, this dreamer becomes the most serious and most accomplished of officers. His bearing, his gesture, his glance, his voice, and one might almost add his stature, undergo a complete change when Pierre Loti of the *Académie Française* becomes a lieutenant in the French navy.

THE TURKISH SALON IN PIERRE LOTI'S HOUSE.

The young commander is adored by his men, who find him devoted to the execution of justice, at once implacable towards a wilful fault, and indulgent towards an unwitting error. Although of small stature, he is so strong that he calls forth the admiration of his men, when, in the case of a manœuvre badly executed or in the removal of some cargo, he indicates with a gesture what is to be done, or lifts or sets in place some object. No one of his subordinates could get the better of him, if he ventured to contend with him as gymnast or as marksman. The sailors ascribe to him a very complex superiority made up of all in him that they can see and understand, as well as of much that is beyond their grasp, and they are devoted and submissive to him to the point of fanaticism.

Lieutenant Julien Viaud, whenever he has the leisure to do so, becomes Pierre Loti from two o'clock until six o'clock in the afternoon. He requires no more time than this to write in his superb, large, correct handwriting a volume in a few months. His study is always full of flowers; he has a passion for them, and in a few seconds he can arrange in a vase an exquisite bouquet of what had appeared to be the most insignificant of flowers. The more perfume his flowers have the more he loves them. The odor of flowers never becomes oppressive to him, even when he is writing.

HOW LOTI LIVES.

If Loti is stationed in a city, it is quite certain that within an hour of his arrival he will have found and selected for his residence the house commanding the widest view, situated in the most original manner, and in which one can find the greatest retirement. In such a house I saw him at Hendaye.

The house was situated on the Bidassoa, a river as much Spanish as French, which serves as frontier to the two countries. When the tide rises, the Bidassoa is an arm of the sea, a gulf.

My readers will permit me to copy a description of Loti's house which I have already made, for I wrote my first impressions of the place on the spot, and I cannot improve it. "Loti's house is small, but is decorated by the fancy of a great artist. Over the white woodwork of the drawing-room, very commonplace and bare in itself, Loti has draped fishing-nets, which are agitated by the warm airs from without, and cause light and mysterious shadows to flit over the walls. The gray of the nets waving over the softened whiteness gives the impression of an evanescent decoration seen in a dream. Huge crab-shells which have become transparent, rough and ugly monsters of the sea, are attached to the netting.

"On every hand, in the many vases, are many beautiful flowers, which Loti can never be denied. Hangings draped in the corners, portières, furnishings disposed with taste, all combine to make one exclaim, on entering for the first time: 'How beautiful this is!' Loti's study, placed above the drawing-room, looks out also on the Bidassoa; one might say at certain hours that the view is over the sea. To write in peace, Loti has condemned the inner door to the room, and his visitors must go up to his sanctum by means of a

PIERRE LOTI IN FANCY COSTUME AS AN ICELANDIC FISHERMAN.

rope ladder, an easy way for sailors, but slightly incommodious for others.

"On the terrace, at the foot of this ladder, is a laurel of Apollo, bushy, enormous, colossal in size.

"'This was an omen,' I said to him, 'that you were to become an academician during your sojourn at Hendaye.'

"'That did not occur to me till after my election,' he answered."

In his address to the Académie Française, Loti has described his impressions while the question of his nomination was under consideration at Paris. He was in a skiff on the sea, returning from his small vessel, the "Zarclot," and was fully persuaded that he, so far away, so great a stranger to the tactics which often have an influence with the learned assembly, could not be proposed. And yet, in spite of his doubts, he had an impulse to stop at the telegraph station before going to his house.

"And," said he, "when I saw the heap of despatches which awaited me, I understood, even before I had opened one of them, that I had been elected."

Pierre Loti is a musician of a high order. He sings in a beautiful, true baritone voice, and as an accompanist he is unrivalled.

He loves quiet life with his family. His mother, Madame Viand—for Pierre Loti is Lieutenant Julien Viand—is the source from which he has drawn the distinction, sensibility, and grace of his mind. She is eighty-two years old, but she is as active as a young woman, and she performed feats of mountain climbing last autumn which were beyond the powers of her daughter, Madame Bou, the sister of Loti. It is a curious fact that Madame Viand, at her present age, has just witnessed for the first time a bull fight at Fontarabia, that adorable little Spanish city, which is on the other side of the river from Hendaye. Loti feared greatly lest the violent impression received from the combat should injure his mother. But she instantly grasped the picturesque side of the spectacle, and was absorbingly interested in it.

Pierre Loti is married, and his young wife loves to bear the name of Madame Pierre Loti, in preference to that of Madame Julien Viand. She admires her husband as much as the most impassioned of his readers, and she is sufficiently literate to understand him. Knowing Loti's love for flowers, it is one of her favorite occupations to renew the flowers on his table and in the drawing-room for the great gratification of Loti's eyes.

Loti lost his first little son, who came prematurely into the world, and he has never ceased to mourn for him. He has given his second son the name borne by the first, Samuel. The young Samuel, although scarcely four years old, is already a person of pronounced character. Of course he intends to be a sailor, and he is always dressed in sailor's costume. Inasmuch as his trousers are white, they must be changed several times daily, for the future admiral is somewhat too fond of playing on all fours with his cats.

Loti is passionately fond of cats. He attracts them to him to such a degree that all the unfortunate cats in a city where he is living seem to give each other the word, and flock about him to enlist his sympathy in their lot, to which he is never insensible. This brings to mind his wonderful "Book of Pity and of Death," in which he has drawn us to participate so deeply in the sufferings of animals. The four pages devoted to the last but one of the cattle slaughtered on the deck of the ship while the officer is on watch, and at whose execution the last of the animals looks on, is man's most elegant protest against the sufferings, the tortures, which we inflict on dumb creatures. After reading these pages one must be wholly without heart not to be moved, at least while the impression of the reading lasts, to become a vegetarian.

It has often been said that a man of letters cannot be a sailor in serious earnest. Such an affirmation may be true in regard to others, although the French navy has counted distinguished authors among its men; it is not true in regard to Loti. No one is more conversant with the occupations of his career, more attentive or skilful in performing his duties. Here again he gratifies the old passion of his childhood for physical exercises, his love of activity. The calling of a sailor has this peculiarity, which would naturally attract Loti's choice, that in it one is always on the eve of a battle between the elements, of an unfolding of moral and physical power, and that it affords many days to be given to dreaming.

I repeat to my readers that if, after this hasty sketch, they feel themselves insufficiently acquainted with Pierre Loti, they may look for him in his works. In any case, I believe I have given them a key by which they may find him.

BISMARCK IN 1894
From a photograph by Karl Hahn, Munich.
(See page 354.)

McCLURE'S MAGAZINE.

Vol. IV.   MAY, 1895.   No. 6.

OUR FIRST ONE HUNDRED THOUSAND.

IN one year and ten months from the issue of the first number, the circulation of McCLURE'S MAGAZINE has grown to 100,000 copies, the increase in twelve months being 65,000 copies.

The growth of the Magazine has been gradual from month to month, and has come from no special effort in pushing or advertising it, but mainly from the acceptability of the Magazine itself. In fact, so continuous has been the increase that only once, during the past eight months, has a sufficient number of copies been printed; and so closely has the Magazine sold out each month that there are on hand few more than sufficient copies to meet the need for bound volumes. Hence the size of each edition is a very accurate measure of the actual circulation. This fact is significant; because, while it is a mere matter of money to print large editions, anybody can do it who has the purse and will, to print them and sell them is quite another affair.

CIRCULATION DOUBLED INSIDE THE FIRST YEAR.

The first issue of McCLURE'S MAGAZINE (June, 1893) consisted of 20,000 copies. The edition gradually grew until, with the December, 1893, number, it was 35,000; this particular number showing an advance of 5,000 copies over any previous sale. The edition for May, 1894, was 40,000 copies, showing another clean advance over previous issues of 5,000 copies.

The increased sale of this number was attributed to the very complete series of portraits of General Grant, as well as to the valuable articles on his life and character by General Horace Porter and others. And at that time it was decided to devote, in a similar way, some pages to the principal portraits of Napoleon, the belief being that, with the revived interest in Napoleon, such a collection, printed in one number, would increase the circulation another 5,000 copies. The circulation fell off somewhat during the summer months of 1894; but with the October number it was found that an edition of 40,000 copies was considerably too small, that number selling out in four or five days.

THE NAPOLEON PICTURES AND PAPERS.

In seeking for portraits of Napoleon, we accidentally learned of Mr. Hubbard's remarkable collection. This collection we were invited to examine and to use, Mr. Hubbard putting it freely at our disposal. Even a cursory examination showed that it would be impossible to do justice to the collection and to the possibilities of the subject in one or even in four numbers of the Magazine. In fact, it was found that the pictures finally selected could not be published, even in very large installments, in less than eight numbers. So the plan first contemplated, of publishing one article with portraits of Napoleon showing him at different periods of his life, developed into a series of articles illustrated in a more interesting and complete manner than any previous publication on Napoleon. At the same time it became necessary to publish a compact, clear, and interesting life of Napoleon to accompany these pictures. The pictures came to us freely, and the historian was luckily at hand in the person of Miss Ida M. Tarbell, who had done a great deal of work for the Magazine previously, and who had spent three years in Paris studying the epoch of the French Revolution, and had just written a life of one of the principal women of that time.

Her studies as well as her inclinations fitted her to undertake the life of Napoleon, and she has written it most satisfactorily. No less a critic than Colonel John C. Ropes, who is probably the greatest authority on Napoleon in the United States, stated in a letter to the editor of this Magazine: "I think Miss Tarbell's 'Life of Napoleon' gives what we most want to know about him. Her account of his administration of the internal affairs of France was very clear and satisfactory." We believe that for its length it is one of the most satisfactory lives of Napoleon ever produced.

MR. HUBBARD'S RARE NAPOLEON COLLECTION.

Mr. Hubbard's collection is well known both here and abroad. He has been fourteen years gathering these pictures, and has spent large sums of money for them. He is known to the principal dealers in prints in America and Europe, and they keep him informed of whatever is worth buying in the way of portraits of Napoleon. His collection is valuable not only because of the individual worth of each picture, but also because of its completeness. It was meant to present Napoleon as he appeared at every important epoch of his life, from youth to death, as painted by the great masters, and also to include the notable masterpieces which show him in the various great scenes of his life. And in presenting the free use of this collection to us, Mr. Hubbard rendered a service that cannot be overestimated.

It was decided to print of the November number 10,000 copies more than the 40,000 that had been printed of the October number. But so rapidly did subscriptions and news-stand orders pour in on the announcement of the Napoleon series, that the order was increased before the plates left the press to 60,000 copies. This edition was exhausted in one week, and subscriptions were coming in at the rate of 150 a day; so that a second edition of 10,000 copies, making 70,000 in all, showing a gain over any previous number of 30,000 copies, was necessary to supply the demand for the first number containing the Life of Napoleon.

A GAIN IN SIX MONTHS OF 60,000.

It is therefore not hard to trace the principal cause of the extraordinary prosperity of the Magazine. Eighty thousand copies were required of the December number, and the Magazine has gone on prospering until with the April number it was found necessary to increase the edition to 100,000 copies, a gain in six months of 60,000 copies.

It is rather an interesting fact that during the three years in which Abbott's "Life of Napoleon" was appearing in "Harper's Magazine," more than forty years ago, the circulation of that magazine increased nearly 100,000. This was one of the results of the first Napoleonic revival, which received a great impulse from the return of Napoleon's body to France. Another result of that revival was the elevation of the third Napoleon to the imperial throne. The extraordinary vitality of Napoleon's fame is well evidenced by this fact that two magazines, established more than forty years apart, have each owed their first great success to a life of Napoleon.

THE BEST LITERATURE BY THE GREATEST WRITERS.

Of course it would be impossible to increase the circulation of a magazine 60,000 copies in six months in the face of the extraordinary competition in the magazine world, unless the magazine possessed many excellences; and while the Life of Napoleon has placed McCLURE'S MAGAZINE in the hands of many thousands of people who otherwise would not have taken it, the whole table of contents has been valuable in retaining their continued support. The Magazine has aimed to publish the best literature by the greatest writers, and while it is no slave to famous names, and has published a great deal of matter by writers heretofore unknown, at the same time there are few contemporary writers of the highest rank who have not contributed to its pages, and some of the very greatest writers have contributed some of their most important matter.

NOTABLE CONTRIBUTORS AND CONTRIBUTIONS.

Mr. Stevenson, besides writing a serial for the Magazine, also contributed an autobiographical article of rare charm and interest, and, at the time of his death, was under engagement to write for the Magazine a long and important novel. This novel, we have reason to believe, was left practically finished, and, if so, it will

THE HON. GARDINER G. HUBBARD IN HIS LIBRARY.

appear in our pages during the next year. Rudyard Kipling, Conan Doyle, Octave Thanet, Walter Besant, Joel Chandler Harris, Thomas Hardy, Robert Barr, Bret Harte, Gilbert Parker, Henry M. Stanley, Ian Maclaren, and others have contributed short stories; and it would be hard to make a list outside of these that contained anything like so many of the greatest writers of our time. Articles of great importance, and such as have commended themselves by their interest and timeliness, have been contributed by the Right Honorable W. E. Gladstone, General Horace Porter, Sara Orne Jewett, Herbert Spencer, Edward Everett Hale, General A. W. Greely, Charles A. Dana, M. de Blowitz, Professor Henry Drummond (who has contributed four very important articles on subjects identified with his name), J. M. Barrie, Washington Gladden, S. R. Crockett, Hamlin Garland, H. H. Boyesen, Beatrice Harraden, and others. Indeed, a glance through the back numbers of the Magazine demonstrates the fact that it has published a great deal of the really great literature produced during its lifetime. In addition to contributions by authors of the first rank, it has had a staff of highly trained writers, who have investigated the most interesting developments of contemporary activities, and have written about subjects in historical, scientific, biographical, and other fields, in a manner to introduce almost a new standard in such matters. In the field of popular science the Magazine has no equal.

THE PIONEER OF CHEAP MAGAZINES.

The list of readers has grown so rapidly that the larger part of the present constituency do not know that McCLURE'S MAGAZINE was the first magazine published at as low a price as 15 cents a copy. It was the pioneer in the field of cheap magazines, and now its imitators actually outnumber the high-priced magazines. Just one month after the first number of McCLURE'S was issued, a prominent 25-cent magazine cut its price in two, and three or four months later, another magazine reduced its price still further; and the aggregate circulation, at the present moment, of the magazines sold at 10 or 15 cents is probably more than twice that of the higher-priced magazines. And this has all come to pass since Mc-CLURE'S MAGAZINE was started, a year ago last June.

FOUNDED WITHOUT CAPITAL.

An interesting fact in regard to the Magazine, aside from its rapid success, is the fact that it was founded practically without capital. It had been regarded in New York as an absolute axiom that not less than $200,000, and probably as much as $500,000, would be required to found an illustrated monthly magazine, and the experience of more than one publisher seemed to prove the soundness of this opinion. Indeed, several magazines have been attempted in recent years which exhausted enormous sums of money without even getting established. It therefore seemed to many a foolhardy enterprise to start a magazine with no capital, and there were times when we ourselves felt that we had undertaken a very large task, especially during the first few months, in the midst of the financial panic of 1893. But, as a matter of fact, the success of the Magazine was so rapid that there was no real discouragement from the publication of the first number, and if the publishers, when they began, had had any money ahead, even a small amount, say $10,000 or $15,000, they really would never have known an anxious moment.

TO BE MADE BETTER AND BETTER.

The Magazine has been singularly fortunate in many ways. It is really a child of the newspaper syndicates established by its proprietors more than ten years ago, and their previous experience as editors enabled them to avoid many mistakes. And, besides, the Magazine was established in a very modest way, and reprinted many of the short stories and articles which its publishers had published previously through the newspaper press, thus reducing its initial charges. This, of course, may have interfered to a certain extent with the growth in circulation; but it was impossible for the publishers to found a magazine in any other manner. But this reprinting of matter has been only an incident of the lack of capital, and is in no way a necessity of the low price of the Magazine; and the publishers' plans do not contemplate the policy of republication to any extent in the future. By another year they will be able to carry out a number of plans for the enlargement and improvement of the Magazine in different directions. The enterprises for the future justify us in expecting continued increase of support and growth in circulation.

Our present circulation has come upon us almost unawares; we were simply conscious of doing our best to make a good magazine, and, before we knew it, the circulation had reached the first stage in our progress, viz., 100,000. We intend to work just as hard for the next 100,000, which, judging by our past experience, will soon be attained.

McCLURE'S QUARTERLY.

This prompt and generous support of McCLURE'S MAGAZINE now enables its publishers to undertake another new enterprise,—a very important departure in the publication of expensive books. On May tenth will appear the first number of McCLURE'S QUARTERLY, the largest and most magnificently illustrated magazine in the world, to appear, as its name indicates, every three months, each number devoted to one subject in the fields of history, biography, science, adventure, portraiture, etc. The price will be fifty cents a copy. It will contain illustrations and text equivalent, if published in the ordinary way, to volumes costing from $5.00 to $8.00.

The first number of the Quarterly will contain the complete Life of Napoleon, by Miss Tarbell, already printed in the Magazine, but with important additions, and illustrated with between two and three hundred pictures. It will contain 256 pages of text, and will be printed on the finest quality of coated paper made expressly for this work.

NAPOLEON AS A LIEUTENANT OF ARTILLERY.

This charming portrait of Napoleon (from McClure's Quarterly is now published for the first time. It is from a water color by an unknown artist, in the collection of Baron Larrey, Paris.

The second number of the Quarterly will be a collection of the series of portraits of distinguished men and women, known as "human documents," which have been appearing in the Magazine since its foundation. It will contain an aggregate of not less than six hundred pictures, including portraits of W. E. Gladstone, Prince Bismarck, General Grant, Oliver Wendell Holmes, John G. Whittier, W. D. Howells, Alphonse Daudet, R. L. Stevenson, Professor Henry Drummond, C. A. Dana, Eugene Field, Thomas A. Edison, Cardinal Gibbons, and others.

THE LIFE OF NAPOLEON.

Miss Tarbell's Life of Napoleon as enlarged will contain an aggregate of about 70,000 words. It tells the story of this extraordinary man's career vividly and dramatically, and yet avoids the fables and inaccuracies that characterize the earlier histories, being written in the light of the most recent publications,— memoirs, letters, and state papers of the period. It is easily read, and easily understood, and gives the average reader a clearer conception of the character and career of Napoleon than he could derive from any other volume.

THE ILLUSTRATIONS.

The chief source of illustrations for the Life of Napoleon in the Quarterly, is still, as in the case of the Napoleon papers in the Magazine, the great collection of Mr. Hubbard, the owner having generously placed the entire collection at the service of the publishers for use in the Quarterly, as he had previously for use in the Magazine. But in order to make it still more comprehensive, a representative of McCLURE'S MAGAZINE and an authorized agent of Mr. Hubbard visited Paris, to seek out there whatever it might yet be desirable to have. They secured the assistance of M. Armand Dayot, *Inspecteur des Beaux-Arts*, who possessed rare qualifications for the task. His official position he owed to his familiarity with the great art collections, both public and private, of France, and his official duties made him especially familiar with the great paintings relating to French history. Besides, he was a specialist in Napoleonic iconography. He had written, among other things, a volume on Raffet and Charlet, whose lithographs are among the most notable representations of the events of Napoleon's life. On account of his qualifications and special knowledge, he had been selected by the great house of Hachette & Company to edit their book on "The Life of Napoleon in Pictures," which was the first attempt to bring together in one volume the most important pictures relating to the military, political, and private life of Napoleon. M. Dayot had just completed this task, and was fresh from his studies of Napoleonic pictures, when his aid was secured by the publishers of McCLURE'S MAGAZINE in supplementing the Hubbard collection.

Josephine, 1796.
This portrait, never before published, is from a miniature by Rochen, now in the collection of the Marquis of Girardin, Paris. It is one of a great number of hitherto unpublished pictures in McClure's Quarterly.

The work was prosecuted with the one aim of omitting no important picture. When great paintings indispensable to a complete pictorial life of Napoleon were found, which had never been either etched or engraved, photographs were obtained, many of these photographs being made especially for our use.

A generous selection of pictures was made from the works of Raffet and Charlet. M. Dayot was able also to add a number of pictures—not less than a score—of unique value, through his personal relations with the owners of the great private Napoleonic collections. Thus were obtained hitherto unpublished pictures, of the highest value, from the collections of Mgr. Duc d'Aumale; of H. I. H., Prince Victor Napoleon; of Prince Roland; of Baron Larrey, the son of the chief surgeon of the army of Napoleon; of the Duke of Bassano, son of the minister and confidant of the emperor; of M. Edmond Taigny, the friend and biographer of Isabey; of M. Albert Christophle, Governor General of the Credit Foncier of France; of M. Paul le Roux, who has perhaps the richest of the Napoleonic collections; and of M. le Marquis de Girardin, son-in-law of the Duc de Gaëte, the faithful Minister of Finance of Napoleon I. It will be easily understood that no doubt can be raised as to the authenticity of documents borrowed from such sources.

It is, therefore, not too much to say that we have here the most complete reunion of important Napoleonic documents which has ever been published. In this magnificent collection of pictures, chronologically presented, we see, in succession, portraits of Napoleon as pupil at Brienne, as lieutenant in the regiment of la Fère, as captain of artillery, as lieutenant-colonel of the volunteers of Corsica, as the hero of Vendémiaire, as conqueror at Arcola, as conqueror at the battle of the Pyramids, as First Consul, and finally at all the different periods of the emperorship, from the solemnities of the *sacre* to the exile and death at St. Helena.

And not only the figure of Napoleon, multiplied to infinity by various interpretations, appears on almost every page of this book, but also the portraits of his most celebrated generals, of his heroic companions in arms: of Ney, Lefebvre, Murat, Junot, Lannes, Bernadotte, Masséna, Kléber, etc.; and of all the members of his family, to which are added the historic figures of his implacable enemies: Alexander I., Francis II., George III., Pitt, Metternich, Wellington, Nelson, and Blücher. Amongst the throng of emperors, empresses, kings, queens, warriors, and statesmen, smiling or grave, appear the faces of well-known artists, poets, actors, scientists, and thinkers: Bernardin de St. Pierre, Berthollet, Chénier, Talma, Girodet, Isabey, Gérard, and others.

It is, in a word, a picturesque and complete *résumé* of the astonishing existence of Napoleon, or, rather, an artistic and captivating *exposé* of the whole history of his reign, presented to the reader under this attractive form of an endless series of pictures, each one of which is accompanied by a commentary as interesting as it is instructive.

Only exceptionally have pictures, statues, or prints by living artists been chosen. It is especially in documents of the Napoleonic epoch that we must seek for historic verity. Gros, Guérin, Boizot, David, Longhi, Isabey, Gérard, Dähling, Girodet, and Vernet (to cite only the best) will always teach us more of the subjects which they painted *de visu* than the most charming work executed at the present day by artists however rich in imagination. It is from the great historical value of Mr. Hubbard's extraordinary collection, to be reproduced almost complete, and supplemented by the *pièces inédites*, from the rare collections named above, and to the reproduction of which their owners have kindly consented, that this Life of Napoleon will derive a most powerful interest.

NAPOLEON AT BRIENNE.   NAPOLEON AS GENERAL OF THE ARMY OF ITALY.   NAPOLEON AS EMPEROR.

A set of crayon sketches by Napoleon's friend, the artist David, now in the collection of M. Chevremy. From McClure's Quarterly.

GASTON TISSANDIER, THE BALLOONIST.

A TALK WITH HIM IN HIS WORK-ROOM—THE PAST AND FUTURE OF THE AIR-SHIP.

By ROBERT H. SHERARD.

THERE is, perhaps, no more charming man in all Paris than M. Gaston Tissandier, the great aëronaut and editor of one of the most successful scientific publications of the day, "La Nature." He is quiet, modest, and reserved, but most cordial, and, when speaking on a subject which interests him, especially when talking on aëronautics, or when showing his wonderful collection of curiosities relating to ballooning, he becomes quite ardent. His eyes light up, he speaks rapidly, and the wonderful energy which has enabled him to do so much in the course of his career is betrayed in every word and gesture.

Gaston Tissandier is a Parisian by birth, and was born on the 21st of November, 1843. On his mother's side he is descended from a remarkable scientist, Lhéritier de Brutelles. He was educated at the Lycée Bonaparte and afterwards entered the Conservatoire des Arts et Metiers, as pupil to P. P. Dehérain. At the age of twenty-one he was appointed director of the Experimental and Analytical Laboratory of the Union Générale, a most important industrial establishment. While here he contributed frequently to the "Moniteur Scientifique," and discovered a new coloring matter in the tar extracted from cider-apple pulp. It was at the age of twenty-five that he began to make the balloon ascensions which have rendered his name famous. His first was undertaken at Calais, on the 16th of August, 1868, in company with the aëronaut Duruof. The result of it was that Tissandier was encouraged to hope that, by the use of the various air currents, it might be possible, after all, to solve the problem of the direction of balloons. By rising and falling in their balloon the two aëronauts, on that occasion, were able to proceed in a given direction a distance of twenty-eight kilometres, and, if this otherwise unremarkable ascension was so greatly discussed at the time, it was because it seemed that at last—that is to say, by a proper application of the natural forces—the problem referred to might be considered to be capable of solution. It may be remarked here that, although M. Tissandier has since that time made no less than forty-five ascensions, he does not consider the problem any nearer solution than

GASTON TISSANDIER.

it was a quarter of a century ago, as transpires in the conversation I have recently had with him.

M. Tissandier lives on the fifth floor of a modern house in the Rue de Chateaudun, in a luxuriously furnished apartment. The ante-chamber is filled with bookshelves, and with cases laden with curiosities relating to the science with which his name is associated. Against the walls of the ante-chamber, as of the passages which lead from it to the various rooms, are pictures, mostly of the last century, depicting the heroes of aërostatics and various historical ascensions. In the fine drawing-room, into which the visitor is shown, are to be remarked a series of drawings representing the various episodes of the terrible ascension of 1875, which nearly cost M. Tissandier his life. This was the ascension of the balloon "Zenith" on the 15th of April, following closely upon the inaugural ascension undertaken in that balloon on March 23d, when M. Tissandier, in company with his brother Albert, a M. Jobert, and MM. Crocé-Spinelli and Sivel, remained over twenty-three hours in the air, thus beating the record of the world in the matter of length of a balloon voyage. Starting at noon on its second voyage, the "Zenith," manned by MM. Gaston Tissandier, Crocé-Spinelli, and Sivel, soon reached an altitude which had never been reached by a balloon before; that is to say, an altitude of twenty-eight thousand two hundred and fifteen feet. Before this height had been reached M. Tissandier lost consciousness and did not recover until the balloon had descended to an altitude of twenty-two thousand nine hundred and sixty-five feet. Then he had the horror to discover that his two companions, less fortunate than himself, had passed from the swoon to death. Not discouraged by this fearful experience Tissandier continued his experiments and ascensions. In 1881 he showed at the exhibition of electricity in the Palais de l'Industrie the model of an electric dirigible balloon, which seemed so satisfactory that some time after, having in vain tried to form a company, he associated himself with his brother Albert; and at their own expense they constructed, in an aërostatic workshop at Auteuil, a working air-ship of the same pattern, in which an ascension was first made on the 8th of October, 1883. Although the results obtained were not such as to allow it to be thought that the problem of steering balloons had been solved, it seemed established that in the use of electrical apparatus the solution of the problem must be expected. Captains Krebs and Rénard, of the government aërostatic service, took up the idea, and at Chalais-Meudon obtained some greatly superior results with improved apparatus.

"It is chiefly because of the success of these gentlemen," said M. Tissandier, "that I have of late abandoned my investigations. My brother and I have been the first to applaud the success of MM. Krebs and Rénard, because where the sacred interests of science or of fatherland are concerned, there can and should be no question of personalities."

A SCIENTIFIC WORK-ROOM AND CURIOSITY SHOP.

M. Gaston Tissandier's work-room—wherein, seated at a table covered with papers and books, with his back to a huge book-case reaching from floor to ceiling, the savant receives his visitors—contains, amongst other objects of interest, the unique plaster cast of a group designed by the sculptor Clodion in 1784, which it was intended to erect on the Place des Tuileries in honor of the brothers Montgolfier. The cast, which was never executed, represents a Genius inflating a balloon by means of a burning torch. Two little Cupids present to a sitting woman, who may

DESCENT OF THE BALLOON "NEPTUNE" AT CAPE GRISNEZ, AUGUST 10, 1868.

be supposed to represent France, or Fame, a medallion on which are designed in profile the heads of the two brothers who discovered ballooning. Behind sits a figure of Time with a scythe, and above him are two other Cupids. The cast is signed by Clodion, and is a unique and highly interesting work of art. M. Tissandier's apartment is full of such curiosities. Adjoining the stand on which this cast is placed is a cabinet filled with bonbon and snuff boxes of the last century, all of which are ornamented with designs and pictures relating to the discovery which, as M. Tissandier says, "was, it was thought, to revolutionize the world." Many of these, apart from this interest, are of great intrinsic beauty and value. In a cupboard in an adjoining room M. Tissandier has a quantity of very rare old books, printed long before the Montgolfiers had made their discovery, proving that the possibility of aërial navigation had long impressed itself on the thinking world. One very curious book, and as rare as curious, is entitled, "L'Homme dans la Lune, ou le Voyage Chimerique fait au Monde de la Lune, nouvellement decouvert, Par Dominique Gonzalés, Aventurier Espagnol, autrement dit Le Courier Volant." This work was published in 1648. Another volume of great interest, forming part of this collection, is a work published in 1757, entitled, "The Art of Navigating in the Air, by Father Galien."

M. Tissandier's aërostatical collection contains upwards of three thousand different objects. In the huge portfolios stored in the dining-room, are hundreds of engravings, colored pictures, posters and handbills of the period of the discovery, amongst which are many most curious and interesting in character. One may mention especially a government announcement dated Tuesday, September 2, 1783, from the "Gazette de France," which was posted all over the environs of Paris, explaining that people had no reason to be frightened by the appearance of a balloon in the air, and should not consider it or its crew as dangerous; giving a brief explanation of what the balloon was and what might be expected of it, and commanding that the lives and apparatus of the aëronauts should be respected. M. Tissandier said : " I have been collecting everything relating to the history of ballooning for upwards of twenty-five years, and have, I think, the most complete collection of the kind in the world. I continue adding to it year by year, and have no difficulty now, as I always hear at once of any curiosity that may be on sale in any part of the world."

Perhaps the piece of his collection which M. Tissandier is proudest of is the original of a letter written by Franklin to Sir Joseph Banks, president of the Royal Society, London, describing the first ascension of the Montgolfiers, which he witnessed from the little house at Passy, where he was then residing. This letter, entirely in Franklin's writing, is dated November 21, 1783. It was bought by M. Tissandier, together with other papers, at a sale in England, a great bargain, for the price of ten guineas. The whole apartment overflows with aëronautic curiosities. In the bedroom is a chest of drawers inlaid in wood mosaic, highly colored, with a representation of the transport of Charles's balloon, the first one to be inflated with hydrogen, in December, 1783, from the Champs de Mars, where the inflation had been executed, to the Place des Tuileries, where the ascension was to take place. There is against the wall a wash-fountain in copper, on which is engraved a balloon bearing the inscription :

A CORNER IN TISSANDIER'S DRAWING-ROOM.

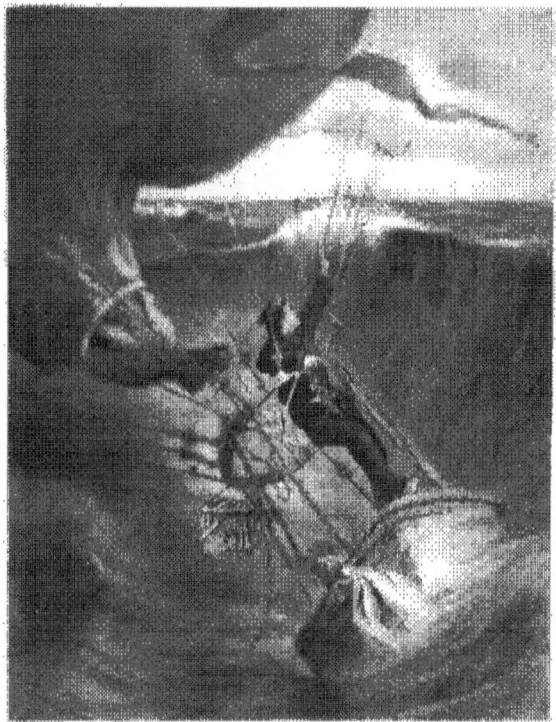

THE "BATAILLE PRINCE" LOST IN THE SEA DURING THE SIEGE OF PARIS. AFTER A DRAWING BY DE MYRBACH.

"Vive la Nation," which dates from 1794. Here may be seen a portrait of Blanchard, here one of Charles, here a colored sheet on which the game of balloons has taken the place of the royal game of goose, here a magic lantern with slides painted in Nuremberg, on which are depicted various ballooning scenes and heroes. The very modern furniture is in harmony with the general character of the place. The chairs in both drawing-room and study are covered with tapestry on which are worked representations of balloon ascensions.

Yet M. Tissandier says that now for some time he has given up research in this field of study, the reason being chiefly that he does not wish to compete with his confrères at Meudon, and also that he is kept very busy with his literary work. He has found time to contribute largely to French literature. Among his most important works, apart from those of a more strictly scientific character, may be enumerated his "Scientific Recreations," which was crowned by the French Academy; "Water," "Martyrs of Science," "Heroes of Labor," "Souvenirs of a Military Aëronaut in the Army of the Loire," the magnificent "History of Ballooning," and "History of my Ascensions." Besides these works, he has written largely for the principal papers and reviews of France. It was shortly after the war that he founded the magazine "La Nature," which he still edits, and which has become so valuable a property in his hands. "I founded that journal," said M. Tissandier, "because I felt that everybody ought to work towards the regeneration of France; that everybody who could do something towards reconstructing our dear country should do so; that everybody who could work should work, according to his abilities; and that was the best way that we could serve the fatherland at a time when it was in such sore distress."

THE FUTURE OF BALLOONING.

In answer to a question as to his opinion on the future of ballooning, M. Tissandier said: "I believe that the sanguine expectations which were aroused at the time of Montgolfier's first experiments will some day be realized, and that the conditions of human life will, in consequence, be completely revolutionized. Already very great progress has been made within recent years towards the solution of the problem of steering balloons, on which the whole question of the future of ballooning, as a science of practical utility to man, entirely depends. The recent experiments at Chalais-Meudon seem to point to the fact that the various conditions of success have at last been discovered, and that it is only a question of time and perseverance now.

"The conditions of success, on which the solution of the problem of steering balloons depends, are four: a motor, a screw, a rudder, and a speed superior to that of the wind. If balloons are to be steered, the balloon must have a motive power by which it can be moved forward and upwards and downwards when it is necessary to take it out of a current of wind superior to its own speed. For, as we discovered, the rate of speed of the wind varies according to the altitude. You find layers of atmosphere, if I may use that expression, one above the other, moving at very different rates of speed. The motor must move a screw, because the screw is the most powerful means known of propelling a body through a fluid. Just as it is the best means of propulsion for a ship in water, it is the best for a ship in the air, which is only a fluid of less density than water. Similarly, the shape of the balloon should resemble that of a ship, because the same conditions are applicable to the one as to the other; that is to say, it should be of an elongated form and should be fitted with a rudder, placed at its stern, made of stuff smooth and taut, and fulfilling the same functions and obeying the same principles as the rudder of a ship. A balloon of elongated shape, fitted with a screw, set in motion by a motor, and with steering gear such as I have described, would sail as surely in any direction that might be desired as a steamship in the sea, so long as the air was still. It is the opposing force of the air currents—that is to say, of the wind—which makes the steering of the air-ship a matter of such difficulty. When the speed of the air, coming in the face of the balloon, is equal to that generated by the balloon itself, the air-ship remains stationary; when it is superior, the balloon is driven back. The problem is to find a motor of sufficient power to maintain a rate of speed superior to that of the strongest air current. All kinds of motors have been tried without result in the past. The first motor essayed was the oar, worked by the aëronaut himself. This was the invention of Blanchard in 1784. He claimed to have solved the problem and to have been able to direct his balloon against the wind by means of his oars, which were worked by hand, much like the oars of a boat. Similar attempts were made in the same year by Guyton de Morveau and Abbé Bertrand at Dijon, the oars in this case being more in the form of paddles, made of silk tightly stretched over a light wood frame, and worked by hand like the wings of a bird. Abbé Miolan and his companion, getting nearer to the truth, about the same time experimented with a balloon which was fitted with one gigantic oar worked like a scull over the stern of a boat. I say that they got nearer to the truth, because it was from the scull worked over the stern of the boat that the idea of the screw was taken as a means of propulsion; and it is in the screw, and the screw only, that the hope of the modern aëronaut lies. But all these experiments were, from the outset, destined to remain impracticable, for the simple reason that man's arm power is too feeble to compete with the wind even at an ordinary rate of speed. As to the next development, which was that of the use of sails, it cannot but have proceeded from a perfect ignorance of the most elementary principles of physics. A M. Tissandier de la Mothe—no, he was no relation of mine—solemnly proposed to the Academy of Sciences an invention for applying to the 'aërostatic globe' the same sails that are applied to ships in the water. It was an absurdity, because the balloon, relatively to the air by which it is surrounded, is in a state of such absolute immobility that the flame of a candle lighted in a balloon

THE BALLOON "ZENITH" PASSING OVER THE RIVER GIRONDE, NEAR ITS MOUTH, MARCH 24, 1875.

does not flicker, and a soap-bubble (I have tried this myself again and again) can be laid down on any part of the balloon and will remain as utterly motionless as a stone-weight. The sails applied to a balloon, even in the strongest hurricane, would not receive a breath of air. It is fair to the Academy of Sciences of the time to say that they at once saw the absurdity of M. de la Mothe's proposal. But De la Mothe was not the only man who, from a want of elementary scientific knowledge, thought to solve the problem of the steering of balloons by the use of sails. An Englishman named Martyn, a certain Guyot—who, by the way, proposed that balloons should be made egg-shaped—a savant named Robertson, who ought to have known better, and a M. Terzuolo, who proposed, as late as 1855, that the sail to be fitted to the balloon should be inflated with air generated by a hand pump, all committed the same error. About as absurd as Terzuolo's idea was that of an inventor who proposed to me that the balloon should be constructed of magnetized material, by reason of which it would be attracted, invariably, in the direction of the North Pole. I think that I have his letter here." M. Tissandier took down a box and opened a number of paper cases which, as he showed me, were impressed with the water-mark of Montgolfier brothers, descendants of the famous Montgolfiers, who are engaged in the manufacture of paper in the centre of France. The water-mark is a balloon.

THE PROBLEM OF STEERING.

"Although it had long been established that it was useless hoping for any practical results in aërial navigation," continued M. Tissandier, "until a motor of sufficient power could be discovered, it was thought that, in the meanwhile, by taking advantage of the very forces which it had to combat, some sort of practical result, as a *pis aller*, might be obtained. I fancy that it was M. Duruof and myself, in our ascent on the 16th of August, 1868, near Calais, who first demonstrated that, by using the various air currents, one might more or less sail in the direction that it was desired to take. At a distance of one thousand nine hundred and sixty-nine feet from the surface of the earth the air current blew from northeast to southwest. Above that height there was an air current which blew in exactly the opposite direction. Between the two was a thick layer of clouds. Thus by rising above or by sinking below this layer of clouds we obtained two absolutely opposed directions. Thanks to this circumstance, we were able to travel a distance of twenty-seven kilometres in one direction, and then, by a mere manœuvre with the ballast, to return to nearly the same spot we had started from. By tacking, moreover, had we dared, we could, I believe, have crossed right over to England and

FLYING MACHINE IN WHICH DR GROOF WAS KILLED, JULY 9, 1874.

returned to France without any danger. Duruof at Cherbourg, Jovis at Nice, and M. Bunelle at Odessa, repeated these experiments with equal success. But, as I say, this taking advantage of the aërial currents for following any given direction can only be considered as a *pis aller* in certain cases. Very often, of course, there are no favorable currents of which advantage can be taken. At other times the winds are entirely adverse, for the phenomena of contrary winds at different heights are not reliable. I have been frequently disappointed, even when setting out with the hope of being able, thanks to a favorable current, to reach a given point, notably on one occasion when, during the war, I travelled from Rouen with letters and official despatches. I ascended with every ground for hoping that the wind would take my balloon to Paris, but was forced to interrupt my journey miles away from the capital.

"What must be the essential is a motor of sufficient power to turn a screw so as to generate a force of propulsion superior to the force of the wind. Of course, nobody expects that there will ever be discovered a motor powerful enough to generate a force superior to that of the strongest winds which may be met with in the air, but certainly one should be practicable of sufficient force to compete with ordinary air currents, such as in nine cases out of ten would be met with by the aëronaut. Tempests are not of such frequent occurrence as to discourage the experiment. A great step was taken by Henri Giffard, and I believe that if that great man had lived—he died by his own hand, discouraged when failing health interrupted his wonderful career, just at a time when he was preparing an experiment of the highest interest—I believe, I say, that the problem would already have been solved. His first experiments were with balloons propelled by a steam motor. He was only twenty-six. It was in 1851 when he took out a patent for a system of balloon navigation by the use of steam power, and on the 24th of September,

1852, he made his first ascent at the Hippodrome. His balloon was elongated in shape, measuring forty-four metres from point to point, and eleven in diameter at its longest diameter.

"It was Giffard who established the fact that the balloon must be of an elongated model, so as to present the least surface to the friction of the air. In 1855 he constructed another balloon of elongated form, containing three thousand two hundred cubic metres of gas. Though winds were unfavorable, and the force of propulsion generated by the steam-motor inferior to that of the winds against which it had to battle, the balloon made a very good fight of it, and at the same time the usefulness of the rudder was established. Giffard was able to tack in the directions he wished, moving from right to left and from left to right in his efforts to escape the full force of the opposing currents. He may be said to have definitely proved the fact that the balloon, to be steered, must be fitted with a rudder, and that this may be made effective by a motor of sufficient power. It is to Giffard, whom I shall always consider as my master and my Mæcenas, that we owe it, that the problem of aërial navigation can no longer be treated as the Utopia of science. M. Dupuy de Lôme confirmed this by the remarkable ascent which he effected in 1872. De Lôme's motor was again of insufficient strength, yet certain results were obtained in the way of deviation from the current, and it was finally made clear that results could be expected from the elongated balloon fitted with steering gear and propelled by a screw. But the motor had yet, and has yet, to be found.

"If the steam-motor, in spite of the results obtained by Giffard and by De Lôme, has been abandoned, it is for a number of practical reasons. In the first place, it is very dangerous. Consider the peril of a furnace placed under a mass so inflammable as an immense body of hydrogen gas. One shudders to think of the accidents which might ensue in the air. For this reason alone the use of the steam-motor must be considered impracticable. Another objection, and a very serious one, is that the balloon worked by a steam-motor would always be diminishing weight as the fuel and the water were consumed; the former dissipating in gas and smoke and the latter in steam. The balloon, accordingly, would be constantly rising in the air, and the only way of lowering it would be by sacrificing its contents; that is to say, by diminishing its volume of gas, the result of which would be that its duration would be singularly shortened. Giffard knew of all these objections and had planned measures for overcoming them, which unfortunately he was never able to execute. Thus, by the use of a condenser, he hoped to collect the steam as it left the boiler, to reduce it to water, and, using it again, to avoid the loss of weight, which was such a fatal objection to the steam-boiler. He also proposed to use hydrogen gas as fuel, using for this purpose the gas which, as the balloon ascends and the pressure of the atmosphere diminishes, is forced from it. The balloon would thus have been self-feeding, and no fuel would have had to be carried, thus still further reducing the inconvenience caused by a constant loss of weight.

"Other experiments have been tried with compressed air-motors, gas-motors, and others. The objection to all these is their enormous weight.

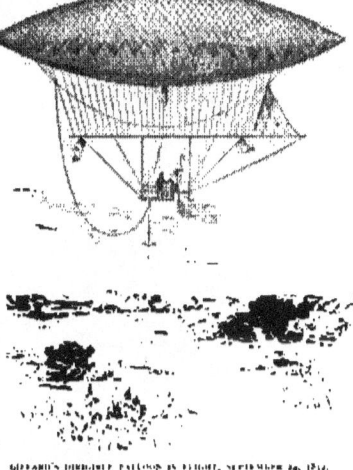

GIFFARD'S DIRIGIBLE BALLOON IN FLIGHT, SEPTEMBER 24, 1852.

THE POSSIBILITIES OF THE ELECTRIC MOTOR.

"My opinion is, that the only motor which will solve the question is the electric motor. It was I who first took out a patent for this idea, my patent being for 'the application of electricity to aërial navigation.' That was in 1881, and in a note communicated to the Academy of Sciences I explained the advantages of the electric motor. In the first place, it works without a furnace. Secondly, its weight never diminishes nor increases during its working, and it is set in motion with the greatest ease. Assisted by M. Gaston Planté and other savants and engineers, I was at last able to realize my project of an electric motor. A reduced model of the electric balloon was exhibited at the Electricity Exhibition in 1881. It was inflated with pure hydrogen, and the screw, worked by an electric motor, attained a speed of three metres a second. It was not, however, until 1883 that, with the help and collaboration of my brother, Albert Tissandier, I was able to construct a balloon worked by an electric motor for actual navigation. Our balloon, following the principles verified by the experiments of De Lôme and of Giffard, was of elongated form, measuring twenty-eight metres from point to point, and having a diameter of nine metres at its broadest part. The tissue was of calico, glazed with a varnish specially invented for the purpose by M. Arnoul of Saint Ouen-l'Aumone. The volume of the balloon was ten hundred and sixty cubic metres. Our motor was not, however, of sufficient force to overcome that of the wind, and the best result obtained was that we remained stationary. When sailing with the wind, however, our screw propelled us in a very satisfactory manner. We were delighted with the easy working of the motor, and the result of this experiment was to confirm absolutely the principle that it is the electric motor that must be used. Although we did not make headway against a wind blowing at a rate of three metres the second, we were able to resist it and to deviate from its current by tacking, with the greatest facility.

"In September, 1884, having in the meanwhile improved our rudder, we made another ascent with an improved machine, and, heading against a wind blowing at the rate of four metres the second, were able to progress against it for about a quarter of an hour. Unfortunately, we had only enough material to work our motor for a limited period, and were driven to interrupt our voyage about an hour too early. At that time the wind was blowing with a force very much inferior to that of our motor,

CAR OF THE "ZENITH" IN THE ASCENSION OF APRIL 15, 1875, WHEN MM. CROCÉ-SPINELLI AND SIVEL WERE KILLED. SIVEL, ON THE LEFT, IS LIFTING LOOSE THE BALLAST-BAGS FILLED WITH SAND. TISSANDIER, IN THE CENTRE, IS OBSERVING THE BAROMETERS. CROCÉ-SPINELLI, HAVING JUST FINISHED SOME OBSERVATIONS OF THE SPECTROSCOPE, IS TAKING A DRAUGHT OF OXYGEN.

which was one of four metres to the second, and had we been able to continue its working we could have sailed back to Paris as easily as if, instead of being in a balloon, we had been in a screw steamer on a calm sea. Altogether, both my brother and myself had every reason to be satisfied with the result of our experiments, and to consider that a step had been taken toward the solution of the problem on which the whole future of ballooning will depend. We were unable to continue our experiments, because we had not the necessary funds; and this was also to a great extent the reason why we did not obtain better results at the time. Our material was altogether insufficient, our motors too weak, but we were not able to afford anything more expensive. Another reason why we do not continue our experiments—for perhaps money could be found for executing them on a really practical scale—is, that we do not wish to enter into competition with the aëronauts at Chalais-Meudon, who are supported by, and work for, the French Ministry of War. The director of the Chalais-Meudon works is Captain Rénard, who, in collaboration with Captain Krebs, took up my screw at the bow, which screw was worked by a very powerful dynamo of special construction. The ascent took place on the 4th of August, the trip lasting twenty-three minutes, during which a space of four and a third miles was covered, the balloon being guided from start to finish with a precision which can only be compared to that with which a screw steamer is manœuvred in the water. Again, in 1885, another ascent was made with a perfected balloon. The balloon was steered towards Paris, and returned to the point of departure with the greatest ease and precision.

"The result of these experiments is, that with elongated balloons fitted with a screw propeller, generating a force of speed of from three to six metres the second, the aëronaut can travel in whatever direction he chooses for a limited space of time, provided that the weather be favorable; that is to say, provided the speed of any head-wind he may encounter be not superior to the speed generated by the motor carried, and working on his balloon. This result shows what remains to be done; we must improve the motors in point both of speed and of weight. It is also clear that the bigger the balloon the better the results to be looked for; because, while the resistance only increases in proportion to the surface presented, the ascensional force increases in proportion to the cube of its dimensions. All the objections made to the possibility of steering balloons have one after another been proved futile. It has been said that balloons cannot resist the pressure of the air, and that, by increasing the solidity of the material of which it is made, this danger can be entirely removed. I think that the balloon which will finally solve the problem will be one of an even more elongated form than any tried up to the present time. It will have a screw, because that is the best means of propulsion known to-day. But while I believe the balloon of the future will be worked by electricity, I do not see why experiments should not be continued with the steam motor; for, by the use of condensers, such as were suggested, and, but for his unfortunate death, would have been experimented on, by Henri Giffard, and by isolating the furnace with metal work, the objections and danger would be reduced to a minimum. Similarly the gas motor might be experimented with further, provided its great intrinsic weight can be reduced to reasonable limits.*

"In conclusion," said M. Tissandier, "I may say that I am extremely hopeful that it may be given to me to see the problem which I have so long worked at solved even in my lifetime. All that is required is time, money, and perseverance."

* The requirement of lightness in the material of construction, it may be added to what M. Tissandier says above, seems to be fully met in aluminium, which has now become a commercial metal. This has only one third the specific gravity of steel, and its tensile strength is equal to that of malleable iron.

THE SECOND FUNERAL OF NAPOLEON.

REMOVAL OF NAPOLEON'S REMAINS FROM ST. HELENA TO THE BANKS OF THE SEINE IN 1840.

BY IDA M. TARBELL.

With engravings from the collection of the Hon. Gardiner G. Hubbard.

It is my wish that my ashes may repose on the banks of the Seine, in the midst of the French people, whom I have loved so well.—TESTAMENT OF NAPOLEON, 2d Clause.

> He wants not this; but France shall feel the want
> Of this last consolation, though so scant;
> Her honor, fame, and faith demand his bones,
> To rear above a pyramid of thrones;
> Or carried onward, in the battle's van,
> To form, like Goeschn's dust, her talisman.
> But be it as it is, the time may come,
> His name shall beat the alarm like Ziska's drum.
> —BYRON, in *The Age of Bronze*.

THE FRENCH CHAMBER OF DEPUTIES SURPRISED.

ON May 12, 1840, Louis Philippe being king of the French people, the Chamber of Deputies was busy with a discussion on sugar tariffs. It had been dragging somewhat, and the members were showing signs of restlessness. Suddenly the Count de Rémusat, then Minister of Interior, appeared, and asked a hearing for a communication from the government.

"Gentlemen," he said, "the king has ordered his Royal Highness Monseigneur the Prince de Joinville* to go with his frigate to the island of St. Helena, there to collect the remains of the Emperor Napoleon."

A tremor ran over the House. The announcement was utterly unexpected. Napoleon to come back! The body seemed electrified, and the voice of the minister was drowned for a moment in applause. When he went on, it was to say:

"We have come to ask for an appropriation which shall enable us to receive the remains in a fitting manner, and to raise an enduring tomb to Napoleon."

"*Très bien! Très bien!*" cried the House.

"The government, anxious to discharge a great national duty, asked England for the precious treasure which fortune had put into her hands.

"The thought of France was welcomed as soon as expressed. Listen to the reply of our magnanimous ally:

"'The government of her Majesty hopes that the promptness of her response will be considered in France as a proof of her desire to efface the last traces of those national animosities which armed France and England against each other in the life of the emperor. The government of her Majesty dares to hope that if such sentiments still exist in certain quarters, they will be buried in the tomb where the remains of Napoleon are to be deposited.'"

The reading of this generous and dignified communi-

*The Prince de Joinville was the third son of Louis Philippe.

COUNT BERTRAND.

cation caused a profound sensation, and cries of "*Bravo! bravo!*" reëchoed through the hall. The minister, so well received, grew eloquent.

"England is right, gentlemen; the noble way in which restitution has been made will knit the bonds which unite us. It will wipe out all traces of a sorrowful past. The time has come when the two nations should remember only their glory. The frigate freighted with the mortal remains of Napoleon will return to the mouth of the Seine. They will be placed in the Invalides. A solemn celebration and grand religious and military ceremonies will consecrate the tomb which must guard them forever.

"It is important, gentlemen, that this august sepulchre should not remain exposed in a public place, in the midst of a noisy and inappreciative populace. It should be in a silent and sacred spot, where all those who honor glory and genius, grandeur and misfortune, can visit it and meditate.

"He was emperor and king. He was the legitimate sovereign of our country. He is entitled to burial at Saint-Denis. But the ordinary royal sepulchre is not enough for Napoleon. He should reign and command forever in the spot where the country's soldiers repose, and where those who are called to defend it will seek their inspiration. His sword will be placed on his tomb.

"Art will raise beneath the dome of the temple consecrated to the god of battles, a tomb worthy, if that be possible, of the name which shall be engraved upon it. This monument must have a simple beauty, grand outlines, and that appearance of eternal strength which defies the action of time. Napoleon must have a monument lasting as his memory. . . .

"Hereafter France, and France alone, will possess all that remains of Napoleon. His tomb, like his fame, will belong to no one but his country. The monarchy of 1830 is the only and the legitimate heir of the past of which France is so proud. It is the duty of this monarchy, which was the first to rally all the forces and to conciliate all the aspirations of the French Revolution, fearlessly to raise and honor the statue and the tomb of the popular hero. There is one thing, one only, which does not fear comparison with glory—that is liberty." [*]

KING LOUIS PHILIPPE.

Throughout this speech, every word of which was an astonishment to the Chamber, sincere and deep emotion prevailed. At intervals enthusiastic applause burst forth. For a moment all party distinctions were forgotten. The whole House was under the sway of that strange and powerful emotion which Napoleon, as no other leader who ever lived, was able to inspire. When the minister followed his speech

[*] "Le Moniteur Universel," May 13, 1840.

by the draft of a law for a special credit of one million francs, a member, beside himself with excitement, moved that rules be laid aside and the law voted without the legal preliminaries. The president refused to put so irregular a motion, but the House would not be quiet. The deputies left their places, formed in groups in the hemicycle, surrounded the minister, congratulating him with fervor. They walked up and down, gesticulating and shouting. It was fully half an hour before the president was able to bring them to order, and then they were in anything but a working mood.

"The president must close the session," cried an agitated member; "the law which has just been proposed has caused too great emotion for us to return now to discussing sugar."

But the president replied very properly, and a little sententiously, that the Chamber owed its time to the country's business, and that it must give it. And, in spite of their excitement, the members had to go back to their sugar.

THE AUTHOR OF THE "GRANDE PENSÉE."

But how had it come about that the French government had dared burst upon the country with so astounding a communication? There were many explanations offered. A curious story which went abroad took the credit from the king and gave it to O'Connell, the Irish agitator.*

As the story went, O'Connell had warned Lord Palmerston that he proposed to present a bill in the Commons for returning Napoleon's remains to France.

"Take care," said Lord Palmerston. "Instead of pleasing the French government, you may embarrass it seriously."

"That is not the question," answered O'Connell. "The question for me is what I ought to do. Now, my duty is to propose to the Commons to return the emperor's bones. England's duty is to welcome the motion. I shall make my proposition, then, without disturbing myself about whom it will flatter or wound."

"So be it," said Lord Palmerston. "Only give me fifteen days."

"Very well," answered O'Connell.

Immediately Lord Palmerston wrote to M. Thiers, then at the head of the French Ministry, that he was about to be forced to tell the country that England had never refused to return the remains of Napoleon to France, because France had never asked that they be returned. As the story goes, M. Thiers advised Louis Philippe to forestall O'Connell, and thus it came about that Napoleon's remains were returned to France.

The *grande pensée*, as the idea was immediately called, seems, however, to have originated with M. Thiers, who saw in it a means of reawakening the waning interest in Louis Philippe. He believed that the very audacity of the act would create admiration and applause. Then, too, it was in harmony with the claim of the régime; that is, that the government of 1830 united all that was best in all the past governments of France, and so was stronger than any one of them. The mania of both king and minister for collecting and restoring made them think favorably of the idea. Already Louis Philippe had inaugurated galleries at Versailles, and hung them with miles of canvas, celebrating the victories of all his predecessors. In the gallery of portraits he had placed Marie Antoinette and Louis XVI. beside Madame Roland, Charlotte Corday, Robespierre, and Napoleon and his marshals.

He had already replaced the statue of Napoleon on the top of the Column Vendôme. He had restored cathedrals,

LORD PALMERSTON.

* "Histoire de la vie politique et privée de Louis Philippe," par M. A. Dumas, vol. II., page 151.

THE SECOND FUNERAL OF NAPOLEON.   507

churches, and chateaux, put up statues and monuments, and all this he had done with studied indifference to the politics of the individuals honored.

Yet while so many little important personages were being exalted, the remains of the greatest leader France had ever known, were lying in a far-away island. Louis Philippe felt that no monument he could build to the heroes of the past would equal the honor of restoring Napoleon's remains.

was almost overpowered by his orders* to sound the British ministry on the subject. Had the Emperor Napoleon no more partisans or heirs? Were the attempts of Joseph in 1830, of Louis Napoleon in 1836, forgotten? Was it the business of Louis Philippe to resurrect a rival? Would Napoleon's tomb be a gage of security within, a symbol of peace without? His first moment of surprise passed, however, Guizot accepted the sentimental explanation of the enterprise, and played his part with zest. "The consequences are none of my business," he told his London friends who were alarmed at the idea. "Free countries are three-decked vessels living in the midst of tempests. They rise and fall, and the very waves which rack them, send them ahead. I like this life, this spectacle. It is worth living for! And there are so few things of which one can say that!"

THIERS.

The matter was simpler, because it was almost certain that England would not block the path. The *entente cordiale*, whose base had been laid by Talleyrand nearly ten years earlier, had become comparatively solid peace, and either nation was willing to go out of the way, if necessary, to do the other a neighborly kindness. France was so full of good will that she was even willing to ask a favor.

The proposal was so sudden that even Guizot, then French ambassador at London,

* "Mémoires pour servir à l'histoire de mon temps," par M. Guizot, v. 5, p. 108.

Two days after Guizot had explained the project to Lord Palmerston, and made his request, he had his reply.

The remains of the "emperor" were at the disposition of the French. Of the "emperor," notice! After twenty-five years England recalled the act of her ministers in July, 1815, and recognized that France made Napoleon emperor as well as general. It is easy to be just where one is not afraid.

HOW THE COUNTRY RECEIVED THE NEWS.

The announcement that Napoleon's remains were to be brought back, produced the same effect upon the country at large that it had upon the Chamber—a moment of acute emotion, of all-forgetting enthusiasm. But in the Chamber and the country the feeling was short-lived. The political aspects of the bold movement were too conspicuous. A chorus of criticisms and forebodings arose. It was more of M. Thiers' claptrap, said those opposed to the English policy of the government. What particularly angered this party, was the words "magnanimous ally" in the minister's address.

The Bonapartes feigned to despise the proposed ceremony. It was insufficient for the greatness of their hero. One million francs could not possibly produce the display the object demanded. Another point of theirs was more serious. The emperor was the legitimate sovereign of the country, they said, quoting from the minister's speech to the Chamber, and they added : " His title was founded on the *senatus consultum* of the year 12, which, by an equal number of suffrages, secured the succession to his brother Joseph. It was then unquestionably Joseph Bonaparte who was proclaimed emperor of the French by the Minister of the Interior, and amid the applause of the deputies."

Scoffers said that Louis Philippe must have discovered that his soft mantle of popularity was about worn out, if he was going to make one of the old gray redingote of a man whom he had called a monster. The Legitimists denied that Napoleon was a legitimate sovereign with a right to sleep at Saint-Denis like a Bourbon or a Valois. The Orleanists were wounded by the hopes they saw inspired in the Bonapartists by this declaration. The Republicans resented the honor done to the man whom they held up as the greatest of all despots.

There was a conviction among many that the restoration was premature, and probably would bring on the country an agitation which would endanger the stability of the throne. It was tempting the Bonaparte pretensions certainly, and perhaps arousing a tremendous popular sentiment to support them. Lamartine warned the Chamber in an eloquent address.

GUIZOT.

"The ministers assure us that the throne will not shrink inside such a tomb. Will these ovations, this cortége, this posthumous crowning of what they call a legitimacy, this great movement given by the impulsion of the government itself to the sentiment of the masses, this shock to the popular imagination, these prolonged and touching spectacles, these recitals, these popular publications, these editions of the Napoleonic idea five hundred million copies strong, these bills of indemnity given to a happy despotism, this adoration of success—will all this have no danger for the future of representative monarchy?"*

While the press and government, the clubs and *cafés*, discussed the political side of the question, the populace quietly revived the Napoleon legend. Within two days after the government had announced its intentions, commerce had begun to take advantage of the financial possibilities in the approaching ceremony. New editions of the "Lives" of Napoleon which Vernet and Raffet had illustrated, were advertised. Dumas' "Life" and Thiers' "Consulate and

* "Le Moniteur Universel." May 15, 1840.

Empire" were announced. Memoirs of the period, like those of the Duchesse d'Abrantès and of Marmont, were revived.

As on the announcement of Napoleon's death in 1821, there was an inundation of pamphlets in verse and prose; of portraits and war compositions, lithographs, engravings, and wood-cuts; of thousands of little objects such as the French know so well how to make. The shops and street carts were heaped with every conceivable article *à la Napoléon*. In a short time the country was experiencing a movement similar in character to that which has swept over France during the last two years, with this difference: In 1840 there was a deep and sincere personal affection for Napoleon still existing among thousands of old soldiers who had served under him. This gave a genuineness to the feeling, quite unlike anything to be seen in France to-day, where there is more or less affectation in the cult professed. There was, too, in 1840, a decided political character to the movement. The imperial cause had hosts of defenders then. To-day there is only the feeblest political force in the Napoleon movement. The present interest is preëminently literary.

Day by day the legend grew among the people. It was fed in a thousand ways. There were numbers of thrilling public presentations, as when Bertrand sent to Louis Philippe his master's sword, to be put upon the coffin when it should reach France. There was a revival of the tales of the Empire, and hundreds of old men related, about the *café* tables, stories like those of General Marbot, rife with heroism, adventure, pathos, and wit. The preparations for the expedition excited great curiosity. Thousands went to see the splendid ebony casket made to receive the remains. The *chambre ardente* prepared in the "Belle Poule," the vessel which was to conduct the Prince de Joinville, the commander of the expedition, and his suite, to St. Helena, was the object of numberless pilgrimages during all the time that the vessel lay in the harbor of Toulon. The Napoleon legend grew as the people gazed.

THE VOYAGE TO ST. HELENA.

On July 7th the "Belle Poule" sailed from Toulon accompanied by the "Favorite." The commander of the expedition, the Prince de Joinville, had not received his orders to go on the expedition with great pleasure. Two of his brothers had just been sent to Africa to fight, and he envied them their opportunities for adventures and glory; and, besides, he was sick of a most plebeian complaint, the measles. "One day as I lay in high fever," he says in his "Memoirs," "I saw my father appear, followed by M. de Rémusat, then Minister of the Interior. This unusual visit filled me with astonishment, and my surprise increased when my father said, 'Joinville, you are to go out to Saint Helena and bring back Napoleon's coffin.' If I had not been in bed already I should have fallen down flat, and at first blush I felt nowise flattered when I compared the warlike campaign my brothers were on with the undertaker's job I was being sent to perform in the other hemisphere. But I served my country, and I had no right to discuss my orders."

If the young prince was privately a little ashamed of his task, publicly he adapted

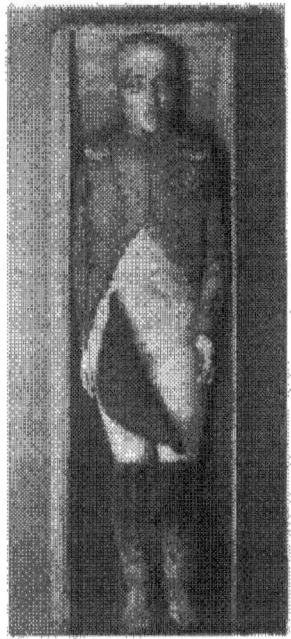

NAPOLEON'S BODY AS IT APPEARED AT THE DISINTERMENT IN ST. HELENA.

FRONTISPIECE TO THE SUCCEEDING SERIES OF ENGRAVINGS AS ORIGINALLY PUBLISHED.

himself admirably to the occasion. In his suite were several old friends of Napoleon: the Baron las Cases, General Gourgaud, Count Bertrand, and four of his former servants. All of these persons had been with him at St. Helena. Marchand, one of the executors of the emperor, was on the "Favorite."

Save once, France heard nothing of the expedition from its sailing on July 7th until its return to Cherbourg on November 30th. But the silence only made the mission loom larger. The mystery and uncertainty gave solemnity and majesty to the enterprise.

A rude blow to the really solemn temper of the country came in August, when Louis Napoleon, son of the ex-King of Holland, afterwards Napoleon III., landed one morning at Boulogne-sur-Mer with some sixty followers and a *tame eagle*, and attempted to excite a revolution. In the proclamations which he scattered, he told the people that he came to discharge the providential mission left him by the martyr of St. Helena, and he assured them that the remains

RECEIVING NAPOLEON'S BODY ON THE "BELLE POULE," AT ST. HELENA, OCTOBER 15, 1840.

of Napoleon returned from exile with sentiments of love and reconciliation. The attempt was a ridiculous fiasco, and the young man was promptly shut up at Havre. He received little sympathy for his weak imitation of the return from Elba—the French only applaud success, and they emphatically oppose any interruption of what promises to be a great spectacle—but the government began seriously to turn public attention into other channels. Trouble with England over the Eastern question assisted them materially in this.

And in the meantime where was the "Belle Poule"? A voyage of sixty-six days brought her, on October 8th, to St. Helena, where she was welcomed by the English with every honor. Indeed, throughout the affair the attitude of the English was dignified and generous. They showed plainly their desire to satisfy and flatter the pride and sentiment of the French.

EXHUMATION OF THE BODY.

It had been decided that the exhumation of the body and its transfer to the French should take place on the twenty-fifth anniversary of the arrival of Napoleon at the island. The disinterment was begun at midnight on October 15th, the English conducting the work, and a number of the French, including those of the party who had been with Napoleon at his death, being present. The work was one of extraordinary difficulty, for the same remarkable precautions against escape were taken in Napoleon's death as had been in his life.

The grave in the valley of Napoleon, as the place had come to be called, was surrounded by an iron railing set in a heavy stone curb. Over the grave was a covering of six-inch stone which admitted to a vault eleven feet deep, eight feet long, and four feet eight inches broad. The vault was apparently filled with earth, but digging down some seven feet a layer of Roman cement was found; this broken, laid bare a layer of rough-hewn stone ten inches thick, and fastened together by iron clamps. It took four and one-half hours to remove this layer. The stone up, the slab forming the lid of the interior sarcophagus was exposed, enclosed in a border of Roman cement strongly attached to the walls of the vault. So stoutly had all these various coverings been sealed with cement and bound by iron bands, that it took the large party of laborers ten hours to reach the coffin.

As soon as exposed the coffin was purified, sprinkled with holy water, consecrated by a *De Profundis*, and then raised with the greatest care, and carried into a tent which had been prepared for it. After the religious ceremonies, the inner coffins were opened. "The outermost coffin was slightly injured," says an eye-witness; "then came one of lead, which was in good condition, and enclosed two others—one of tin and one of wood. The last coffin was lined inside with white satin, which, having become detached by the effect of time, had fallen upon the body and enveloped it like a winding-sheet, and had become slightly attached to it.

"It is difficult to describe with what anxiety and emotion those who were present waited for the moment which was to expose to them all that was left of the Emperor Napoleon. Notwithstanding the singular state of preservation of the tomb and coffins, we could scarcely hope to find anything but some misshapen remains of the least perishable part of the costume to evidence the identity of the body. But when Dr. Guillard raised the sheet of satin, an indescribable feeling of surprise and affection was expressed by the spectators, many of whom burst into tears. The emperor himself was before their eyes! The features of the face, though changed, were perfectly recognizable; the hands extremely beautiful; his well-known costume had suffered but little, and the colors were easily distinguished. The attitude itself was full of ease, and but for the fragments of satin lining which covered, as with fine gauze, several parts of the uniform, we might have believed we still saw Napoleon lying on his bed of state." *

A solemn procession was now formed, and the coffin borne over the rugged hills of St. Helena to the quay. "We were all deeply impressed," says the Prince de Joinville, "when the coffin was seen coming slowly down the mountain side to the firing of cannon, escorted by British infantry with arms reversed, the band playing, to the dull rolling accompaniment of the drums, that splendid funeral march which English people call the *Dead March in Saul*."

At the head of the quay, the Prince de Joinville, attended by the officers of the French vessels, was waiting to receive the remains of the emperor. In the midst of the most solemn military funeral rites the French embarked with their precious charge. "The scene at that moment was very fine," continues the prince. "A magnificent sunset had been succeeded by a twilight of the deepest calm. The British authorities and the troops stood motionless on the beach, while our ship's guns fired a royal salute. I stood in the stern of my long boat, over which floated a magnificent tricolor flag, worked by the ladies of St. Helena. Beside me were the generals and superior officers. The pick of my topmen, all in white, with crape on their arms, and bareheaded like ourselves, rowed the boat in silence, and with the most admirable precision. We advanced with majestic slowness, escorted by the boats bearing the staff. It was very touching, and a deep national sentiment seemed to hover over the whole scene."

* "Le Moniteur Universel," December 13, 1840.

REMOVAL OF NAPOLEON'S BODY FROM THE TOMB AT THE FUNERAL CAR AT PARIS, DECEMBER 15, 1840.

But no sooner did the coffin reach the French cutter than mourning was changed to triumph. Flags were unfurled, masts squared, drums set a-beating, and *salvos* poured from forts and vessels. The emperor had come back to his own!

RETURN TO FRANCE.

Three days later the "Belle Poule" was *en route* for France. One incident alone marked her return. A passing vessel brought the news that war had been declared between France and England. The Prince de Joinville was only twenty-two, a hot-headed youth, and the news of war immediately convinced him that England had her fleet out watching for him, ready to carry off Napoleon again. He rose to the height of his fears. The elegant furnishings of the saloons of his vessel were torn out and thrown overboard to make room to put in batteries; the men were made ready for fighting, and everybody on board was compelled to take an oath to sink the vessel before allowing the remains to be taken. This done, the "Belle Poule" went her way peacefully to Cherbourg, where she arrived on November 30th, forty-three days after leaving St. Helena.

The town of Cherbourg owes much to Napoleon—her splendid harbors, and great tracts of land rescued from the sea—and she honored the return of his remains with every pomp. Even the poor of the town were made to rejoice by lavish gifts in the emperor's honor; and one of the chief squares—one he had redeemed from the sea—became the Place Napoleon.

The vessels lay eight days at Cherbourg, for the arrival had been a fortnight earlier than was anticipated, and nothing was ready for the celebration in Paris; but the time was none too long for the thousands who flocked in interminable processions to the vessels. When the vessels left for Havre, Cherbourg was so excited that she did what must have seemed to the nervous inhabitants an extravagance, even in Napoleon's honor. She fired a *thousand* guns!

FROM CHERBOURG TO PARIS.

The passage of the flotilla from Cherbourg to Paris took seven days. At almost every town and hamlet elaborate demonstrations were made. At Havre and Rouen they were especially magnificent.

A striking feature of the river cortège was the ceremonies at the various bridges under which the vessels passed. The most elaborate of these was at Rouen, where the central arch of the suspension bridge had been formed into an immense arch of triumph. The decorations were the exclusive work of wounded legionary officers and soldiers of the Empire. When the vessel bearing the coffin passed under, the veterans showered down upon it wreaths of flowers and branches of laurel.

These elaborate and grandiose ceremonies were not, however, the really touching feature of the passage. The hill-sides and river-banks were crowded with people from all the surrounding country, who sometimes even pressed into the river in order better to see the vessels. Those on the flotilla saw aged peasants firing salutes with ancient muskets, old men kneeling with uncovered heads on the sod, and others their heads in their hands weeping —these men were veterans of the Empire paying homage to the passage of their hero.

It was on the afternoon of December 14th, just as the sun was setting radiantly behind Mt. Valerian, that the flotilla reached Courbevoie, a few miles from Paris, where Napoleon's body was first to touch French soil. The bridge at Courbevoie, the islands of Neuilly, the hills which rise from the Seine, were crowded, far as the eye could reach, with a throng drawn from the entire country around.

The flotilla as it approached was a brilliant sight. At the head was the "Dorade," a cross at her prow, and, behind, the coffin. It was dressed in purple velvet, surrounded by flags and garlands of oak and cypress, surmounted by a canopy of black velvet ornamented with silver and masses of floating black plumes. Between cross and coffin stood the Prince de Joinville in full uniform, and behind him Generals Bertrand and Gourgaud and the Abbé Coquereau, almoner of the expedition. The vessels following the "Dorade" bore the crews of the "Belle Poule" and the "Favorite" and the military bands. A magnificent funeral boat, on whose deck there was a temple of bronzed wood, hung with splendid draperies of purple and gold, brought up the official procession. Behind followed numberless craft of all descriptions. Majestic funeral marches and *salvos* of artillery accompanied the advance.

At Courbevoie the flotilla anchored. Notwithstanding the intense cold, thousands of people camped all night on the hill-sides and shores, their bivouac fires illuminating the landscape.

DECEMBER 15, 1840.

Only those who have seen Paris on the day of a great *fête* or ceremony can picture to themselves the 15th of December, 1840. The day was intensely cold, eight degrees below the freezing point, but at five o'clock in the morning, when the drums began beating, and the guns booming, the populace poured forth, taking up their positions along the line of the expected procession. This line was fully three miles in length,

THE FUNERAL PROCESSION OF PARIS. FUNERAL CAR PASSING UNDER THE ARC DE TRIOMPHE.

and ran from Courbevoie to the Arc de Triomphe by way of Neuilly, thence down the Champs Elysées, across the Place and Bridge de la Concorde, and along the *quai* to the Esplanade des Invalides. From one end to the other it was packed on either side a hundred deep, before nine o'clock. The journals of the day compute the number of visitors expected in Paris as about half a million. Inside and outside of the Hôtel des Invalides alone, thirty-six thousand places were given to the Minister of

THE SECOND FUNERAL OF NAPOLEON.

THE FUNERAL PROCESSION IN PARIS. FUNERAL CAR PASSING DOWN THE CHAMPS ELYSÉES.

the Interior, and that did not cover one-tenth of the requests he received. It is certain that nearly a million persons saw the entry of Napoleon's remains. The people hung from the trees, crowded the roofs, stood on ladders of every description, filled the windows, and literally swarmed over the walks and grass plots. A brisk business went on in elevated positions. A ladder rung cost five francs ($1.00); the man who had a cart across which he had laid boards, rented standing-room at from

THE FUNERAL PROCESSION IN PARIS. FUNERAL CAR LEAVING THE FOOT OF LA CONCORDE.

five to ten francs. As for windows and balconies—they sold for fabulous prices, in spite of the fact that the placard *fenêtres et balcons à louer* appeared in almost every house from Neuilly to the Invalides, even in many a magnificent hotel of the Champs Elysées. Fifty francs ($10.00) was the price of the meanest window; a good one cost one hundred francs ($20.00); three thousand francs ($600.00) were paid for good balconies. One speculator rented a vacant house for the day for five thousand francs ($1,000.00), and made money on his investment.

The crowd made every preparation to keep warm; some of them carried footstoves filled with live coals, others little hand-warmers. At intervals along the procession great masses of the spectators danced to keep up their circulation. Venders of all sorts of articles did a thriving business. Every article was, of course, Napoleonized; one even bought *gauffrettes* and *Madeleines* cut out in the shape of Napoleons. There were badges of every form, imperial eagles, It's, crowns, even the *petit chapeau*. Many pamphlets in prose and verse had a great sale, especially those of Casimir Delavigne, Victor Hugo, and Barthélemy; though all these stately odes were far outstripped by one song, thousands upon thousands of copies of which were sold. It ran:

" Premier capitaine du monde
Depuis le siège de Toulon,
Tant sur la terre que sur l'onde
Tout redoutait Napoléon,
Du Nil au nord de la Tamise !
Devant lui l'ennemi fuyait.
Avant de combattre, il tremblait
Voyant sa redingote grise." *

The cortége which had brought this crowd together was magnificent in the extreme. A brilliant military display formed the first portion; *gendarmerie*, municipal guards, officers, infantry, cavalry, artillery, cadets from the important schools, national guards. But this had little effect on the crowd. The genuine interest began when Marengo, Napoleon's famous battlehorse, appeared—it was not Marengo, but it looked like him, which for spectacular purposes was just as well; and the saddle and bridle were genuine—the defile now became exciting. The commission of St. Helena appeared in carriages, then the Marshals of France, the Prince de Joinville, the crews of the vessels which had been to St. Helena, finally the funeral car, a magnificent creation over thirty feet high, its design and ornaments symbolic. Sixteen black horses in splendid trappings drew the car, whose funeral pall was held by a marshal and an admiral of France, by the Duc de Reggio and General Bertrand.

The passing of the car was everywhere greeted with sincere emotion, profound reverence.

* The greatest captain, all agree,
Since the siege of Toulon ;
On the earth, as on the sea,
All yielded to Napoleon.
His enemies fled, full of dismay,
Beyond the Thames from off the Nile,
Before the fight; trembling the while
If they but saw his redingote gray.

Even the opposition recognized the genuineness of the feeling; many of them owned to sharing it for one moment of self-forgetfulness, and they began to ask themselves, as Lamartine had asked the Chamber six months before, what they had been thinking to allow the French heart and imagination to be so fired? Even cynical Englishmen who looked on with stern or contemptuous countenances, said to themselves meditatively that night, as they sat by their fire resting, " Something good must have been in this man, something loving and kindly, that has kept his name so cherished in the popular memory and gained him such lasting reverence and affection." *

Following the car came those who had been intimately associated with the emperor in his life—his aides-de-camp and civil and military officers. Many of them had been with him in famous battles ; some were at Fontainebleau in 1814, others at Malmaison in 1815. The veterans of the Imperial Guard followed; behind them a deputation from Ajaccio.

From Courbevoie to the Hôtel des Invalides, one walked through a hedge of elaborate decorations—of bees, eagles, crowns, N's; of bucklers, banners, and wreaths bearing the names of famous victories; of urns blazing with incense ; of rostral columns ; masts bearing trophies of arms and clusters of flags ; flaming tripods; allegorical statues ; triumphal arches ; great banks of seats draped in imperial purple and packed with spectators, and phalanges of soldiers. On the top of the Arc de Triomphe was an imposing apotheosis of Napoleon. Each side of the Pont de la Concorde was adorned with huge statues. On the Esplanade des Invalides the car passed between an avenue of thirty-two statues of great French kings, heroes and heroines—Charles Martel, Charlemagne, Clovis, Bayard, Jean d'Arc, Latour d'Auvergne, Ney. The chivalry and valor of France welcomed Napoleon home. Oddly enough, this hedge of statues ended in one of Napoleon himself ; the incongruity of the arrangement struck even the *gamins*. " Tiens," cried one urchin, " voilà comme l'empereur fait la queue à lui-même." † (" Hello, see there how the emperor brings up his own procession.")

The effect of the pageant was greatly increased by the splendor of the day. A " Napoleonic day," said the crowd, and they recalled how the emperor was said in his

* " Second Funeral of Napoleon." By Michael Angelo Tamarch (Thackeray).
† " The London Times," December 18, 1840.

THE SECOND FUNERAL OF NAPOLEON. 519

THE FUNERAL OF NAPOLEON IN PARIS. FUNERAL CAR PASSING UP THE AVENUE OF KINGS IN THE ESPLANADE DES INVALIDES.

lifetime invariably to have had the sunshine at the critical point of his *fêtes*. It certainly was so on the return from St. Helena. The day that the body was exhumed was dreary until the transfer was made to the French; then the sun shone out gloriously. At Havre, at the moment the vessel entered the Seine, the sun arose. "Napoleon reëntered France encircled by glory," said Montholon. "The sun of Austerlitz saluted the return of the hero." At Courbevoie, on the morning of

¹ THE FUNERAL PROCESSION IN PARIS TRANSFERRING THE COFFIN INTO THE CHURCH OF THE HÔTEL DES INVALIDES.

the 15th, the sun came out just as the coffin was taken from the boat first to touch the soil of France.

DISTURBANCES DURING THE CEREMONY.

The procession passed quietly from one end to the other of the route, to the great relief of the authorities. Difficulty was anticipated from several sources: from the Anglophobes, the Revolutionists, the Legitimists, the Bonapartists, and the great mass of dissatisfied, who, no matter what form of rule they are under, are always against the government. The greatest fear seems to have been on the part of the

English. Thackeray, who was in town at the time, gives an amusing picture of his own nervousness on the morning of the 15th.

"Did the French nation, or did they not, intend to offer up some of us English over the imperial grave? And were the games to be concluded by a massacre? It was said in the newspapers that Lord Granville had despatched circulars to all the English residents in Paris, begging them to keep their homes. The French journals announced this news, and warned us charitably of the fate intended for us. Had Lord Granville written? Certainly not to me. Or had he written to all *except me*? And was I *the victim*—the doomed one?—to be seized directly I showed my face in the Champs Elysées, and torn in pieces by French patriotism to the frantic chorus of the Marseillaise? I depend on it, Madame, that high and low in this city on Tuesday were not altogether at their ease, and that the bravest felt no small tremor. And be sure of this, that as his Majesty Louis Philippe took his nightcap off his royal head that morning, he prayed heartily that he might at night put it on in safety."

Fortunately Thackeray's courage conquered, and so we have the entertaining "Second Funeral of Napoleon," by Michael Angelo Titmarsh.

In spite of all forebodings, the hostile displays were nothing more than occasional cries of "*A bas les Anglais*," a few attempts to promenade the tricolor flag and drown *le premier capitaine du monde* by the Marseillaise, and a strong indignation when it was learned that the representatives of the Allies had refused to be present at the final ceremony.

Most of the observers of the funeral attributed the good order of the crowd to the cold. A correspondent of the "National Intelligence" of that date says:

"If this business had fallen in the month of June or July, with all its excitements, spontaneous and elaborate, I should have deemed a sanguinary struggle between the government and the mob certain or highly probable. The present military array might answer for an approaching army of Cossacks. Forty or fifty thousand troops remain in the barracks within and camps without, besides the regular soldiery and National Guards in the field, ready to act against the domestic enemy.

"*Providentially* the cold increased to the utmost keenness; the genial currents of the insurrectionary and revolutionary soul were frozen."

AT THE CHURCH OF THE INVALIDES.

The climax of the pageant was the temple of the Invalides. The spacious church was draped in the most magnificent and lavish fashion, and adorned with a perfect bewilderment of imperial emblems. The light was shut out by hangings of violet velvet; tripods blazing with colored flames, and thousands upon thousands of waxen candles in brilliant candelabra lighted the temple. Under the dome, in the place of the altar, stood the catafalque which was to receive the coffin.

From early in the morning the galleries, choir, and tribunes of the Invalides were packed by a distinguished company. There were the Chambers of Deputies and Lords—neither of which had been represented in the cortége—the judicial and educational bodies, the officers of army and navy, the ambassadors and representatives of foreign governments, the king, and the court.

But none of these dignitaries were of more than passing interest that day. The centre of attention, until the coffin entered, was the few old soldiers of the Empire to be seen in the company; most prominent of these was Marshal Moncey, the decrepit governor of the Invalides. His history was one of the greatest valor, and Napoleon never had a more devoted soldier. He was ill when the remains of the emperor returned. It was believed he would die, and, for days before the funeral, he asked his physician every morning: "Doctor, shall I live till the 15th?" And then he would beg: "Give me until then, and I will die contented." He was alive, and just before the cannon announced the arrival of the coffin, he was wheeled into the church.

It was two o'clock in the afternoon when the Archbishop of Paris, preceded by a splendid cross-bearer, and followed by sixteen incense boys and long rows of white-clad priests, left the church to meet the procession. They returned soon. Following them were the Prince de Joinville and a select few from the grand cortége without; in their midst, Napoleon's coffin.

As it passed, the great assemblage was swayed by an extraordinary emotion. There is no one of those who have described the day who does not speak of the sudden, intense agitation which thrilled the company, whether he refers to it half-humorously as Thackeray, who told how "everybody's heart was thumping as hard as possible," or cries with Victor Hugo:

"Sire: En ce moment-là, vous aurez pour royaume,
Tous les fronts, tous les cœurs qui battront sous le ciel.
Les nations feront asseoir votre fantôme,
Au trône universel."*

* Sire, in that moment your kingdom will be on every brow, in every heart which beats under heaven. The nations will seat your phantom on a universal throne.

THE FUNERAL MASS IN THE CHURCH OF THE HÔTEL DES INVALIDES. THE CATAFALQUE ON WHICH THE COFFIN RESTS IS SEEN IN THE DISTANCE.

The king descended from his throne and advanced to meet the cortége. "Sire," said the Prince de Joinville, "I present to you the body of Napoleon, which, in accordance with your commands, I have brought back to France."

"I receive it in the name of France," replied Louis Philippe.

Such at least is what the "Moniteur" affirms was said, but the "Moniteur" is an official journal whose business is, not to tell what really happened, but what would have happened if the government had had its way. The Prince de Joinville gives a different version: "The king received the body at the entrance to the nave, and there

NAPOLEON'S TOMB IN THE CHURCH OF THE HOTEL DES INVALIDES AS IT APPEARS AT THE PRESENT DAY.

rather a comical scene took place. It appears that a little speech which I was to have delivered when I met my father, and also the answer he was to give me, had been drawn up in council, only the authorities had omitted to inform me concerning it. So when I arrived I simply saluted with my sword, and then stood aside. I saw, indeed, that this silent salute, followed by retreat, had thrown something out; but my father, after a moment's hesitation, improvised some appropriate sentence, and the matter was afterwards arranged in the 'Moniteur.'"

Beside the king stood an officer, bearing a cushion; on it lay the sword of Austerlitz. Marshal Soult handed it to the king, who, turning to Bertrand, said:

"General, I commission you to place the emperor's glorious sword on the bier."

And Bertrand, trembling with emotion, laid the sword reverently on his idol's coffin. The great company watched the scene in deepest silence. The only sound which broke the stillness was the half-stifled sobs of the gray-haired soldiers of the Invalides, who stood in places of honor near the catafalque.

The king and the procession returned to their places, and then followed a majestic funeral mass. The *requiem* of Mozart, as rendered that day by all the great singers of Paris, is one of the historic musical performances of France. The archbishop then sprinkled the coffin with holy water, the king taking the brush from him for the same sacred duty.

The funeral was over. Napoleon lay at last "on the banks of the Seine, among the people whom he had so loved."

AFTER THE FUNERAL.

For eight days after the ceremony the church remained open to the public, and in spite of the terrible cold thousands stood from morning until night waiting patiently their turn to enter. After hours of waiting, they frequently were sent away, only to come back earlier the next day. In this company were numbers of veterans of the imperial army who had made the journey to Paris from distant parts of the kingdom. In the delegation of old soldiers from Belgium were many who had walked part of the way, not being able to pay the coach fare the entire distance.

Banquets and dinners followed the funeral. At one of these, a "sacred toast to the immortal memory" was drunk *knee-ling*. In a dozen theatres of Paris the translation of the remains was dramatized. At the Porte Saint-Martin, the actor who took the part of Sir Hudson Lowe had a season of terror, he being in constant danger of violence from the wrought-up audience.

The advertising columns of the newspapers of the day blazed for weeks with announcements of Napoleonized articles; the holiday gifts prepared for the booths of the boulevards and squares, and for the magnificent shops of the Palais Royal and the fashionable streets, whatever their nature — to eat, to wear, to look at — were made up as memorials. Paris seemed to be Napoleon-mad.

In the February following the funeral, the coffin of Napoleon was transferred from the catafalque in the centre of the church to a *chapelle ardente* in the basement at one side. The chapel was richly draped in silk and gold, and hung with trophies. On the coffin lay the imperial crown, the emperor's sword, and the hat which he had worn at Eylau, and which he had given to Gros when he ordered the battle of Eylau painted. Over the coffin waved the flags taken at Austerlitz.

Here Napoleon's body lay until the mausoleum was finished. This magnificent structure was designed by Visconti, the eminent architect, who had also planned the entire decorations of the 15th of December. Visconti utterly ignored the appropriations in executing the monument, ordering what he wanted, regardless of its cost. For the marble from which Pradier made the twelve colossal figures around the tomb, he sent to Carrara; the porphyry which was used to inclose the coffin, he obtained in Finland.

In this magnificent sepulchre Napoleon still sleeps. Duroc and Bertrand lie on either side of the entrance to the chamber, guarding him in death as in life; and to the right and left of the entrance to the church are the tombs of his brothers Jerome and Joseph. On the stones about him are inscribed the names he made glorious; over him are draped scores of trophies; attending him are the veterans of the Invalides.

"Qu'il dorme en paix sous cette voûte !
C'est un casque bien fait, sans doute,
Pour cette tête de géant." *

---

* "Let him rest in peace beneath this dome. It is a helmet made for a giant's head".

"HUMAN DOCUMENTS."

PRINCE BISMARCK.

Prince Otto Edward Leopold von Bismarck was born April 1, 1815, of a very old and sturdy German family. He was put early to school, attended several universities, and served his term in the army. His political life began in 1846, when he was elected a member of the diet of his province, Saxony. The next year he went to Berlin as a representative in the General Diet, and immediately attracted attention by the force and boldness of his speeches. In 1851 he began his diplomatic career as secretary to the Prussian member of the representative Assembly of German Sovereigns at Frankfort. He has been described at this time as "in the bloom of early manhood; of very tall, stalwart, and imposing mien, with blue gray, penetrating, fearless eyes; of a bright, fresh countenance, with blond hair and beard." In 1859 he was sent as ambassador to Russia. In 1862 he was transferred to Paris; but a few months later he was made minister of foreign affairs. He inaugurated his ministry by the summary dissolution of the Prussian Chamber of Deputies, because it refused to pass the budget proposed by the throne, curtly informing the body that the king's government would be obliged to do without its sanction. Five times the deputies were dismissed in this fashion. Bismarck was denounced on all sides as a usurper and despot, and for the time was bitterly hated. But as his profound project, already conceived, of uniting the German states into a compact empire, with Prussia at the head, and the King of Prussia emperor, unfolded itself, and advanced, by one brilliant stroke of statesmanship after another, toward fulfilment, the early distrust was forgotten, and he became, in spite of his "iron hand" and his apparent contempt for popular rights, a popular idol. The short, sharp war of 1866, which ended in the humiliation of Austria at Königgrätz, and the termination of Austrian dominance in Germany, began a national progress, under Bismarck's sagacious and strong direction, which came to its consummation at the close of the war with France, when, on January 18, 1871, in the palace of the French kings, at Versailles, William I., King of Prussia, was proclaimed Emperor of united Germany. In 1890, differences with the present Emperor, William II., led to Bismarck's retirement from public life. There are at the present moment, however, signs of a reconciliation, and it may be that, despite his eighty years, he will again become the guiding spirit of the German state.

1859. AGE 39. STILL MINING AT FRANKFORT.

1866, THE YEAR OF THE WAR WITH AUSTRIA. AGE 51.

BISMARCK IN 1871. AGE 56.

From a photograph by Loescher & Petsch, Berlin. On January 18, 1871, the war with France having been brought to a triumphant close, Bismarck had the satisfaction of seeing King William of Prussia crowned Emperor of united Germany in the palace of the French kings, at Versailles, himself becoming at the same time Chancellor of the German Empire. The formal treaty of peace with France was signed a month later.

PRINCE BISMARCK.

BISMARCK IN 1871. AGE 56.

BISMARCK IN 1877. AGE 62.

On the eve of the Congress of Berlin, wherein the European powers, largely under Bismarck's guidance, fixed the relations of Turkey. From a photograph by Loescher & Petsch, Berlin.

PRINCE BISMARCK.

BISMARCK IN 1880, AGE 65.
From a photograph by Ad. Braun & Co., Paris.

1883, AGE 68.

1885, AGE 70.

PRINCE BISMARCK.

PRINCE BISMARCK.

BISMARCK IN 1886, AGE 71.
From a photograph taken at Friedrichsruh by A. Bockmann, Strasburg.

EMPEROR FREDERICK AND PRINCE BISMARCK. 1888
From a photograph by M. Ziesler, Berlin.

1889. AGE 74.
From a photograph by M. Ziesler, Berlin.

1889. AGE 74.
From a photograph by Jul. Braatz, Berlin.

BISMARCK IN 1890. AGE 75.

In the spring of this year Bismarck's differences with William II. culminated in a retirement from office, which was practically a dismissal, after a continuous unbroken service of nearly thirty years. This portrait was taken at Friedrichsruh two months after his resignation. From a photograph by A. Bockmann, Hamburg.

BISMARCK IN 1890, AGE 75.
From a copyright photograph owned by Strumper & Co., Hamburg.

BISMARCK IN 1894. AGE 79.
From a photograph by Karl Hahn, Munich.

WHAT SHE COULD.

By Ian Maclaren,

Author of "Beside the Bonnie Briar Bush."

MAUD TREVOR was a genuine woman, and kept her accounts with the aid of six purses. One was an ancient housewife of her grandmother's, which used to be equipped with silk and thread and needles and buttons, and from a secret place yielded to the third generation a bank note of value. This capacious receptacle was evidently intended for the household exchequer, whose transactions were innumerable, and whose monthly budget depended for success on an unfailing supply of copper. Another had come from her mother, and was of obsolete design—a bag closed at both extremities, with a long, narrow slit in the middle, and two rings which compressed the gold into one end and the silver into the other. This was marked out by Providence for charity, since it made no provision for pennies, and laid a handicap of inconvenience on threepenny bits. It retained a subtle trace of an old-fashioned scent her mother loved, and recalled her mother going out on some errand of mercy—a St. Clare in her sacrifices and devotion. Purse three descended from her father, and was an incarnation of business—of chamois leather with a steel clasp that closed with a click, having three compartments within, one of which had its own clasp, and was reserved for gold. In this bank Maud kept the funds of a clothing society, whose more masterly bargains ran sometimes into farthings, and she was always haunted with anxiety lest a new farthing and a half sovereign should some day change places. A pretty little purse with ivory sides and silver hinges—a birthday gift of her girlhood—was large enough to hold her dress allowance, which Trevor had fixed at a most generous rate when he had barely four hundred a year, and had since forgotten to increase. One in sealskin had been a gift of engagement days, and held the savings of the year against birthday and Christmas presents—whose contents were the subject of many calculations. A cast-off purse of Trevor's had been devoted to Bertie, their only child, and from its resources came one way or other all he needed, but it happened that number six was constantly reënforced from the purse with the ivory sides.

Saturday forenoon was sacred to bookkeeping, and Maud used her bed as a table for this critical operation, partly because it was so much larger than an *escritoire*, but chiefly because you could empty the purses into little pools with steep protecting banks. Of course, if one sat down hurriedly, there was great danger of amalgamation, with quite hopeless consequences; and Trevor held over Maud's head the chance of his making this mistake. It was his way, till he grew too busy, to watch till the anxious face would suddenly brighten and a rapid change be made in the pools—the household contributing something to presents, and the dress purse to Bertie, while private and public charity would accommodate each other with change. Caresses were strictly forbidden in those times of abstruse calculation; and the Evil One, who stands at every man's elbow, once tempted Trevor to roll the counterpane into a bundle—purses, money, and all—but Maud, when he confessed, said that no human being would be allowed to fall into such wickedness.

Trevor was obliged to open her wardrobe fourteen days after the funeral, and the first thing he lighted upon was the purses. They lay in a row on an old account-book, a motley set indeed; but so absurd and tricky a spirit is pathos, they affected him more swiftly than the sight of a portrait. Was ever any one so faithful and conscientious, so self-forgetful and kind, so capable also and clever in her own sphere? Latterly he had sneered at the purses, and once, being vexed at something in a letter, he had told Maud she ought to have done with that folly and keep her accounts like an educated woman. "A girl of twelve would be ashamed." . . . What a merciless power memory wields! She only drooped her head, . . . it was on the sealskin purse the tear fell, and he saw the bend of the Wye at Tintern where he had surprised her with that purse. He was moved to kiss away that tear, but his heart hardened. Why could she not be like the women he knew? . . . Well, he would not be troubled any longer with her simple ways . . . he could do as he pleased now with the purses. . . . A bitter madness of grief took possession of him, and he arranged them on the bed.

One was empty, the present purse, and he understood. . . . the dress purse, of course, a little silver only . . . the rest had gone that he might have something beautiful, . . . He knew that it must be done sooner or later, and to-day was best, for his heart could be no sorer. . . . Yes, here they were, the ungiven gifts. For every person, from himself to the nurse; all wrapped in soft white paper and ready in good time. . . . She used to arrange everything on Christmas Eve . . . this year he had intended to stay at Cannes, . . . there would just have been Bertie and his mother, now. . . . But he must open it—an inkstand for his study in solid brass, with pens and other things complete; he noted every detail as if to estimate its value. It came back to him how she had cunningly questioned him about his needs before he left for Cannes, till he grew impatient. "Don't bother me about ink-bottles." Yes, the very words, and others . . . the secret writing of memory came out in this fire of sorrow. "Why won't women understand that a man can't answer questions about trifles when he has work on hand?" He could swear to the words, and he knew how Maud looked, although he did not see.

"Don't go away; you promised that you would sit beside me when I worked—hinder me? I suppose you are bidding for a kiss; you know the sight of your face inspires me." . . . That was ten years ago . . . he might have borne with her presence a little longer. . . . She never would come again . . . he would have no interruptions of that kind. . . .

Her gloves, sixes—what a perfect hand it was (smooths out the glove). His memory brings up a dinner-table. Mrs. Chatterby gives her opinion on Meredith's last novel and helps herself to salt; he sees a disgusting hand, with stumpy fingers and, for impudence, a street arab of a thumb. A vulgar little woman through and through, and yet because she picked up scraps from the monthlies, and had the trick of catchwords, people paid her court. And he had sometimes thought, but he knew better to-day . . . of all things in the world a glove is the surest symbol. Mended, too, very neatly . . . that he might have his hansoms.

It was the last thing he ever could have imagined, and yet it must be a diary—Maud's diary! Turns over the leaves, and catches that woman's name against whom he has suddenly taken a violent dislike.

"January 25. Was at Mrs. Chatterby's—how strange one does not say anything of her husband, yet he is the nicer of the two—and I think it will be better not to go again to dinner. One can always make some excuse that will not be quite untrue.

"'The dinner is in honor of Mr. Fynical, who is leaving his college and coming to live in London to do literary work,' as Mrs. Chatterby has been explaining for weeks, 'and to give tone to the weeklies.

"'The younger men are quite devoted to him, and we ought all to be so thankful that he is to be within reach. His touch reminds one of'—I don't know the French writer, but she does not always give the same name. 'We hope to see a great deal of him. So delightfully cynical, you know, and hates the *bourgeoisie*.'

"I was terrified lest I should sit next Mr. Fynical, but Mrs. Chatterby was merciful, and gave me Janie Godfrey's father. Edward says that he is a very able man, and will be Lord Chancellor some day; but he is so quiet and modest that one feels quite at home with him. Last summer he was yachting on the west coast of Scotland, and he described the sunset over the Skye hills; and I tried to give him a Devonshire sunrise. We both forgot where we were, and then Mrs. Chatterby asked me quite loud, so that every one looked, what I thought of 'Smudges.'

"The dinner-table seemed to wait for my answer, and I wish that the book had never come from the library; but I said that I had sent it back because it seemed so bitter and cruel, and one ought to read books which showed the noble side of life.

"'You are one of the old-fashioned women,' she replied. 'You believe in a novel for the young person,' with a smile that hurt me; and I told her that I had been brought up on Sir Walter Scott. I was trying to say something about his purity and chivalry, when I caught Mr. Fynical's eye, and blushed red. If I had only been silent, for I'm afraid every one was laughing, and Edward did not say one word to me all the way home.

"February 20. Another ordeal, but not

so unfortunate as the last. The Browne-Smythes are very kind friends, but I do think they are too much concerned about having clever people at their house. One evening Mrs. Browne-Smythe said she was happy because nothing had been talked about except translations of Homer. A certain guest was so miserable on that occasion that I begged Edward to leave me at home this time, but he said it would not be Greek again. It was science, however, and when we came in Mrs. Browne-Smythe was telling a very learned-looking person that she simply lived for fossils. A young lady beside me was talking about gases to a nervous man, who grew quite red, and tried to escape behind a table. I think she was wrong in her words, and he was too polite to correct her. To my horror, he was obliged to take me in to dinner, and there never could have been two people more deserving of pity, for I was terrified of his knowledge, and he was afraid of my ignorance. We sat in perfect silence till a fatherly old man, quite like a farmer, on my left, began to talk to me so pleasantly that I described our country people, and was really sorry when the ladies had to leave. Edward says that he is one of the greatest discoverers in the world, and has all kinds of honors. We became so friendly that he has promised to take tea with me, and I think he does not despise my simplicity. How I long to be cleverer for Edward's sake, for I'm sure he must be ashamed of me among those brilliant women. I cannot blame him; I am proud of my husband.

"May 15. I am quite discouraged, and have resolved never to go to any charitable committee again. Miss Tabitha Primmer used shameful language at the Magdalene meeting to-day, and Mrs. Wood-Ruler showed me that I had broken Law forty-three by giving a poor girl personal aid. It seems presumptuous on my part to criticise such able and diligent workers, but my mother never spoke about certain subjects, and it is agony for me to discuss them. When the vicar insisted on Sunday that thoughtful women were required for Christian service to-day, and that we must read up all kinds of books, and know all kinds of painful things, my heart sank. It does not seem as if there was any place left for simple folks like me. Perhaps it would be better to give up going out altogether, and live for Edward and Bertie. I can always do something for them, and their love will be enough reward.

"November 30. I have not slept all night, for I made a dreadful mistake about a new book that every one is reading, and Edward was so angry. He did not mean all he said, but he never called me a fool before. Perhaps he is right, and it is hard on him, who is so bright. Sometimes I wish—" And then there was no writing, only a tear mark. . . .

Afterwards he opened the letters that had come since her death, and this is what he read:

"MY DEAR TREVOR: The intelligence of Mrs. Trevor's death has given me a great shock of regret, and you will allow me to express my sympathy. Many men not given to enthusiasm had told me of her face and goodness, and before I had seen your wife I knew she was a very perfect type of womanliness. The few times I met her, Mrs. Trevor cast a certain spell over me—the nameless grace of the former days—and I felt myself unworthy in her presence. Once when a silly woman referred to one of the most miserable examples of decadent fiction, your wife spoke so nobly of true literature that I was moved to thank her; but I gathered from her face that this would not be acceptable. It seemed to me that the mask had fallen from a beautiful soul, and one man, at least, in whom there is too little reverence, took the shoes from off his feet. Pardon me if I have exceeded, and believe me,
"Yours faithfully,
"BERNARD FYSICAL."

The next was from the F. R. S.:

"MY DEAR SIR: It is quite wrong for me, a stranger, to intrude on your grief, but I am compelled to tell you that an old fellow who only spoke to your wife once, had to wipe his spectacles over the 'Times' this morning. It came about this way. The lady I had taken in to dinner at the Browne-Smythes' gabbled about science till I lost my temper, and told her it would be a good thing if women would keep to their own sphere. Your wife was on the other side, and I turned to her in despair. She delighted me by confessing utter ignorance of my subject, and then she won my heart by some of the loveliest stories of peasant life in Devonshire I ever heard, so full of insight and delicacy. If the parsons preached like that I would be in church next Sunday. She put me in mind of a sister I lost long ago, who had the same low, soft voice and honest, trusty eyes. When she found I was a lonely man, your wife had pity on me, and asked me to call on her. But I had to go to America, and only returned two days ago. I intended to wish her a Happy New Year, but it's too late. I cannot get you out of my mind, and I thought it might comfort you to know how a fossil like myself was melted by that kind heart.
"Believe me, my dear sir,
"Your obedient servant,
"ARCHIBALD GILMORE."

The third was also from a man, but this time a lad in rooms whom Trevor had seen at the house:

"DEAR MR. TREVOR: You perhaps know that Mrs. Trevor allowed me to spend an hour with her of an evening, when I felt down-hearted or had any

540   WHAT SHE COULD.

trouble, but no one will ever know how much she did for me. When I came up to London my faith began to go, and I saw that in a short time I would be an Agnostic. This did not trouble me so much on my own account as my mother's, who is dead, and made me promise something on her deathbed. So I bought books and heard sermons on unbelief till I was quite sick of the whole business. Mrs. Trevor took me to hear your own clergyman, who did not help me one bit, for he was too clever and logical; but you remember I came home with you, and after you had gone to your study, I told Mrs. Trevor my difficulties, and she did me more good than all the books. She never argued nor preached, but when I was with her, one felt that religion was a reality, and that she knew more about it than any one I had met since I lost my mother. It is a shame to trouble you with my story when you are in such sorrow, and no one need tell you how noble a woman Mrs. Trevor was; but I could not help letting you know that her goodness has saved one young fellow, at least, from infidelity and worse.

"You will not mind my sending a cross to put on the coffin; it was all I could do.

"Yours gratefully,
"GEORGE BENSON."

There was neither beginning nor end to the fourth letter, but it was written in a lady's hand:

"I am a clergyman's daughter, who left her father's house and went astray. I have been in the Inferno, and have seen what I read in Dante while I was innocent. One day the old rectory rose up before my eyes, the roses hanging over my bedroom window, the birds flying in and out of the ivy, my father on the lawn, aged and broken through my sin, and I resolved that my womanhood should no longer be dragged in the mire. My home was closed years ago; I had no friends, so I went In my desperation to a certain Institute, and told my case to a matron. She was not unkindly, but the committee were awful, without either sympathy or manners; and when an unmarried woman wished to pry into the details of my degradation—but I can't tell a man the shame they would have put upon me—my heart turned to flint, and I left the place. I would have gone back to my life and perished, had it not been for one woman who followed me out and asked me to go home with her for afternoon tea. Had she said one word about my past, I had flung myself away; but because she spoke to me as if I were still in the rectory, I could not refuse. Mrs. Trevor never once mentioned my sin, and she saved my soul. I am now a nurse in one of the hospitals, and full of peace. As long as I live I shall lay white flowers on her grave, who surely was the wisest and tenderest of women."

Trevor's fortitude was failing fast before this weight of unconscious condemnation, and he was only able to read one more, an amazing production, that had cost the writer great pains.

"HONORED SIR: Bill says as its tyking too much on the likes o' me to be addressing you on your missus' death, but it's out her husband that will despise a pore working woman oo's lost her best friend. When Bill 'ad the rumatiks and couldn't do no work, and Byby was a-growing that thin you could see thro' 'im, Mrs. Byles says to me, 'Mrs. 'Awkes, you goes to the Society for the 'Organisation of Female Toilers.' Says I, 'Wot is that?' and she declares, 'It's a set of ladies oo wants to 'elp women to work, and they 'ill see you gets it.' So I goes, and I saw a set of ladies sitting at a table, and they looks at me; and one with spectacles and a vice like an 'and-saw arsks me, 'Wot's yer name?' and 'Ow old are you?' and 'Ow many children have you?' and 'Are your 'abits temperate?' and then she says, 'If you pay a shilling we 'ill put your nyme down for work has an unskilled worker.' 'I ain't got a shilling, and Byby's dyin' for want of food.' 'This ain't a poor 'ouse,' says she; 'this is a Bureau.' When I was a-going down the stairs, a lady comes after me. 'Don't cry, Mrs. 'Awkes,' for she had picked up my name. 'I've some charring for you, and we 'ill go to get somethink for Byby.' If ever there was a hangel in a sealskin jacket and a plain little bonnet, but the true lady hall hover, 'er name was Mrs. Trevor. Bill, he looked up from that day, and was on his keb in a week, and little Jim is the biggest Byby in the court. Mrs. Trevor never rested till I got three hoffices to clean, to say nothing of 'elping at cleanings and parties in 'ouses. She was that kind too, and free, when she'd come hin with nuns of some hoffice. 'We're horganizin' you, Missus 'Awkes, just splendid,' with the prettiest bit smile. Bill, he used to say, ''Er 'usband's a proud man, for I never saw the like o' her for a downright lady in 'er wys;' and 'e knows, does Bill, being a kebman. When I told 'im, he wos that bad that 'e never put a match to pipe the 'ole night. 'Mariar,' 'e says to me, 'you an' me 'as seen somethink of her, but you bet nobudy knew wot a saint she was 'acept 'er 'usband.'" ...

Trevor could read no more, for it had dawned at last upon him that Christ had lived with him for more than ten years, and his eyes had been holden.

COLLEGE BUILDINGS AND CAMPUS FROM THE BASEBALL FIELD.

A PRAIRIE COLLEGE.

AN EMINENT FRENCHWOMAN'S STUDY OF CO-EDUCATION IN AMERICA.

BY MADAME BLANC (TH. BENTZON) OF THE "REVUE DES DEUX MONDES."

[The author of the following article, Madame Blanc, or, as she is better known to French readers, Th. Bentzon, is one of the ablest and most delightful writers among the literary women of the day in France. For many years her short stories and novels have been regular features of the *Revue des Deux Mondes*.

Madame Blanc is even better known in her own country, however, as an authority on contemporary American literature than as a writer of fiction. For years she has been presenting one after another of our writers to the cultivated readers of France, until a great constituency has learned to look to her for information on the literary output of the United States.

The knowledge of our life which she has obtained through our books has been increased by her constant intercourse with Americans travelling in France. She never fails to extend gracious courtesies to literary Americans who seek her in Paris, and she never fails to charm them by her sincere interest in all that concerns our country. Indeed, I never met in Paris a French person who understood our social life so well, or who was so well able to ask intelligent questions about it.

For several years Madame Blanc had cherished the idea of visiting this country, in order to observe for herself what we were like. "I want to see Americans in their homes and at their work," she told me in talking of her plans. "I do not want to see the cosmopolitan life of the few, but the life of the mass of the people."

She carried out her plan in 1893, coming over in October, and remaining until the next June. In this visit of some eight months, she went to nearly all our great cities east of the Mississippi, and from them made numerous excursions out of the beaten paths of sight-seers. She studied all the great institutions, not only of the East, but of the West. She saw all classes, and talked with people of all conditions. She gathered documents on numerous enterprises peculiar to the country, examined statistics, cross-examined leading men and women. Although interested in all phases of our life, Madame Blanc studied with particular care the effect of our institutions upon women. The one original and peculiar thing which most foreigners believe the United States to have produced, is the American woman, and there is no subject which interests them more. To see the American woman in all stages of her development, and in all lights and shades, and to study her present tendencies, was Madame Blanc's desire. She did her work of observation and note-taking with the fidelity, sincerity, and good sense which characterize all her literary efforts, and when she returned to Paris, she had an astonishing amount of material. This material Madame Blanc has already used in a series of articles just completed in the *Revue des Deux Mondes*. The following article is typical of that series.—IDA M. TARBELL.]

WE have yet to become acquainted with co-educational colleges, stranger to our eyes than all the others. It is almost exclusively to the West that one must go to find them. A man of high position in the Bureau of Education spoke to me enthusiastically of the results, from the beginning to the end, of studies pursued under this plan, which in France has recently been the subject of so many earnest discussions, where, however, it could not possibly be established without a complete change in customs and manners.

Perhaps the story of a week or two spent at a prairie college, that of Galesburg, will give my readers the best idea of what co-education, in its most interesting phases, may be. The picture of the college is inseparable in my memory from that of the little town and its inhabitants. I will therefore copy a few fragments from the journal in which I wrote each evening.

A journey of about five hours takes us from Chicago to Galesburg, where I am received into the home of one of the college professors, who, like all Americans, is faithful to the principle, "The friends of our friends are our friends." Rich or poor, they offer you, under this maxim, a share in their family life as easily as we invite to dinner. It is a simple wooden house placed almost at the edge of the town. Before it, leading to the college, lies a street planted with maples, and with board walks upon its two sides. There are three or four rooms upon the first floor; upon the second as many more, with sloping ceilings. That is all. But this modest interior suggests at first sight ideas of order, scrupulous neatness, and studious retirement. The study is full of books, and they are all over the house. In the little parlor there are no mirrors, only very simple furniture, family photographs, good engravings, and flowers; a singular dignity pervades the whole.

This is the frame for one of the most energetic and noble faces I have seen, that of an old man, robust as a young man, a disinterested scholar, whose labor-filled career has been consecrated from beginning to end to the same college, in spite of what ambition may have counselled him. He is, so to speak, one of its pillars.

REV. GEORGE GALE, FOUNDER OF THE TOWN OF GALESBURG, ILLINOIS, AND OF KNOX COLLEGE.

THE FOUNDATION.

The founding of Knox College, as it is described to me, presents unique features. A band of patriotic and Christian pioneers laid its foundation. Their declared aim was to establish a college which might furnish well prepared recruits for the evangelical ministry, and which should make women worthy educators of the future generation. On January 7, 1836, a meet-

A PRAIRIE COLLEGE.

ing was held at Whitesboro, New York, at which a sum of twenty thousand dollars was voted to pay for fifteen thousand acres of land, the sale of which represented the first gift to the college; and in the spring of that same year the colonists, led by the Rev. George Gale, promoter of the project and head of the colony to which he gave his name, turned toward the prairie. By autumn thirty families, composing a homogeneous nucleus, descended from the Pilgrim Fathers of the past, had already built rude cabins upon the place where afterwards was to rise the town. . . .

Alumni Hall, a building of brick and red sandstone, in modified Roman style, has a fine appearance. Its auditorium, which always been especially interested in religion and science. The residence quarter is full of very pretty houses, the most of them built of wood and painted, and affecting all styles of architecture. Grassy borders surround them. They might be described as scattered over a lawn. The whole town is scrupulously neat, with the sidewalks, very ugly by the way, which everywhere in America, along the roads, in the public parks, and about the houses, permit one to avoid the dust or mud, according to the season. A few streets are paved with an improved brick. One feels a pleasant intimacy with the interior of the houses seen through the flower-decked bay windows. We come to a suburb formed of little houses painted in

COLLEGE BUILDINGS FROM THE CITY PARK.

will hold nearly one thousand people, serves each morning as a chapel, where a service of prayer unites the whole college, and where in turn the professors read the Bible and give a brief instruction. I hear the professor of English literature speak upon "Comparisons" apropos of the mote and beam of the Gospel. This custom does not exist in the universities of the East; it seems to me that it contributes largely to the moral atmosphere of Galesburg.

We visit the town, very charming with its shady avenues and green boulevards. It covers a large area, trees and gardens occupying much space. Trees surround the principal buildings. There are a few business streets, but they have a tranquil activity, as is fitting in a town in which traffic is a secondary matter, and which has

light colors, well varnished, like new toys; it is the Swedish quarter. They are an honest people, forming quite an important part of the population, and quickly obtaining a competency through their industry. Passing the college we see a vast drill ground for the three companies commanded by an officer of the United States army, delegated as professor of science and military tactics. The service is obligatory, each student being required to procure a uniform.

There are numerous churches, representing all Protestant sects, and also—a small fraction—the Catholic religion. It was the efforts and sacrifices of the two Congregational and the Presbyterian churches which founded the college. Their influence, therefore, dominates in the council of adminis-

DR. JOHN H. FINLEY, PRESIDENT OF THE COLLEGE.

Dr. Finley was born at Grand Ridge, Illinois, in 1863, and spent his early life on a farm. After graduating from Knox College in 1887, he pursued a post graduate course at Johns Hopkins University. He was associated with Professor Ely in the authorship of "Taxation in American States and Cities," and has been for some years editor of the "Charities Review." He was elected president of Knox in 1892, and is the youngest college president in the United States.

good faces express at once energy and purity. They tell me that they come from distant parts of the West, and that before entering college they earned the necessary money by the labor of their hands. The editor of an important magazine said to me one day, while travelling with me : "I used to pass over all this country on foot during vacations, year after year, a pack of goods on my back, to pay my college expenses. They called me the honest little peddler." And I saw that this epithet would always remain among those that had pleased him most, although he has since attained great success. A good many of the students at Knox College are made of the same solid stuff. It is found that these students who are late in beginning, are likely to show superior talents. Several are pointed out to me who, during the exposition at Chicago, without any foolish shame, used their vacation of two months and a half serving in the restaurants of the Fair, and in pushing the wheel-chairs. Now behold them buried in the "Æneid."

tration, but without any narrowness. A true Christian spirit alone is required as a fundamental and indispensable foundation to an education at Knox. The students are expected to frequent their respective churches on the Sabbath.

A STURDY TYPE OF STUDENT.

I was present at a Latin class conducted by a young woman with an expressive and resolute face, who seemed to exercise great power over her pupils. There were grouped about her almost as many boys as girls. Although no rule requires it, the two sexes are separate, and occupy different sides of the room. In general the girls are more advanced in their knowledge. They smile a little maliciously at each blunder of the boys, who, on the other hand, do not appear sorry to find them in fault. There is no coquetry on the one side or gallantry on the other. I notice the sunburned complexions, the rustic appearance of several of the students, grown men ; their

DR. NEWTON BATEMAN, FORMER PRESIDENT OF THE COLLEGE.

Dr. Bateman was born in New Jersey, July 17, 1822, and went to Illinois in his boyhood. He has had a most important part in the educational development of the State. He served five terms as State superintendent of instruction, in addition to his long connection with Knox College as professor and president. He resigned the presidency in 1892, but he still retains his professorship. Dr. Bateman enjoyed an intimate acquaintance with Lincoln, and when he was State superintendent of instruction they had an office together.

The kind and bright influence of the young girls upon these country boys is most happy. The whip of emulation inspires them; they are ashamed to allow themselves to be distanced by their frail comrades; and, moreover, feminine kindliness polishes them without their knowing it.

If the professor who teaches the chemistry lesson with remarkable animation and clearness had not, on my account, purposely questioned the girl-students that they might show a foreigner (very incapable of judging in the matter) how much they knew, I should think that here, perhaps, the boys would have the advantage. But on this subject our preconceived opinions are apparently belied by the aptitudes of American women.

SOCIETY IN A WESTERN COLLEGE TOWN.

I was invited to several houses of the town, where I found the best society; women at the same time simple and educated, talking of everything, questioning with intelligence. Evidently contact with the college is a perpetual stimulus, and the society of the professors a precious resource. Some of them have travelled, but they are not possessed by that feverish desire for change which I have noticed elsewhere—a thing which is restful. The diversity of denominations in that little town, so religious as a whole, is curious. At a certain luncheon I met half a dozen ladies, all warm friends, although belonging to different churches. Opposite me sat a Baptist; at my side a pleasant Universalist, whose religion pleased me, since it permitted her to be as sure of my eternal salvation as she was of her own. Universalists damn no one.

Professor Hurd was born at Kemptville, Ontario. He worked on his father's farm, and fitted himself for college. Graduating in 1850 from Middlebury College, Vermont, he served a year as principal of the Vermont Literary and Scientific Institution, at Brandon, Vermont. Then he was called to Knox College. Before taking up his work there, however, he studied for a time with Agassiz. He has held the chair of professor of chemistry for forty-one years; for sixteen has acted also as professor of Latin, and for three was acting president.

The French lessons attracted me. The pupils were reading, translating, and explaining a play of Victor Hugo's, "Hernani," and nothing could be more droll than the accent given to those grand, impetuous verses and to those Spanish names, which they spoke with hesitation and robbed of their beauty. But they understood, they understood quite well enough, I believe, to find the character of Hernani that of a fool. I gave them real satisfaction by telling them that even in France his sentiments appeared a little exaggerated. There were some among them who were evidently bewildered by the intricate scene: some of those fine, swarthy fellows, simple and solid, of whom I have already spoken, young giants from distant farms, who have left the plough for their books. One of them accosted me with hesitation, and asked in a tone of passionate curiosity if it was true that the admiration for such a great man as Napoleon was growing less in France? Emboldened by my response, he expressed his conviction, shared by many others, that an obscure soldier had been shot in the place of Marshal Ney, and that Ney had taken refuge in America. The questions of the young girls touched upon more personal subjects: they wanted to know if the education of women in France was making any progress; if we were always shut up in convents; if co-education really did not exist with us.

We took supper at the seminary, where the young ladies from out of town live together. Around the table were assembled professors, men and women, and a few women guests. The dining-room where we were, communicated with another, a larger one, in which the boarders had

A PRAIRIE COLLEGE.

PROFESSOR GEORGE CHURCHILL.

Professor Churchill has been principal of the preparatory department of Knox College since 1855. He was born in New York State in 1820; but his parents were of the colony which in 1836 established the town of Galesburg and founded Knox College, and in the town and the college his life since his tenth year has been mainly passed.

velvety air, which, before the winter winds, accompanies that exquisite season so well named Indian summer. The landscape in its monotony was new to me, who had never seen the steppes. It was the immense, rolling prairie, its short little waves cut only by fences, barriers sometimes straight and sometimes zigzag, which all over America separate fields and confine cattle. Their silvery color, like that of the aging fir, harmonizes well with the brown tone of the soil. The corn had been harvested; there only remained the stalks and long leaves stacked for the cattle. Strange long lines of stumps, which no one takes the trouble to remove, were rotting here and there where once stood groves. They are one of the general characteristics of the American landscape as they rise rudely from the newly-cleared plain. The farmhouse, toward which we were going, was situated in the midst of three thousand acres, part cultivated and part in prairie. We stop before a wooden structure built

taken their places about small separate tables in groups of six or eight. The principal presided. A few of the young men students came in to take their meals with the young ladies. After supper, in the large, handsome drawing-room, all the pupils in the seminary were presented to me, one after another. It was a long line of very different types, often very pleasant to look upon. They came from all quarters of the United States—from Kansas, Colorado, California, Texas, from everywhere. While telling me their names, they told me also their native States. Several were from Utah, from Salt Lake City. I shuddered, thinking myself before Mormons; and they, laughing, explained to me that their parents were "Gentiles."

A VISIT TO AN ILLINOIS FARM.

I was invited to spend an afternoon upon a great farm in the suburbs. The name "farm" is given in America to all rural estates. With more than ordinary hospitality the proprietor of the farm came for me himself in his buggy. Carried along by two excellent horses, we rolled across the prairie, filling our lungs with the soft,

PROFESSOR MILTON L. COMSTOCK.

Professor Comstock was born October 19, 1824, in Hamilton County, Ohio, and graduated from Knox College in 1851. Under the necessity of making his own way he became a teacher some years before his graduation. He was principal of Knox Academy from 1851 to 1854, when he removed to Iowa, where he was for a time editor of the "Iowa Farmer." In 1858 he returned to Knox College an assistant professor of mathematics. He became full professor in 1860, and has served in that capacity ever since.

on the usual plan, with a stoop leading to it, and the indispensable walks. The mistress of the house comes to meet us. There is not a shadow of provincial ceremony in her greeting. She takes us into a drawing-room furnished in black haircloth, and we are immediately engaged in conversation upon interesting subjects.

About one o'clock dinner was served, a strictly American dinner: soup of canned oysters, roast meats, stewed corn, raw celery, rhubarb pie, wild grapes that tasted like black currants, hickory nuts, tea or coffee, as you preferred. Two young girls waited on the table; they were presented to me as the children of the house. They are obliged to assist with the housework during one of these domestic crises so common in the West and nearly everywhere.

As we talk, I discover that the life of a farmer's wife is rather severe in America, where the farm-houses are at great distances from each other, and are upon such an immense scale that the housewife's duties are by no means small. She has no distractions, no neighbors. But in winter my hostess finds compensation at Galesburg, where she belongs to a literary club. The ladies who are members of it, can read much during the summer in connection with the proposed subjects of the coming meetings. I inquired about the subjects, and learned a number of them: the Troubadours and the Trouvères (the Romance languages being held in great honor in the United States, and many people who do not speak French fluently going into ecstasies over our old Provençal literature); the influence of the *salons* of the fourteenth century; French women in politics; origin of Greek art, etc. Would one expect such interest in the affairs of the Old World in a prairie village? For a town of eighteen thousand inhabitants is little more than a village in the United States. But this village has certainly a mind superior in quality to that of many large towns.

In one of our drives a buggy crossed our path carrying a young man and a young girl. I asked the professor who drove me, if they were engaged. "They may become so," he replied, "but not necessarily." And I see that this austere man comprehends, approves this state of things; and upon this point he is of the opinion of all fathers of families whom I have met, in New York and elsewhere, finding it quite natural for their daughters to ride horseback, to go and come, accompanied by a friend. Still I do not know that his tolerance would be equal to that of many others, in case some one ventured to put the theory into practice in his own family.

The longer I stayed in Galesburg, the more I felt its resemblance to some little university town in Germany, as they were before the annexation of Prussia. There is the same simplicity, the same veneration for science and its representatives, the same patriarchal manners. The German spirit, shown by a general knowledge of the language, prevails here, too, as in many other American towns, the result of immigration, of a more or less pronounced stay made by the professors in Germany, and also of that prestige inseparable from the victorious when seen from afar. The most of the inhabitants do not speak French, though a few recall with delight a hurried visit to Paris.

COLLEGE MARRIAGES.

My questions were always about the system of co-education with its advantages and dangers. The pretty wife of the president replied to me: "We, my husband and I, can say no harm of it, since we met and loved at college." The elder daughter of my host married in the same way, after having received all the diplomas of the college.

"Yes, many marriages are decided at college; is there any harm in it? Would it be better to meet in society, in the midst of frivolity? Do they not become much better acquainted, and in a more interesting way, when they study together for years?"

"But these marriages are premature!"

"Not at all; they do not take place until the man's position is secure. The constancy of the two parties is often put to a long test."

My conclusion, after having heard all, is that the system would not succeed in a larger city where an incessant moral surveillance could not be exercised, or where religious influences would be less direct, or where there would be temptations, or even distractions. The still primitive manners of the West permit the realization of what would elsewhere be a Utopia. Many other colleges are founded upon the same basis as Knox, and this proves an uprightness of soul, fresh and robust virtues, to which it has seemed to me that the more Europeanized America of the East does not give

A RESIDENCE STREET IN GALESBURG.

"And does not love distract you from work?"

This very French reflection caused a smile. An American thinks of a wife only after having thought of his serious duties and first of the means of supporting her. The brilliant and almost unique example of the very young president of Knox, who at thirty years of age has lately succeeded a universally esteemed man, forced by his age to a comparative leisure, proves that college engagements do not prevent great efforts and great success.

I was asked if I had seen anything either in the college or the town which suggested any of the disadvantages of which I spoke. Assuredly no. It was because they did not exist. The atmosphere of Knox is clear and healthful. Each respects the dignity of his neighbor without the intervention of strict rules.

sufficient justice. Between the two sections, in the West as in the East, there are prejudices, because they are not well enough acquainted.

The wild odors of the prairie do not prevent me from appreciating certain drawing-rooms in Boston or New York. But I have often been shocked at the willing ignorance which Americans who have crossed the ocean ten times, profess for the still new portions of their own country, as if the treasures of the future were not buried there. I left Galesburg with regret. I afterwards returned to it from a long distance. I think of it yet with respect and with sympathy. It would be a great pleasure for me to take my "knitting" there, as I was invited to do in the frank parlance of the West.

THE DESTRUCTION OF THE RENO GANG.

STORIES FROM THE ARCHIVES OF THE PINKERTON DETECTIVE AGENCY.

BY CLEVELAND MOFFETT.

THE first, and probably the most daring, band of train robbers that ever operated in the United States was the notorious Reno gang, an association of desperate outlaws who, in the years immediately following the war, committed crimes without number in Missouri and Indiana, and for some years terrorized several counties in the region about Seymour in the last-named State. The leaders of this band were four brothers, John Reno, Frank Reno, "Sim" Reno, and William Reno, who rivalled each other in a spirit of lawlessness that must have been born in their blood through the union of a hardy Swiss emigrant with a woman sprung from the Pennsylvania Dutch. Of the six children from this marriage only one escaped the restless, law-despising taint that made the others desperate characters, this single white sheep being "Clint" Reno, familiarly known as "Honest" Reno, and much despised by the rest of the family for his peaceful ways. Even Laura Reno, the one daughter, famed throughout the West for her beauty, loved danger and adventure, was an expert horsewoman, an unerring shot, and as quick with her gun as any man. Laura fairly worshipped her desperado brothers, whom she aided in more than one of their criminal undertakings, shielding them from justice when hard-pressed, and swearing to avenge them when retribution overtook them after their day of triumph.

During the war the Renos had become notorious as "bounty jumpers," and at its close, with a fine scorn for the ways of commonplace industry, these fierce-hearted, dashing young fellows, all well-built, handsome boys, cast about for further means of excitement and opportunities to make an easy living. Beginning their operations in a small way with house-breaking and store robberies, they soon proved themselves so reckless in their daring, so fertile in expedients, so successful in their *coups*, that they quickly extended their field until, in the early part of 1866, they had placed a wide region under contribution, setting all forms of law at defiance.

John Reno and Frank Reno, the elder brothers, were at this time the dominating spirits of the band, and they soon associated with them several of the most skilful and notorious counterfeiters and safe burglars in the country, among these being Peter McCartney, James and Robert Rittenhouse, George McKay, John Dean, *alias* "California Nelse," and William Hopkins. The band soon came to be named with the greatest dread and awe, good citizens fearing to speak a word of censure lest swift punishment be visited upon them. The Reno influence made itself felt even in local politics, corrupt officials being elected at the instigation of the outlaws; so that their conviction became practically impossible.

A SERIES OF DARING TRAIN ROBBERIES.

The Renos, toward the end of 1866, began a series of train robberies which were carried out with such perfection of organization, such amazing coolness, and such uniform success as to attract national attention. The first of these robberies took place on the Ohio and Mississippi Railroad, being accomplished by only four men, Frank and John Reno, assisted by William Sparks and Charles Gerroll. Other train robberies followed in quick succession, the same methods being used in each, with the same immunity from capture, so that people in this region would say to each other, quite as a matter of course: "The Reno boys got away with another train yesterday."

But while indulging in its own acts of outlawry, the Reno band strenuously objected to any rivalry or competition on the part of other highwaymen. A train robbery was perpetrated on the Jeffersonville Railroad early in 1867. The Renos had no connection with this robbery. It was accomplished by two young men named Michael Collins and Walker Hammond, the two men escaping with six thousand dollars, taken from a messenger of the Adams Express Company. But their horses had carried them only a short distance from the looted train when they found themselves surrounded by the formidable Renos, who had quietly watched the robbery from a place of concealment, and now unceremoniously relieved the robbers of their plunder. Not content with this, and as if to intimidate others from like trespasses on their preserves, the Renos used their influence to have their rivals arrested for the crime by which they had profited so little, and both were subsequently tried, convicted, and sentenced to long terms in the Indiana Penitentiary. The Renos meantime, although they were known to have secured and kept the six thousand dollars, were allowed to go unmolested, and continued their depredations.

Up to this time the Reno gang had confined their operations, for the most part, to Indiana, but now they began to make themselves felt in Missouri, where a number of daring crimes were committed; notably, the robbing of the county treasurer's safe at Gallatin, in Daviess County. In this last act John Reno was known to have been personally concerned. The case was placed in the hands of Allan Pinkerton.

THE ADROIT CAPTURE OF JOHN RENO.

Taking up the investigation with his accustomed energy, Mr. Pinkerton traced John Reno back to Seymour, Indiana, where the gang was so strongly intrenched in the midst of corrupt officials and an intimidated populace, that any plan of open arrest was out of the question. Recognizing this, Allan Pinkerton had recourse to the cunning of his craft. He began by stationing in Seymour a trustworthy assistant, who was instructed on a given day, and at a given hour, to decoy John Reno to the railroad station on any pretence that might suggest itself. Then he arranged to have half a dozen Missourians, the biggest and most powerful fellows he could find, led by the sheriff of Daviess County, board an express train on the Ohio and Mississippi Railroad, at Cincinnati, and ride through to Seymour, arriving there at the time agreed upon with his assistant. Along with them was to be a constable bearing all the papers necessary to execute a requisition.

When the train reached Seymour there was the usual crowd lounging about the station, and in it were John Reno and Mr. Pinkerton's lieutenant, who had entirely succeeded in his task. While Reno was staring at the passengers as they left the train, he was suddenly surrounded and seized by a dozen strong arms, and before his friends could rally to his aid, or realize what was happening, he was clapped in irons, carried aboard the train, and soon was rolling away to Missouri under arrest.

Reno's friends stoutly contested the case in the Missouri courts, arguing that the prisoner had been kidnapped and that the law had therefore been violated by his captors. The courts decided against them on this point, however, and John Reno, with several less important members of the gang, was tried and convicted. He was sentenced to twenty-five years of hard labor in the Missouri Penitentiary.

THE BANDITS GROW BOLDER AND BOLDER.

This was the first break in the ranks of the band, the first instance in which they had suffered for their crimes. But the bold spirit of the organization was still unbroken. Three brothers still remained to replace the one who was gone, and, so far from learning caution, the band launched forthwith into still more daring and frequent offences. Trains were "held up" right and left, robberies were committed, and early in 1868 the gang made a famous raid across the country through Indiana and Illinois, robbing safes in county treasurers' offices in a number of places. In several instances some of the members were arrested, but they always managed to have the prosecution quashed or in some way to escape conviction. In the spring of 1868 their operations became so outrageous, and the situation so serious, that Allan Pinkerton was again called upon to do something in the cause of public safety.

In March of this year the safe of the county treasurer at Magnolia, Harrison County, Iowa, was robbed of about fourteen thousand dollars, and Allan Pinkerton detailed his son, William A. Pinkerton, and two assistants to run down the burglars. Arrived at the scene of the robbery, William A. Pinkerton found that the thieves had made their escape on a hand-car, and had gone in the direction of Council Bluffs. At this time, in Council Bluffs, there was a low saloon kept by a man who had formerly lived in Seymour, and who was known as a bad character. It was decided to keep a sharp watch on this resort, William A. Pinkerton reasoning that since Seymour was the friendly refuge of the Renos, it was altogether likely that the outlaws would have a friend, and perhaps an abettor, in the saloon-keeper who had once lived there. After two days' watching, the detectives observed a large man of dark complexion enter the saloon and engage in close conversation with the proprietor, having with him, evidently, some mysterious business.

A SUBSTANTIAL CITIZEN OF COUNCIL BLUFFS COMPROMISED.

Investigation disclosed this man to be Michael Rogers, a prominent and wealthy citizen of Council Bluffs, and the owner of an extensive property in the adjoining counties. Puzzled, but still persuaded that he had found a clue, Mr. Pinkerton put a "shadow" on Rogers, and hurried back to Magnolia, where he learned that, on the day preceding the robbery, Rogers had been seen in Magnolia, where he had paid his taxes, and in doing so had loitered for some time in the treasurer's office. This also looked suspicious. But, on the other hand, search as he might, the detective could find nothing against Rogers's character, every one testifying to his entire respectability.

Still unconvinced, Mr. Pinkerton returned to Council Bluffs, where he was informed by the man who had been "shadowing" Rogers that several strange men had been seen to enter Rogers's house, and had not been seen to come out again. The watch was continued more closely than ever, and after four days of patient waiting, Rogers, accompanied by three strangers, was seen to leave the house cautiously and take a west-bound train on the Pacific Railroad. One of these men, a brawny, athletic fellow, nearly six feet tall, and about twenty-eight years of age, Mr. Pinkerton shrewdly suspected was Frank Reno, although he could not be certain, never having seen Frank Reno. Feeling sure that, if his suspicions were correct, the men would ultimately return to Rogers's house, Mr. Pinkerton did not follow them on the train, but contented himself with keeping the strictest watch for their return. The very next morning the same four men were discovered coming back to the house from the direction of the railroad. But at that hour no train was due, which was a little curious; and another curious point was that they were all covered with mud, and bore marks of having been engaged in some severe, rough labor. The hour was early. The dwellers in Council Bluffs were not yet astir. A little later the city was thrown into a fever of excitement by the news that the safe of the county treasurer at Glenwood, in Mills County, about thirty miles distant, had been robbed the previous night. No trace had yet been got of the thieves, but everything indicated that they were the same men who had robbed the safe at Magnolia. One remarkable point of similarity in the two cases was the means employed by the robbers in escaping, a hand-car having been used also by the Glenwood thieves. And they, too, were believed to have fled in the direction of Council Bluffs. Investigation soon made this absolutely certain, for the missing hand-car was found lying beside the railroad, a short distance from the Council Bluffs station.

ROGERS AND HIS GUESTS ARRESTED.

Putting these new disclosures beside his previous suspicions and discoveries, Mr. Pinkerton was further strengthened in his distrust of the man Rogers, and, although he revealed his suspicions, laughed at him, declaring that Rogers was one of the most respectable citizens of the State, he resolved to attempt an arrest. Proceeding to Rogers's house with all the force he could command, he placed a guard at front and rear, and then, with a few attendants, made his way inside. The first person he met was Mr. Rogers himself, who affected to be very indignant at the intrusion.

"Who have you in this house?" asked Mr. Pinkerton.

"Nobody but my family," answered Mr. Rogers.

"We'll see about that," answered Mr. Pinkerton, and then, turning to his men, he ordered them to search the premises.

They did so, and soon came upon the three strangers, who were taken so completely by surprise that they made no effort at resistance. They were about to sit down to breakfast, which was spread for them in the kitchen. A comparison with photographs and descriptions left no doubt that one of the three was Frank Reno. A second—a man of dark complexion, tall, and well built—proved to be Albert Perkins, a well-known member of the Reno gang. The third was none other than the notorious Miles Ogle, the youngest member of the band, who afterwards came to be known as the most expert counterfeiter in the United States. Ogle, at the present time, is in the Ohio Penitentiary, serving his third term of imprisonment. At his last capture there were found in his possession some of the best counterfeit plates ever made.

While they were securing the four men, the detectives noticed that smoke was curling out of the kitchen stove, accompanied by a sudden blaze. Mr. Pinkerton pulled off a lid, and found on the coals several packages of banknotes, already on fire. Fortunately, the notes had been so tightly wrapped together that only a few of them were destroyed before the packages were got out. Those that remained were afterwards identified as of the money that had been stolen from the Glenwood safe. There was thus no question that these were the robbers so long sought for. A further search of the house brought to light two sets of burglars' tools, which served as cumulative evidence.

The men were carried to Glenwood by the next train. They were met by a great and excited crowd, and for a time were in danger of lynching. Better counsel prevailed, however, and they were placed in the jail to await trial.

A MYSTERIOUS ESCAPE.

With the men in secure, safe custody, there was no doubt of their ultimate conviction, and everyone was breathing easier at the thought that at last the Reno gang was robbed of its terrors. Then suddenly —no one will ever know how it happened —the prisoners made their escape. Great was the surprise and chagrin of the sheriff of Mills County, when, on the morning of April 1, 1868, he entered the jail only to find their cells empty. A big hole sawed through the wall told by what way they had made their exit. They left behind the mocking salutation " April Fool," scrawled in chalk over the floors and walls of the jail.

A large reward was offered for the capture of the robbers, but nothing was heard of them until two months later when an express car on the Ohio and Mississippi Railroad was boarded at Marshfield, Indiana, by a gang of masked men, and robbed of ninety-eight thousand dollars. The messenger made a brave resistance, but could not cope with the robbers, who lifted him bodily and hurled him out of the car, down a steep embankment, while the train was running at high speed.

All the facts in the case pointed to the Reno brothers as the authors of this outrage, for, by frequent repetition, their methods of robbery had become familiar. Allan Pinkerton, furthermore, obtained precise evidence that it was the work of the Renos, from secret agents whom he had stationed at Seymour to watch the doings of the gang. Two of these agents engaged apparently in business at Seymour, one setting up as a saloon-keeper in a rough part of the town, another taking railroad employment which kept him constantly near the station. A third made a wide acquaintance by passing off for a gambler and general good fellow. So successful were they that Allan Pinkerton was soon in possession of facts proving not only that the Marshfield robbery had been committed by the Renos, but that another train robbery which followed was executed by John Moore, Charles Gerroll, William Sparks, and three others, all members of the Reno organization. Moore, Gerroll, and Sparks were arrested shortly after, and placed on a train to be taken from Seymour to Brownstown, the county seat. But they never reached their destination. As the train stopped at a small station some miles from Brownstown, a band of masked men, well armed, rushed on board, overpowered the officers, hurried the three outlaws away to a neighboring farm-yard, and there strung them up to a beech tree, while an old German, who owned the farm, looked on approvingly.

THE VIGILANCE COMMITTEE OF SOUTHERN INDIANA.

This was the first act of retributive justice done by the Secret Vigilance Committee of Southern Indiana, an organization as extraordinary as the situation it was created to deal with. The entire population of that part of Indiana seemed to have risen in self-defence to crush out lawlessness. A second act followed several days later, when three other men who had been concerned in the latest train robbery, having been captured by the county officials, were taken from their hands and condemned to the same fate as their companions. Each one, as he was about to be swung off, was asked by the maskers if he had anything to say. The first two shook their heads sullenly and died without speaking. The third, standing on a barrel with the rope round his neck, looked over the crowd with contemptuous bravado, and addressing them as a lot of "mossback Hoosiers," said he was glad he was not of their class, and was proud to die as a good Republican. The barrel was kicked away, the rope stiffened with his weight, and there ended the career of the sixth member of the band.

Hard times followed for the surviving Renos. Realizing that their power was broken, they fled in various directions. The three brothers—Frank, William, and "Sim"—though still at large, were not left long to enjoy their liberty. A large price was placed on their heads, and betrayal came quickly. William and "Sim" were arrested soon after in Indianapolis and turned over to the local authorities, who, in order to avoid the Vigilance Committee, took the prisoners to New Albany, in an adjoining county, where they were placed in jail.

The Vigilance Committee, growing stronger and more determined every day, now scoured the whole country for other members of the gang or for persons believed to be in sympathy with it. They literally went on the "war path" through this whole region of Indiana, and it went ill with any poor wretch who incurred their suspicion. Like the "White Caps" of the present day, they sent warnings to all who came on their black list, and administered by night, and sometimes by day, such promiscuous floggings and other forms of punishment that the tough and criminal element of the region was entirely cowed, and feared to raise a hand in defence of the Renos as it had previously done. Up to the time the Vigilance Committee was formed, not a member of the Reno gang had been convicted in that locality, largely because the people were afraid to testify against them. They knew that if they should testify their stock would be killed, their barns burned, and they themselves waylaid and beaten. This was the reason offered for the formation of the Vigilance Committee of Southern Indiana. Whether a justification or not, the committee must certainly be credited with having rid the State of a monstrous evil.

THE MEN WHO ESCAPED AT GLENWOOD.

In the excitement of other events the Pinkertons had not forgotten the men who had escaped from the Glenwood jail. They finally traced Miles Ogle and Albert Perkins to Indianapolis, and there Ogle was captured, but Perkins escaped. Frank Reno was discovered a little later in Windsor, Canada, where he was living with Charles Anderson, a professional burglar, safe-blower, and "short-card" gambler, who had fled to Canada to escape prosecution. Reno, operating with Anderson, made a practice of registering as "Frank Going," if the enterprise in which he was engaged was prospering, and as "Frank Coming," if it was not prospering. He and Anderson were now arrested on a charge of robbery and of assault with intent to kill, in the case of the express messenger hurled from his car at Marshfield, Indiana. Under this form their offence became extraditable, and after a long trial before the stipendiary or government magistrate, Gilbert McMicken, at Windsor, the men were ordered for extradition. Aided by the ablest lawyers, they carried their case, however, to the highest court in Canada. But the decision of the lower court was affirmed, and in October, 1868, the men were surrendered into the hands of Allan Pinkerton, who was delegated by the United States Government to receive them. It was due to the patience and persistence of Mr. Alfred Gaither, the Western manager of the Adams Express Company, and his then assistant, Mr. L. C. Weir, now president of the company, and to the general policy of the company to permit no compromise with thieves, that, regardless of cost and time, the prosecution was continued until it issued thus successfully.

Michael Rogers was also discovered to be in Windsor at this time, and he was known to have had a hand in the Marshfield robbery. But he escaped arrest and remained securely in Windsor for a year or two. Later, though, he reached the penitentiary, being brought to grief by a burglary done at Tolono, Illinois. On coming out, he joined the notorious McCartney gang of counterfeiters, and had many narrow escapes. The last known of him, grown an old man, he was living quietly on a farm in Texas.

Made at last secure of Reno and Anderson, Allan Pinkerton chartered a tug to carry them to Cleveland, and thus avoid the friends who, as he had reason to know, were waiting across the river in Detroit to effect a rescue. When the tug had gone about twenty miles it was run down by a large steamer and sunk, the passengers, including the prisoners, being saved from drowning with the greatest difficulty. The prisoners were carried on to Cleveland by another boat, and from there were hurried on by rail to New Albany, where they were placed in jail along with "Sim" and William Reno.

The final passage in the history of the Reno gang occurred about a month later, in the latter part of November, 1868, when one day a passenger car was dropped off at Seymour, Indiana, some distance from the station. There was nothing remarkable in this, nor did the car attract any attention. That night a train passing through Seymour took up the car and drew it away. A few people about the station when the car was taken up remembered afterwards that this car was filled with strange looking men, who wore Scotch caps and black cloth masks, and seemed to be under the command of a tall, dark-haired man addressed by every one as "No. 1." Although there were at least fifty of these men, it is a remarkable fact, developed in a subsequent investigation, that the conductor of the train could remember nothing about the incident, declaring that he did not enter the car, and knew nothing of its being attached to his train. It is certain the company of masked men did everything in their power to avoid attention, scarcely speaking to each other during the ride, and making all their movements as noiseless as possible.

SWIFT JUSTICE AT LAST.

The train reached New Albany at two o'clock in the morning. The car was detached, and was presently emptied of its fifty men as silently and mysteriously as it had been filled. A few hurried commands were given by "No. 1," and then the company marched in quiet order to the jail. Arrived there they summoned the jailer to open the doors, but were met with a firm refusal and the shining barrel of a revolver. There followed an exchange of shots, in which the sheriff received a ball in the arm, and two local police officers were captured. Without loss of time the jail doors were battered down; the company entered, and taking the three Reno brothers and their friend, Charles Anderson, from their cells, placed nooses that they had ready around the men's necks, and hung them to the rafters in the corridors of the jail. Then having locked the doors of the jail, leaving the prisoners secure, they made their way silently back to the New Albany station, reaching there in time to catch the train that drew out at half past three A. M. The same special car in which they had come was coupled to this train, and dropped off at the switch when Seymour was reached. This was just before daybreak on a dreary November morning.

Who these fifty men were was never discovered, although, because of the fact that Reno and Anderson had been extradited from Great Britain, the general government made an investigation. It was rumored, however, and generally understood, that the company included some of the most prominent people in Seymour, among others a number of railroad and express employees. It was found that at the time of the lynching all the telegraph wires leading from New Albany had been cut, so that it was noon of the following day before the country learned of it.

The newspapers described the leader of the party as a man of unusual stature, who wore a handsome diamond ring on the little finger of his right hand. Later some significance was attached to the fact that a well-known railroad official, who answered this description as to stature, and who had always worn a handsome diamond ring previous to the lynching, ceased to wear his ring for several years afterward.

After the execution of her brothers it was rumored that Laura Reno had taken an oath to devote the rest of her life to avenging them; and for a moment there were threats and mutterings of reprisals from allies or surviving members of the gang. But these latter were not heard again after a certain morning, the third day after the execution, when the people of Seymour, on leaving their homes, were startled to see on the walls and in other public places large posters proclaiming that if any property was injured or destroyed, or any persons molested or assaulted, or if there was any further talk in regard to recent happenings, some twenty-five persons, therein frankly named, who were known to be sympathizers with the Renos, or to be more or less intimately connected with them, had better beware. And as for the sister's deadly oath, she did no act in proof of the violent intentions imputed to her, but instead subsequently became the wife of a respectable man, and settled down to a useful life, though a much more commonplace one than she had previously known. John Reno, after serving fifteen years in the Missouri Penitentiary, was released, and is said to be at present living on the old farm. "Clint" Reno, or "Honest" Reno, always stayed at the old homestead, and has never been willing to speak of his brothers or of what happened to them. Seymour, purged of the evil influences that corrupted it, has grown into a thriving and beautiful little city, and is to-day one of the model towns of Indiana.

JOURNALISM.

A LECTURE DELIVERED TO THE STUDENTS OF UNION COLLEGE.

BY CHARLES A. DANA, EDITOR OF "THE SUN."

MR. PRESIDENT, GENERAL BUTTERFIELD AND GENTLEMEN: I am intensely grateful to General Butterfield and President Webster for the opportunity of appearing before you to-day. If there is anything in life that is delightful to an old man, it is the opportunity of meeting intelligent and earnest young men, and telling them something out of his experience that may be useful to them; and as our desire is that this shall be a practical occasion, I want to say at the beginning that if any part of the subject, as I go over it, shall not seem to any one of you to be sufficiently explained and elucidated, I shall be very much obliged if you will get up and ask the questions that you wish to have answered.

The profession of journalism is comparatively new. It really is, as it exists to-day, an affair of the last forty or fifty years. When I began to practise it in a weekly paper the apparatus which we have now, and which General Butterfield has referred to, was quite unknown. The sheets which we daily take in our hands, and from which we gather a view of the whole world, and of all that has been going on in it—all the sciences, all the ideas, all the achievements, all the new lights that influence the destiny of mankind—all that was entirely out of the question. There was no such apparatus; and it has been created by the necessities of the public and by the genius of a few men, who have invented, step by step, the machinery and the methods that are indispensable, and without which we could not undertake to do what we do.

PROMOTION IN JOURNALISM IS ACCORDING TO ONE'S FACULTY.

Of course, the most essential part of this great mechanism is not the mechanism itself; it is the intelligence, the brains, and the sense of truth and honor that reside in the men who conduct it and make it a vehicle of usefulness, or, it may be, of mischief; because what is useful can just as easily be turned to mischief if the engineer who stands behind and lets on the steam is of an erroneous disposition.

The number of intellectual young men who are looking at this new profession, which, for the want of a better name, we call the profession of journalism, is very great. I suppose that I receive myself every day, taking one day with another, half a dozen letters from men, many of them college graduates, asking for employment, and for an opportunity of showing what is in them. Of course, they cannot all get in in the same paper. Now and then one obtains a place, but generally the rule that is observed in all well-organized newspaper offices is that the boys who began at the beginning are taken up step by step, in accordance with their faculties and their merits. This is so because, as we know in college, it is impossible that there should be any imposture which sets a man's abilities above their real value, since in the daily intercourse and the daily competition of study and of recitation the real worth of a man's brain is demonstrated, so that there is never any doubt. So it is in a newspaper office. The boys who begin at the bottom come out at the top. At the same time, these boys do not all start out with the best outfit, that is to say, with the best education; and I have known very distinguished authorities who doubted whether high education was of any great use to a journalist. Horace Greeley told me several times that the real newspaper man was the boy who had slept on newspapers and ate ink. Although I served him for years, and we were very near in our personal relations, I think he always had a little grudge against me because I came up through a college.

Now, here before us are a number of young gentlemen who, I have no doubt, will be led to embrace this profession. We know that among a certain number of students there are so many doctors, so many clergymen, so many lawyers—sometimes too many lawyers—and there are also, of course, a considerable number who are looking forward to this great civilizing engine of the press; and it is a great engine.

Just consider the clergyman. He preaches two or three times in a week, and he has for his congregation two hundred, three hundred, five hundred, and, if he is a great popular orator in a great city, he may have a thousand hearers; but the newspaper man is the stronger, because, throughout all the avenues of newspaper communication, how many does he preach to? A million, half a million, two hundred thousand people; and his preaching is not on Sundays only, but it is every day. He reiterates, he says it over and over, and finally the thing gets fixed in men's minds from the mere habit of saying it and hearing it; and, without criticising, without inquiring whether it is really so, the newspaper dictum gets established and is taken for gospel; and perhaps it is not gospel at all.

SCHOOLS OF JOURNALISM.

In regard to this profession there are two stages, and we will consider each of them separately. The first is the stage of preparation. What sort of preparation, what sort of preliminary education, should a man have who means to devote himself to this business? There are some colleges which have lately introduced schools of journalism, or departments of journalism, where they propose to teach the art of newspaper making, to instruct the student in the methods that he should employ, and to fit him out so that he can go to a newspaper office and make a newspaper.

Well, I will not say that is not useful. I do not know that there is, in any intellectual study, or in any intellectual pursuit, or in any intellectual occupation that is followed with zeal and attention, anything that can be described as useless. No, I do not know of anything, if you really learn it, although it may seem to your next neighbor around the corner rather trivial, that is not useful after all. There is certainly a great utility and a profound science in baseball, and the man who pursues it and acquires it has acquired something that will be useful to him. He has got a knowledge, he has got an intellectual discipline, that will be valuable all his life through. So it is with every study that a man may pursue, so that we cannot say that anything is useless. But as for these departments of journalism in the colleges, I have never found that a student or graduate who had pursued that department, instead of pursuing other studies, was of any great value as a practical worker in the newspaper work that he had been trying to learn.

In fact, it seems to me, if I may be allowed a little criticism, that the colleges generally are rather branching out too much, until they are inclined to take the whole universe into their curriculum, and to teach things which do not exactly belong there. Give the young man a first-class course of general education; and if I could have my way, every young man who is going to be a newspaper man, and who is not absolutely rebellious against it, should learn Greek and Latin after the good old fashion. I had rather take a young fellow who knows the Ajax of Sophocles, and who has read Tacitus, and can scan every ode of Horace, I would rather take him to report a prize-fight or a spelling match, for instance, than to take one who has never had those advantages. I believe in the colleges; I believe in high education; but I do not believe in scattering your fire before you are in the face of the enemy.

THE BEST TIME TO BEGIN TO LEARN JOURNALISM.

When you begin to practise the profession of a newspaper man, then is the best time to begin to learn it; but while you are in college, with the daily series of professors and all the appliances of study that belong to the college, make the best of them, and pursue vigorously those studies that give accuracy in learning, and that give fidelity and accuracy in recitation. The great end of education, President Walker used to say, is to be able to tell what you know; and he used to say, too, that some bright men carried it so far that they were able to tell a great deal they did not know.

There is no question that accuracy, the faculty of seeing a thing as it is, of knowing, for instance, that it is two and one-quarter and not two and three-eighths, and saying so, is one of the first and most precious ends of a good education. Next to that I would put the ability to know how and where most promptly to look for what you don't know, and what you want to know. Thirdly, I would put Dr. Walker's great object, being able to tell what you know, and to tell it accurately, precisely, without exaggeration, without prejudice, the fact just as it is, whether it be a report of a baseball game or of a sermon or of a lecture on electricity; whatever it may be, to get the thing exactly as it is. The man

CHARLES A. DANA. FROM A PHOTOGRAPH BY ANDERSON, NEW YORK.

who can do that is a very well educated man.

In addition come the qualities of personal talent and genius. Now, genius is a great factor. When we think of such a genius as the one I have just mentioned, the late Mr. Greeley, why, our minds may well be filled with admiration. I do not suppose more than one or two gentlemen here ever knew Mr. Greeley personally; but he was a man of immense ability, of instincts of extraordinary correctness in many respects, and of the power of expression, of telling what he knew, in a delightfully picturesque, humorous way which not merely instructed the hearer and reader, but gave him a sense of delight and satisfaction from the mere art that was applied in the telling. He had had no great advantages of education. He had to pick up his education as he went along, reading in the winter evenings by the firelight, and never wasting a chance of learning something. But he lacked one of the most precious faculties, which it is another great object of the college education to cultivate and bring out, and that is what we will call the critical faculty, the judgment which, when a proposition is stated to you or a fact is reported, looks at it calmly and says: "That is true," or else, "That is false;" the judgment, the instinct—the developed and cultivated instinct—which knows the truth when it is presented, and detects error when it comes masquerading before you, without the necessity of any long examination to ascertain whether it is truth or error. This great man of whom I am speaking, this great and brilliant journalist, one of the greatest we have produced, was deficient in that faculty, so that sometimes he was mistaken. We are all of us mistaken occasionally, I dare say, but perhaps his mistakes were more conspicuous because of his great power in writing and his rare genius.

Now, as for the preliminary studies of the journalist, apart from the ancient languages, whose importance, I think, cannot be overestimated; and the reason why this importance, in my judgment, is so great, is that they lie at the foundation of our own language; and the man who does not know three or four of those old languages, or, at least, two of them—if he knows three, if he knows the old Teutonic, all the better—the man who has not that knowledge does not really know the English language, and does not command its wonderful resources, all the subtleties and abilities of expression which are in it. Certainly, without Greek and Latin no man knows English; and without Teutonic no man's knowledge of English is perfect.

A THOROUGH KNOWLEDGE OF ENGLISH THE FIRST REQUISITE.

The first thing for the man who is looking forward to this profession, in which the use of the English language is the main thing—since it is the instrument that he must apply continually for the expression of ideas and for the dissemination of knowledge—is to know this language thoroughly; and that is the very cornerstone of the education that a journalist should look forward to and should labor after, and should neglect no opportunity of improving himself in.

After a knowledge of the English language comes, of course, in regular order, the practice, the cultivation of the ability to use it, the development of that art which in its latest form we call style, and which distinguishes one writer from another. This style is something of such evanescent, intangible nature that it is difficult to tell in what it consists. I suppose it is in the combination of imagination and humor, with the entire command of the word-resources of the language, all applied together in the construction of sentences. I suppose that is what makes style. It is a very precious gift, but it is not a gift that can always be acquired by practice or by study.

It may be added that certainly, in its highest perfection, it can never be acquired by practice. I do not believe, for instance, that everybody who should endeavor to acquire such a style as the late Dr. Channing possessed could succeed in doing so. He was a famous writer fifty years ago in Boston, and his style is of the most beautiful and remarkable character. As a specimen of it, let me suggest to you his essay on Napoleon Bonaparte. That was, perhaps, the very best of the critical analysis of Napoleon that succeeded the period of Napoleon worship which had run all over the world. Channing's style was sweet, pure, and delightful, without having those surprises, those extraordinary felicities, that mark the styles of some writers. It was perfectly simple, translucent throughout, without effort, never leaving you in any doubt as to the idea; and you closed the book with the feeling that you had fallen in with a most sympathetic mind, whose instructions you might sometimes accept or sometimes reject, but whom you could not regard without entire respect and admiration.

Another example of a very beautiful and admirable style which is well worth study is that of Nathaniel Hawthorne. In his writings we are charmed with the new sense and meaning that he seems to give to familiar words. It is like reading a new language to take a chapter of Hawthorne; yet it is perfectly lovely, because, with all its suggestiveness, it is perfectly clear; and when you have done with it you wish you could do it yourself.

A KNOWLEDGE OF POLITICS THE SECOND REQUISITE.

The next thing that I would dwell upon would be the knowledge of politics, and especially of American politics. This is a very hard subject. Its history is difficult. If you go back to the foundation of the republic, you find it was extremely complicated even then; and it requires very careful study and a very elevated impartiality to make your analysis at all satisfactory to yourself as you go through the work.

Still, it is indispensable to a man who means to fill an important place in journalism, and all who begin upon it certainly have that intention. No young man goes into any profession without a good degree of ambition; no young man can carry his ambition very far in journalism—I mean, in general, universal journalism, not in special; no man can carry his ambition very far who does not know politics, and in order to know politics there must be in the man some natural disposition for politics. I have often been appealed to by friends, who said: "Can't you take this young man and give him employment?"

Then I will watch that young man for a month or so, and see what it is that he takes up in the morning. If he takes up the newspaper and turns to the political part of the paper, and is interested in that, why, that is a good symptom of his intellectual tendencies; but if, instead of that, he takes up a magazine and sits down to read a love story, why, you cannot make a newspaper man out of him.

And yet he may make a very good writer of love stories; and as that is a sort of merchandise which seems to be always in demand, and to bring pretty fair prices, why, if you have a talent in that direction, go ahead. You may make a good living, I have no doubt; but you will not play any momentous part upon the stage of public affairs, and that is the sphere of activity which the generoushearted and courageous youth looks forward to.

In order to be of importance in the affairs of this world in the newspaper profession you must be a politician, and you must know not merely the theories and doctrines of parties, not merely the recondite part of politics, but you must know practical politics, the history, the men, the individuals, their ideas, their purposes, and their deeds; know them, if you can, as they really are, not as the blind and the prejudiced may imagine them to be.

Now, Mr. Greeley is my great exemplar in journalism. He thought a newspaper man was of little use who did not know just the number of votes in every township in the State of New York, and in every voting precinct, and who could not tell whether the returns from the second district of Pound Ridge, in Westchester County, were correctly reported or not, without sending to the place to find out how many votes had really been cast. That was one of his great points of distinction and success; but I would not advise you to labor after that sort of knowledge unless you have inherited a natural talent for it. But you should understand and appreciate the theory of the American Government, you should know where this Republic began, where it came from, and where it belongs in the history of mankind, and what part it is destined to play in the vast drama of human existence. That is the sort of politics that must appeal to any intelligent man, and that will surely test his utmost powers. And while we are on this point, we may say in passing that an American who thinks another into journalism. You must be for the Stars and Stripes every time, or the people of this country won't be for you, and you won't sell enough papers to pay your expenses.

STUDY THE CONSTITUTION.

In order to understand the theory of the American Government, the most serious, calm, persistent study should be given to the Constitution of the United States. I don't mean learning it by heart, committing it to memory. What you want is to understand it, to know the principles at the bottom of it, to feel the impulse of it, to feel the heart-beat that thrills through the whole American people. That is the vitality that is worth knowing; that is the sort of politics that excels all the mysteries of ward elections, and lifts you up into a view where you can see the clear skies, the unknown expanse of the future. And besides the Constitution of the United States, it is well to be acquainted with the Constitutions of all the States. All these Constitutions are more or less modelled upon the central Constitution; but there are differences, and those differences a man ought to know. The citizen of New York ought to understand the Constitution of New York, and for himself get at the reason for this and that provision. Take, for instance, the great question which has occupied the people of New York so long, the question of an elective judiciary or of a judiciary appointed by the governor; which is better, which is right? That is better and that is right, evidently, which gives better judges, and which produces a more equable, steady, consistent, and just administration of law. Well, now, the young man who sets to work and studies out that question has accomplished a great deal; he has got a light in his mind that will go with him a great way, and that will help out his judgment in other things. Supposing that he is conducting a newspaper, and is responsible to the people for conducting it in an instructive and useful manner, and for having it such that when he says a thing is so the people will know that it is so; the man who knows the Constitutions of the States, of his own State, and of all the principal States, as well as the Constitution of the United States, is well fitted for conducting a newspaper, or even for administering a government.

The modern newspaper, however, is not

country. You have got to look beyond your own land; you have got to study the history of every European country. You must know, first of all, the history of England. We came from England; the American Constitution is rooted in English principles and in English history. You want to know where it started from. You want to go into the garden where the seed was first sown, and watch the growth of this great product of wisdom and beneficence which we call the American Constitution. You see, the course of preparatory study is pretty large; and it is not very easy; it must be carried on in earnest. It is not a matter of fancy or of play. And so not merely with the history of England, but with the history of all of Europe, of every great and every little country. The course of human history offers a safe guide for human action, and especially for political action. The history of France is a chapter that is worthy of the utmost attention that can be given to it. Why have such and such results been produced? What is there from which this or that effect has proceeded? These are the sort of questions that careful study can bring an answer to; and without careful study you will never get the answer.

But I do not propose all these things as a course of preparatory study for a young man. You cannot learn everything in a day. It is as much as many men can do to learn a few things in the lapse of a long life; but at least try to learn something solid, to add to your stock of efficacious knowledge, to add to your understanding of principles, and to feel that as little effort as possible has been wasted and as little time as possible flung away.

THE NEWSPAPER MAN SHOULD KNOW THE BIBLE, SHAKESPEARE, AND MILTON.

The next point to be attended to is this: what books ought you to read? There are some books that are indispensable—a few books. Almost all books have their use, even the silly ones, and an omnivorous reader, if he reads intelligently, need never feel that his time is wasted, even when he bestows it on the flimsiest trash that is printed. But there are some books that are absolutely indispensable to the kind of education that we are contemplating, and to the profession that we are considering; and of all these the most indispensable, the most useful, the one whose knowledge is most effective, is the Bible. There is no book from which more valuable lessons can be learned. I am considering it now not as a religious book, but as a manual of utility, of professional preparation and professional use for a journalist. There is perhaps no book whose style is more suggestive and more instructive, from which you learn more directly that sublime simplicity which never exaggerates, which recounts the greatest event with solemnity, of course, but without sentimentality or affectation, none which you open with such confidence and lay down with such reverence; there is no book like the Bible. When you get into a controversy and want exactly the right answer, when you are looking for an expression, what is there that closes a dispute like a verse from the Bible? What is it that sets up the right principle for you, which pleads for a policy, for a cause, so much as the right passage of Holy Scripture?

Then, everybody who is going to practise the newspaper profession ought to know Shakespeare. He is the chief master of English speech. He is the head of English literature. Considered as a writer, considered as a poet, considered as a philosopher, I do not know another who can be named with him. He is not merely a constructor of plays that are powerful and impressive when they are shown upon the stage, with all the auxiliaries of lights and scenery and characters; he is a high literary treasure, a mighty storehouse of wisdom, the great glory of the literature of our language; and, if you don't know him, knowing the language may not be of much avail after all. Perhaps that is an exaggeration, and I take it back; but it is an object to know Shakespeare; it is indispensable to a journalist.

Then there is another English author who ought not to be neglected by any young man who means to succeed in this profession. I mean John Milton, and I invite your attention to that immortal essay of his, too little known in our day, the Speech for the Liberty of Unlicensed Printing. It is a treasury of the highest wisdom, of the noblest sentiments, and of the greatest instruction; study that, and you will get at once the philosophy of English liberty and the highest doctrine that has ever been promulgated, to my knowledge, with regard to the freedom of the press.

When I advise you to make yourselves familiar with these glories of English literature, I do not say that these writers ought to be taken as models. Do not take any model. Every man has his own natural style, and the thing to do is to develop it into simplicity and clearness. Do not, for instance, labor after such a style as Matthew Arnold's, one of the most beautiful styles that has ever been seen in any literature. It is no use to try to get another man's style, or to imitate the wit or the mannerisms of another writer. The late Mr. Carlyle, for example, did, in my judgment, a considerable mischief in his day because he led everybody to write after the style of his "French Revolution," and it became pretty tedious. They got over it after a time, however. But it was not a good thing. Let every man write in his own style, taking care only not to be led into any affectation, but to be perfectly clear, perfectly simple, or, in other words, to follow the honored and noble traditions of Union College.

REPORTING.

That is all that it seems to me necessary to say with regard to the studies and the education of the journalist. Now, let us turn to the practice of this profession. One of the parts of the newspaper profession which employs the greatest number of men, and I may also say the greatest amount of talent, is the business of reporting. In a large newspaper office, as in the "Tribune" in New York, for example, where there may be one hundred men who are attached to the paper as writers, as correspondents, as reporters, and to the strictly editorial department, out of this one hundred, sixty or seventy will be reporters, that is, men who are sent out when any event of interest occurs, when a bank breaks, when a great fire takes place, when there is an earthquake, to inquire into the facts and collect information, and to put that information into form, so that it can be printed the next day. That is one of the most important branches of the profession, and it is paid very liberally, I am glad to say. For instance, I know many reporters who earn ten or fifteen dollars a day, and some who earn more. They have constant employment, and their labor is entirely agreeable to themselves. That is one of the first things, when a young man comes for employment, and you take him on and give him a chance, that he is set to do. There, you see, all this culture that we have been considering is at once brought into action. He must learn accurately the facts, and he must state them exactly as they are; and if he can state them with a little degree of life, a little approach to eloquence, or a little humor in his style, why, his report will be perfect. It must be accurate; it must be free from affectation; it must be well set forth, so that there shall not be any doubt as to any part or detail of it; and then, if it is enlivened with imagination or with feeling or with humor, why, you have got a literary product that no one need be ashamed of. Thus we see this department of the newspaper is really a high art, and it may be carried to an extraordinary degree towards perfection. At the same time, the cultivated man is not in every case the best reporter. One of the best I ever knew was a man who could not spell four words correctly to save his life, and his verb did not always agree with the subject in person and number; but he always got the fact so exactly, and he saw the picturesque, the interesting, and important aspect of it so vividly, that it was worth another man's while, who possessed the knowledge of grammar and spelling, to go over the report and write it out. Now, that was a man who had genius; he had a talent the most indubitable, and he got handsomely paid in spite of his lack of grammar, because, after his work had been done over by a scholar, it was really beautiful. But any man who is sincere and earnest, and not always thinking about himself, can learn to be a good reporter. He can learn to ascertain the truth; he can acquire the habit of seeing. When he looks at a fire, what is the most important thing about that fire? Here, let us say, are five houses burning; which is the greatest? whose store is that which is burning? and who has met with the greatest loss? Has any individual perished in the conflagration? Are there any very interesting circumstances about the fire? How did it occur? Was it like Chicago, where a cow kicked over a spirit lamp and burned up the city? All these things the reporter has to judge about. He is the eye of the paper, and he is there to see which is the vital fact in the story, and to produce it, tell it, write it out.

THE EXCHANGE READER.

Next to the reporter, a very important functionary in the newspaper is the man who reads the other newspapers and makes extracts from them. Mr. Greeley used to think that it was enough to make a good paper if he had an able man to read the exchanges, provided he himself was there in person to add up the returns of the elections. The man who reads the exchanges is a very important man; and, let me say, too, he is a pretty highly paid man. He has to read, we will say, three thousand papers regularly. All the newspapers in the country come into the office, and he does not do anything else. He sits at his desk all day, and a pile of newspapers, or, say, a cord of newspapers, is laid before him every morning; he starts to work and turns them over and over to see what is in them. He has to know what it is that should be taken from them and put into his paper. What is the interesting story? It requires judgment to know this; it requires knowledge and experience as well as talent. It also requires a sense of humor, because there are a great many things that are really important that may not seem so at the first glance, and the newspaper reader has got to judge about that. He must always be on hand and spend a great many hours at his desk; and he is pretty tired when he gets through with his day's task. It is a hard duty, but he has lots of amusement, and, as I said, he is very well paid. So he is happy.

THE MANUSCRIPT READER.

Next to the exchange reader in the newspaper organization comes the man whose duty it is to receive manuscripts and examine them and prepare them for the press, to edit them, correct them; where the writer has made a little slip of rhetoric, to put the right word in or the right turn of the phrase; to clarify it all; to make the sentences clean. That is a hard job in the writing of a great many persons. They interject; they put sub-sentences in parentheses. They do not begin and say the thing in its exact order, taking first the man and then what he did, and where he went; but they mix it up and complicate it. The editor who examines the manuscripts has got to go through all these things and straighten them out and disentangle the facts that the writer has twisted up; and then he must correct the punctuation, mark the paragraphs where one idea is finished and a new idea begins. He also receives the correspondence. Letters from all over the world go into his hands. You will get a letter from Madagascar, perhaps. Ought it to be published? There is a lot of news in it, perhaps, that is of no interest in New York or in Schenectady. He has got to determine whether it is worth while to put that in or to leave it out, although you may have to pay for it and not use it. Masses of matter are paid for in a large newspaper office that are never used. So you see he is a very important functionary, and it requires a great deal of knowledge, a great deal of judgment, a great deal of literary cultivation, to be able to fill that position.

Then finally you come to the editor-in-chief, and he is always a man who gets into his place by a natural process of selection. He comes there because he can do the work; and I have known some young men who had no idea that they would ever have control of a newspaper, who have risen to that place, and who have filled it with wisdom and success and force. Yet at the bottom of it all, it is always a question of character as well as of talent. A fellow that is practising arts of deception may last a little while, but he cannot last long. The man who stays is the man who has the staying power; and the staying power is not merely intellectual, it is moral. It is in the character; and people believe in him because they are sure he does not mean to say anything that is not so.

Now, every one who has written or talked about newspapers has made a great account of the matter of news, and in these remarks that it has been my opportunity to make, I have not said anything yet on that subject. News is undoubtedly a great thing in a newspaper. A newspaper without news is no newspaper. The main function of a newspaper is to give the news and tell you what has happened in the world, what events have occurred of all sorts, political, scientific, and nonsensical. By the way, one person that I have not mentioned is the scientific man. That is also a place that has to be filled by special cultivation. A scientific man, one who knows electricity and chemistry; one who can really understand the inventions of Edison, and who can tell what is going on in the scientific world, where so many men of genius are incessantly at work bringing out and developing new things: there must be a man of that sort on a newspaper. That is a department of news of supreme consequence.

NEWS COLLECTING DECLINING INTO SECOND PLACE.

But the business of collecting news, which has always been regarded as of prime importance, is rather declining into a second place. It is a necessity, and it is very costly, to collect and to bring here to Schenectady, for instance, for printing to-morrow morning, the news of the whole world; from England, from Germany, from Russia, from France, from Africa, from South America, from the Pacific, so that it may be presented to the reader who takes up the paper to-morrow, and he may have a panorama of all the events of the preceding day. What a wonder, what a marvel it is, that here, for one or two cents, you buy a history of the entire globe of the day before! It is something that is miraculous, really, when you consider it. All brought here to Schenectady and printed! All brought here by electricity, by means of the telegraph! So that the man who has knowledge enough to read, can tell what was done in France yesterday, or in Turkey or in Persia. That is a wonderful thing. But the very necessity of bringing all this matter together, and the immense expense attendant upon it, have led to the formation of associations among newspapers and to the organization of agencies. I won't undertake to say now how much the expense is, because I do not remember it with absolute certainty; but it is an enormous sum, say perhaps three to five thousand dollars a day; but when it is divided among the four or five or six thousand newspapers in the United States, first divided among all the great cities and then among the cities of the second class, which pay less, and so on until finally it is distributed all around, why, it costs each individual newspaper very little; and the system which is most perfectly organized is the establishment in Chicago and New York, known as the United Press. It supplies the news of the whole world, so that the individual editor sitting at his desk has only to look after the news of his own locality. When he has got that, he gets from the United Press the news of all the rest of the world, and, putting them together, his report of the day's history of the globe is complete. That is an institution which has revolutionized and is revolutionizing the operations of the profession, so that instead of the struggle to hunt after the news, to appreciate the importance of events that people generally do not see, and to report them so that you may have in your journal something that the others have not got, that struggle is mainly obviated by this organization of the United Press. The news of the entire world is brought to you, and the editor, the newspaper, is put back into the position which the thinker occupied before the supreme attention to news was regarded as indispensable. The editors and writers of the newspapers are now emancipated from all that drudgery, and have become intellectual beings again. The work of news getting is performed by this great and wide-reaching agency of the United Press, and the individual editor here in Schenectady or in Chicago or New Orleans has no anxiety on that subject any longer. He devotes himself to the intellectual part of his business, and is able to carry that on with a nearer approach to perfection than he has ever been able to attain before. That, I think, is a revolution that is going to make a great change in the profession of newspaper making, raising it to a higher dignity than it has ever occupied. I look forward to the effects of this revolution with the greatest hope and confidence, and I think you young gentlemen who have not yet embarked in the profession may be congratulated on being able to come into it under such auspicious circumstances.

Gentlemen, I am greatly indebted to you for your kind attention, and I bid you farewell!

A GAME POSTPONED.

By GERTRUDE SMITH,

Author of "The Rousing of Mrs. Porter, and Other Stories."

IT had been snowing for two days, and now the snow-ploughs were out, and the first really good sleighing of the winter would begin.

The great fields lay in unbroken whiteness. The woods along the banks of the Iowa River were billows of snow. The large farm-houses, and the number and size of the barns and other outlying buildings, gave evidence of the richness of the soil that lay buried and resting for another harvest.

Judge Hilton's house had the distinction of being built of brick. There was a dignity in its solidity over the usual white frame houses on the surrounding farms that well became the dignity of the judge.

The judge was New England born and bred. There is the veneration for Puritan ancestry in the entirely Western soul that the Puritan mind still has for good old English blood.

Isabel Hilton was her father's housekeeper and only child. The mother had died while she was a baby, and she had ruled the house and been ruled by her father since that time.

She had all her father's reserve and pride of family, and at the same time his happy nature and gracious manner, that won her friends when she desired to make friends. Those who found it impossible to win their way into her favor, called this reserve in Isabel, her "down East airs." There was a discouraging belief among the young men in the country around, some of whose fathers owned farms and herds of cattle large enough to divide and establish them in enviable beginnings, that if the judge thought any of them worthy to win his daughter's love there would never be an opportunity to gain the consent of the young lady.

The judge had theories against Isabel's entertaining young men alone, nor would he permit her to go with any escort but himself.

The privilege of spending the evening with Isabel, in the presence of her father, was considered a mark of distinction, and held the one so honored on the wave of hope.

"If a fellow had the backbone to out-sit the judge some night, he might propose to the daughter," was the comment Mr. Holderman made to his son one day. Clint Holderman had been one of Isabel's most persistent admirers.

"The trouble with all of you is, you go there shaking in your boots, and talk to the judge, and come away with the big head because you dared do that; but I tell you, if I was a young fellow I'd out-sit him if I sat till the break of day. It's some such pluck as that the judge is looking for. He raised her, and he knows her value; and she ain't going cheap to none of you. If you can go in ahead of the other fellows and tow her in, I'll give you ten thousand dollars and deed you a section of land.

CLINT.

A GAME POSTPONED.

Come, now, let's see what you're made of?"

In some way this lordly promise got adrift the current of country gossip, and roused the admirers of Isabel, one and all, to new interest in the contest. Large stories were told of the late hours the judge kept that winter with Isabel's suitors.

Clint Holderman drove over to the brick house early on the evening that he had set his mind with flint-like determination to give his father's advice the trial.

It was a cold night, and as he sped along in his new cutter, drawn by a handsome span of black horses, and well tucked in with buffalo robes, his heart was warm with hope.

He had spent many evenings of the winter playing chess with the judge, so he was sure of his welcome; but to-night he looked beyond all this. He thought of the hour when, at last, with his heart and understanding touched, the judge would bid them good night, and he should be left alone with Isabel.

There was no handsomer young man in the country than Clint Holderman; none who danced better, or who drove better horses; but more than all this, the judge had repeatedly told him that he had never known a man who played a better hand at chess.

This was an encouragement indeed; for if the judge had a weakness, it was for chess, and it would be decidedly pleasant to have a son-in-law who could be to him such a ready source of entertainment. As he drove into the yard, the judge came out on the side piazza.

"Good evening," he called out. "Just drive on to the barn; the man will put out your horses."

One of the farm hands came out of the stable as he spoke, and Clint threw him the reins and followed the judge into the house.

"Snapping cold, but splendid sleighing," the judge said, while Clint was pulling off his overcoat in the hall.

"Yes. I believe my ears are touched," Clint answered, rubbing them.

"Isabel is popping some corn. She'll be glad you happened over to help eat it."

He led the way into the long sitting-room at the end of the hall.

Isabel was on her knees before an open wood fire, shaking a corn-popper.

The white kernels snapped and expanded with a pleasant sound,

The lamp had not been lit, but the firelight made the room bright and cosy.

"Isabel, here is Mr. Holderman, my dear."

She sprang up.

"I didn't hear you come in. Good even-

ISABEL.

ing. Come over here by the fire. Why, it's Clint!" she said, as he came into the glow. "I thought father meant your father. I never think of you as Mr. Holderman. Have some corn."

She held the popper open before him.

"I'm sure I never think of you as Miss Hilton," he said, plunging his hand into the corn, and laughing. "That would be a little too much like strangers, as long as we've known each other."

The judge cleared his throat.

"I have always decidedly disliked the informality of country people in calling every one by their Christian names," he said. "It leaves no degree in intimacy. But I suppose it is impossible to know where to draw the line."

Isabel went back and knelt before the fire again.

"Oh, I don't know," she said, shaking the popper vigorously. "As long as it is a custom I don't think any one feels it a mark of special intimacy, and so the custom is protected by being a custom."

The young man sat awkwardly in his chair, and was silent.

They seemed to be closing the doors against any thought he might have of closer intimacy with the family.

The judge left the room for a moment, and came back with a lighted lamp, and placed it on the claw-legged table in the centre of the room. He had put on a long dressing-gown faced with crimson quilted silk, and now he drew his great chair up before the fire, and stretched himself out in it.

"Come, Clint, I will let you shake the popper for me, and I'll go down cellar and get some apples." Isabel looked at him with a merry twinkle in her eyes, as she held the handle towards him, and then ran out of the room.

Clint grasped the handle of the popper with the delight of success flooding his veins. Isabel had never before given him a reason to believe that she cared for him that could compare with that look.

Daylight would find him sitting right there, but he would beat the judge's watch and gain the opportunity of speaking to her.

It was a delightful evening. The judge partook of the popcorn, and the conversation was more than usually affable and entertaining.

Isabel sat on the opposite side of the fireplace and crocheted on a blue wool scarf. There were pink spots burning her cheeks, and her eyes were very sweet.

The time passed on until the noisy clock on the mantel clearly and forcibly announced the hour of ten.

It had been comparatively easy this far, but now was the time when Clint usually went home.

The real contest was about to begin.

The judge shoved his chair back to the table, picked up a paper, and began to read.

From time to time he glanced over the top of his paper at the two talking before the fire, but still read on.

When the clock struck eleven, he threw the paper down, pulled his chair back to the fire, and drew the young man into an animated political discussion.

Isabel stirred about the room, putting things in order for the night.

It was nearing midnight. For the last fifteen minutes the conversation had begun to lag.

There were cold moments of complete silence.

"Had you noticed that I had traded horses?" Clint asked in one painful pause.

"No; have you?" Isabel asked, coming forward with interest.

"Yes. I've traded the grays for George Merwin's blacks. Of course there was considerable to boot. They go like the wind in my new cutter."

"I should think they would." Isabel drew a deep breath. "I do like black horses. I never cared for gray ones. I always think of having to look for a red-headed girl," she laughed. "I should think you'd always be on the outlook for one when you ride behind them."

"Perhaps Mr. Holderman is looking for a red-headed girl," the judge said, with a queer look in the direction of the young man. "There's a superstition that a red-headed girl has a violent temper. Now, that isn't always true," he said, after a moment's silence, in which his thought seemed to have been far away. "Isabel's mother had as sweet a disposition as any woman that ever lived, and her hair was the color of that deep flame there."

Isabel was leaning on the back of her father's chair. "Why, father, you've always said my hair was almost the color of mother's. I'm sure no one would think of calling mine red."

"I don't know about that," the judge laughed; "and I don't know about the temper, either," he added, reaching up and pinching her cheek.

"I never liked red hair, but I'm sure I don't believe in that sign," Clint said clumsily. He gazed fixedly into the fire, and felt as though he were turning to stone.

The clock struck twelve with a resonant, defiant stroke, as though it understood the contest in which it held the stakes, and refused to commit itself as to whose side would win.

At a quarter past twelve the judge stood up.

Clint felt his heart beating wildly. The moment of triumph was at hand.

The judge crossed to the bay window at the other end of the room. Isabel's eyes followed him nervously.

A GAME POSTPONED.

From one side, among the geraniums and ivy, he drew the chess-table, and pushed it before him toward the fire.

"I think it would be pleasant for us to have a game of chess," he said affably.

Clint sprang to his feet.

"Oh, thank you, sir. I think I must be going home."

"Oh, must you? Well, come over again and we'll get at it earlier in the evening."

It seemed hours before Clint finally found himself out on the smooth snow-beaten road, spinning along toward home.

He would have been completely wretched in his defeat if it had not been for that look in Isabel's eyes when she handed him the corn-popper. He could endure his father's ridicule and wait his time, remembering that look.

And so he made a good story of it at breakfast the next morning, and added, elevating his voice above the roaring laugh of his father and the shrieks of his mother and sister:

"Never you mind. The judge isn't through with me yet. I've only fired my first gun. I'll own when I came out of the house I was out of shot, but I haven't given up the fight yet."

"Oh, you'll let some other bantam rooster carry her off. I guess I'm safe enough on the cash and land I promised you," his father answered with a provoking laugh.

"Don't you count on it," Clint said, springing up from the table with fire in his eyes. "I'm not downed yet, I tell you."

"All right, sonny; we'll give a big dance to celebrate your engagement, and an oyster supper. I suppose there's no rush about ordering the oysters?"

"I'll hold you to that," Clint said, bringing his fist up against the door. "If the thing's settled by Saturday week, we'll have the dance. If it isn't—well, it won't be. I'm going over to town after the mail."

He turned and went out of the room. As the door closed, he heard his sister say, tittering:

"Clint has about as hard a time courting Isabel as you had courting mother."

This was a warm thought of comfort to him. At least Isabel had never denied him her love, and he knew that his mother had been hardly won.

It was a bright winter morning. Before him was a clear stretch of road to the Iowa River, three miles away.

The white fields on either side sparkled in the sunlight. The great drifts, rolled up along the fences, looked blue in the shadows of their fantastic terracings. The sleighing never was better.

All at once Clint heard the noise of sleigh-bells, and a voice called to him: "Give me the road."

He turned and saw Isabel Hilton coming toward him, driving her own bay ponies at a fearful rate.

Clint drove quickly out at one side of the road, and she sped by him.

He saw that her horses were running away.

There had been no alarm in Isabel's face, though she was holding the reins with all her strength, and had looked neither to the right nor the left as she passed him. If there was one thing more than another that the Holdermans prided themselves in, it was their knowledge of a good horse and splendid horsemanship.

Isabel Hilton's love of horses and her daring in driving them had been one of the first things that had won Clint's admiration. Her control and courage now appealed to him tremendously. His own horses seemed to have caught the spirit of the runaway pair ahead, as they flew along over the snow after them.

Clint knew that at any moment Isabel's slight arms might lose the power to hold those tense reins so securely, and the horses dash to one side and the crash come, and there was nothing he could do. On went the cutter ahead of him, swaying to the left and the right, but still keeping the road. The bridge across the Iowa River was just ahead. Clint thought of the bridge with terror. If the cutter swayed to one side, as it was doing now, the crash would come on entering.

He saw Isabel's strength tightening on the reins, and knew that she felt the danger.

Her horses flew up the slight incline to the bridge, and Clint braced his nerves to withstand the shock. But to his amazement he saw that the horses were slowing up, and entering the bridge with all the respect of well-trained horses; and by the time they were over the frozen current below, they were walking as quietly as though they had decided on that point as the end of their excitement.

Clint entered the bridge as Isabel was leaving it. She drove out to one side of the road and waited for him to come up to her. "I'll let you go on ahead of me now, if you want to," she called out, as he stopped.

"Look here," Clint called back, "did you think of those horses stopping at the bridge that way, I'd like to know?"

"Yes; didn't you? I knew they might

not, but I thought they would if I could keep them in the road. Didn't you think of their doing it?"

"Well, no. I had something else to think about," he answered, looking at her admiringly.

Isabel's face flushed, but she looked at him smiling.

"I wasn't afraid as long as the road was clear, but I should have lost all courage if I had seen a team coming."

"Talk of pluck!" Clint said, driving a little nearer to her cutter. "Isabel, what did you think of last night? What did you think of me, anyway?"

She drove out into the road ahead of him, and then looked back over her shoulder, laughing. "I thought if you had only waited half an hour longer I would have been eighteen. It is my birthday to-day. I'm of age." And with that she touched her ponies with the whip, and kept well ahead of him all the way to the village.

When they met again, it was before the fire in the sitting-room at the brick house, where they had held the hours the night before. But the contest with the judge had lost its seriousness.

Between them he sat, imperturbable, as he had sat the night before; but to-night he was only an amusing barrier, and not a serious obstruction. Love had leaped the bounds, and was free. It triumphed in their eyes as they looked across him, and over him, smiling knowingly at each other.

"We're going to have a dance over at our house Saturday week, and an oyster supper. It is going to be a celebration of a great event in our family," Clint announced with a meaning gesture to Isabel.

"What's the event you're celebrating?" the judge asked, looking over his spectacles.

"Well, that's something of a secret until to-morrow. I hope I can tell you then. You must be sure and come. We're going to have a great time."

The judge looked at Isabel. "Do you think we can go, my dear?"

Her cheeks were rosy. "Why, yes, I should think we could, father."

"Thank you, then. We'll come," the judge said, leaning back in his chair, and looking at the ceiling. "And now would you like to play that game of chess we didn't have last night?"

It was evident he had no intention of giving up the field. Clint did not answer. He was not as fearless of the judge as he had supposed. His heart throbbed excitedly.

Isabel pressed her hands together hard and looked into the fire. The clock ticked loudly, emphasizing the silence.

Finally the judge brought his eyes from the ceiling, and looked at the young man.

"Didn't you hear what I said to you?" he asked, running his hand through his forelock and grasping the arm of his chair.

"Yes, sir, I did," said Clint respectfully.

"Well, then?"

"If you'll allow me to say it, sir, I think I've won the game already."

"What's that?"

"I believe, sir, I've won the game."

The judge glared at him for a moment, and then his eyes fell on Isabel.

He looked from one to the other. The ticks of the clock seemed to choke each other.

"Well, my boy," he said, drawing a deep breath—the tears had started to his eyes—"I don't know but you have." He held out his hand. "I don't know but you have, my boy."

"Thank you, sir, thank you."

Her father reached the other hand to Isabel, and stood up and drew her into his arms, then pushed her from him, and crossed the room to the door leading into the hall.

Isabel's eyes followed him lovingly. He turned and looked back at them and smiled.

"Well, children, I'm feeling a little tired to-night," he said, "and I think, if you'll be kind enough to excuse me, I'll go to bed."

He went out and shut the door.

TAMMANY.

EARLY SPOILSMEN, AND THE REIGN OF THE PLUG-UGLIES.

BY E. J. EDWARDS.

With portraits and other Illustrations.

The Public Offices Become Tammany Spoils.—Birth of the Campaign Fund and of the Lobby.—An Early Tammany Official a Defaulter for upwards of a Million.—Riot between Rival Police Forces.—Marshal Rynders and his High-handed Rule.

PRESIDENT JACKSON, before many months of his first administration had passed, made it clear that in two important matters he was influenced by his Secretary of State, Martin Van Buren. This influence caused the President to depart from the policy which he had in his letter of 1824 declared to be the just and patriotic method of appointment to public office. It also led to his opposition to the Bank of the United States. Up to Jackson's first administration the Federal appointments on the whole were based upon merit, although the important administrative offices were necessarily filled by men in sympathy with the national Administration. John Quincy Adams, for instance, refused to remove the collector at the port of New York, although urged to do so for the reason that this officer supported Jackson in 1824 against Adams. The President declared that, so long as the officer was faithful in his service, it made no difference what his personal preferences were.

After Jackson's advent to the chief magistracy, it soon became apparent that he proposed in the administration of the patronage to adopt the custom which had for some ten or twelve years been followed in New York State and City. There the offices were looked upon as the perquisites of politics, and the levers by which personal ambition and party success could be attained. Nowhere else in the Union was this view adopted, excepting possibly in Virginia, where the association of politicians then called the "Richmond Junta" parcelled out the patronage with a view to partisan supremacy. That President Jackson proposed to follow the same plan was indicated even before his inauguration. The Washington "Telegraph," a few days before the presidential election of 1828, said: "We take it for granted that General Jackson will reward his friends and punish his enemies." That mere announcement seems to have been sufficient to bring a great crowd of office-seekers, and for the first time, to Washington, as soon as Jackson was inaugurated, and what Colonel Benton wrote thirty years afterwards in his recollections of public life was especially true of the early days of Jackson's administration. Colonel Benton said: "The crowds which congregate at the

HENRY CLAY.

capital with every change of administration, as suppliants for office, are humiliating, and threaten to change the contest of the parties from a contest for principle into a struggle for plunder."

The practice then begun, leading to scenes which Colonel Benton calls humiliating, was due directly to the New York influence. The public offices were awarded by the President as rewards for services done in the campaign of 1828, and in the expectation of further aid. In New York City, the "Bucktails," or "Anti-Clintonians," names which characterized different elements all associated with Tammany Hall, received every one of the Federal offices. The Secretary of State, Mr. Van Buren, who was the warm friend of and associate with Tammany, and his subordinates controlled this patronage. Speedily this new policy caused much criticism, and it became necessary to defend the New York system, even in so important a place as the Federal Senate.

TESTIMONY AGAINST VAN BUREN.

Upon the break-up of President Jackson's first cabinet, Van Buren was nominated for minister to the court of St. James. The Senate declined to confirm the nomination; but no sooner had the Senate finally adjourned, than the President sent Van Buren on to his post. This action when the Senate met again was the subject of warm debate, and Henry Clay in speaking of it took occasion to denounce "the pernicious system of party politics adopted by the present Administration, by which the honors and the offices were put up to be scrambled for by partisans; a system," he said, "which the minister to London had brought from the State in which he formerly lived, and had for so long a time practised a part in its political transactions." This was a direct charge that for adopting the "spoils" system into national politics, which it is the bad distinction of the Jackson administration to have accomplished, chief credit was due to Mr. Van Buren, an associate of Tammany, and that he had therein but expanded a system long practised by him and other New York politicians.

Senator Marcy, a man long associated with Tammany, replied to Clay. But his reply was little more than a frank admission "It may be that the politicians of New York," said he, "are not so fastidious as some gentlemen are. They boldly preach what they practise. When they are contending for victory, they avow their intention of enjoying the fruits of it. If they fail, they will not murmur. If they win, they expect to reap all the advantages. They see nothing wrong in the rule, that to the victors belong the spoils of the enemy."

The policy thus boldly avowed and defended, was from that time steadfastly maintained, and the influences flowing from it are in no small measure responsible for the later Tammany.

As for Tammany's association with the Jackson administration in the war on the United States Bank, William H. Seward, writing long afterwards, said: "The existing institution [the Bank of the United States] was obnoxious to the State banks [in New York City], which desired to secure for themselves the pecuniary profits derived by the Bank of the United States from deposits, transfers, and management of the public funds. The Republicans [Democrats] of New York, under the lead of Mr. Van Buren, encouraged President Jackson in his premature demonstration against the bank, and thus raised a party issue for the approaching presidential election." Thurlow Weed, in his "Memoirs," makes the charge yet more directly, declaring that Van Buren persuaded President Jackson to oppose the bank. And once, in conversation with the late August Belmont, Mr. Weed said that the New York City bankers, at least those of them who were associated with the "Bucktails," or Tammany men, were the first to suggest to Van Buren that it would be a good thing if the Bank of the United States were refused a new charter. That President Jackson's attitude was enthusiastically indorsed by Tammany, is indicated by the fact that the organization sent to Albany almost the full delegation of members of the legislature from New York City, and that these members secured the passage of a resolution indorsing the President's policy, and afterwards, in caucus, nominated Jackson to the presidency for a second term.

THE BEGINNING OF THE LOBBY.

In an earlier article, mention was made of the fact that Aaron Burr, then a Tammany leader, procured a charter for a State bank in a questionable way. This bank proved so profitable that capital was attracted largely to the banking business. Other charters were obtained, and there was always suspicion as to the means by which they were secured. April 19, 1832, William

H. Seward, at that time a member of the State Senate, wrote from Albany: "The lobby are becoming corrupt and impudent. Yesterday, after I had made up my mind to vote for the Leather Manufacturers' Bank charter, I received a letter requesting me to vote for it because it would be to the interest of the writer. I threw the letter into the fire, and told Mr. Tracey that I was almost disposed to vote against the bank. The bill passed. To-day the

On the whole, the representatives of Tammany in the legislature and the higher elective offices were men of standing. It sent, for instance, to the legislature, between 1835 and 1840, such men as A. C. Wheeler, Prosper M. Wetmore, James T. Roosevelt, and Charles P. Clinch. Of these the last is perhaps the best known to this generation. He served for many years as Deputy Collector of the Port, was an author of some reputation, and the

THE FIRST TAMMANY HALL AS FIRST REBUILT—THE PRESENT "SUN" BUILDING.

gentleman appeared and told me that any amount of stock I wanted in the bank I could have at ten per cent. He said he could not offer it before the Bank Bill passed. I told him I wanted no stock in his bank." In the winter of 1880, Mr. A. D. Barbour, who had been familiar with legislative matters for more than forty years, speaking of the lobby, said that it began when the "Ducktails," or Tammany men, got into the habit of sending men up to the capital to try to influence legislators, and that that was as much as fifty years before the time when he was speaking.

intimate friend of Fitz-Greene Halleck, J. Rodman Drake, and Washington Irving.
Perhaps the most prominent of the Tammany men of that time was Nathaniel P. Tallmadge. He had been elected to the United States Senate, having the favor both of Tammany and the Albany Regency. The policy of President Jackson with respect to the United States Bank caused him to sever his association with the Jackson men. Others began to organize into opposition. They called themselves Conservatives, and at the charter election in New York City, in 1834, the opposition took

the name of Whigs, and was the nucleus of what six years later became the triumphant party in national politics.

THE GLENTWORTH CASE.

The political tactics of the "Loco-focos," as the Tammany Democrats were now called—a name that soon afterwards extended to Democrats throughout the Eastern and Middle States—is illustrated by what is known in history as the Glentworth case. A few weeks before the presidential election of 1840, a man of the name of Glentworth was arrested on the charge, made by the Loco-foco politicians, of having been hired by R. M. Blatchford, Moses H. Grinnell, Simeon E. Draper, and James Bowen, to import illegal voters from Philadelphia. He was taken before a Tammany recorder, Robert H. Morris, and a Tammany justice, Matsell. The city rang with the story, says W. H. Seward, in his "Memoirs." "Handbills were sent out ; the newspapers were full of the sensation. It was charged that Governor Seward had fled." The citizens named in the accusation were among the most prominent merchants and lawyers of New York. Mr. Grinnell was perhaps the ablest shipping merchant New York has ever had. His name is perpetuated in that of a land discovered by an explorer whom Mr. Grinnell had aided to equip his expedition. Simeon E. Draper was afterwards Collector of the Port ; and R. M. Blatchford was the father of the late Justice Blatchford of the Supreme Court. In an investigation by the grand jury, it was shown that Glentworth, who had formerly lived in Philadelphia, had informed the persons named in the accusation that Loco-foco politicians had arranged to bring a large number of men from Philadelphia to cast illegal votes. Glentworth declared that he could prevent it, and he was furnished with money by these persons to do so. Grinnell, Blatchford, and the others, upon examination, stated that they had paid the money, not to bring fraudulent voters to support the Whig ticket, but to prevent the importation of them for the support of the Loco-foco ticket.

The grand jury, instead of holding Glentworth, censured the recorder. Public sentiment was roused to such a pitch that a procession of more than fifteen thousand men marched to Mr. Grinnell's house and tendered him the nomination for Congress. He accepted it, and was elected, running far ahead of his ticket. Glentworth made oath that the Loco-focos had offered him money and the Consulate of Havre, if he would implicate the Whigs in this plot. In 1841 he was accused again, and was indicted; but on the trial the jury disagreed.

Among Glentworth's papers, which were seized in course of the investigation, was found a letter, in which it was said that the men who were to be imported into New York as repeaters, were to represent that they had been employed to lay pipes upon the new Croton aqueduct. This was speedily seized by the political writers of the day, and "pipe-laying" became the convenient term, as it still remains, to designate self-seeking political intrigue.

In 1838, when Nathaniel P. Tallmadge had withdrawn from the Jackson party because he disagreed with it on the United States Bank question, the Whigs, as a matter of policy, made him their candidate for the United States Senate. The Whigs had a majority in the Assembly large enough to overcome the Loco-foco majority in the Senate. To prevent Tallmadge's election the Tammany men and their friends in the Senate decided to support no candidate. For a time they scattered their votes, and then refrained from voting at all. The Senate thus failed to choose a United States Senator, and, as the law then was, there could be, under such circumstances, no joint ballot. For nearly two years New York had but one representative in the United States Senate.

There sprang up within Tammany during the bank controversy a faction which called itself the "Equal Rights party." This element opposed all banks, all paper money, and began the agitation for the use of coin, and nothing else, as the money of the country, which was continued for years. The principle was accepted by many Democrats, and is the main reason for the tradition that the Democratic party is a hard money party. In 1835 this Equal Rights faction made a very earnest attempt to become predominant in Tammany. It was as earnestly opposed. Finally the contest was brought to an issue at a caucus held in Tammany Hall, which proved a most violent and noisy demonstration. When the confusion was at its height, the great crowd found itself in darkness. Some of those who opposed the Equal Rights faction had put out the gas. The Equal Rights men were not taken wholly by surprise, however. Immediately there appeared a multitude of flickering flames from a hundred candles which the Equal Rights party had brought with them, and were

now lighting with "Loco-foco matches."
Within twenty-four hours the name Loco-
foco was applied to Tammany, irrespective
of its factions, and the word passed from
mouth to mouth, so that within a month it
was very rarely that any one heard the organization called by any other name.

VAN BUREN'S ELECTION AND THE FINANCIAL PANIC OF 1837.

The policy respecting the patronage
which Mr. Van Buren had persuaded
Jackson to adopt, also served Van Buren's
ambition well. He was personally not a
man of wide popularity. Even in New
York State it is very
doubtful whether,
without the aid of
Federal and State
patronage, and the
powerful purpose of
President Jackson
to force his nomi-
nation, he could
have commanded
the New York dele-
gation to the con-
vention which nom-
inated him. Those
delegates were ap-
pointed by a con-
vention controlled
by Federal and State
office-holders. In
that convention
forty-eight office-
holders, or a con-
trolling number,
took part, and twen-
ty of these were
postmasters. Of
the delegation then
appointed, more than one-third were office-
holders.

But Mr. Van Buren, winning the nomination, and gaining the election with ease,
since no earnest opposition had been developed into a national party, was nevertheless to be confronted almost at the
threshold of his administration by embar-
rassments which he never overcame. The
year of 1836, or the presidential year, was
a season of magnificent speculation. The
city of New York had never enjoyed such a
time of activity in trade, and in all channels.
The increase in public and private building was enormous, and the city was found
to be growing with a rapidity which even
the magic-like development of Western
towns in later years did not match. Railways and canals were being planned and
developed. The era of travel began, and
capital was so abundant that immense
quantities of it were furnished for speculative enterprise all over the United States.
This abundant capital was provided by
banks which, with the certainty that the
Bank of the United States would expire
by limitation in 1836, had sprung up in
such numbers as to alarm true financiers.
Governor Marcy himself was forced to
warn against this impulse, and in a message to the legislature in 1835, he urged
that body not to increase banks and
banking capital further, because, as he
said, this would be "aiding an unregu-
lated spirit of specu-
lation." No heed
was paid to this re-
monstrance. Im-
migration itself
received a mighty
impetus at this time,
and during Van
Buren's administra-
tion it was still fur-
ther quickened by
the successful ex-
periment of ocean
steam navigation.
To this day there
are traditions of the
scenes of excitement
and enthusiasm at a
Tammany celebra-
tion in honor of the
arrival in New York
harbor of the steam-
ship "Great West-
ern." This, though,
was in 1838.

WILLIAM H. SEWARD.

In February, 1837,
however, there came
ominous portents of financial distress.
Even a month before Mr. Van Buren's
inauguration, money commanded four and
five per cent. Failures in the cotton and
sugar trade in New York City were reported. A month after Van Buren entered
the White House, two hundred and fifty
business houses in New York stopped payment. A run on the banks began. A committee of New York merchants hastened to
Washington and appealed to Van Buren
to summon Congress into extraordinary
session. This committee asserted that
real estate in New York had been depreci-
ated in six months by so much as forty
million dollars, and that stocks had fallen
in price in the aggregate by a sum fully as
great. The President was told that twenty

thousand men were out of employment. All the banks suspended specie payment in May, and the Federal Government itself was practically bankrupt. The administration both of Jackson and Van Buren had announced in effect that the government would receive and pay only in specie, but it had no specie to pay with, since all that it possessed was in the vaults of the suspended banks. Mr. Van Buren later summoned Congress into extra session, and he asked for legislation which would make the government independent of any banks, either State or National. To his amazement and chagrin the President found that his party in Congress could not be controlled. His administration could command support in neither house; and the only aid Congress gave him, was the right to issue ten millions in treasury notes.

Of course such a financial convulsion as this had immediate effect upon the party which Mr. Van Buren represented. The signs of disintegration were alarming. The cry throughout the country was that New York methods and New York politics had brought about this unhappy condition. The Whigs, and especially those in New York, gained recruits every day. Tammany itself was demoralized, since many of its ablest and most respected men were leaving it.

PECULATIONS BY EARLY TAMMANY OFFICE-HOLDERS.

In 1837 there came the revelation that two Federal office-holders, both Tammany men and ardent politicians, were defaulters. The disclosure was made just at a moment when the panic and excitement entailed by the widespread financial disasters of the time were at their height. The offenders were Samuel Swartwout, Collector of the Port of New York, and William M. Price, the United States District Attorney for the Southern District of New York. A committee of Congress made as thorough an investigation as was possible, but its work was made difficult because Swartwout and Price had both fled to Europe. The report showed that Swartwout had embezzled one million two hundred thousand dollars, and Price as much as seventy-five thousand dollars. It was the first conspicuous scandal of a pecuniary kind in which Federal office-holders were involved. Charges were made that it was the inevitable result of the practice which began with Jackson's administration, and which had been taught to Jackson by Van Buren, of distributing the offices as political rewards. As both Swartwout and Price were Tammany appointees, Tammany politicians, named for office by President Jackson because they had Tammany indorsement, of course the revelations brought shame to that organization. Mr. Van Buren was humiliated, and he was frank enough to confess that this scandal, going hand in hand with the financial convulsions, would be likely to create opposition which might, at least for a time, be fatal to the party.

It is anticipating a little, but I will mention here another defalcation, which was exposed some years later. Isaac V. Fowler, a Tammany sachem, and one of the most influential politicians of that organization, was appointed by President Pierce Postmaster of New York. He received his office as a reward for his political service, and with the expectation that he would use it to aid the party. After Buchanan was nominated for the Presidency, Mr. Fowler was visited by certain Pennsylvania politicians, and solicited for a large subscription to the campaign in that State. The custom had prevailed for some years, among politicians in other parts of the country, of seeking large money contributions for campaign purposes from the rich men and politicians of New York. Patronage in New York City had so greatly extended, and the emoluments were so large, that it was easy to raise a considerable sum by assessments upon the office-holders. The Pennsylvania

GOVERNOR MARCY.

THE REIGN OF THE PLUG-UGLIES.

ISAAC V. FOWLER.

politicians told Mr. Fowler that they needed as much as two hundred and fifty thousand dollars to carry Pennsylvania for Buchanan.

"But I have not so much money as that, and don't know how I can raise it," Mr. Fowler replied.

They told him that he must raise it, and their pleadings were too urgent for him to resist. He proposed to them that he would advance the money from Post Office funds in his control, if they would agree to make the sum good after the election. Of course they made the promise, and of course it was never fulfilled.

Some years later, Mr. August Belmont, who at one time was chairman of the National Democratic Committee, in speaking of the Fowler defalcation to General Thomas L. James, then Postmaster-General, told him that the Post Office Department in Washington discovered the defalcation soon after Buchanan's inauguration, but that political influences in New York and Pennsylvania were strong enough to protect Mr. Fowler, chief among them being the influence of certain prominent Tammany men. Later, however, in 1860, Mr. Fowler came to grief. He was faithful to his Tammany associations, and Tammany favored the nomination of Stephen A. Douglas for the Presidency. The Post Office Department was controlled in the interest of John C. Breckenridge, and when Mr. Fowler declined to use the New York Post Office to aid the Breckenridge party, the Post Office Department exposed him as a defaulter. He fled to Mexico, and his bondsmen were called upon to make good the loss. Then it was discovered that, after his re-appointment by President Buchanan, he had failed to renew his official bond. The Government, therefore, was unable to recover a penny. During the excitement of the civil war, the Government was persuaded to dismiss the prosecution, and Fowler returned to the United States, the Government still recovering not a dollar.

MARSHAL RYNDERS AND THE EMPIRE CLUB.

How well Tammany men had learned by this time to stand together, was rather amusingly revealed at the time of the exposure of Fowler's crime. The warrant for his arrest was given to United States Marshal Rynders, the potent leader of the turbulent and lawless element which had now grown strong in Tammany Hall. Rynders went to the New York Hotel, where Fowler lived, and entering the lobby at a time when he knew Fowler would be there, he shouted in a loud voice, "I am United States Marshal Rynders, and I have a warrant for the arrest of Postmaster Isaac V. Fowler." Every eye in that lobby, excepting Rynders's, was fixed on Fowler, who was chatting with a friend. Fowler turned, walked to the rear of the hotel, went to the street by a back door, and fled to Mexico, while the mar-

JOHN MORRISSEY.

shal returned to the District Attorney's office, reporting that Fowler could not be found.

Rynders came from the South, and but little is known of his early history. He was accounted a man of great courage; he had some political skill of the smaller kind; and he became the idol of the Empire Club, which he organized, and which was closely allied with Tammany. Most of the members of the Empire Club were mere rowdies, some of them of the sort named "Bowery Plug-Uglies," a peculiar type, whose haunts were the saloons (very hot-beds of politics); who lived to fight, and run to fires, and train immigrants to political activity, and who commanded the approaches to the polls upon election day. It was the Empire Club, indeed, which taught the political value of the newly arrived foreigner. Its members approached the immigrants at the piers on the arrival of every steamship or packet; conducted them into congenial districts; found them employment in the city works, or perhaps helped them to set up in business as keepers of grog-shops. The effect of these attentions was speedily apparent, and the person who, a few months before, had seemed the meekest of aliens became the most enthusiastic of politicians, believing that success was the criterion in politics, and that anything was justifiable to win it.

EARLY ELECTION FRAUDS.

Fraudulent naturalization on a scale theretofore undreamed of is said to have been practised by the Empire Club under Rynders's leadership, in the presidential campaign of '44. Thousands of immigrants were rushed through the courts, and naturalization papers issued to men in no wise entitled to them, men, often, who had been in the country but a few months. Nathan Sargent, writing at this time, says: "The course pursued by the Free-Soilers [in the nomination of James G. Birney for the Presidency] was one of the causes of Mr. Polk's obtaining the vote of New York State. But there was one other cause which I can never forget—the frauds perpetrated by the Empire Club, managed by one not less celebrated in his day than William M. Tweed has been since—the notorious Isaiah M. Rynders. That these frauds were tremendous is now well known, as it is that this Rynders was a fit instrument with which to perpetrate them, and that he was paid therefor by being appointed to an important office in the Custom House."

Daniel Webster said in a public address soon after the election: "But why should New York go against us? I approach the subject at once, for it is useless to keep it back, and I say that, in my mind, there is a great necessity for a thorough reformation of the naturalization laws." Mr. Sargent, commenting upon Webster's speech, says: "Webster's allusion to the fraudulent votes given in the city of New York by foreigners, large numbers of whom had received dishonest naturalization papers just previous to election day, and most if not all of whom had voted early and often, was fully understood."

Roscoe Conkling once said, chatting with a group of friends, that Governor Seward had told him that the Tammany frauds committed by the Empire Club in New York City in 1844 unquestionably gave Polk the meagre majority of five thousand which he obtained in New York State, and by which he was brought to the Presidency.

Tammany politics as employed in organization, in the making of voters, in the controlling of districts, and the direction of the machinery of elections, developed, from 1840 to the outbreak of the civil war, as picturesque and peculiar conditions as ever existed in a mining camp of the West. Had there lived then in New York some one who painted with the pen of Bret Harte, we should have had pictures as highly colored and as weird as any that Harte ever painted of the California camps, and pictures, too, of men who were making and unmaking administrations, and by their votes, honest and dishonest, were exerting a mighty influence upon the political life of the nation. Strange associations were organized, sometimes affiliated with Tammany as its servants, sometimes in factional quarrel against it. In these associations John Kelly, William M. Tweed, Richard Croker (then a mere lad), Daniel E. Sickles, Fernando Wood, and other men who afterwards gained national prominence, were taught their first lesson in politics. If there is any censure to be passed for these conditions, it should attach especially to the men of intelligence and high personal character who tolerated, and in fact encouraged such things, because by their aid strength was given to the national party of Tammany.

The "Dead Rabbits" of the Bowery, the Empire Club, the Apollo Hall Association, and the various volunteer fire companies

THE REIGN OF THE PLUG-UGLIES.

FERNANDO WOOD.

were political organizations, whose members lived to fight, to pack caucuses, to run in voters, and to make them as well. Important among these associations was a fire company organized in the sixth ward, which was then the very heart of the city. They called their company "Big Six," and it was among them that William M. Tweed, a young chairmaker, gained his first influence, and learned politics. He had the qualities of leadership essential to the command of such rough company, and he was speedily promoted, until at last he became chief of "Big Six," and grew into more than local repute. He organized his district so that it delivered a certain, agreed-on Tammany majority upon election day. But the Great Captain in this strange epoch was always Marshal Rynders. His name inspired terror in the hearts of all reputable citizens. His followers violently broke up the meetings of the opposition party. On one occasion they went to the Tabernacle where Wendell Phillips was to speak, with the intention of mobbing him.

"MIKE" WALSH AND HIS WAR ON TAMMANY.

But they raised up enemies of their own kind. One rough fellow there was, a man of great force and courage, a natural orator, who steadily opposed crat. He was "Mike" Walsh, the founder of the "Subterranean Club," which was the persistent and often the bloody foe of the Empire Club of Rynders. Walsh himself was a slender man, an inch or two above medium height, and did not suggest in his physical appearance his great strength. He was the bitterest foe in the Democratic party that Tammany had ever met. He was a warm friend of John Morrissey, and it was at Walsh's suggestion that Morrissey turned from prize-fighting to politics—so prosperous a transfer of his abilities that he was sent for one term to Congress, and afterwards was maintained for a number of years as a member of the State Senate. Walsh, as a public speaker, was esteemed a fair rival of Daniel E. Sickles, whom Tammany sent to Congress, and of Fernando Wood, who was elected mayor by Tammany in 1854, though during his term of office he quarrelled with the organization.

We may surely take Walsh's word for

the condition of political morals in his day. He knew, if any one did. Standing before a great crowd of Democrats in Knickerbocker Hall, a few years before the war, he said, "I tell you now, and I say it boldly, that in this body politic of New York, there is not political or personal honesty enough left to drive a nail into to hang a hat upon." And he meant by that remark to characterize the condition which Tammany politics had created. Walsh it was who first publicly charged that there was corruption of the ballot-box after the votes had been delivered. He was named as a Democratic Anti-Tammany candidate for Congress in 1854; John Kelly, afterwards the famous leader of Tammany Hall, being the Tammany candidate against him. The contest was very close. There was rioting and fighting throughout the district. Walsh was everywhere, fearing no danger, but he was always surrounded by groups of his faithful club members, who would have died for him had he been attacked. When the polls closed, the vote was known to be very close, and as the counting of the ballots went on it became manifest that the result would not be decided until the ballots in the last box were counted. But that box was found to have been stolen. It was kept hidden for more than three days; then it was produced, and the count gave Kelly a majority of fourteen. Walsh denounced this result as a corruptly procured one, and declared that the ballot-box had either been stuffed, or votes which belonged to him had not been counted. A year or two later he was confirmed in this assertion by the statement of one of the inspectors, who admitted that he had put himself in danger of State's prison because of what he had done with that ballot-box.

Fernando Wood, a man of iron will, great political cunning, and absorbing ambition, a man, too, of some cultivation and very attractive manners and speech, was chosen as the Tammany mayor in the election of 1854. During his administration he quarrelled with some of the Tammany leaders, and he was reëlected as the candidate of a democratic faction called the Apollo Hall party, which was opposed to Tammany. The quarrel was one of those periodical splits of which the history of Tammany shows so many.

TWO BODIES OF POLICE FIGHTING FOR SUPREMACY.

To cripple Wood, and to take the police department from under those malign influences which even then had sway in it, the legislature (then Republican) created a new police system called the metropolitan police. Its jurisdiction covered not only New York City, but Brooklyn, and some of the other suburbs. Mayor Wood ignored the legislature, and kept his own police force in uniform and on duty. It was called the municipal police. The chief was George W. Matsell, a warm friend of Wood's and a devoted Tammany man. Matsell furnished the mayor with a sufficient force of municipal police, and Mr. Wood intrenched himself in the City Hall. A collision was inevitable, and on June 16 it occurred.

Mr. Wood had under his control, in and about the City Hall, some eight hundred "municipal" policemen. The commissioner appointed by the legislature, Mr. Gardner, sent fifty "metropolitan" policemen to disperse the illegal force, and assume authority in and about the hall. As many as ten thousand persons, most of them bent upon violence, were assembled in City Hall Park and the adjacent streets. An eye-witness, describing the scene, said, in the New York "Tribune" of June 17: " About two o'clock, having business with Judge French, whose office is in the City Hall, I proceeded to that place. I observed a great number of policemen in the halls and upon the steps and around the park, whose appearance was more that of a mob than of law-abiding citizens. As I passed through the crowd in the hall I saw a man

GENERAL MATSELL

PARKE GODWIN, ABOUT 1855.

whom I knew well, a man conspicuous in Tammany Hall, and an office-holder under the mayor. I heard him say, 'There goes one of those Black Republicans.' As Judge French was not in, I went out and met him upon Nassau Street, and afterwards called upon him. A little after I saw the metropolitan police coming into the park. I turned around to watch the result. As the metropolitan men advanced towards the steps in the rear of the building, the excitement of the crowd became very intense. Threats and imprecations, and the foulest language known to the Five Points vocabulary, were heard. The crowd was a mob animated by the single desire to beat down the metropolitan police. They were prepared for the most desperate and bloody deeds. . . .

"The mayor's men were arranged in a very advantageous position. They presented a solid, compact front, completely covering the steps and extending back into the hall, which was literally filled with policemen and desperate men.

"The metropolitan men advanced in a solid body and in perfect order, and were met about midway upon the steps, when one of the mayor's men struck one of them. I am positive that it was one of the mayor's men who struck first. If necessary, I can testify to this fact in any court of justice.

"After this blow was struck a promiscuous fight commenced. I watched the movements of Mr. Smith of the fifth worthy and brave officer and excellent citizen. He fought with a valor worthy of the most gallant champion of the age of chivalry. He was attacked by four or five men, and repeatedly felled to the earth, and after the blood was streaming from his wounds, his club was finally wrested from him, and then he was clubbed in a most barbarous and inhuman manner.

"I saw two Irishmen break a limb from a tree, and, taking each a club, knock every and any body they could reach who had the badge of the metropolitan police.

"The mayor's men, completely surrounding the metropolitan police, attacked them in flank and rear. I suppose, being known to some of the politicians present, I was pointed out as a Black Republican. At any rate, a man came up to me, and, applying that epithet, attempted to strike me. I was on my guard, however, and parrying his blow knocked him off and escaped from the crowd."

THE SEVENTH REGIMENT SUPPRESSES THE RIOT.

It happened that just about this time the Seventh Regiment was marching down Broadway, intending to take a steamboat for Boston, to participate in the Bunker Hill celebration of the next day. Commissioner Gardner, finding that the metropolitan police were likely to be overpow-

ered, and many of them perhaps killed, caused the militia to be called out, and its orders to the front were received by the Seventh Regiment only a little way up Broadway from the City Hall. Turning instantly from an expedition altogether of pleasure to one of the gravest business, the regiment fixed its bayonets and dispersed the mob.

Mayor Wood, seeing that the militia had arrived, and perhaps appalled at the spectacle before him, suggested that there be an amnesty until the courts could decide upon the constitutionality of the new law. That proposition was agreed to, and soon after the Court of Appeals decided that the metropolitan police were properly appointed, and, inferentially, that the resistance to them was an act of rebellion against the State.

Mr. Parke Godwin, then one of the editors of the "Evening Post," had been very outspoken in his newspaper writings and also in public speech, in denunciation of the political methods in common practice. Thereby Mr. Godwin had aroused the hatred of Isaiah Rynders and his associates. His denunciation of Tammany in particular, and its methods, had greatly angered the whole organization, but he had incurred the especial hostility of Rynders, and one day word was brought to him that Rynders and his associates were threatening to kill him, and he should have a care.

RYNDERS LIES IN WAIT FOR PARKE GODWIN.

One afternoon, having left his office to go home, Mr. Godwin stopped, as was his custom, in Florence's restaurant for some oysters. As he stood at the oyster-stand, he saw in the remote part of the room Rynders and some of his men. He at once suspected that they proposed to assault him before he could leave the building. He realized that it would not do for him to run, however; so he began to eat his oysters, while deliberating upon his course in case he should be attacked. Suddenly he noticed that a man stood beside him, and looking up he saw "Mike" Walsh, who said to him: "Go on eating your oysters, Mr. Godwin, but do it as quickly as you can, and then go away. Rynders and his men have been waiting here for you and intend to kill you, but they won't attack you as long as I am by your side."

The advice was followed. After Mr. Godwin, having finished his oysters, had gone out, Rynders stepped up to Walsh and said: "What do you mean by interfering in this matter? It is none of your affair."

"Well, Godwin did me a good turn once, and I don't propose to see him stabbed in the back. You were going to do a sneaking thing; you were going to assassinate him, and any man who will do that is a coward."

"No man ever called me a coward, Mike Walsh, and you can't."

"But I do, and I will prove that you are a coward. If you are not one, come up-stairs with me now. We will lock ourselves into a room; I will take a knife and you take one; and the man who is alive after we have got through, will unlock the door and go out."

Rynders accepted the challenge. They went to an upper room. Walsh locked the door, gave Rynders a large bowie-knife, took one himself, and said: "You stand in that corner, and I'll stand in this. Then we will walk toward the centre of the room, and we won't stop until one or the other of us is finished."

Each took his corner. Then Walsh turned and approached the centre of the room. But Rynders did not stir. "Why don't you come out?" said Walsh. Rynders, turning in his corner, faced his antagonist, and said: "Mike, you and I have always been friends; what is the use of our fighting now? If we get at it, we shall both be killed, and there is no good in that,". Walsh for a moment said not a word; but his lip curled, and he looked upon Rynders with an expression of utter contempt. Then he said: "I told you you were a coward, and now I prove it. Never speak to me again."

The intense excitement that prevailed throughout the nation as the election of 1860 approached, caused these demoralizing conditions in New York to be for a time overlooked. A few of the Tammany leaders either openly supported the action of the Southern States in seceding from the Union, or else gave sullen and indifferent aid to those who were preparing to take up arms in defence of the Union. Tammany as a body favored the nomination of Stephen A. Douglas, and it should be said that in the crisis of 1861, as in every other time in its history, Tammany as a whole was staunch, loyal, devoted, and fervent in its support of national sovereignty and the Union.

www.ingramcontent.com/pod-product-compliance
Lightning Source LLC
Chambersburg PA
CBHW031936290426
44108CB00011B/578